iWork

the missing manual®

The book that should have been in the box®

Jessica Thornsby & Josh Clark

O'REILLY®

Beijing | Cambridge | Farnham | Köln | Sebastopol | Tokyo

iWork: The Missing Manual

by Jessica Thornsby and Josh Clark

Copyright © 2014 Jessica Thornsby. All rights reserved.
Printed in the United States of America.

Published by O'Reilly Media, Inc.,
1005 Gravenstein Highway North, Sebastopol, CA 95472.

O'Reilly books may be purchased for educational, business, or sales promotional use. Online editions are also available for most titles (*http://my.safaribooksonline.com*). For more information, contact our corporate/institutional sales department: (800) 998-9938 or *corporate@oreilly.com*.

March 2014:   First Edition.

Revision History for the First Edition:

　2014-03-11　　First release

See *http://www.oreilly.com/catalog/errata.csp?isbn=0636920012832* for release details.

ISBN-13: 978-1-4493-9331-1

[M]

Contents

Part One: Pages for Mac

Part Two: Keynote for Mac

Part Six: **Appendix**

The Missing Credits

ABOUT THE AUTHOR

 Jessica Thornsby is a technical writer based in sunny Sheffield, England. She writes about Android, app development, rooting and flashing mobile devices, Eclipse, Java, and all things Apple. When not wordsmithing about technology, she writes about her local food scene, and for various animal magazines. On the rare occasions when she's dragged away from her keyboard, she enjoys beer gardens, going to concerts, cooking tongue-blistering curries, and obsessively researching her family tree.

 Josh Clark (author, previous edition) is a designer specializing in multi-device design, strategy, and user experience. He's the author of many books including *Tapworthy: Designing Great iPhone Apps* and *Designing for Touch*. When he's not writing about clever design and humane software, he's building it. Josh's agency, Global Moxie, offers design services, strategic consulting, and training to help creative organizations build tapworthy apps and responsive websites. His clients include AOL, Time Inc., eBay, and many others. In a previous life, Josh worked on a slew of national PBS programs at Boston's WGBH. He shared his three words of Russian with Mikhail Gorbachev, strolled the ranch with Nancy Reagan, and wrote trivia questions for a prime-time game show. In 1996, he created the uber-popular Couch-to-5K (C25K) running program, which has helped millions of skeptical would-be exercisers take up jogging. (His motto is the same for fitness as it is for using software: no pain, no pain.)

ABOUT THE CREATIVE TEAM

Dawn Mann (editor) is assistant editor for the Missing Manual series. When not working, she plays soccer, beads, and causes trouble. Email: *dawn@oreilly.com*.

Kara Ebrahim (production editor) lives, works, and plays in Cambridge, MA. She loves graphic design and all things outdoors. Email: *kebrahim@oreilly.com*.

Julie Van Keuren (proofreader) quit her newspaper job in 2006 to move to Montana and live the freelancing dream. She and her husband, M.H. (who is living the novel-writing dream), have two sons, Dexter and Michael. Email: *little_media@yahoo.com*.

Ron Strauss (indexer) specializes in the indexing of information technology publications of all kinds. Ron is also an accomplished classical violist and lives in Northern California with his wife and fellow indexer, Annie, and his miniature pinscher, Kanga. Email: *rstrauss@mchsi.com*.

Tina Spargo (technical reviewer), her husband (and professional musician) Ed, their children, Max and Lorelei, and two silly Spaniels, Parker (Clumber) and Piper (Sussex), all share time and space in their suburban Boston home. Tina juggles being an at-home mom with promoting and marketing Ed's musical projects and freelancing as a virtual assistant. Tina has over 20 years' experience supporting top-level executives in a variety of industries. Website: *www.tinaspargo.com.*

ACKNOWLEDGMENTS

I would like to thank the entire team at O'Reilly for their support and encouragement, and for generally being such awesome people to work with. Thank you to Dawn Mann for guiding this manuscript through the writing process; technical reviewer Tina Spargo; production editor Kara Ebrahim; and all the other talented people I've been lucky enough to work with on this project.

I'd like to thank my friends and family for putting up with me during the writing process (and in general!), but special thanks have to go to Pauline, Peter, and Toby. Last but not least, I'd like to thank my menagerie and writing-buddies for keeping me entertained even when I'm shackled to my keyboard: my house bunnies Stewart and Peanut, and chinchillas Taco and Buca.

THE MISSING MANUAL SERIES

Missing Manuals are witty, superbly written guides to computer products that don't come with printed manuals (which is just about all of them). Each book features a handcrafted index and cross-references to specific pages (not just chapters). For a full list of current and upcoming Missing Manuals, head to *www.missingmanuals.com.*

Introduction

The words "productivity software" don't exactly make your skin tingle. Most of us use a word-processing or spreadsheet program because we *have* to. It's how we get our day-to-day work done, pushing through the words and numbers that office, school, or household demands impose. What's to get excited about?

Until recently, not much. For decades, word-processing, spreadsheet, and presentation programs have been blandly efficient tools that solemnly transferred your work to page and screen. Bland gets the job done, but it doesn't inspire. You and your ideas deserve an environment that's more stirring than that. Dreary work tools don't cut it.

An inspiring spreadsheet program? A rousing word processor? The concepts seem improbable—but as usual, Apple beats the odds. When the company originally unveiled its iWork collection of programs, Apple proved that doing serious work doesn't have to *feel* serious. And with all the subsequent updates, Apple has remained true to that mission. The iWork package includes Pages, Keynote, and Numbers: iWork's word processor, presentation program, and spreadsheet program, respectively.

All the iWork programs put an unprecedented emphasis on the design and polish of your final documents, making it easy to create results that look not only professional, but actually stunning. It's like you've got an entire art department on the payroll—and, in fact, that's not far from the truth. Pages, Keynote, and Numbers all come stacked high with prebuilt templates that you can put to use right away, letting the skill of Apple's talented designers shine through in your own work. Although the template concept isn't anything new, the quality of Apple's design raises the bar to a whole new level.

But iWork is more than just a collection of glossy templates. The latest version of iWork makes some big changes to the '09 version. It may be hard to believe, but when iWork was last updated in 2009, mobile apps were still a pretty new concept. And although slimmed-down versions of the iWork for Mac apps made it onto the iPhone, iPad, and iPod Touch back then, this latest release finally brings the iWork for Mac and iWork for iOS apps together in one uniform update. And then there's the small matter of iWork for iCloud, a new online service that debuted in late 2013, which makes it easy to share documents among the various versions of iWork.

Clearly, there's a lot of new stuff to wrap your brain around. The next few sections get you ready for the ride by making sure you understand the three programs that make up iWork, as well as the three different flavors of iWork.

■ The Three *Parts* of iWork

As mentioned above, iWork isn't just a single program—it's a collection of three different programs: Pages, Keynote, and Numbers. When used in combination, they can turn you into an unstoppable word-processing, presentation-giving, spreadsheet-creating powerhouse! Here's a quick overview of what each program can do.

Pages: Word Processing Meets Graphic Design

When words are your game, Pages has you covered. As a *word processor,* Pages' most basic job is to make it easy to get words onto the screen and, once there, coax and refine them into irresistible prose for the printed page. Use Pages to write letters, pen the Great American Novel, draw up contracts, or write a term paper. The program gives you all the power-editing tools you're likely to need: spell checking, styles, images, guidelines, and lots of other goodies.

But Pages has a whole separate career beyond word processing: The program moonlights as a graphic designer. Pages makes it almost embarrassingly easy to create gorgeous page layouts for glossy newsletters, catalogs, brochures, flyers, posters, greeting cards—you name it. You can deck out any document with photos or graphics with drag-and-drop simplicity.

You can create professionally designed documents quickly and easily, thanks to Pages' collection of templates. Pick the design that you want to use and then drop in your own pictures and text, as easy as filling in the blanks. Just like that, *you're* the artsy designer (and you didn't even have to grow a goatee or buy a beret).

Keynote: Presentations with Gusto

Keynote is a *presentation program* for making slideshows, usually to accompany a talk or other live presentation. The program helps you build screens of text and graphics to illustrate important points as you roam the stage earning the awe and admiration of your audience. As you flip from slide to slide, Keynote shimmies and shakes with cinematic transitions and all the supporting razzle-dazzle that your presentation deserves.

More than just a pretty face, though, Keynote is also an elegantly simple program to use. There's an awful lot of complexity behind the scenes of the program's eye-popping effects, but Keynote modestly keeps the hard stuff to itself. For you, the presenter, the design process is always simple and straightforward. And like all iWork programs, Keynote gets you started with a collection of themes that make your slides look great even when you don't use a single special effect. Whether subdued or busy, your slideshow's design is always polished and consistent.

Numbers: Crunching Data with Style

Numbers is a *spreadsheet program,* tuned for organizing data and juggling numbers. The program has a special talent for math, of course—it eats balance sheets and financial models for breakfast. But like any spreadsheet program, Numbers can also bring order to just about any kind of information. Use it for contact lists, team rosters, product inventories, invoices, or to-do lists. Once you've loaded up your data, Numbers can flip it every which way: sort it, filter it, and analyze it.

As usual with iWork programs, the thing that makes Numbers special is its remarkable talent for stylish design. Traditionally, formatting spreadsheets has been an ugly, time-consuming process, and many people simply don't bother. With Numbers, however, it's easy—even addictive—to transform your data into a multimedia report by mixing tables with colorful charts, photos, and illustrations. The program's chart tools are especially dazzling, turning your stodgy figures into impressive infographics.

■ The Three *Flavors* of iWork

Now that you know what Pages, Keynote, and Numbers are capable of, it's time to take a closer look at the various versions of iWork that Apple now offers. It's a lot to keep track of, but it's worth understanding the advantages of each flavor.

iWork for Mac

If you've been using a Mac for a while, then you're probably already familiar with this version of iWork. iWork for Mac works just like any other Mac software: You download it and then install it on your computer.

In the past, you had to pay for each iWork for Mac program separately (and, if you have an older Mac, you still do). But if you have a new Mac—one you purchased in October 2013 or later—then you can get all three iWork programs for free. (See page 798 in Appendix A for details.)

This version of iWork is also the most robust—it has the most features of the three. That's why coverage of iWork for Mac makes up the majority of this book: Part One (page 3) covers Pages for Mac (version 5.1), Part Two (page 279) covers Keynote for Mac (version 6.1), and Part Three (page 431) covers Numbers for Mac (version 3.1).

iWork for iOS

The days of having to sit at a computer to get your fix of nerdy goodness is a thing of the past. If you need easy access to spreadsheets, presentations, or word-processing documents (whether you're on the go or just too comfy on the sofa to fetch your laptop from upstairs), the iWork for iOS apps are the answer. This version of iWork brings the fun Pages, Keynote, and Numbers to your iPad, iPhone, and iPod Touch. (This book uses the term iDevice as shorthand for all three Apple gadgets.)

NOTE *iOS* is the name of the operating system used by all iDevices. What's an operating system, you ask? It's the underlying software that makes all the programs on the iDevice work; it's the equivalent of OS X on a Mac.

The iWork for iOS apps are basically pared-down versions of the iWork programs that run on your Mac. Page 799 in Appendix A explains how to install these apps. And Part Four of this book (which starts on page 675) takes you on a tour of Pages (Chapter 24), Keynote (Chapter 25), and Numbers (Chapter 26) as you'll encounter them on your iDevice. (Specifically, this book covers version 2.1 of each app.)

iWork for iCloud

So, iWork fans can now create and edit word-processing documents, presentations, and spreadsheets on their Macs *and* iDevices. But could too much choice can be a bad thing?

Imagine it's drawing dangerously close to the end of the workday, and there's a margarita with your name on it at the pub across the road. But before you can enjoy it, you need to print out an invoice for your manager. You know you created the invoice in Pages, but was that on your Mac or your iPad? You also have Pages on your iPod Touch, and can't rule out the possibility that you created the invoice on your iPhone while waiting for the train. It looks like that margarita will just have to wait while you track down that pesky invoice...

If only there were a place where you could store *all* your iWork documents, regardless of whether you created them on your Mac, iPad, iPhone, or iPod Touch.

Enter iWork for iCloud, an online service that lets you create and edit iWork documents in a web browser and save them in "the cloud." (See page 257 for details about cloud computing; for now, think of it as saving your documents online, in the same way services like Gmail save emails online.) iWork for iCloud is basically iWork in website form. If you already have an Apple-approved web browser installed on your computer (see page 756 for a list of those browsers), you don't need to install any new software to use this version of iWork. You can even access iWork for iCloud from a PC!

As you'll learn in Part Five of this book, iWork for iCloud is a *free* version of iWork that lets you create basic word-processing documents (Chapter 28), presentations (Chapter 29), and spreadsheets (Chapter 30)—although, as of this writing, it doesn't boast *all* the features you get in the Mac and iOS versions. But iWork for iCloud also serves a more important purpose: It can be the central hub for *all* your iWork documents. Once you introduce your iWork for Mac and iWork for iOS apps to your iCloud account, every iWork document you create and every change you make is automatically synced with your iWork for iCloud account, and vice versa. Syncing your documents with iCloud also means that if your Mac or iDevice spontaneously combusts, you don't lose all of your documents—they're still safely stored in your iCloud account.

This book shows you how to create and edit documents using iWork for iCloud, as well as how to link iWork for Mac, iOS, and iCloud to create one, big, interconnected iWork family.

> **NOTE** This book covers iWork for iCloud as it existed at the time this book was being written (spring 2014). But Apple will likely make regular updates to iWork for iCloud, so some features may work differently than described in these pages.

■ What's New in iWork

The latest version of iWork (see the previous section for the exact version numbers covered in this book) is nothing short of a complete overhaul, with one clear aim: Giving you the same experience regardless of whether you're using iWork on your Mac, iDevice, or web browser—and that's no easy feat.

The biggest change in the latest version of iWork is that all the versions of the program can now connect via iCloud, which means you can share, save, and collaborate on documents across all of Apple's gadgets. Naturally, this leveling-the-playing-field approach means that some features have been lost in translation, but what the iWork community has gained is a set of sleek, simplified, and uniform programs that you can master once, and then use across all of your Apple devices.

In addition to these major changes, Apple has added a few extras to this latest update. Here are some of the most important:

- **Bubble charts.** These charts display three dimensions of data in one lovely chart. The first two sets are represented by the traditional x and y-axes, while the third set is represented by the size of a circle (and all these circles kind of look like bubbles, hence the name). Bubble charts are really easy to use—if you've ever worked with a scatter chart, then you know how to create a bubble chart. (As of this writing, bubble charts weren't available in iWork for iCloud).

- **Interactive charts.** These charts let you see how your data changes over time. Just drag the slider underneath an interactive chart to move among data sets in your series. (Interactive charts are also not available in iWork for iCloud—at least, they weren't when this book was written).

- **Star ratings.** Nothing lets you know what's hot or not quicker than a star rating. This new data format means you can transform boring old numbers in a table into 0–5 star ratings.

- **Simplified interface.** iWork's new look (see Figure 1-2 on page 6) may seem simple, but it ensures that everything you need is always right at your fingertips. Not content with giving iWork a consistent look across Macs, iDevices, and web browsers, Apple has also made the programs easier to navigate than ever before. For example, whenever you select an object, the Format panel (page 23) appears with all the settings you need to edit that object.

The toolbar at the top of each program is also more stripped down than ever before: Simply click one of its buttons to open a drop-down menu containing everything you need. Click the Chart button, for example, and you get access to iWork's entire arsenal of 2D, 3D, and interactive charts. Or click the Media button to add images, videos, and audio clips from a wide range of online and offline sources.

■ The Very Basics

You'll find very little jargon or geeky terminology in this book. You will, however, encounter a few terms and concepts that you'll come across frequently in your computing life:

- **Clicking.** This book gives you three kinds of instructions that require you to use your computer's mouse or trackpad. To *click* means to point the arrow cursor at something on the screen and then—without moving the cursor—to press and release the clicker button on the mouse (or laptop trackpad). To *double-click,* of course, means to click twice in rapid succession, again without moving the cursor. And to *drag* means to move the cursor while holding the clicker button continuously.

  When you're told to *Shift-click* something, you click while pressing the Shift key. Related procedures, like *Control-clicking,* work the same way—just click while pressing the corresponding key.

- **Menus.** The *menus* are the words at the top of your screen: File, Edit, and so on. Click one to make a list of commands appear as though they're written on a window shade you've just pulled down. Some people click to open a menu and then release the mouse button; after reading the menu choices, they click the option they want. Other people like to press the mouse button continuously as they click the menu title and drag down the list to the desired command; only then do they release the mouse button. Both methods work, so use whichever one you prefer.

- **Keyboard shortcuts.** Every time you take your hand off the keyboard to move the mouse, you lose time and potentially disrupt your creative flow. That's why many experienced computer fans use keystroke combinations instead of menu commands wherever possible. ⌘-B, for example, is the keyboard shortcut for boldface type in iWork (and most other programs).

  When you see a shortcut like ⌘-S (which saves changes to the current document), it's telling you to hold down the ⌘ key, and, while it's down, type the letter S, and then release both keys.

- **Choice is good.** iWork frequently gives you several ways to trigger a particular command—by choosing a menu command, *or* by clicking a toolbar button, *or* by pressing a key combination, for example. Some people prefer the speed of keyboard shortcuts; others like the satisfaction of a visual command array available in menus or toolbars. This book lists all the alternatives, but by no means are you expected to memorize them all.

About This Book

Despite the many improvements in software over the years, one feature has grown consistently worse: documentation. When you purchase most programs these days, you don't get a single page of printed instructions. To learn about the hundreds of features in a program, you're expected to use online help or to download a manual from the company's website. (Apple has an entire section of its website dedicated to all the different incarnations of iWork: *www.apple.com/support/iwork*.)

But even if you're comfortable reading a help screen in one window as you try to work in another, something is still missing. At times, the terse electronic help screens assume you already understand the discussion at hand and hurriedly skip over important topics that require an in-depth presentation. In addition, you don't always get an objective evaluation of the program's features. (Engineers often add technically sophisticated features to a program because they *can*, not because you need them.) You shouldn't have to waste time learning features that don't help you get your work done.

The purpose of this book is to serve as the manual that should have come with iWork. In this book's pages, you'll find step-by-step instructions for using every feature in Pages, Keynote, and Numbers. Because many features appear in all three programs (not to mention all three *versions* of the programs) some features get in-depth treatment for one program but not another; when that's the case, the book points you to the page where you'll find the full scoop. In addition, you'll always find clear evaluations of each feature to help you determine which ones are useful to you, as well as how and when to use them. Shortcuts and workarounds save you time and headaches, and you'll even unearth features that the online help doesn't mention.

Beyond just the mechanical aspects of using iWork, however, this book also gives you practical aesthetic advice about document design and presentation. Pages, Keynote, and Numbers give you amazing technical tools to create luxurious layouts—or shoot yourself in the foot. This book helps keep the lead out of your sneakers with simple, good-natured tips for planning and preparing your document layout, based on tried-and-true principles of graphic design.

Throughout this book, you'll find carefully constructed sample documents showing how to put iWork's tools to best effect and, hopefully, provide a hint of inspiration for your own work. Most of these documents follow the adventures of an ill-conceived and very un-amusing amusement park, Crazyland Wonderpark (recently under new management); a place where visitors can experience "unique" attractions that revolve around squirrels, pencil sharpeners, plastic dinosaurs, beans, and public toilets, all while enjoying equally questionable food. If this book inspires you to open your own theme park (or you just want to try out some of the techniques discussed), you can download some of these sample files from this book's Missing CD page at *www. missingmanuals.com/cds.*

iWork: The Missing Manual is designed to accommodate readers of every technical level. The primary discussions are written for advanced-beginner or intermediate computer users. But if you're a first-timer, special sidebar articles labeled "Up to Speed" provide the introductory information you need to understand the topic at hand. If you're an advanced user, keep your eye out for similar boxes called Power Users' Clinics, which offer more technical tips, tricks, and shortcuts.

■ About the Outline

This book is divided into six parts, each containing several chapters:

- **Part One** covers Pages for Mac. You'll learn the basics of entering and formatting text, as well as how to add some graphic-design wizardry to your word processing by creating glossy reports, newsletters, posters, and much more. By the time you finish this section of the book, you'll be able to bend word-processing documents to your will.

- **Part Two** explains the ins and outs of Keynote for Mac. You'll find out how to format slides, customize them every which way, and add animations worthy of a Hollywood blockbuster. This section even explains how to connect your Mac to an external monitor or projector so you'll have no trouble wowing your audience.

- **Part Three** delves into Numbers for Mac. If you've ever used Microsoft Excel, you'll be pleasantly surprised at how easy and *fun* Numbers is to work with. Numbers spreadsheets can contain much more than just boring old tables—you'll learn how to jazz up your data with images, charts, and even videos.

- **Part Four** covers iWork for iOS, so you can use iWork on the go. Each app gets its own chapter: Chapter 24 covers Pages for iOS, Chapter 25 is dedicated to Keynote for iOS, and Chapter 26 explains Numbers for iOS.

- **Part Five** provides all the info you need to get started with iWork for iCloud. Just like Part Four, Part Five dedicates a chapter to each part of iWork: Pages (Chapter 28), Keynote (Chapter 29), and Numbers (Chapter 30).

- **Part Six** contains just one thing: Appendix A, which explains how to install and upgrade iWork for Mac and iWork for iOS.

About→These→Arrows

In this book, and throughout the Missing Manual series, you'll find sentences like this one: "Go to →System Preferences→iCloud." That's shorthand for a much longer set of instructions that direct you to three places in sequence, like this: "At the top-left corner of your screen, you'll see the symbol. Click it to open a menu. In that menu, click System Preferences. In the System Preferences window that opens, click the iCloud icon."

Similarly, this kind of arrow shorthand helps simplify the business of choosing commands in iWork menus. Figure I-1 has the details.

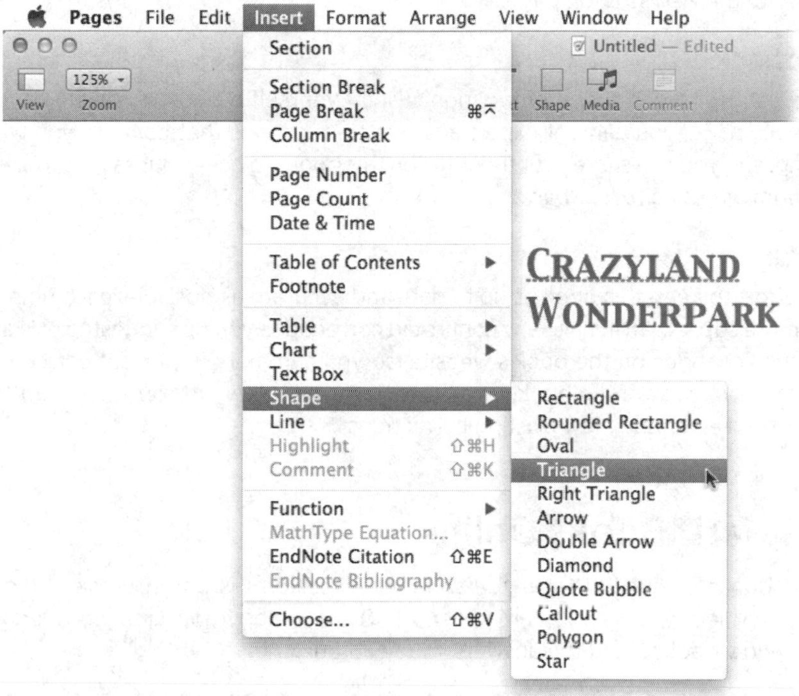

FIGURE I-1

The instruction "Choose Insert→Shape→Triangle" means "Open the Insert menu at the top of your screen, and then choose the Shape option. On the submenu that appears, select Triangle."

■ About the Online Resources

As the owner of a Missing Manual, you've got more than just a book to read. Online, you'll find example files so you can get some hands-on experience with the techniques described in this book. You can also communicate with the Missing Manual team and tell us what you love (or hate) about the book. Head over to *www.missingmanuals. com*, or go directly to one of the following sections.

Missing CD

This book doesn't have a CD pasted inside the back cover, but you're not missing out on anything. Go to *www.missingmanuals.com/cds* and click the "Missing CD-ROM" link for this book to find all the sample files. And so you don't wear down your fingers typing long web addresses, the Missing CD page also offers a list of clickable links to the websites mentioned in this book.

Registration

If you register this book at oreilly.com, you'll be eligible for special offers—like discounts on future editions of *iWork: The Missing Manual.* Registering takes only a few clicks. To get started, type *http://oreilly.com/register* into your browser to hop directly to the Registration page.

Feedback

Got questions? Need more information? Fancy yourself a book reviewer? On our Feedback page, you can get expert answers to questions that come to you while reading, and you can share your thoughts on this book. To have your say, go to *www. missingmanuals.com/feedback.*

Errata

In an effort to keep this book as up to date and accurate as possible, each time we print more copies, we'll make any confirmed corrections you've suggested. We also note such changes on the book's website, so you can mark important corrections into your own copy of the book, if you like. Go to *http://tinyurl.com/iworkmm2014* to report an error and view existing corrections.

■ Safari® Books Online

Safari® Books Online (*http://my.safaribooksonline.com*) is an on-demand digital library that lets you easily search over 7,500 technology and creative reference books and videos to find the answers you need quickly.

With a subscription, you can read any page and watch any video from our library online. Read books on your cellphone and mobile devices. Access new titles before they are available for print, and get exclusive access to manuscripts in development and post feedback for the authors. Copy and paste code samples, organize your favorites, download chapters, bookmark key sections, create notes, print out pages, and benefit from tons of other time-saving features.

Pages for Mac

Creating a Pages Document

Most of us think of a word processor as a glorified typewriter, a simple way to organize ideas and arguments for the printed page. You craft words into paragraphs, juggle them, refine them, and then you're done. Tap, tap, tap, print, and then it's time to put your feet up.

Pages goes a step further, making it easy not only to *compose* your documents, but to *design* them, too. Whether you're publishing a glossy newsletter or just writing a thank-you note to Aunt Peg, Pages lets you give your documents the visual pizzazz they deserve.

This chapter guides you through your new word-processing digs and gets you creating your own basic documents and simple projects—which just so happen to highlight Pages' main features.

NOTE If you need help installing Pages for Mac, see Appendix A.

■ Getting Started with Pages

Launch Pages by opening your Finder window and locating the Applications folder in the left-hand sidebar. Click the Applications folder to open it, and then scroll until you find the Pages icon. Double-click the icon to launch Pages. Alternatively, if you've added Pages to your Mac's Dock (the strip of icons that runs along the bottom of your screen), you can jump straight into Pages by clicking the Dock's Pages icon.

TIP On a Mac, you launch every program in exactly the same way. So, now that you know how to launch Pages, you know how to launch Keynote and Numbers (and any other program), too.

The first time you launch Pages, you're greeted by a "Welcome to Pages" screen, followed by a "New in Pages" screen. To take a look at your existing documents, select View My Documents (page 17 has more info about opening existing documents).

To jump straight in and create a new document, click the New Document button, which launches the *Template Chooser*. The Template Chooser is where you, well, choose a template (glad that's cleared up...).

Templates contain a mix of fancy things like images, tables, and shapes, not to mention dummy text, so you're never confronted with a terrifyingly blank page (unless you want a blank page, of course, in which case take a deep breath and select the Blank template; page 16 has details). Templates can save you oodles of time. For example, if you're organizing your local Small Animal Olympics event (hamsters vaulting through rings, rabbits doing the long jump—the usual), you could simply select the Event Poster template, type out a bit of text, replace the image placeholders with shots of fuzzy little animals, and you're done.

Pages boasts 60 professionally designed templates to meet all of your wordsmithing needs, from newsletters to For Rent flyers, letters, cards, and everything in between. To make it easier to root out the template of your dreams, the Template Chooser is divided into categories (as shown in Figure 1-1). Select any category in the left-hand pane to see what that category has to offer. To ensure you pick the right template every time, the Template Chooser shows you miniature previews, or *thumbnails*, of each template. When you spy a template you want to use, either double-click its thumbnail, or click the thumbnail once and then click the Choose button.

FIGURE 1-1

To browse the available templates, click a category in the window's left pane, or choose All to see everything the Template Chooser has to offer. Use the arrow keys on your keyboard to browse the thumbnails for your chosen category.

Pages responds by opening a new document (in a new window) that's based on your chosen template and gives it the riveting name "Untitled" (you'll learn how to give it a new name on page 12). In addition to offering you lots of design options, these templates are built to last: When you choose a template, Pages actually opens a *copy* of the original, meaning you're not editing the actual template itself. So feel free to work on your document, safe in the knowledge that the blueprint is locked away—unmodified—and will be right there waiting for you the next time you need it. (You *can* modify templates if you really need to, and you can create templates of your own, too. For all the ins and outs of template creation and manipulation, see Chapter 10.)

TIP Got cold feet? If you're no longer crazy about the template now that you've seen it up close and personal, you can throw it back and start over by closing the window (click the red Close button in the upper-left corner of the document window), and then going to File→New or pressing ⌘-N to pick a new template.

That was the warm-up; now it's time to really dive in! The following sections show you how to put Pages' templates to good use and start creating beautiful documents straight away. These quick-start introductions provide a high-level overview of Pages' key features, but don't fret: You'll get acquainted with the program's nuts and bolts in the following chapters.

■ Creating Pages Documents

Uh-oh, earnings are down at Crazyland Wonderpark (the less-than-amusing amusement park you grudgingly inherited from your Aunt Ethel)—time to get on the campaign trail and really market the park's strong points. Who knows, if you design some great word-processing documents, maybe even that guy who wrote the really mean online review won't be able to resist a repeat visit? Here's hoping.

To create your first Pages document, launch the Template Chooser as explained above or by going to File→New, and hunt through the categories until you find the perfect template for your soon-to-be award-winning marketing campaign (the Elegant Brochure template in the Miscellaneous category looks perfect). Double-click your chosen template to create a new document based on it. The resulting new document, complete with dummy text and placeholder images, is shown in Figure 1-2.

TIP If you decide that none of the templates are what you need, you can start with a blank document instead. For info on how to do that, flip to page 16. And if you want Pages to use the same template every time you create a document (unless you specifically tell it to choose another template), page 16 explains how to set that up.

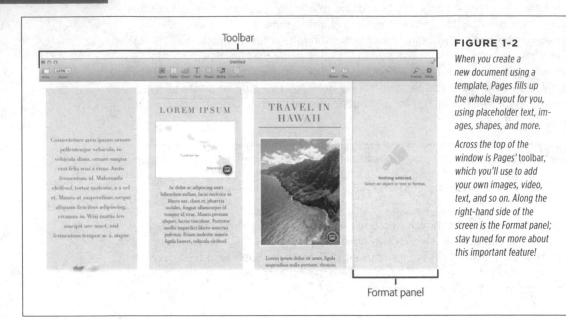

Toolbar

FIGURE 1-2

When you create a new document using a template, Pages fills up the whole layout for you, using placeholder text, images, shapes, and more.

Across the top of the window is Pages' toolbar, which you'll use to add your own images, video, text, and so on. Along the right-hand side of the screen is the Format panel; stay tuned for more about this important feature!

Format panel

Replacing Placeholder Text

Unless you opted for the Blank template (page 16), your newly created document is composed of a collection of design elements called *objects:* text, shapes, images, movies, and even audio. Each object is contained in its own little box that you can drag, resize, and customize. At the most basic level, creating a document is all about filling these boxes with words and pictures.

Chapter 6 explores the ins and outs of working with objects. For now, though, the Elegant Brochure template has given you a leg up by providing you with a document that's already bursting with nicely formatted objects. All that remains is to fill in your content.

■ SELECTING AND EDITING TEXT

Nearly all of Pages' templates include *placeholder text* that shows where you can add text of your very own, and the Elegant Brochure template is no exception. Just click any placeholder text, and Pages selects the entire text block (as shown in Figure 1-3). Start typing, and the block disappears, replaced with your newly typed text.

The next chapter digs into all the nitty-gritty options for editing and formatting text. For now, we'll keep it simple. If you've ever used a computer before, you already know how this works: Click to place the insertion point where you want to add or delete text, type your smooth-and-seductive prose promoting everything that's good and wholesome about Crazyland Wonderpark, and hit the Return key every time you want to start a new paragraph or add a blank line.

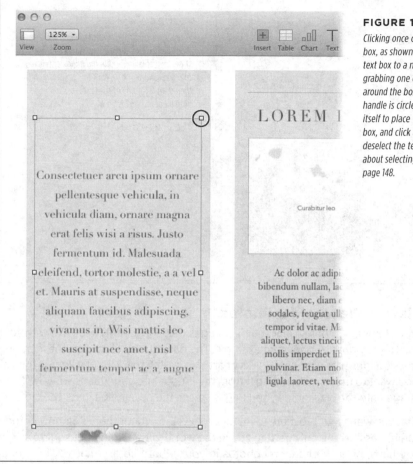

FIGURE 1-3

Clicking once on a text box selects the entire box, as shown here. You can then drag the text box to a new location, or resize it by grabbing one of the eight square handles around the box's perimeter (the upper-right handle is circled here). Double-click the text itself to place your cursor inside the text box, and click anywhere outside the box to deselect the text box completely. For more about selecting and editing text boxes, see page 148.

If you've gotten carried away singing the praises of Crazyland Wonderpark and your text box is overflowing, Pages lets you know by adding a *clipping indicator*, a + sign at the bottom of the text box (see Figure 1-4). This indicator gives you a heads-up that the box contains more text than it can display. To get out of this pickle, click anywhere inside the text box, and then drag any of the selection handles (or the clipping indicator) until all the text is visible. Or, if you don't want to make the text box any bigger (or there isn't any room to do so), simply edit your text down until it fits.

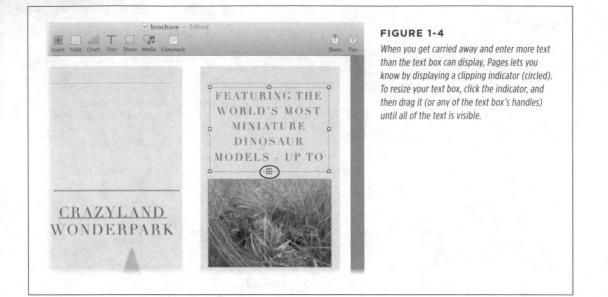

FIGURE 1-4

When you get carried away and enter more text than the text box can display, Pages lets you know by displaying a clipping indicator (circled). To resize your text box, click the indicator, and then drag it (or any of the text box's handles) until all of the text is visible.

Replacing Placeholder Photos

Nearly all templates contain placeholder images that you'll want to replace with your own pictures; Figure 1-5 shows an example. The easiest way to replace these boring old stock images with your own works of art is to switch to the Finder, locate the image you want to use, and then drag it from the Finder into your Pages window. Drop the image onto the placeholder, and Pages swaps the new image in for the old one.

Say that you want your brochure to feature Crazyland Wonderpark's all-new petting zoo, quite possibly the only petting zoo in the world with nothing but squirrels. You already have a bunch of squirrel photos in your iPhoto library that you're itching to add to your brochure, and happily, all the iWork programs make it easy to plop pictures from iPhoto straight into your documents:

1. **Click the icon in the placeholder image's bottom-right corner.**

   Pages opens the Media Browser window, where you can browse your collections of audio, photos, and movies, as shown in Figure 1-6.

The Case of the Clever Cursor

As you use Pages, you'll see the cursor morph into new shapes as it moves around your document—don't let that throw you. For such a tiny thing, your mouse pointer is surprisingly intelligent, changing appearance in response to what it's pointing at.

When there's no document open, the cursor maintains its traditional arrow-pointer shape. But when it's positioned over something you've typed in a word-processing document, the pointer changes into an *I-beam cursor*—so called due to its resemblance to the cross-section of a steel I-beam. (If you're working with a page-layout document, you need to place your cursor inside a text box or a shape by double-clicking it before the I-beam cursor makes an appearance). The cursor is shaped this way so that you can precisely position it between two letters in a line of text. Then, when you click the mouse, the blinking *insertion point* jumps to that spot so you can add or delete text at that specific point.

When you start typing, the cursor *disappears*, leaving only the blinking insertion point, which is simply a vertical bar (|). Pages does this so that the cursor doesn't distract you when you're typing.

If you move the mouse a fraction of an inch, however, the cursor reappears. (This distinction between I-beam cursor and insertion point challenges beginners. Many folks feel compelled to carefully position the I-beam cursor *over* the insertion point before typing—a pointless effort.)

As soon as you move the I-beam cursor beyond a text-editing area in a page-layout document (or put your cursor over a non-text object, such as an image, in a word-processing document), the cursor resumes its arrow shape, ready to manipulate scroll bars, buttons, and menus.

As you get acquainted with Pages, pay attention to your clever cursor: It's giving you constant hints about what you can do at any given moment.

FIGURE 1-5

Media placeholders—which can contain photos, music files, and videos—are easy to identify because they have little icons in their bottom-right corners (circled). To replace a placeholder image, simply drag a new image onto it. When you drop the new picture on top of the placeholder, Pages makes the switch. You can drag pictures onto the placeholder from your desktop or directly from your iPhoto collection, as explained below.

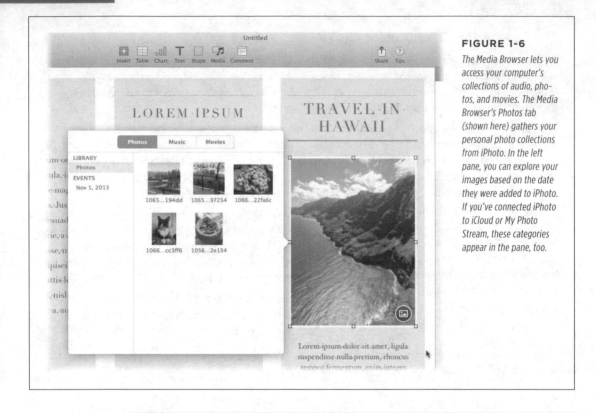

FIGURE 1-6

The Media Browser lets you access your computer's collections of audio, photos, and movies. The Media Browser's Photos tab (shown here) gathers your personal photo collections from iPhoto. In the left pane, you can explore your images based on the date they were added to iPhoto. If you've connected iPhoto to iCloud or My Photo Stream, these categories appear in the pane, too.

NOTE iPhoto is free with every new Mac. If iPhoto didn't come preinstalled on your shiny new Mac, you can download it for free from the App Store (see Appendix A for more about downloading iPhoto and other free apps). If you don't own a new Mac, you can buy iPhoto (as of this writing, it cost $14.99). Learn more about iPhoto at *www.apple.com/mac/iphoto.*

2. **In the Media Browser window, choose your photo.**

   Click the thumbnail preview of the photo you want to use.

3. **The new photo appears in your document.**

   Pages replaces the placeholder image with your photo, automatically resizing it to fit the placeholder's dimensions.

TIP Once you replace a placeholder image with an image of your very own, the media placeholder icon (circled in Figure 1-5) disappears. Not to worry: If you want to replace this photo at any point, Control-click the photo and select Replace Image from the shortcut menu to relaunch the Media Browser window. Choose your new image, and Pages performs its placeholder squeezery again, formatting the new picture to fit the existing layout.

■ COPING WITH SNIPPED IMAGES

When you replace a placeholder image with one of your own, Pages sizes and crops your picture until it's the right size to fit the existing space, hiding parts of the image that don't quite fit, as shown in Figure 1-7.

FIGURE 1-7

Top: Here's a photo of one of the cute critters from Crazyland Wonderpark's petting zoo.

Bottom: When the image was inserted into the brochure, Pages sliced off the right-hand side of the photo to fit the original placeholder's dimensions.

Never fear: The missing bits of the photo aren't gone for good; they're just hidden by a *mask*. You can use masks to crop pictures throughout iWork. Think of a mask as a window with curtains that allow only part of the image to peek through. You can adjust the curtains or resize the picture under the mask to control the exact portion of the picture that's visible.

Time to draw back those curtains! Figure 1-8 shows how Pages' mask-editing features let you temporarily uncover the hidden portions of an image. To edit the mask, double-click the image to reveal the Edit Mask controls, along with two buttons: Edit Mask and Resize. When you're in mask-editing mode, Pages reveals the entire photo, with the hidden parts of the image dimmed and transparent so that you can see what's masked and what's not. To change the mask, click the Edit Mask button and drag the slider.

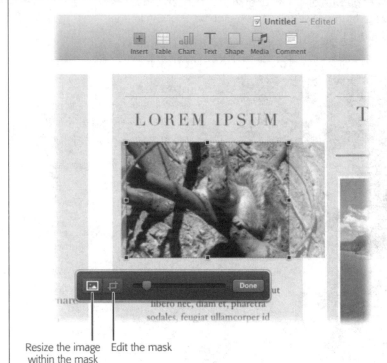

FIGURE 1-8

Editing a mask lets you change which part of the picture you reveal and which parts you keep hidden. Zoom the image in or out by dragging the slider next to the Edit Mask button. You may also want to try resizing the image within the mask by clicking the Resize button and then using the selection handles (which turn black to let you know that you're editing the image and not the mask). When you put your cursor over the image, the cursor turns into a hand, and you can then drag the image to a new position behind the mask.

If you accidentally drag the picture while mucking around with the mask controls, you can undo this change by pressing ⌘-Z or choosing Edit→Undo.

Resize the image   Edit the mask
within the mask

When you're done editing the mask, hit Return, click Done, or click anywhere outside the image, and Pages proudly displays the final result. For complete details about adding, editing, and removing image masks, see page 158.

Saving and Printing

After replacing the dummy text

and placeholder images, it's time to save your document so you can come back and continue working on it later:

1. **Choose File→Save or press ⌘-S.**

   The Save dialog box appears (Figure 1-9).

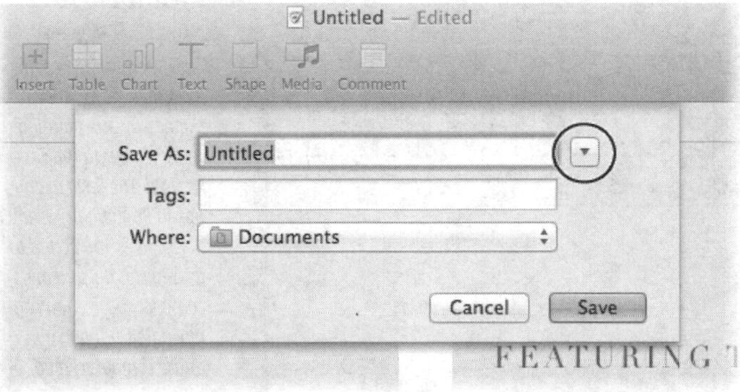

FIGURE 1-9

The compact version of the Save dialog box (shown here) has three fields: Save As, Tags, and Where. Type the name of your document in the Save As field. Tags are an optional extra that can help you find a file in a hurry; see the box on page 15 for more information on tags. Use the Where field to tell Pages where to save your document.

If you want to take a look at the expanded version of the Save dialog box (it's shown in Figure 1-10), click the downward-pointing triangle circled here.

2. **Type a title for the document in the Save As field, and tell Pages where to save your document.**

   The Save As field is already highlighted, so just start typing. Click the Where menu and choose Documents (if it's not already selected) to store this Pages file in your Documents folder. If you're interested in tags, then see the box on page 15 for more info.

TIP   To see more options in the Save dialog box, click the button circled in Figure 1-9 to expand the dialog box as shown in Figure 1-10.

---

3. **Click Save.**

   The Save dialog box vanishes, and Pages stores your document in the location you chose in the Where field. You can now continue to work on your document, periodically choosing File→Save (or, to save yourself some time, ⌘-S) to update the saved file with any changes.

TIP   Save often! Pages automatically saves your document at regular intervals, but you'll want to get into the habit of saving your work every few minutes to make extra sure Pages is committing your most recent changes to memory. To find out more about these automatic backups, check out page 39.

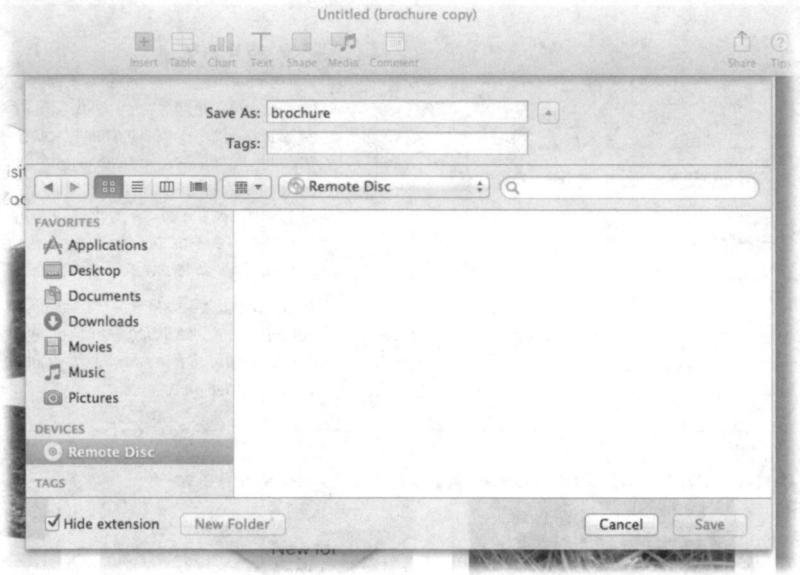

FIGURE 1-10

To take a peek at the expanded version of the Save dialog box, click the downward-pointing triangle next to the Save As field. The Save dialog box in its full glory (shown here) gives you access to locations not listed in its compact cousin. You can navigate through your entire computer—and even other computers on your network—to find the perfect destination for your document.

When you're ready to unleash your marketing prowess on the world, print your document:

1. **Choose File→Print or press ⌘-P.**

   The Print dialog box appears.

2. **Make sure the right printer is selected.**

   If you have more than one printer connected to your computer, check that the correct one is selected in the Printer drop-down menu.

3. **Type the number of copies you need in the Copies box.**

   If you just want one copy, there's no need to make any changes.

4. **Click Print.**

   Your printer starts whirring and chirping and, in short order, delivers the hard copy.

Now that you've finished creating your brochure, you can close its document window by clicking the red Close button in its upper-left corner. If Pages asks whether you want to save your changes, click Save. Your documents vanishes from the screen but remains safely stored away on your hard drive, ready to be reopened if you ever want to revise it or to print more copies.

Tagging Your Files

When you save a document, the Save dialog box gives you the option to add *tags* to it. Tags are useful for organizing and cross-referencing your files. For example, say you have a dedicated Brochures folder on your computer. You can store all your brochure documents there and then add tags to each one to make it clear which brochures are for the summer 2013 season, the autumn 2013 season, spring 2014, and so on.

Tags aren't just part of Pages—you can assign them to any file anywhere on your computer. Open the Finder and take a look at the left-hand sidebar—yup, there's a Tags section. Click any of the tags listed there to see all the files marked with that tag. Imagine you have brochures tagged as Spring 2014, and you have posters, leaflets, and newsletters scattered all across your computer that *also* have the Spring 2014 tag. If you want to see all the marketing goodies you've created for spring 2014, just click this tag in the Finder's sidebar.

Out of the box, your Mac has several tags ready and raring to go—but they're limited to colors (a red tag named Red, an orange tag named Orange, and so on). To use these tags, in Pages, open the Save dialog box by choosing File→Save, click the Tags field, and then select any tags to apply them to your file. However, to really get the most out of tags, you need to create your own (such as the aforementioned Spring 2014).

To create a custom tag, open the Finder and select the file you want to apply a new custom tag to. You'll notice that the toolbar at the top of the Finder contains a row of icons, which includes an Edit Tags button (if you're not sure which button this is, put your cursor over each button to see a tooltip with the button's name). Click the Edit Tags button, type out the text of your new tag, and then either press Return or click "Create new tag." After that, assigning your new tag works in exactly the same way as the predefined tags: To apply it to a Pages document, open the program's Save dialog box, click the Tags field, and then choose your custom tag.

Adding Pages

After you've finished updating your brochure with your own text and photos, you're ready to add more pages.

If you're working with a *word-processing document* (a document that's all about the text—such as the Note Taking, Blank, or Essay template) then when you hit the bottom of a page, Pages adds a new page automatically. But if you're working with a *page-layout document* (a template that includes funkier objects, like placeholder images, tables, charts, or shapes), then you have to create new pages yourself.

TIP Unsure whether you're dealing with a word-processing document or a page-layout document? A surefire way to check is to click a blank area of your document. If the cursor turns into the I-beam cursor, ready for you to start typing, then you have a word-processing document on your hands. If nothing happens, then it's a page-layout document. Another way to check is to click the Insert button in the toolbar: If you see a Page option, you're working with a page-layout document. If the Page option is missing, you're working with a word-processing document.

Adding a new page to a page-layout document is easy: Choose Insert→Page or click the Insert button in the toolbar and then click Page. To add a new page to a word-processing document, either continue typing until you reach the bottom of the page (at which point, the program automatically creates a new page) or click Insert in the toolbar and choose Page Break (page breaks are covered in more detail on page 60).

And so it goes: Keep adding pages and filling them with your own text, photos of squirrels, and snaps from your forthcoming exhibit: The World's Greatest Round-abouts and Where to Find Them.

In the Buff: The Blank Template

Templates are particularly useful for getting off to a flying start with complex layouts. But let's face it: Not all documents require a fancy, elegant design. If you're dashing off a quick shopping list, organizing your thoughts, crafting a short story, or building a page layout from scratch, the best starting point is often a blank page.

Pages offers two blank templates for your word-processing delight—Blank and Blank Landscape—which you can find in the Template Chooser's aptly named Basic category. Unlike all the program's other templates, you won't find any placeholder text or images in these two templates. Simply double-click whichever blank template suits your fancy, and Pages creates an empty document for you.

As you settle into a routine with Pages, the Blank template may become your go-to template, the fastest route to getting something down on paper. If you do fall into the habit of choosing Blank every time—or any other template, for that matter—there's really no reason to go through the middle man Template Chooser every time you want to start a new document. Sure, it's only trying to help, but couldn't Pages just cut to the chase and automatically use your favorite template when you want a new document? Yep, you just have to ask nicely.

Setting Your Default Template

You can relieve the Template Chooser of its duties and nominate a default template at the same time. After that, whenever you go to File→New, Pages creates a new document based on your preferred template. Here's how to set this up:

1. **Choose Pages→Preferences, and Pages displays the Preferences window.**

2. **Click the General button (if it's not already selected).**

3. **Next to the For New Documents heading, turn on the "Use template" option.**

4. **Click the Change Template button to display the Template Chooser, and then select your preferred template.**

   Double-click a template's preview image, or click it once and then click the Choose button. Either way, the For New Documents setting updates to show the name of your new go-to template: "Use template: [Template name]."

5. Close the Preferences window by clicking the red Close button.

If you have a change of heart and want the Template Chooser back in your life, go to Pages→Preferences→General, and change the For New Documents setting back to Show Template Chooser.

■ Opening an Existing Document

After this flurry of creating and saving documents, you now have a tidy collection of Pages files on your hard drive. When you're ready to get at 'em again, use any of these techniques to open a saved file:

- In the Finder, double-click a Pages document.

TIP　If the Pages icon is visible in your Mac's Dock (that's the bar that runs along the very bottom of your screen), then you can also drag a Pages document from the Finder or your desktop onto this icon to open it.

- In Pages, choose File→Open, or press ⌘-O. Pages displays the Open dialog box (Figure 1-11), which is your doorway to browsing all the Pages (and Pages-compatible) files on your hard drive and choosing which one you want to open.

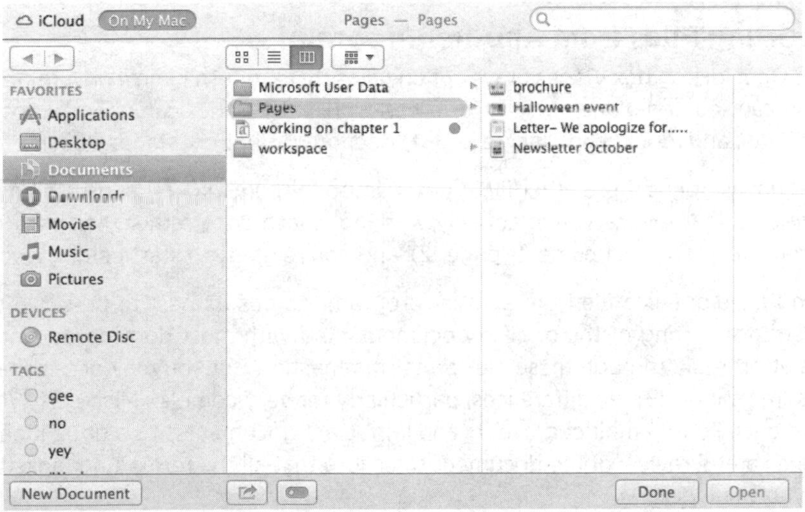

FIGURE 1-11

The Open dialog box lets you browse your computer, iCloud, or any other computer on your network to find your file. If you've forgotten exactly where you stashed the file you're hankering after, use the search box at the top right to hunt down your file. Select the file that you want to open, and then click the Open button.

- If you're looking for the document you were working on 10 minutes ago, you can find it in Pages' File→Open Recent submenu (Figure 1-12), which gives you fast access to the last 10 files you've dabbled with.

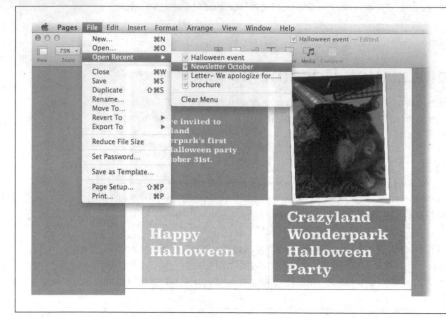

FIGURE 1-12

The Open Recent submenu contains a list of your most recently used Pages documents. Select the document you want, and Pages opens it for you in a new window. If other people are using your computer and you prefer them to not see that you've been editing a file named "Plans for Super Secret New Attraction," then choose File→Open Recent→Clear Menu to make Pages forget your editing history.

Importing Files from Another Program

In the Open dialog box, Pages grays out any files that it doesn't know how to open, so you can see at a glance which files it can work with. Pages can open Microsoft Word (.doc and .docx) and plain text (.txt) documents, not just Pages documents.

When Pages opens these other file types, it imports them into a brand-new Pages document. That means you're actually working with a *copy* rather than with the original file. Save the document (page 12), and you're ready to start editing away.

When Pages opens a file from another program, it does its best to preserve the text and formatting of the original document. And with most documents, Pages spins effortlessly through these file-format gymnastics. But you may occasionally find some minor display differences, particularly for very complex Microsoft Word documents. So for ambitious layouts and important documents, it's a good idea to make a careful review of the document to ensure that all the formatting looks the way you want.

■ THE DOCUMENT WARNINGS WINDOW

Pages doesn't stay quiet if it can't cope with parts of an imported document. When it suspects some elements might not have made the transfer intact, it lets you know. Specifically, the Document Warnings window, shown in Figure 1-13, tells you what's wrong with your imported document.

FIGURE 1-13

The Document Warnings window details any problems that occur when you import a document from another program. Here, for example, Pages is letting you know that it deleted some elements that it didn't understand, so you should check the imported document extra carefully to make sure nothing vital is missing.

Reports

Insert Table Chart Text Shape Media Comment   Share Tips

Some changes were made to your document.

Form components aren't supported and were removed.

Cancel   OK

■ Controlling the Document Window

Even though you've already tried your hand at creating your own documents in this chapter, you might have noticed that you've barely touched Pages' menus and toolbar buttons. As you've seen, the nuts-and-bolts editing of text and images takes place directly in the document window's main work area with lots of typing and a bit of light mousework.

Over the next few chapters, as you get acquainted with Pages' more advanced formatting and layout tools, you'll get more hands-on with other parts of the program. Mastering the different buttons and menus is the next step to creating and editing show-stopping documents. Fortunately, Apple has gone easy on you. Rather than cramming every possible tool and button into Pages' document window, it's gone for a less-is-more approach.

In fact, when you opened your first Pages document, you may have thought, "Where is everything?" Don't panic—it's all there. Despite its minimalist design, Pages offers easy access to the tools and features you're most likely to need by placing them in the toolbar and the Format panel, while keeping the ones you need less often hidden beneath the surface. See Figure 1-14 for a quick tour around the more interesting parts of your document-window cockpit.

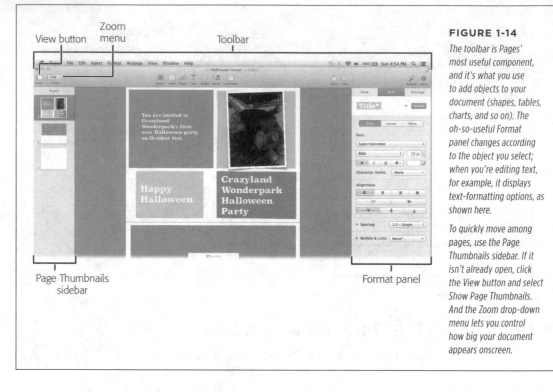

View button · Zoom menu · Toolbar

Page Thumbnails sidebar · Format panel

FIGURE 1-14

The toolbar is Pages' most useful component, and it's what you use to add objects to your document (shapes, tables, charts, and so on). The oh-so-useful Format panel changes according to the object you select; when you're editing text, for example, it displays text-formatting options, as shown here.

To quickly move among pages, use the Page Thumbnails sidebar. If it isn't already open, click the View button and select Show Page Thumbnails. And the Zoom drop-down menu lets you control how big your document appears onscreen.

Using the Toolbar

The toolbar runs along the top of the document window, complete with a set of colorful buttons for one-click access to common features, saving mileage on your mouse and strain on your memory. You'll learn more about each of these buttons in the coming chapters, but here's the condensed version:

- **View.** The first button opens a drop-down menu that lets you show and hide parts of the document window. You can use it to display the Page Thumbnails sidebar, open the Find & Replace dialog box (page 27), show or hide the ruler (see page 53), and make Pages display your current word count to help you keep track of how much (or little!) you've typed.

- **Zoom.** Click this button to make the onscreen size of your document bigger or smaller (see page 24).

- **Insert.** This drop-down menu lets you add non-object goodies to your document, such as new pages, page numbers, a page count, and column breaks (see page 119).

- **Table.** This button inserts a table into your document (see page 205).

- **Chart.** Click this button to insert a variety of 2D, 3D, and interactive charts (see page 233).

- **Text.** This button inserts a text box into your document (see page 148).

- **Shape.** The Shapes drop-down menu lets you add lines, arrows, and geometric shapes to your document (see page 168).

- **Media.** Insert images, audio clips, and video clips by clicking this button (see page 156).

- **Comment.** This button adds a note to your text, letting you annotate your document, which is handy for collaboration and tag-team editing (see page 103).

- **Share.** If you're in the mood to share, click this button to access a ton of options. Want to share this document via email? How about Twitter, Facebook, or AirDrop? Your sharing options are discussed on page 256. You can even share your document via iCloud; page 256 has the skinny on the exciting new world of iCloud.

- **Tips.** This button is your ticket to handy hints about Pages. When you click this button, Pages draws your attention to important menus and buttons by plastering sticky notes all over your screen. If you see an arrow inside a sticky note, click it to see additional info about whatever's mentioned in the sticky note. To hide the sticky notes, simply click this button again.

- **Format.** Click this button to hide or reveal the Format panel, which is covered in more detail on page 23.

- **Setup.** Click this button to open the Document and Section tabs (see page 105).

■ CUSTOMIZING THE TOOLBAR

If you find the toolbar too distracting, you can banish it by choosing View→Hide Toolbar; by pressing Option-⌘-T, or by Control-clicking the toolbar, and then selecting Hide Toolbar. Hiding the toolbar also lets you see more of your document without needing to scroll.

Chances are, though, you'll want to keep the toolbar around while you're working on most documents. If you want to coax the toolbar back into your life, either repeat the keyboard shortcut listed above, select View→Show Toolbar, or Control-click the gray band that runs along the top of Pages' document window and then select Hide Toolbar.

The toolbar is pretty slimmed down compared with what it looked like in Pages '09, but you can still fully customize this sleek little bar. To add and remove icons from the toolbar, either Control-click the toolbar and choose Customize Toolbar or choose View→Customize Toolbar. Either way, Pages opens the Customize Toolbar window shown in Figure 1-15 and puts faint boxes around the parts of the toolbar that you can drag and drop additional icons onto.

To remove an icon from the toolbar, grab the icon and drag it down, off the toolbar; when you release it, the icon vanishes in a puff of smoke. To add icons to the toolbar, grab any icon from the Customize Toolbar window, and then drop it onto one of the empty boxes on the toolbar. Once the toolbar is full, Pages adds scrolling arrows to the toolbar, so you can continue to pack in icons. Once you're happy with the toolbar, click Done.

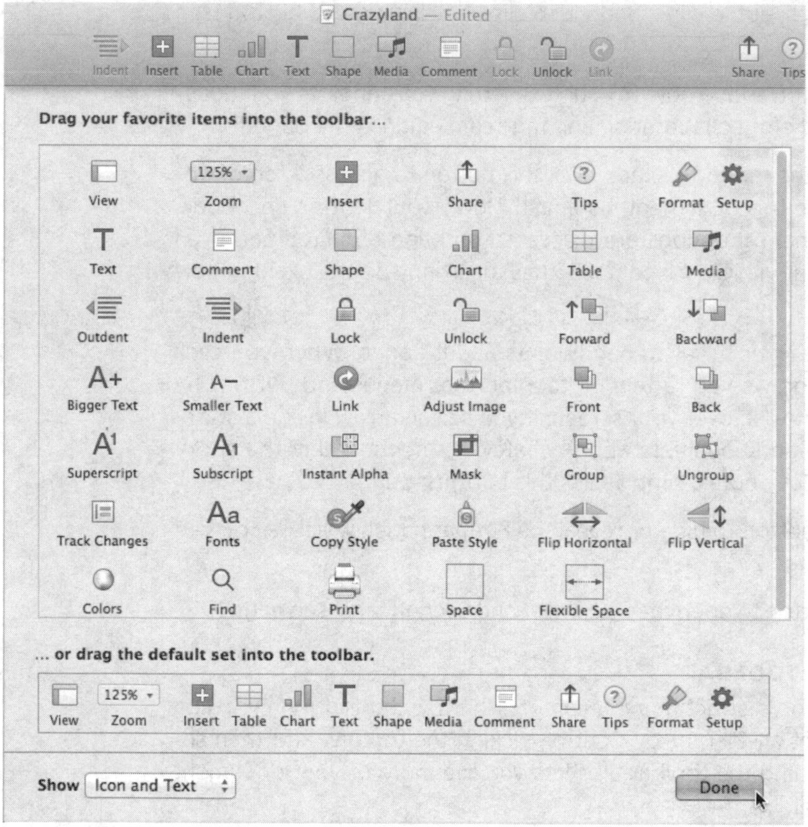

FIGURE 1-15

You can add more icons to the toolbar by opening the Customize Toolbar window and dragging icons from this window onto the toolbar. If the toolbar is beginning to look a bit unruly, you can restore it to its original state by dragging the "default icon set" (the boxed set of icons near the bottom of the window) onto the toolbar. When you're finished, click Done.

You can also remove the labels from underneath the toolbar's icons. Doing so makes the toolbar even sleeker, if you're a fan of that less-is-more look. To hide the labels, Control-click the toolbar, and then select Icon Only from the drop-down menu shown in Figure 1-16. If you're racking your brain to remember what an icon means, you can get the labels back by Control-clicking the toolbar and then selecting "Icon and Text." You can also change these labels by opening the Customize Toolbar window and choosing Icon Only from the drop-down menu in the window's bottom-left corner.

FIGURE 1-16

You can hide the labels that appear underneath each icon in the toolbar (in this screenshot, the labels are visible). To hide these labels, Control-click the toolbar, and then choose Icon Only. To display them again, choose "Icon and Text" instead. You can access further toolbar-customizing options by clicking Customize Toolbar.

Shape Shifter: The Format Panel

The Format panel is one of the most important and useful tools Pages has to offer; an ever-changing shape shifter that always has just the right options you need to edit the currently selected object. For example, if you select an image, the Format panel contains options for adjusting the image's exposure, swapping in a new image, and adding a drop shadow. No matter what part of the document you're editing, the Format panel keeps up with you, dispatching tools that are no longer relevant to make room for options you're more likely to use.

> **NOTE** Technically, Apple calls the Format panel the "Format inspector." But since it looks like a panel, this book calls it the Format panel. Just don't be confused if you read a tutorial from Apple that mentions the Format inspector—it's referring to the Format panel.

Since it contains only relevant buttons, sliders, and checkboxes, the Format panel is uncluttered and easy to navigate, with nothing hidden away in strange nooks and crannies. Figure 1-17 shows the Format panel in action.

Depending on the object you select, the Format panel may be split into two or more tabs. In Figure 1-17, for instance, the Format panel is displaying the Style, Text, and Arrange tabs. To move among the different tabs, simply click the tab you're interested in. The Arrange tab is a permanent fixture when you're dealing with objects, as it contains controls for resizing, repositioning, and rotating objects. You may also see additional tabs, such as Shape and Text, when you select a shape.

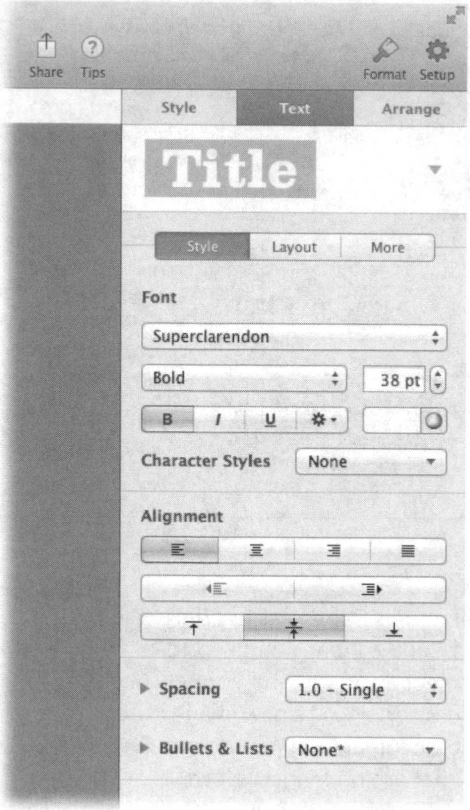

FIGURE 1-17

The Format panel lets you fine-tune the appearance of whatever object is currently selected. For example, if you're typing inside a text box, the Format panel shows options for formatting text, such as changing the font; adding a bold, italic, or underlined effect; changing the font size; and so on.

If the panel's slim silhouette requires more space than you care to give up, you can send it packin' by clicking the Format button in the toolbar. Had a change of heart? Bring it back by clicking the Format button once again.

Changing Your Page View

Pages always displays your document just the way it will look on the printed page, complete with margins, page breaks, and the like. When Pages opens a document, it sets the zoom level to 125% magnification, a comfortable, medium-sized view that's about the size of your printed document.

To shrink or magnify how your document appears on your screen, click the Zoom button in the toolbar, and then select the percentage you want to use. Or, if you're in a hurry, you can use keyboard shortcuts to change the zoom level:

- Enlarge the page to the next zoom level: ⌘-> (that's the ⌘ key, the Shift key, and the > key)

- Zoom out: ⌘-< (that's the ⌘ key, the Shift key, and the < key)

- Zoom to actual size (100%): ⌘-0 (that's the number zero, not the letter O). See the box below for more about this option.

These options are also available from the View→Zoom submenu.

Zooming in and out doesn't affect the *actual* size of your document, only the way that Pages *previews* it for you onscreen. Think of zooming as holding up a sheet of paper for a close look or pushing it away—it doesn't change the size of the document, just how much detail you see.

UP TO SPEED

Why Isn't "Actual Size" the Actual Size?

When you choose 100% in the Zoom drop-down menu, your document shrinks to a mighty small size—certainly smaller than how it looks printed out. In the View→Zoom menu, Pages even lists this 100 percent size as "Actual Size," which clearly isn't the case. What gives?

Welcome to the exciting world of screen resolution, where nothing is quite what it seems. In days of yore, all Mac monitors displayed at a resolution of 72 *dots* (or pixels) *per inch*

(dpi). So, if a document displayed onscreen at 100 percent, you could actually take a ruler out of your pencil case, measure the document ruler displayed on the screen, and the two would match perfectly. Apple used to make a big deal about this—but nowadays the resolution of most LCD displays is over 200 dpi. The result is that everything appears at a reduced size onscreen, which is why Pages overcompensates by opening documents at 125 percent zoom.

At the bottom of the Zoom drop-down menu (and in the View→Zoom submenu), you'll find two automatic zoom settings that you can use as alternatives to the percentage settings. *Fit Width* adjusts the zoom level so the page fills the full width of the document window—no matter how narrow or wide (don't you wish that your pants had this setting at Thanksgiving?). *Fit Page*, on the other hand, adjusts the zoom level so that an entire page fits into your window. Select either of these settings, and Pages automatically changes the zoom level as you adjust the size of the document window by dragging any edge or switching to Full Screen view (page 28).

Navigating Your Document

Scooting around a one-page brochure isn't too much of a challenge, but finding your way around a 200-page manifesto is much tougher. Pages provides a number of tools that help keep you oriented, and let you move quickly through even the chubbiest of documents. To bring earlier parts of your document into view (known as *scrolling up*), press the up arrow key on your keyboard. To bring later parts of your document into view (*scrolling down*), use the down arrow key. When you're scrolling, a scroll bar briefly appears along the left-hand side of the Format panel to give you some idea of your position within your document.

TIP If you're using Pages on a laptop, you can also scroll using gestures. Place two fingers on your Mac's touchpad and drag up and down to move around your document. For more on Mac gestures, see *http://support. apple.com/kb/ht4721*.

But why bother with all this mousing around when Pages has kindly provided you with all sorts of keyboard shortcuts? Table 1-1 reveals all.

TABLE 1-1 *Pages keyboard shortcuts*

PRESS THIS...	...TO DO THIS.
← or →	Move insertion point one character to the left or right.
↑ or ↓	Move insertion point to the line above or below.
Option-←	Move insertion point to the beginning of the current word; if the insertion point is already at the beginning of a word, then it jumps to the beginning of the *previous* word.
Option-→	Move insertion point to the end of the current word; if the insertion point is already at the beginning of a word, then it jumps to the beginning of the *next* word.
⌘-← or →	Move insertion point to the beginning or end of the current line.
⌘-↑ or ↓	In a word-processing document, move insertion point to the beginning or end of the document. In a page-layout document, this shortcut moves the insertion point to the beginning or end of the text in the selected object (such as a shape or text box).
Option-↑ or ↓	Move insertion point to the beginning or end of the current paragraph.

■ PAGE THUMBNAILS SIDEBAR

Think of the *Page Thumbnails sidebar* as a visual table of contents for your document. This sidebar is turned off when you open a document, but you can toggle it on and off using the View button in the toolbar or by selecting View→Show/Hide Page Thumbnails. If you're in a hurry, you can press Option-⌘-P to show/hide the Page Thumbnails sidebar. Whichever method you use, the sidebar opens along the left side of the document window (Figure 1-18).

The sidebar shows numbered thumbnail images of each page within your document; use the up and down arrow keys on your keyboard to move through the pages in your document. The Thumbnails sidebar makes it easy to find the exact page you're looking for—especially if your document features big, colorful pictures or distinctive page layouts. You can recognize the page you're after at a glance, since the thumbnails are images of the pages themselves—including headlines, columns of text, pictures, and so on.

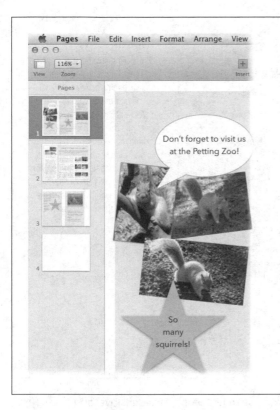

FIGURE 1-18

The Pages Thumbnail sidebar contains miniature previews of all the pages in your document. Click any thumbnail image to jump to the corresponding page, or use the up and down arrow keys to move between pages. Pages' highlights the selected thumbnail with a yellow border.

You can adjust the width of the Page Thumbnails sidebar by putting your cursor over the line where the sidebar meets the main editing area. When the cursor turns into a double-headed arrow, drag left or right to resize the sidebar. The thumbnails grow as you make the sidebar wider, so this is a handy way to get a closer look at those page previews.

To jump to a specific page, click its thumbnail in the sidebar. The page then appears in the main viewing area, ready for editing. In the sidebar, Pages highlights the current page, so you can see your exact position within the document. As you'll learn later, you can also use these thumbnails to delete pages—or even entire sections—of your document (see page 115).

■ THE FIND & REPLACE DIALOG BOX

The *Find & Replace dialog box* trawls through every last word in your document and pinpoints specific words you tell it to look for. To open this handy feature, click the View button and select Show Find & Replace; go to Edit→Find→Find; or simply press ⌘-F (that's F for "find"). Whatever method you use, the Find & Replace dialog box appears smack-bang in the middle of your screen. Happily, you can drag it to a more convenient location so you can keep it open and continue editing your document. Type a word or a phrase into the dialog box's text field, and as you type, the field displays a grayed-out tally of how many matching words it has zeroed in on, as shown in Figure 1-19.

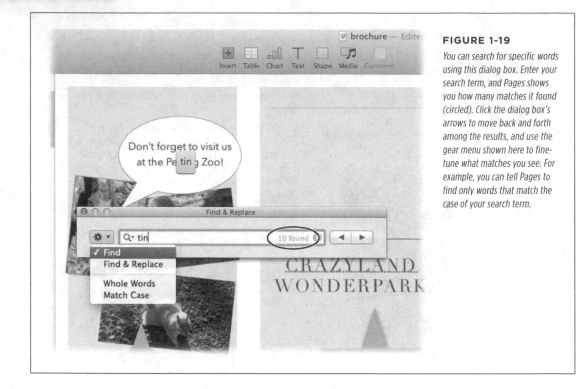

FIGURE 1-19

You can search for specific words using this dialog box. Enter your search term, and Pages shows you how many matches it found (circled). Click the dialog box's arrows to move back and forth among the results, and use the gear menu shown here to fine-tune what matches you see. For example, you can tell Pages to find only words that match the case of your search term.

When you first open this dialog box, its searches aren't case-sensitive, and it also finds matches in the middle of words. So if you type *tin*, for example, it will find matches in the words "Tiny" and "petting." To make the dialog box pickier, click the gear icon on its left side, and then click Whole Words (to strip out results from the middle of words) or Match Case (to see results only if they have the same capitalization as what you typed). You can tell which search settings the dialog box is using because Pages puts a checkmark next to each option in the gear menu. If you change your mind, you can turn any option off by clicking the gear icon again and reselecting whatever option is giving you grief.

Once you're happy with your settings, you can scroll through the matches by clicking the dialog box's arrow buttons.

NOTE This section just scratched the surface of what the Find & Replace dialog box has to offer. Page 85 takes a closer look at this handy feature.

Editing in Full-Screen View

The marvelous curse of your Mac is that it plays so many roles. Your word-processing machine is also an engine for entertainment, communication, news, and—if you're not disciplined—rampant procrastination. When you're trying to buckle down and actually do some work, your Mac's many tools and toys can be distracting. Pages' *full-screen view* helps you remain focused by making your document the one and only thing on your screen, hushing the siren calls of Facebook, Twitter, and all the other goodies vying for your attention.

Choose View→Enter Full Screen, click the double-arrow icon in the upper-right corner of the Pages window, or press Control-⌘-F, and Pages banishes everything except your current document. Even the menu bar disappears, leaving you with only the bare bones you need to really concentrate on creating the perfect document (Figure 1-20).

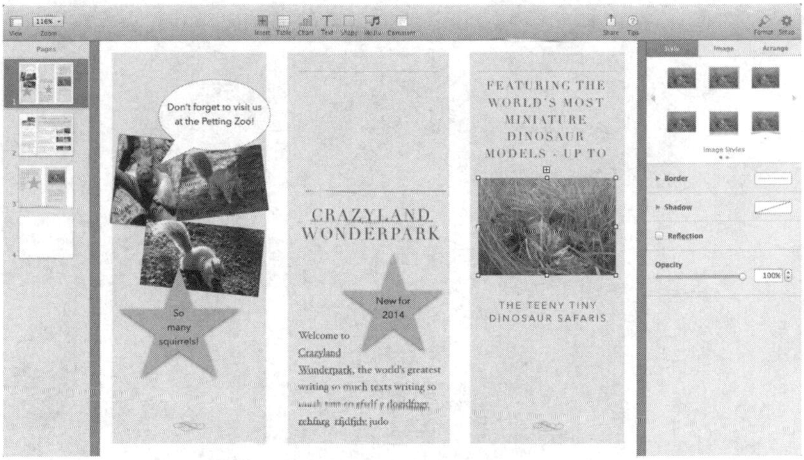

FIGURE 1-20

Pages' full-screen mode lets you focus exclusively on your document. This mode is also handy for reviewing documents in meetings, as it makes your document big enough for several people to see while huddled around your Mac.

If this stripped-down look makes you feel a bit naked, don't get nervous. The menus at the top of your screen haven't gone far; they're waiting quietly behind the scenes, and you can get them back at any time by moving the pointer to the top of the screen.

Even in full-screen view, you can adjust the zoom as usual (page 24). With all this screen space devoted only to your Pages document, you may want to choose a more magnified view.

When you're done with full-screen view and want to return to the regular window view, press Esc. Or move your pointer to the top of the screen to temporarily uncover the menu bar, and then choose View→Exit Full Screen or click the double-arrow icon at the right end of the menu bar.

With this newfound ability for extraordinary focus, you're ready to start cranking out words. The next chapter gives you a leg up by exploring everything you need to know about adding, editing, and formatting text.

Editing Text in Pages

With Pages' flashy arsenal of design features, it's tempting to take the program's mild-mannered writing tools for granted. The graphic-design flourishes certainly set Pages apart from other word-processing programs, but the gang at Apple hasn't forgotten that, in the end, it's words that tell the story. Beneath the program's stylish veneer beats the heart of a full-featured word processor that can polish your prose to a squeaky-clean shine. Along the way, you can shape every aspect of your text's visual presentation, from the sublime (subtle typography tweaks) to the ridiculous (smiley faces as bullet points? Why not!). This chapter covers everything you need to know about editing and formatting your text.

■ Word-Processor Text vs. Text Boxes

As you learned in the previous chapter (on page 15), Pages presents your text in one of two forms. In word-processing documents, the main text flows through your document in one continuous outpouring of words. In page-layout documents, on the other hand, text shows up in independent *text boxes* that you can slide around your page, freestyle.

> **NOTE** In Chapter 7, you'll learn that word-processing documents can contain both a main body of text *and* text boxes, in the form of callouts and sidebars (see page 154). For now, though, it's simpler to think of your text as either a main body of free-flowing text or a text box.

The important thing to remember is that whether your words are a big chunk of text in a word-processing document or isolated in a text box, text is text, and Pages offers the same editing and formatting options no matter what form your text is in. A text box is mobile, and word-processor text isn't; other than that, editing text inside those elements works exactly the same way.

Once you've mastered text editing in Pages, you've got it nailed in Keynote and Numbers, too. Both programs include text boxes, just like Pages. Although Pages gives you a few more text-formatting options than its iWork cousins, the essentials remain the same across all three programs, right down to the interface buttons and tools that you use to format your text.

■ Basic Text Editing in iWork

Pages, Keynote, and Numbers all follow the Mac's basic conventions for adding, editing, selecting, and moving text. If you're familiar with other Mac software, you'll feel right at home here. But even if you're a longtime Mac user, you might not be aware of all the handy shortcuts that can make this writing thing easier. Here's the skinny.

Inserting Text

Inserting text or spaces in a document is the most basic editing task of all. To do so, move the I-beam cursor (page 9) to wherever you want to insert text, click once, and then start typing.

NOTE If you're dealing with a text box, click the box once to select it, and then *double*-click to place your cursor inside the box, ready to start churning out those words. When you're done, click anywhere outside the box to deselect it. See page 148 for all the secrets of selecting and editing text boxes.

Deleting Text

More word-processing basics: If you make a typo, press Delete to backspace and remove the offending characters. If you have to jump back a few words to make your correction, *hold down* the Delete key and watch the letters disappear until you snip out that mistake and then retype.

TIP Delete whole words at a time by holding down the Option key while you delete. Option-Delete zaps the word to the left of the insertion point.

If you use a desktop computer with a full keyboard, you can *forward delete*, too, which removes the text to the *right* of the insertion point. To forward delete, press the forward-delete key (⌦). Mac laptops and Mac keyboards without a number pad don't have this key, but you can get the same effect by pressing Function-Delete (the Function key is labeled "fn"). You can forward delete whole words by pressing Function-Option-Delete.

Word-Processor Masterclass

Even though most computer owners haven't touched a type-writer in years—if ever—many bad habits persist from that earlier technology. Here are a few bad habits that you may not even be aware have their roots in the type-writing era:

- Underlining: Pages makes it simple to underline text, but it's a bad idea to underline for emphasis. For one thing, if people are reading your document on a computer screen, they may think that underlined words are hyperlinks to web pages. Use **bold** or *italic* instead—they're much more 21st century, and just as easy to apply. (Seriously, when's the last time you saw something underlined in a book or a magazine?)

- Spacing with the space bar: Use the space bar to add a space between words *only*. Never use the space bar to align your text. Why? Because spacing can appear differently on the printed page than it does onscreen, so

that beautifully spaced poster you spent hours creating could look like a complete mess as soon as it passes through your printer. Instead, use Pages' tab feature (page 52) or use tables (see Chapter 8).

- Leaving out special characters and accents: Special characters and accents are easy to produce correctly on a computer. So don't write *resume* if you mean *résumé*. Are you making copies or using the Xerox™? Don't put it off until mañana—take that vacation to Curaçao today! Page 64 shows you how to insert symbols, accents, and other special characters.

- Using the wrong dash character: Using two hyphens (--) to represent a dash is old school. What you want is an *em dash* (—), so called because it's the width of an uppercase M. Create one with the Shift-Option-hyphen key combination.

If you realize that you made an error way back in the distant mists of time (page 1, say), you don't need to delete half your document for the sake of one misspelling. Step away from the Delete key! Instead, use the mouse to zero in on the slip-up in one of two ways:

- **Click and then press Delete.** Position the I-beam cursor to the immediate right of the error, click once, and then press Delete until those offending letters are no more. Type your correction, move the I-beam cursor back to where you left off, and resume typing.

- **Select text and then retype.** If the error you want to delete is more than a few letters long, use the select-then-retype method instead. Start by dragging carefully from the beginning to the end (or from the end to the beginning) of the offending text. Sometimes this method means dragging perfectly horizontally, carefully staying on the same line; other times it means dragging diagonally from the beginning of a passage to the end. Either way, Pages highlights the text you've selected so you can make sure you've got everything you want. After you release the mouse, hit Delete to vaporize all of the highlighted text. Or, you can just type your replacement text—anything you type instantly replaces the highlighted text, so you don't need to press the Delete key.

NOTE Apparently iWork's designers think there are people out there who want to do *everything* with the mouse. To honor the mouse-obsessed, they've included the Edit→Delete command. It does exactly the same thing to highlighted text as the Delete key but, y'know, with more effort.

Making a Selection

To edit text, follow a two-step process: First *select* the text, and then retype (or use menu commands) to *change* it. You can select as little as a single character or as much as an entire document:

- **Select a word or a passage.** Position your I-beam cursor at one end of your intended selection, drag to the other end, and then release the mouse button. Pages selects everything between those two points and highlights the text so you can tell it's selected.

- **Select an individual letter.** Drag across the letter, and Pages highlights it to show that it's selected.

You can *deselect* highlighted text by clicking once, either inside or outside the highlighted text. Or, if you're determined to do things in the most roundabout way possible, choose Edit→Deselect All.

■ MASS SELECTION TECHNIQUES

While selecting text with a drag of the mouse works just fine, your Mac has several tricks for speeding things up:

- **Select one word.** Double-click any part of the word.

- **Select several consecutive words.** Double-click anywhere in the first word; on the second click, keep the mouse button pressed, and then drag to select additional words. As you drag, Pages selects the text in whole-word chunks, so you can be faster (and sloppier) in your selection effort.

- **Select a whole paragraph.** *Triple*-click anywhere in the paragraph. To select multiple paragraphs, triple-click the first one and then, on the third click, drag to select your text paragraph by paragraph.

- **Select a block of text.** Click to place the insertion point at one end of the block. Then, while pressing the Shift key, click the far end of the block you want to select. This works even if the far end is many pages away.

- **Select the entire document.** In a word-processing document, choose Edit→ Select All, or press ⌘-A. (In a page-layout document, this command selects all the text within the current text box or shape.) Use this technique when you want to make a global change, such as changing the font or the margin settings. (Before you do this, though, check out Chapter 3 to see how styles can help you make global changes in a more savvy fashion.)

■ KEYBOARD SELECTION TECHNIQUES

Why interrupt your typing flow to use the mouse at all? Black belts in keyboard kung fu know every keyboard-based shortcut and rarely resort to something as uncool as the mouse (or trackpad). It's actually possible to create basic Pages documents without lifting a finger from the keyboard!

Even if you don't want to abandon the mouse completely, learning keyboard shortcuts for common tasks saves time and keeps your mind focused on the actual typing. Pages has a bunch of shortcuts that can help you select text; the most common are shown in Table 2-1.

TABLE 2-1 *Mac text-selection shortcuts*

TO SELECT THIS...	...USE THIS SHORTCUT.
Character before/after insertion point*	Shift-right arrow or -left arrow
Word before/after insertion point	Shift-Option-right arrow or -left arrow
From insertion point to next/previous line	Shift-up arrow or -down arrow
From insertion point to beginning/end of line	Shift-⌘-right arrow or -left arrow
From insertion point to beginning/end of paragraph	Shift-Option-up arrow or -down arrow
All the text in a word-processing document, or—in a page-layout document—all the text in the selected object.	⌘-A

* Quick reminder: The insertion point is the spot in your document where you see a blinking | character; in other words, it's the spot where the next thing you type will appear.

No matter how you go about selecting text, the next action you perform applies to all the selected text, whether you change the text's formatting or delete it.

> **TIP** Remember, if you have some text selected, then anything you type *replaces* the selected text. This phenomenon can be helpful when, for example, you want to replace a sentence. On the other hand, it can get you into trouble. If you've selected your entire document, for example, typing a single letter (or even pressing the space bar) replaces all your carefully crafted text. Don't panic, though: The Edit→Undo command is standing by to save the day (page 37 has details).

Cutting, Copying, and Pasting

Back in the BC era (that's Before Computers), moving text around your paper document was a bona fide arts-and-crafts project: Cutting and pasting involved real scissors and real paste. Now, thanks to the Cut, Copy, and Paste commands, you're free to move text around as much as you like without ever getting your fingers sticky.

You'll find these three commands in the Edit menu, but do yourself a favor and memorize their keyboard shortcuts. You'll repeat the Cut, Copy, and Paste routine so many times that your mouse would rack up some serious frequent-flier miles. So save yourself some time and get into the habit of using the keyboard commands:

- **Key combination ⌘-X** *cuts*, or removes the selected text. Your computer whisks the deleted material onto its invisible *Clipboard* (see the box below), ready to be redeposited when you use the Paste command. (To help remember this shortcut, think of the X as a tiny pair of scissors that's ready to cut some text.)

- **Key combination ⌘-C** *copies* the selected text—leaving the original text untouched, but cloning an exact copy onto the invisible Clipboard. (Think "C as in *copy*.")

- **Key combination ⌘-V** *pastes* the cut or copied text back into your document wherever your blinking insertion point is. (Think V as in, "Voilà, there it is!"). If you select any text before running this command, Pages pastes the cut or copied text *over* the selected text, replacing it.

NOTE In case you hadn't noticed, the X, C, and V keys form a neat row on your keyboard, making these shortcuts even easier to use (and remember).

When you copy text from one part of an iWork document and paste it into another, the text stubbornly hangs onto its original formatting—sometimes with unhappy results. For example, if you copy a few words out of an *italicized caption* and paste them into a **large, bold headline**, the result is a headline with a few small italic words. Yuck. To scoot around this problem, all three iWork programs offer a style-conscious pasting option: Choose Edit→"Paste and Match Style" (or press Shift-Option-⌘-V), and the pasted words assume the style of the paragraph where they land. In the example just mentioned, the small italic words automatically take on the big, bold headline style when pasted into the headline. Much nicer.

UP TO SPEED

Clipboard Crash Course

The Cut, Copy, and Paste commands rely on an invisible temporary storage locker called the Clipboard.

The Clipboard is a single-minded assistant: It can hold only one thing at a time. Hand it something else, and it immediately drops whatever it was holding, forgetting that thing for good. The Clipboard then clutches this new item, ready for your command to paste—until you give it a new item or shut down your computer.

Put another way, whenever you cut or copy something, you obliterate whatever was already on the Clipboard. On the other hand, you can paste whatever is currently on the Clipboard an infinite number of times without wearing it out.

Because the Clipboard is part of the Mac operating system and not an iWork-specific feature, it's your gateway to transferring information between programs. Say that you're designing a new poster for Crazyland Wonderpark, and you need some customer quotes to jazz it up. The customer who wrote a negative online review actually paid a repeat visit, and then sent you an email admitting "it wasn't as bad as the first time, really." (It's not every day you get praise like that!) You can copy this glowing endorsement from the email and then switch to the Pages document and press ⌘-V (or choose Edit→Paste) to paste it into your poster.

Using Drag-and-Drop Editing

Drag-and-drop is a one-step alternative to the cut-and-paste two-step:

1. **Select the section of text you want to move.**

   You can use any of the methods discussed on page 34.

2. **Position your pointer over the chunk of highlighted text, and then drag that selection to its new location within the document.**

   Release your mouse to drop the text in its new home.

3. **The text you dragged appears in its new location at the insertion point**

If you change your mind mid-drag, call the whole thing off by pressing the Esc key, and your selection zips back to its original position.

TIP The drag-and-drop method is most useful when you're dragging text a short distance, so that you don't have to scroll to find the new location. You can force Pages to scroll by dragging to the top or bottom edge of the window, but even that technique can be clumsy. So if you can't see both your original text and its intended destination onscreen, do yourself a favor and use Cut (or Copy) and Paste instead.

You can also use the drag-and-drop technique to *copy* selected text. Hold down the Option key and keep it pressed while dragging your text (if you've done this correctly, you'll notice a little green button next to your pointer). When you release the mouse button, Pages drops the copy into position, leaving the original untouched.

TIP You can even drag text from one program and drop it into another—or onto your desktop. When you drag to the desktop, you create a *text clipping*, a standalone file that you can open and read, or drag back into your document at any time.

Using Shortcut Menus

Along with an ever-shifting cast of other commands, Cut, Copy, and Paste are also available via *shortcut menus* (a.k.a. context menus)—handy pop-ups that give you instant access to many common commands. Control-click (or right-click—see the box on page 38) just about anything onscreen to check out its shortcut menu; different items appear in the menu depending on the context (hence why it's also called a context menu). The shortcut menu for a text selection is shown in Figure 2-1, but you get a completely different set of commands when you Control-click a picture, for example. If you ever get stumped about how to handle a particular text or design element, bringing up the context can often point you in the right direction.

■ Undoing and Backing Up

All iWork programs offer a few special tools to save you from yourself—or from your hamster trotting across your keyboard immediately after you run the Select All command (goodbye, novel!).

When you have one of those "Oh no!" moments, reach for the Edit→Undo command (or press ⌘-Z), and Pages scrubs out your last action. Whether you've accidentally changed a word, deleted a page, or applied a new font color, ⌘-Z lets you take it back. (If you learn only one keyboard shortcut, you owe it to yourself to master ⌘-Z. It'll get you out of sticky situations time and time again.)

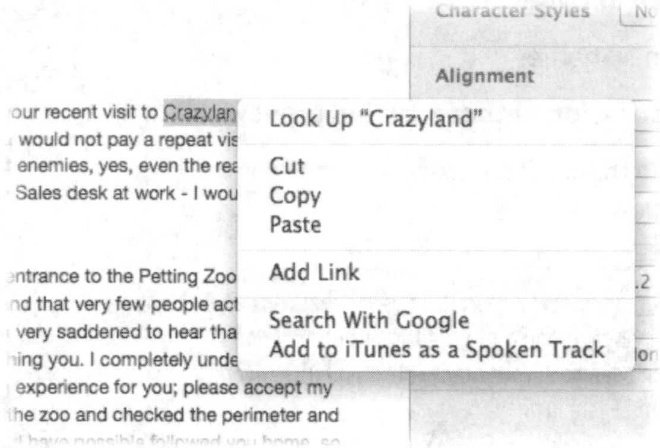

FIGURE 2-1

Shortcut menus change depending on what you've Control-clicked. Control-click any element in your document (here the word "Crazyland"), and its shortcut menu appears, containing a selection of common commands related to what you clicked. When you click text, as was the case here, the menu includes the Cut, Copy, and Paste commands, along with other commands and features that are explored in the coming chapters.

The Right to Right-Click

If you're a Windows refugee, you'll recognize your Mac's shortcut menus as *right-click menus*, summoned by clicking the right button on a two-button mouse. In the old days, Apple's standard mice had only one button, so right clicks didn't normally exist. That's why, even today, this book suggests Control-clicking to display shortcut menus (see page 37). But if you happen to have a two-button mouse, you can open shortcut menus by right-clicking, just as you would in Windows.

Even if your mouse or trackpad doesn't literally have two buttons, you can still get the right-click effect with a trip to your Mac's System Preferences. Go to →System Preferences,

and then choose either Trackpad or Mouse. There you can add a *secondary click* setting to trigger the shortcut menu. ("Secondary click" doesn't exactly roll off the tongue like "right click," but this mouthful makes it less confusing for lefties, who often prefer to flip the left and right functions.)

On recent laptops, for example, you can set things up so that shortcut menus appear when you tap the trackpad with two fingers, or when you click the right side of a multitouch trackpad. Recent vintages of Apple mice (such as the Mighty Mouse) can also be configured to trigger shortcut menus.

The iWork programs all give you unlimited multiple undos, which means that as you repeatedly press ⌘-Z, you can watch Pages peel away the changes you've made to your document, one after another. Even if you've saved the document (which you should do frequently, of course) you can still undo changes you made before saving. But there's one thing you need to bear in mind: When you *close* a document, Pages forgets all about your changes. So the next time you open that document, you have to start moving forward again—there's nothing for the Undo command to undo.

After you perform an undo (and breathe a sigh of relief), the Edit menu's Redo command becomes selectable—which lets you redo whatever you just undid. If you've performed multiple undos, you can get back to square one by performing the same number of redos. On the keyboard, Redo is a Shift key away from undo: Shift-⌘-Z.

If you've *really* made a mess of your document and you're suffering finger fatigue from pressing ⌘-Z over and over, you can leap back to the last saved version of your file. Choose File→Revert To, and then pick Last Saved, Last Opened, or Browse All Versions (you may not see all of these options; it depends on what you've been up to). The first two options are pretty self-explanatory, but Browse All Versions takes a bit of extra explaining.

Basically, the clever software that runs your Mac (known as the *operating system*) has been secretly saving a version of your document every hour, building a hidden history of your Pages file. While this may sound like a good way to clog up your computer's memory, your Mac keeps hourly versions of your document for only a day. After that, it hangs onto daily versions for a month, and then weekly versions for all the previous months.

When you click Browse All Versions, your Mac responds by transporting you to the *Versions browser* shown in Figure 2-2. In this browser, you can rifle through the entire history of your documents and restore previous versions, if necessary. To swap your current document for a previous version, select the version you're after (you can use the timeline on the right side of the screen), and then click Restore. When you've finished with the Versions browser, click Done.

Current version of your document   Previous versions

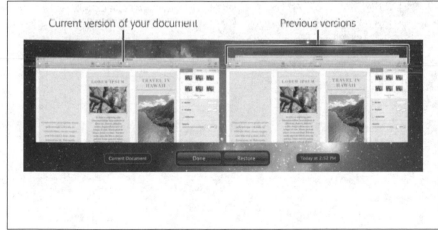

FIGURE 2-2

The Versions browser shows you the current version of your document on the left side and all the past versions of it on the right side. Click any version to put it center stage. The really clever thing is that all the different versions are live documents, so you can move text, photos, or whatever between current and past versions.

■ Changing Font Styles and Appearance

Now that you've mastered basic editing techniques, you may already have all the prose polishing know-how you need. But like any word processor, Pages lets you do much more than simply type and edit your words: You can change the way they look, too. Dress up your text with a new font, make it larger or smaller, mix in some color, or tweak the type style.

You can apply your font changes to as much or as little of your text as you like—from single characters to several words, paragraphs, pages, or the whole document. Simply select the text and then make your formatting changes. When you select text or an object that holds text (such as a text box or shape), the Format panel offers fast access to all the most common font-formatting settings. However, depending on the object you select, the Format panel may not automatically show you the text-formatting options; in that case, you'll need to click the Text tab to get at them. Throughout the rest of this chapter, assume that the Text tab is open and the Style button is selected (as shown in Figure 2-3), unless explicitly stated otherwise.

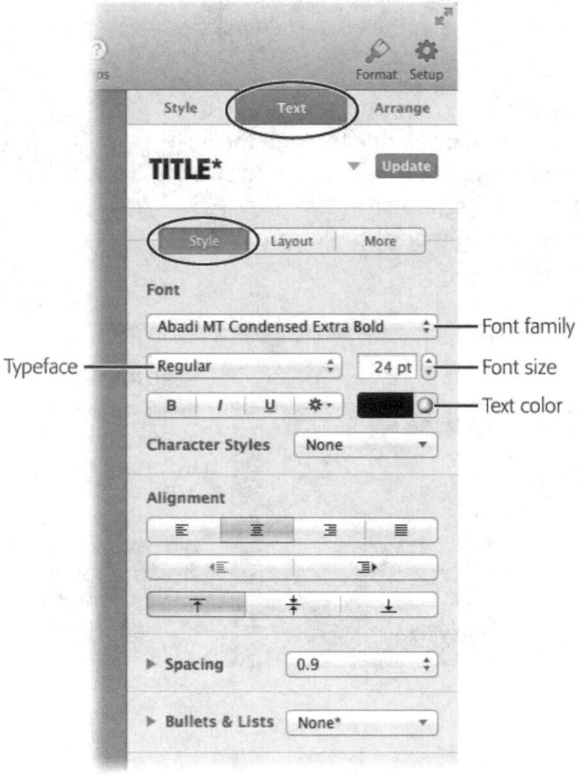

FIGURE 2-3

If you've selected the text you want to change (or your insertion point is ready and waiting inside an object that can hold text) but the Format panel isn't displaying the text-formatting options, you may need to do a bit of clicking. Make sure the Text tab is selected (circled, top), and then click the Style button (circled, bottom).

Once you've displayed the Style settings, you'll see everything you need to create beautifully formatted text. Change the font using the font family drop-down menu; select a typeface as explained in the box on page 41; change the text's size and/or color; or make the text bold, italic, or underlined.

To change the font, click the *font family* drop-down menu and Pages lists all the available typefaces alphabetically from Abadi to Zapfino, and displays each one in the font itself so you get a preview. Change the font size by using the arrow buttons labeled in Figure 2-3, or type a point size directly into the font size field.

Be **bold** by clicking the Format panel's B button, *italicize* with the I button, and underline with the U button. (To remove any of these styles, simply click the button in question a second time.) You can also apply these common font styles by pressing ⌘-B, ⌘-I, and ⌘-U respectively, or choose them from the Format→Font submenu, which also offers options for adding strikethrough or outline styles to your text.

POWER USERS' CLINIC

Fonts, Families, and Faces

Most of us think of a font as a label for a particular lettering design. As it turns out, a font is more specifically a particular style (bold or italic, for instance) within a *typeface*. Although the words "font" and "typeface" are commonly used interchangeably, they actually have distinct meanings that are often important when you're choosing a font in iWork.

The combination of a *typeface family* (Times, Helvetica, Courier, and so on) and a *font* determines the appearance of the text you see. Times, for example, is a typeface family that consists of these fonts: Regular, Italic, Bold, and Bold Italic. In this case—and for most other typefaces, too—this family of fonts simply gives you bold and italic variations of the typeface. When you select a typeface family from the Typeface drop-down menu (Times, for example), you can leave the Font drop-down menu set to Regular or choose a different option. Choosing Bold, for instance, lets you create text that has the Times typeface

and the Bold font; choosing Italic gives you Times and Italic font; and so on. You can also apply bold, italic, or underlined formatting by clicking the B, I, and U buttons in this section.

When applying variations such as bold and italic, you'll usually see a strong family resemblance. But just like in human families, siblings can be remarkably different. Font styles for some typeface families go beyond simple bold or italic and very nearly stray off into entirely new typefaces altogether. While these font versions share similar features of shape and style, they squeeze, stretch, and strain into *dramatically* different forms, as the Futura typeface demonstrates in Figure 2-4.

As you choose your font, especially for big display fonts and headlines, it's worth peeking in the typeface drop-down menu (labeled in Figure 2-3) to see what variations Pages offers. You may find some pleasant surprises.

FIGURE 2-4

The Futura typeface family includes Medium, Medium Italic, Condensed Medium, and Condensed ExtraBold variations. These typefaces offer dramatically different variations on Futura's basic letterforms.

Pages applies your formatting changes to the currently selected text, but if nothing is selected, the formatting is applied to the *entire word* where the blinking insertion point is currently located. This is handy if you want to italicize one word, for example: Just click anywhere inside the word and then press the keystroke for italic (⌘-I). If the insertion point isn't inside a word, Pages applies the formatting to *whatever you type next*. This lets you set the formatting as you type: Immediately before typing a word you want to italicize, press ⌘-I, type the word, and then press the keystroke *again* to turn off italics and return to typing un-italicized text.

The Fonts Window

The Format panel scratches most of your font-formatting itches, but when you need fine-tuned control over your fonts—or want to add zany effects—it's all about the Fonts window shown in Figure 2-5. To open this window, choose Format→Font→Show Fonts or press ⌘-T (T for "Type").

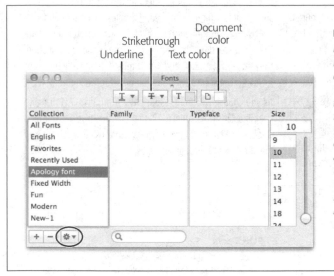

FIGURE 2-5

Use the Fonts window to add a range of special effects to your text. The Underline button lets you add single or double underlines and choose a color for the underline. The Strikethrough button puts a single or double line through your text and lets you choose the color. Click the Text Color button, and the Color Picker pops up so you can choose a text color (see page 192 for details). A click of the misleadingly named Document Color button also launches the Color Picker, but this time it applies the color you choose to the background of the paragraph where your insertion point is. Use the window's + and – buttons to create or remove font collections, and click the Action button (the gear icon, circled) to access even more formatting options.

> **TIP** If Pages places the Fonts window right on top of the text you're formatting, no problem—simply click the bar along the top of the Fonts window and drag it to a different spot.

The heart of the Fonts window is the columns that list your font collections (font groupings that came on your computer or that you created), font families (the typeface names, like Helvetica or Times), the typeface (plain, bold, italic, and so on), and the size. In the Collection column, choose All Fonts to see *every* font available on your computer, and then work your way through the columns from left to right to select a font, style, and size.

You can control the Fonts window's behavior and access some of its more unusual font settings through the Action menu. Click the gear icon at the bottom of the Fonts window, and then choose from the following:

- **Add to Favorites.** After you choose a font family, typeface, and size, use this command to add this custom "font" to a special collection called Favorites. Your Mac saves the font, style, and size in the Fonts window's Favorites collection. You can use these font collections in any program that uses OS X's Fonts window, such as Keynote, Numbers, and Mail—all at no extra cost.

- **Show/Hide Preview.** As you create your font, the Preview pane at the top of the Fonts window displays a preview of text written in your custom font. However, the Format panel's Text tab does exactly the same job, so save yourself some space and keep the Preview pane hidden.

- **Hide/Show Effects.** Choose this command to hide the window's buttons that control the text's underline, strikethrough, and color, and the document's color. If you're certain that you don't want to apply these effects to your text, hiding these buttons gives the rest of the Fonts window more breathing room.

- **Color.** Launches the Color Picker, where you can choose your text color (useful if you hide the color effects buttons, as described above). See page 192 for more about the Color Picker.

- **Characters.** Forget about trying to remember keyboard combinations for special symbols. This command brings up the *Characters window*, OS X's built-in cheat sheet for selecting math and currency symbols, Greek letters, copyright signs, smiley faces, and so on. See page 64 for more info about the Characters window.

- **Typography.** Some fonts, such as Zapfino and Hoefler, have advanced typography features, which let you create different effects. Select this menu item to launch a little box that controls these features. If the current font doesn't include any such goodies, you'll just see a message that reads, "No typographic features for this font." But you may find that your font includes all kinds of interesting options. This box spins quickly into obscure realms like diacritics, Yiddish digraphs, and glyph variants. If such typographical exotica sound useful to you, give the Typography command a spin. And if you need more information about any of these topics (which are beyond the scope of this book), enlightenment is just a quick Google search away!

- **Edit Sizes.** Select this command to open a pane where you can make changes to the Fonts window's font-size list and slider. To hide the list or slider, turn off the Fixed List or Adjustable Slider checkbox. Use the Min and Max boxes to change the minimum and maximum font sizes available in the Fonts window's Size list. You can also add a new size by entering a number in the New Size field and then clicking the + button. To remove a size, select it in the list and then click the – button. If you go a bit overboard with adding and removing font sizes, you can put things back the way they were by clicking Reset Sizes. Once you finish, click Done to close the Edit Sizes pane.

- **Manage Fonts.** Choose the final command in the Action menu to open Font Book, the heart of OS X's font-management system. In Font Book you can add or remove fonts, activate or disable fonts, search for duplicate fonts, and generally manage your collections.

Serve Up the Serifs

Serifs are the little points or lines at the ends of strokes that form certain typefaces—the "feet" at the bottom of H, I, or T, for example. They're remnants of the time before printing presses, when all type was inscribed by hand with a broad-tipped pen and ink. Over the past 500 years, type designers have retained serifs in many font designs—not out of a reverence for tradition, but because serifs make type more readable in print. Serif-style typefaces like Garamond, Palatino, and Times are much easier to read in blocks of printed text than *sans serif* typefaces like Helvetica, Arial, or Verdana. Many books (though, strangely, not this one) use serif fonts as their primary typefaces, reserving

sans-serif fonts for headlines, titles, and the like. Assuming that your documents are destined for print, do your readers a favor by following this convention, whether you're writing a letter, a newsletter, or a doctoral dissertation.

On the other hand, studies show that *on computer screens*, sans-serif fonts are more legible, particularly at smaller sizes. Fortunately, you can have it both ways when working in Pages: Set your body text in a serif font, but pamper your eyeballs by zooming in 150 percent or more (see page 24 for more info about zoom).

Setting Colors and Character Spacing

You already know that the Format panel's Text tab offers lots of options for formatting text. It also includes sundries for applying alignment and list formatting, which you'll learn about later in this chapter. For now, we'll take a quick look at the panel's text controls for color and character spacing, so make sure you have the Text tab open, and then click the Style button (see Figure 2-3 if you need a reminder of where this tab and button are located).

■ THE COLOR PICKER

The Format panel's Text tab includes two controls for setting text color: the *color well* and the color wheel icon, which launches the Color Picker (both labeled in Figure 2-6). Clicking the color well calls up the Color Picker, the OS X palette of millions of colors that you can use in your text. Choose a color, and Pages pours your selected color into the color well, while applying the new color to your highlighted text. See page 192 for a full tour of the Color Picker's features.

■ SPREAD THE WORD: CHARACTER SPACING

The Format panel's Text tab also includes an Advanced Options drop-down menu that contains the *Character Spacing* setting, which adjusts the amount of space between letters. You can use this setting to, for example, expand or contract a headline to perfectly fit above a column. Used judiciously—just a few percent—the effect is nearly invisible, yet it can make your documents look *much* better. Make more extreme character-spacing adjustments only if you're trying to attract attention.

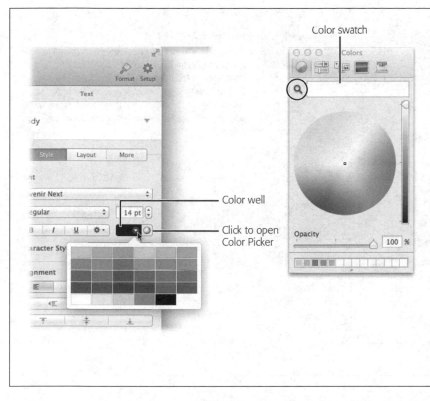

FIGURE 2-6

Left: Click the color well to open this drop-down list of just some of the colors you can select. If you want to see all your color options, launch the Color Picker by clicking the color wheel icon labeled here.

Right: The Color Picker gives you several color-related tools: Click the magnifying glass (circled) to turn your cursor into a color-sampling tool, and then click any color on your screen to select it. The color swatch shows the currently selected color, and the Opacity slider controls the color's opacity. You can store your favorite colors for later use by dragging them from the swatch into the little squares at the bottom of the window.

To access the Character Spacing setting, click the gear icon next to the Format panel's B, I, and U buttons (it's circled in Figure 2-7). This opens the Advanced Options menu (also shown in Figure 2-7), which lists the current character spacing as a percentage. Click the setting's arrow buttons to increase or decrease the percentage, or type your desired percentage directly into the text field.

NOTE You can also adjust character spacing via the Format→Font→Character Spacing submenu to increase (Loosen), decrease (Tighten), or reset the character spacing (Use None). But because the Tighten and Loosen commands nudge characters only one percent at a time, they're not the quickest of methods. If big spacing changes are your goal, you're far better off using the Format tab's Advanced Options drop-down menu.

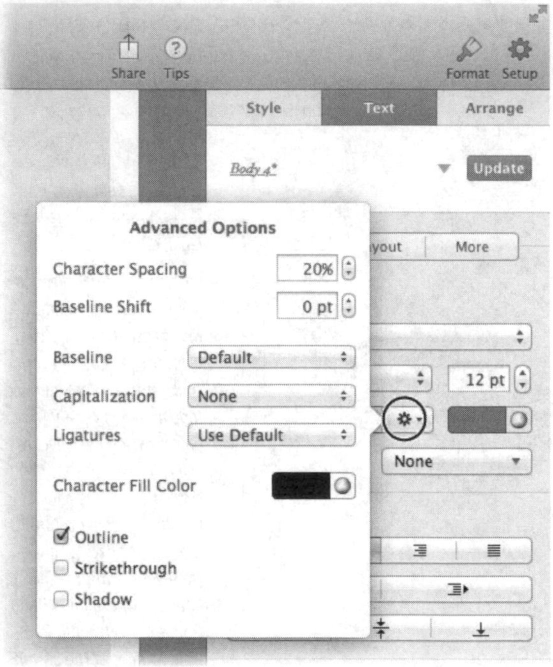

FIGURE 2-7

To adjust the amount of space between letters (known to typographers as tracking), open the Advanced Options drop-down menu and then tweak the Character Spacing setting. It's best to select some text before adjusting this setting so you can see how the text changes. If you don't have any text selected, Pages applies the new setting to whatever you type next.

■ LIFTING LETTERS WITH BASELINE SHIFT

The Advanced Options drop-down menu also includes another spacing option: *Baseline Shift.* Use this setting to raise or lower the selected text relative to other text on the same line. Click the up arrow button or enter a number of points in the box to raise the text; use the down arrow button or enter a negative number in the box to lower the text. This setting might be just what you need for precision character tweaking when you're mixing different fonts on the same line, or when you need to adjust a trademark symbol (™).

If you're in the mood for more baseline-related fun, the Format→Font→Baseline menu holds commands for raising and lowering the baseline in one-point increments and for creating preset *superscripts* and *subscripts*—text with raised or lowered baselines, respectively, *and* a smaller font size—which are useful for creating end-note reference numbers and chemical formulas. Those superscript and subscript commands typically give you the effect you're after when you need a dash of mc^2 or a drink of H_2O.

NOTE If you raise or lower one or more characters' baselines, Pages increases the line spacing above or below that line, respectively, unless you've set a fixed line spacing (see page 51).

The Format→Font Menu

As you've seen, you can use the Format→Font menu to access some of the same settings found in the Format panel and the Fonts window. This submenu knows a few other neat tricks, too:

- **Bigger/Smaller.** These commands nudge the font size of the selected text up or down by one point. You can also use the keyboard shortcuts ⌘-+ for Bigger and ⌘-– for Smaller (that's ⌘-minus).

- **Ligature.** The commands in this sub-submenu let you turn *ligatures* (see the box on page 48) on or off for the selected text, though you can use these commands only if the font you're using actually *has* ligatures (otherwise, they're grayed out). Choose Use Default to use the "normal" settings for your font, or choose Use All to turn on all available ligatures for the selected text. (Note that these commands have no effect if you've turned off ligatures for the entire document using the instructions on page 112). Choose Use None to turn off ligatures for the selected text.

- **Capitalization.** This sub-submenu's commands change the case of the selected text; you can choose None, All Caps, Small Caps, and Title Case. The normal state of affairs is None, which displays your text exactly as you type it. All Caps capitalizes EVERY LETTER of the selected text. Small Caps also capitalizes every letter capital but observes your original capitalization by making CAPITAL LETTERS larger. Choose Title to capitalize The First Letter Of Every Word in the selection. These options don't actually change the text you originally typed—they only change how the text is *displayed*. So if you change text to All Caps and then back to None, for example, the text displays your original capitalization.

◼ Formatting Paragraphs

All the text styling you've seen so far can be applied to any selected text—as little as a single character—but Pages offers another category of formatting options that apply to whole paragraphs at a time. These settings include line spacing, tabs, indentation, and background color. (Formatting lists with bullets and numbering is also a type of paragraph formatting, and you'll learn more about that later in this chapter, starting on page 66.)

Ligatures: The Art of Linked Letters

Ligatures are pairs of letters that share common components when printed next to each other. Scribes writing with pen and ink in the Middle Ages originally created ligatures to save space on their parchment and to increase writing speed—just like how you probably cross both T's at once when you write the word "butter," for example.

Typographers now create these special combination characters to improve printed text's appearance. The most common ligatures are ff, fi, fl, ffi, and ffl. In most typefaces, ligatures provide very subtle typographic differences, but some typefaces have much more dramatic ligatures, as demonstrated by the Zapfino typeface, shown here with ligatures (top) and without (bottom).

Since these formatting styles apply to entire paragraphs, all you have to do is put your insertion point *anywhere* within the paragraph you want to change—there's no need to highlight the whole thing precisely from start to finish. You can highlight any part of the paragraph, or you can just click anywhere inside the paragraph. To apply this formatting to *several* paragraphs, select part of each paragraph you want to change, such as grabbing the last few words of one paragraph and the first few of the next. Bottom line: When it comes to paragraph formatting, it's OK to be sloppy with your selecting because, when you make a change, Pages updates all the text in all the paragraphs included in your selection.

When you're typing away and press Return to start a new paragraph, that paragraph inherits the formatting of its predecessor. That means you can type merrily away and your formatting stays the same from paragraph to paragraph until you decide to change it.

Aligning Text

You can use one of the most basic paragraph formatting options—*text alignment*—to enhance the overall appearance and readability of your text. Two of the four alignment styles look "normal" (left aligned and justified)—the other two (right aligned and centered) are better reserved for headings and other special occasions. To adjust paragraph alignment, head to the Text tab's Alignment section, and then click one of the four text-alignment buttons to get the effects shown in Figure 2-8. (You can also find these same settings in Format→Text menu.)

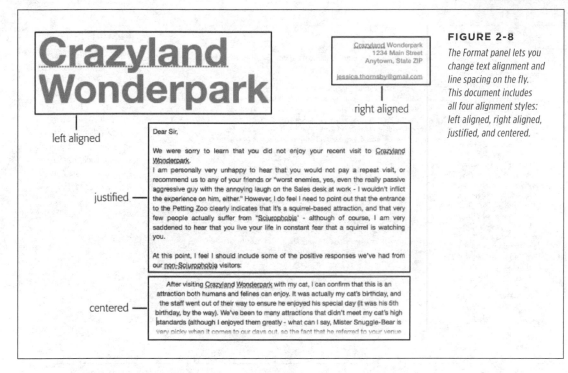

FIGURE 2-8

The Format panel lets you change text alignment and line spacing on the fly. This document includes all four alignment styles: left aligned, right aligned, justified, and centered.

Here are your options:

- **Align left.** Most people use this familiar, standard typewriter style (which is also called *flush left* or *ragged right*) for the majority of their text because it looks "normal" to most people. In fact, experts give the Best Readability Award to left-aligned text because every line starts at the same point, words have uniform spacing, and hey, people are used to it, so it doesn't distract them. This style is typical for letters and manuscripts—in fact, for anything that you don't want to be considered "different."

- **Justified.** Next on the readability scale is *justified*, a.k.a. *force justified* or *fully justified*. This style stretches all lines so that their ends line up neatly with both the left and right margins. Every line is exactly the same width, creating a clean, well-ordered, and distinctly non-ragged appearance. You often see justified style used in magazines, newspapers, and books (including this one).

  Pages teases lines all the way to the margin by varying the spacing between words. When the columns are wide enough and the words aren't too long, justified works well. But if the columns are too narrow, you can end up with an uneven look and/or awkward gaps between words, as shown in the stretched text in Figure 2-9. Hyphenating long words helps reduce this problem, but it can still look messy if you're not careful.

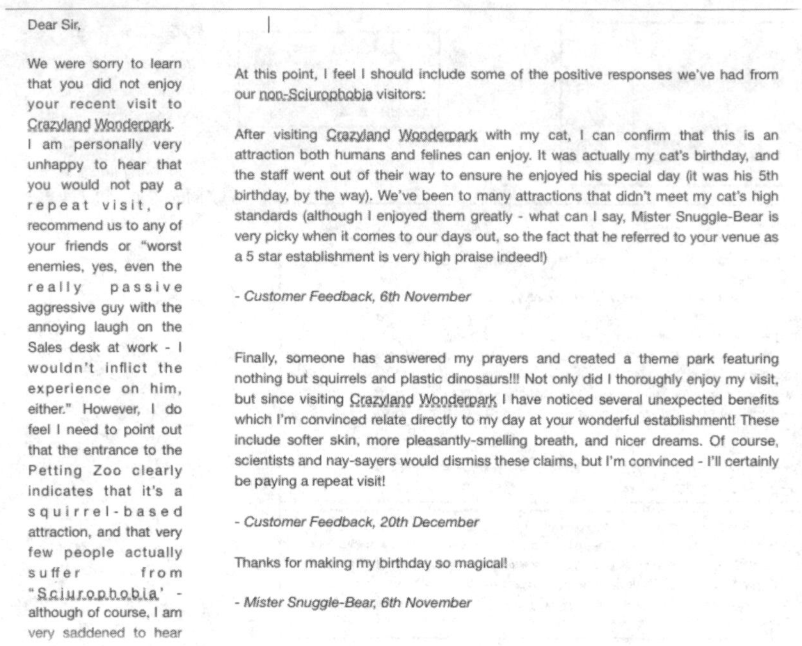

Dear Sir,

We were sorry to learn that you did not enjoy your recent visit to Crazyland Wonderpark. I am personally very unhappy to hear that you would not pay a repeat visit, or recommend us to any of your friends or "worst enemies, yes, even the really passive aggressive guy with the annoying laugh on the Sales desk at work - I wouldn't inflict the experience on him, either." However, I do feel I need to point out that the entrance to the Petting Zoo clearly indicates that it's a squirrel-based attraction, and that very few people actually suffer from "Sciurophobia' - although of course, I am very saddened to hear

At this point, I feel I should include some of the positive responses we've had from our non-Sciurophobia visitors:

After visiting Crazyland Wonderpark with my cat, I can confirm that this is an attraction both humans and felines can enjoy. It was actually my cat's birthday, and the staff went out of their way to ensure he enjoyed his special day (it was his 5th birthday, by the way). We've been to many attractions that didn't meet my cat's high standards (although I enjoyed them greatly - what can I say, Mister Snuggle-Bear is very picky when it comes to our days out, so the fact that he referred to your venue as a 5 star establishment is very high praise indeed!)

- Customer Feedback, 6th November

Finally, someone has answered my prayers and created a theme park featuring nothing but squirrels and plastic dinosaurs!!! Not only did I thoroughly enjoy my visit, but since visiting Crazyland Wonderpark I have noticed several unexpected benefits which I'm convinced relate directly to my day at your wonderful establishment! These include softer skin, more pleasantly-smelling breath, and nicer dreams. Of course, scientists and nay-sayers would dismiss these claims, but I'm convinced - I'll certainly be paying a repeat visit!

- Customer Feedback, 20th December

Thanks for making my birthday so magical!

- Mister Snuggle-Bear, 6th November

FIGURE 2-9

Under the right conditions, justified text makes your pages look especially tidy, but be on the lookout for the gaps of white space that tend to crop up in narrow columns (left). The remedy: Make your columns wider (right) and turn on automatic hyphenation (see page 112).

TIP The secret to successfully using justified alignment is to make your columns wide enough, and the recipe for minimum column width is this: Font size (in points) divided by 3 equals the minimum column width in inches. So for 12-point type, the narrowest column should be four inches (12 ÷ 3 = 4).

- **Align right.** Although difficult to read for more than a few lines, *right-aligned* text can be useful as a design flourish for headings and callouts. Also known as *flush right, ragged left, right justified*, or just plain weird, a paragraph formatted in this way demands attention. Remember, though, that readers have their limits when it comes to this sort of crazy behavior. Like centered text (described next), flush-right text can be effective when you use it selectively, but scary in excess.

- **Centered.** Give someone access to paragraph-alignment controls, and it seems like they're magnetically drawn to *centered* text. Centering can indeed bring an elegant and formal look to small amounts of text, but please, show some restraint. Like right-aligned text, this style is at the bottom of the heap for readability—every line begins and ends in a different spot, creating a real tracking problem for your poor reader's eyeballs. If your document is longer than a few lines, think thrice about centering anything except headings and special display text.

Between the Lines: Line Spacing

Give your words some breathing room by opening up the space between lines, or go the other way to cram more words onto the page. Unless you tell it otherwise, Pages uses single-spaced lines but lets you set the *line spacing* anywhere from 0.1 to 10 lines, where 1 is standard single-spaced lines, 2 is double-spaced, and so on.

To quickly change line spacing, place your pointer inside the paragraph you want to update, or select multiple paragraphs. In the Format panel's Text tab, find the Spacing section, click the drop-down menu there, and then choose a new spacing number. However, this method only gives you options between 1 and 2, which is just the tip of what the Spacing section has to offer: Click the Spacing heading (or the triangle next to it) and the section expands to reveal all sorts of extra goodies (see Figure 2-10).

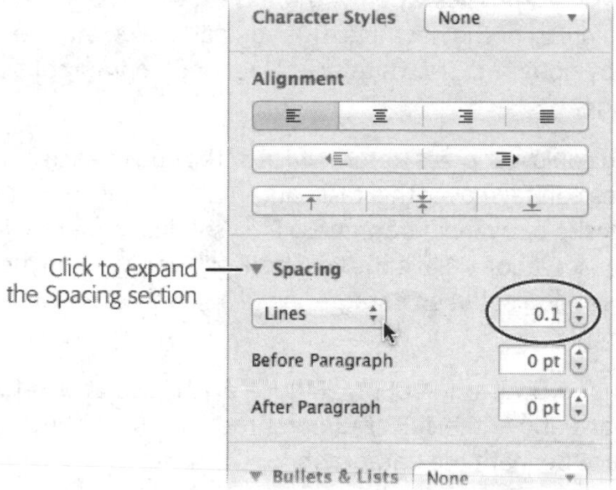

FIGURE 2-10

Click the Spacing heading to see these additional spacing options. To further tweak line spacing, open the Lines drop-down menu (where the cursor is pointing here), and then choose from Exactly, At Least, and Between.

The first text field in this expanded section (it's circled in Figure 2-10) is where you can choose more dramatic numbers for your line spacing. Be careful though: Crank the line spacing down *too* low (below 1) and you'll end up with a dense thicket of overlapping, illegible scribbles. You can adjust line spacing with the up and down arrows, or by typing a number into this box.

If you click the Lines button, you can choose among these options:

- **Exactly.** This option gives you *fixed* line spacing, where every line is spaced at the same interval regardless of the font size. In truth, this setting doesn't really control line *spacing* but rather line *height* (that's the distance from one line's baseline to the next). Choosing Exactly and setting the text field to the right of this menu to 12, for example, sets the height of each line to 12 points, rather than adding an *additional* 12 points between each line.

- **At Least.** As with Exactly, this option applies to height rather than spacing. When you choose this option, Pages adjusts the line height based on font size as it would with single-spaced text but guarantees a minimum height—all line heights will be *at least* the measurement defined here. If you have one line set at a smaller font size than the value entered here, for example, then Pages bumps up the spacing for that line to meet this minimum height—handy for ensuring that your lines never end up squished together!

- **Between.** This setting lets you define the exact spacing *between* each line. When you choose this option, Pages sets line heights as it would for single-spaced text, and then adds or subtracts the spacing set here. A value of zero points results in single line spacing. A negative value decreases line spacing, eventually overlapping the lines of text.

Spacing Paragraphs

Pages observes the usual keyboard physics when you press Return: The insertion point moves down to the beginning of the next line. But you can make your documents more reader-friendly by adding *extra* white space between paragraphs, to help break up a text-filled page.

To create this extra space, you *could* just press Return twice at the end of each paragraph, but why bother? Pages can take over this task, automatically inserting any amount of white space you desire between paragraphs. This isn't just a timesaving convenience or a matter of conservation ("Save the keystrokes!"); it gives you more flexibility, letting you set the spacing between paragraphs to a bit more or a bit less than a full line break, for example.

In the Format panel's extended Spacing section (Figure 2-10), use the Before Paragraph setting to add space above the selected paragraph, and use the After Paragraph setting to add space beneath the paragraph.

■ LINE BREAKS VS. PARAGRAPH BREAKS

Great, so you've added some paragraph spacing, and now you're flying through your document, trailing gorgeous plumes of white space behind every paragraph. But what if you just want a new line—a quick trip down to the next row of text, not a full-blown paragraph with that extra spacing? In that case, you need a *line break*. Until now, you might have thought that's what the Return key gives you, but as you've seen, pressing the Return key actually buys you a new *paragraph*, which is more than a new line. To get a simple line break, press Shift-Return. Pages bumps the insertion point down to the next line, but you're still within the same paragraph—the same formatting rules apply, and you keep any automatic paragraph spacing at bay.

Setting Tabs

Back in the mechanical era of the typewriter, the most efficient way to create tables was to use *tabs*, short for "tabulations." Instead of painstakingly tapping just the right number of spaces to line up every column, the typist set a mechanical lever at each column position, or *tab stop*, on the page. Pressing the Tab key zipped the typewriter carriage to the next stop, making column layout and paragraph indentation faster, easier, and more accurate.

Tabs are still with us, and they remain a handy way to make simple tables and line up columns on an invoice, resumé, or expense report. Just like its typewriter ancestors, Pages jumps your insertion point to the next tab stop every time you press the Tab key—until you reach the right margin, when pressing the Tab key moves the insertion point down to the first tab stop on the next line. This transition to the next line typically brings the last word of text along with it too, so it's a pretty sloppy way to go about things. When you're adding tab stops to individual lines, you're usually better off pressing Return at the end of each line, a rare exception to the "don't treat it like a typewriter" rule.

TIP For all but the most simple tables, you'll find Pages' built-in table tools much more powerful than the humble tab. If you use a table, it's easy to make quick adjustments, add borders and shading—and the table can even manage your math for you. For more info on using tables, see Chapter 8.

As with other paragraph-formatting options, tab-stop settings apply to entire paragraphs at a time, and you can have different tab stops for individual paragraphs. To see the tab stops for the selected paragraph(s), first you have to display the *ruler* (shown in Figure 2-11) by pressing ⌘-R or clicking the View button in the toolbar and selecting Show Ruler. To hide the ruler, repeat the same technique but note that the command now says Hide Ruler.

TIP Unless you change things, Pages sets the ruler's units to inches. To swap inches for centimeters or points, go to Pages→Preferences→Rulers and change the Ruler Units setting.

When you open a new document, the ruler is scrubbed clean, featuring no tab markers at all, which might lead you to believe that pressing the Tab key will have no effect. Wrong! Until you create your own custom tab stops, Pages provides "invisible" stops every half-inch, so pressing the Tab key jumps you ahead to the next half-inch tab stop. However, once you create your very first tab stop, all the invisible tab stops to the *left* of your custom tab stop evaporate (the ones to the right of it stick around, though).

NOTE If you prefer different spacing for the out-of-the-box tab stops, it's easy enough to change this setting. In the Format panel's Text tab, click the Layout button (it's to the right of the Style button you've been using up until this point), and then click the Tabs heading to expand that section. Adjust the Default Spacing however you like. Just keep in mind that this changes the tab stops for the selected paragraph(s) only.

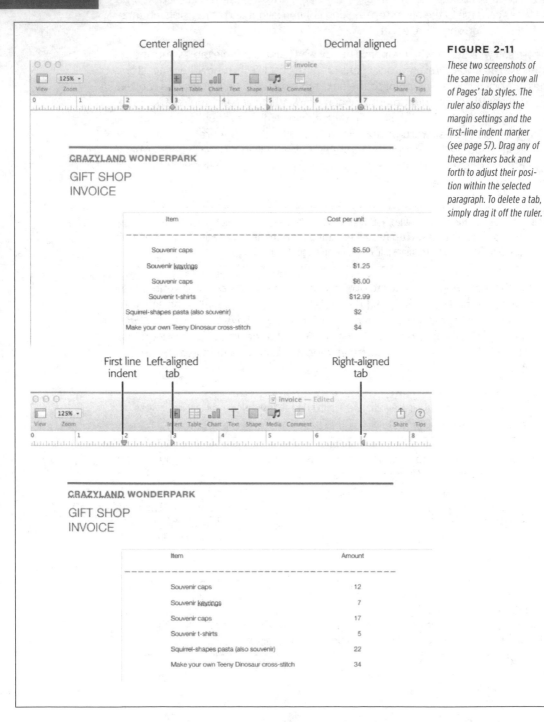

FIGURE 2-11

These two screenshots of the same invoice show all of Pages' tab styles. The ruler also displays the margin settings and the first-line indent marker (see page 57). Drag any of these markers back and forth to adjust their position within the selected paragraph. To delete a tab, simply drag it off the ruler.

■ WORKING WITH CUSTOM TAB STOPS

To add a new tab to the selected paragraph or object that can hold text (basically, a shape or a text box), open the ruler (if it isn't already visible) by choosing View→Show Ruler, and then click anywhere on the ruler. Pages initially adds a *left-aligned* tab stop at that location, but you can choose from four different tab styles; each style is represented on the ruler by a different icon, as shown in Figure 2-11. Control-click a tab marker to choose a tab style, or double-click the marker to get a new style—keep double-clicking, and Pages cycles through all the styles, in this order:

- **Left tab.** This is the "normal" type of tab, familiar to former typewriter users worldwide. These tab markers look like triangles that point to the right. When you tab to a left-aligned tab stop and start typing, the left end of whatever you type next starts at this tab and continues to the right.

- **Center tab.** After tabbing to this tab stop, whose marker looks like a diamond, your subsequent typing remains centered under the tab.

- **Right tab.** When you tab to a right-aligned tab stop (whose marker looks like a triangle pointing to the left), what you type next flows to the *left* of the tab stop; the right end of the text remains aligned with the tab stop.

- **Decimal tab.** This kind of tab stop (whose marker looks like a circle with a dot in the middle) is the secret to keeping columns of numbers under control. When you press Tab and the insertion point lands under a decimal tab stop, it behaves like a right-aligned tab until you press the period key on your keyboard to add a decimal point. That decimal point remains directly underneath the tab stop—and exactly under the decimal point in the line above. In other words, this tab stop lets you align columns of numbers perfectly on the decimal point. Be aware, though, that this kind of tab stop interprets *any* period as a decimal point—even if it's the period at the end of a sentence.

> **TIP** You can make other symbols besides decimal points align beneath a decimal tab. In the Format panel's Text tab, click the Layout button, and then click the Tabs heading to reveal the Decimal Character setting (see Figure 2-12). Any character you type here—such as a comma, an asterisk, a percent sign, or even a letter—replaces the decimal as the balancing point between numbers on the left and numbers on the right (so you could have 1.2, or 1x2, or 1*2, for example).

To remove a tab stop, drag its marker off the ruler, and it disappears in a puff of smoke. To change a tab's position, drag its marker to a new spot along the ruler. While you're dragging, Pages helpfully displays a vertical guideline through your document to help you line up the tab in your text. When you drop the marker at its new location, Pages automatically updates your tabbed text to reflect the change.

> **TIP** Tabs snap to the nearest ruler mark when you drag them. You can get more ruler marks by zooming in on the page using the Zoom drop-down menu (page 24).

■ FINE-TUNING TABS

In most cases, clicking around the ruler gives you all the control you'll need over tabs, but if you want more, you can head to the Format panel's Text tab, click the Layout button, and then click the Tabs heading to expand that section. The Tabs section contains all of Pages' tab settings, including a few that aren't available on the ruler (see Figure 2-12). The section's table lists all of your custom tab stops by their distance from the left edge of your document's text.

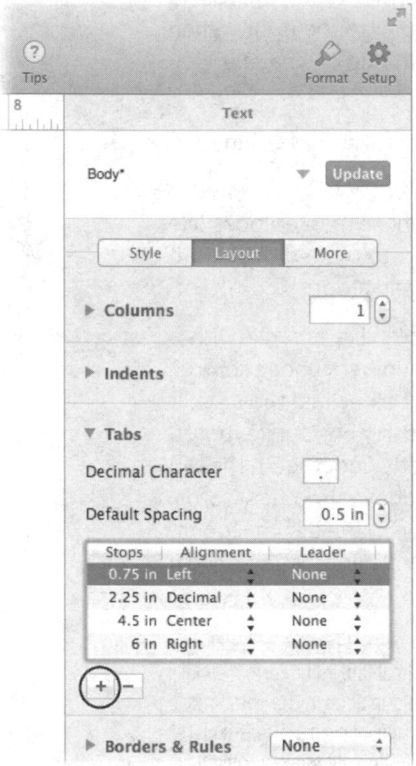

FIGURE 2-12

The Tabs section offers the mathematically inclined an alternative to the ruler. Here you can control the spacing of Pages' default tabs, change the character that provides the alignment point for decimal tabs, and control whether Pages adds leader lines between tabs, as explained in Figure 2-13.

To add a new tab stop, click the + button (circled). To remove a tab stop, select it in the table, and then click the – button).

If you're really observant, you may have noticed that the values in the Stops column of the Tabs section's table don't match what you see on the ruler. What gives? The ruler shows the distance from the edge of the paper, while the Stops column lists the distances from the left edge of your text—in other words, the Stops column's distances don't include the document's margins.

To add a new tab stop from the Tabs section, click the + sign at its bottom-left corner (circled in Figure 2-12). If you're adding the first custom tab stop for a paragraph, Pages adds the new stop at the same location as the first "invisible" tab stop (the increment value shown in the Default Spacing field). If the paragraph already has custom tab stops, then Pages adds the new tab stop after all of your other tabs, using the default increment value. For example, if the Default Spacing field is set to "0.5 in" and you already have a tab at the 1-inch mark, then the new tab appears at 1.5 inches.

To edit a tab stop's position via the Tabs section's table, simply double-click the number in the Stops column, type a new number, and then press Return. To change a tab's alignment style, click the arrows in the Alignment column, and then choose a new style. To remove a tab stop, click anywhere in its row in the table, and then click the – (minus) button below the table or press the Delete key.

The Tabs section's table also contains a Leaders column, which is where you can create a *leader line* of dots, hyphens, dashes, arrows, or underlines between your tab stops. When you add a leader to a tab, it leaves a streaming trail behind it, leading the eye to the next tab stop. You'll commonly find leader lines in menus, tables of contents, price lists, theater programs, and so on. The leader characters fill the space to the left of the tab that's been assigned to the leader; Figure 2-13 shows this effect.

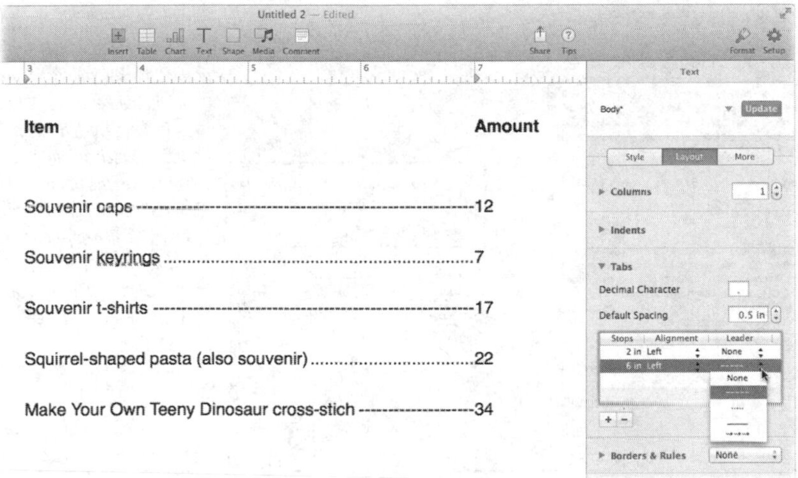

FIGURE 2-13

Don't be a hero and try to duplicate this look by pressing the period or hyphen key over and over again. Instead, use leader lines to lead the eye smoothly from one column to the next. To add a leader line, head to the Tabs section's table and, in the tab's row, click the arrows in the Leader column, and then choose one of the four styles.

NOTE Using leader lines isn't just the right way to do this particular job, it's the *easy* way. You might feel the urge to attempt this effect just by typing a line of periods, but just say no. Why? Because this will eventually backfire horribly when you edit the text on either side of the periods, or change the font size of the document. You'll constantly find yourself trying to get things lined up again, cleaning up dots like some kind of manic Pac-Man.

Indenting Text

Now that you've mastered the art of the tab, you might be tempted to use tabs to indent the first lines of your paragraphs. Resist! Although tabs were once the preferred way for generations of old-school typists to indent lines of text, Pages has a more streamlined approach to indenting lines or paragraphs. Just like tab stops, you can change indentation by dragging the indentation controls on the ruler, or by opening the Text tab, selecting the Layout button, and then using the settings in the Indents section (click its heading to expand it).

The ruler displays the left and right boundaries of the current text as downward-pointing blue triangles; these are the left and right *indent markers,* shown in Figure 2-14. To change the left or right indentation of the selected paragraph, drag the appropriate indent marker to a new spot. Just like when you move a tab, Pages shows a vertical guideline while you drag to help you pinpoint the best location.

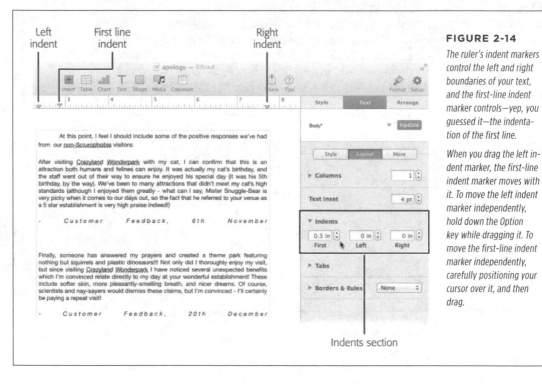

FIGURE 2-14

The ruler's indent markers control the left and right boundaries of your text, and the first-line indent marker controls—yep, you guessed it—the indentation of the first line.

When you drag the left indent marker, the first-line indent marker moves with it. To move the left indent marker independently, hold down the Option key while dragging it. To move the first-line indent marker independently, carefully positioning your cursor over it, and then drag.

The left indent marker travels with a companion, the *first-line indent marker,* shown on the ruler as a horizontal bar. This marker controls where the first line of the paragraph begins. If you like to indent the first line of your paragraphs, you can adjust this control and Pages will then handle that indentation automatically. For a traditional paragraph indentation, for example, drag the marker to the right of the left indent marker. You can also *outdent* the first line of text, to create a *hanging indent,* by moving the marker to the *left* of the left indent marker, so that the first line of text hangs out into the left margin.

The ruler gives you a fast, visual way to make changes, but the Format panel's Indents section gives you more precise controls over indentation. In the expanded Indents section, make your adjustments to the First, Left, and Right settings. (As with tabs, these settings reflect the distance from the edge of the document's margins, not from the edge of the paper.)

Setting Paragraph Borders and Background Color

Judicious use of background colors and borders can highlight portions of text, visually setting it apart from the main body of your document. You might put this trick to use, for example, for side notes, or contact information on a flyer, or an author bio at the bottom of an article.

■ ADDING BORDERS AND RULES

Pages lets you add lines around your text in two different styles: as *borders* and as *rules.* A border is a box that surrounds the selected text, while a rule is a line that appears between paragraphs.

To create a box around one or more paragraphs, you add a border:

1. **Place the insertion point inside the paragraph or, to draw the box around several paragraphs, select them all.**

2. **In the Format panel's Text tab, click the Layout button, and then click the Borders & Rules heading to expand this section, as shown in Figure 2-15.**

3. **Choose a line style from the drop-down menu labeled in Figure 2-15.**

4. **Choose where you want the line to appear by clicking one of the Position buttons (see Figure 2-15).**

   To add a border around all four sides of a paragraph, click the rightmost Position button.

> **TIP** To *remove* a border (not to mention all the rules) from a paragraph, choose None from the line style drop-down menu.

There are a few tweaks you can make to a border once you've created it. Change its color by clicking the first color well in this section or the color wheel icon next to it. Widen or narrow the border using the line thickness setting. The Offset field controls the amount of padding between the text and the border, so increase this setting to give your text some breathing room, or decrease it to tighten the border.

To add lines between paragraphs instead of a box around them, click the appropriate Position button. From left to right, these buttons put a line above, above *and* below, and below the selected paragraph(s). (The icons on each button show what they do.) As you learned above, the final position button puts lines on all sides of the selected paragraph(s), creating a border effect.

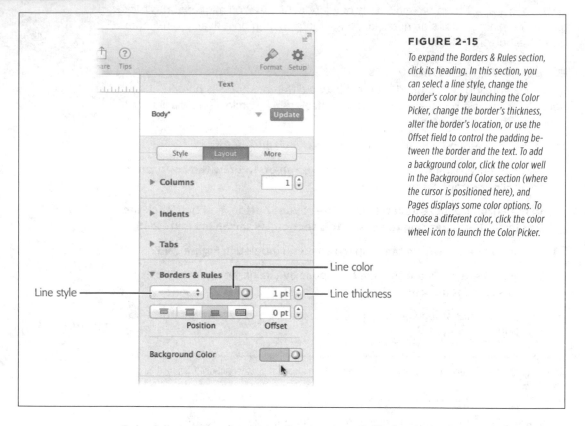

FIGURE 2-15

To expand the Borders & Rules section, click its heading. In this section, you can select a line style, change the border's color by launching the Color Picker, change the border's thickness, alter the border's location, or use the Offset field to control the padding between the border and the text. To add a background color, click the color well in the Background Color section (where the cursor is positioned here), and Pages displays some color options. To choose a different color, click the color wheel icon to launch the Color Picker.

Rules follow different, er, rules than borders. Unlike borders, which can draw a single box around multiple paragraphs, rules stick to individual paragraphs only. So if you highlight several paragraphs and click the Position button that adds a top-line rule, for example, the rule shows up above *each* of the selected paragraphs, giving you lines between all your paragraphs. In this example, to add a line above only the top paragraph, select only that first paragraph and then click the top-line Position button.

Also in the extended Borders & Rules section, you can add a splash of color behind the selected paragraph(s). Choose a color by clicking the Background Color color well or the color wheel icon next to it.

Coping with Breakups

Carefully crafted words split asunder, paragraphs separated, headings introducing nothing at all, widows and orphans left behind—oh, the inhumanity! Who knew turning the page could be so violent?

Most of the time, of course, page breaks are unremarkable, and your word processor does you a service by quietly and automatically continuing your text to a new page. Every so often, though, a page break conspires to split up a paragraph that should be kept whole (the caption for a picture, for example). Other common page-break fractures: two paragraphs that should stick together (a heading and the text it introduces, say) or a single lonely line of text.

Them's the breaks, but don't despair. Pages gives you tools to prevent ugly breakups.

■ INSERTING A PAGE BREAK

Page breaks give you explicit control over when a new page begins. Choose Insert→Page Break in either the menu bar at the top of your screen or from Pages' toolbar—or use the keyboard shortcut ⌘-fn-Return—and Pages starts a new page at the insertion point. (Pages also offers section breaks and column breaks, both of which are described in Chapter 5.)

You can get a similar effect by specifying that a paragraph should always start on a new page. To do this, select a paragraph and, in the Format panel's Text tab, click the More button (to the right of the Layout button you've used before), and then turn on the "Start paragraph on a new page" checkbox.

> **TIP** In practice, you're usually better off inserting an actual page break than turning on the "Start paragraph on a new page" setting. That's because a manual page break makes it more obvious why a new page is starting—the page break shows up as a formatting character when you select it or turn on invisible characters (see page 62), while the "Start paragraph on a new page" option is hidden away in the Format panel. The exception, however, is when you want to create a recurring style—like a chapter heading—that should always start a new page. You'll learn all about styles in Chapter 3.

A manual page break is best used to separate different parts of your document—like chapters of a book or sections of a report—but it's a blunt instrument at best when it comes to fine-tuning page breaks for specific paragraphs. If the text you want to keep together is getting split, then sure, you can fix that by forcing a page break before the paragraph, but at a price: When you make changes to the document down the road, your page break could slip to the middle of the page, leaving you with a gaping hole of white space. For situations like this, Pages lets you attach rules to paragraphs that control how they behave when a new page comes along.

■ CARING FOR WIDOWS AND ORPHANS

In typesetting lingo, *widows* and *orphans* are single lines of text isolated from the other lines of their paragraphs by a page break. (A widow is a line that continues alone at the top of the next page, and an orphan is a line abandoned at the bottom of a page by the rest of its paragraph.) These dangling darlings are considered poor form in page design, and Pages prevents them with a no-line-left-behind policy, shifting page breaks as necessary to avoid chopping off a paragraph at its first or last line. You can turn this option on or off for the selected paragraph by heading to the Format panel's Text tab, clicking the More button, and then turning the "Prevent widows and orphans" checkbox on or off.

■ KEEPING LINES AND PARAGRAPHS TOGETHER

Preventing widows and orphans is all well and good, but what about keeping the whole family together? You can tell Pages that it should keep a paragraph whole by turning on the "Keep lines on same page" option in the Format panel's Text tab; click the More button to see this setting. With that checkbox turned on, Pages will never split up the selected paragraph, instead starting a new page before the paragraph when necessary to keep the family together.

You can similarly ask Pages to keep paragraphs together with the "Keep with next paragraph" checkbox. As its name suggests, this setting prevents page breaks from separating the selected paragraph from the next one. This is especially useful for gluing headings to the text they introduce (see "Herculean Headings" on page 82).

■ Spaces, Invisibles, and Special Characters

So far, this chapter has explained how to format text to make it more pleasing to the eye. But what about what the eye *can't* see? Don't look now, but your Pages document and your keyboard are both teeming with hidden symbols. Here's how to unleash these mysterious characters.

Viewing Invisibles

While you're crafting your words and paragraphs, you probably don't give much thought to the spaces between them, but they're not as empty as you might think. There's a whole universe of invisible characters living in that white space. Every time you press the space bar, the Tab key, or the Return key, for example, Pages adds a formatting character to your document. These formatting marks are called *invisibles* because, you guessed it, you can't normally see them; you just see the spaces they leave behind. They're conspicuous by their absence.

> **NOTE** Joining these rather ordinary spacing characters are several other invisibles, which stand in for more complex formatting. These include page breaks, section breaks, and column breaks, which you'll learn about in the coming chapters.

As you format a document, it can be helpful to see the details of these spacing characters: Are those line breaks or paragraph breaks? Spaces or tabs? Is that an extra space between those two words?

The challenge with seeing invisibles is, of course, their invisibility. Many of these characters—specifically, all the "breaks," including paragraph breaks, line breaks, page breaks, and so on—show up when you highlight them as part of a selection. But spaces and tabs still remain invisible even under the highlight. To make *all* unseen characters drop their cloaking, choose View→Show Invisibles. Pages instantly peppers your document with arrows, dots, and paragraph marks for every behind-the-scenes element you've typed or inserted, as shown in Figure 2-16. Table 2-2 decodes these hieroglyphs.

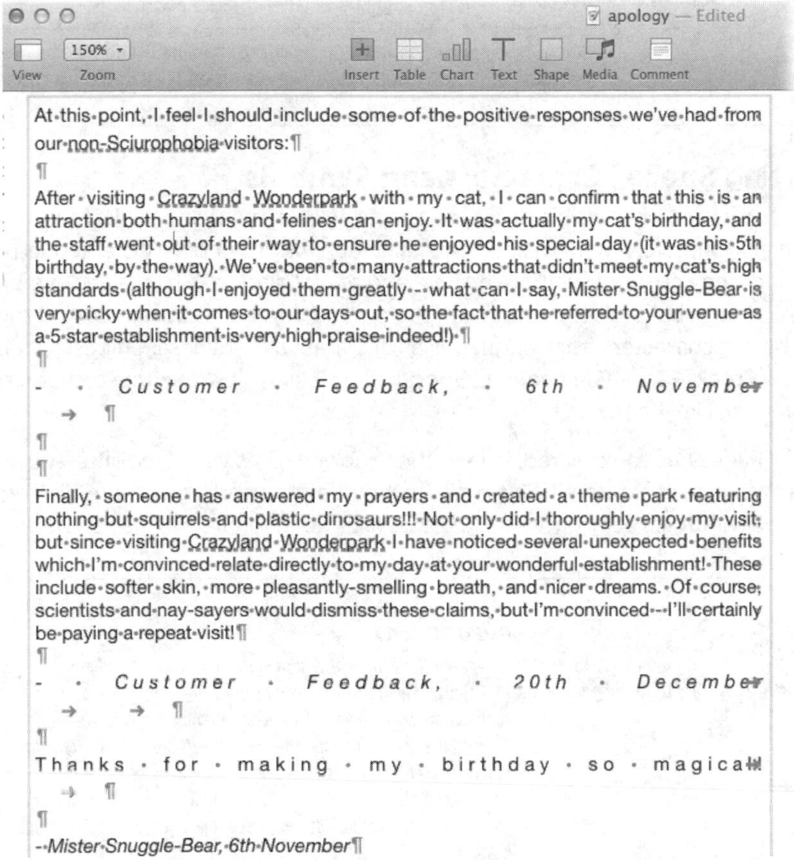

FIGURE 2-16

Choose View→Show Invisibles to make Pages uncover its formatting characters, which are otherwise rendered in invisible ink. Normally Pages reveals these characters in baby blue, but you can choose your own color. Choose Pages→Preferences, click the General button, and then click the color well labeled Invisibles. The Color Picker appears, at the ready to transform your invisibles to gothic gray, lipstick red, or whatever tickles your fancy.

TABLE 2-2 *Invisible characters*

INVISIBLE CHARACTER	REPRESENTS	TO INSERT
•	Space	Space bar
⋮	Nonbreaking space	Option-space bar
→	Tab	Tab
¶	Paragraph break	Return
↵	Line break	Shift-Return
◻	Page break	Insert→Page Break

INVISIBLE CHARACTER	REPRESENTS	TO INSERT
⑪	Column break	Insert→Column Break
▤	Section break	Insert→Section Break
⚓	Anchor point (for inline objects with text wrapping)	Insert an inline object (page 146) and turn on text wrapping (page 181)

Inserting Special Characters and Symbols

Other characters, while visible on your screen, can't be found on your keyboard and are certainly elusive, if not invisible. These include math symbols, accented letters, trademark and copyright symbols, arrows, and other "dingbat" shapes and symbols. Throw in the babel of every human language, and you have thousands and thousands of text characters from languages as disparate as Japanese, Chinese, Arabic, Hebrew, Greek, Farsi—you name it. Good luck tracking down all those characters on a standard keyboard.

Happily, Pages has you covered. In fact, the program gives you *three* different ways to insert special characters. The fastest technique for inserting accented letters is a bit sneaky, but it's easy once you know how to do it. Figure 2-17 has the details.

FIGURE 2-17

To type a letter with an accent mark, simply press the letter on your keyboard and hold it down. (Don't worry: Pages won't add a zillion copies of the letter to your document.) After a brief pause, Pages displays a little pop-up that includes various versions of that letter with different accent marks, as shown here. To choose one, either click it or press the number key that corresponds to the number below it. Either way, Pages adds the accented version of the letter to your document.

NOTE Pages doesn't include accented versions of *all* letters. It has lots of different versions of vowels, but not most consonants. So if you press and hold a key and don't see a pop-up, that just means that Pages only includes the plain vanilla version of that letter.

Here's how to insert just about any character you might desire:

1. **Place the insertion point where you want to add the special character.**

2. **Choose Edit→Special Characters to call up the OS X *Characters window,* shown in Figure 2-18.**

FIGURE 2-18

The Characters window gives you access to thousands of symbols, accents, smiley faces, and special characters, including a whimsical collection of dingbats. If you frequently use one or more special characters, you can find it in the Recents & Favorites category (click the little clock icon at the bottom left of the Characters window).

3. **The different categories of characters each have their own icon at the bottom of the Characters window. Click any of these icons to see what each category contains.**

   Recent characters appear in the first category, Recents & Favorites. From left to right, the categories are Recents & Favorites, People, Nature, Objects, Places, Symbols, Letterlike Symbols, Pictographs, Bullet/Stars, Technical Symbols, and Sign/Standard Symbols. (Don't worry: If you forget what one of these icons represents, put your cursor over it and Pages displays a little tooltip with the name of that category.) Not all of these categories can fit on a single page, so if you can't find the category you're looking for, click the double-arrow symbol in the bottom-right corner of this window to see more.

   To insert a character or symbol into your document, click it once.

   Pages pops the character into your document at the insertion point and closes the Characters window.

TIP The Characters window lets you insert only one character at a time. If you want to insert additional characters, you need to *reopen* the Characters window. The window also vanishes if you click anywhere outside of it.

POWER USERS' CLINIC

The Missing Equation Editor

If you routinely work with equations featuring more Greek characters than a Euripides play, turning to the Characters window for each and every character is a surefire way to get your gammas and deltas in a twist. What you need is an equation editor.

None of the iWork applications are themselves particularly clever when it comes to sophisticated mathematical notation, but they're on good speaking terms with a program that is. Pages, Numbers, and Keynote can all work alongside MathType, a program specifically designed for editing equations. You can buy a copy from *www.mathtype.com*.

If you have MathType 6.9 installed, you can use it from inside any iWork program to create a mathematical expression and insert it into your document. Here's how:

1. Place the insertion point where you want the equation to appear.

2. Choose Insert→MathType Equation.

3. Type or paste the equation you want, using MathType's tools.

4. When you finish typing your equation, choose File→ "Close and Return to Pages," and then save your equation by clicking Yes when prompted.

5. The equation appears at the insertion point. To edit the equation, double-click it to reopen MathType.

After you close MathType, Pages treats the equation just as it does normal text, and you can change the font and the color, for example.

If navigating around the Characters window using the category icons is too footloose and fancy free for you, or you can't find the symbol you're after, there's another version of the Characters window lurking behind the scenes (shown in Figure 2-19). To access this other version, drag the Characters window a little ways in any direction to uncover a new icon in its upper-right corner (it looks just like the icon that's circled in Figure 2-19, top right). Click this icon, and Pages transports you to the expanded Characters window, where all the categories are listed on the left-hand side (oddly, these categories are different from the ones in the smaller Characters window). Click a category to see all the symbols that fall into it.

■ Working with Lists

Our brains love a good list. We itemize, rank, categorize, outline, and catalog (and, apparently, some of us even list the ways we list). Different types of lists typically require different levels of attention—you dash off shopping lists quickly, work through recipe instructions step by step, and painstakingly revise and reorder the outline for a research paper. Pages provides simple but flexible tools for managing all kinds of lists, from quick and casual bullet lists to complex *nested lists*, dense with topics and indented sub-sub-subtopics.

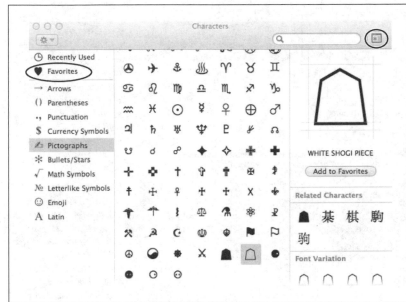

FIGURE 2-19

Click any symbol here and Pages provides you with some more info about it, including available variations. Once you find the right symbol, you can add it to your document by either double-clicking it or dragging and dropping it into your document. To declare a symbol one of your favorites, click it, and then click the "Add to Favorites" button. After you designate your first favorite symbol, the Characters window gains a Favorites category (circled, left).

To return to the smaller Characters window, click the icon in the window's upper right (circled, right).

If Pages sees you making a list, it slips quietly into a special mode tuned for managing list items. Pages calls this *automatic list detection,* which is fancy talk for, "I saw you start a paragraph with a number—I bet you're making a list." Pages recognizes that most of us make lists in the same way: one item per line, usually preceded with a number, a bullet, or a bullet point (see Figure 2-20). Specifically, Pages bumps you automatically into list mode when you do either of the following:

- Start a paragraph with a hyphen (-) or a bullet (•), followed by a space, some text, and then the Return key. (To type a bullet, press Option-8.)

- Start a paragraph with a number or letter, followed by a period, a space, some text, and then the Return key.

After you press Return at the end of that first item, Pages gives you a new paragraph as usual, but this time the paragraph is preceded with another *bullet,* which is a label that marks each item in your list. This is called, naturally, a *bulleted list.* If you used a number or a letter to start your first list item, then Pages starts your next line with the next number or letter in the series—1 is followed by 2; A is followed by B. This is called a *numbered list.* As the name suggests, in a *dashed list,* every item starts with a dash (-) of exactly the same length and thickness.

No need to do anything special—just keep listing away, pressing Return after each item, and Pages keeps giving you bullets on the next line. For numbered lists, Pages keeps advancing the number or letter, and if you go back and add or delete an item earlier in your list, Pages adjusts your list on the fly.

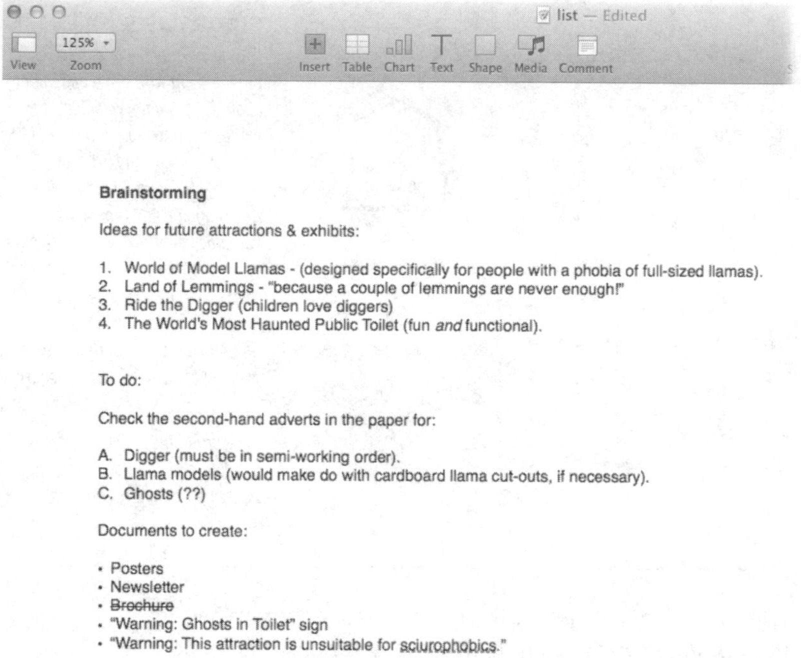

FIGURE 2-20

When your paragraph starts with a number (top), letter (middle), or bullet (bottom), a space, some text, and then the Return key, Pages quietly shifts into list mode, and remains in that mode until you press the Return key twice.

Pressing Return always starts a new list item with its own bullet. If you want to add a second paragraph under an item without creating a new bullet or number, press Shift-Return to add a line break, and Pages gives you a new line under the same list item, without bumping you out of list mode.

When you're done with your list, press Return twice, and Pages releases you from list mode, returning you gracefully to normal text entry.

Using List Styles

You don't have to rely on Pages' automatic list detection to start your list. Head to the Format panel's Text tab, click the Style button, and then click the Bullets & Lists drop-down menu to choose a preformatted list style. When you do that, Pages changes your current paragraph to a list item in the style you selected. You can also use this technique to convert a run of paragraphs into a list—select all the paragraphs, and then choose your list style. You can likewise change one type of list into another, morphing a bulleted list into a numbered list, or vice versa. Or convert list items into plain old paragraphs by selecting them and then choosing None from this drop-down menu.

In addition to the list styles you learned about in the previous section, the Bullets & Lists drop-down menu gives you access to some other preformatted list styles: Bullet Big, Image, Harvard, Dash, and Note Taking (see Figure 2-21 for some examples). The Harvard style is a specialized numbered list that offers special formatting options for labeling nested lists, described later in this chapter.

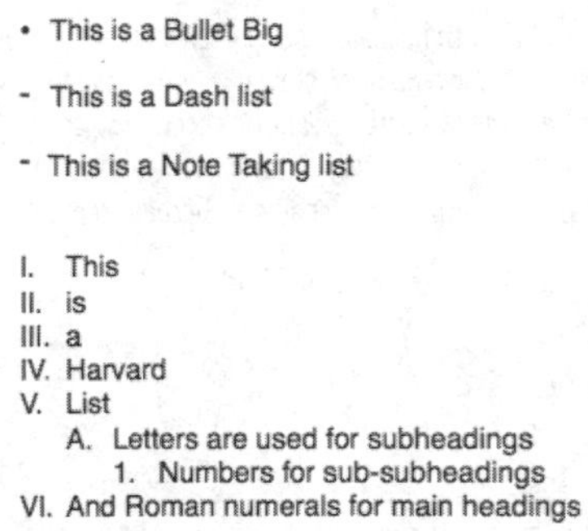

FIGURE 2-21

- This is a Bullet Big

- This is a Dash list

- This is a Note Taking list

I. This
II. is
III. a
IV. Harvard
V. List
    A. Letters are used for subheadings
       1. Numbers for sub-subheadings
VI. And Roman numerals for main headings

Pages has several preset list styles you can choose from, including Harvard, which uses Roman numerals for each main heading, letters for subheadings, and Arabic numerals for sub-subheadings.

As you can see in this screenshot, Dash lists and Note Taking lists are very similar, so in most cases it doesn't matter which one you choose.

If you create your own list styles, you can add them to the Bullets & Lists drop-down menu by opening this menu and clicking the + that appears in its upper-right corner.

After you've chosen a list style, you can change the amount of space (or indent) between the edge of your page and the bullet character, and the indent between the bullet character and the first letter of your item. To change the indent or list style for a particular item or several items, highlight the item(s), and then, in the Format panel, click the Bullets & Lists heading to expand this section as shown in Figure 2-22. The Indent setting there has two text fields: one labeled Bullet or Number (depending on what kind of list style you chose) controls the amount of space between the edge of your page and your bullet character; and one labeled Text controls the amount of space between the bullet character and the first letter of your first item.

Depending on the list style you select, the expanded Bullets & Lists section contains some additional options.

- **Bulleted lists.** If you chose a list style that includes bullet characters (Bullet, Bullet Big, Dash, or Note Taking), you can actually change the bullet character Pages uses. To do so, click the Bullet field and choose from one of the suggested characters (as shown in Figure 2-22), or type a character directly into the text field. You could even use a special character by placing the insertion point in the Bullet field, opening the Characters window, and then choosing a character as described on page 64. You can also change the size of the bullet character using the Size setting below the Bullet field, or change where the bullet appears vertically on the page using the Align setting next to that (when it comes to Align, a subtle tweak works better than moving the bullet point a million miles away from its list item).

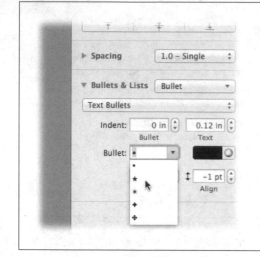

FIGURE 2-22

Create your own bullet characters, either by selecting a new bullet style from this drop-down menu, typing in your own character, or choosing one from the Characters window. You can also change the color of your bullet character using the color well next to the Bullet field (note that this doesn't work for all special characters).

- **Image lists.** If your basic bullet characters seem a bit buttoned-up for your taste, Pages provides 64 more informal bullets—or you can create your own. To create an image list, click the first drop-down menu in the Format panel's Bullets & Lists section, select Image, and a Current Image setting appears in the Bullets & Lists section. Click the Current Image thumbnail to see what Pages has to offer out of the box (scroll down to see them all). If you don't like the look of any of these images, then create your own by clicking the Custom Image button and then choosing an image that's stored on your computer. Large, high-resolution photograph files really slow things down, and since Pages displays the pictures at a very small size anyway, you might want to use a copy of any large graphics files in a small, thumbnail size better suited for bullets.

> **TIP** If the image you want is close by—on your desktop, for example—cut to the chase by dragging and dropping the image file onto the Current Image thumbnail.

- **Ordered lists.** These can be either numerical or alphabetical, but you don't have to restrict yourself to 1, 2, 3 and A, B, C. You can make order more interesting by using different characters and formatting. To see your options, select either Numbered or Lettered from the first Bullets & Lists drop-down menu. When you do that, a few new settings appear in the Bullets & Lists section:

    — **Character.** The first new option is a drop-down menu that's labeled "A. B. C. D." or "1. 2. 3. 4." depending on what list style you selected. Open this drop-down menu to see what other characters you can use in your list. You can also make the number or letter character bigger or smaller using the

Number setting above this drop-down menu—increase the percentage to make the character bigger; decrease it to make it smaller.

— **Tiered numbers.** A *tiered number list* is used in outline lists to number subtopics (you'll learn how to create subtopics in the following section). A tiered number list item adds the number label of its "parent" item. So, if list item 3 has subtopics, they'll be numbered 3.1, 3.2, 3.3, and so on. If your tiered number list has no parent items, it looks exactly the same as a regular numbered list—1, 2, 3. To turn a normal list into a tiered number list, turn on the Tiered Numbers checkbox.

— **Starting character.** Pages automatically turns on the "Continue from previous" radio button. That means that, each time you add a new ordered list item, Pages will continue numbering or lettering it by incrementing from the letter or number of the last list item you created (1, 2, 3 or A, B, C and so on). But if you want to use a different number or letter for your list item, then turn on the "Start from" radio button and then choose your starting point.

Organizing and Nesting Lists

You've seen that Pages can help you create straight-up, single-level lists, but it can also manage lists with depth, turning simple lists into *nested lists* of topics and subtopics. These are lists whose items happen to contain other list items indented within them.

You probably learned about nested lists way back in grade school, when your third-grade teacher taught you about outlines. You remember: You used Roman numerals and capital letters to summarize papers about Egyptian mummies, koala bears, and the state flower.

Nested lists are handy when you have lots of information you want to organize into a hierarchy, such as a meticulously-planned shopping list where each aisle is a topic (Fruit & Veg; Frozen Goods; and so on) and the actual items are the subtopics. Nested lists are useful for creating a document outline for a longer project, as you can quickly add and delete topics or move them around using drag and drop (see this in action in Figure 2-23) until you've created the perfect roadmap for your document.

When you're just after a simple indented list, or when you want to include an outline inside your regular text, a nested list is the right tool for the job. You create a nested list just like an ordinary list, pressing Return after each list item to create another topic at the same level. Press the Tab key or ⌘-] (right-bracket) to indent, or *demote*, an item and turn it into a subtopic of the previous line. Press Shift-Tab or ⌘-[(left-indent) to "outdent," or *promote*, the item, moving it to the left and back up the outline's hierarchy.

> **NOTE** Pressing the Tab key anywhere inside a list item always indents it. If you instead want to use the Tab key to advance to the next tab stop, press Option-Tab.

These keyboard shortcuts are, as usual, the most efficient way to manage the indent level of outline items. So if you plan to do a lot of nesting, it pays to get familiar with using them to weave in and out of your hierarchy. But Pages also offers several other methods for changing the indent level of a list item:

- **Drag-and-drop.** Grab a list item by its bullet or number and drag to the right to indent or to the left to outdent. A guide arrow appears as you drag to show you where the item will land when you drop it.

- **Format panel.** In the panel's Bullets & Lists section, use the Indent setting to move the list item in or out.

- **Format menu.** Choose Format→Text→Increase List Indent Level or Decrease List Indent Level to move the selected item.

■ MOVING LIST ITEMS

Did you catch that drag-and-drop option in the list above? It turns out that list items' bullets aren't just decorative—*they're handles.* Click any list item's bullet, and Pages selects the entire item. Drag the bullet, and Pages moves the entire item to a new location, showing you a blue guideline and an arrow where the item will wind up when you drop it (see Figure 2-23). When you drag an item that contains indented subtopics below it, Pages brings those items along, too, letting you move an entire branch of your list's "tree" to a new location. If you drag an item out of its current list and into a new spot in the document, Pages turns it into its own new list.

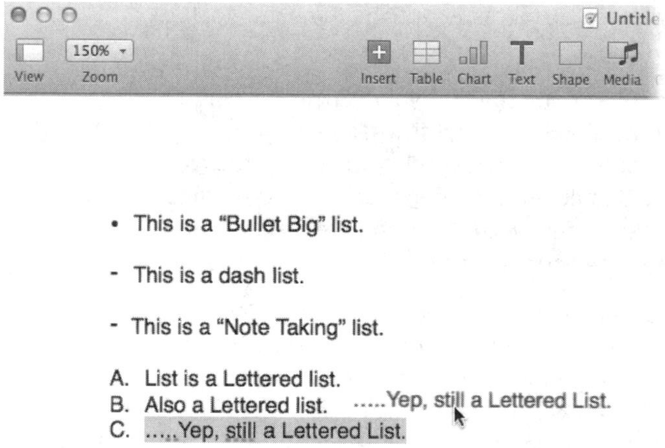

FIGURE 2-23

Pages makes it easy to shuffle your list items with simple drag-and-drop. Grab an item by its bullet character and drag it to its new location. Pages displays a line while you drag to show you where the item will land in the list when you drop it, as shown here.

■ LABELING NESTED LISTS

You can use any of Pages' list styles with nested lists, but Pages provides one style that's particularly well suited to nesting: Harvard. This style (which you apply from the Format panel's Bullets & Lists drop-down menu) is the outline style that your grade-school English teacher taught. Harvard style uses Roman numerals for each main heading, letters for subheadings, Arabic numerals for sub-subheadings, and so on, as shown back in Figure 2-21. With this style, you can easily follow a hierarchy—at least for the first four or five levels. Harvard labels the items in your list and, like numbered lists, automatically updates these notations as you make changes to your outline.

To change a list to Harvard style (or any list style, for that matter), highlight the list items and then, in the Format panel, choose your new style from the Bullets & Lists drop-down menu. You can also design your own custom outline notation by creating a new list style (see page 91). Figure 2-24 shows an example of how you can mix and match list styles with a nested list.

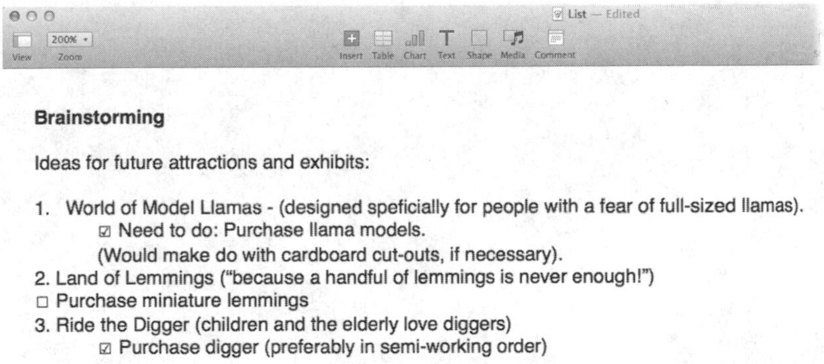

FIGURE 2-24

You can create subtopics in a nested list that are styled differently from other items—for example to insert notes or checklist boxes into the middle of a list. To create a checklist, select the entries you want to modify, and then expand the Format panel's Bullets & Lists section. Next, set the first drop-down menu in that section to Image, set the second drop-down menu to Image Bullets, and then click the Current Image thumbnail and choose your image. The various squares work well as checklist boxes. Just print out your checklist, and add a tick to those boxes when you're done.

Creating and Using Styles

When you create a word-processing document in Pages, you tend to use a small assortment of formatting styles over and over again. In a short piece, formatting your titles or the occasional quote is no big deal; just highlight each and use the Format panel to change its size, color, and so on.

But consider the longer document. What if your manuscript contains 200 headings, plus another 50 sidebar boxes and a slew of footnotes, captions, long quotations, and other heavily formatted elements? In such documents—this book, for example— manually formatting every heading, subheading, sidebar, and caption to make them all consistent would drive you nuts. Add to that the headache of accidentally pasting in fonts and styles from other documents or other portions of your text, and it's all too easy to spend more time toggling formatting buttons than actually writing.

Styles ease the pain. Here's the concept: You format a chunk of text exactly the way you want it—font, paragraph formatting, color, spacing, and so on—and then tell Pages to memorize all that formatting as a *style*. A style is a prepackaged bundle of formatting rules that you can apply with a click of the mouse: Highlight some text, choose a saved style, and you're done. Repeat the process for all the styles you need—headings, sidebars, captions, whatever. You end up with a collection of custom-tailored styles for each of the repeating elements in your document. Figure 3-1 gives you a taste of how helpful styles can be.

TIP When you create a style, it's available only within that document—unless you save the document as a template, as explained on page 263. When you save a custom style as part of a template, every document you create from that template has access to that style.

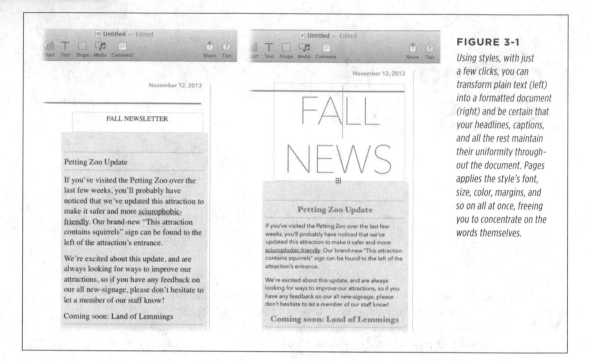

FIGURE 3-1

Using styles, with just a few clicks, you can transform plain text (left) into a formatted document (right) and be certain that your headlines, captions, and all the rest maintain their uniformity through-out the document. Pages applies the style's font, size, color, margins, and so on all at once, freeing you to concentrate on the words themselves.

Once you've created your styles (details start on page 77), you've done the hard part. After that, when you type, you can choose styles as you need them. Since you're no longer formatting by hand, Pages guarantees consistent page elements throughout the document. And as you go through your document during the editing process, if you happen to notice that you accidentally styled, for example, a headline using the subheading style, you can fix the problem by applying the correct style with a single click. Select the text you want to update, click the headline style, and your errant heading automatically falls in line with the correct formatting.

Even better, if you later decide that you want to use a different font for all your headings, you can just update the style definition, and Pages updates every heading faster than you can say "Helvetica bold"—there's no need to go back through your document and change each and every heading manually.

■ When You Need Styles

Styles are more than just a handy tool—they're an essential part of good document hygiene. They keep your text clean, tidy, and consistent. If you've never used styles in your word processing—and most people haven't—it's time to start. Seriously: It's a bad habit to manually format every kind of text in your document (headings, body text, and so on). Break that habit and use styles instead.

If you're still not sure that styles are for you, you should at least get to know the warning signs. You know you need a style makeover when:

- The first thing you do when you open a document is go to the Format panel to change the font or the text size.

- You frequently find yourself selecting the entire document to apply (or reapply) new formatting.

- You repeat the same formatting tasks over and over again when you add headings or other elements.

- You battle constantly with fonts—you change the font of your text, for example, only to find that the old font pops back up when you type a new paragraph.

- You're always reformatting text pasted into your document to fix font and size differences.

- You want to use Pages' built-in tools to automatically build a table of contents (see page 122).

If any of these symptoms sound familiar, styles are the remedy. In fact—surprise!— every time you use Pages, you're already using styles. Every Pages template, including the Blank templates, comes stocked with a prefab selection of styles, including the default font that Pages gives you when you create a new document from that template (see page 5).

■ Style Central: The Text Tab

The Format panel's good old Text tab is where you can apply and modify existing styles and create styles of your own. To get started, make sure that the tab's Style button is selected (it's near the top of the tab).

The white box at the very top of the Text tab is a preview area—called the *Paragraph Styles pane*—that displays the name of the style that's applied to the text where your cursor is currently located. Not surprisingly, the style's name is formatted just like the style itself.

On the right side of the Paragraph Styles pane is a gray triangle (circled in Figure 3-2); click it to open the Paragraph Styles drop-down menu (also shown in Figure 3-2). As their name suggests, *paragraph styles* apply to entire paragraphs, letting you paint entire swaths of text with any combination of font, text, and paragraph formatting. Use paragraph styles to shape the look of the major structural elements of your document: body text, headings, captions, footnotes, page headers and footers, and so on.

To apply a paragraph style, click anywhere inside an existing paragraph, and then head to the Format panel and open the Paragraph Styles drop-down menu. The menu contains all the built-in paragraph styles available for the template that the current document is based on (even the Blank templates come with paragraph styles). When you click a style's name in the menu, Pages applies it to the text of the *entire* paragraph no matter how much or little of it you selected. If you have a selection that includes text from multiple paragraphs, then Pages applies the style to all of them.

FIGURE 3-2

Click the triangle circled here to open the Paragraph Styles drop-down menu, where the current style is marked with a checkmark.

You can rename or delete any of the styles in this menu by putting your cursor over a style's name and then clicking the little arrow that appears to open a small menu. To rename the style, click Rename Style and type out your new title. To remove the style completely, click Delete Style. (If you try to delete a style that's used in the current document, Pages displays a dialog box asking you to choose a style to replace the one you're deleting.)

To remove a paragraph style, you can replace it with another style, or, if you just applied a style, choose Edit→Undo to reverse your style change.

NOTE Pages also includes *character styles*, which apply to text inside a paragraph. They let you dress up individual sentences, words, or even a single character. These styles relate only to font and text formatting—typeface, size, color, and so on—and can't be used to set paragraph formatting like line spacing, alignment, borders, and the like. See page 81 for the scoop on character styles.

Style Overrides

Just because you've applied a style to some text, that doesn't mean you can't add additional formatting. You're free to apply italic, bold, or other *character* formatting to some of the words in the paragraph; or you can change the paragraph's alignment, line spacing, background color, or other *paragraph* formatting options.

When you tweak a paragraph that already has a style applied to it, you create what's called a *style override*. Pages lets you know that the style has been changed by adding an asterisk and/or an Update button to the style's name in the Paragraph Styles pane at the top of the Format panel's Text tab, as shown in Figure 3-3. An asterisk appears whenever you update text that has a paragraph style applied to it (whether you update a single letter or 15 pages of text), but the Update button appears only when you update an *entire* paragraph.

FIGURE 3-3

If you select an entire paragraph and then make formatting changes such as the font color, size, or typeface, an Update button appears next to the style's name (circled, right). When you change the formatting of text (whether it's a single letter or an entire paragraph) that has a paragraph style applied to it, an asterisk appears instead (circled, left). If you've done both, then you see both the Update button and an asterisk, as is the case here.

You can ignore the Update button and asterisk completely—you have a right to tweak a paragraph style whenever you want, after all—but it's still important to understand what these features do, in case you need them in the future. If you decide that you don't want to keep the changes you've made (a.k.a. overrides), you can revert to the original style by opening the Paragraph Styles drop-down menu and then clicking the style name that has a checkmark next to it. To incorporate your tweaks into the original style, click the Update button. From then on, whenever you use this updated style, it includes your changes. To save your changes as a new, separate style, select some text that's formatted with the new style, open the Paragraph Styles drop-down menu, click the + button in the menu's upper-right corner, and then give your style a name.

TIP If you didn't select an entire paragraph when you made changes, you won't see the Update button, but you can still update the paragraph's style. Click the paragraph that uses the style you want to update, and then click the gray triangle at the top right of the Format panel to open the Paragraph Styles drop-down menu. In the menu, put your cursor over the current style's name (it's the one with the checkmark), click the arrow that appears to its right, and then select Update Style. If you're having second thoughts and want to throw out all your tweaks in favor of the style's original formatting, then click Clear Override instead.

■ Creating Styles

Whether you're modifying an existing style or building a new one from scratch, Pages lets you "create by example"—in other words, you format the text the way you want it to look and then tell Pages to memorize that formatting as a new style that you can then apply to entire paragraphs or to individual characters.

Creating Paragraph Styles

Paragraph styles apply their formatting to entire paragraphs, and they're easy to create. To get started, choose a paragraph in your document you'd like to format with a new style, or just type a new paragraph so you have some text to play with. Then:

1. **Place your insertion point in the paragraph and make sure the Format panel's Text tab is open and that you've clicked the tab's Style button.**

   The Style button is right below the current style's preview at the top of the Format panel.

2. **Click the gray triangle in the Paragraph Styles pane at the top of the Format panel and choose the style that's the closest to what you had in mind.**

   Pages updates your paragraph to match the selected style.

3. **Make all your modifications to the paragraph, tweaking the font, size, color, indentation, spacing, tabs, you name it.**

   You can use any of the character and paragraph formatting options described in Chapter 3 (pages 77–82). Mold the paragraph to your whim. When you make changes to the paragraph, an Update button appears next to your style's name in the Paragraph Styles pane at the top of the Format panel.

4. **Decide how to handle the new style you've just created.**

   To update your original style to match the new formatting you applied in step 3, click the Update button. When you do that, Pages applies your freshly modified style to *all occurrences* of that style throughout your document, and forgets the original paragraph style. In other words, you should click the Update button only if you have no more use for the old style.

   Or, instead of updating the existing style, you can save the style as a brand-new, custom style. To do so, click the gray triangle at the top of the Format panel, and then in the Paragraph Styles menu that appears, click the + button. Pages saves this style with a boring placeholder name, but the name is already selected and ready for editing. Simply type a better name, and then click anywhere outside the title-editing box to save your paragraph style with its new name.

TIP   Want to see the sort of effects you can create with custom styles? Visit this book's Missing CD page at *www.missingmanuals.com/cds* and grab *Custom_styles.pages*, a blank sample document that contains lots of custom paragraph styles for you to play with.

Creating Character Styles

You'll typically use character styles for emphasis; for example, you might create a Citation style to italicize book titles, or an Our Company style to call out your company's name in shadowed, electric-blue, 64-point text (you're tacky, but at least you're consistent).

To apply one of Pages' ready-and-raring-to-go character styles, select some text—for example drag across a word or two. Then head to the Text tab, make sure the Style button is selected, click the Character Styles drop-down menu, and choose a style. (If you don't select any text before choosing a character style, then Pages applies the style to whatever you type next.)

The process of creating and modifying character styles is almost the same as creating paragraph styles. To update one of Pages' ready-made character styles, select some text, and then choose an option from the Character Styles drop-down menu (it's best to choose a style that's close to the effect you have in mind). Then use the Font section's various settings to tweak the text until it looks the way you want. Finally, open the Character Styles menu again, and then click the Update button that appears next to the current style's name.

To create a brand-new character style instead, type some text and then apply all the formatting you want to bundle into your new style. Then, open the Character Styles drop-down menu, click the + button in the menu's upper-right corner, and type a name for your style. From this point onward, you can apply your custom character style exactly the same way as Pages' default character styles: Select some text, open the Character Styles drop-down menu, and select your style. If you need to update your character style at any point, apply the style to some text, and then make your formatting changes to that text. You'll notice that an asterisk (*) appears next to the style's name in the Character Styles drop-down menu; open the menu and save your changes by clicking the Update button next to the style's name.

Copying Styles

You don't necessarily need to save a style in order to reuse that formatting throughout your text. You can also copy and paste paragraph styles using commands in the Format menu. Unlike the normal copy-and-paste maneuver, copying a style doesn't copy the *text* of your selection, only its *formatting*.

To copy a paragraph style, place your insertion point anywhere within the paragraph and choose Format→Copy Style; then place your insertion point in another paragraph where you want to use that style and choose Format→Paste Style. Shazam! The text takes on the formatting of the pasted style, while the words themselves remain unchanged. This technique copies not only the style, but also any style overrides (page 78) that you've applied to the paragraph style.

Herculean Headings

Paragraph styles are especially useful for formatting text headings—and not just for the usual font-size and color differences that set headings apart from body text. You can save yourself some time—and pain around the temples—by giving your heading styles some special paragraph formatting that take note of a heading's typical status as the start of a new section of text.

When you define paragraph styles for headings, consider putting these options to good use (unless otherwise stated, you can find them in the Format panel's Text tab by clicking the More button):

- **Keep lines on same page.** Page breaks should never carve up your headings. This setting guarantees that multiline headings stick together.

- **Keep with next paragraph.** Don't leave your headings hanging out alone at the bottom of a page. This setting ensures that headings are always on the same page as the text they introduce.

- **Start paragraph on a new page.** Use this setting to automatically create a new page when kicking off major new sections. If you turn this option on for a Title style,

for example, Pages puts each chapter heading at the top of a new page.

- **Prevent widows and orphans.** Whenever you reach the end of a page, Pages makes adjustments to prevent widows and orphans (page 60 looks at widows and orphans in more detail).

- **Paragraph spacing.** Open up some space before and/ or after a heading to separate it visually from the surrounding text and to mark the leap into a new section. To do so, in the Format panel's Text tab, click the Style button, and then look for the Spacing heading. Click the heading to expand that section, which includes the Before Paragraph and After Paragraph settings. For example, in this book, headings have more space before them than after them; that spacing indicates that the headings are related to the text that follows them.

Better yet, you can copy and paste styles *between documents*. In other words you can pick and choose styles from any of your Pages documents and paste them into other Pages documents. Not only does this technique reformat the selected text, but after a style is in your document, you can also save it as a new style (see page 80 to learn how), ready to use in other parts of your document.

■ Changing the Default Font

All Pages templates come with their own set of styles that define the document's default fonts and styles. For example, the Blank templates use 11-point Helvetica as their default font. If your personal font fondness lies elsewhere, you can use the techniques you've learned so far to customize this built-in style and use your preferred font instead. But, ugh, that means you have to customize this default style *every time* you open a new document by manually redefining all the paragraph styles or copy/pasting styles from another document. No thanks.

With most other word processors, you can just change a preference setting and choose a new standard font. But Pages' emphasis on professionally designed templates means that the default font rides along with each template, not in a global preference. Because of that, the easiest way to have your favorite font and styles handy in every new document is to create your *own* template with your preferred default font. Chapter 10 explores all the details of custom templates, but here's the quick and dirty version:

1. **Create a new document from the Blank template.**

   Pages displays your new document and selects the default Body style.

2. **In the Format panel's Text tab, click the Style button (if it's not already selected) and then use the tab's settings to choose your preferred typeface and font size for body text.**

   Make any other formatting changes—tabs, indentation, line spacing, and so on—that you would like to be the standard for body text.

3. **In the Paragraph Styles pane at the top of the Format panel, click the Update button to override the original Body style.**

4. **Repeat steps 2 and 3 for any other styles you want to customize: Headings, Subheadings, and so on.**

   Click the gray triangle at the top of the Format panel, choose the style you want to modify, and then use the Text tab's settings to customize it.

5. **Choose File→Save as Template, and then click "Add to Template Chooser."**

   Give the template a name, and then save it by pressing the Return key or clicking anywhere outside of the title-editing box.

Your newly minted template appears in the Template Chooser in the My Templates category, ready to take the Blank template's place as your new starting point.

Typo-Busting Power Tools

The last chapters introduced you to Pages, the faithful transcriber of words, an able assistant for capturing your ideas and juggling them into presentable shape. Like any good assistant, though, Pages does more than just take down your words—it catalogs them, quietly fixes errors, and serves as a dictionary *and* a thesaurus, all rolled into one.

Pages juggles all of these roles by giving you a set of power tools to buzz through the jobs that support your writing: editing, sharing, and gathering feedback. The program's Find & Replace feature makes short work of sifting through long documents; the built-in dictionary, thesaurus, and encyclopedia help you catch errors or find the perfect word; Pages' in-house grammarian offers advice for sharpening your writing; and change tracking eases collaboration by keeping up with the edits and comments of multiple authors.

Together, this pit crew of support services adds up to a mean collection of typo busters, protecting you from careless mistakes while helping you find or solicit the right words to get your ideas across. This chapter explores them all.

■ Changing Your Mind: Find & Replace

Whether you're completing your 400-page novel or just polishing a three-page letter, you often have to change a word, a phrase, or even a single character that appears repeatedly throughout the text. For example, as newsletter editor for Crazyland Wonderpark, you've been asked to write a book: *Marketing Your Theme Park: The Missing Manual* (congratulations!). As you zoom into your final chapters, your editor asks you to make a few changes:

- You use the word "squirrel" far too often throughout the book (seriously—is there *really* nothing else in that petting zoo?) and it's insensitive to the sciurophobics of the world. Now you have to change all 273 mentions of the word "squirrel" to something less likely to give sciurophobics palpitations. You opt for "rodent," a much cuddlier word.

- It's great that the Teeny Tiny Dinosaur Safari features a model of the "Irritator" species of dinosaur, but please make sure Irritator is capitalized whenever it's mentioned. (This isn't a widely known species of dinosaur, and without the capitalization it sounds as though you're saying derogatory things about your own attraction).

- Your café menu has some unfortunate auto-corrections. For example, your burgers, soups, and salads are made with fresh *cilantro* and not fresh *cement*, right?

- Half of your mentions of *The World's Most Haunted Public Toilet* are in quotation marks, but you should instead italicize them with the *Emphasis* style and delete the quotes.

It's Find & Replace to the rescue! Hunting through hundreds of manuscript pages for these changes would require some serious patience, but Find & Replace saves you the trouble, sifting through your document and making changes in the blink of an eye.

Finding

Pages' Find & Replace feature is really two commands rolled into one: *Find* and *Find & Replace*. Sometimes you just need to find a word or phrase in your document. For example, you might want to find the pages where you use the phrase "everyone loves an irritator." Here's how to do that:

1. **To open the Find & Replace window, choose Edit→Find→Find, press ⌘-F, or click the View button in the toolbar and then select Show Find & Replace.**

   The Find & Replace window appears, as shown in Figure 4-1.

2. **Enter the word or phrase you're looking for in the Find field:** *everyone loves an irritator.*

   As you type, Pages highlights the first instance of the word or phrase that it finds and, at the right end of the Find field, displays a message that indicates how many instances it found ("8 found," for example). Click the window's gear icon and make sure Match Case is turned off (in other words, make sure it doesn't have a checkmark next to it), because you want to find both capitalized *and* lowercase occurrences of this unfortunate phrase. In some cases, you'll also want to turn on the Whole Words setting to prevent the search from turning up words that include merely part of your search term.

3. **Click the window's right-arrow button (or press Return), and Pages jumps to the next instance of your search term(s).**

The right-arrow button tells Pages to search forward from your current selection. You can search *backward* from your present location by clicking the left-arrow button or by pressing Shift-Return.

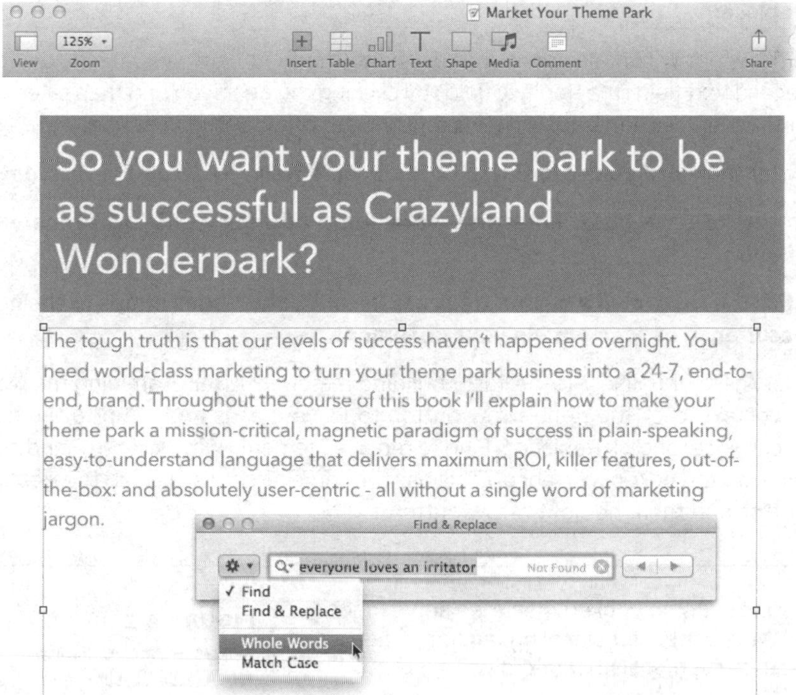

FIGURE 4-1

To toggle the Match Case and Whole Words settings on and off, click the gear icon to display the menu shown here. When either of these options is turned on, it has a checkmark next to it, like the Find command here.

If you can't see the found word highlighted in your document, it could be hidden behind the Find & Replace window. To prevent this inconvenience, drag the Find & Replace window to one side before starting your search.

Work your way through your whole document by clicking the right-arrow button repeatedly (or pressing Return) to leap from result to result. If you want to make things more difficult for yourself, you can move backward and forward through your matches by clicking Edit→Find→Find Next/Find Previous.

Finding and Replacing

On its own, the Find tool is a nifty way to zip straight to specific portions of your document. But things really get interesting when you mix in Replace. The Find & Replace feature can save you so much time and hassle that a better name might be Search & Rescue—it lets you motor through edits, telling Pages to automatically change matching words to something else. You can review each of these changes before applying them, or you can just take the leap and tell Pages to go ahead and change *all* matches across the board.

■ **REVIEWING EACH CHANGE**

Some changes require a yes-or-no decision from you. For example, you might want to review every occurrence of the words "cement" and "cilantro" to make sure you're using the right word in the right context. When you do find a mistake, you can either tell Pages to correct it or leave it untouched. Here's how:

1. **Call up the Find & Replace window by choosing Edit→Find→Find, pressing ⌘-F, or clicking the View button in the toolbar and selecting Show Find & Replace.**

   If the window contains only one text field (the Find field), you need to add a second text field (the Replace field) by clicking the gear icon and then selecting Find & Replace. Figure 4-2 shows this two-text-field setup in action.

2. **Enter the word you're looking for in the Find field: for example, *cement*.**

3. **In the Replace field, enter the word that you *may* want to use instead: *cilantro*.**

4. **Click the right-arrow button (or press Return), and Pages jumps to the next occurrence of "cement" in your document.**

   Tasty herb or unlikely-to-be-tasty building material? After examining the word in context, click the right-arrow button to leave it as is and jump to the next occurrence, or click Replace & Find to replace "cement" with "cilantro" and *then* move to the next occurrence. (This has the same effect as clicking the Replace button and then the right-arrow button.)

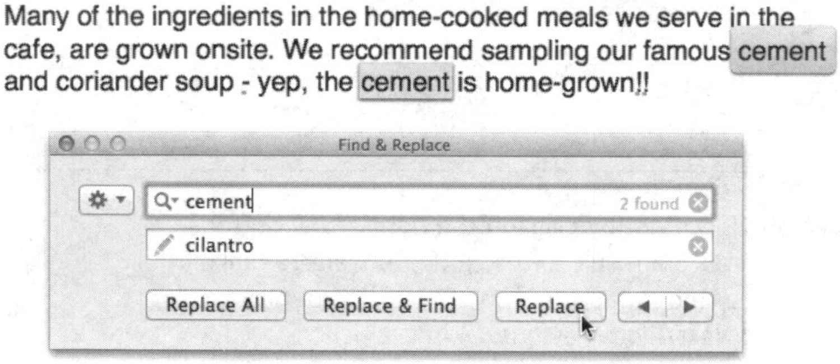

FIGURE 4-2

If you're certain about the terms you've set up for your Find & Replace, click Replace All and Pages makes the change everywhere in your document and tells you how many occurrences it found. Click Replace to replace only the currently highlighted word, or click Replace & Find to replace the current word and move on to the next occurrence so you can evaluate it.

TIP If you want to *remove* all occurrences of a word, leave the Replace field empty when you perform your search. When you click Replace, Pages deletes the found text—replacing it with nothing at all.

■ REPLACE ALL AUTOMATICALLY

Some circumstances don't require you to review every change. When you know that you definitely want to replace all instances of a word or phrase, the *Replace All* button is the answer. To capitalize every lowercase instance of "irritator" in your document, for example, type *irritator* in the Find field and *Irritator* in the Replace field, and then click Replace All. Pages instantly fixes all the irritators within your document, without asking for your opinion on each occurrence.

■ WHOLE WORDS VS. PARTIAL MATCHES

When working with Replace All, it's particularly important to be clear about what you're replacing. When you want to change only a specific word, click the Find & Replace window's gear icon and click Whole Words. This tells Pages not to confuse the word you're searching for with parts of other words. That way, when you want to change *Sue* to *Betty*, the words *issue* and *Suez* don't turn into *isBetty* and *Bettyz*.

> **NOTE** Searching for a word with the Whole Words option turned on won't find the plural and possessive forms that may be lurking in your document. To catch these, you need to perform extra searches, one for the plural and one for the possessive—and perhaps one for the plural possessive.

■ SEARCHING FOR SPACES AND INVISIBLE CHARACTERS

Pages' Find & Replace feature doesn't limit you to "normal" words and characters—you can just as easily search for spaces, tabs, line breaks, and a range of other invisible characters (for more on "invisibles," see page 62). Say that you want to sweep out extra spaces from your document, replacing two or more spaces with a single space. No problem: Type two spaces in the Find field, type one space in the Replace field, and then click Replace All. Pages replaces all your double spaces with single spaces. But what if, in a space bar-addled frenzy, you typed *three* or more spaces? Just click Replace All again to replace those extra spaces. Continue clicking Replace All until the indicator at the right end of the Find field reads "0 found."

■ Spell Checking

One of the most appreciated features of the modern word processor is its ability to corect embarassing misspellings. Pages can't save you from choosing the *wrong* word—it still can't tell a "heroine" from "heroin," or "there" from "their" from "they're"—but it can at least let you know when you've misspelled "correct" or "embarrassing."

Make a *spell check* the last stop before you consider any document finished. Even if you're a spelling bee champ, typos eventually befall anyone who puts fingers to keyboard. To catch these gaffes, Pages makes use of OS X's systemwide spell checker—tapping into the same dictionary used by other Apple programs like Mail, Keynote, Numbers, TextEdit, and iPhoto.

Checking Spelling As You Type

Unless you tell it otherwise, Pages quietly watches as you type. If you misspell a word, Pages tries to help you out in a couple of different ways.

When you first install Pages, the program's Correct Spelling Automatically feature is turned on. So if you type a word that Pages doesn't recognize, the program displays the word it thinks you were *trying* to spell in a little pop-up like the one in Figure 4-3 (unless Pages has absolutely no idea what word you're trying to spell!) For example, if you type "erally," Pages might suggest "really." If you press the space bar on your keyboard, Pages assumes you're OK with its correction and updates your misspelling to what it suggested. If you disagree with the replacement, click the x in the pop-up window to keep your entry as it is, and then you can hit the space bar and continue on your way. (If Pages changes the spelling of a word, it indicates this by underlining the corrected word in blue—but only until you type the next word. So if you aren't careful, Pages may make changes that you don't notice.)

Fortunately, you're not stuck with this feature if you think it's more trouble than it's worth (and you may very well think that—there are whole websites dedicated to embarrassing typos caused by auto-correct features like this). To turn it off, click Edit→Spelling and Grammar→Correct Spelling Automatically, which removes the checkmark next to this option.

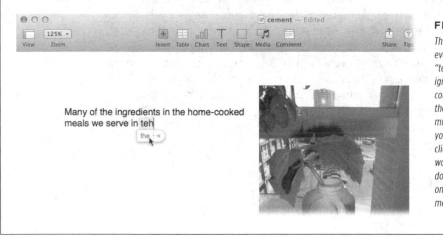

FIGURE 4-3

This screenshot shows everyone's favorite typo: "teh" instead of "the." To ignore Pages' suggested correction, click the x in the pop-up window. To admit that Pages is right and you're in the wrong, either click the correctly spelled word in the pop-up window or press the space bar on your keyboard—both methods give you "the."

If you turn off Correct Spelling Automatically (or if you leave it on but you type a word that Pages doesn't know *and* doesn't have a suggestion for), the program flags words it doesn't recognize with a red dashed underline and provides fast access to spelling suggestions—if you want them. This *Check Spelling While Typing* feature is turned on by default, but you can toggle it on and off by choosing Edit→Spelling and Grammar→Check Spelling While Typing.

When Pages adds a red underline to a suspicious spelling, Control-click the word. A shortcut menu appears, topped with the spell checker's guesses at correct spellings (Figure 4-4). Click the word you're after, and Pages makes the correction.

NOTE If you want Pages to check your grammar, too, head to Edit→Spelling and Grammar→Check Grammar with Spelling. From then on, when you see a word marked with a *green* underline, it means Pages is questioning your grammar.

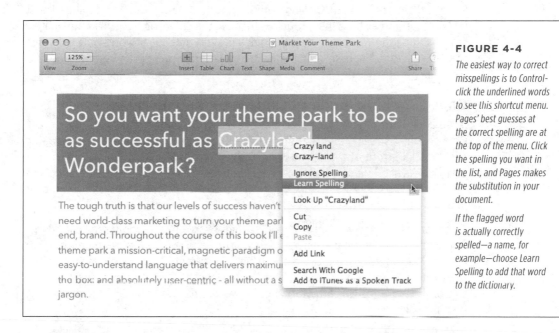

FIGURE 4-4

The easiest way to correct misspellings is to Control-click the underlined words to see this shortcut menu. Pages' best guesses at the correct spelling are at the top of the menu. Click the spelling you want in the list, and Pages makes the substitution in your document.

If the flagged word is actually correctly spelled—a name, for example—choose Learn Spelling to add that word to the dictionary.

Just because Pages flags a word doesn't necessarily mean that it's misspelled—only that the spell checker doesn't recognize it. This is common, for example, with names, addresses, or specialized technical lingo not included in your Mac's dictionary. (This also happens with foreign words, but that's a special case—more on that in a moment.) You can teach the spell checker a new word by Control-clicking a red-underlined word and choosing Learn Spelling from the shortcut menu. Pages adds the word to your Mac's dictionary so that it stops getting flagged—not only by Pages but also by every other program that uses the Mac operating system's spell checker.

Another choice in the shortcut menu is Ignore Spelling. Choose this setting when you don't want the highlighted word flagged in the current document, but you don't want to add it to the dictionary either. For example, say your chapter titled "Marketing Your Theme Park Cafe" makes several mentions of Ghoulash, Boo-Nilla milkshakes, and Pooooooultery-Geist Chicken sandwiches, in honor of the World's Most Haunted Public Toilet attraction. If you choose Ignore Spelling when Pages first stumbles across one of these frightening foodstuffs, Pages will stay quiet about these words—as well as their lowercase variations—for the remainder of the document. In new documents, however, it will continue to catch these words as misspellings.

NOTE   Your Ignore Spelling commands last until you close the document. When you reopen the file later, Pages once again flags your previously ignored words as unrecognized.

Once you've chosen the correct spelling, Learn Spelling, or Ignore Spelling from the shortcut menu, Pages removes the red underline.

Whoops! You accidentally told the spell checker to learn the word "Boo-Nilla," and now none of your programs spot this as a misspelling. No problem: Control-click the word and choose Unlearn Spelling from the shortcut menu. Ah, the red underline is back. Pages and all the other programs that use the OS X spell checker immediately start flagging the word as a misspelling again. (This maneuver works only for words that you've added yourself—OS X doesn't let you remove words from its standard dictionary.)

Check Spelling in the Document or Selection

If red underlines are derailing your creative train of thought, you can turn them off. Choose Edit→Spelling and Grammar→Check Spelling While Typing to remove the checkmark in front of that menu item. The red lines vanish and you can turn your attention back to your masterpiece. When you're ready to accept the spell checker's help again, you can ask it to take you through all the unknown words in your document one by one.

To get started, place your insertion point where you'd like to begin spell checking—at the beginning of the document, for example—and then press ⌘-; (semicolon) or choose Edit→Spelling and Grammar→Check Document Now to tell Pages to point out the first word it doesn't recognize. Control-click the word to choose an alternative or to tell Pages to learn or ignore the word. Press ⌘-; again to move onto the next misspelled word.

If all this Control-clicking is wearing you down, you can call on the Spelling and Grammar window to guide you through your document, showing you each unrecognized word and its suggested replacements simultaneously. Open this window by putting your insertion point where you'd like to start spell checking, and then choosing Edit→Spelling and Grammar→Show Spelling and Grammar. The Spelling and Grammar window shows you the first misspelled word and suggests fixes, as shown in Figure 4-5.

Pages offers its recommendations with a list of suggested spellings. If you see the correct word, double-click it (or click once to select it and then click Change)—Pages replaces it in the document and moves on to the next misspelling. The Ignore button skips this word for the rest of the document; the Learn button adds it to the dictionary. If you just want to skip over the word and move on to the next misspelling, click Find Next (or press ⌘-;).

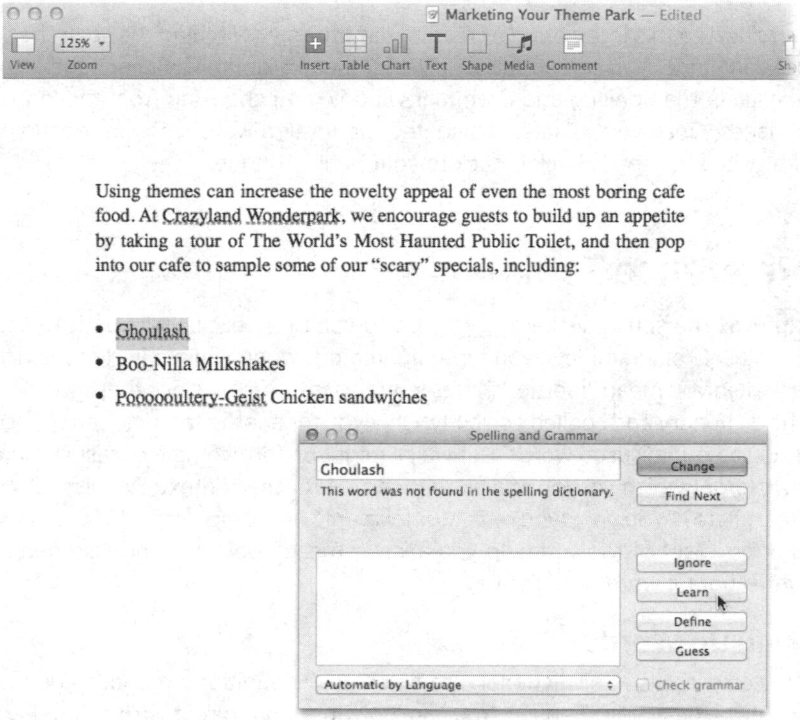

FIGURE 4-5

*The Spelling and Grammar
window lets you click your
way through the mis-
spelled words Pages has
flagged, see its guesses,
correct misspellings, teach
the dictionary new words,
and ignore certain words.
Click Define to launch
the dictionary and learn
more about the currently
selected word. Pages highlights each unrecognized
word in the document as
you do this, so you can see
the word's context.*

If none of the alternative spellings that Pages displays is correct, or if the program doesn't provide any suggestions, you can type the correct spelling yourself in the field at the top of the Spelling and Grammar window, and then click Change. You can also tell Pages to check your document for questionable grammar by turning on the Check Grammar checkbox at the bottom of the window.

Using Foreign-Language Dictionaries

Your Mac knows lots of languages and has a dictionary for each of them. Normally, the spell checker uses the dictionary that matches your system-wide language set-ting. (If you change that setting in ⌘→System Preferences→"Language and Region," you also change the language for your menus and dialog boxes.)

But say that you write multilingual documents, or perhaps you're known to sprinkle your prose with languages of the world to demonstrate your cosmopolitan credentials. When Pages spell checks your document, it doesn't find those foreign-language words in your standard dictionary and incorrectly marks them as misspelled.

You can sidestep this international crisis by temporarily switching the spell checker to a new language. You can do this by clicking the "Automatic by Language" dropdown menu in the Spelling and Grammar window and choosing from the long list of languages. Once you've safely navigated the foreign waters of your document, you can switch the spell checker back to your native tongue.

◼ Reference Tools

As helpful as the spell checker might be, you can't rely exclusively on it to catch every mistake. For example, if you type "lightening" when you mean "lightning," or "metal" when you mean "mettle," Pages won't spot the error, since these words are all in the dictionary and spelled correctly. Only you (or another reader) can spot correctly spelled but misused words. But we all might be forgiven the occasional lapse when we forget which version of a word is correct for the context: Do I use "affect" or "effect" here? "Your" or "you're"? "Compliment" or "complement"? Fortunately, Pages offers a set of tools to help you answer those questions and also find lots more info about a word or phrase.

Looking Up Words

Your Mac comes with a full dictionary, complete with definitions, pronunciation, and usage notes—the whole shebang. You can look up a word directly from your Pages document by Control-clicking it and choosing "Look Up [word]" from the shortcut menu. Doing so opens a window showing you the dictionary definition, the related thesaurus entry, and the Wikipedia definition (discussed in more detail in the next section), as shown in Figure 4-6. Click any of these entries to expand it; for example, click the word "Dictionary" to see the *full* dictionary entry.

Finding Info on the Web

Say that the simple definition of "nausea" just doesn't cut it, and imagine that you need all the facts, figures, and finer details to prove that Crazyland Wonderpark *isn't* responsible for a recent visitor's sudden bout of sickness. In such situations, Pages gives you a few easy ways to find detailed information from the Web about any topic.

When it comes to the dictionary/thesaurus/Wikipedia window, the Wikipedia section is particularly interesting. When you're connected to the Internet, click this section's heading to expand it and call up the encyclopedia entry for your word or phrase from *Wikipedia*, the Web's free encyclopedia (as shown in Figure 4-7).

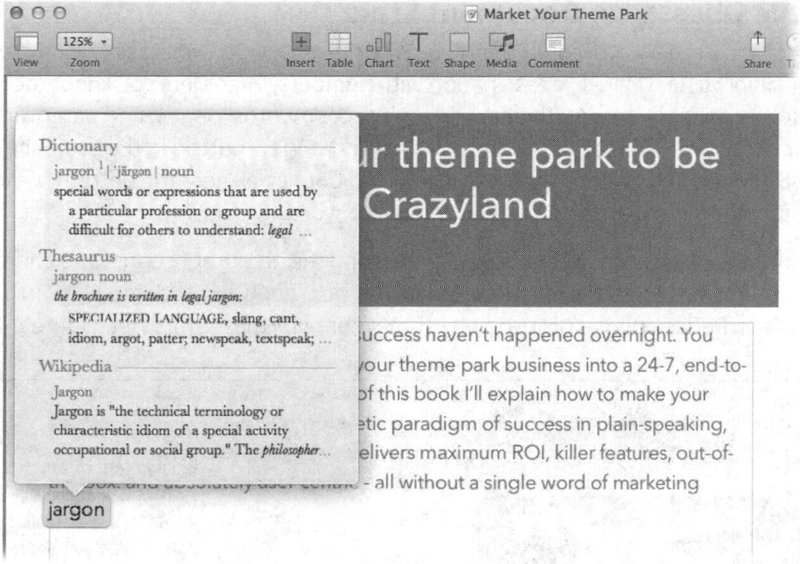

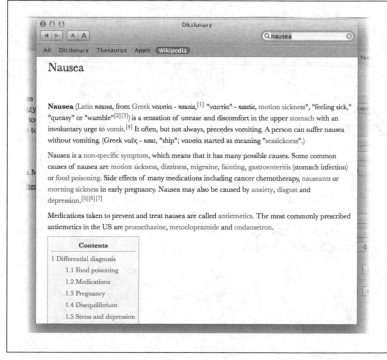

FIGURE 4-6

Control-click any word to read up on its meaning in the dictionary, look up synonyms and antonyms in the thesaurus, or read more background information on it by clicking the word "Wikipedia."

FIGURE 4-7

The Dictionary window features a Wikipedia tab, which lets you read the Wikipedia encyclopedia entry for any word or phrase. Just keep in mind that Wikipedia is written by volunteers, so it's always wise to check at least one other source to make sure Wikipedia's info is correct.

Pages offers a similar shortcut for performing a Google search: Control-click the word in question, and then select Search With Google. Pages opens Safari and takes you straight to the Google search results for the word you Control-clicked.

For the Obsessive: Document Stats

Whether you have a word-count goal (you're writing a 5,000-word essay for a class, say) or simply a Rain Man–like fascination with numbers, Pages lets you keep track of the number of characters (with and without spaces), words, pages, and paragraphs in your documents. To see these statistics, click the View button in the toolbar and select Show Word Count. This adds a little Word Count box near the bottom of your document that updates as you add and remove words.

The Word Count box is also your ticket to checking the paragraph, page, and character count. Put your cursor over the Word Count box, and then click the little arrows that appear. Pages opens a drop-down list that contains these stats (see Figure 4-8).

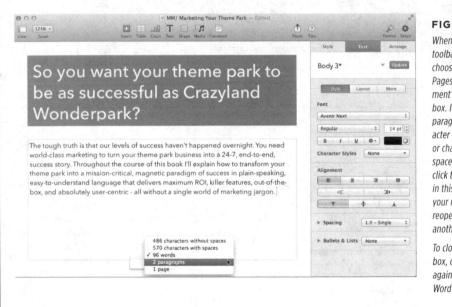

FIGURE 4-8

When you first click the toolbar's View button and choose Show Word Count, Pages displays your document's word count in this box. If you'd rather see paragraph, page, or character count with spaces, or character count without spaces, instead, simply click the appropriate items in this list. (If you change your mind, you can always reopen this list and choose another item.)

To close the Word Count box, click the View button again and select Hide Word Count.

If you want to see the statistics for a specific passage of your document, select the text you want to tally. The Word Count box updates to show you how many words, characters, pages, and paragraphs you've selected. To return to the figures for the entire document, just click anywhere outside the highlighted text to deselect it.

■ Auto-Correction and Text Substitution

Pages offers one final automatic safety net to save you from fat-finger foibles on the keyboard. Most of the time, auto-correct chugs along quite happily on its own, but there are a couple of tweaks you can make to get even more out of it. To tweak the auto-correct's settings, go to Edit→Substitutions→Show Substitutions. This opens the Substitutions window, where you can turn on, turn off, or update the following options:

- **Smart Quotes.** *Smart quotes* (also known as *curly quotes*) are usually "" and '', but did you know there's a whole world of exotic quotation marks out there? When this checkbox is turned on, you can use the two drop-down menus shown in Figure 4-9 to specify exactly what Pages should make double and single quotation marks look like.

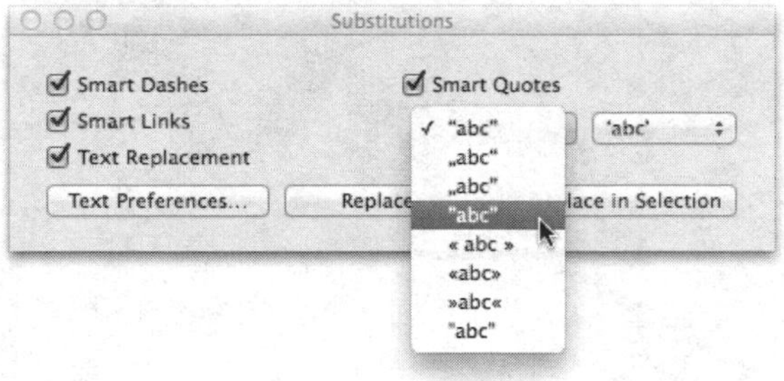

FIGURE 4-9

Tell Pages to automatically convert double and single quotation marks (" and ', respectively) to smart quotes by turning on the Smart Quotes checkbox. Set a style for the double quotation marks using the Substitution window's first drop-down menu (the one that's open in this screenshot), and set a style for single quotation marks using the second drop-down menu.

- **Smart Dashes.** When this checkbox is turned on, Pages converts double dashes (--) to *em dashes* (—).

- **Smart Links.** With this setting turned on, Pages turns all email and web addresses into hyperlinks (see page 126).

- **Text Replacement.** This option lets you create your own rules for substituting one set of text for another. It's particularly handy for inserting frequently used symbols such as © or ™ without having to memorize their keyboard shortcuts or resorting to the Characters window. Once you've turned on this checkbox, click the Text Preferences button to display a table of replacements (Figure 4-10). In this window, the Replace column lists text that Pages will automatically substitute for the corresponding text in the With column. Create your own replacement rules by clicking the + button in the lower-left corner of the window. To remove a rule, select it in the table and then click the – button. To disable all rules, close this window and return to the main Substitutes window, and then turn off the Text Replacements checkbox.

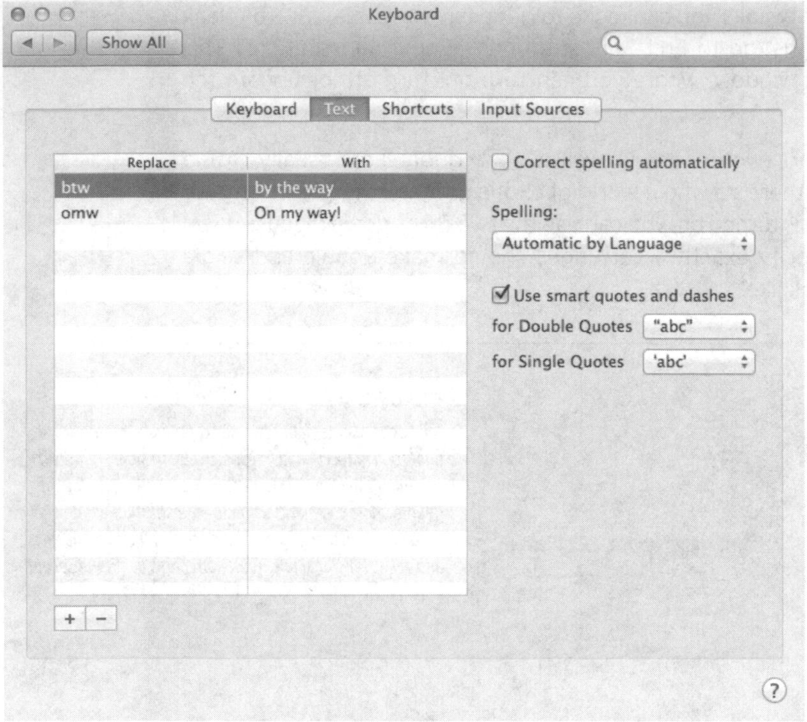

FIGURE 4-10

To create a new rule, click the + button in this window's bottom left. Then, in the Replace column, type the text that you want Pages to replace, and in the With column type the replacement text. In this example, whenever you type "omw," Pages will step in and replace it with "On my way!"

Tracking Changes

As you've seen, Pages provides a whole arsenal of tools to help you spot, prevent, and correct errors in your documents. In the end, though, these automated services can go only so far. No matter how cleverly programmed, a bucket-of-bolts wordbot is no substitute for the critical eye and creative mind of a living, breathing human editor. That's especially true when you move beyond mechanical considerations of spelling or typos and into more writerly concerns of style and substance. Even there, though, Pages can be helpful: When you're ready to solicit feedback from others, Pages plays traffic cop to keep the editing process flowing smoothly, monitoring every change made to your document.

NOTE You may be able to use iCloud to share a Pages document that has change tracking turned on (see page 749 for more on iCloud) but change tracking stops working as soon as you share your document via iCloud. However, you can share a copy of a document that has change tracking turned on; see page 256 for details.

Light-Speed Typing with Text Substitution

Although pretty empty when you first start using Pages, the Text Replacement option is a hidden powerhouse of productivity. You might be under the impression that this feature is useful only for subtle typographic corrections that turn (c) into © or 1/2 into ½. While those are handy enough, text substitution becomes really powerful when you tailor it for the words, phrases, or even *paragraphs* that you use all the time.

For example, as the owner of Crazyland Wonderpark, you notice that you frequently begin letters with the same sentence: "I'm sorry to hear that you did not enjoy your recent visit to Crazyland Wonderpark." It's tough to be sincere day after day—so cut yourself some slack and let Pages apologize for you:

1. Choose Edit→Substitutions→Show Substitutions, make sure the Text Replacement checkbox is turned on, and then click the Text Preferences button.

2. Click the + button to create a new text-substitution rule.

3. In the Replace column, enter some easy-to-remember shortcut text.

4. It's a good idea to use a string of characters that you're unlikely to type normally—otherwise, Pages might make your substitution when you don't want it. One strategy is to start your substitution with some punctuation, like a colon or a period. For example, *:sorry* might be a good shortcut for your apologetic replacement text.

5. In the With column, type your long-form text—in this example, that's your smooth-talking apology.

Now whenever you type *:sorry* followed by a space or punctuation, Pages automatically replaces that shortcut text with your full sentence.

Cleverly deployed text substitutions effectively turn you into the world's fastest typist when it comes to a range of frequently used phrases:

- **Habitual typos.** Always typing "teh" instead of "the" or "becuase" instead of "because"? Add these to your text-substitution list, and Pages manages the corrections automatically.

- **Web or email addresses.** If you often type the same email addresses or lengthy web addresses, save yourself time and errors by creating shortcuts. Now *:comp* automatically gives you *complaints@crazylandwonderpark.co.uk*—and if you have the Smart Links option turned on (page 97), Pages even turns this text into a hyperlink. Neat.

- **Phone numbers.** Like speed dial for your keyboard.

- **Product names or industry lingo.** If you're always forgetting exactly how to spell sciurophobia, create *:phobia* as a quick, easy-to-spell shortcut.

- **Boilerplate text.** Most of us have text—like the letter's apologetic intro—that we type or paste over and over again. Driving directions, company descriptions, personal introductions, and letter sign-offs are all good candidates for text substitution.

With *change tracking*, Pages quietly catalogs every edit made to your document, letting you review all additions, deletions, and replacements before accepting revisions into the final draft. While this can be handy even when you're working on text all by your lonesome, it becomes invaluable when you're collaborating with an editor, co-writing a document with others, or being critiqued by your boss. Change tracking builds a paper trail of a document's edit history so that you and others can see exactly who changed what and when.

NOTE   Pages' change tracking works seamlessly with Microsoft Word. So when you export a Pages document to Word format (page 251)—or use Pages to open a Word document (page 18)—Pages preserves the edit history. Word users can review your changes and vice versa.

Starting and Stopping Change Tracking

To turn on change tracking, choose Edit→Track Changes. Pages reveals the *review toolbar* (shown in Figure 4-11) just below the regular toolbar, where you can scroll through comments and changes, and accept and reject changes. Pages calls attention to each change by adding a *change bar*, a vertical bar in the left margin next to each edit. (The line is color-coded to match the author who made that change.)

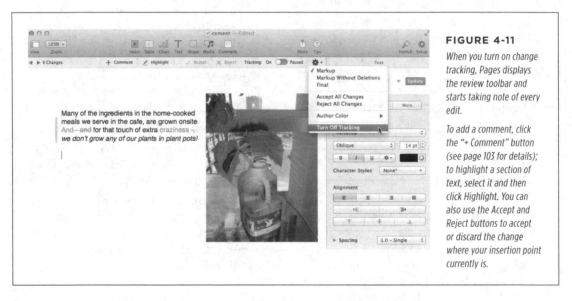

FIGURE 4-11

When you turn on change tracking, Pages displays the review toolbar and starts taking note of every edit.

To add a comment, click the "+ Comment" button (see page 103 for details); to highlight a section of text, select it and then click Highlight. You can also use the Accept and Reject buttons to accept or discard the change where your insertion point currently is.

The number of changes waiting to be accepted or rejected is shown on the left end of the review toolbar. To review these changes, click the arrow buttons to move from one change to the next. When you're looking at a change, a pop-up appears with more information about that change, and Pages highlights the relevant area in your document.

To turn off change tracking completely, click the gear icon, and then choose Turn Off Tracking. But be careful: When you turn off change tracking, you not only stop tracking future changes, you also *lose the current change history*. Pages pauses to ask if you really want to do this and, if so, lets you decide what to do with the current batch of changes, as shown in Figure 4-12.

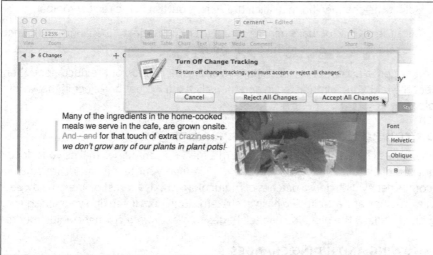

FIGURE 4-12

When you turn off change tracking, Pages asks what it should do with the current set of changes. Clicking Accept All Changes keeps the current version as is. Clicking Reject All Changes throws out the edits and reverts to the original text. (Of course, if you click the wrong button, you can always choose Edit→Undo to turn change tracking back on and fix your mistake.)

A gentler way to shut down change tracking is to put it on *pause*. This temporarily puts the tracking on hold while maintaining the current edit history; Pages doesn't track any changes that you make in paused mode. To pause change tracking, click the Tracking slider in the review toolbar to set it to Paused. To resume, click the slider to set it to the On position.

Reviewing, Accepting, and Rejecting Changes

With change tracking on, you can step through every edit and decide whether you want to *accept* or *reject* each one. When you accept an edit, it becomes a permanent part of the text. When you reject an edit, Pages peels it back, reverting to the original, unedited text. In both cases, Pages removes the change from the edit history. Think of accepting or rejecting changes like checking off items on your editorial to-do list: Once you review a change and make your decision, Pages considers the edit closed and removes it from sight.

Use any of these methods to accept a change:

- Cycle through the changes using the arrow buttons at the left end of the review toolbar. When you're looking at a change's pop-up, click the Accept icon.

- Place the insertion point inside the edited text, and then click the Accept button in the review toolbar or the pop-up that appears.

- Click the review toolbar's gear icon, and then click Accept All Changes (this command does exactly what it says: accepts *all* changes).

Pages likewise gives you three ways to reject changes:

- Click the Reject button in the change pop-up.

- Select the change and then click the Reject button in the review toolbar.

- Click the review toolbar's gear icon, and then click Reject All Changes (note that this rejects *all* changes in the document!).

If you prefer to accept or reject changes from just a *portion* of the document, then select the text you're interested in and then click the Accept or Reject in the review toolbar.

Controlling How Pages Displays Changes

As handy as change tracking can be, all this markup sometimes makes your document too busy to let you focus on your work. When your text is thick with edits, it becomes heavy with dense patches of multicolored text, a forest of lines, a crowded review toolbar, and a confusing hash of strikethrough text. If you find yourself squinting just to follow the plot, you can tell Pages to make some cosmetic adjustments.

■ SHOWING AND HIDING CHANGES

The review toolbar's gear drop-down menu (shown in Figure 4-11) offers three options for dialing Pages' markup detail up or down:

- **Markup.** Pages displays deleted text with the strikethrough style, and new text is bolded. Both new text and deletions are color-coded by author. To change the color Pages uses, open the gear menu in the review toolbar and choose a new hue from the Author Color submenu.

- **Markup Without Deletions.** Pages hides deletions and displays only new text. However, Pages still displays change bars to the left of lines where text was deleted.

- **Final.** Pages displays text without markup. The result is that you see your document as it would look if you accepted all changes. You may be wondering how this is change tracking at all, but Pages actually continues to track the changes behind the scenes, so if you want to switch to Markup or Markup Without Deletions at a later date, you can.

■ CHANGING YOUR COLOR AND NAME

If seeing your own text edits in a sickly yellow is getting you down, you can choose a new author color. In the review toolbar's gear drop-down menu, choose Author Color and pick a new hue. Alas, you can't choose colors for other authors, so you can't impose your creative vision on others, but at least you have control over your own personal style.

While you're busy overhauling your personal branding, you can also change your author handle. Unless you tell it otherwise, Pages labels your changes with your name from Address Book, but you can use any name you like. Go to Pages→Preferences, click the General button, and then enter your preferred moniker in the Author field.

Adding Comments

Besides keeping a record of changes, Pages' change-tracking feature also lets you and other editors leave *comments* about the text. Comments are notes that don't appear in the actual body of the text, but Pages lets you know these comments exist by highlighting the related text and adding a tally in the upper-left corner of the reviews toolbar (for example, "4 Changes & Comments"). To open a comment, put your cursor over the highlighted text. Like change pop-ups, comments are tethered to a particular text selection, making them a useful way to ask questions, offer suggestions, or leave yourself a reminder about a particular passage. They're like Post-It notes that you slap on the document—temporary messages fixed to your text while also remaining separate from it. Comments have a colored band that matches your author color, so you can easily see who's saying what.

To add a comment, select the text you want to annotate, and then click the "+ Comment" button in the review toolbar. Pages displays a comment pop-up and adds a colored square in the margin to the left of the original text (see Figure 4-13). Type your comment in the pop-up, which grows and shrinks to fit your text, and then click outside the pop-up when you're done. To edit a comment, click its colored square (or click the text it's attached to) to display it, and then click inside its pop-up and type away (you can edit other editors' comments as well as your own). To delete a comment, click the Delete button in the comment's pop-up, or delete the annotated text from your document.

FIGURE 4-13

Comments let you add notes and annotations to your text, a useful way to leave yourself research notes and reminders, or to gather suggestions as you pass a document around to a group for feedback. Every comment is anchored to a specific passage of text, which Pages highlights (as shown here). Pages also adds a colored square to the left of this text (circled).

You can hide all comments by choosing View→Comments and Changes→Hide Comments. To coax your document's comments back into the open, go to View→ Comments and Changes→Show Comments.

Although comments look similar to change pop-ups, they're not technically part of change tracking. So you can leave comments when change tracking is turned off, and when you accept or reject all changes, your comments remain intact.

Wiping the Change History

Before you email your business proposal to the client, it's probably best to clear out the comments making fun of the ridiculous shirt he wore to the meeting last Thursday. Ditto for the change tracking that shows that you arbitrarily doubled your fee five minutes before sending the proposal. You get the idea: After you've gathered and reviewed all the edits and finally rounded the corner into final-draft territory, turn off change tracking by going to Edit→Turn Off Tracking, and then remove all those incriminating comments by going to Edit→"Remove Highlights and Comments."

Now your scrubbed and typo-free document is ready to be shared with the world. But before you do that...wouldn't your masterpiece look better with a table of contents, some numbered page footers, or perhaps a multicolumn layout? That's the stuff of document formatting, which just happens to be the subject of the next chapter.

Formatting and Organizing Documents

The last few chapters focused on editing and formatting your prose, with an eye on refining the details of your document at the word, sentence, and paragraph level. This chapter takes the big-picture view, turning to the layout and organization of your entire document. That includes nitty-gritty housekeeping tasks like setting page margins, headers, footnotes, and page size, and the grander architectural work of dividing hard-to-swallow blocks of text into more manageable columns and creating a table of contents. These features benefit both you and your readers, making it easy for everyone to navigate your text.

As you'll see, most of Pages' document-management tools—such as page numbering and tables of contents—are geared toward longer documents. However, some of the options you'll encounter throughout this chapter, like protecting your document with a password or adding hyperlinks, come in handy for documents of all sizes.

This chapter covers all these advanced organizational issues and more, but first, you'll dip a toe in the waters with some basic page formatting.

◾ Document Formatting

The overall layout of an individual page—and your entire document—depends on what's known as *document formatting*. This high-level formatting determines how Pages handles things like your document's page margins, hyphenation, and footnotes.

To change document formatting, use the aptly named *Document tab*. At the right end of Pages' toolbar, click the Setup button to replace the Format panel with the

Setup panel, which contains two tabs: Document and Section. If it isn't already open, click the Document tab to get your grubby paws on the document-formatting settings (Figure 5-1).

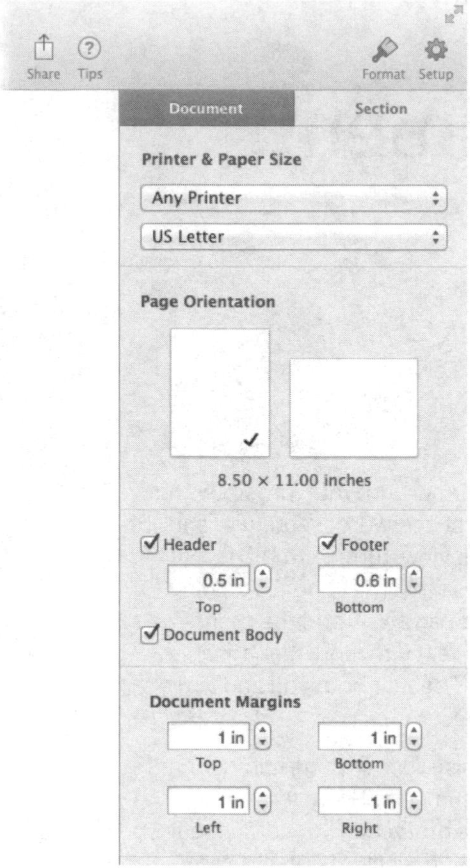

FIGURE 5-1

Pages' Document settings are your key to changing the overall layout of a document: page size, margins, header and footer size, and so on. This is also where you find the master switches for hyphenation and ligatures.

The Document tab also contains a Document Body checkbox that lets you remove the document's body (complete with all inline objects and body text). Unless you're absolutely sure you want a document that's practically nothing but headers and footers, leave this checkbox turned on.

(Technically, Apple calls the Setup panel the Document Setup Inspector, and choosing View→Inspector→Document Setup hides or shows the panel. This book uses the term "Setup panel" consistently because the button at the right end of Pages' toolbar is labeled "Setup," so don't be confused if you read a tutorial that mentions the Document Setup Inspector.)

Page Setup

At the top of the Setup panel's Document tab, the Printer & Paper Size section lets you control the paper size you'll use to print your document. To change the paper size, click the second drop-down menu (which is initially set to US Letter) and choose the size you want. You can also change the document's *page orientation—portrait* (vertical) or *landscape* (horizontal)—by clicking either of the page thumbnails in the Document tab's Page Orientation section.

You can access these same options via File→Page Setup, which also offers some additional page setup-related goodies. In the File→Page Setup window, you can change the document's *scale* to print at a reduced size (less than 100 percent) or a magnified size (more than 100 percent). And if none of the paper sizes that Pages offers fit the bill, you can create a custom paper size. Simply open the Paper Size drop-down menu, and then select Manage Custom Sizes to open the Custom Paper Sizes window (shown in Figure 5-2).

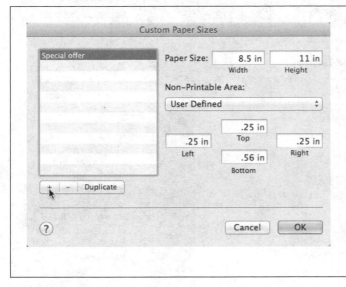

FIGURE 5-2

If none of the provided paper sizes meet your high standards, you can create your own in this window. Start by clicking the + button (where the cursor is here) to add a new, untitled paper size. Double-click the word "Untitled" and enter a more memorable name. Then type your custom sizes in the Width and Height boxes, and type margin measurements in the Top, Left, Right, and Bottom boxes (there's more about margins in the next section). Once you're happy with the info you've entered, click OK to save this custom size. From this point onward, this paper size appears in the File→Page Setup window's Paper Sizes drop-down menu.

To delete a custom size, reopen the Custom Paper Sizes window, select the size in question, and then click the – (minus) button.

Adjusting Page Margins

The margins are the blank space that appears all the way around your pages. To change your margin settings, head to the Setup panel (if it's not open, click the Setup button in the toolbar) and select the Document tab. In the panel's Document Margins section, use the up and down arrows to change the margins, or type a new value in the measurement fields for any of the four sides—Top, Bottom, Left, or Right.

NOTE The top and bottom margins set the spacing between the edge of the paper and your body text. These margin settings don't affect the document's headers or footers, which are *inside* the document margin that you set here.

The numbers you type into these fields have to be in decimal form (.75 equals three-quarters, for example); fractions aren't accepted. And don't bother with entering the "in" for inches—Pages assumes you're using the ruler's current unit of measurement (page 459).

Working with Headers and Footers

Use headers and footers to display information about your document at the top or bottom of the page. You can use these repeating strips to hold anything you want: a logo or other image, a date, a legal warning or copyright notice, or even an ad (see Figure 5-3 for an example).

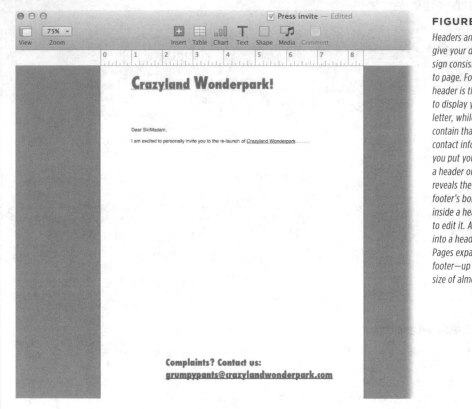

FIGURE 5-3
Headers and footers can give your document design consistency from page to page. For example, a header is the perfect place to display your logo in a letter, while the footer can contain that all-important contact information. When you put your cursor over a header or footer, Pages reveals the header and footer's borders. Just click inside a header or footer to edit it. As you enter text into a header or footer, Pages expands the header/footer—up to a maximum size of almost half a page.

Glance down at the bottom of this book's pages for another example of a footer. Here, headers and footers are different on right and left pages; both include page numbers, but left pages display the book's title, while right pages display the chapter title. You can also add headers and footers to much shorter documents to include your letterhead or return address, the date or time you created the document, the name of the Pages file, and so on.

Headers and footers are always turned on in new documents, but you can get rid of them (or bring them back again) by going to the Setup tab's Document tab (shown in Figure 5-1) and turning the Headers and Footers checkboxes on or off. But be careful: These settings affect *every* page of your document, and when you turn off headers or footers, you also delete the text they contain. Turning them back on gives you only empty fields, and you'll need to start from square one.

The Document tab also lets you change the margins for headers and footers. Use the up and down arrows next to the Header and Footer boxes, or enter a new value to adjust the space between the edge of the paper and the start of the header or footer.

NOTE If you create a perfectly formatted document, complete with headers and footers, you can easily create stationery from it by removing the body text. The safest way is to save a copy of the document: Choose File→Duplicate, and then save the copy. Next, make sure you're working on the duplicate, head to the Setup panel's Document tab, and turn off the Document Body checkbox. Pages asks if you really want to remove the body of the document; click Convert, and your body text disappears. You now have yourself some lovely stationery.

To add a header or footer to any Pages document, make sure that headers and footers are turned on in the Setup panel's Document tab, and then choose View→Show Layout. Pages reveals ghostlike outlines around the header and footer (as well as the other areas in your document). Click inside any of the six header or footer sections, and then enter and format your text just as you would any other text in your document (to get access to all the usual character and paragraph formatting options, click the Format button in the toolbar).

Strictly speaking, you don't actually *have* to choose Show Layout to enter header and footer text—doing so simply reveals the header or footer outlines so you have a target to aim for. You could instead put your cursor over one of the header or footer areas; when the cursor's in the right position, Pages reveals the header/footer outline. But if you find yourself waving the cursor around trying to find the header/footer, then the Show Layout command is your friend.

TIP To add a page number to your header or footer, choose Insert→Page Number. You'll learn more about numbering pages, and other auto-formatted text, on page 119.

Headers and footers aren't just for text. You can add photos or artwork—a logo perhaps—and these objects behave the same in headers and footers as they do in the body of the page.

As mentioned earlier, whatever you add to a header or footer shows up on *every* page of your document, unless you specifically tell Pages otherwise. To change the layout or content of headers or footers in different parts of your document, or to make headers and footers appear only in part of your document, you first need to break the document into sections using section breaks. You'll learn about section breaks and how to customize individual sections of your document later in this chapter (see page 114). For now, just know that you can hide the headers and footers on the first page of a multipage document by using the options in the Setup panel's Section tab (Figure 5-4).

NOTE To see the kinds of effects you can achieve by dividing a document into sections and creating different headers and footers for each section, go to this book's Missing CD page at *www.missingmanuals.com/cds* and download the file *headers_footers.pages*.

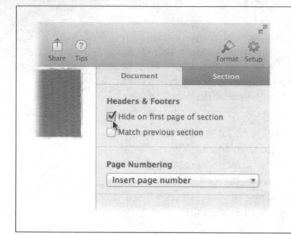

FIGURE 5-4

The Setup panel's section tab includes some handy settings. The "Hide on first page of section" checkbox lets you hide headers and footers on the first page of your document (or, more specifically, the first page of the current section).

The Fine Print: Footnotes and Endnotes

If you're the scholarly type or have a fetish for fine print, you can use *footnotes* or *endnotes* (collectively known simply as *notes*) to cite your sources or add a comment to your text. Pages inserts a superscript number or symbol—the *reference mark*—into your text and then adds the actual note text either to the bottom of the same page, just above the page footer (for footnotes), or to the end of the section or document (for endnotes). Figure 5-5 shows a footnote.

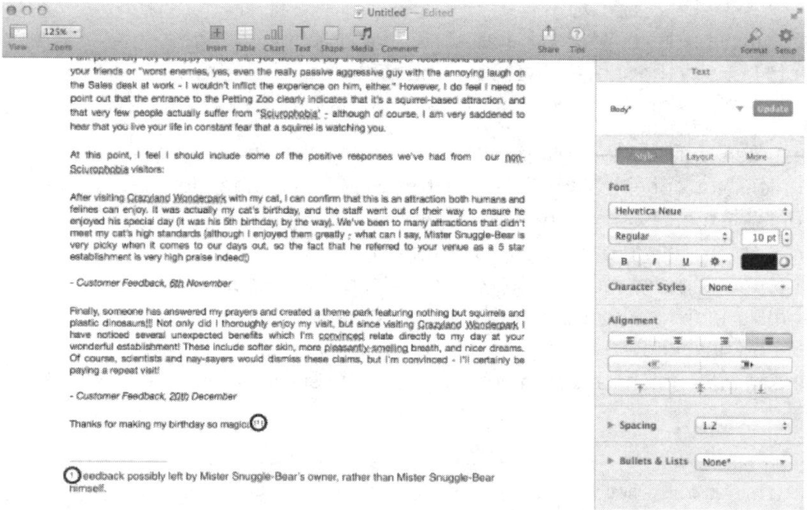

FIGURE 5-5

Footnotes appear at the bottom of the same page where you insert the reference mark into your text. Pages inserts a superscript number or symbol (circled, top) into the text and then adds a corresponding note field (circled, bottom) to the bottom of the page. When you create a footnote, Pages takes you directly to the corresponding note field, ready for you to start typing your note. You can change the footnote at any time by clicking inside the note field and typing away.

> **NOTE** You can add notes only to the main text of word-processing documents—you can't add them to text that appears in text boxes, shapes, graphs, or tables. (See page 15 for a reminder on the differences between word-processing and page layout documents.) You can't add notes to page-layout documents at all.

■ ADDING NOTES

Odd as it sounds, in Pages, all notes start off as footnotes. Even if your goal is to add an endnote, you first add a footnote and then transform it *into* an endnote. To add a footnote, place the insertion point where you want the reference mark to appear and then choose Insert→Footnote. Pages adds the reference mark to your text and takes you straight to the note's *note field*, a text box where you can type your note. To turn this footnote into an endnote, make sure your insertion point is inside the note field; next, open the Format panel's Footnotes tab, open the Type drop-down menu, and then choose Document Endnotes or Section Endnotes.

Pages styles footnotes and endnotes with the built-in Footnote paragraph style, but you can format the text however you like in exactly the same way you format any other text (by clicking the Format button in the toolbar, and then, in the Format panel's Text tab, applying the usual formatting changes). To delete a note, simply delete its reference mark in the body of your text. To move a note to a new location, cut (⌘-X) its reference mark, and then paste (⌘-V) it into a new location. As you add, move, and delete notes, Pages automatically renumbers your notes so they're all kept ordered and tidy. For footnotes, Pages also does the necessary content contortions to keep the notes on the same page as the text they're referring to.

■ SETTING YOUR DISPLAY PREFERENCES FOR NOTES

When you select a footnote or endnote, the Footnotes tab appears in the Format panel. (If the Format panel is closed, click the Format button in Pages' toolbar to open it.) This tab contains settings that control how your notes appear in your document. The Type drop-down menu offers three options:

- **Footnotes.** Choose this option to display footnotes at the bottom of the page where you insert them.

- **Document Endnotes.** Choose this option to show notes only at the very end of your document. Pages inserts a section break at the end of the document to create a new page for the endnotes. If you like, you can add extra text to this endnotes page—a header or introductory text, for example. If you prefer not to have the endnotes in their own page or section, then simply delete the section break that Pages adds (see page 114 for info about section breaks).

- **Section Endnotes.** This setting tells Pages to hold your notes until the end of each section of your document (for when you're creating chapter endnotes, say). Pages adds the endnotes to the last page of the section. For more about sections, see page 114.

> **TIP** The box on page 113 describes another option for adding endnotes to Pages documents.

Pages provides three numbering styles for notes: Arabic (1, 2, 3), Roman (i, ii, iii), and symbol (*, †, ‡, and so on). Choose the style you prefer from the Footnotes tab's Format drop-down menu.

The tab's Numbering drop-down menu controls how Pages numbers your footnotes. Choose Continuous to number all footnotes from the beginning of the document to the end. "Restarts on Each Page" starts the number sequence over again on each new page that contains footnotes. And "Restarts on Each Section" restarts the numbering sequence after each section break (page 114 has more about sections).

The last option on the Footnotes tab is the Space Between Notes setting, which lets you add or reduce the white space between each note. Click the up or down arrow to change the value, or type a new value directly into the text field.

All of these settings apply to your entire document. This means that you can't mix and match endnotes and footnotes in the same document, or switch numbering styles midway through a document. Also, changing any of these settings instantly converts all notes in your document to the new setting. For example, if you choose Document Endnotes from the Type drop-down menu, Pages shuffles *all* of your footnotes to the back of the document. Likewise, changing the Format or Numbering settings renumbers all notes to match the new setting.

Automatic Hyphenation

Near the bottom of the Setup panel's Document tab (to see it, click the Setup button in Pages' toolbar, and then click the Document tab) is a Hyphenation checkbox that lets you turn automatic hyphenation on or off for your entire document. Turning on this checkbox tells Pages to squeeze as much text as possible onto each line by hyphenating words and splitting them onto the next line. Pages' standard setting for hyphenation is "off," which is just as well because this feature is aggressive about splitting words—even short ones—which can make your text more difficult to read. For typical word-processing documents with wide columns of text, hyphenation isn't really necessary. But it becomes really useful when you have narrow columns with justified alignment (page 49) that would otherwise create unsightly wrinkles and bulges of white space in your text.

Turning on the Hyphenation checkbox tells Pages to add hyphens for your entire document whenever it deems them necessary. However, even with this setting turned on, you can turn hyphenation off for individual paragraphs: Place your insertion point inside the paragraph in question, click the toolbar's Format button to open the Format panel, click the Text tab (if it's not already selected), and then click the More button. Finally, turn on the "Remove paragraph hyphenation" checkbox.

Using Ligatures

If you're a fan of ligatures (the box on page 48 explains what they are), you'll be pleased to know that Pages automatically turns on ligatures for new documents. Why? Because, while not all fonts include ligatures, those that do generally look better when you use these connected characters. To turn ligatures off for a whole document, head to the Setup panel's Document tab and turn off the Ligatures checkbox.

Citations and Bibliographies with EndNote

For students, researchers, and academics, writing projects are typically chock-full of citations and bibliographic references—so much so that most scholars create elaborate systems to track and manage the articles and books they reference in their work. EndNote is an especially popular program for creating a personal database of relevant readings. Pages works hand in hand with EndNote X6 or later to insert citations into your document, automatically adding and updating a bibliography of referenced works along the way. To learn more about End-Note or to buy the program, visit *www.endnote.com*. Before EndNote can communicate with Pages, you need to install the Pages EndNote plug-in; head over to *http://support.apple.com/kb/DL1692* to download the installer. Once the installer has finished downloading, track it down in your Finder, and double-click it to begin the installation.

If a citation is just a traffic ticket as far as you're concerned, move along. But if you have EndNote X6 or later installed on your Mac, Pages adds the EndNote Citation and EndNote Bibliography commands to Pages' Insert menu. Before using them, though, be sure that you've assigned a default library in EndNote that the program should use whenever it launches. (In EndNote, a *library* is a collection of references to books, articles, and other sources; Pages always uses the default library when it adds citations.) To add or edit a citation:

1. In Pages, place the insertion point where you want the citation to appear in your document—a footnote, perhaps—and then choose Insert→EndNote Citation. EndNote opens and displays its Find EndNote Citations window.

2. In the Find field, type part of the name of the source you want to cite, and then press Return to search EndNote for the citation to use.

3. Use the Find EndNote Citations window's controls to choose how the citation appears in your Pages document.

4. If applicable, enter a page range in the Citation Range field. To add the citation to the document's bibliography without including the citation text in the document, turn on the "Only insert into the bibliography" checkbox.

5. Select a citation from the list, and then click Insert.

When you add a document's first citation, Pages automatically adds a bibliography to the end of the file, with the citation as its first entry. As you add more citations, Pages updates the bibliography with the new info. To change the citation format, choose Edit→EndNote Citations→Bibliography Format and pick a style.

To delete a citation in your document, select the citation, and then press Delete.

Like hyphenation, this feature is document-wide, but you can turn ligatures off for individual paragraphs by placing your insertion point inside a paragraph and then going to the Format panel's Text tab, clicking the More button, and then turning on the "Remove ligatures" checkbox.

■ Organizing Your Document with Sections

In Pages, you can use *sections* to mark divisions between your document's main topics in the same way that newspaper sections or book chapters create clear breaks in subject matter. In fact, sections are exactly how you'd go about dividing chapters of a book in Pages—in your manuscript for *Marketing Your Theme Park: The Missing Manual*, for example. Starting a new section for each chapter lets you make subtle formatting changes to each one. For example, you can change the page footer so your reader knows that she's reading "Chapter 3: Launching Your First PR campaign" or "Chapter 4: Recovering from Your First PR Disaster."

Specifically, you can use sections to change any of the following formatting elements from one part of your document to the next: headers, footers, page numbering, margins, and column layout. (Hang in there, you'll learn about columns later in this chapter—specifically, on page 116.) Sections let you move, delete, or apply changes to an entire group of pages all at once.

> **NOTE** If you're not sure whether to use sections or to simply create multiple documents, the box below can help you decide.

ORGANIZATION STATION

New Sections or Separate Files?

When you create lengthy, complex word-processing documents—books, reports, dissertations, and so on—you may find it convenient to break them up into chapters, and have one chapter per file. For example, a book with 10 chapters would be composed of 10 separate files. You can then format each file differently to reflect the kind of information it contains, while using styles to keep the overall appearance similar. Backup bonus: You don't put all your eggs in one basket—if one of your files goes south, you don't lose your entire manuscript.

But there are also good arguments for keeping your entire manuscript in one file. For example, doing so lets you use the Find or Find & Replace commands to search your entire manuscript at once; and making style changes across the entire document is a one-step process. Using Pages' sections feature, you can break your document into as many sections as you like, each with distinct formatting.

So what's the right solution? It really comes down to personal preference, but it's generally a good idea to split documents into separate files under these conditions:

- **Very long documents.** Finding your way through hundreds of pages of text can become a slog. Dividing documents of more than, say, 100 pages into smaller files makes maintenance and editing easier.

- **Many authors.** When different people are writing different sections of your document, give each author his own file for his portion of the text.

- **Rolling editorial process.** If you want to send chapters of your book to your editor as you finish them, splitting them into separate files means that she can make revisions to one file while you forge ahead with the rest.

Under most other conditions, it's better to keep your document in one file, even when you have a complex collection of layout elements. For example, you might write a business report that contains an introductory narrative; a section with lots of facts, figures, tables, and footnotes that's set in two columns; another section featuring customer endorsements with photographs that's set in three columns; and a concluding narrative. For this type of job, divide (into sections) and conquer!

Adding Sections

You can insert a section break anywhere in a Pages document. Put your insertion point at the beginning of the text that should be in the new section, and then choose Insert→Section Break. Pages adds the break and moves the text that follows it onto the next page.

Pages makes it easy to review where your document's different sections begin and end. In the toolbar, click the View button and select Show Page Thumbnails (or choose View→Show Page Thumbnails) to display the Page Thumbnails sidebar. This sidebar shows every page of your document as little page-by-page snapshots. Clicking any page highlights its entire section in a yellow border, as shown in Figure 5-6.

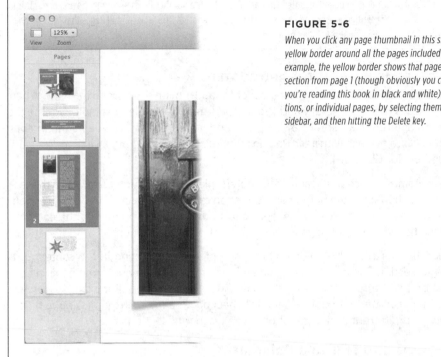

FIGURE 5-6

When you click any page thumbnail in this sidebar, Pages puts a yellow border around all the pages included in that section. In this example, the yellow border shows that pages 2 and 3 are in a separate section from page 1 (though obviously you can't see that border if you're reading this book in black and white). You can also delete sections, or individual pages, by selecting them in the Page Thumbnails sidebar, and then hitting the Delete key.

Section breaks are like page breaks on steroids, giving you not only a new page but also a new set of display rules that you can customize for the new section of text. The new section starts life as a clone of the previous section, with the exact same layout, headers, footers, and so on. Once you've created a new section, it's time to start customizing its layout and formatting.

■ PAGE NUMBERING

To add page numbers to this new section, put your insertion point anywhere in its text; next, click the toolbar's Setup button, and then click the Setup panel's Section tab. Choose a page numbering format from the Page Numbering drop-down menu, and the Section tab changes to include all the options you need to specify exactly how Pages should handle page numbering within your new section.

Choose your preferred numbering scheme from the Page Numbering drop-down menu (1, 2, 3 or i, ii, iii, for instance). If you leave the "Continue from previous section" radio button turned on, Pages keeps rolling with the same page numbering.

For example, if the previous section ended on page 14, your new section starts with page 15. If you prefer to start at a different number, choose "Start at" instead, and then enter the page number you want the section to begin counting from.

> **TIP** You can use the Section tab's settings to adjust the page numbering of the first section of a document, too, or even in a document that doesn't have any section breaks at all. If you want to start numbering your pages from anywhere other than page 1, choose "Start at" and enter the number for the document's first page. This is useful when you're writing a book and have your chapters in separate files: You can tell Pages that the first page of your Chapter 4 document is actually page 136.

■ CUSTOMIZING HEADERS AND FOOTERS

It's often helpful to change the header or footer from one section to the next. When you're designing the Crazyland Wonderpark newsletter, for example, you might have a different header for News, Events, and Visitor Letters. Or you might number your book's preface with italic Roman numerals in the footer but switch to "regular" numbers for Chapter 1.

To customize a section's headers and footers, place the insertion point within the section and then go to the Setup panel's Section tab. In the Headers & Footers section, turn off the "Match previous section" checkbox. Now, as you modify the contents of the header and footer, your changes affect only this section.

Page 110 describes the "Hide on first page of section" setting in the context of a single-section document. For documents with multiple sections, turning this checkbox on or off affects the headers in the current section *only*. For example, turning on the "Hide on first page of section" checkbox means that the first page of the *section* is different from the rest of the pages in that section.

Layouts and Multiple Columns

Pages' layout settings let you control the number of text columns in a section, and that section's margins. In word-processing documents, every section has its own layout, and changing the layout settings lets you have one column of text in the first section, three in the next, and so on. And if you're using objects such as shapes or text boxes (see Chapter 7 for more info), each object has its own layout, so you can set a different number of columns in each one (this applies to both word-processing and page-layout documents).

Adding columns to a document can dramatically improve readability by making it easier to track from one line to the next. A narrow text column means less distance for your eyes to sweep back across the page to find the beginning of the next line. By dividing text into narrower columns, readers' eyes don't have to zig and zag quite so far. The wider the page and the smaller the type, the more important columns are for reducing line length. (For exhibit A, check out any newspaper.)

TIP Readability studies show that a comfortable reading width is 50 to 80 characters per line. With words averaging between 5 and 10 letters, that means that your columns should ideally have approximately 8 to 12 words per line.

■ ADDING COLUMNS

Pages makes creating columns effortless. Put your insertion point anywhere in the *layout* that you want to format (such as a section in a word-processing document or in an object like a text box), open the Format panel to the Text tab, and then click the Layout button. Use the arrows next to the Columns heading to increase or decrease the number of columns, as shown in Figure 5-7.

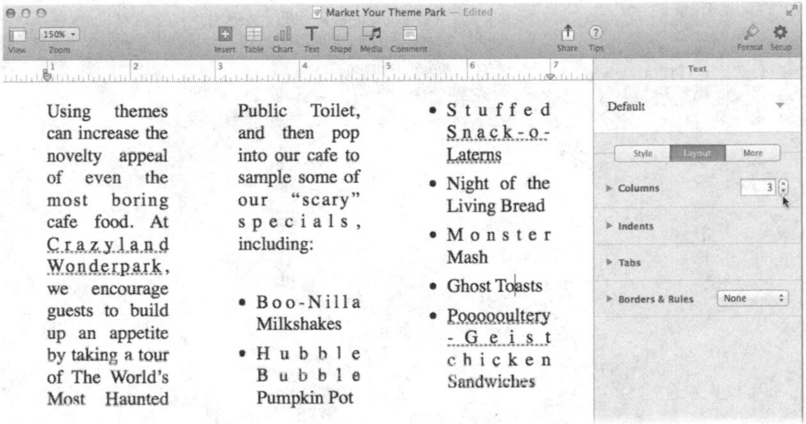

FIGURE 5-7

The Format panel's Columns section lets you slice your text into columns. Choose the number of columns you want, and Pages organizes your document's text into evenly spaced columns. (The number of columns you can create depends on the dimensions of your page.)

NOTE If you haven't added any section breaks to your word-processing document, changing the number of columns affects the entire document.

But what if you want your columns to be of varying widths, or you need to add more space between them? The Format panel has you covered.

■ ADJUSTING THE NUMBER AND WIDTH OF COLUMNS

Thought the Format panel's Columns section was just a single text field and a couple of arrows? Think again! Click the Columns heading to expand this section and uncover a mini table that gives you complete control over your columns (Figure 5-8).

To change the number of columns, enter a new number in the Columns field or click its arrow buttons. Pages lets you create up to 10 columns, but the maximum for each document depends on the document's page size and orientation. For example, Pages will create up to seven columns on a Classic Letter-size sheet—but in reality, the maximum you'd actually want to use is more like four.

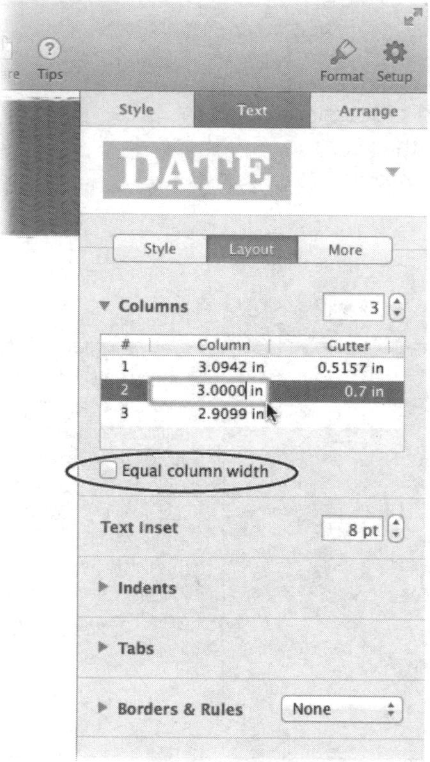

FIGURE 5-8

The expanded Columns section gives you precise control over the number and size of your columns and gutters (the space between columns). Each column is listed in the table, along with its width and the width of its gutter.

To change the size of a gutter or the width of a column, first make sure the "Equal column width" checkbox (circled) is turned off—if it isn't, Pages will apply your edits to all of the columns or gutters. (If you want to apply your change to all your columns or gutters, then leave the "Equal column width" setting turned on.) Then, in the table, double-click the width or gutter measurement of any column, and then type your preferred width. In this screenshot, the width of the second column is being changed.

■ **COLUMN BREAKS**

Use a *column break* to end one column's text and force the text to continue at the top of the next column, as shown in Figure 5-9. Without column breaks, columns continue all the way down to the bottom of the page before moving to the next column; adding a break is the only way to jump text to the next column before reaching the bottom of the page.

Column breaks are a good way to add white space at the bottom of a page or layout, or to even out columns when the last column doesn't quite reach the bottom of the page. You can also use column breaks to prevent *"almost" orphans* and *"almost" widows*—two unsightly lines of a paragraph left behind at the bottom or top of a column.

To create a column break, place the insertion point where you want the column to end, and then choose Insert→Column Break. Pages shifts the insertion point and any text below it to the top of the next column. You can also add a column break by clicking the Insert button in the toolbar, and then selecting Column Break.

To remove a column break, first you have to turn on invisibles so you can actually see it; choose View→Show Invisibles. Select the column-break character (circled in Figure 5-9), and then press Delete. Alternatively, you could Control-click the icon and then choose Cut.

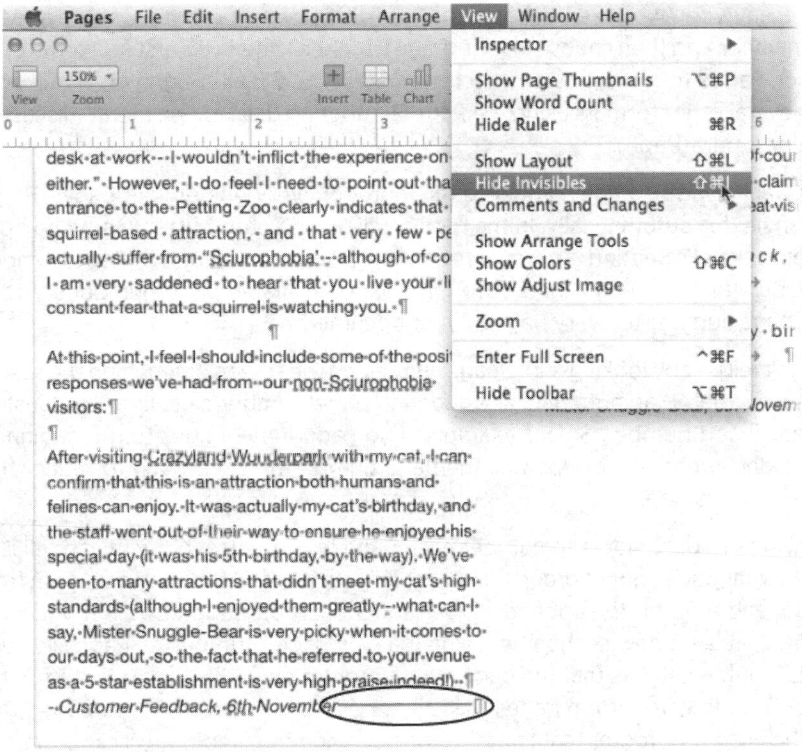

FIGURE 5-9

Column breaks control where the text in a column ends. You could, for example, end a column at a paragraph break, or start a new column to correspond with a heading that launches into a new subject.

To see the column-break character (circled), choose View→Show Invisibles. To make the Invisibles, er, in-visible again, click Choose View→Hide Invisibles.

■ Auto-Entry: Formatted Text Fields

Need to include repeating informational tidbits (things like page number, date, and so on) that show stats about your document? Pages offers three flavors of special auto-entry text called *formatted text fields*. You simply add these handy items to your document, and then Pages automatically fills in the blank with the relevant info. These are the three kinds of formatted text fields:

- **Page Number.** The number of the current page; particularly useful to add to your document's header or footer.

- **Page Count.** The total number of pages in your document.

- **Date and Time.** The current date and/or time, formatted the way you like.

The following sections explain each of these options in detail.

Page Numbers and Page Counts

What is hands down the most popular form of automatic text entry, usually found in headers and footers? The *page number*. Pages lets you insert the current page number anywhere you like: Just place the insertion point where you want to add the page number and then choose Insert→Page Number. When you first insert the page number, Pages formats it as an Arabic numeral (1, 2, 3), although you can choose from several other formats using the Page Numbering drop-down menu (discussed in the next paragraph).

If you want to add a page number to the footer of every one of your pages, Pages can handle this automatically. In the toolbar, click the Setup button, and then open the Setup panel's Section tab. You'll see a drop-down menu labeled "Page Numbering." Open this menu and choose from the list of available page-number styles to add a page number to every page of your document.

You can't tell just by looking at the page number on the screen, but behind the scenes Pages has created an automatically updating page-number calculator—not just an ordinary typed number. So, for example, if you add a few pages to the beginning of your document, Pages updates the page number on each page to reflect that page's new position.

Pages' default behavior is to number each page in sequence, but you can tell it to number your pages out of order. For example, your page numbering could run from 1–1,000, and then hit the appendix. Your appendix is on page 1,001, but you want to show that it's a new section by giving it a new page "number": i. Pages lets you do this, but the catch is that the page number (or letter, in this case) must be in the header or footer. To inform Pages that page 1,001 is now page i, go to page 1,001, click the header or footer that contains the page number, and then click "Start new header/footer here" in the pop-up. This breaks the link with the previous headers and footers, so you're free to go to the Setup panel's Section tab, select the "Start at" option, and then enter a new number or choose a new format (such as Roman numerals) without affecting any of the headers or footers that come before it.

The "Start at" setting is handy if you want to start your page-numbering sequence at a number other than 1 if, say, this document is the third chapter of a larger work. In the Setup panel's Section tab, turn on the "Start at" radio button, and then enter a starting number in the box.

To remove a page number, select it and then press Delete. Pages removes the page number from *all* the pages of the current section (or, if your document doesn't include any section breaks, the entire document).

NOTE When you insert a page number or page count field into a document, it looks just like any other number you type into a document. Even if you display invisibles (View→Show Invisibles), Pages gives you no indication that these numbers are actually formatted text fields. And if you highlight the number and type another number to replace it, you actually completely delete the formatted text field and replace it with a regular ol' number character. So you just have to remember where you added formatted text fields (or keep them out of harm's way by putting them in the header or footer).

■ ADDING A PAGE COUNT

You can also add a *page count field* to your text by choosing Insert→Page Count. The Page Count text field reports the total number of pages in your document...kind of.

More specifically, the page count is the page number of the last page in the current run of page numbers. Most documents start at page 1 and never reset their page numbers; in those cases, the page count is indeed the number of pages in the document—the same as the page number of the last page in your document.

However, if you add a new section to your document and reset the page number (as explained on page 115), the page count gets reset, too. So, if you create a new section on page 10 and then tell Pages that the page numbering for this section should restart at 1, then the page count field forgets everything that's come before and shows a page count of 1. Page counts are handy if you want to reassure busy readers that there aren't *too* many pages in your brochure.

Inserting the Date and Time

When you choose Insert→Date & Time, Pages adds a *date and time field*, which at first lives up to only the first half of its name—the field shows today's date in this format: Friday, November 14, 2014.

You'll quickly discover that you can't edit a date and time text field; it appears in your document as a solid, unbreakable block of text that resists your efforts to click inside it. Instead, when you click the field, Pages opens a little window where you can edit the date's format, or even change the date and time that's displayed, as shown in Figure 5-10.

When you're done making changes in the editing window, you're ready to send it away. But like a late-night guest or a chatty officemate, the window doesn't always know when to leave. There's no Close button or other obvious way to get rid of it. The secret (and you can use this tip for that guest and officemate, too) is to ignore it: Click anywhere outside the editing window to make it disappear.

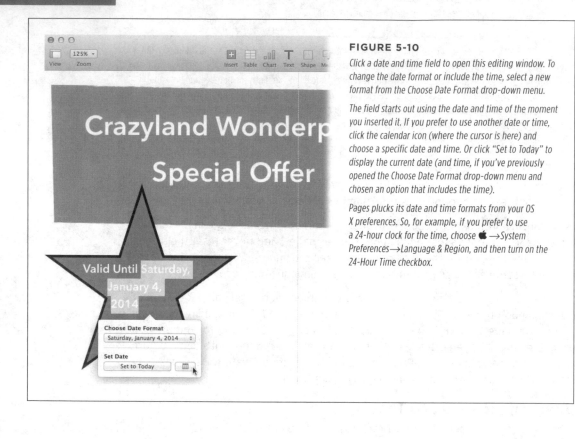

FIGURE 5-10
Click a date and time field to open this editing window. To change the date format or include the time, select a new format from the Choose Date Format drop-down menu.

The field starts out using the date and time of the moment you inserted it. If you prefer to use another date or time, click the calendar icon (where the cursor is here) and choose a specific date and time. Or click "Set to Today" to display the current date (and time, if you've previously opened the Choose Date Format drop-down menu and chosen an option that includes the time).

Pages plucks its date and time formats from your OS X preferences. So, for example, if you prefer to use a 24-hour clock for the time, choose →System Preferences→Language & Region, and then turn on the 24-Hour Time checkbox.

Adding a Table of Contents

With a little advance planning as you design your word-processing document, Pages can automatically generate a *table of contents* for you with one click. The secret is to format all your headings and subheadings using *styles*. In fact, that's the only way to do it—to let Pages build a table of contents (or *TOC* for short), you have to consistently use styles so that Pages can identify your headings and subheadings. If you're not yet converted to the church of styles, it's high time to become a believer; see page 77.

> **NOTE** You can add tables of contents only to word-processing documents, not page-layout documents (see page 15 for a reminder on the difference). Also, TOCs can't pull headings from more than one Pages document. So, if you want your literary masterpiece to have an all-encompassing TOC, you need to pen all your words in a single document.

Before adding a table of contents to your book, for example, make sure you've applied paragraph styles to all the chapter titles, headings, and subheadings throughout the manuscript document.

With your heading styles to guide the way, Pages can now rocket through the document, noting those headings and their page numbers, and assembling them all into a tidy list. To create a table of contents, place your insertion point where you want the TOC to appear (typically, near the beginning of the document). Then choose Insert→"Table of Contents," and select one of these options:

- **Document.** Pages scours the entire document.

- **Section.** Pages gathers information only from the section where your insertion point is positioned.

- **To Next Occurrence.** Pages gathers entries from between this table of contents and the next table of contents only.

Pages then generates your table of contents. Select the newly created TOC, and then make sure the Format panel is open (if not, click the Format button in the toolbar) and open the Table of Contents tab (as shown in Figure 5-11).

In the Table of Contents tab's list, turn on the checkbox to the left of each paragraph style you want in your table of contents. For example, in your book, you'll certainly want to include every chapter title. So if you use Title style for your chapter titles, turn on the Title checkbox. Do the same for all the styles you want to include—Heading 1 and Heading 2, perhaps. If you also want page numbers included in the TOC for a certain type of heading, turn on the checkbox to the right of the style's name. You might want to include page numbers for main headings for each chapter title, for example, but list subheadings without page numbers.

> **TIP** You may want to add a page break or section break after the table of contents to separate it from the rest of your document.

In Pages, a table of contents can look ahead and behind, and it doesn't stop listing headings when it runs into another table of contents, unless you tell it to do so by selecting Insert→"Table of Contents"→"To Next Occurrence."

As you edit your document, Pages keeps track of page numbering changes, new headings, text edits, and rearranged sections. So once you create a table of contents, you can forget about it—Pages has everything under control.

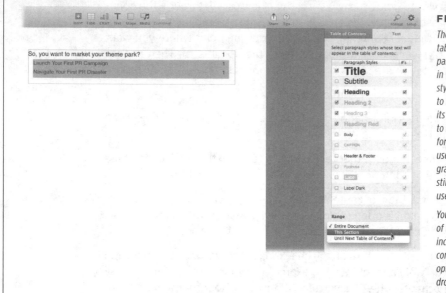

FIGURE 5-11

The Table of Contents tab lets you select the paragraph styles you want in your TOC. Turn on a style's left-hand checkbox to include it, and turn on its right-hand checkbox to include page numbers for that style. Styles not used in the document are grayed out, but you can still add them in case you use them later.

You can control which part of the document Pages includes in your table of contents by choosing an option from the Range drop-down menu.

Modifying a Table of Contents

Pages lets you apply the usual round of text formatting to your table of contents—but you can't edit its *text*. The TOC is actually a special breed of formatted text field, and so defies your attempts to edit its contents. The only way to change its text is to change the original heading (for example) elsewhere in your document.

Since you can't directly edit the text in a table of contents, that means that you can't add or remove words, or format individual pieces of text by selecting a word and then changing its font size, for instance. In fact, you can't style individual words at all—changes you apply to an item in the TOC apply to every other TOC item that uses that style.

Here's the only way to go about changing the formatting of your table of contents:

1. **In the TOC, click an entry you'd like to format—one of the Heading 2 entries, for example.**

   Pages highlights *all* the headings in the table of contents that use that style. In other words, you can't highlight an individual entry in the table of contents (unless it's the only entry using that style).

2. **Make sure the Text tab is open in the Format panel (as shown in Figure 5-12), and then use the tab's settings to edit the entries' formatting.**

See Chapter 2 for a reminder on how to format text. You can also use the ruler (page 53) to adjust tabs and margins.

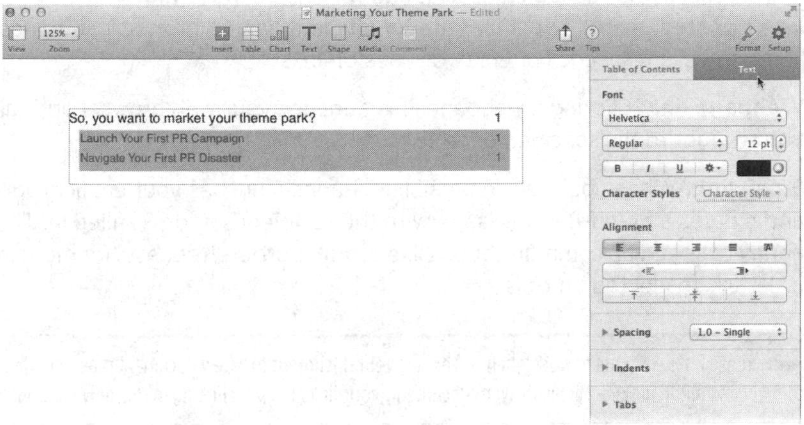

FIGURE 5-12

Pages creates its table of contents from the styled headings you've used in your document. If you select an item in the TOC, Pages highlights all the items that use the same paragraph style (here, Heading 2). You can then modify all this text using the Text tab's settings.

NOTE To remove all of a certain kind of TOC entry in one go (all Heading 2 entries, say), head to the Format panel's Table of Contents tab. There, click the checkbox to the left of the style's name to turn it off, and Pages deletes all those entries.

3. **To change the placement and display of page numbers, adjust the Style tab's settings.**

If your selected style—Heading 2, in this example—includes page numbers in the TOC, Pages inserts a tab between the text title and the page number. To adjust the size of the tab, use the ruler (see page 52 for more about creating and editing tab stops). You can also edit the tab in the Format panel's Text tab; click the Tabs heading to expand that section. There, you can adjust the tab's size and make edits such as adding and deleting *leader lines*—the string of dots or dashes that leads your eyes from the text on the left to the page number on the right. See page 55 for a reminder of how to adjust tabs and leader lines.

TIP Remember, if you're not happy with your changes, you can take it all back by choosing Edit→Undo.

■ Hyperlinks

While a table of contents is the most traditional method for helping readers find their way around a document, the Internet has made another type of navigation familiar to all: *hyperlinks* (or *links* for short). Just as they do in web pages, hyperlinks in Pages documents let you hop, skip, and jump to new content by clicking a linked word or phrase. If your document is destined for onscreen viewing—such as a PDF document posted online—hyperlinks are an efficient way to browse web pages or send email messages. Pages offers two types of links:

- **Webpage link.** Clicking a webpage link launches your web browser and takes you straight to the specified page.

- **Email link.** When you click an email link, Pages launches your email program and creates a brand-new message with the recipient's address filled in. This is handy to speed up communications like product orders, requests for more info, or letters to elected officials.

NOTE These links continue to work when you export your document to a new document type. Whether you save your work as a PDF file or a Microsoft Word document, your links keep on linking in this new environment.

Adding Webpage Links

No document needs to be an island; you can add a link from your file to anywhere on the Web. In fact, unless you tell it otherwise, Pages does this *for* you anytime you type a web address that starts with *www*, automatically converting the address into a clickable hyperlink. You can also add a webpage link to any other text, using the following steps:

1. **Select the text you want to link.**

   For example, if you're creating a PDF flyer that you intend to post on various websites, you might include the phrase, "For more info, visit our website!" Rather than following this with your web address typed out in full, you can simply select the words "our website" and turn them into a hyperlink.

2. **Choose Format→Add Link, or press ⌘-K.**

   Either way, Pages opens the Link window. In the "Link to" drop-down list, select Webpage, and in the Link text box type out the web address you want to link to. (If you're linking to a website with a really long address, it might be quicker to copy the address from your browser's address bar and then paste it into the Link window.) If you have second thoughts about the text you're turning into a link (or you realize you left a letter off the end of your text selection), you can change this *display text* by modifying what's in the Display field (see Figure 5-13).

NOTE *URL*, which stands for Uniform Resource Locator, is just a high-falutin' term for a web page address like *www.missingmanuals.com*.

Writing your first newsletter

Offers your~~~~~~~~~~~~~~~~~~able to res

Link to: Webpage

Link: www.missingmanuals.com

Display: Missing Manuals

Remove   Open

For more info, go to the Missing Manuals website!

FIGURE 5-13

If your Pages document is destined to be viewed on a computer, you can create hyperlinks to open web pages. In your document, select the text you want to link, and then go to Format→Add Link or press ⌘-K to open the Link window shown here. In this screenshot, the display text "Missing Manuals" links to www.missingmanuals. com. You can also edit the display text (for example, you could replace "Missing Manuals" with "Click here").

3. **Once everything looks good, click anywhere outside of the Link window to save your changes.**

   Pages adds an underline to your display text to let you know that it's a fully functioning hyperlink. You can check to make sure the link is working correctly by clicking the display text and then clicking the Open button that appears.

4. **If you need to edit the hyperlink, click the display text and then choose Edit to reopen the Link window.**

   Make your changes, and then click anywhere outside the Link window to save them.

To remove a hyperlink, either delete the display text or click the display text, click the Edit button that appears, and then in the Link window, click Remove.

If you type a web address into your document, Pages automatically sees it for what it really is and links it up *for* you (and adds an underline beneath the text so you know what it has done). If you'd rather not have Pages automatically link up all your web addresses, you can turn this feature off by going to Edit→Substitutions and clicking Smart Links once to remove the checkmark next to it.

Adding Email Links

You can add email links to your document to make it easy for readers to contact you or to follow a call to action (encouraging the citizenry to contact their elected officials, for example). Select the text you want to turn into an email link ("email Governor Jones," say), and then choose Format→Add Link, or press ⌘-K. In the

Link window, set the "Link to" drop-down menu to Email. In the To field, enter the recipient's email address and, if you want, enter a subject line for the email message in the Subject field. You can also alter the Display text as described in the previous section. When you're done, click outside the Link window, and Pages adds the link to your document text. From then on, clicking the link opens a preaddressed message in your email program, ready to accept your eager prose.

> **NOTE** As with web addresses, Pages normally converts email addresses in your text into hyperlinks. You can stop this behavior by going to Edit→Substitutions and clicking Smart Links once to remove the checkmark next to it. You can also edit and remove email links in exactly the same way as webpage links.

Beyond Text: Laying Out Documents

Way back in Chapter 1, you heard lots of talk about how Pages' graphic-design kung fu sets it apart from other word processors. Since then, though, you've learned only about Pages' more traditional word-processing features—not a peep about graphic design. Patience, Grasshopper. Now that you've learned the basics, you're ready to stretch your legs and move beyond text and into the stylish, colorful world of page layout.

Like most word processors, Pages lets you add images and free-floating text boxes to your documents. But Pages goes several steps beyond the typical offerings, letting you do more than just prettify your text. The program gives you a full-blown set of layout tools in what amounts to a consumer-level version of heavyweight design software like Quark or InDesign. Whether you're making a brochure, a newsletter, a poster, or an elegant annual report, Pages helps you create documents designed for visual impact.

In Pages, your creative focus shifts from words to the overall design. Your text becomes just one of many elements as you compose your document into a symphony of images, tables, charts, shapes, and even sound and video. These design elements are known collectively as *objects* in Pages, Keynote, and Numbers. In the next few chapters you'll dig into the details of working with these building blocks.

If you've got all the design savvy of a platypus, don't be daunted. Although graphic design is a sophisticated field with infinite levels of nuance, the basic principles are uncomplicated. Even the most style-challenged can create a clean, clear design by following a few fundamental guidelines covered in the next several pages. And Pages' elegant collection of design tools makes it easy to pull it all together with grace and aplomb.

But first, a moment to breathe. Black-belt graphic designers don't just jump in and start slinging design elements around the page. Great design always starts with a little prep work to plan your overall page composition and to establish a few ground rules for your design. Doing this saves time and promotes visual consistency, especially when you're developing a design spanning several pages. This groundwork phase includes making decisions about fonts, colors, white space, column widths, and the overall visual structure of your document. This chapter explores all those areas, helping you lay the foundation for a great design.

■ Templates: The Key to Prefab Page Designs

First things first: If all this gentle encouragement isn't enough to convince you that you *can* create your own design from scratch—or if you're just feeling impatient—the templates that come bundled with Pages are your ticket to an instant, polished, and professional design. Apple's already done all the heavy lifting for you by selecting the fonts and color palette, creating areas for images and text, and much more. Figure 6-1 shows a couple of examples.

FIGURE 6-1

Pages' built-in templates offer attractive, ready-to-go designs (unless you opt for a Blank template, of course!) Every non-blank template comes with predefined text styles, placeholder text, and placeholder objects. Here, you see two of Pages' templates: Serif Newsletter (left) and For Sale Flyer (right).

Chapter 1 gave you a jump-start on using templates to quickly drop your own text and images into a ready-to-go page design (see page 5). As you make your way through this chapter and the two that follow, you'll learn how to work with the various objects included in Pages' templates, and how to add your own objects to enhance the design and make it your own. First, though, a few quick pointers to help you get started with templates.

Working with Placeholder Text

Unless you opt for one of the Blank templates, your Pages template comes prefilled with *placeholder text* to help you visualize how your document will look once it's complete. However, it's unlikely that you'll want to send out a newsletter that's filled with "lorem ipsum dolor" text, so your first task when you create a new document is replacing this "Greek" text with your own words. (To learn where this placeholder text comes from, see the box on page 132.)

Page 150 has the lowdown on editing text boxes, but placeholder text puts a slight twist on things. You can't *edit* placeholder text, you can only replace it. Click anywhere in the placeholder text, and you select the entire clump of text at once. Just start typing, and your new text replaces the whole shebang. With the placeholder text out of the way, you're back in the world of normal word processing. Some templates include several placeholder-text areas within a single text box, so you have to click and replace each one separately, as shown in Figure 6-2.

FIGURE 6-2

Pages' templates provide placeholder text and images that show you how to use the template to the best effect. Text boxes sometimes contain one or more placeholder text areas. In the Lost & Found template, for example, the text box in the lower third of the layout has separate placeholders for the main body text (selected in this screenshot); the What, When, and Where subheadings in the bottom right; and the information that's written beside each of these subheadings. Click anywhere inside any of these placeholder areas and start typing to replace it with your own info.

The dog image is also a placeholder. You can replace his smiling face by clicking the icon in the image's bottom-right corner or dragging and dropping your own image from the Finder or your desktop onto the placeholder image. No matter which method you use, Pages automatically sizes and formats your image to fit the placeholder's layout.

TIP If you add text to a template by copying and pasting it from another document, rather than simply pasting it in by choosing Edit→Paste or pressing ⌘-V, choose Edit→"Paste and Match Style" (or press Option-Shift-⌘-V) to force your text to fall into line with the template's style. See page 36 for more about this useful pasting option.

UP TO SPEED

Lorem Ipsum Dolor?

As you just learned, the text that initially appears in all Pages templates is simply placeholder text, intended to be replaced by whatever text you wish to place there. Typesetters call this kind of placeholder "Greek text"—even though the standard filler isn't actually Greek. Instead, it's loosely derived from a 2,000-year-old Latin treatise on ethics by Cicero, *de Finibus Bonorum et Malorum* (*The Extremes of Good and Evil*).

Designers use this dummy text when creating layouts so that (non-Latin) readers aren't distracted by the text's content—and instead pay attention to the page design. This practice goes back to the 1500s, when it first appeared in a type specimen book, and it continues—using that same chunk of text—to this day.

Working with Media Placeholders

Most photos that are included in templates, like the smiley dog in Figure 6-2, are also placeholders—*media placeholders*. You can hang onto these placeholders or replace them with a picture of your choosing.

To replace a media placeholder, click the placeholder to select it, and then click the round icon in the placeholder's bottom-right corner. This displays the Media Browser; click the Photos tab and then select a picture from your iPhoto library, iCloud, or My Photo Stream. Find the image you want to use, and then click it once to swap it in for the placeholder graphic. Alternatively, if your new image is close by, you can simply drag it from its original location and drop it onto the media placeholder.

However you replace a media placeholder, Pages resizes your new image and applies the same borders, effects, and rotation as the placeholder image had. (To find out more about working with images, flip to page 156.)

NOTE You can add placeholder text and images to your own documents—useful when you create templates for yourself or your buddies. For details, see page 273.

Immovable Objects: Locked, Background, and Master Objects

An area that frequently puzzles newcomers about templates is when objects won't budge. You click and you click, but the shape, picture, or text box remains completely oblivious to your efforts to get its attention. What gives?

If you click an image (or any other object), and the selection border appears, but it's decorated with little X marks where the square selection handles normally are, this means that the object is *locked*—fixed on the page and uneditable. Many templates use shapes or images to add background colors or visual "containers" around other content, and lock these objects so that you don't inadvertently sweep them to an off-kilter location on the page and ruin the whole layout. In Figure 6-2, for example, the yellow rectangles at the top and bottom of the page provide a nice backdrop for the text, but these shapes are locked, so you can't move, delete, or replace them.

To unlock an object, click it, head to the Format panel and click the Arrange tab, and then click the Unlock button (you may have to scroll down the Format panel to see it). To learn more about locking and unlocking objects, see page 191.

If you can't even select an image or other object to make its border appear, it's probably a *background object* or *master object*, which means that it's been added as a background element of one or more pages. To make it so you can select (and therefore edit) these kinds of objects, click the Arrange menu at the top of your screen, and then choose Section Masters→Make Master Objects Selectable. You can then select and edit these objects as normal. For more about working with background and master objects, see page 188.

NOTE Want to experiment with all these different object types and settings for yourself? You can grab the sample document *object_examples.pages*, which contains a background object, a locked object, a media placeholder, and a text box with placeholder text. To download it, go to this book's Missing CD page at *www. missingmanuals.com/cds*.

■ Planning a Layout from Scratch

Templates are a nifty way to learn by example, giving you a pre-designed document to dissect and examine to figure out how it all hangs together. But there's nothing like building your *own* layout from scratch to learn the principles and pitfalls of graphic design firsthand. The rest of this chapter gets you started on that process, taking you from blank page to lively layout. You'll finish the job in the next chapter as you learn the details of working with objects. Here's your assignment:

At long last, Crazyland Wonderpark is launching a series of custom birthday and special-occasion packages. From supernatural overnight experiences in the World's Most Haunted Public Toilet, to an Extreme Digger Driving Experience, to the all-new Squirrel Apocalypse survival game (kind of like Zombie Apocalypse, but you're chased by people dressed up as squirrels rather than zombies), people have lots of options to choose from. Your goal is to create a catalog that showcases the various packages you have to offer, to help drive this new part of your business. It may sound like a lot of work, but Pages is on standby to take the hassle out of designing and cataloging this exciting new service.

The catalog will have a brochure-style layout, with big, splashy photos showing children, adults, and the elderly all finally fulfilling their dreams of driving a digger, as well as visitors running from people in fluffy squirrel costumes—along with some slick marketing text. Brief articles scattered throughout will advertise extras that can be added to each package to make an already-special experience super-mega special. You'll need several different page types: the cover, a few layouts to showcase each experience, and a couple of article pages.

In your enthusiasm for your new project, you might be tempted to jump straight in. Resist that urge. Take a few minutes to sketch some design options *on paper*. Yes, even in this digital age, it's tough to beat pen and paper when it comes to working through visual ideas. Some great ideas started out as scrawls on a cocktail napkin or the back of an envelope, so your page-layout sketches are in good company. The goal here isn't to draw anything terribly refined. Instead, you're trying to capture some big-picture options for blocking out your pages and, along the way, identifying the page elements that you want to include: images, shapes, headlines, text, captions, and so on. Figure 6-3 shows some examples.

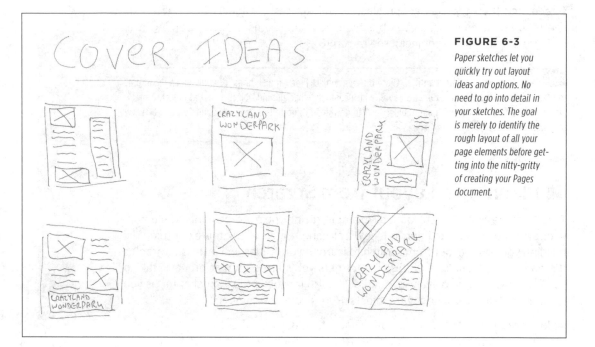

FIGURE 6-3

Paper sketches let you quickly try out layout ideas and options. No need to go into detail in your sketches. The goal is merely to identify the rough layout of all your page elements before getting into the nitty-gritty of creating your Pages document.

Designing a Page Layout

As you make your line-drawing sketches, focus on keeping the layout as simple and uncluttered as possible. A common mistake among novice designers is to use *every* option and nifty trick that the software offers, cramming your document full of graphics, wacky fonts, and every color in the spectrum. When you're trying to get noticed, this approach seems completely logical: To make noise, make a noisy design. The reality, though, is that noisy designs have less impact than more restrained, orderly visuals.

This doesn't necessarily mean that your goal should be to create a spare, minimalist design—only that you should avoid a busy layout by removing elements that add complexity without adding meaning. Architect Ludwig Mies van der Rohe gave us the familiar phrase "Less is more," but designer Milton Glaser later offered a more practical (if less elegant) version: "Just enough is more." As you make your sketches, keep asking yourself, "What can I take away? Does my logo really need to be *that* big?" Our brains naturally seek out order and rhythm—by creating a design with *just enough* information and imagery, you can get your message across efficiently without distracting your reader.

Here are some guidelines to keep in mind as you're planning and sketching your layout:

- **White space is important.** Don't assume that you have to fill every inch of the page. Designers consider *white space*, the unused portions of the page, to be a design element as important as the text and images they surround. Well deployed white space gives your design room to breathe and guides the viewer's eye to the page's important elements. When you open up space between text and image, or even between lines of text, you relax the design, making it easier to read and lending it an air of elegance. (Take a peek at any luxury ad campaign, and you'll see that it's chock-full of empty space.)

  Alas, white space is not some magic pixie dust that you can sprinkle willy-nilly on your page. Poorly placed white space simply leaves scattershot gaps in the layout, making your design appear incomplete. It takes practice to get it right. The main thing to remember is that in *most* design projects, your job *isn't* to cram as much as possible onto the page; instead, the goal is to make the information you're presenting readable and clear. White space helps to do that.

- **When it comes to fonts, practice restraint.** Just because there are lots of fonts on your computer doesn't mean that you need to use them all. And please, whatever you do, for the love of your reader, *don't use them all in the same document.*

  Consistency is far more important in a well-designed layout than variety. Use just one or two fonts throughout your document, varying only their size or style for specific uses. For example, you might choose a sans-serif font for headings—like Helvetica, Futura, or Gill Sans—and pick a serif font—like Hoefler, Georgia, or Times—for body text (see "Serve Up the Serifs" on page 44 for a refresher on what these terms mean). You can then work with these fonts in varying forms to suit these different roles. Make your headings and subheadings large and bold, for example, and shrink or italicize your body text to turn it into a photo caption.

  On a related note, when you're ready to start working with your document in Pages, one of the first things you should do is set up its *styles*. Create a paragraph style for every type of text element you'll use in your pages: headings, subheadings, body text, captions, and so on. By using only these preset styles to format your text, you'll ensure consistency throughout your document and make it easy to apply changes across your entire design. (For more info on styles, see page 75 in Chapter 3).

- **Don't include the whole rainbow.** You're catching on: Keep the color palette—you guessed it—simple. The *palette* is the primary collection of colors that you assemble in your design—whether in subdued balance or noisy contrast. When you're choosing colors, the basic ideas aren't that different from the ones you follow when you get dressed in the morning. Use no more than three or four colors for the text, backgrounds, and non-photo elements of your design. These colors should have visual harmony together, and it's a good idea to pick them when you *first* start working on a document, so that you know your full palette when you make those first strokes on your document's canvas. The box below has more tips on choosing a color palette.

Color Me Inspired

When seeking inspiration for your color palette, one place to look is in your own photo collection, or in that remarkable photo gallery known as the World Wide Web (plant and nature photos are an especially rich resource). With a little help from your Mac's Color Picker, you can swipe those colors for your own design. Here's how to build a color palette from a photo:

1. Create a new Pages document using one of the Blank templates.

2. Pick a photo you want to swipe colors from. This could be a photo you snapped yourself, or it could be one you found online using flickr.com or Google's image search (search for "purple flower," for example). If you're using a photo that's already on your computer, drag it into your iPhoto library so Pages can find it (see page 138 for more on working with an iPhoto library). If you're using a photo you find online, download it to your computer, and *then* add it to your iPhoto library.

3. In Pages, click the Media button in the toolbar to open the Media Browser, and then click the Photos button.

4. Find the photo you want to use, and click it once to add it to your document.

5. Open the Color Picker by choosing View→Show Colors.

6. In the Color Picker, click the magnifying glass icon to transform your cursor into a magnifying glass. Position your new cursor over a portion of the picture whose color you like, and then click to capture this hue, as shown in Figure 6-4.

7. Drag this newly captured color from the rectangular color well near the top of the Color Picker (labeled in Figure 6-4), and drop it into one of the little squares at the bottom of the Color Picker for later use. (For more about choosing colors with the Color Picker, see page 192).

8. Repeat steps 6 and 7 to continue gathering your collection of colors.

Alternatively, several websites are devoted entirely to color palettes and provide ready-made color combos. So while you're thinking about color, why not do a little window shopping? Try *www.colourlovers.com*, *www.colorcombos.com*, or *http://kuler.adobe.com*.

Collecting Your Materials

Behold the mighty hunter-gatherer, foraging the wilderness for sustenance. That's you, scavenging the vast savanna of your hard drive for the text and images to nourish your design. Thanks to your layout sketches, you even have a rough shopping list for your hunt, a visual inventory of the layout elements that you need to make your design work. Take this expedition seriously: By collecting the raw materials for your layout in advance, you'll be able to focus on designing and assembling your document without having to break away and go in search of more. (If you're building a house, you don't want to be going to Home Depot every time you need a nail or a plank, right?)

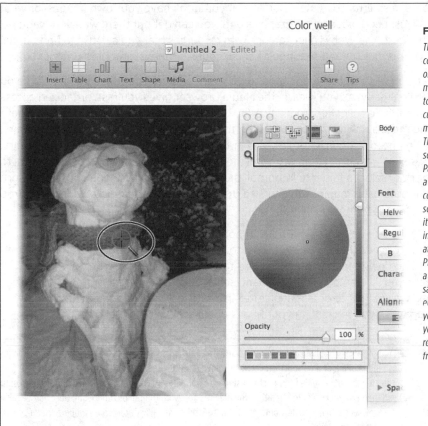

Color well

FIGURE 6-4

The OS X Color Picker lets you collect colors from anywhere on your screen. Click the magnifying-glass icon next to the color well to turn your cursor into a color-collecting magnifying glass (circled). Then click anywhere on your screen (even outside the Pages window) to capture a color in the Color Picker's color well. To save the color so you can use it again, drag it from the color well down into one of the little squares at the bottom of the Color Picker window. To remove a color from your palette of saved colors, drag one of the empty saved-color squares (if you have any) onto the color you want to zap, or simply replace it with another color from the color well.

■ WRITING YOUR TEXT

Writing and designing are two *very* different disciplines, and it's best not to tackle them both at the same time. Pages recognizes this with its two-format approach to document files: word-processing versus page-layout (see page 15 for a reminder on the sometimes-subtle differences between the two). Embrace this distinction and write your text ahead of time in a plain-vanilla word-processing document (use the Blank or Note Taking template, for example). You can use all of Pages' text-editing tools in page-layout documents, too, but a word-processing document is simply a friendlier place for spinning prose because you can compose your initial drafts without being distracted by stuff like image placeholders and master objects.

With your text ready to go before you even start your layout, you'll also have a better sense of exactly what you're designing. Images and even entire page layouts will suggest themselves more readily once you have the text locked down.

■ ASSEMBLING AN ALBUM OF IMAGES

With a project like the Crazyland Wonderpark catalog, you're likely to have all the pictures you need of guests hunting for ghosts in public toilets and running from people in squirrel costumes. But what if you *don't* have your own images, or what if you just need placeholder graphics until you can get out there with your camera? In that case, the Web is chockablock with resources that you can use to find photos for your layout (page 331 suggests some sources for eye-grabbing photos).

Once you've collected your images onto your computer, put them into iPhoto if you haven't already. As you'll learn, the Media Browser gives you fast, organized access to your iPhoto collection from any iWork program, and having your images in iPhoto is the most efficient way to work with them. To add photos to your iPhoto library, you first need to open iPhoto: In the Finder window, go to Pictures→iPhoto Library, choose File→"Import to Library," and then select the individual photo(s) you want to import, or select a folder to import all the photos it contains in one go. Click Import, and iPhoto hauls 'em in. You can also drag photos into the iPhoto window or drop them onto the iPhoto icon in the Dock.

Finally, create an album in iPhoto to hold all the images you think you might use in your project (Figure 6-5 explains how). Don't focus too much at this point on whittling down the selection—it's hard to predict what might work best in a layout before you've created your document, so it's best to keep your options open. Once you have your set of potential pictures in a single album, you can focus on just that group when you're creating your Pages document.

> **NOTE** You can also grab photos from My Photo Stream, which gives you access to all the photos and images stored on any iPhone, iPad, or iPod Touch (collectively known as "iDevices") associated with your Apple ID (see page 796 for the lowdown on Apple IDs). To start using My Photo Stream, you need to create an iCloud account (page 750) and then turn on My Photo Stream on the iDevices you want to grab pictures from. Once you've done that, the Media Browser contains two new options: My Photo Stream (see *www.apple.com/support/icloud/photo-stream* for more info) and iCloud.

■ BUILDING A PLAYLIST OF MUSIC AND MOVIES

If your document is destined to be viewed onscreen, you can add sound and video, too. If that's your plan, go ahead and gather the music and videos that you'd like to use. Pages looks in your computer's Movies folder and iPhoto library to find video—so organize your videos into their own subfolder inside the Movies folder, or add your movies to your project's iPhoto album. When it comes to audio, Pages peeks at your iTunes account, so create a playlist for your project in iTunes.

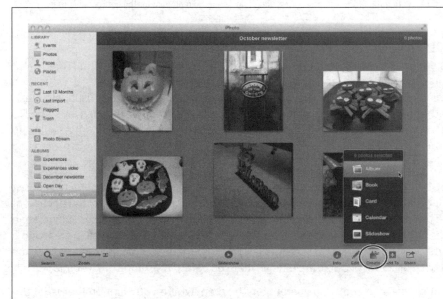

FIGURE 6-5

To create an album in iPhoto, click the Create button (circled) and select Album. A new album appears in the left sidebar, with the title already selected and ready for editing. Give the album a memorable title, and then hit Return.

If you already have a bunch of photos in iPhoto that you want to add to your new album, highlight them in the main photo-viewing area, and then click the Add To button in the bottom-right corner of the iPhoto window. Select Album, and then choose the album you want to move them to.

◼ Creating a Page-Layout Document

You've blocked out some rough layouts on paper, you've created an inventory of design elements, and you've gathered your raw materials. Hallelujah—you're finally ready to start building your design in Pages!

Start by creating a new document: Go to File→New and select a template to use. Since you're building a new document from scratch, the Blank template is a good place to start (you'll find it in the Basic category).

Fine-Tuning Your Document Settings

Before taking this baby out for a spin, check your cockpit controls. Run through some of the basics of document setup to ensure that your end product comes out the way you want. What paper size will you print on? Will it be a vertical (portrait) or horizontal (landscape) layout? Is it going to require page numbers, sections, or a table of contents? Work out your requirements and make the necessary adjustments before you begin entering text and inserting pictures (Chapter 5 has all the info on formatting your document).

Page Layout vs. Word Processing

As you'll learn over the course of the next two chapters, you can add page-layout elements (such as images, shapes, text boxes, tables, and charts) to word-processing documents. That said, when you're working on documents with a visual emphasis (rather than a textual one), page-layout documents are typically the way to go. To reflect that, the next couple of chapters focus on page-layout documents—just keep in mind that you can use all the techniques described there in your word-processing documents, too.

The big difference between the two file types is that page-layout documents consist solely of free-floating elements—there's no text built into the fabric of the document like there is in word-processing documents. Instead, you add text boxes, images, and other objects as you need them, on a page-by-page basis. Rather than following a constantly flowing river of text, the design of a page-layout document is built on an ad hoc collection of discrete elements that you carefully arrange on the page canvas.

That's what's so cool: You can put anything anywhere you want on the page! But that's also the rub. When *anything* is possible, there are an infinite number of directions your design can take (not all of them good), which makes the blank page especially intimidating. Without a dash of discipline, your layout can devolve into a chaotic jumble of images and text scattered on the page.

All designers benefit from a bit of structure. So before you start cajoling your design into place, it's a good idea to get up to speed on *guides,* which can help you keep objects in check.

Using Alignment Guides

When you have multiple objects on the same page, you often want to align them in some way. Happily, you don't need to dig out your old shatterproof ruler to get that perfectly aligned look. Pages can supply guides that appear whenever it looks like you're trying to get your objects lined up (see Figure 6-6).

To turn guides on (or off, if they're getting on your nerves), go to Pages→Preferences, and then click the Rulers button. In the Alignment Guides section, turn the following settings on or off, as desired:

- **Show guides at object center.** Turn this option on to show guides when the object you're dragging is center aligned with other objects on the page, or with the center of the page itself.

- **Show guides at object edges.** Turn this option on to show the guides when the object you're dragging is aligned with the edges of another object or with one of the four edges (margins) of your page.

- **Color.** To change the color of the guides to something other than Pages' standard yellow, click the Alignment Guides color well and choose a new hue.

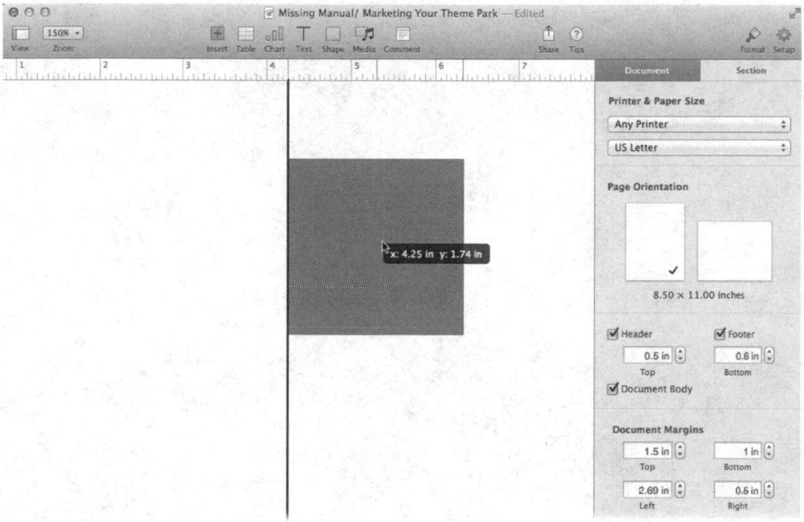

FIGURE 6-6

Flickering guides appear when you're dragging an object into a new position and that object is either precariously close to aligning with other objects on the same page, or it's approaching the edges or center of your page. To achieve perfect alignment, follow the guides and drop your object into position.

In this screenshot, the square is approaching the center of the page, so Pages is displaying a vertical alignment guide. (Here, the guide's color has been set to black to make it easier to see, but when you first start using Pages, guides are yellow).

To *temporarily* hide the alignment guides when they're turned on, hold down the Command (⌘) key while you're dragging an object. This is handy if you want to place an image close to an alignment guide but not exactly on it. In this scenario, guides are an annoying distraction, and the ⌘-drag approach is your friend.

> **TIP** Guides work with or without the ruler, but if you're fussing over the alignment of objects, chances are you'd benefit from being able to see the ruler. If the ruler isn't already open, display it by clicking View→Show Rulers.

Now that you have a plan for your document and have collected all the images, audio files, and video files you'll be using, it's time to compose your first page.

Objects Up Close: Adding, Modifying, and More

P ages, Keynote, and Numbers all give you a wide range of design elements to choose from: text boxes, pictures, movies, sounds, shapes, tables, and charts. As varied as these visual components might seem, they're much more alike than you might think. In iWork, all these elements are called *objects*, and you move, layer, and adjust them using exactly the same techniques. It's like one of those cheesy televised talent contests: Although each contestant has her own distinct talent, they all follow the same rules.

Throughout this chapter, you'll meet most of iWork's objects (you'll get to know more about tables and charts in the next chapter), and then see how to make your objects more stylish using things like borders and shadow effects. From workaday actions like selecting and moving objects to spinning them 360 degrees or adding shadows, reflections, and borders, this chapter gives you the know-how to build sophisticated layouts with ease.

And here's the best part: Once you get the hang of working with objects in one iWork program, you've got it down in the others, too. Designing a presentation slideshow in Keynote, for example, is very much like designing a leaflet in Pages. You use the same tools in both programs to arrange your images, text, charts, and so on. This chapter introduces you to all of these object-editing tools using Crazyland Wonderpark's Experiences catalog as an example.

■ Floating vs. Inline Objects

Objects are the building blocks of Pages documents (unless you're designing a word-processing document made up of nothing but free-flowing text, of course).

Every object on the page is contained in its own invisible box, and you grab an object's box to resize, move, or shuffle it. At its most basic level, creating a page layout is about arranging these boxes to your liking—a text box here, an image over there, a table down below, and a shape behind the whole thing to add a splash of color. But objects aren't limited to flashy page-layout documents. They live happily in word-processing documents, too, where you can use them to illustrate your text with pictures, charts, sidebars, and more.

Most objects in a page layout are free-floating elements that you nudge around the page independent of the others. But you can also *anchor* an object within a table or a specific part of your text so that an image, for example, always appears with the same paragraph or even acts like a word within a sentence. Pages manages this distinction with two categories of objects:

- **Floating objects** are placed on the page independent of the objects or text around them. When you add a floating object to a document, it stays stubbornly in the same spot even as you add new text or other objects around it. Calling this kind of object "floating" might seem counterintuitive, since that term tends to mean "drifting" or "on the move," but in iWork it means fixed to a specific location. One way to think of it is that floating objects hover in place above the page. As your text moves and shifts below them, these objects *float* above the fray, their positions unperturbed by changes to text or objects elsewhere in the document. If you add your logo to the top left of your letterhead, for example, it stays on the top left even when you add text before or after it. There's more on how floating objects work in just a moment.

- **Inline objects** behave like a word or character in a line of text. If you add more text to your document prior to an inline object, for example, the object gets pushed along with the text, always remaining tied to the words next to it. You'll find inline objects to be a good choice for text boxes containing a short quote that needs to stay connected to the surrounding text, or images that you want to include in a table or to illustrate a particular paragraph.

> **NOTE** You can only create inline objects in word-processing documents.

In general, all this means that floating objects are more useful in page-layout documents, and inline objects tend to be more useful in word-processing documents. That's because floating objects are ideal for placing objects in a precise location on the page (perfect for page layout), while inline objects let you tell Pages, "Keep this object lined up with this text no matter what" (ideal for word-processing documents, where text is always on the move).

Whether it's floating or inline, when you insert an object on a text-filled page, you can determine how surrounding text *wraps* around it—flowing around the object to its left or right, or jumping down to continue below the object. For floating objects, you can choose not to have any text-wrapping at all, letting the text flow right over the object, or under it so that the object obscures the text. (For more on wrapping, see page 181.)

NOTE Just because you can't create inline objects in page-layout documents doesn't mean you can't use text-wrapping. Text-wrapping works in both page-layout and word-processing documents.

Since floating objects are distinct from the rest of the elements on the page, you can stack them in *layers*—just like you might arrange printed snapshots on a scrapbook page, where one picture is on top, overlapping portions of other pictures beneath. Besides shifting the vertical or horizontal position of a floating object, you can also shift the *depth* of its layer, moving it in front of or behind other objects that it over-laps. (Inline objects, on the other hand, always remain on the same layer as the text in which they're embedded.)

Pages also lets you adjust the *opacity* of each object, making it partly transparent so you can see the objects in the layers below (see page 202).

After you place objects on the page, you can resize, rotate, and layer them on top of one another. You can add shadows, adjust each object's opacity, or group sev-eral objects together so you can reposition them simultaneously. For the full story on object manipulation, see "Working with Objects" on page 178 and "Modifying Object Styles" on page 191.

Floating Objects

Floating objects like the ones shown in Figure 7-1 give you precise control over exactly where the object appears on the page. Drop a floating object into your layout, and it stays put, no matter how you might add or move other text and objects around it. This fine control makes floating objects the tool of choice for page-layout docu-ments, letting you arrange every picture and text box exactly where you want it. Pages prefers floating objects, too: When you add an object to a word-processing document, Pages makes it a floating object; if you want an inline object instead, you have to manually convert the object as explained in the next section. (Since floating objects are the only option in page-layout documents, all objects added to them are floating objects.)

To add an image as a floating object, for example, open the Media Browser (in Pages' toolbar, click Media), and then select a photo. You can then drag this photo anywhere on the page—that's the whole idea. The image is contained in a box that has eight square *selection handles* on its sides and corners. Drag any of the handles to resize the picture.

You can also add floating objects by going to the Insert menu and choosing Table, Text Box, Shape, or Chart. To insert any kind of file that Pages understand (an image or a video, say), go to Insert→Choose, and Pages opens a window that lets you pluck a file straight from your hard drive. Click Insert to finish the job, or double-click the file to drop it straight into your document. (You'll learn the nuts and bolts of adding and editing these different object types later in this chapter.)

Inline Objects

In contrast to freewheeling floating objects, inline objects are stuck inside the main body of word-processing documents. Think of inline objects like another character or word in a sentence. Once you turn an object into an inline object, it remains anchored to that portion of the text, adjusting its location as you add and edit text around it—just like any other character in a sentence.

To create an inline picture, for example, first add the image to your document (either by dragging it into Pages from your desktop or the Finder, or by selecting it in the Media Browser). Position the image where you want it to appear in your text, and then head to the Format panel and open the Arrange tab. At the top of that tab, make sure the "Move with Text" button is selected (if not, click it). Then click the Text Wrap drop-down menu and select "Inline with Text," as shown in Figure 7-2. From now on, no matter how much text you add or delete, the object shifts along with your text so that it remains in the same position.

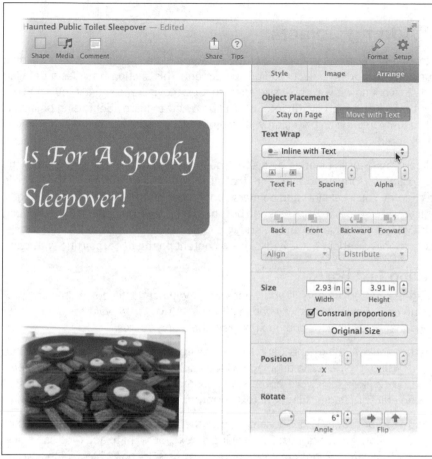

FIGURE 7-2

To anchor an object within free-flowing text, select the object and head to the Format panel's Arrange tab. Make sure that "Move with Text" is selected (as shown here), and then click the Text Wrap drop-down menu (where the cursor is here). Select "Inline with Text" to make your object shift along with the text, like it's just another character in your lines of text.

Inline objects have only three selection handles: at the bottom, right, and bottom-right corner. Drag any of these handles to resize the object. Also, you can move inline objects to different layers in your document using the technique described on page 187.

NOTE If you're going to be making lots of adjustments to your object's position and how it interacts with other objects, you may want to keep the Arrange settings permanently onscreen. To do so, open the Arrange *window*, which floats independent of the Format panel, by going to View→Show Arrange Tools. If the Arrange window is getting in your way, you can drag it somewhere more convenient, or click the red button at its top left to close it.

To turn an inline object back into a floating object, select the object, open the Arrange tab in the Format panel, and then either open the Text Wrap drop-down menu and choose any option *other* than "Inline with Text," or simply click the "Stay on Page" button. You can then treat the object just as you would any floating object.

Adding Objects

With all that basic orientation out of the way, you're finally ready to start building your page by adding objects to your document. This section provides a detailed guide to working with text boxes, images, shapes, movies, and sound (you'll find out about tables and charts in Chapter 8). The best way to learn about using objects is just to jump in and start working with them, which is what the next several pages are all about.

To keep you focused on adding objects, you won't find detailed descriptions of the shared actions, formatting, and styles that all objects have in common until later on in the chapter. You'll get hints and pointers about those features in the next few pages, but if you prefer to learn those ins and outs first, feel free to jump ahead to "Working with Objects" on page 178 and "Modifying Object Styles" on page 191. Meanwhile, this section is all about actually designing content on the page, starting with text.

Adding Text Boxes

In page-layout documents, if you want words, you need text boxes. In word-processing documents, you don't *need* text boxes, but you may want to use them for things that dress up your body text, like sidebars and quotes.

Whether you're adding a headline to your design, inserting a lengthy article into your newsletter, or labeling an image with a caption, text boxes get the job done. A text box is like a mini word-processing document—a little window of words that you can edit with Pages' full set of text-formatting features.

To add a text box to any Pages document, click the Text button in the toolbar, and then click the option that looks most like the kind of text you want to add (you can adjust its formatting later). Pages creates your text box as a floating object, plunking it in the center of your screen with the imaginative placeholder text "Text." Start typing, and Pages replaces the word "Text" with your (hopefully) more imaginative words.

NOTE You can also add a text box by choosing Insert→Text Box.

A text box can hold as much text as you can muster, but the volume of verbiage that it can *display* is limited by its physical dimensions. If you type or paste more content into a text box than it has room to display, Pages adds the plus-shaped *clipping indicator* to the bottom of the text box, like the one circled in Figure 7-3. Simply resize the text box to make it large enough to display the hidden text, or whittle down the text a bit.

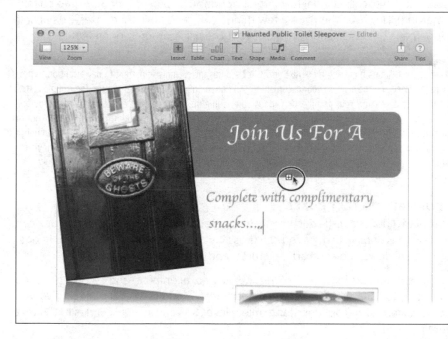

FIGURE 7-3

In addition to resizing handles, text boxes sometimes feature a clipping indicator (the + circled here), which shows that there's more text than can fit in the text box.

Here's the thing: While you're editing the contents of a text box, you can't resize the text box or move it to a new location. If you want to move or resize the text box, first *deselect* it by clicking outside it, and then click the text box once. Pages highlights the text box's boundary and adds eight selection handles. These handles signal that you're editing the text box at the *object level*—think of it as editing the box itself rather than the text inside it. You can now move the text box, resize it, add a border around it, change its opacity, rotate it, and more. Drag the text box to wherever you want, and resize it by dragging its selection handles. Click inside the text box again to start editing its text; now you're editing at the *text level* again.

TIP Instead of doing the deselect/reselect hokey pokey to switch from text editing to object editing, press ⌘-Return once you've finished typing in the box. Pages sweeps away the insertion point, selects the text box, and displays its selection handles.

Be careful here: If you start typing while a text box is sporting selection handles, your new text completely replaces the contents of the text box. A better, more foolproof way to start editing the contents of a text box is to double-click anywhere inside the box.

You can format text inside a text box as you would any other text: apply styles, change colors, add shadows, and so on. When you're editing text, the Format panel displays its usual collection of formatting options (see page 39 for more info on text formatting). However, there are a few things you *can't* do in text boxes: They can't include page breaks, section breaks, layout breaks, footnotes, or endnotes.

> **TIP** As you amass more and more text boxes, it becomes increasingly important to pay attention to how they're positioned on the page, so your document doesn't descend into disorganized clutter. The trouble is that it's difficult to guess how your document's various objects line up with its layout elements (headers, footers, and margins). When you're lining up a text box, wouldn't it be helpful if you could actually see the layout of your document? That's where *Layout view* comes in. It lets you see the structural skeleton of your page. Choose View→Show Layout to turn it on, and View→Hide Layout to make those headers, footers, and margins invisible again.

■ FORMATTING TEXT BOXES

Think of text boxes as little documents within your bigger document: A text box can be a few lines of plain text, or you can dress it up with a background color or image, borders, shadows, tables, charts, pictures, and even columns.

You format the text itself (its color, fonts, styles, alignment, and so on) using the formatting tools in the Format panel and Fonts window. But text boxes give you *additional* formatting options at the object level, so you can apply styles to the text container itself.

The Format panel's Text tab lets you specify the position of text inside the text box, using the vertical alignment buttons indicated in Figure 7-4 (click the tab's Style button to see them). And the Text Inset field (shown in Figure 7-5—click the Text tab's Layout button to see it) controls the amount of padding between the boundary of the text box and its content.

> **NOTE** Pages also lets you control the way the surrounding text wraps *around* a text box. See page 181 for the lowdown on text wrapping.

You can add a solid color, a *gradient* (a fill color that gradually blends one hue into another), or an image to the background of a text box; you can also add a border, a shadow, or a reflection, or adjust the text box's opacity (some of these style changes are shown in Figure 7-6). The Format panel is your go-to place for making all of these style changes; you can find all the details in "Modifying Object Styles," starting on page 191.

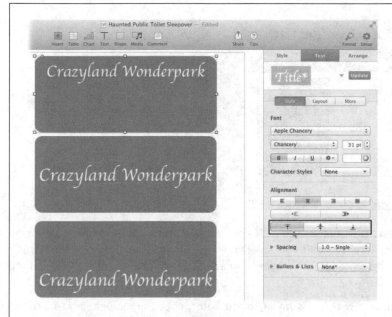

FIGURE 7-4

On the Format panel's Text tab, click the Style button to see these settings, which include the usual horizontal alignment controls (Align Left, Align Right, Center, and Justified; see page 48 for more info). However, if you select a text box or a shape, you can also use the vertical alignment buttons (indicated) to tell Pages how to position the text vertically within the text box or shape: top, middle, or bottom, as shown here.

FIGURE 7-5

To change the amount of padding between the text box's boundary and its contents, click the Text tab's Layout button, and then look for the Text Inset field, which affects all four sides equally. Use the up- and down-arrow buttons to change the point value of this setting, or type a number directly into the field. This image shows two text boxes with different settings: a smaller text inset (top) and a larger text inset (bottom).

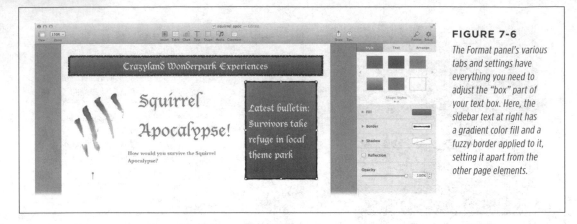

FIGURE 7-6

The Format panel's various tabs and settings have everything you need to adjust the "box" part of your text box. Here, the sidebar text at right has a gradient color fill and a fuzzy border applied to it, setting it apart from the other page elements.

To style a text box, first select it (if you've been editing the text inside the text box, press ⌘-Return to shift your selection to the object level). Then, in the Format panel, click the Style tab, where you can adjust the following settings (which are shown in Figure 7-6):

- **To change a text box's background color,** click the Fill heading to expand that section. Then click the drop-down menu that appears and choose Color Fill. Finally, below the drop-down menu, click the color well to choose from a few default colors, or click the color wheel icon to create your own hue using the Color Picker (see page 192). Page 192 also has more info about object fills.

- **To add a line around your text box,** click the Border heading, click the drop-down menu that appears, and then choose Line. (Picture Frame borders are covered on page 166.) When you do that, a few new settings appear so you can customize your border. Click the unlabeled drop-down menu in the Border section's bottom left to choose from a range of dashed, dotted, and blurred borders; change the border's color using the color well and color-wheel icon; or change how thick the border is using the text field.

- **To add a shadow to a text box,** click the Shadow heading, click the drop-down menu that appears, and then choose Drop Shadow to create a floating effect (all the shadow styles are covered on page 199). Once you've chosen a style, you can use the settings that appear to customize it by, for example, changing its opacity or even its color (page 201 has all the info you need on modifying shadows).

TIP Does customizing a border or shadow effect feel too much like hard work? No problem. Pages has several ready-made styles that you can grab whenever you need a nicely formatted border or shadow in a hurry. To see what's available, click the box to the right of either the Shadow or Border heading to display a drop-down list of built-in options. Simply click any style to apply it to your object. To quickly remove either effect, select No Border or No Shadow.

- **To add a reflection to your text box,** turn on the Reflection checkbox. You can then use the settings that appear to change how opaque the reflection is.

- **To adjust the opacity of the entire text box**—background, border, *and* text—adjust the Opacity setting.

■ COMBINING TEXT BOXES WITH OTHER OBJECTS

Whether you're working on a word-processing document or a page-layout document, you can combine floating text boxes with other floating objects. First, make sure you have at least one text box in your document (choose Insert→Text Box). Then, to add another floating object to it, click the toolbar button for the type of object you want to add (Table, Chart, and so on) or grab an existing object that's floating around in your document. Next, resize the object (or simply drag it) so that it overlaps the text box. (What you're actually doing is *layering* another floating object over your text box.)

> **NOTE** You can't make the text in an *inline* text box wrap around a floating object. As you learned on page 144, inline objects can't overlap with other objects.

To change how the text fits around your overlapping object, head to the Format panel's Arrange tab, and then select a wrapping style for your object from the Text Wrap menu. You may also want to adjust the Text Fit setting (see page 182). The text in the text box wraps around your new object according to the settings you choose, as shown in Figure 7-7.

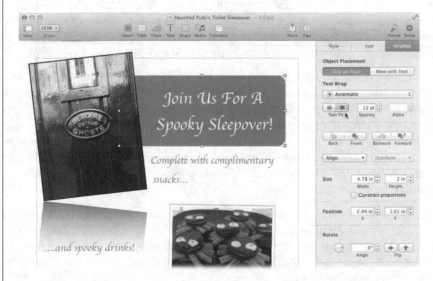

FIGURE 7-7

Floating objects have an impact on floating text boxes. Here, the text "Complete with complimentary snacks..." is pushed farther down the page by the rounded rectangle shape and the "Beware of the Ghosts" image. The text wraps around the shape and image based on your Text Wrap settings.

NOTE Combining two floating text boxes can create some interesting effects. For example, you can make the contents of one text box wrap around an overlapping text box to create a pull quote.

Although your new floating object affects any overlapping floating text boxes, it's still a separate object, with its own life outside of the text box—the two move independently. If you want to make sure that two floating objects always travel together as a unit, you need to *group* them. To do that, ⌘-click each of the objects you want to smoosh together into a group, and then go to the Format panel's Arrange tab and click the Group button (you may need to scroll down to see it). Now if you move the text box, the other object comes along for the ride and vice versa—the group behaves like one big object. (For more on grouping objects, see page 190.)

NOTE When you group objects together, you can no longer resize them individually or change any of their display properties (background color, border, shadow, and so on). If you select an object group, the selection handles appear around the entire group, and dragging them resizes *all* objects in the group. You can still edit the text within grouped text boxes (and shapes, too) by double-clicking the text and typing away, but other changes to individual elements are blocked until you *ungroup* the objects. To break up the band, select the grouped object, open the Format panel's Arrange tab, and click the Ungroup button. You can then make your changes. (To stick the objects back together again when you're done, select the objects, and then click the Arrange tab's Group button.)

■ PULL QUOTES AND SIDEBARS

If you want to include text in a page-layout document, text boxes are where it's at. Whether you're creating long passages or a couple of brief callouts, you use text boxes for nearly all text-related goings-on (although shapes can hold text too, as you'll learn on page 174). In word-processing documents, however, text boxes are most useful for highlighting or isolating some text from the main body text. *Pull quotes* and *sidebars* are two common examples. Figure 7-8 shows a pull quote.

In a word-processing document, you can create a sidebar or pull quote as either a floating or inline text box, but one advantage to going with the inline style for a pull quote is that it will always appear next to the relevant text. If you make it a floating object, on the other hand, it remains in exactly the same position on the page—even if subsequent edits move the section it came from to a new location, or even onto a different page entirely. Making a pull quote inline in a word-processing document means you don't have to worry about it getting abandoned by the related text as you edit your document.

Pull quotes and sidebars are close cousins that differ only in length and font style—a pull quote is typically brief and set in large type, while a sidebar is usually longer and set in the same font size as the main text (or close to it). In any case, the process of creating them is essentially the same. Here's how to add an inline pull quote or sidebar to a word-processing document:

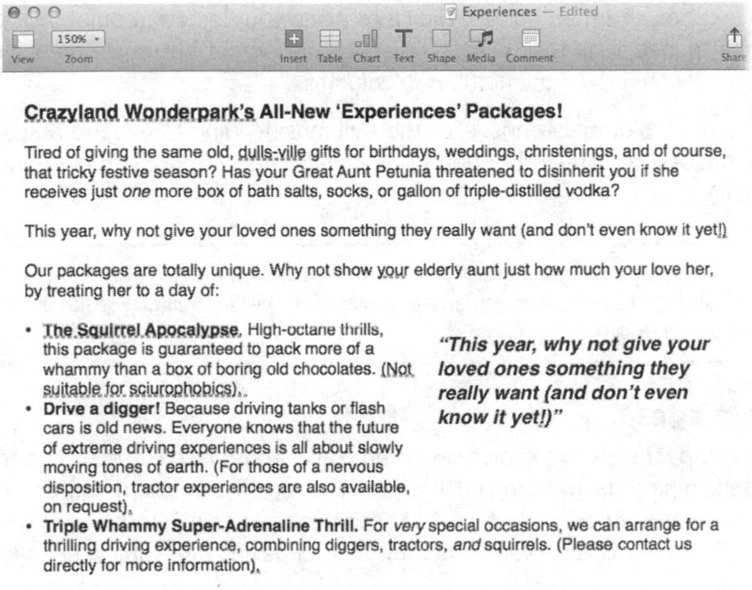

FIGURE 7-8

Pull quotes (a.k.a. callouts) highlight an important point that's in the main text. Since they relate directly to part of the text, they need to be placed near the relevant passage. Magazine articles often have pull quotes to add visual interest to the page by breaking up the columns of plain text.

Sidebars hold a paragraph or more that's related to, but not really part of, the flow of the main text. Sidebars can stand alone as a little chapter or chunk of information. This book uses sidebars to hold these kinds of digressions; the box on page 136 is an example of a sidebar.

1. **Add a text box to your document by choosing Insert→Text or clicking the Text button in the toolbar.**

   Either way, Pages inserts a *floating* text box, which isn't quite what you want.

2. **Drag the text box to where you want it to appear in your main body text.**

3. **Open the Format panel's Arrange tab.**

4. **In the Arrange tab, click the "Move with Text" button, and then click the Text Wrap drop-down menu and select "Inline with Text."**

NOTE Pages can automatically create a text box from copied text, which is handy for pull quotes that repeat a portion of your main text. Start by copying the text for your pull quote (⌘-C), and then click *outside* the edge of the document so the insertion point disappears (and the Format panel says "Nothing selected"). Next, choose Edit→Paste or press ⌘-V, and Pages inserts a new floating text box containing your copied text. All you have to do is resize or reposition the text box and format the text.

Shape objects make for attractive alternatives to text boxes for pull quotes and callouts. Shapes let you put a callout in a curvy container—a circle or rounded rectangle, perhaps—or a variety of other forms including stars and arrows. See page 168 to learn more about shapes.

■ ADDING COLUMNS TO TEXT BOXES

You can set text boxes to display content in multiple columns, which is handy for newsletter or magazine articles in a page-layout document, or wide multicolumn sidebars in word-processing documents. To set the column layout of a text box, select the text box and then double-click it to place your insertion point inside it. In the Format panel, open the Text tab and click the Layout button. Then use the Columns text field to adjust the number of columns.

To fine-tune your column settings, click the Columns heading to expand that section and get access to some other options (see page 116 for more info on working with columns).

> **NOTE** Columns work pretty much the same in text boxes as they do in the body of a word-processing document, except that text boxes can have only a single column layout. In other words, no section breaks are allowed in text boxes (or shapes).

Adding Images

When visual impact is the goal, pictures often play a larger role in the design than the text itself. In page-layout projects like the Crazyland Wonderpark Experiences catalog, for example, photos are the primary content, and text is reduced to a secondary role. Pages gives you a variety of tools to arrange and fine-tune your images.

■ MEET THE MEDIA BROWSER

All the iWork programs provide fast access to your photos, movies, and audio via the Media Browser, which lets you access the following:

- Photos, videos, and graphics stored in iPhoto, iCloud, and My Photo Stream.

- Music, movies, and sound files stored in iTunes.

- Movies stored in iMovie and your Movies folder.

To open the Media Browser (Figure 7-9), click the Media button in the toolbar. Use the tabs at the top of the Media Browser to browse audio, photos, or movies stored both on your Mac and online. Choose a folder or album in the Media Browser's sidebar, and the main pane displays the songs, photos, or movies that are in that folder or album you select in the sidebar.

To add a picture to your document, click the Media Browser's Photos tab and browse through your collection. When you find the photo you want to use, click it. Pages adds the picture to your document as a floating object. Drag the image to move it into position, or resize it by dragging its selection handles. (With Pages' standard settings, the image keeps its original proportions even if you resize it. If you prefer to stretch or squeeze the image into new dimensions, make sure the image is selected, and then open the Format panel's Arrange tab and turn off the "Constrain proportions" checkbox (see page 179 for more details.)

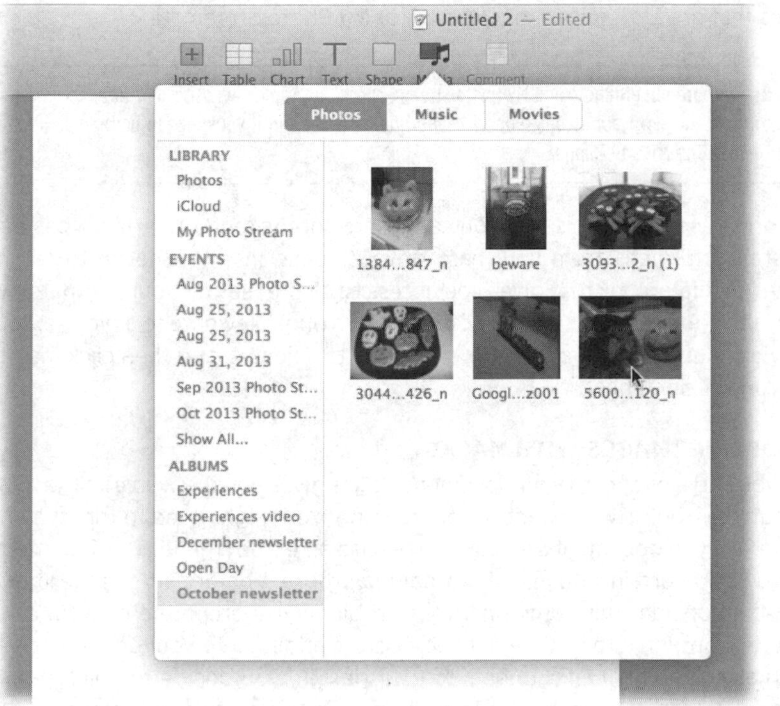

FIGURE 7-9

Click the Media button in the toolbar to reveal the Media Browser, which opens a wormhole into your personal collection of photos, audio, and video. Use the tabs at the top of the window to switch from one type of media to another. In the left-hand sidebar, choose a playlist, iPhoto album, or folder to browse its contents.

When you locate the picture, song, or movie you want to use, click it to add it to your document.

TIP If you need to replace an image in a hurry, Control-click the image and select Replace Image to open—you guessed it—the Media Browser.

To turn a floating image into an inline object, go to the Format panel's Arrange tab, select the "Move with Text" button, and then, from the Text Wrap drop-down menu, choose "Inline with Text." For more on floating versus inline objects, review page 143.

NOTE When you add a photo to a Pages document, Pages technically inserts a *copy* of the picture into your document—it becomes part of the document file. That means any changes that you make to the picture in Pages don't affect the original picture file. Plus, if you move your Pages document to another computer or email it to a colleague, any images go along for the ride.

■ CHOOSING A FILE FROM YOUR HARD DISK

Pages can handle a broad range of image formats, including JPEG, TIFF, GIF, PSD, PICT, EPS, and PDF. The Media Browser is a quick and easy way to insert pictures into your document—but it's not the only way. The Media Browser displays only pictures that are stored in iPhoto, iCloud, or My Photo Stream.

> **NOTE** For more about iPhoto and My Photo Stream, check out Apple's website: *www.apple.com/support/mac-apps/iphoto* and *www.apple.com/support/icloud/photo-stream*. Or, if you'd like to become an iPhoto pro, check out *iPhoto: The Missing Manual*.

If you don't use any of this trio, you can insert photos (and other file types Pages understands) directly from your hard drive. Choose Insert→Choose to call up a Finder-style dialog box that gives you access to all the files on your computer, your iCloud, and your network (if you're connected to one). Navigate to a picture, sound, or movie file and double-click it (or click once to select it, and then click Insert) to add it to your document.

■ CROPPING IMAGES WITH MASKS

When you add a picture to your document, Pages gives you the *whole* image to work with, but you don't always want the entire thing. You might need to trim the image to make it fit the document's layout or to excise an ex-boyfriend. This is something that you could certainly do in a photo-editing program before adding the image to Pages, but consider this common layout problem: You prepare a picture for your brochure, cropping it to just the right size before adding it to your document. Later, when making the final adjustments to your design, you decide the picture needs to be a quarter inch taller and half an inch narrower. So you delete the picture, go back to your photo-editing program, open the original image again, recrop it, save the new cropped version, and reinsert it into your document. Or, even worse, you go back to open the original picture and discover you saved only the cropped version. (Fortunately, this heartbreaking scenario can't happen if you use iPhoto to crop, as it always saves your original. Open iPhoto, select the photo, click Edit at the bottom of the iPhoto window, and then click "Revert to Original.")

With Pages, you don't need a photo-editing program to crop. You can simply *mask* your photos right in your Pages document, cropping them by selecting the portion of the picture to display while hiding the rest of it. Just like a fuzzy squirrel mask hides *part* of the face of a Squirrel Apocalypse actor while letting his blood-thirsty eyes peek through, a mask in iWork hides part of your image.

> **NOTE** This book plays it a little fast and loose by using the word *crop* interchangeably with *mask*. Image impresarios will know that cropping and masking are technically very different things. Cropping an image permanently removes a portion of it, while masking merely hides a portion of it. Masking, in other words, creates the illusion of cropping without actually changing the original image—and that's how all iWork programs work. So when this book refers to cropping an image, it's meant in the sense generally understood by regular folks— "Show me only part of the image"—not the technical sense of permanently removing a portion of the image, something iWork doesn't do.

The original picture always remains untouched when you add a mask—the only thing that changes is what portion shows through the *masking shape* (think of this as the space in your mask, where the image shows through—kind of like the eye holes in a Halloween mask). If you ever want to get the original image back, simply *unmask* the photo to reveal the entire image.

NOTE Only *floating* images have adjustable masks. If you turn an image into an inline object, you lose the ability to tweak and change the mask—so make sure your image is masked exactly the way you want it before turning it into an inline object (see page 143 for more on inline objects).

Here's how to crop an image in Pages with a mask:

1. **Insert a picture into your document (see page 156).**

2. **Double-click the image to open the mask controls shown in Figure 7-10.**

   Pages initially makes the mask the same size as your image, so don't be surprised if you can't actually see the mask when you double-click an image—as long as the mini toolbar with the mask controls is open, you've uncovered the image's mask.

Adjust image   Edit mask

FIGURE 7-10

Instead of cropping pictures before you import them into Pages, use a mask. Double-click an image to display the mask controls shown here. To adjust the size of the image within the mask, click the Adjust Image button and then drag the image's selection handles. You can also use the slider to resize the image. Alternatively, click the Edit Mask button and then drag the selection handles to change the mask's dimensions.

Finish by pressing Return to hide the masked (transparent) part of the picture. (Alternatively, click anywhere outside of the image, and Pages applies your changes.) If you decide you don't like your first crop attempt, simply double-click the picture to reopen the mask controls.

If you want to rotate your image, page 183 explains how.

3. **In the mini toolbar, click the Edit Mask button, and then adjust the size of the masking shape using its selection handles, until you're happy with the part of the image that's peeking through the mask.**

As you resize, Pages shows the dimensions of the mask as a dotted outline. Once parts of your image venture beyond this mask, they turn transparent to indicate that they'll be invisible once you close the mask controls.

> **TIP** You can tell whether you have the mask or the image selected by the color of the resizing handles: When the image is selected, the handles are white; when the mask is selected, they're black (as in Figure 7-10).

4. **To shift the mask's position on your picture, drag it by its border. To move the picture beneath the masking shape, move the cursor over any part of the picture and, when the cursor turns into a hand icon, drag.**

When you drag the picture under the mask, the selection handles for that image appear. You can use them to resize the picture independent of the mask. To return to editing the mask shape, click the Edit Mask button in the mini toolbar.

5. **When you're happy with your cropping efforts, you can apply the mask in one of three ways: Press Return, click anywhere outside the image, or click Done in the mask controls.**

6. **If you need to recrop the picture, double-click it again to reopen the mask controls.**

Repeat steps 3–5 until you have a mask effect you're happy with.

> **TIP** You can add white space around a picture by making a mask larger than the actual picture. Using this method, you can create asymmetrical white space around a picture—something you can't otherwise achieve. To do so, click the Edit Mask button and then drag the mask so that it reaches *beyond* the edges of your image.

A masked picture effectively has two editing modes—one for adjusting the overall image, and one for adjusting the size and position of the mask:

- **Moving or resizing a masked image** works just like editing a regular image—you don't even see the mask. Simply click the image once to select it, and then drag it to a new location, or drag its selection handles to resize it. When you resize an image, its masking shape stays the same, and the same portion of the image is shown; it's just a different size.

- **Editing the mask's size and position** works just like cropping: Double-click the image to reveal the mask controls.

> **TIP** Made a big mistake with your mask edits? No problem. You can get the original mask effect back by going to Format→Image→Reset Mask.

■ MORPHING PICTURES INTO NEW SHAPES WITH MASKS

Photos are rectangular. Sure, you can rotate them, or you can crop them with masks to change their proportions. But since the standard image mask in Pages is rectangular, too, you're still stuck with a four-cornered picture.

If all this feels a little square, Pages lets you break the mold and reshape pictures into all kinds of funky shapes. The difference can be subtle, like adding rounded corners to an image, or bold, like shaping your picture into a circle, star, quote bubble, or any shape you can imagine, as shown in Figure 7-11.

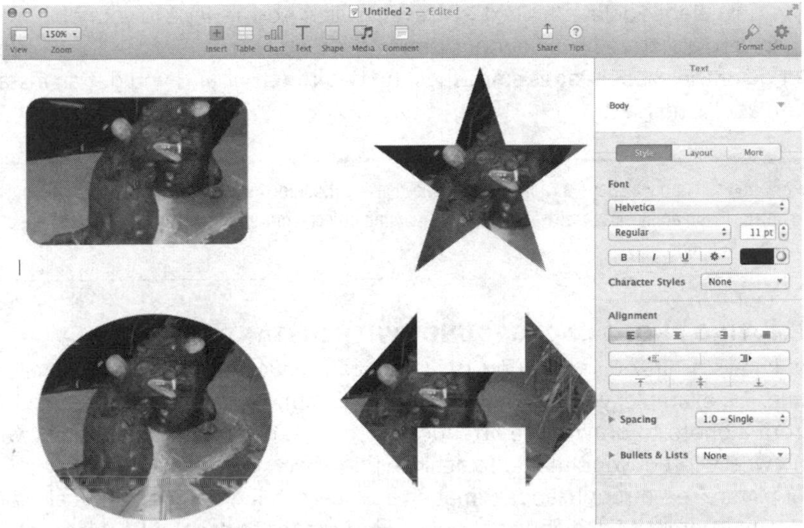

FIGURE 7-11

You can mask a picture with a shape to give the image a range of forms. Here, the same scary image has been masked with a rounded rectangle, a star, an oval, and a double-headed arrow. Mask a picture with the shape of your choice by selecting the image and then choosing a shape from the Format→Image→"Mask with Shape" submenu.

It turns out this is just fancy cropping. Instead of using the standard rectangular masking shape, however, you apply a mask with a custom shape. Here's how:

1. **Insert a picture into your document (page 156).**

2. **Select the picture, and then choose Format→Image→"Mask with Shape" and pick a shape from the list of options.**

   To add rounded corners, for example, choose Rounded Rectangle. To add a circle, choose Oval (weirdly, this option does in fact add a circle—so you'll need to resize and squish it a bit if you're after an oval). Whatever shape you choose, Pages displays the masking shape on your image, with the same familiar selection handles and mask controls that you encountered with the standard rectangular mask.

3. **Drag, resize, and adjust the mask just as you would with the standard rectangle (page 158).**

4. **When you're done, click outside the image, and the image shows off its shapely new form.**

When you apply a mask via the Format→Image→"Mask with Shape" submenu, you take the shape as is. When you choose Star, for example, Pages always gives you a five-pointed star, and Polygon always buys you a pentagon. But what if you want more points in your star, more sides to your polygon, or a different shape entirely? Happily, you can use any shape you like by creating a custom shape (see page 172), and then positioning it on top of the picture you'd like to mask. Select both the shape and the picture by ⌘-clicking each of them, and then choose Format→Image→"Mask with Selection," and Pages applies your custom shape as a mask. (If the shape contains any text, Pages delete this text.) Or, even easier: Add a shape to your document, and then drag a picture from your desktop or the Finder on top of the shape. When you let go of the shape, Pages smooshes the two together and you get an instant, shape-masked image.

> **NOTE** You can apply a shape as a mask using the "Mask with Selection" command only if the image is a *floating* object. If you apply "Mask with Selection" to an inline object, your image will vanish—probably not the effect you had in mind!

■ REMOVING PHOTO BACKGROUNDS WITH INSTANT ALPHA

Pages knows a nifty disappearing trick that can make portions of your pictures invisible. For example, you can remove the background of an image, or cut out the sky from a photo to draw more attention to the foreground and make text wrap around what's left of your image. To achieve this effect, Pages makes certain colors in your picture see-through, approximating a process that graphics geeks call *alpha-channel transparency*. For a phrase about making images transparent, "alpha-channel transparency" is decidedly opaque, but Apple nevertheless embraced this technical lingo when it named this iWork feature *Instant Alpha*.

To give Instant Alpha a spin, select an image, open the Format panel's Image tab, and then click the Instant Alpha button (or choose Format→Image→Instant Alpha). When you move your cursor over the image, the cursor turns into a big square with a crosshairs in it (the cursor is circled in Figure 7-12, top). Click and drag this cursor over the area of your image that you want to remove.

As you drag, Pages highlights the region that it will remove from the image, covering the soon-to-be-removed portion in a contrasting color, so there's no confusion about what section is slated for deletion. The farther you drag, the more you select for deletion. Pages figures out which areas to select by choosing similar colors that touch the region you drag over. When you release the mouse button, Pages dims the area it plans to remove. If you like, you can continue selecting additional areas by repeating the click-and-drag process. When you're done, click the Done button floating around in the middle of your screen, or press the Return key on your keyboard.

If you're not happy with the result, the quickest way to undo your changes is by going to Edit→Undo (or pressing ⌘-Z). Or you can get the original image back by selecting the picture, choosing Format→Image→Instant Alpha, and then clicking the Reset button that appears in the middle of your screen. Alternatively, select the image and then choose Format→Image→Remove Instant Alpha.

Using Instant Alpha takes a bit of practice, and it works best in areas with solid colors and clear boundaries—clear blue skies or photos taken against a solid background, for example. Pages has less success with complex patterns, so you'll likely run into some frustration when cutting out busy backgrounds. Often, you can eventually get the effect you're looking for by sticking to it, working through the area you want to remove bit by bit.

TIP Speaking of clear boundaries, Instant Alpha normally detects where your background color meets an edge and stops there, working its magic only on the field of color that touches your selection. In other words, it removes only adjacent patches of color. But if you hold down the Option key while you drag, you can select *all* occurrences of the chosen color anywhere in your image, even if they're *not* adjacent to your current selection.

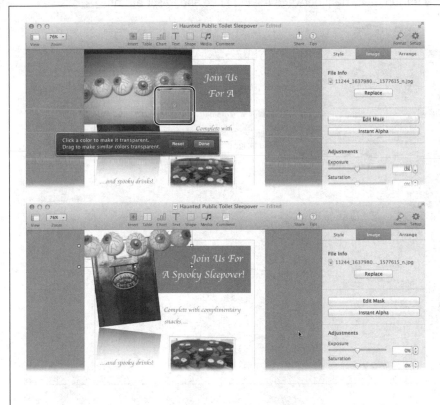

FIGURE 7-12

Instant Alpha gives the iWork programs their own green-screen special effects, letting you make certain colors and regions of a picture transparent. Select the image, choose Format panel→Image→Instant Alpha, and then drag the special cursor (circled, top) over the area you want to hide. Press Return, and Pages makes the selected region invisible, letting the background shine through. This screenshot shows an eyeball image before (top) and after (bottom) Instant Alpha.

You can now make the surrounding text flow through the parts of the image you removed and hug the contours of your image; for details, see page 182.

■ THE ADJUST IMAGE WINDOW

Pages is hardly a full-fledged image editor—it's no Photoshop—but it does give you a set of sliders that let you adjust pictures' appearance and quality. For simple tweaks, these settings can save you a roundtrip to a more sophisticated image-editing program. You can find the first two of these sliders by selecting an image and then opening the Format panel's Image tab:

- **Exposure** adjusts the picture's shadows and highlights.

- **Saturation** makes the colors more or less intense.

Just grab a slider and drag it left or right to see the effect on your image, or use the arrows and the accompanying text field to choose a specific percentage of exposure or saturation. After making your changes, if you decide that the picture looked better before you started mucking around with it, simply click the Image tab's Reset button to return to the original image.

But wait, there's more! To get even more control over your image, choose View→Show Adjust Image to open the Adjust Image window shown in Figure 7-13. (You can also open this window by heading to the Format panel's Image tab and then clicking the lined button that's right between the Enhance and Reset buttons.)

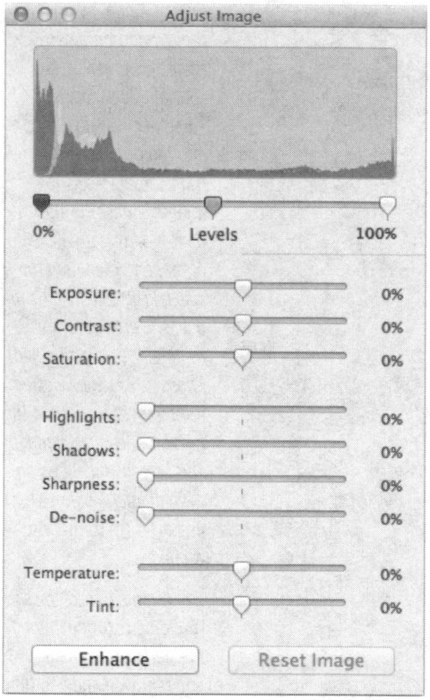

FIGURE 7-13

The Adjust Image window lets you change a variety of color settings for a picture. Select an image, go to View→Show Adjust Image, and then nudge these sliders to your heart's content. Or go the easy route: Click the Enhance button, and Pages chooses settings for you.

If you get carried away and want the old image back, then click the Reset Image button.

The Adjust Image window gives you lots of control over your picture. Here's what the various sliders do:

- **Levels** changes the levels of light and dark tones in the image. Just above the levels slider, the colorful *histogram* charts the relative levels of shadows and highlights in the red, blue, and green tones of your image. The left side of the histogram shows the levels of the darker tones, and the right shows the lighter. As you adjust any of the sliders in this window, the histogram updates to reflect your changes, showing how much color information is in each range from darkest to lightest. (If you're confused, don't fret—histograms are pretty complicated. Just keep an eye on your image as you drag the Adjust Image window's sliders and go with whatever looks best to you.)

    The Levels slider is actually *three* settings in one. The little knob in the middle of the slider controls the image's midtones. The knobs on the left and right ends of the slider let you adjust the darkest and lightest tones in the image: Drag the left knob to tweak darker tones (shadows), and drag the right slider to adjust lighter tones (highlights).

> **NOTE** The Exposure and Saturation sliders are described on page 164.

- **Contrast** controls the difference between the light and dark tones in the picture. Boosting contrast makes shadows darker and highlights lighter, which makes colors pop and tends to sharpen the edges of objects. Turning the contrast way up gives pictures a graphic, almost cartoony, effect that washes away subtle details. Turning it way down tends to make images murky.

- **Highlights** can correct overexposed areas by darkening your image.

- **Shadows** can correct underexposed areas by brightening your image

- **Sharpness** makes the image, well, sharper or more blurred. Adjusting this setting too high can cause weird outlines around objects in your image.

- **De-noise.** In image-editing circles, "noise" is the term for strange spots and blurs in images. Increase this setting to remove this unwanted interference.

- **Temperature** controls the amount of orange versus blue tones in the picture. Move this slider left to make the image "warmer" (more orange), or right to make it "cooler" (more blue).

- **Tint** controls the amount of red versus green tones in the picture: Drag this slider left for more red or right for more green.

Totally confused? If tinkering with image attributes isn't your idea of fun, you can just hand the whole thing over to Pages. Click the Enhance button, and Pages adjusts all the sliders automatically, choosing settings that it thinks will show your picture to best effect. If you're using a completely undoctored photo—straight from your digital camera, for example—using the Enhance button is a quick and easy way to clean it up and give it some extra pop.

■ FRAME IT

Pages gives you several picture frames that you can use with your images to dress them up or give them a *trompe l'oeil* 3D effect, like an actual paper photograph on the page. These frames are a special category of border that you can apply to pictures, shapes, and text boxes. They're not limited to images—you can add a picture frame to *any* object except tables and charts. You browse and apply these frames directly from the Format panel's Style tab:

1. **Select the picture, movie, shape, or text box you want to frame.**

2. **In the Format panel, click the Style tab.**

3. **Click the Border heading to expand that section, and then select Picture Frame from the drop-down menu that appears.**

   Pages adds some more options to the Borders section, as shown in Figure 7-14.

4. **Click the thumbnail in the Border section's lower left (it's circled in Figure 7-14) to open a drop-down menu of picture frame styles.**

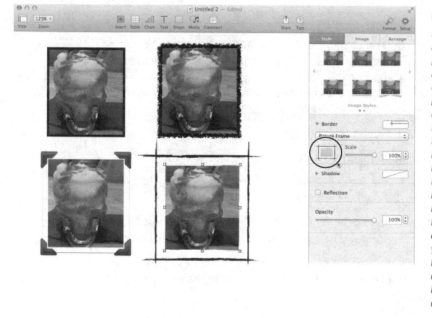

FIGURE 7-14

Here's the same skull image sporting four different picture frame styles. To add a frame, select the object, open the Format panel's Style tab, and then click the Border heading to expand that section. Set the drop-down menu to Picture Frame (as shown here), and then click the thumbnail that's circled here to open a drop-down menu of all the different frame styles. Make your choice, and Pages frames your object. To remove a frame, click the thumbnail once again and choose No Border from the drop-down menu.

5. **Click one of these styles to apply it to your image.**

6. **If you like, use the Scale slider to change the picture frame's size.**

   Frames start at full scale (100%), but you can make them narrower by dragging this slider to the left or entering a lower percentage.

If you change your mind, you can remove the picture frame by selecting the object and then clicking the thumbnail in the Border section and choosing No Border from the drop-down menu.

> **TIP** Many of the picture frames are designed to make your picture look like a paper photograph. You can enhance this effect by adding a shadow and setting the picture slightly askew, like a photo fixed to the page by human hands. Subtlety is a good goal here—just a slight angle and a light shadow give the best result. To rotate a picture, ⌘-drag one of its selection handles. To add a shadow, open the Format panel's Style tab, click the Shadow heading to expand this section, and then build your perfect shadow effect (see page 199 for more info).

■ REDUCING IMAGE FILE SIZES

Don't skimp on great imagery. Pictures give your graphic design visual impact and draw readers into your work. But they do come at a cost, at least as far as your hard drive or Internet connection is concerned. As you pile high-resolution images into your Pages document, its file size inevitably grows—sometimes enormously. That's not necessarily a big deal if the document is going no farther than your own computer and printer, but if you plan to share the document by email or online (see Chapter 9), image-heavy documents become bandwidth busters. Fortunately, Pages has a way to trim the flab.

When you add a picture to your document, Pages normally puts a copy of the entire original image inside your document—at full size and full resolution. That can mean several megabytes per image. But are you really using every last one of those precious bits and bytes? Chances are, you've reduced the size of most of your pictures or masked them to crop out parts of the original. If you're happy with your image-editing work, and don't need to go back to the original, you can tell Pages to throw out the clipped portions of your pictures. That way, Pages keeps only the smaller version of the pictures, reducing your file's waistline along the way.

To reduce the file size of all the media files within your document, choose File→Reduce File Size. Pages provides a file-size savings estimate (Figure 7-15) or, if the file size of the image(s) can't be further reduced, Pages lets you know that the document is already at fighting weight. To proceed with the size-reduction process, click Reduce.

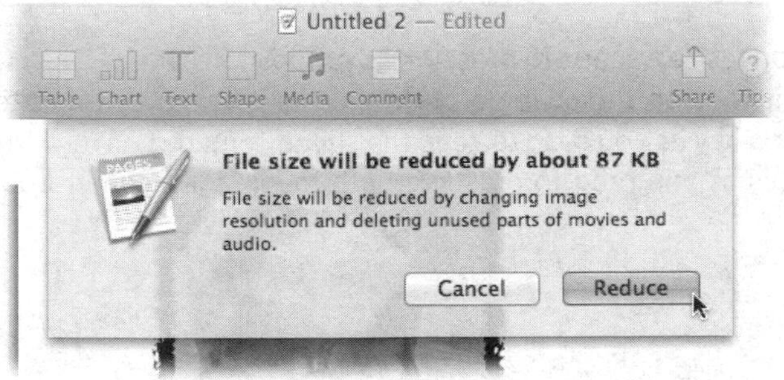

FIGURE 7-15

When you tell Pages to reduce file sizes of all the media files within your document by choosing File→Reduce File Size, Pages asks you to confirm the action and lets you know how much space you'll save. Click Reduce to continue.

NOTE The Reduce File Size command also compresses any audio and video files in your document. For details, see page 177.

But there's a downside to reducing image file size: Your file no longer contains the original images, which means that cropped portions are gone for good, and trying to make the picture larger may give you grainy or blurry results. To avoid unpleasant surprises when you want to make changes, it's a good idea to save the Reduce File Size command for when you've completed your design, or at least the current draft. If you do need to go back to the original, you've always got a fallback, though: The *real* original image remains untouched on your hard drive or in your iPhoto collection, so you can simply go back and add the picture to the document again.

Also, keep in mind that this technique slims down the overall *resolution* of images too, optimizing them for onscreen display but reducing their printed quality. So if your goal is a gorgeous print, don't use this feature—or at least save a separate copy for printing.

Adding Shapes

Pages supplies a collection of lines, arrows, and geometric shapes that you can add to your document as objects. You can use shapes as graphic elements to add fields of color behind portions of your page, for example, or as containers for text. The flyer back in Figure 7-1 (page 146), for example includes a rounded rectangle that peeks out from behind an image and provides a container for the "Join Us" headline.

To add a shape, click the Shape button in the toolbar. Pages opens a drop-down menu with thumbnails of all the shapes you can choose from (Figure 7-16). Each shape is available in several different colors; to see them all, click the arrow buttons on the left and right of the drop-down menu. Once you find a shape you're happy with, click it to add it to your document.

Drag the shape to position it, and drag its selection handles to resize it. See "Modifying Object Styles" on page 191 for details about changing a shape's color and opacity, filling the shape with a picture, and so on.

TIP If none of Pages' default shapes suit your fancy, you can draw your *own* shape. Page 172 explains how.

Hold the Shift key as you resize a shape to preserve its proportions; this is especially helpful when you want to keep the shape a perfect circle, square, or equilateral triangle. Hold the Option key as you drag to keep the shape centered on its current position. Hold *both* keys as you drag to preserve both the image's center and its proportions.

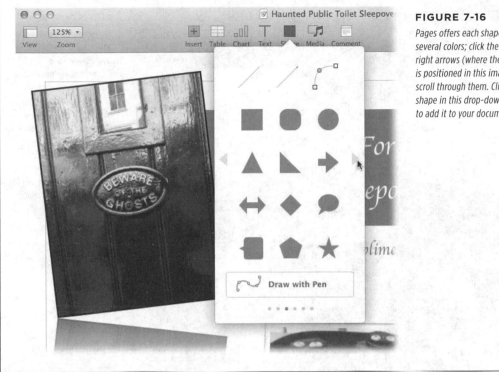

FIGURE 7-16

Pages offers each shape in several colors; click the left and right arrows (where the cursor is positioned in this image) to scroll through them. Click any shape in this drop-down menu to add it to your document.

Here's a rundown of the various options in the Shape drop-down menu shown in Figure 7-16 from top to bottom, left to right:

- **Lines.** When you click the Shape button in Pages' toolbar, the first two shapes in the drop-down menu are variations on that paragon of straight-and-narrow: the line. You can choose a plain line or one with an arrow on it. When you insert either type of line into your document, it sports one selection handle at each end. Drag these handles to change the line's length or angle. Hold the Shift key while you drag to constrain the angle to 45-degree increments.

> **NOTE** The item in the top-right corner of the Shapes drop-down menu is a *connection line* that lets you link two objects together. See page 184 for more on connection lines.

To adjust the line's thickness, color, and *stroke* (solid, dashed, dotted, or a variety of other brushstroke types), go to the Format panel's Style tab and click the Stroke heading to expand that section. You can then use the two Endpoints drop-down menus to choose various arrow and endpoint styles for your line, as shown in Figure 7-17.

FIGURE 7-17

You adjust the style, size, and shape of the two line styles in the Style tab's Stroke section. The line shown here has an arrow as its right endpoint and nothing for its left endpoint. Select the shapes of the endpoints from the Endpoints drop-down menus (where the cursor is here). For a simple line with no special endpoints, set both drop-down menus to None.

- **Geometric shapes.** Basic geometric shapes are next in the shapes lineup. Choose from a rectangle, circle, triangle, and more. Pages inserts these shapes in their most regular forms: square, circle, equilateral triangle, right isosceles triangle, and so on. Hold the Shift key while you drag a shape's selection handle to preserve the shape's proportions while you resize.

> **TIP** To change the curvy corners of a rounded rectangle (or add curves to a regular rectangle), select the shape, and you'll notice that one of the selection handles is a little green dot. Drag this circular *control handle* left or right to straighten or round the corners, respectively.

- **Arrow shapes.** Pages provides two big fat arrow shapes—one single-headed and one double-headed. Instead of being *lines* with arrowheads, like the ones you learned about at the beginning of this list, these shapes can have an outline stroke and a color, or image fill just like the other geometric shapes. You can adjust the size of the arrowhead and the width of the line using the green control handle inside the arrowhead.

- **Speech bubbles.** Pages gives you two familiar comic-style speech bubbles—an oval with a point tumbling out of it, and the same thing with a rounded rectangle. Like the arrow shapes, these shapes give you extra, circular control handles that you can use to adjust the shape. This time, you get *three* control handles, which respectively control the length of the bubble's point, the width of its point, and the shape of the bubble.

- **Stars and polygons.** If the regular geometric shapes seem too confining, Pages lets you add as many sides as you like to your shapes with the polygon and star options. You can vary the number and depth of points on a star as explained in Figure 7-18. To change the number of sides on a polygon, select the shape, grab the green control handle that appears, and then drag clockwise to increase the number of sides or counterclockwise to decrease the number of sides. A polygon can have anywhere from 3 to 11 sides.

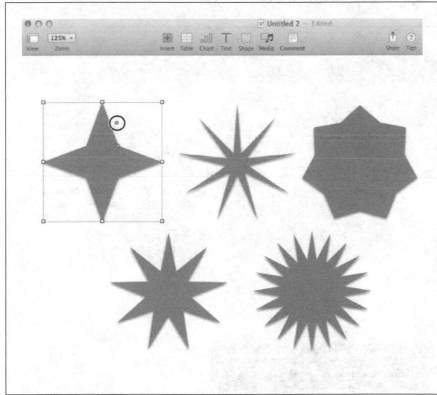

FIGURE 7-18

To change the number of points on a star shape, select it, and then grab the outer control handle (circled) and drag clockwise to add more points or counterclockwise to remove points. Your star can have anywhere from 3 to 20 points, and as you drag a little information box appears to help you keep track of just how pointy your star is.

To change the depth of your star's points, grab the inner control handle (the one on the edge of the star) and pull outward for shallower points or inward for more dramatic points. Again, an information box appears so you can keep track of the radius of your points.

■ DRAWING CUSTOM SHAPES

All the built-in shapes are familiar, uniform silhouettes. If you're after something a bit more unusual, you can draw your own shape. You simply plot your shape point by point, and Pages follows along, playing connect the dots:

1. **Click the Shape button in the toolbar, and select "Draw with Pen."**

   Your cursor turns into a pen nib.

2. **Click anywhere in your document to create the first point.**

3. **Continue clicking to add the second point, the third point, and so on.**

   Pages draws a line from point to point, as shown in Figure 7-19. To create a curve instead of a straight line, click and then drag the mouse to adjust the shape and angle of the curve. To delete the point you've just created, press Delete.

4. **Complete your shape by clicking the first point.**

   Pages pulls you out of drawing mode and, from this point on, treats your custom shape just like any built-in shape.

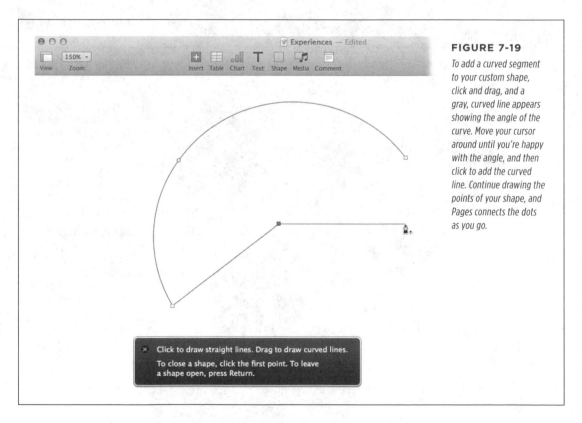

FIGURE 7-19

To add a curved segment to your custom shape, click and drag, and a gray, curved line appears showing the angle of the curve. Move your cursor around until you're happy with the angle, and then click to add the curved line. Continue drawing the points of your shape, and Pages connects the dots as you go.

NOTE Until you close a custom shape by clicking its starting point, Pages considers your creation a line instead. You can leave it as a line—keeping your rendering "open" so that there's no line between the first and last points—and even add endpoints. To stop drawing without completing the shape, press Esc; Pages pulls you out of drawing mode, and you're left with a line.

Custom shapes are created with their fill color set to transparent, so that background objects show through. To add a fill, go to the Format panel's Style tab, click the Fill heading to expand that section, and then choose a fill color (see page 192 for details).

■ EDITING SHAPES

Whether you've added a built-in shape to your document or drawn your own custom shape, you can nudge and cajole the shape into a new form by adding, deleting, or reshaping its points. But before you can edit a shape, you have to tell Pages that you want permission to do so: Select the shape and then choose Format→Shapes and Lines→Make Editable.

When a shape is editable, tiny red handles appear around its edges, marking its adjustment points. (Square handles appear at the end of each line segment in the shape, and round handles appear at the midpoint of each line when you move your cursor over a segment.) Drag these handles to change its shape. Dragging square handles simply adjusts the angle of the line segments; dragging round handles lets you curve the lines. You can move several handles at once by Shift-clicking multiple handles and then dragging. (A selected handle is red in the middle, while unselected handles are white in the middle.)

To add a new circular handle, put your cursor over the shape's border and, when your cursor sprouts a + sign; click to add a handle. Once you've added a circular handle, you can turn it into a square handle by Control-clicking it and then selecting Make Sharp Point from the shortcut menu (there's more on sharp points vs. smooth points vs. Bézier points in the Tip on page 174). To delete a handle, click it to select it, and then press Delete.

Just like when you're drawing a shape, handles can be corners or curves. When a curve is attached to a circular handle, the line segments on either side curve through it (Figure 7-19 shows an example). You can convert a corner handle into a curved handle and vice versa by double-clicking the handle. To adjust a curved line segment, grab its circular handle and drag to adjust the length and angle of the curve.

When you're done editing a shape, deselect it or press Return.

To do the reverse and change all curved points into corner points, make the shape editable, select all the handles for the points that you want to turn into corners, and then go to Format→Shapes and Lines→Make Sharp Point.

You can also access the Make Sharp Point/Make Smooth Point options by Shift-clicking all the selection handles you want to change and then Control-clicking one of these handles to open a shortcut menu that includes the Make Sharp Point and Make Smooth Point commands.

■ CREATING HOLES IN SHAPES

You can give any shape in Pages a funky makeover by punching a hole in it—using another shape as the hole-punch! For example, you could add a circle circle and then punch a hole through it with a smaller circle. You could even get really creative and design your own geometric logos using Pages' shapes. To try this new feature for yourself, add all of the shapes you want to combine into a single shape, and make sure the shape(s) you wish to use as hole-punches are on the top object layer (see page 187).

TIP To make it easier for you to gauge the final effect, you may find it helpful to give your objects contrasting fill colors (see page 192).

Position your hole-punch object(s) on top of the object that's about to be punched full of holes. When you're happy with the positioning Shift-click all of the objects, open the Format panel's Arrange tab, and then click Subtract. Voilà—you have a new, unique shape! This feature is definitely worth experimenting with. Take some time to see what different effects you can create.

If simply punching a hole in a shape isn't adventurous enough for you, you'll find two other options alongside the Subtract button:

- **Intersect.** When two shapes overlap, Shift-click the shapes and then click this button to preserve only the overlapping portions of said shapes.

- **Exclude.** When two shapes overlap, select both shapes and then click Exclude to delete the overlapping portions.

NOTE The Arrange tab's Unite button does something similar to grouping objects. See page 190 for more info.

■ TEXT IN SHAPES

Behind its mild-mannered facade, the humble shape has (nearly) all the powers of a text box: You can add and format text in a shape just as you can in a regular text box. This makes shapes a playful alternative to text boxes for callouts and pull quotes (see page 154 for pointers on creating inline pull quotes).

To add text to a shape, simply double-click it and start typing. Enter your text, and format it as usual using the Format panel. If you enter more text than the shape can display, a + sign clipping indicator appears at the bottom of the shape. To reveal the rest of the text, resize the shape by selecting it and dragging one of its selection handles.

It's common to rotate or flip speech-bubble shapes and arrows to make them point at a specific location and better fit your layout (see page 183 for details about how to rotate objects). But when you do this to a shape that contains text, the text makes the same transformation. When you flip a shape horizontally, for example, the text inside it flips, too, as if you're reading it in a mirror. Chances are, that's not what you had in mind. After you've flipped or rotated the containing shape, you can tell Pages to reset the text back to its plain old horizontal, left-to-right orientation: Select the shape, and then choose Format→"Shape and Lines"→"Reset Text and Object Handles."

■ **APPLYING SHAPE STYLES**

To change a shape's color and border, select the shape, and then head to the Format panel's Style tab and choose a new fill color (page 192) or border effect (page 198). You can also give a shape a quick makeover using any of Pages' ready-made shape styles. These styles include only various fill colors and border effects, but they're so quick to apply that they're worth checking out. Simply click any of the colored thumbnails at the top of the Styles tab to apply that style to the selected shape.

TIP These ready-made styles aren't restricted to shapes—you can find them in the Style tab whether you select an image, video, table, chart, or text box.

If you can't find a style you like in the Format panel's selection of ready-made styles, why not create your own? Start by using the settings in the Format panel's Style tab to create the border, color, shadow, reflection, and opacity effects you want. Then, near the top of the Style tab, click the little left or right arrow next to the style thumbnails to display several blank thumbnails. (This section of the Style tab is called the *Styles pane*.) Save your style to one of these blank slots by clicking the thumbnail with the + on it. Pages saves your style and adds a thumbnail of it to the Styles pane, and from now on you can click this thumbnail to apply your style to any shape in your document. Annoyingly, you can't use custom styles across documents, so if you want to use your style in a second Pages document, then you need to create a template that features this new object style. See Chapter 10 (page 263) for details on how to create a template.

Adding Sound and Video

If you're just going to print out your documents, you don't need to add sound and video clips. But if you're designing documents for people to view onscreen, Pages has features that let your viewers start and stop the playback of movies, narration, and music. For the best interactive environment, though, you're better off creating this kind of multimedia presentation in Keynote, which is better equipped for that kind of thing (see page 279). But, hey, if you're still determined to put a video in your word-processing document, Pages lets you do that.

Adding sound or video works just like adding a picture. You can select an audio or video clip in the Media Browser's Music or Movies tab. When you add a sound or video file to your document, click the triangular Play button once to play it, and then click anywhere within the object to pause it.

You can also drag a sound or movie file directly from a folder into your document. Pages can work with any file type that QuickTime and iTunes understand, including MOV, MP3, MP4, AAC, AIFF, and others. Instead of dragging the file into your document, you can also select Insert→Choose, and Pages opens a window where you can pick your file.

> **TIP** It's a good idea to lock a video or audio file to prevent your viewers from accidentally resizing or repositioning it when they click it to play or pause. To do so, select the media file in your document, go to the Format panel's Arrange tab, and then click the Lock button (you may need to scroll down to see it). This ban on changes affects you, too. To get permission to edit the video or audio object once again, head back to the Arrange tab and click Unlock.

When you add an audio or video clip, the Format panel sports a new tab that matches the kind of clip you inserted: an Audio tab if you added a sound clip, or a Movie and Audio tabs (shown in Figure 7-20) if you added a video clip. The settings are almost identical in both tabs, and they give you several ways to control the playback of audio and video clips in your document:

- **Replace** opens Pages' file-choosing window so you can pick a new video or audio file.

- The **Controls** section gives you traditional playback controls to play/pause, fast-forward, and rewind your clip. These are handy when the click-to-play and click-to-stop controls in the document itself aren't quite enough. (Alas, you can't add these controls to your document; they're available only in the Movie and Audio tabs.)

- **Volume** controls the loudness of the clip.

- Click the Edit Audio or Edit Movie heading (depending on the type of object you're working with) to see some extra options, including the **Trim** slider shown in Figure 7-20, which lets you control where the clip begins and ends so you can bracket a specific portion of the audio or video. Drag the left-hand handle to where you want the clip to start and the right-hand handle to where you want it to end.

- The **Poster Frame** slider (which is available only for video clips and resides in the Edit Movie section) determines which frame of the movie Pages displays before you start playing the clip (and when you print your document). Pages starts out using the very first frame of the movie, but you can change it to any other frame by dragging the slider to the frame of your choice. This is useful if the first frame of your movie is plain black, or if another frame better represents the movie's subject. No matter which frame you select here, when you play the movie in the document, Pages plays it from the beginning.

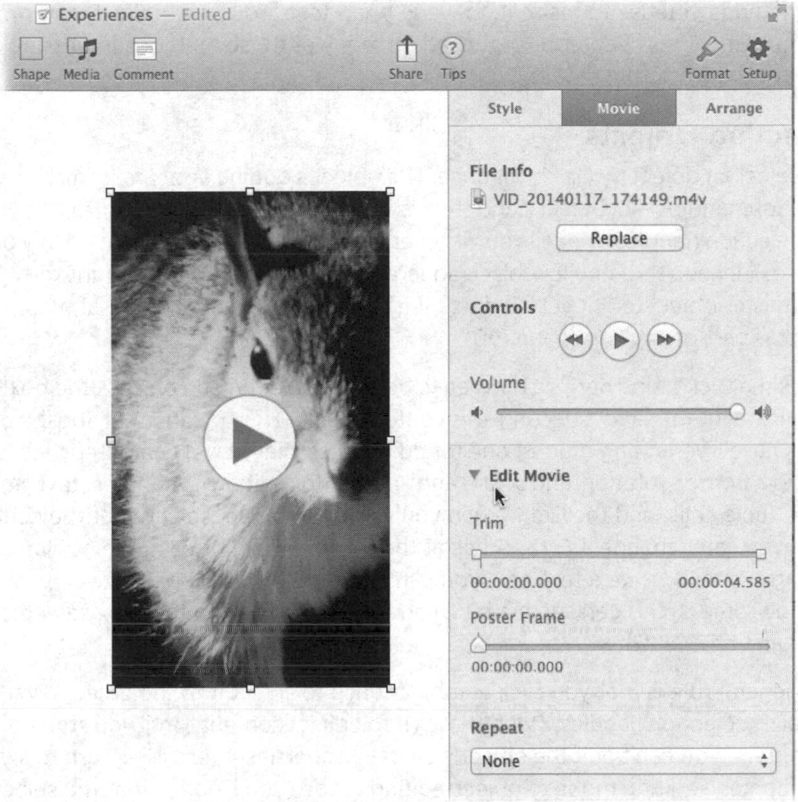

FIGURE 7-20
The Format panel controls the playback of audio and video in your document. Select the audio or video object, and then click the Audio or Movie tab in the Format panel to see these settings. In this screenshot, the Edit Movie heading has been clicked to expand that section.

- **Repeat.** This drop-down menu is where you tell Pages what to do with the audio or video when it reaches the end. Choose None to simply make the video or audio clip stop playing when it's over, choose Loop to make your clip start again at the beginning, or choose "Loop Back and Forth" to make it start playing backward when it hits the end, then forward when it hits the beginning, bouncing back and forth.

■ MANAGING MOVIE AND SOUND FILE SIZES

You can let a little air out of swelling multimedia files with the File→Reduce File Size command, described on page 167. When you do this, Pages removes any audio or video from before or after the start and stop points you set using the Trim slider shown in Figure 7-20. Just keep in mind that, after running this command, you can't get that clipped media back unless you add the original file again from scratch.

■ Working with Objects

As you've explored the ins and outs of adding pictures, text, shapes, audio, and video, you've no doubt noticed the similarities in how all these objects work. While the content of these object types may be very different, they share many of the same properties and behaviors. Whether an object contains a movie or a passage of text, the methods you use to resize it, move it, wrap text around it, poke it, and prod it are the same. This chapter has touched on many of those methods in passing, but now you'll dig into the details.

Selecting Objects

You select an object by clicking it once. The object's outline appears, complete with selection handles—in Object Land, this is the equivalent of standing to attention. The selection handles also tell you whether the object is floating (eight hollow black squares), inline (three hollow black squares), locked on the page (eight gray X's), or a master object (eight yellow dots). If an object's outline is blue, that means the object is part of a group (page 190).

Here's the tricky bit: There's a difference between selecting an object—the box that contains content—and selecting the content itself. That means that most object types have two editing modes: one for editing its object-level characteristics (size, position, border, rotation, and so on) and another for editing its content (text, image mask, table cells, and the like). When you've got an object selected at the content level, you can't change its properties at the object level. For example, while you're editing the text *inside* a text box, you can't change the text box's size or position. For newcomers, this can seem a bit frustrating: "I've got the text box selected, so why can't I move it?!"

The general rule is that you click an object once to select it at the object level and reveal its selection handles. *Double-click* it to edit its content. Until you stop editing its content, you can't edit the object's overall properties. Press ⌘-Return to switch from content-editing mode to object-editing mode (you'll notice that the selection handles return). In other words, double-click to drill down into the content, and then press ⌘-Return to withdraw to the object level. Or you can simply click outside the object to deselect it, and then click it once to reselect it at the object level.

To select several objects at once, hold down the Shift key as you click objects. You can also select several floating objects by dragging: Position your pointer in the corner of your document and drag it across your objects. When you release the mouse, Pages selects all the objects you dragged across. To select *all* the objects in your document, choose Edit→Select All (⌘-A). (In a word-processing document, this command selects all the free-flowing body text, too.)

Moving Objects

As long as an object isn't locked (page 132) or fixed in the background (page 188), you can move it by clicking and dragging. You can drag floating objects anywhere in your document—or nudge them along one point at a time with your keyboard's arrow keys (bump your objects 10 points at a time by holding down the Shift key at the same time). Hold down the Shift key while you drag a floating object to limit its motion to a strictly vertical, horizontal, or 45-degree path.

> **NOTE** With Pages' standard settings, a little gray box pops up to show you the object's position in the document as you move it. You can get rid of this box by going to Pages→Preferences→Rulers and then turning off the "Show size and position when moving objects" checkbox.

Inline objects have a more limited range of motion. When you drag inline objects, you can only drop them into a line of text in the same text area. Watch the insertion point as you drag, and then drop the object when your insertion point reaches the spot in the text where you want to put the object. If you want to move an inline object *outside* its parent text, you have to convert it into a floating object first; head back to page 147 for details.

If you're using guides—and for careful page-layout work, you should—you may occasionally find that you want to position an object very close to, but not exactly on, a guide. In this case, Pages' guides may be getting in the way of your positioning efforts. To put the object right where you want it, temporarily turn off guides by pressing ⌘ while you drag. For more info on guides, see page 140.

Hold down the Option key while you drag an object to make a copy instead of moving the original—the duplicate springs right out of the original, and you can drop it wherever you like. You can also copy an object by selecting it and choosing Edit→Duplicate Selection. If you have to move an object a significant distance—to another page or to the other end of your document, say—select the object and then do one of the following:

- Choose Edit→Cut, or use the shortcut ⌘-X.
- Choose Edit→Copy, or use the shortcut ⌘-C.

Scroll to where you want to insert the object, and then choose Edit→Paste (or use the shortcut ⌘-V) and the object appears in the middle of the current page. You can then drag the object into its final position. For more on copying objects (or just their styles), see page 203.

Resizing Objects

When you select an object and put your cursor over one of its selection handles, the cursor changes into a double-headed arrow to indicate that you can resize the object by dragging that handle. If the object is a picture or a movie, Pages locks its proportions to prevent you from stretching or squashing it while you resize, but you're free to alter the proportions of other objects like shapes and tables. To force Pages to preserve an object's proportions, hold down the Shift key while you resize. To resize an object so that its center stays put, press the Option key as you drag.

If you want to stretch or squash a picture or video clip, open the Format panel's Arrange tab and turn off the "Constrain proportions" checkbox, as shown in Figure 7-21. If you don't care for the funhouse-mirror look you've created for your picture or movie, you can always click the Original Size button to return to square one.

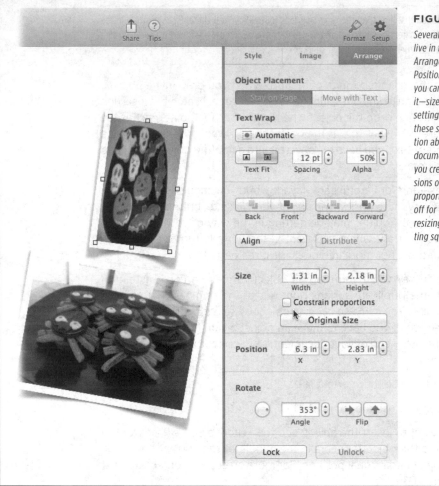

FIGURE 7-21

Several handy object controls live in the lower half of the Arrange tab. In the tab's Size, Position, and Rotate sections, you can enter—you guessed it—size, position, and rotation settings. Or you can just consult these sections for information about the objects in your document. The Flip buttons let you create mirror-image versions of objects. The "Constrain proportions" checkbox is turned off for the selected image, so resizing has resulted in it getting squished.

The Arrange tab gives you detailed control over an object's measurements. If you want to give an object precise dimensions instead of eyeballing it by dragging its selection handles, you can enter measurements in the Width and Height fields. This is handy, for example, when you need two or more pictures to have the same dimensions. Simply select the two (or more) objects, and then enter width and/or height measurements. Presto—all the selected objects are now the same size. (If the "Constrain proportions" is turned on, the Width and Height fields update simultaneously to maintain the object's original dimensions. If you want to change a single dimension, turn off this checkbox.)

You can also use the Arrange tab to set an object's position on the page via the X and Y fields. X is the distance from the left edge of the object to the left edge of the page; Y is the distance from the top of the object to the top of the page.

NOTE When you're working with lines, Pages updates the Arrange tab to include *two* sets of X and Y fields—one for the line's start and one for the line's end—letting you position a line by setting these coordinates. When you add the line to your document, Pages assigns the Start coordinates to the line's upper-left endpoint and the End coordinates to the line's lower-right endpoint. These coordinates always apply to the same end of the line—even if you later rotate or flip it.

Wrapping Text Around Objects

When you include objects—whether inline or floating—on a page containing text, you can control whether and how that text is going to flow, or *wrap*, around the object. Think of your object as a stone lodged in the middle of your stream of words: As your text flows past the object, how does it get around? Does the text flow to the right of the object? To the left? Both? As your words pass by, do they hug the object's contours to outline its shape? Or maybe the text doesn't flow around the object at all, instead hopping over it to continue on the other side—or running directly below so that the text is hidden by the object above. If you're not exactly sure how all this might look, Figure 7-23 shows examples of several wrapping styles.

Pages gives you fine-tuned control over how text flows around objects by letting you choose text-wrapping settings for each object. You'll find these options in the Format panel's Arrange tab, as shown in Figure 7-22.

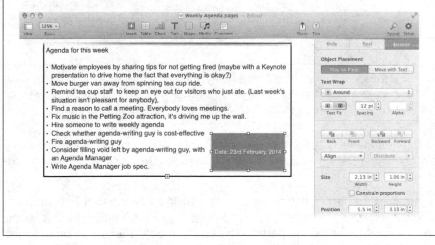

FIGURE 7-22

To control the way text floats around an object, select the object and then choose an option from Arrange tab's Text Wrap drop-down menu.

Here, the text is set to wrap Around the rectangle shape, but you can also choose from Automatic text wrapping, and Above and Below text wrapping.

Wrapping works differently for inline versus floating objects. Text wraps around a floating object only when the object is on top of the text in the layer stack; otherwise, the text just plows right over it (see page 187 for more about layering objects). In word-processing documents, a floating object is *always* on top of the body text, so the main text always wraps around it, unless you send the object to the *background* (see page 132) or turn wrapping off for the object.

Inline-object wrapping styles differ from their floating-object cousins, but in many cases they can still produce wrapping results that are visually identical. Their vital distinction is that, with inline objects, the object is tied to the text at the anchor point indicator and stays linked to that text, no matter how much you edit the text around it.

To change the text wrapping settings for an object, select the object, and open the Format panel's Arrange tab. Click the Text Wrap drop-down menu, and choose a wrapping style. Figure 7-23 compares a couple of different wrapping styles. (You can experiment with text wrapping for yourself by going to this book's Missing CD page at *www.missingmanuals.com/cds* and downloading the file *text_wrap.pages*.)

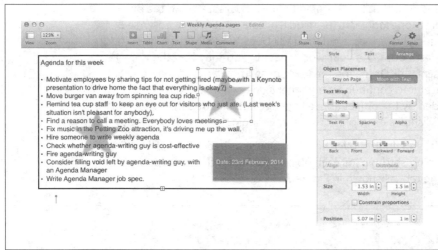

FIGURE 7-23

You can determine exactly how text wraps around objects—or have your text ignore the objects completely and plow straight across them—using the Arrange tab's settings.

Here, the text is set to wrap around the rectangle, as you saw in Figure 7-22. Meanwhile, the text wrap for the two stars is set to None so that the text runs across both of them.

> **NOTE** If your text won't wrap around a floating object no matter what settings you apply to it, try selecting the object and then choosing Arrange→"Bring to Front." Text wraps around floating objects only when the floating object is on top of the text in the layer stack. For more about layers, see page 187.

Use the Arrange tab's Spacing setting to control how tightly text wraps around an object. A higher setting creates a larger gap between the object and the surrounding text.

The Arrange tab's Text Fit buttons and the Alpha field apply only to objects with non-rectangular shapes: rotated objects, shape objects, pictures masked with a shape, and images with transparent portions. As you learned in the discussion of Pages' Instant Alpha feature on page 162, images can contain transparent regions called an *alpha channel*. You can add this transparency in Pages by using the Instant Alpha feature, or you can do it in a separate image-editing program. (If you do it with an external image editor, the exact procedures for adding transparency vary according to the program, and only some image formats—like PNG, PSD, and PDF—can include alpha channels.) Clicking the right-hand Text Fit button tells Pages to ignore the image's transparent regions and let text flow right through them. If an image includes areas of partial transparency, the Alpha setting controls *how* transparent the region has to be in order for text to flow through it.

> **NOTE** When you add transparency using Pages' Instant Alpha feature, text does indeed wrap to the image's contours as described above, but it's a little buggy. Sometimes it doesn't work unless you set the Arrange tab's Spacing field to zero. So if you're having trouble fitting text to the contours of your Instant-Alpha'd image, try zeroing out the Spacing setting.

Rotating and Flipping Objects

Objects are normally upstanding citizens. When you add an object, Pages props it upright, aligning it vertically and horizontally with the page's edge. But if all this feels a bit too conventional, you can tip objects askew by *rotating* them. Nudge an image ever so slightly, for example, to give it a jaunty, dynamic feel. Or you might spin a headline 90 degrees to run up the side of the page, flip an arrow shape to face the opposite direction, or display the upside-down answer key to your newsletter's quiz.

To wrest objects from the horizontal straight and narrow, select the object and then ⌘-drag one of its selection handles. (Figure 7-24). Drag to swivel the object clockwise or counterclockwise; press ⌘-Shift to rotate the object in 45-degree increments.

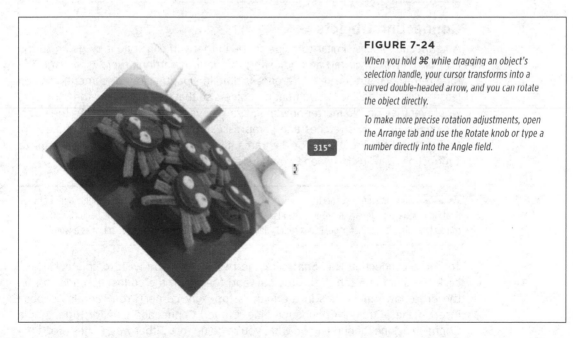

FIGURE 7-24

When you hold ⌘ while dragging an object's selection handle, your cursor transforms into a curved double-headed arrow, and you can rotate the object directly.

To make more precise rotation adjustments, open the Arrange tab and use the Rotate knob or type a number directly into the Angle field.

315°

Pages normally rotates an object around its center point, but you can get it to instead pivot around the selection handle opposite the one you're dragging by pressing the

⌘ and Option keys while you drag. And, yes, you can press Shift-Option-⌘ to pivot the object in 45-degree increments from the opposing selection handle.

The Format panel's Arrange tab puts another spin on rotation: Select an object and then adjust the Arrange tab's Rotate knob. You can also enter an angle measurement directly into the Angle field, or use the up and down arrows next to it to rotate in one-degree increments. The standard (right-side-up) position for an object is zero degrees, and the angle increases as you rotate counterclockwise. In addition to dragging the Rotate knob, you can click the knob and the angle-indicator dot jumps to that position. Unlike a compass where zero degrees occupies the top (north) position, Pages puts the zero degree indicator at the right (east) position to indicate horizontality.

Finally, the Arrange tab contains two Flip buttons. You can flip a selected object horizontally or vertically with these buttons, turning the object into its mirror image. (You can also choose Arrange→Flip Horizontally or Arrange→Flip Vertically to do the same thing.)

NOTE As mentioned earlier, if you flip or rotate a shape containing text, the text gets flipped or rotated, too. You can reset the text and make it readable again by choosing Format→"Shapes and Lines"→"Reset Text and Object Handles." Even if you decide to keep the text as is, it remains editable—although you might struggle to edit upside-down text!

Connecting Objects

A *connection line* is similar to a line shape in that you can style it by going to the Format panel's Style tab and adjusting the various settings there (see page 169 for a refresher). But the key difference is that, in a page-layout document, you can leash a connection line to two floating objects so that its ends follow these objects wherever they go. No matter how much you move these objects around the page, the connection line stretches and compresses to keep the two objects linked up. Connection lines are useful for diagrams, flowcharts, and anywhere you want to suggest a visual link between two objects.

NOTE You can't draw connection lines between objects in a word-processing document, only between floating objects in page-layout documents. Also, the two objects have to be on the same page (if you move a connected object to another page, Pages rudely deletes the connection line without so much as a word).

To add a connection line, Shift-click the two objects you wish to connect. Next, click the Shape button in the toolbar, and then click the connection-line icon in the drop-down menu (it's in the menu's top-right corner). You can also choose Insert→Line→Straight Connection Line, Curved Connection Line, or Right Angle Connection Line (depending on what you're going for). Either way, Pages drops the connection line into your document and attaches it to the two objects you selected.

TIP Straight and curved connection lines are pretty self-explanatory, but right-angle connection lines could use a little more explanation. Basically, this kind of connection line links up your objects with a right angle in between—regardless of where the objects are positioned. If you have two objects side by side, for example, the connection line juts dramatically from the first object so it can create that all-important right angle before heading over to your second object. No matter how much you click or drag a right-angle connection line, it refuses to curve.

You can change the route a connection line takes to your objects by selecting the line and then dragging its green control handle, as shown in Figure 7-25.

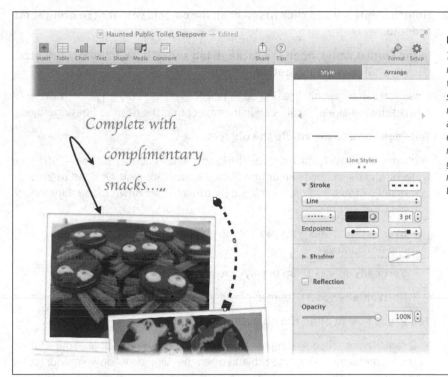

FIGURE 7-25

These two photos are connected to the "Complete with complimentary snacks" text box with connection lines. You can add stroke styles and endpoints to your connection lines and drag the green control handle in the middle of a line to change the line's shape.

NOTE When you draw a connection line to one or more objects with instant-alpha transparency (page 162), the connection line goes right up to the edge of the visible area: It doesn't stop at the object's invisible, Instant Alpha'd border.

Once in place, you can change the stroke, endpoints, and color of the connection line in the Format panel's Style tab (remember, click the Stroke heading to expand this section), just as you would a regular line shape. To remove the connection line, select it, and then press Delete.

Distributing and Aligning Objects

Sometimes being spaced out is a good thing. Say you have four floating objects and you want them evenly spaced across a page. Pages can handle the spacing and alignment for you automatically with the Distribute Objects and Align Objects commands, as shown in Figure 7-26. Here's how to use these commands to organize floating objects:

1. **Drag the objects into the approximate arrangement you want, placing the first and last objects precisely at the edges of the space where you want to arrange the group.**

2. **Hold the Shift key and click to select all the objects you want to bring some order to.**

3. **In the Format panel, open the Arrange tab and, if it isn't already selected, click the "Stay on Page" button.**

   Since you can align only floating objects, clicking the "Stay on Page" button (if it isn't selected already) turns an inline object into the desired floating object.

4. **Tell Pages how to distribute the objects.**

   You've got two ways to do this. If you're a fan of menus, choose Arrange→Distribute Objects, and then choose an option from the sub-submenu. Or head to the Format panel's Arrange tab and click the Distribute drop-down menu. Either way, you get three options:

   — **Evenly** distributes your objects evenly across the page, both vertically and horizontally.

   — **Vertically** spaces them evenly across the vertical axis.

   — **Horizontally** spaces them evenly across the horizontal axis.

5. **Tell Pages how to align the objects.**

   You can either choose Arrange→Align Objects and then pick an option or go to the Format panel's Arrange tab and open the Align drop-down menu. Either way, you get lots of options:

   — The **Left**, **Center**, and **Right** commands align the objects vertically along their left sides, vertical centerlines, or right sides, respectively.

   — The **Top**, **Middle**, and **Bottom** commands align objects horizontally along their tops, horizontal centerlines, and bottom sides, respectively.

   Keep in mind that Pages always aligns objects along the edge of the object group, in the current direction: When aligning left, for example, the objects align along the left edge of the leftmost object in the selection; when aligning top, they line up with the top edge of the top object in the selection; and so on.

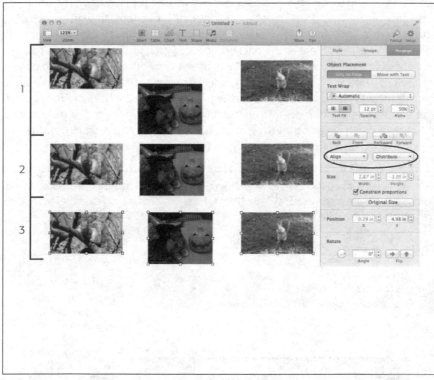

FIGURE 7-26

1. The photos in this group aren't aligned or distributed evenly.

2. This group shows what happens when you select all three objects, and then choose Arrange→Align Objects→Top or use the Align menu circled here. Pages hoists the objects up so they're all aligned with the highest object in the selection.

3. To distribute the photos, choose Arrange→Distribute Objects→Horizontally or make a selection from the Distribute menu circled here. Pages moves the middle object so that it's evenly spaced between the other two.

TIP   You can also access the object alignment and distribution commands via shortcut menus: Select all the objects you want to align, Control-click one of them, and then choose the alignment or distribution you want.

Arranging Objects

Much of this chapter has focused on how to format individual objects independent of the other objects around them. But as you fill your layout with objects, they start to bump into one another, overlap, and wrap around one another. As that happens, you have to start playing traffic cop, laying down the law for how objects relate to those around them. This section explains how to do that.

■ LAYERING OBJECTS

Think of objects as cards scattered across your page. When two cards overlap, one lays on top of the other, partially covering it or perhaps even obscuring it completely. That's because the cards are on different *layers*. Pages lets you shuffle the order of your objects, so you can control which one winds up on top. This is important not only for controlling whether one object covers another, but for text wrapping, too. Text wraps around a floating object only when that object appears on top of the text in the *layer stack*; otherwise the text just flows straight across that object.

Each time you add a new object to your document, Pages places it on the top layer, so the new object covers up any other object that it overlaps. In word-processing documents, the body-text layer is always the bottom layer (but you can slip objects beneath it by sending them to the background, as you'll see in a moment). You can move objects forward or backward one layer at a time by opening the Format panel's Arrange tab and clicking the Backward and Forward buttons. Move the selected object *all* the way to the front or back of the pile by clicking the Back or Front button instead (see page 187 for more info on layering objects). Better yet, Control-click (or right-click, if you have a two-button mouse) an object and then, from the shortcut menu, choose a layering command (Figure 7-27).

> **NOTE** You can also rearrange layers using the Arrange menu. The Bring Forward and Send Backward commands move objects one layer at a time, while the "Bring to Front" and "Send to Back" commands move objects to the very top or bottom of the layer stack, respectively.

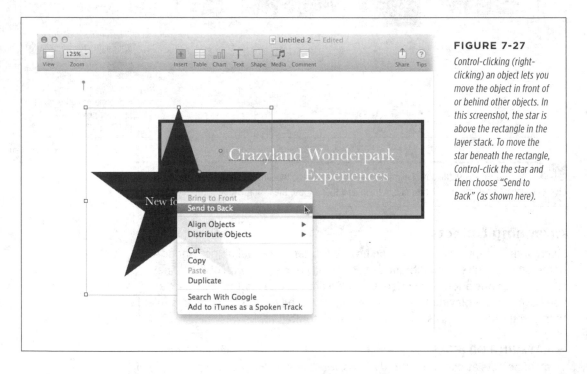

FIGURE 7-27

Control-clicking (right-clicking) an object lets you move the object in front of or behind other objects. In this screenshot, the star is above the rectangle in the layer stack. To move the star beneath the rectangle, Control-click the star and then choose "Send to Back" (as shown here).

■ SENDING OBJECTS TO THE BACKGROUND

In word-processing documents, floating objects are always above your document's body text in the layer stack—in other words, the body text is always the bottom layer. That means that even if you use the "Send to Back" command or the Back button in the Arrange tab, the object doesn't actually go to the *very* bottom layer—that honor is reserved for the body text. To get around this limitation, you need to use a workaround: You can slip the object beneath everything else on the page (even the main body text) by turning the object into a *master object*. This is useful when you want to create a *watermark* effect, for example, adding an image, graphic, or even other text as a ghostly image behind your words. (You can get that phantom effect by turning down the object's opacity after you send it to the background; see page 202.)

> **NOTE** What is a master object, anyway? The following section has all the details. For now, just think of it as the very bottom layer in a word-processing document.

To create a master object, select an object, and then choose Arrange→Section Masters→"Move Object to Section Master." The object turns into a wallflower, slipping behind the scenes as everything else floats above it.

Once you turn an object into a master object, it's no longer selectable, no matter how many times you click it. To convert a master object back into a regular object, you first need to make it selectable, so select Arrange→Section Masters→Make Master Objects Selectable. You can then select the object and choose Arrange→Section Masters→"Move Object to Page," which turns the object back into a normal object.

However, this workaround comes at a cost: When you turn an object into a master object, it appears in the background of *every* page throughout that section. That's annoying, but it's the only way to slip an object beneath that bottom text layer.

■ REPEATING ELEMENTS WITH MASTER OBJECTS

As you just learned, master objects appear on every page in a given section. That's slightly annoying when you want to add a watermark to only a single page, but that behavior is super handy if, for example, you want your logo to appear in the background of every page of your 200-page prospectus. Pages can add an image (or any other object) to every page of a word-processing document by turning that image into a *master object*, making it a fixed part of every page throughout the current section. Better yet, Pages doesn't limit master objects to the background—they can interact with text and other objects on your page, too.

Master objects behave like headers and footers: They turn up again and again on every page, always in the same location and always with the same content. But unlike headers and footers, master objects can appear *anywhere* on the page; they're not limited to the top or bottom.

To turn a regular object into a master object, select it and then choose Arrange→Section Masters→"Move Object[s] to Section Master." As soon as you run that command, you can no longer select or edit the object—it's now fixed in the layout, like wallpaper on every page of your document (or the current section, if you have section breaks). Pages makes master objects unselectable so they don't get in your way as you work through your document.

But what if you want to tweak a master object by changing its fill color, say, or giving it a border? You can't even select it! To edit a master object (or even delete it entirely), choose Arrange→Section Masters→Make Master Objects Selectable. Pages adds a checkmark to the Make Master Objects Selectable menu item to indicate that this feature is on; click the command again to turn it off.

When master objects are selectable, you can edit, resize, or move them just like regular objects. (Pages indicates that master objects are special by making their selection handles yellow circles rather than white squares.) Changes you make to a master object filter through every page of your document. Likewise, if you delete the master object, Pages deletes it from every page in your document.

You can transform a master object back into a regular floating object by selecting it and then choosing Arrange→Section Masters→"Move Object to Page." Pages exchanges the yellow, circular handles of a master object for the white, square handles of a regular object—and now you can maneuver it like any other floating object. But there's a twist: When you change a master object back to a regular object, Pages changes *every occurrence* of that master object in your document into a regular floating object, and selects all of them. In other words, if you have a 20-page document featuring your logo as a master object on every page, choosing "Move Object to Page" creates 20 separate logo images, one for each page, all of them selected (press Delete to delete them all at once).

■ GROUPING OBJECTS

After going to the trouble of precisely positioning floating objects relative to one another, you'll often wish you could move, rotate, resize, or copy them as if they were a single object. Happily, Pages gives you the power to group objects in this way. (And if you need to adjust them individually later on, you can ungroup them.)

> **NOTE** You can't group inline objects, only floating objects.

Hold down the Shift key as you click each object you want to include in the group (all the objects have to be on the same page). Then choose Arrange→Group, or open the Format panel's Arrange tab and click Group (you may need to scroll down to see this button). Pages replaces the individual selection rectangles around each object with one *big* rectangle that encloses the whole group (see Figure 7-28). Pages treats grouped objects like a single entity. You can apply all the usual object manipulations and adjustments to a group of objects.

> **NOTE** If you're trying to combine shapes into a group, you'll get an extra option in the Arrange tab: Unite. Uniting objects is similar to grouping them; the only difference is that you can't split united shapes back into separate entities, so think carefully before clicking the Unite button!

This all-for-one group approach means that you lose the ability to style or edit objects individually. The exception is editing text inside text boxes or shapes—you can continue to do that by double-clicking the text to edit it. To make other changes to single objects within a group, you first have to disband your little club. To restore the grouped objects' individuality, select the group, and then choose Arrange→Ungroup or go to the Format panel's Arrange tab and click Ungroup.

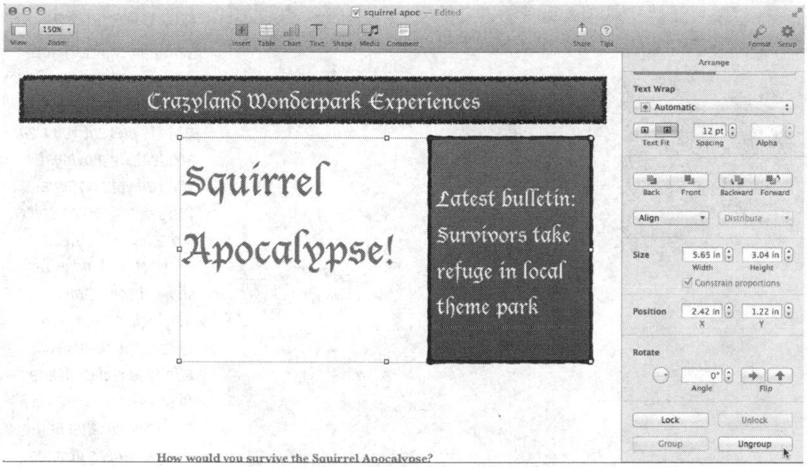

FIGURE 7-28

When you click any object in a group, Pages displays a selection rectangle around the entire group to indicate that it treats them as a single unit. Dragging grouped objects moves all of them at once, and dragging the selection handles resizes all objects within that group. And just like when you resize individual objects, resizing grouped text boxes and shapes with text in them doesn't change the size of the text, just the size of the object it's inside.

■ LOCKING OBJECTS

You can lock a floating object to the page to ensure you don't accidentally shift it out of position as you work on your layout. To lock an object, select it and then choose Arrange→Lock, press ⌘-L, or go to the Format panel's Arrange tab and click Lock. Pages nails your object to the page, replacing its selection handles with X marks to indicate that it's off the market for editing (Figure 7-29). You can select locked objects, but you can't change them in any way until you unlock them.

> **NOTE** You can't lock inline objects in a word-processing document.

Unlock an object by selecting it and then choosing Arrange→Unlock, pressing Option-⌘-L, or opening the Format panel's Arrange tab and clicking the Unlock button. No matter which method you use, Pages unchains the object and you're free to edit it as normal.

■ Modifying Object Styles

Besides controlling objects' size and placement on the page, you can also adjust the way each object looks by changing its various *properties*. Object properties include things like background color or image, line color and style, reflections, shadows, and opacity. As this section explains, the Format panel and Color Picker are your command centers for adjusting these properties.

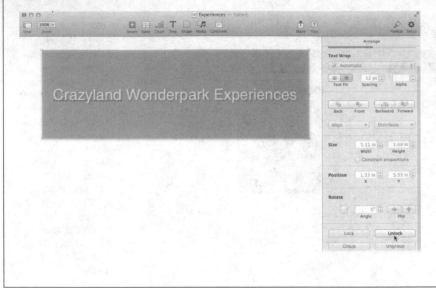

FIGURE 7-29

Select an object, choose Arrange→Lock, and Pages fastens the object to the page to prevent you from accidentally moving it as you edit your document. If you select a locked object, it displays X's instead of selection handles (as shown here—though they're faint and hard to see) and resists your efforts to edit or delete it. To unlock an object, click the Unlock button in the Format panel's Arrange tab (where the cursor is here).

TIP If your object styling goes awry and you wind up with an object painted with garish colors and egregious effects, remember that the Undo command is always on hand to get you out of a pickle: Either go to Edit→Undo, or use the ⌘-Z shortcut.

Filling Objects with Colors, Gradients, and Images

You can change an object's color using the Format panel's Style tab—both its *fill* (interior) color and its border color. As this section explains, you have several options when it comes to filling objects.

■ COLOR FILLS

You can add a fill color to any shape or text box. To change an object's fill color, select the object, open the Format panel's Style tab, and then click the Fill heading to expand that section. In the first unlabeled drop-down menu in that section, choose Color Fill, and then pick one of Pages' default colors by clicking the color well and making a selection from the drop-down menu. Or, if none of these default colors float your boat, you can create your own using the Color Picker.

As you've learned, the Color Picker is a part of OS X and comes into play in many different programs when you need to adjust colors. Open the Color Picker by going to View→Show Colors or by clicking the color wheel icon in the Fill section of the Format panel's Style tab (shown in Figure 7-30). You can then use all of the Color Picker's options to create your perfect, custom color.

Figure 7-30 shows the standard version of the Color Picker, but if you're not thrilled by it, you have four other ways to choose colors. Switch between them by clicking the buttons above the color well. Once you find a color you like, apply it to your shape either by dragging it from the color well at the top of the Color Picker, or from one of the palette squares at the bottom of the Color Picker, and dropping it onto your object.

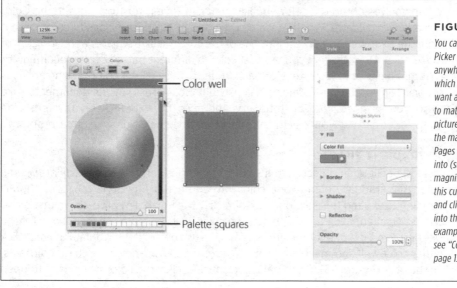

FIGURE 7-30

You can use the Color Picker to copy a color from anywhere on your screen, which is handy if you want a text box's color to match the color in a picture, for example. Click the magnifying glass, and Pages turns your cursor into (surprise, surprise) a magnifying glass. Place this cursor over a color and click to load that color into the color well. For an example of this technique, see "Color Me Inspired" on page 136.

NOTE   If you open the Color Picker via the Format panel's Style tab, you don't need to drag colors from the Color Picker to update your object: The selected object changes automatically as you select different colors, shades, and opacities in the Color Picker.

Once you've chosen your color, you can make it more (or less) transparent by dragging the Opacity slider at the bottom of the Color Picker. As you adjust the opacity, Pages splits the color well diagonally and displays the reduced-opacity color in the bottom half. The upper half of the color well displays shades of gray—this is actually the mask that Pages applies to the selected color to reduce its opacity (or increase its transparency). In other words, if you set the opacity to zero, the upper part of the color well is pure black, masking out all the color and resulting in no color. Increase the opacity, and that black turns into lighter and lighter gray, letting more of the color show through, resulting in more opaque colors—until you hit 100 percent opacity.

TIP   When you make an object's fill color transparent (in other words, when you set the Color Picker's Opacity slider to anything less than 100%), text and objects behind it show through. You can get a similar effect by increasing the object's transparency—just lower its opacity in the Format panel's Style tab (see page 202). The difference, though, is that changing an object's opacity makes its contents transparent, too (including any text). Making just the fill color transparent allows the contents to remain completely opaque.

Instead of whipping up your own colors with the Color Picker, you can just find a color in any document or any object on your screen (even outside of Pages) and load it into the Color Picker. For this trick, click the magnifying glass icon next to the color well. Pages turns your cursor into a magnifying glass with a crosshairs in the middle, which lets you pinpoint individual pixels. Maneuver the magnifying glass over any part of your screen until the color you want appears as the central pixel in the crosshairs, and then click to load that pixel's color into the Color Picker.

When you've captured a color you like, you can save it for future use in the Color Picker's *color palette*. Whether it's a pure color or a reduced-opacity color, grab it from the color well and drag it into one of the color palette squares at the bottom of the window. Doing so lets you use that color in different parts of your document for different types of objects, text, or backgrounds. This custom color-picking ability is especially helpful for maintaining a consistent look across several documents—like a brochure, business card, or stationery. And since the Color Picker is a system-wide feature, you can use your saved colors in other documents or even other *programs*.

■ GRADIENT FILLS

Instead of filling an object with a solid color, Pages can create a *gradient fill*, a fill color that gradually blends one color into another. In the Style tab, click the Fill heading to expand this section, and then click the unlabeled drop-down menu and choose Gradient Fill. Pages displays two color wells beneath the menu: one for the starting color and one for the ending color. To use one of Pages' default colors, click either color well and make your selection from the drop-down menu that appears, as shown in Figure 7-31. Or, to get more specific, click the color wheel icon to open the Color Picker.

You could choose, for example, red and yellow to create a sunset gradient that transitions from red through all the shades of orange to yellow. But it turns out that the most effective gradient is one you barely notice. A subtle color shift that maintains the same color but shifts just a few degrees of brightness often creates the illusion of a translucent inner glow that lends real elegance to an object. In the Color Picker, try using the Brightness slider (where the cursor is back in Figure 7-30) to pick your second gradient color. For the best effect, give the slider only a little nudge. Reducing the opacity of one of the colors also lets you create a gradient that becomes gradually transparent, which gives an object the appearance of fading into the background.

A gradient starts at one side of an object and ends at the opposite side. In the Fill section of the Format panel's Style tab, click the arrow buttons to change the gradient's direction from top to bottom or left to right. Use the Angle knob or enter an angle directly into the Angle field to set any other gradient direction. Click the curved, double-headed arrow to flip the gradient, swapping the starting and ending colors.

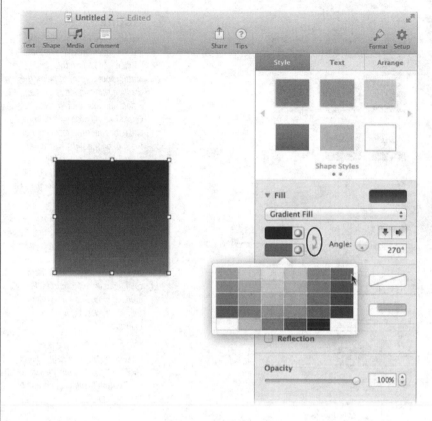

FIGURE 7-31

To fill a shape or text box with a gradient that blends gradually from one color into another, click the Fill heading to expand that section, and then choose Gradient Fill from the drop-down menu. Click each of the color wells that appears to select a starting and ending color for your gradient (to swap these colors, click the curved arrows circled here), and then use the arrow buttons or the Angle knob to determine the gradient's direction.

The Gradient Fill option is a good place to get acquainted with gradients, but Pages lets you use several more gradient features when you choose *Advanced Gradient Fill* from the Fill section's drop-down menu. These advanced options let you add more colors, so instead of making a simple linear transition from one color to another, you can step through an entire spectrum of colors. You can also change how sharply the gradient shifts from one color to another. Figure 7-32 shows you how it works.

Finally, the Advanced Gradient Fill option lets you choose a *radial gradient,* as opposed to the *linear gradients* you've seen so far. Linear gradients change the color from one side of the object to the other in a straight line, whereas radial gradients change color from a central focal point that radiates outward in a circle. Change the center point of the radial gradient by dragging the object's *blend point* (the green circle control that appears when you click the Radial button; this button is labeled in Figure 7-32).

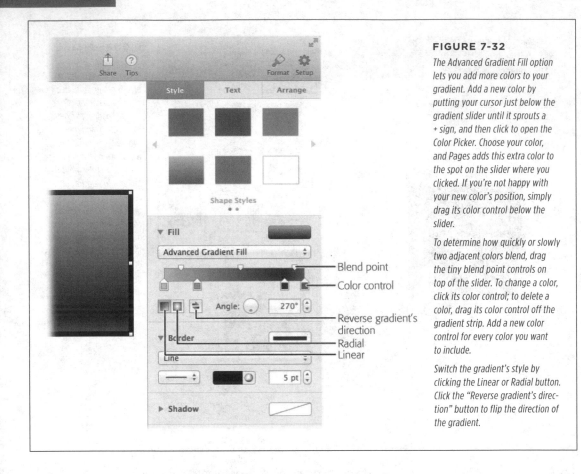

FIGURE 7-32

The Advanced Gradient Fill option lets you add more colors to your gradient. Add a new color by putting your cursor just below the gradient slider until it sprouts a + sign, and then click to open the Color Picker. Choose your color, and Pages adds this extra color to the spot on the slider where you clicked. If you're not happy with your new color's position, simply drag its color control below the slider.

To determine how quickly or slowly two adjacent colors blend, drag the tiny blend point controls on top of the slider. To change a color, click its color control; to delete a color, drag its color control off the gradient strip. Add a new color control for every color you want to include.

Switch the gradient's style by clicking the Linear or Radial button. Click the "Reverse gradient's direction" button to flip the direction of the gradient.

■ FILLING WITH IMAGES

Pages lets you use images instead of colors to fill objects. This is one technique for applying a background image to a text box or a table cell, or to fill a shape with an image (although you might be better off using the "Mask with Shape" command for that; see page 161).

Select a shape or text box, for example, and, in the Fill section of the Format panel's Style tab (click the Fill heading to expand it), open the drop-down menu and choose Image Fill. Then, to select an image, click the Choose button and pick an image file from your hard drive. Pages adds the image to your selected object, and you can then scale this image according to your choice in the Fill section's second drop-down menu:

- **Original Size.** Choose this menu item and Pages places the image into the object at its exact original size. If the image is large—like a high-resolution photograph—you'll see only a tiny portion of the picture, and unfortunately you can't control which part of the picture Pages displays. If the original image is smaller than the object you're filling, Pages places it in the center of the object, and you can't shift the position of the image within the object.

- **Stretch.** Pages stretches the image, distorting it a little or a lot as it transforms the image's proportions to conform to the object's dimensions.

- **Tile.** If the image is smaller than the object, Pages fills the object with multiple copies of the image (like tiles on a countertop). If the image is larger than the object, Pages cuts a section from the upper-left corner of the image and pastes it into the object at its original size. As you can see in Figure 7-33 (top right), when this happens, you may end up with a fill that's just an unrecognizable part of your image (depending on what's in the upper-left corner of your image).

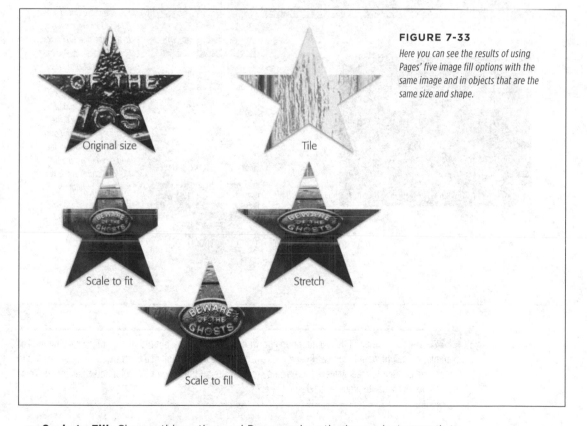

FIGURE 7-33

Here you can see the results of using Pages' five image fill options with the same image and in objects that are the same size and shape.

Original size

Tile

Scale to fit

Stretch

Scale to fill

- **Scale to Fill.** Choose this option and Pages resizes the image just enough to completely fill the object's shape. This option never leaves any blank space in the image's background, but it often means that portions of the image get cropped. If you fill a horizontal shape with a vertical image, for example, the top and bottom of the vertical image aren't visible.

- **Scale to Fit.** Pages attempts to fit the entire image into the object by making the image the same height and width as the object and then cropping anything that doesn't fit. When the object doesn't match the proportions of the image, this often results in some empty space within the object.

Once you've filled an object with an image, you can add a color tint to the image to impart, for example, a rosy glow or a ghoulish green overcast. In the Style tab's Fill section, open the first drop-down menu and choose Advanced Image Fill. Select an image and a scaling method (if you haven't already), and then click either the color well or the color wheel icon. Select a color and adjust its opacity, and Pages applies the filter to your image (see Figure 7-34).

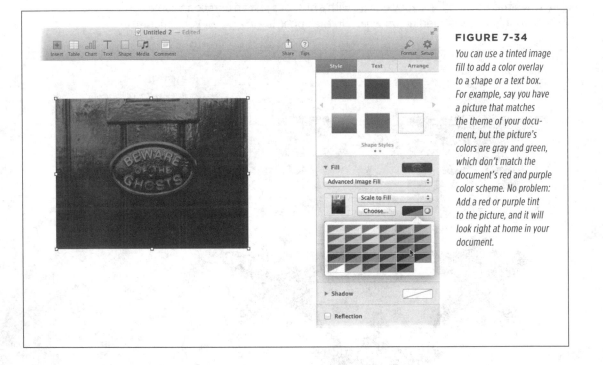

FIGURE 7-34

You can use a tinted image fill to add a color overlay to a shape or a text box. For example, say you have a picture that matches the theme of your document, but the picture's colors are gray and green, which don't match the document's red and purple color scheme. No problem: Add a red or purple tint to the picture, and it will look right at home in your document.

TIP Use tinted image fills to fade an image without affecting the opacity of the image's container. For example, you might want to fade an image you're using as the background in a text box, so that the text in the foreground is easier to read. Achieve this effect by using white for the image's tint color and adjusting the Color Picker's Opacity slider to produce the desired effect.

Adjusting Line Styles

Pages uses border lines as standard or optional components in most objects. You can even get fancy by replacing a simple border with a graphical picture frame. You can make all of these line adjustments in the Format panel's Style tab. Click the Border heading to see all the controls that are on offer (Figure 7-35).

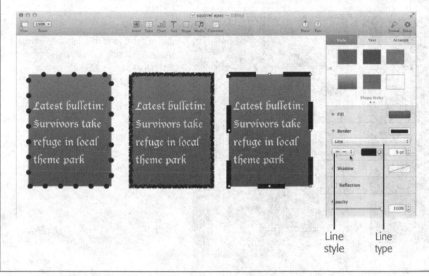

FIGURE 7-35

Use the Border settings to select the line style, line weight, and color for an object's border. Here, the three rectangle shapes each have a different line style.

You can apply border lines to any object, but picture frames aren't available for tables or charts. (On behalf of the Council on Good Design, thank you, Apple.) This section focuses on adding border lines; for details about picture frames, see page 166.

To adjust an object's border line style, select the object, open the Format panel's Style tab, and then click the Border heading to expand that section. Open the Line Type drop-down menu (labeled in Figure 7-35) and choose Line. Next, open the Line Style drop-down menu and choose your desired style (dashed, dotted, blurred, or whatever). Click the color well to choose from Pages' default colors, or click the color wheel icon to open the Color Picker. Set the border's thickness using the field in the bottom-right corner of the Border section.

To remove an object's border altogether, open the Line Type drop-down menu and select No Border.

Adding Shadows and Reflections

Shadows and reflections are perhaps the most popular ways to make graphics really pop. Adding a shadow to a page element seems to lift it off the page, setting it apart from everything else and subtly adding an extra dimension to your design. A reflection adds an illusion of depth to the page by adding a dimmed mirror-image below the original object, as if you were looking at it across a wet or glossy surface. Figure 7-36 shows a couple of examples.

Just don't overdo it. When you add special effects to *every* picture on the page, they're no longer special, are they? Good design is often more about restraint than showy effects, so use these effects judiciously or to call out just one or two elements in your document. Carefully choose the elements that you want to highlight and then apply your effects with a light touch.

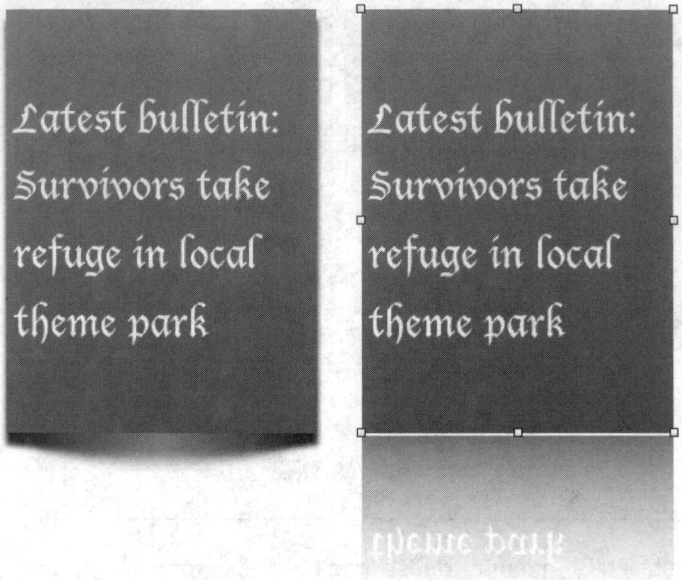

FIGURE 7-36

Adding a shadow or reflection to an image creates the illusion of depth. A shadow makes the image look like it's floating above the page (left), while a mirror-image reflection makes the image appear as though you're seeing it across a glossy floor (right).

> **NOTE** You can add reflections to images, text boxes, shapes, and movies—but not to tables or charts. Also, if you add a shadow to a text box, you probably want to add a fill color (perhaps just white—see page 192); and be wary of the text itself casting the reflection.

Pages makes it easy to add these effects. To add a reflection, select the object, open the Format panel's Style tab, and then turn on the Reflection checkbox. You can then use the Reflection slider to adjust the reflection's opacity. To remove a reflection, select the object, and then turn off the Reflection checkbox.

To add a shadow, head to the Format panel's Style tab, click the Shadow heading, and then choose a style from the drop-down menu (Figure 7-37 shows all three styles):

- **Drop Shadow** creates the impression that your object is floating above the page.

- **Contact Shadow** makes it look like your object is standing on the page.

- **Curved Shadow** creates the impression that the object's edges are curled. You can control the curve of the shadow using the Inward/Outward slider. For a dramatic effect, nudge the slider in the Outward direction; for something more subtle, push the slider in the Inward direction.

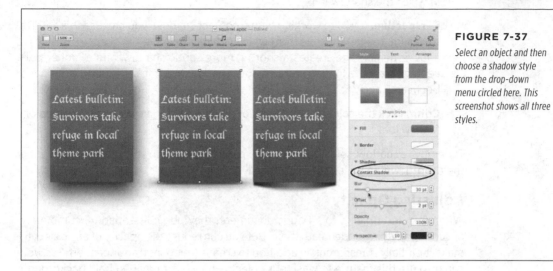

FIGURE 7-37

Select an object and then choose a shadow style from the drop-down menu circled here. This screenshot shows all three styles.

Once you choose your shadow style, the Style tab's Shadow section offers several settings you can use to customize your shadow (the exact settings you see depend on the style you choose):

- **Blur.** Adjust the softness of the shadow with this setting. (For curved shadows, you see the Inward/Outward slider instead of this slider.) The minimum setting creates a hard-edged shadow with a very slightly soft edge. Higher numbers increase the virtual cloud cover, blurring the shadow and eventually producing an indistinct haze beneath the object.

- **Offset.** Adjust this slider to set the distance between the shadow's outline and the object. An offset of zero results in the kind of shadow you'd cast at high noon on the equator: The virtual light source is directly overhead, casting an equal shadow on all sides and rendering any angle setting moot (unless you have Curved Shadow selected). Increasing or decreasing the offset shifts the shadow in the direction of the Angle setting (described below), making the image appear to float higher off the page.

TIP When the Offset setting for a Drop Shadow is zero, the shadow creates a glow effect. To give a picture a red glow, for example, choose red from the color well or Color Picker, set the Offset setting to zero, and boost the Blur value to increase the size of the glow.

- **Opacity.** Turning this setting up makes the shadow darker and bolder, and turning it down makes it more transparent. This opacity setting affects only the shadow, not the object.

- **Angle.** This setting, which appears for drop shadows and curved shadows, controls the direction of the virtual light source, which in turn controls the direction in which the shadow falls.

- **Perspective.** If you're working with a contact shadow, you can use this setting to change the perspective from which you're looking at the shadow. Basically, a lower percentage creates a shorter, more subtle shadow, and a higher percentage creates a longer, more obvious shadow. You can select any percentage between 5 and 35.

- **Color.** Click the color well or the color wheel icon to give your shadow a colorful new look.

To remove a shadow, select the object, expand the Style tab's Shadow section, open the drop-down menu, and then choose None.

Adjusting Opacity

When you add objects to a Pages document, they begin life opaque, completely obscuring anything underneath them. But you can reduce the opacity of any object to make it partially transparent. In addition to creating elegant translucent effects, you can also use this feature to wash out objects—handy for creating pale background images or de-emphasizing an object to direct the reader's attention to another, bolder page element.

To adjust opacity, select an object and then head to the Format panel's Style tab and adjust the Opacity setting as shown in Figure 7-38.

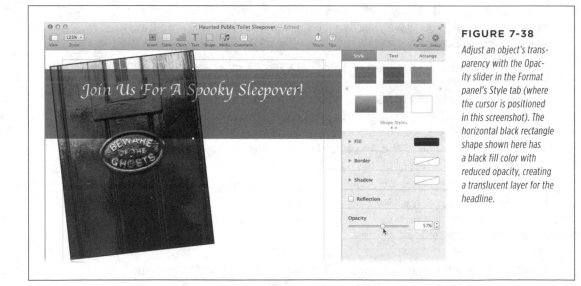

FIGURE 7-38

Adjust an object's transparency with the Opacity slider in the Format panel's Style tab (where the cursor is positioned in this screenshot). The horizontal black rectangle shape shown here has a black fill color with reduced opacity, creating a translucent layer for the headline.

NOTE   Pages includes three opacity controls: The Opacity slider in the Format panel's Style tab affects entire objects; the Color Picker's Opacity slider adjusts opacity of an object's fill, border line, or text; and the Opacity slider in the Shadow section of the Format panel's Style tab is strictly for shadows.

■ Copying Objects and Graphic Styles

When you design longer documents, you'll often find yourself including similar objects over and over again, like the pull quotes and sidebars in the Crazyland Won-derpark Experiences catalog. For consistency, it's important for these elements to have the same color, shadow, border, text alignment, and so on. But who wants to repeat all those formatting steps every time you add a new pull quote? Thankfully, Pages doesn't expect you to.

When you want to create a new object, the easiest way to duplicate the look of another object you've added and styled is to clone the original and then edit the copy as necessary. For example, you could copy a sidebar's text box and then add some new text. Pages provides three ways to copy an object:

- **Copy and paste.** Select the object you want to copy and then choose Edit→Copy or press ⌘-C. Next, choose Edit→Paste or press ⌘-V, and then drag the object to its new location.

- **Option-drag.** Hold down the Option key and drag the original object, and Pages creates a copy.

- **Duplicate.** Select the object you want to copy and then choose Edit→Duplicate Selection or press ⌘-D. Pages clones the object and adds the copy on top of the original, slightly offset, so you can drag it wherever you want.

Making a brand-new copy of an object is all well and good when you want to add a *new* object to your document. But what about when the object already exists and you just want to restyle it to match another object? Pages lets you copy one object's *graphic style*—all its object-level settings—to another object, quickly and effectively repainting the second object with the look of the first.

Select the object whose style you want to copy and choose Format→Copy Style or press Option-⌘-C. Then select the object that's going to receive the style and choose Format→Paste Style or press Option-⌘-V. Voilà—the second object inherits all the settings of the original: its border, fill, shadow, reflection, text wrap, and any other object-level settings. Unlike the regular Paste command, Paste Style doesn't touch the object's content, just its style and formatting.

NOTE   In addition to object-level settings, using Paste Style on text boxes and shapes brings along all the font and text formatting of the original, too.

And with that last nifty trick, you've now got all the know-how you need to juggle and finesse your document's words and pictures. But what about numbers? Pages gives you a sleek collection of tools to add tables, mini-spreadsheets, and charts to your document. These are objects, too, but they're different enough to merit a chapter of their very own. Pull up a chair and turn to the next chapter to learn all about tables.

Building Tables and Charts

Numbers often spell out an idea even better than words can. When you're writing an annual report, for example, or charting the monthly ebb of visitors to your amusement park, the actual figures add up to much more than a lengthy written description. Pages might be a *word* processor, but it does a fine job at slinging numbers, too, giving you the tools to present data and other complex information clearly and efficiently.

Numbers? As you know, this also happens to be the name of a certain spreadsheet program included in iWork. In fact, the way that Pages uses tables and charts to manage your data reveals a strong family resemblance to its math-minded cousin. As you'll learn when you dig into Numbers later in this book, tables are central to Numbers documents, where every table acts as its own standalone spreadsheet. In Pages (and Keynote, too), tables are lightweight versions of the full-featured tables in Numbers; the same goes for charts.

Like the images, shapes, and text boxes explored in Chapter 7, tables and charts are *objects*, so you can move, resize, and manipulate them like you can any other object. You'll learn all the advanced details of building tables and charts in the Numbers section of this book, but this chapter gets you started on the fundamentals as it takes you through Pages' table and chart features.

■ Creating Tables

Tables are efficient containers for displaying large amounts of data or creating forms. A table is a grid of information constructed from rows and columns that slice and dice the table into blocks called *cells*. Table cells have some special math know-how, as you'll see on page 228, but you can use them to organize just about any kind of info. Each cell can contain a chunk of text or numbers, and Pages can dress up tables or individual cells with borders and color, or with image fills for backgrounds. You can create very simple, plain-text tables or more elaborate ones, complete with color and background pictures, that look nothing like a table at first glance. Figure 8-1 shows a few examples.

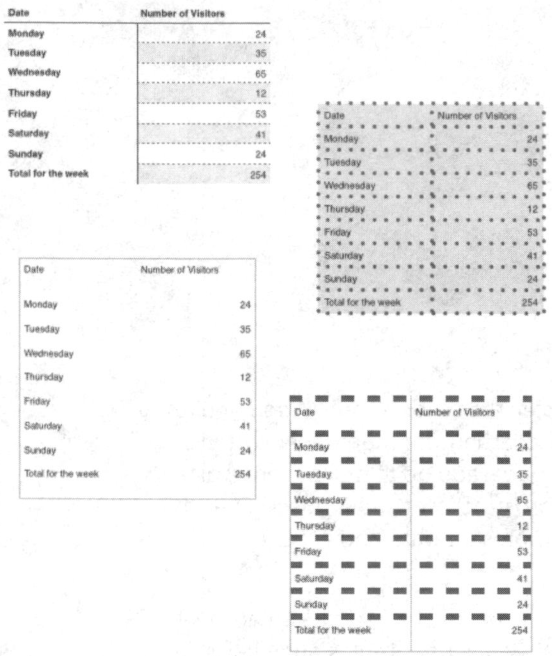

FIGURE 8-1

You can make tables that are just columns of facts and figures, but with Pages' table-making abilities—combined with your imagination—it's easy to create forms, catalogs, photo layouts, and oodles more. The tables pictured here are just some examples of what you can create.

You can get a closer look at them (plus some other example tables) by downloading the sample document example_tables.pages *from this book's Missing CD page at* www.missingmanuals.com/cds.

Tables can either be floating or inline objects, with one important distinction: Floating tables are limited to *one* page, while inline tables can span *several* pages. (Pop back to page 143 for a recap of the difference between floating and inline objects.)

How many cells can you put in a table? Though you'd be hard-pressed to think up a need for such a table, a table can be as small as one cell (that's a measly one column wide by one row high!). At the other extreme, a floating table can fill an entire page with as many rows as you can squeeze in, while an inline table can stretch across many pages and columns, with a virtually unlimited number of rows—for a catalog product list, for example. Massive tables, however, can slow down Pages as it manages thousands of cells—especially when those cells contain arithmetic calculations, something you'll learn about on page 228. If you need a table that's more than a few pages long, consider breaking it up into two or more tables, or use Numbers instead.

Inserting Inline Tables

When you add a table to a word-processing document, it always starts out as an inline object. To add an inline table to a word-processing document, just click the Table button in the toolbar and choose from one of the formats in the drop-down menu, or choose Insert→Table and then select one of the options in the Table submenu:

- **Headers.** Adds a table with a header row and a header column (see page 215 for more about headers).

- **Basic.** Adds a table with a header row but no header column.

- **Plain.** Adds a table with no headers.

- **Sums.** Adds a table with a header row, header column, and footer row (perfect for adding formulas to).

> **TIP** Remember that Pages offers each object in a range of colors. So when you add a table using the Table button in the toolbar, you can click the left- and right-arrow buttons in the drop-down menu to browse through the different colors. Or, after you've added a table to your document, you can also give the table object an instant makeover by selecting it, opening the Format panel's Table tab, and then selecting one of the table styles.

Pages starts you off with a table that occupies the entire width of a text column, as shown in Figure 8-2. Select your table by clicking it once (OK, so this actually just selects a single cell, but don't worry about this for now). When you select the table, the Table tab appears in the Format panel. This tab lets you tailor the number of rows and columns or adjust the column width and row height to suit your needs. The Table tab offers a bunch of other options, too, which you'll explore over the next few pages.

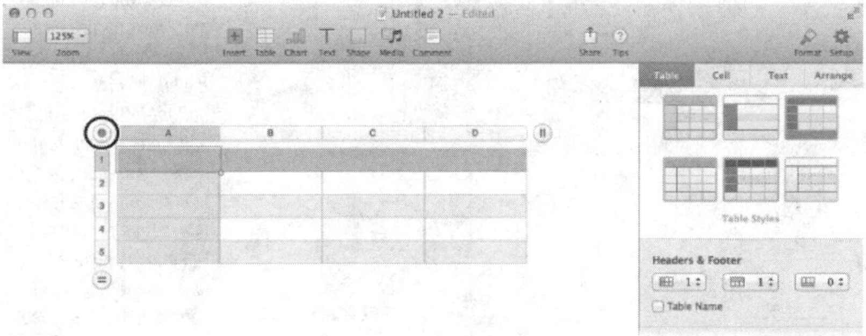

FIGURE 8-2

When you add a new table, it starts out blank. Depending on the type of table you chose, it may contain shaded header rows and header columns, intended for labeling your cells. For more about header rows and columns, see page 215.

Like other inline objects, inline tables of one page or less in height have only three active selection handles: at the bottom edge, right edge, and bottom-right corner (they're shown in Figure 8-3). To display a table's selection handles, click the circle icon in the table's upper-left corner (this icon is circled in Figure 8-2). Drag these handles to resize the table as you would any other object.

NOTE If an inline table extends onto another page or another column, all of its selection handles disappear. So if you want to resize an inline table that spans several pages or columns, you need to temporarily turn it back into a floating object (page 147) in order to recover its selection handles.

Unless and until you specifically change the width of an inline table or any of its columns, the table always spans the width of the surrounding text. If you change the text margins, for example, the table automatically becomes narrower or wider to fit. But this behavior changes when you step in and manually change the width of the table's cells. Narrowing the text margins still narrows the table, but when you subsequently make the text margins *wider*, the table width increases until the table reaches your specified width, at which point the table stops expanding.

Inserting Floating Tables

When you add a table to a page-layout document, the table starts out as a floating object. Adding a floating table to a *word-processing* document involves a few extra steps. Start by adding a standard, inline table by clicking the Table button in the toolbar or by choosing Insert→Table. Then select any part of the table, open the Format panel's Arrange tab, and then click the "Stay on Page" button.

You can then tailor the number and size of rows and columns to your needs, by opening the Format panel's Table tab, as shown in Figure 8-3. To resize your table, click the circle icon in its upper-left corner, and then drag any of the selection handles that appears.

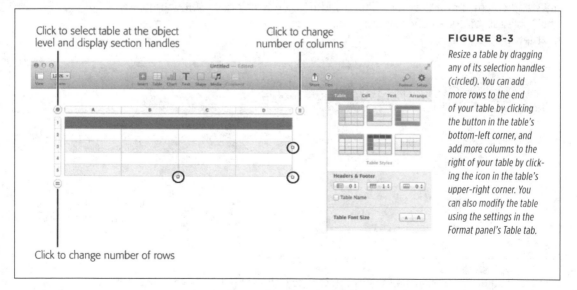

Click to select table at the object level and display section handles

Click to change number of columns

Click to change number of rows

FIGURE 8-3

Resize a table by dragging any of its selection handles (circled). You can add more rows to the end of your table by clicking the button in the table's bottom-left corner, and add more columns to the right of your table by clicking the icon in the table's upper-right corner. You can also modify the table using the settings in the Format panel's Table tab.

Dragging a floating table's selection handles is the easiest way to resize it, but you can also change the size of a table by resizing its columns and rows. For more on this, see page 222.

> **NOTE** When you make a floating table taller than the page it's on, the rest of the table juts out beyond the bottom or top page margins—in digital limbo. You can get at these "invisible" rows or columns by dragging the table up or down the page, reducing the height of its rows, or deleting some rows. But if you want a table that spans multiple pages, it's best to use an inline table instead.

Selecting Tables, Cells, and Text

When you work with tables, you can select and edit them at three different levels:

- **The object level.** To select a table at the object level, click the circle icon in its upper-left corner. Pages selects the entire table and displays the three selection handles. Font, style, and formatting changes you make when the table is selected at this level apply to all of its cells and the text within them—and of course you can apply all the usual object formatting to the table, changing its size, position, and so on.

- **The cell level.** To select a cell, simply click it once (you don't have to select the table at the object level first). Pages makes it clear that the cell is selected by adding a blue border around the cell's edges. When you have a cell selected, all changes you make apply only to the selected cell and the text within it, and you can't move the table or edit its object-level settings. You can set the background and borders of individual cells, for example. Be careful here, though: When you select a cell, Pages implicitly selects all the text within that cell (but doesn't visually indicate this in any way)—so if you start typing at this point, you'll replace *all* text in that cell. If that's not what you want to do, you should instead switch to editing the table at…

- **The text level.** This is the level where you actually edit the text within an individual cell. Double-click a cell or, if you've already selected a cell, click it once more to place your cursor inside that cell. You're now ready to make changes at a specific point in the cell's text.

> **TIP** As described above, keep on clicking a table to continue drilling further down into its content from the table level, to the cell level, to the text level. To reverse direction, press ⌘-Return; pressing ⌘-Return while editing text inside a cell selects the entire cell, and pressing it again selects the entire table.

When you have a table selected at the cell level, you can move through the cells from left to right by pressing Tab, which selects the next cell. When you reach the last cell in a row, pressing Tab bumps you down to the first cell in the next row. If you're already at the last row of the table, Pages adds a new row and takes you down to its first cell. This is an easy way to enlarge your table organically, row by row, as you add new content.

Whether you have a cell selected at the cell or text level, you can throw the cell-selecting machinery into reverse by pressing Shift-Tab, which moves through your cells from right to left. When you're in the very first cell in the table, click Shift-Tab to teleport down to the very last cell.

You can also use the arrow keys to skip from cell to cell. When you have a cell selected at the cell level, use any of the arrow keys to move to the next cell in that direction. When you're editing a cell at the text level, the arrow keys move you around the text as usual. But when you reach either the beginning or end of the text, the arrow key skips over to the next cell, selecting the whole thing at the cell level. As when you use the Tab or Shift-Tab keys, the right and left arrow keys bump you to the next or previous row when you hit the end of the line; the up and down arrow keys move you to the previous or next column when you reach the start or end of a column.

You can select several cells at once in order to, for example, change their background color or delete all their content. Pages gives you a few ways to select groups of cells:

- Shift-click cells or drag the mouse across them to select a block of neighboring cells.

- You can ⌘-click individual cells anywhere in the table—the cells don't have to be adjacent to one another. You also use ⌘-click to deselect cells that you've already selected.

- To select an entire row or column, click the corresponding *reference tab*, as shown in Figure 8-4.

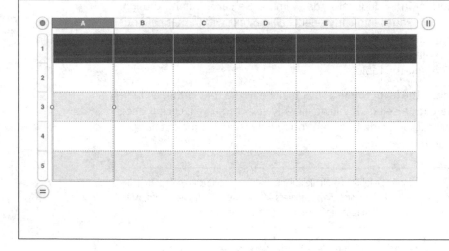

FIGURE 8-4

To select a whole column or row, click the column or row's reference tab. The row reference tabs are labeled 1, 2, 3, and so on. The column reference tabs are labeled A, B, C, D... In this screenshot, the reference tab for column A is selected. As with cells, you can select several columns or rows by Shift-clicking or ⌘-clicking their reference tabs.

Typing into Table Cells

A table is essentially a cluster of text boxes, so adding and editing text in a table cell works the same as in a text box. When you first select a table at the cell level or tab into a new cell, Pages selects all the text in the selected cell. Start typing to replace *all* the text in that cell, or click again to select the cell at the text level and place the insertion point where you want to add text to the cell. Then type away.

You edit text within a cell just as you would anywhere else in Pages: Click once to place the insertion point in a particular spot, double-click to select a word, triple-click to select a paragraph. Choose Edit→Copy to copy some selected text from a cell, and choose Edit→Paste and paste that text at the insertion point in the same cell, a different cell, or outside the table. Format the text using any of the options available in the Format panel or the Fonts window (for the full overview, review Chapter 2 starting on page 39).

Aligning text inside table cells works the same as aligning text inside a text box. However, in addition to the usual horizontal alignment styles—left-aligned, centered, right-aligned, or justified—table cells also have an *automatic alignment* option. This setting changes the alignment based on the type of content within the cell: Pages left-aligns text and right-aligns numbers. To change this alignment, select either the entire table or one or more individual cells, and then head to the Format panel's Text tab, click the Style button, and then choose any of the alignment options shown in Figure 8-5. The Text tab's Alignment section also includes vertical controls that let you align text to the top, bottom, or middle of the cell.

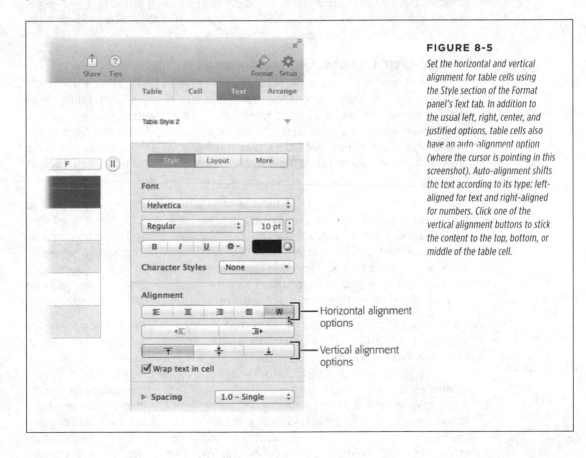

FIGURE 8-5

Set the horizontal and vertical alignment for table cells using the Style section of the Format panel's Text tab. In addition to the usual left, right, center, and justified options, table cells also have an auto-alignment option (where the cursor is pointing in this screenshot). Auto-alignment shifts the text according to its type: left-aligned for text and right-aligned for numbers. Click one of the vertical alignment buttons to stick the content to the top, bottom, or middle of the table cell.

Vertical alignment applies to *all* the text in the selected cell. But if a cell contains more than one paragraph of text, you can apply horizontal alignment on a paragraph-by-paragraph basis.

You can control the distance between the text within a cell and the cell's edges by opening the Format panel's Text tab and clicking the Layout button, which gives you access to the Text Inset setting. Tighten the gap between the text and the cell's edges by entering a lower number in the Text Inset field. (Pages applies the text inset around all four sides of the cell.)

The Text Inset setting determines the outer boundaries of the text area for a cell, but you can also adjust a cell's text margins using Pages' ruler. If the ruler isn't already open, choose View→Show Ruler, press ⌘-R, or click the View button in the toolbar and select Show Ruler. You can then adjust the right and left margins inward from the text inset—as well as create first-line indents and tabs for the selected cell in exactly the same way as regular text (see page 52 for more on tabs and first-line indents). You can use the ruler on only one cell at a time and only when you've selected that cell at the text level (you know you're editing at the text level when the insertion point is visible or the cell's text is highlighted). See page 55 for more about changing insets and tabs with the ruler.

■ AUTOMATICALLY RESIZING TABLE ROWS

As you add new text to a cell, Pages keeps up with you by expanding the height of the cell's row so that it has enough room to display all of your text. When Pages makes room in the row as you add more content, the rows below it get nudged down, making the entire table taller. While floating tables can spread out onto more than one page or column, these extra rows and columns hang off the page and are impossible to edit. Inline tables, on the other hand, simply continue onto the next page or column.

If you prefer to have a row stay a fixed height no matter how much content you pour into it, open the Format panel's Table tab, click the Row & Column Size heading to expand that section (you may have to scroll down to see it), and then turn off the "Resize rows to fit cell contents" checkbox. With this setting turned off, Pages hides any overflow text, and you have to trim the text or adjust its font size to bring the extra text back into view. You might turn this setting off if you're working with tables that don't need to display much text, in order to maintain uniform row height.

When you add more text than can fit on one line of a cell, Pages normally wraps your text to a new line, just like it would in any text column. If you don't want Pages to do this, open the Format panel's Text tab, click the Style button, and then turn off the "Wrap text in cell" checkbox to limit cell text to one line. If the cell next door is empty, the extra content spills over into that cell (the contents actually remain in the original cell, and that's where you'll need to edit the text, but the text is no longer penned in by its cell boundaries). If the neighboring cell has its own content, then the text doesn't spill over and is clipped to the cell's width. The extra data is still there; it's just hidden. To show the whole thing, turn on the "Wrap text in cell" checkbox again. You can apply this setting on a cell-by-cell basis, wrapping the text in some cells in your table and not wrapping the text in others.

■ MOVING CELL CONTENT

You can move the contents of a cell, along with all its formatting, to another cell by dragging or by cutting and pasting. The trick is to first make sure that the cell is selected at the *cell* level, not at the text level: If the insertion point is visible in the cell, press ⌘-Return so that the blue border appears around the cell and the insertion point disappears. Then simply drag the cell's contents to another cell. As you drag, a blue border appears around the cell in which Pages intends to drop your selection. When you release the mouse, the contents of the first cell appear in the second one, replacing any content that used to exist there, and Pages empties out the first cell. You can get the same result with Cut and Paste: Select the cell you want to move, press Edit→Cut to remove its contents, select the target cell, and then press Edit→Paste.

If you want to *copy* a cell's content instead of moving it, follow the same drag-and-drop maneuver, but hold down the Option key while you drag. The pointer sprouts a green circle with a + sign on it, and Pages copies the contents of the first cell into the second, replacing the contents of the second cell (if any). Copying and pasting does the same thing: Choose Edit→Copy to copy the selected cell to the Clipboard (page 36), select the destination cell, and then choose Edit→Paste.

> **TIP** If you want to strip a cell of all of its formatting as well as its content—to remove its background color, for example—select the cell, and then choose Edit→Clear All or Control-click the cell and choose Clear All. Choosing Edit→Cut will give you the same effect. Both commands are more effective than pressing Delete, which removes text but not formatting.

You can also use these moving and copying techniques to create new tables. When you drag cells from a table and into any other part of the page, Pages moves those cell(s) from the original table and creates a new table out of them. If you want to copy the data into a new table instead, then hold down the Option key while you drag, and the original content remains untouched. This technique works for both inline and floating tables, although the new table Pages creates is always a floating table.

Adding and Deleting Rows and Columns

If your table has exactly the right number of rows and columns when you insert it, congratulations! You can skip ahead to the next section. Usually, though, you'll find it necessary to adjust the number of rows and columns as you work on a table.

You can add more rows and columns to your table at any time. To add a new row above or below the selected cell, choose Format→Table→Add Row Above or Add Row Below. Or, to add a new column before or after the selected cell, choose Format→Table→Add Column Before or →Add Column After. (You'll also find these commands in the shortcut menu: Control-click anywhere in the table and choose the command you want.) When you use one of these commands, Pages duplicates the backgrounds and other formatting of the selected cell's row or column, but not the text within those cells.

> **TIP** Because adding rows and columns is so common when you're working on a table, get to know the Option-arrow keyboard combinations for these commands: Option–up arrow adds a row above the selected cell, and Option–down arrow adds a row below; Option–left arrow adds a column to the left of the selected cell, and Option–right arrow adds a column to the right.

You can also add more rows to the bottom of the table or more columns to the right side by using the icons in the table's lower-left and upper-right corners, respectively (these icons are labeled back in Figure 8-3). Click either of these buttons to open a little menu where you can click the up and down arrows to add or remove rows or columns. Pages tacks on the new cells, duplicating the bottom row's or right column's background fill and other formatting. If you *lower* the numbers in these little menus, Pages trims cells from the bottom or the right side of the table, unless those cells contain data—in that case, Pages won't let you reduce the number any further.

Finally, you can get specific about where your new column or row should appear. To add a new column, decide where you want to insert it, and then put your cursor over the reference tab of the column directly to the right or left of where the new column should go. For example, if you want to insert a new column between columns B and C, place your cursor over either column B's or C's reference tab. When you do that, a tiny triangle appears on the right side of the tab. Click this triangle, and then choose either Add Column After or Add Column Before. Figure 8-6 shows how to add rows using this technique.

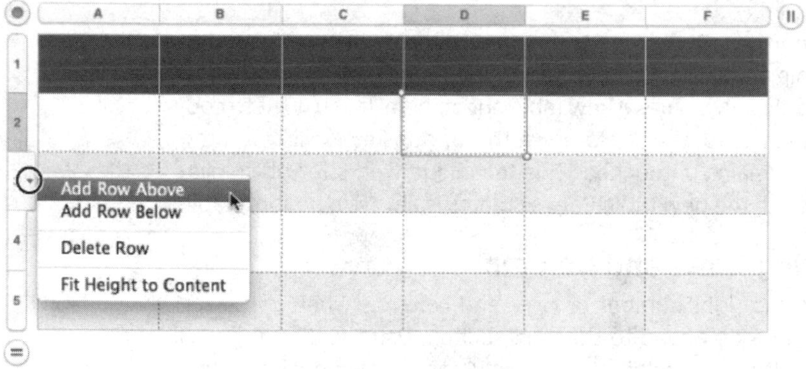

FIGURE 8-6

You can add columns and rows using the table's reference tabs. To add a new row, put your cursor over the reference tab that's above or below where you want to insert the row. When the triangle button appears on the tab (circled), click it, and then select Add Row Below or Add Row Above.

To delete a row or a column, select a cell within it, and then choose Format→Table→ Delete Row or →Delete Column. You can delete multiple rows or columns by selecting two or more cells in neighboring rows or columns and then choosing the same commands, which now read "Delete Rows" and "Delete Columns." These commands are also available via shortcut menu: Select your cell(s), and then Control-click to open the shortcut menu. You can also put your pointer over the column's or row's reference tab; when the tiny triangle appears on the tab, click it, and then choose Delete Row or Delete Column.

■ LABELING TABLES WITH HEADER ROWS, HEADER COLUMNS, AND FOOTER ROWS

Tables typically sport labels on their rows or columns to advertise their contents, and Pages provides *header rows* and *header columns* for just that purpose—in fact, all newborn tables (except the ones in the bottom-left corner of the Tables drop-down menu) start out with a header row. A header row is the very first row in a table, and a header column is the leftmost column. You can format header rows and columns however you like, but Pages starts off by shading them differently than the rest of the table to make them stand out. (Pages calls non-header rows and columns *body rows* and *body columns*.)

Header rows and columns act just like body rows and columns, but with a few special perks. For one thing, header rows keep coming back. Just like page headers appear on every page of a document, a table header row appears at the top of each page or text column when an inline table continues across a break, as shown in Figure 8-7. This helps your reader stay oriented after flipping the page or dragging her eyes up to a new column—the table's columns are always neatly labeled. You can edit the text inside a repeated header row, but doing so also updates every *other* instance of the row in other pages or columns.

As you'll see when you learn about using formulas on page 228, header rows and columns are also clever with math, providing shortcuts to apply automatic calculations to their row or column. This is particularly handy with *footer rows*, which appear as the very last row in the table; they're frequently used to provide tallies for each of the table's columns. Header rows and columns also provide coordinates for your rows and columns that you can use to identify individual cells when you refer to them in formulas. You'll learn more about this in the section "Making Mini-Spreadsheets with Formulas" starting on page 228.

To add header rows, header columns, or footer rows, open the Format panel's Table tab and use the drop-down menus in the Headers & Footers section, as shown in Figure 8-8. Choose the number of rows or columns to display from the three drop-down menus. To remove a table header or footer, reduce the number in the corresponding drop-down menu—set it to *0* to remove all rows or columns of that type.

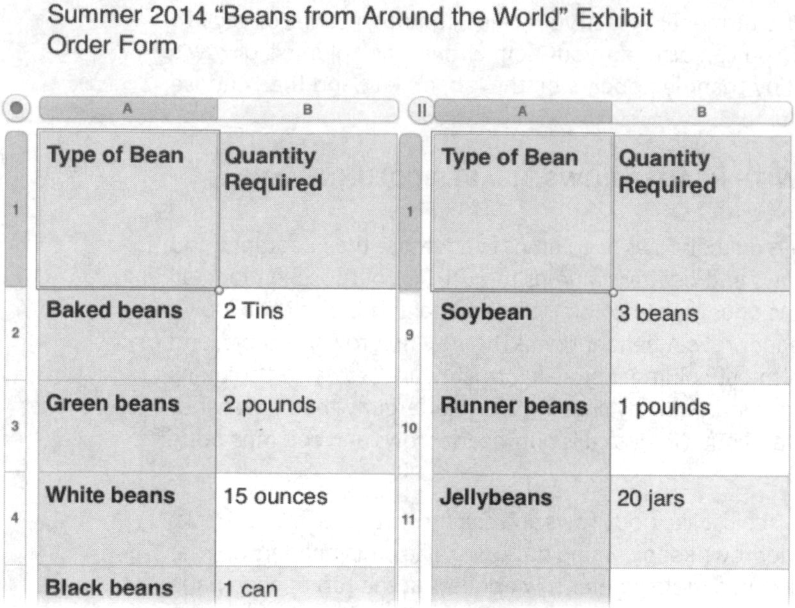

Summer 2014 "Beans from Around the World" Exhibit
Order Form

FIGURE 8-7

When an inline table crosses onto a new page or column, the header row makes the leap, too, automatically relabeling the table in its new context. Here, a table of beans spans two columns, repeating its header at the top of each one.

	A	B			A	B
1	Type of Bean	Quantity Required		1	Type of Bean	Quantity Required
2	Baked beans	2 Tins		9	Soybean	3 beans
3	Green beans	2 pounds		10	Runner beans	1 pounds
4	White beans	15 ounces		11	Jellybeans	20 jars
	Black beans	1 can				

Although Pages creates row and column headers with a background fill to differentiate them from the rest of the table, you can remove that fill or replace it with another that better suits your table design. For more on changing the background color of cells, see page 220.

Setting the Data Type with Cell Format

Pages recognizes that the data in your table cells has more meaning than just a collection of typed letters and numbers—there are *kinds* of data. A monetary value is different from a plain number, and a date is different from regular text. To help format, sort, and organize the various kinds of data in a table, you can tell Pages exactly what type of data is in each cell and how you'd like Pages to display it. For example, you can format cells with monetary values to include a currency symbol ($, ¥, £, and so on), and you can tell Pages to display all dates in a consistent manner no matter how you enter them (1/6/14, Jan 6, 2014, and so on).

You do all this by selecting the Format panel's Cell tab and then opening the Data Format drop-down menu and choosing the appropriate data type. (Figure 8-9 shows the settings that appear when you choose Currency.) Select the cell(s) you want to format, and then choose one of these options from the Data Format menu:

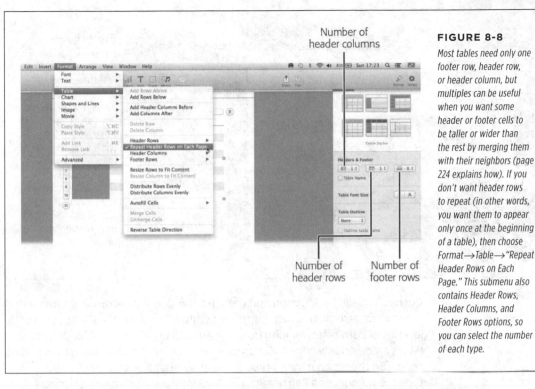

Number of
header columns

FIGURE 8-8

*Most tables need only one
footer row, header row,
or header column, but
multiples can be useful
when you want some
header or footer cells to
be taller or wider than
the rest by merging them
with their neighbors (page
224 explains how). If you
don't want header rows
to repeat (in other words,
you want them to appear
only once at the beginning
of a table), then choose
Format→Table→"Repeat
Header Rows on Each
Page." This submenu also
contains Header Rows,
Header Columns, and
Footer Rows options, so
you can select the number
of each type.*

Number of
header rows

Number of
footer rows

- **Automatic.** This free-form setting tells Pages to try to figure out what kind of data you're entering. The program recognizes currency, numbers, text, dates, and percentages as you type them. When you select one or more cells with Automatic formatting that all contain the same type of data, the Cell tab cleverly shows preferences for displaying that data type—if all the cells happen to be dates, for example, then picking Automatic shows you options for choosing the display format for date and time.

- **Number.** Choose this setting to deal with digits, and then select from the number-specific options that appear to fine-tune how the digits are displayed. Select the number of decimal points to include onscreen, and Pages manages the rounding for you. When you want a cell to display a value rounded to the nearest integer, for example, set the Decimals field to zero; that way, if the cell's value is 1.264, Pages displays 1. But this is only what's *displayed*. Behind the scenes, Pages remembers the full value, so if you later change the number of decimal points, Pages will display 1.3 for one decimal place, 1.26 for two decimal places, and so on. The Number settings also let you choose the format to use for negative numbers and whether to include a thousands separator (1,000 vs. 1000).

- **Currency.** Select this option and then use the Currency drop-down menu that appears to determine which currency symbol Pages displays. Choose from a long list of currencies, ranging from the Australian dollar to the Polish zloty, and Pages automatically adds the appropriate symbol to the numbers in the selected cell(s). So there's no need to type a $ sign before all of your dollar values—just type the number and Pages adds the $ for you when you move to another cell. Turn on the Accounting Style checkbox to display the currency symbol on the left side of the cell, and the number on the right.

- **Percentage.** This setting is also similar to Number and offers the exact same options. The difference is that, with this setting selected, Pages displays decimal numbers as percentages. Type *0.5* into a cell with this format, for example, and Pages displays it as 50%; type *10* and Pages displays it as 1000%; and so on.

- **Fraction.** Choose this option to display decimal numbers as their fractional equivalents—or at least their rough equivalents. Enter 0.25 into a fraction cell, for example, and Pages turns it into 1/4. When you choose Fraction, the Cell tab offers up the Accuracy drop-down menu, which lets you choose how detailed you'd like the fraction to be, from one digit (7/8) to two digits (23/24) to three digits (445/553). You can also choose to have Pages display fractions with a fixed denominator (halves, quarters, eights, sixteenths, and so on), and the program rounds your numbers to the nearest fraction. As with rounding in Number and Percentage cells, this is just for display purposes—Pages always remembers the "real" value for you.

- **Numeral System.** Choose this option to switch your cell to a whole different number system to count in base 2 (binary), base 16 (hexadecimal), or some other numeral system. If that sentence made no sense to you, don't worry—that almost certainly means that you don't need this particular cell format, which is generally reserved for hard-core math folks. Pick the base value of the system you want to use in the Base field, and then choose the number of digits to display in the Places field. If you select Base 2, 8, or 16, you can also tell Pages how to display negative values.

- **Scientific.** This option displays numbers in *scientific notation*, a numbering scheme that's useful for very, very minuscule numbers or super-massive numbers. This setting lets you choose how many decimal places you want to display, and Pages rounds as necessary.

- **Text.** Just as its name suggests, this setting indicates that the cell contains regular text—numbers get no special treatment in fields with this formatting.

- **Date & Time.** This setting lets you display a date and time in a variety of different formats, no matter how you enter the date. You can enter the date as 12/6/14, for example, and depending on your settings, have Pages display it as "Saturday, December 6, 2014." Make your selections from the Date and Time drop-down menu.

- **Duration.** This format displays an amount of time (weeks, hours, seconds, and so on). Duration fields can display a variety of time units, from hours and minutes to milliseconds and weeks. Click the Custom Units button, select all the time units you want to display, and then use the Style drop-down menu to tell Pages how to display these units (see Figure 8-10).

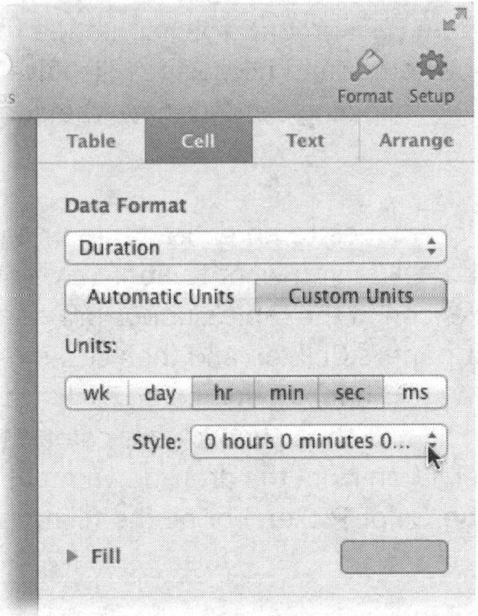

FIGURE 8-10

When you choose the Duration format, Pages lets you pick the units to display as well as their format. The Custom Units button lets you select all the units you want to use. Here, Pages is set to display hours, minutes, and seconds, but you can choose as many units as you want. To dictate how Pages displays this info, open the Style drop-down menu and choose a format; for example, "1 week" can be displayed as 1, 1w, or 1 week.

Sorting Table Rows

Tables are designed to organize and communicate data—and chances are, you want that data to appear in a certain order. If you have a table listing all the members of the Crazyland Wonderpark Fan Club, for example, you might want to sort the list alphabetically by name, or chronologically by the date members joined, or in descending order by the number of times they've asked to be removed from your mailing list.

You can do just that by choosing a column to use to reorder the table's rows. In the column you want to order, put your cursor over that column's reference tab, click the little triangle when it appears, and then choose one of these options:

- **Sort Ascending** reorders all the rows alphabetically by name, from A to Z.

- **Sort Descending** flips the order so the rows are sorted from Z to A.

Pages sorts your rows differently depending on the type of data in the sort column. As you might expect, text is sorted alphabetically, numbers are sorted numerically, and dates are sorted chronologically. When cells contain a mix of text and numbers, numbers come first in ascending sort order, followed by letters (the reverse is true in descending order). Rows with empty cells in the sort column are basically ignored, dismissed to the bottom of the table to bring up the rear behind the sorted rows. And header cells aren't sorted at all.

> **TIP** To sort your data the way you want, you may have to give Pages a nudge in the right direction. Dates, for example, don't sort chronologically until you set the column's cells to use the Date & Time data format (hop back to page 216 for a reminder of how to do that).

Formatting Tables

When the time comes to move beyond basic text tables, Pages is ready with a host of table formatting options. You can add a background color or image fill to the entire table or to individual cells; control whether and how Pages displays cell borders; adjust opacity, rotation, and so on. The following sections have the details.

■ ADDING BACKGROUNDS

You can add background colors, gradients, or images to an entire table or to individual cells. To get started, either select the cell(s) you want to apply a color to or select the entire table by clicking the circle icon in the table's upper-left corner. Choose your fill color by opening the Format panel's Cell tab and then clicking the Fill heading to expand that section. To add a solid background color, click the Fill section's drop-down menu and select Color Fill, and then choose your color either by clicking the color well and making your selection from the drop-down menu, or by clicking the color wheel icon to launch the Color Picker. For all the filling possibilities, see page 192.

You can also apply background colors to individual cells by dragging and dropping: Choose View→Show Colors to display the Color Picker. Select a color, adjust its opacity, and then drag your custom color from the Color Picker's color well or color palette squares and drop it in the table. Pages outlines the table cell beneath your cursor in blue as you drag, indicating its readiness to receive the color as soon as you release the mouse button. (See page 192 for a complete tour of the Color Picker.)

When working with particularly lengthy, multicolumn tables, you can increase readability by adding an *alternating row color* so that odd rows are one color and even rows are another. This creates a subtle visual distinction between each entry and helps readers more easily scan individual rows. To achieve this effect, open the Format panel's Table tab and turn on the Alternating Row Color checkbox. You can then choose a color by clicking the color well or by launching the Color Picker.

NOTE If you want alternating backgrounds that use another fill style—a gradient fill, for example—you have to do it manually. Turn on the Alternating Row Color setting, and style the in-between rows by clicking their reference tabs and then making your style changes in the Cell tab's Fill section.

■ FORMATTING CELL BORDERS

Most new Pages tables feature a one-point black border around every cell. That may be fine for a bare-bones, quick-and-dirty table, but a little time spent modifying your table's borders can pay off with a more readable and visually appealing table. You can change the color, opacity, and thickness of cell borders—or remove the border entirely for the whole table, individual cells, or even a single side of a cell.

To change the border that runs around your table's exterior, select the table at the table level so its selection handles are visible. Then open the Format panel's Table tab, click the Table Outline drop-down menu, and then choose a line style for your border (or choose None to remove borders entirely). Set the border width by typing a number into the accompanying text field. Change the color of your border by clicking the color well and choosing a color from the drop-down menu, or by launching the Color Picker.

To access additional options for styling a table's border, open the Format panel's Cell tab, and then click the Border heading to expand that section. The Border section's settings let you style some borders differently from others—adding a bold border to the four sides of the table, for example, while having a more subtle border between rows. These settings apply to whatever part of the table you select, so if you want to update the borders for an entire table, select the table at the object level; if you want to update only a range of cells, select that range; and so on.

In the Border section, you choose a line style for your border by opening the unlabeled drop-down menu, and change the thickness and color of your border using the section's other settings. Once you've found border settings you like, apply the border to your selection by clicking one of the tiny icons shown in Figure 8-11. If you need to update the border at any point, make your changes and then click the border icon once again to reapply the border effect.

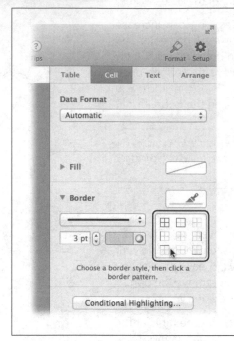

FIGURE 8-11

Once you're happy with the border settings you've chosen, apply them to your selection by clicking one of the thumbnails in the "Apply style to" section (indicated). Each thumbnail is actually a miniature grid that shows where Pages will apply your border if you click it: Around all sides of the selected cells, only around the edge of the outermost cells in your selection, and so on.

As mentioned above, if you're not keen on the border effect you just applied, you can't modify it. To completely remove a border effect, select the cell(s) in question (or the whole table), open the unlabeled drop-down menu below the Border heading, and choose No Border. To undo all of your customizations and revert to the table's original border, click the Border section's paintbrush icon and, in the drop-down menu shown in Figure 8-12, click the Reset button.

If you're in a hurry, you can create a basic border by selecting the table, cell, or range of cells whose borders you want to customize and then clicking the paintbrush icon in the upper-right of the Cell tab's Border section (see Figure 8-12). Choose a border style from the "Choose a border style" drop-down menu, and then click an icon to indicate which parts of your selection you want to apply the border to. You can also remove and reset your borders in this drop-down menu; however, you can't tweak the border's width or fine-tune its color like you can in the expanded Border section.

■ RESIZING CELLS, ROWS, AND COLUMNS

If the regularity of your table's cells makes you feel a little square, loosen things up by resizing individual cells or entire rows and columns. Simply select the table at the cell level by clicking any cell (it doesn't matter exactly which cell you click), and then put your cursor over the border of the reference tab of the column or row you want to resize. When your cursor turns into a double-headed arrow, drag to resize that entire column or row.

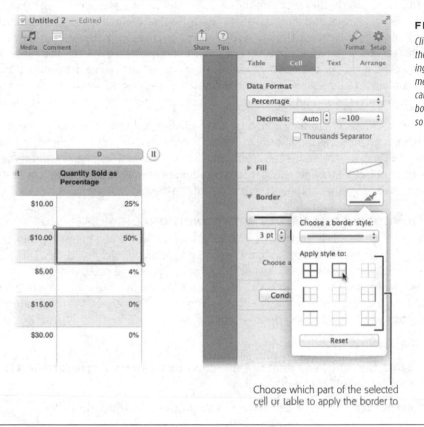

FIGURE 8-12
Click the paintbrush icon to the right of the Border heading to display the drop-down menu shown here, where you can choose a style for your border (lined, dotted, and so on).

Choose which part of the selected cell or table to apply the border to

You can also use the Format panel's Table tab to manually adjust the dimensions of rows and columns. Click the Row & Column Size heading to expand that section (you may have to scroll down to see it), select one or more cells, and then enter measurements in the Row and Column fields.

If you've made lots of sizing changes to your table's cells and the result looks a bit lopsided, Pages provides two commands that can tidy things up for you. Select a group of cells and then choose Format→Table→Distribute Rows Evenly, and Pages adjusts the heights of the selected cells so that they all match. Similarly, the Distribute Columns Evenly command tells Pages to adjust the selected cells to make their widths match. If you select the entire table and then use both of these commands, Pages makes every cell in the table the same size. (If the Table tab's "Resize rows to fit cell contents" checkbox is turned on, the Distribute Rows Evenly command makes all the rows the same height as the cell that contains the most text. If this checkbox is turned off, Pages keeps the dimensions of the entire table the same while equalizing the heights of the rows, so some text winds up being hidden.)

■ MERGING CELLS

Pages can merge two or more cells into one—as long as the cells you're bringing together form a rectangular shape (in other words, don't try to merge cells that are arranged diagonally, that aren't neighbors, or that form an L shape). Start by selecting two or more cells, and then choose Format→Table→Merge Cells or Control-click one of the cells and choose the same command from the shortcut menu. Either way, Pages tears down the wall and fuses the neighboring cells into one, and applies the background image or color of the upper, left, or upper-left cell of the group. If the cells contain text, Pages combines it in the new cell, separating text from cells in the same row with tabs and separating text from separate rows with paragraph breaks.

Restore merged cells to their gotta-be-me individual cells by selecting the cells in question, and then choosing Format→Table→Unmerge Cells, or Control-clicking the cells and choosing Unmerge Cells from the shortcut menu. This doesn't "unmerge" the content inside, though; any content that had been merged from two separate cells remains together in the left or top cell of the freshly split group.

■ MONITORING CELL VALUES WITH CONDITIONAL HIGHLIGHTING

You can light up a cell with colors of your choice when the cell meets certain criteria. This nifty visual alarm system is called *conditional highlighting.* In a table of Crazyland Wonderpark Fan Club members, for example, you could use this feature to highlight folks who want to be taken off your mailing list. In a table showing the number of visitors, for example, you could color-code days where the total number of visitors went into dizzying double-digit figures.

To add conditional formatting to a table:

1. **Select the cell(s) you want to apply conditional formatting to (or select the table at the object level).**

2. **In the Format panel's Cell tab, click Conditional Highlighting.**

   The Conditional Highlighting tab appears, showing any rules you've already applied to the selected cells.

3. **To add a new condition, click the "Add a Rule" button and then choose a condition from the drop-down menu.**

   The drop-down menu includes several categories: Numbers, Text, Dates, Durations, and Blank. Click a category heading to see the various types of conditions in that category, and then click the one that matches what you're after. (The options in the Blank category let you highlight cells based on whether they're empty.)

4. **Back in the Conditional Highlighting tab, provide any additional info Pages needs to create the condition.**

   For example, in Figure 8-13, the "greater than" condition is selected, and so Pages displays a text field where you can enter the number you're interested in (10, in this example). If you choose a condition from the Date category, you'll see drop-down menus that let you specify exact dates.

TIP Your conditional formatting rule can use the value of a table cell as the test value. To achieve this, click the blue circle at the right end of the value field; a cell-reference field pops up (it looks a little bit like the Formula Editor described on page 229). Add a cell reference by clicking a table cell in your document or by typing the reference directly into the cell-reference field, and then click the green checkmark to save it. You'll learn all about cell references on page 230.

5. **Click the Conditional Highlighting tab's final drop-down menu to choose the formatting you want Pages to apply when a cell meets the conditions.**

   As you can see in Figure 8-13, this menu includes various fill colors, as well as text formatting like italics and different font colors.

   If none of the menu's options are what you're looking for, click Custom Style at the very bottom of the menu (you may need to scroll to see it). When you do that, a host of familiar text-formatting settings appear in the Conditional Formatting tab so you can create your own style.

NOTE The "between" condition (which you can find in both the Numbers and Dates categories) requires you to specify two test values. The condition is met if either of the numbers or any value in between them appears in the cell(s).

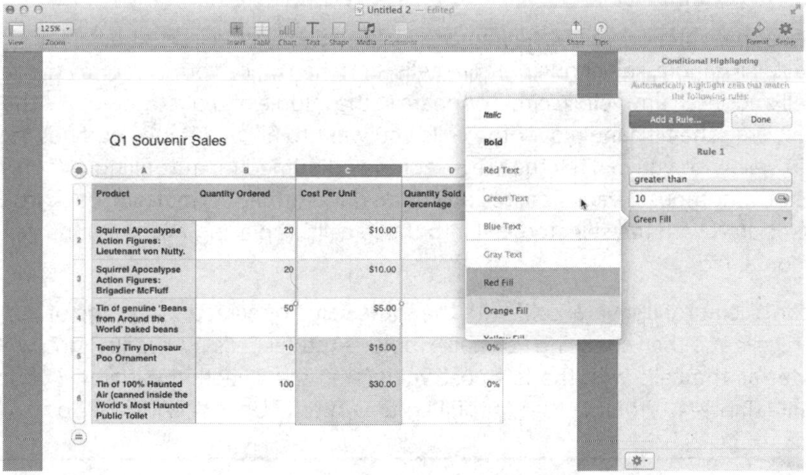

FIGURE 8-13

Conditional highlighting lets you highlight cells that meet certain criteria. Here, the Cost Per Unit column is set to highlight cells containing any number higher than 10.

Once you tell Pages what to look for, use the drop-down menu shown here to tell it how to format the cells that meet your criteria.

6. **To add another rule, click the "Add a Rule" button and repeat steps 3–5.**

You can add as many rules as you like, setting a bright green color for cells that match one condition, for example, and dull red for cells that match another. Just keep in mind that Pages applies only the first matching rule in a list. For example, if a cell matches rule 1 (green fill, say) *and* rule 2 (red text), the cell will display a green fill only, with no red text. So make sure your most important rule is at the top of your list.

To change the order of your rules, put your cursor over a rule until a lined icon appears in its upper-left corner; grab this icon and drag your rule into a new position within the menu. To delete a rule, put your cursor over it and then click the trash-can icon that appears. To delete *all* the rules for the selected cells, click the gear icon at the bottom of the Conditional Highlighting tab and select Clear All Rules.

After you've set conditional formatting rules for a cell, you can go back and edit the rules anytime by selecting the cell, opening the Format panel's Cell tab, and then clicking Show Highlighting Rules. To find all the cells in a table that have the same conditional formatting rules as a particular cell, select the cell, click the Show Highlighting Rules button, click the gear icon at the bottom of the Conditional Highlighting tab, and then click "Select Cells with Matching Rules."

Autofilling Table Cells

Autofilling lets you use the content in one or more cells to automatically add values to neighboring cells. This is particularly handy when you want to add cells that increment dates or numbers from cell to cell—like a counter.

Every cell has magical yellow *fill handles*, like the one circled in Figure 8-14, top. To display a fill handle, select one or more cells, and then place your cursor over one of the cell's edges; a tiny yellow circle appears in the middle of that edge—that's the fill handle. Drag the fill handle over the cells you want to fill, and Pages outlines those cells in yellow so you can tell they're selected and primed for autofilling. When you let go of your mouse, Pages pastes any data, data format, formula, or background fill associated with the selected cell into those cells, replacing any previous values they contained.

You can also autofill several cells with the same value by selecting a range of neighboring cells and then choosing Format→Table→Autofill Cells→Autofill Right, which replaces all the cells with the leftmost value(s) in the selection. Similarly, choose Format→Table→Autofill Cells→Autofill Left, →Autofill Up, or →Autofill Down.

NOTE When you copy a formula into a new cell—whether by moving, pasting, or autofilling—Pages updates the formula's cell references to reflect its new location. You'll learn all about formulas in just a moment (for more details, see "Moving Formulas" on page 233).

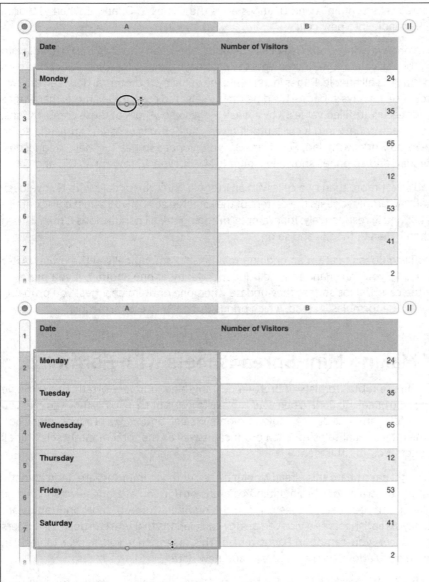

FIGURE 8-14

Drag the fill handle of your selected cell(s) (circled, top) to copy content or to apply a pattern of values to the neighboring cells (bottom).

You can drag the fill handle of two numeric cells to continue the count into neighboring cells; drag the fill handle of cells with an irregular interval (or text values) to repeat their values; drag the fill handle of a date/time value to increment the date by one day for every cell; or drag the fill handle of two date/time cells to increment the value by the interval between the two dates.

This alone is useful enough when you're setting up a table to copy cell formatting or initial cell values. But autofilling gets especially interesting when it fills values based on detected patterns, letting you increment or cycle through values as you drag the fill handle into adjacent cells. To take advantage of this feature, select two or more cells before dragging. For example, if two selected cells contain 1 and 2,

Pages adds the values 3 and 4 when you drag through the two adjacent cells. But, if the two selected cells contain 1 and 4, Pages adds the values 7 and 10 when you drag through the adjacent two cells (values are incremented by 3). Likewise, if two selected cells contain A and B, Pages adds the values C, D, and E when you drag the fill handle into new cells.

This works with dates, too: Select one date cell, and when you drag the fill handle into neighboring cells, Pages increments the date day by day. When you select two cells and drag the fill handle, Pages increments the value by the interval between the two dates. If seven days separate the dates in the selected cells, for example, then Pages bumps each autofilled value up by a week. Pages knows lots of these combinations: If you type *January* into a cell, autofill gives you February, March, April, and so on (the same works with Jan, Feb, Mar, …). Type *Monday* to get Tuesday, Wednesday, Thursday, and so on (as shown in Figure 8-14), or type *Q1* to get Q2, Q3, and Q4.

If you select more than two cells with an irregular interval (or cells with text values), autofilling simply repeats the pattern of the selected cells: If you select cells containing 1, 2, and 5, respectively, for example, dragging the fill handle adds 1, then 2, then 5, then 1, then 2, then 5, and so on.

Autofilling doesn't set up an ongoing relationship among cells in the group. After autofilling, you can change the cells independently of one another. If you prefer to link the cells' values so that they update when one of them changes, you probably want to use formulas instead, which brings us neatly to the next topic.

■ Making Mini-Spreadsheets with Formulas

You can use tables for lists of pretty much anything, but very often tables involve some kind of calculation. When your table lists items in an invoice, for example, you have a total amount due. A table of monthly sales figures by product might add up the total annual sales for each product, as well as the total monthly sales for all products. You get the idea.

You might have heard this already, but it turns out that computers are good at math. No need to strain your brain adding columns or figuring averages—when you use tables to list your data, Pages can run the numbers for you. In iWork, tables are actually spreadsheets and vice versa—any calculations that you can do in a Numbers spreadsheet, you can do in Pages tables. This means that your clever tables can update calculations on the fly as you add new data.

When you add a calculated value to a cell, Pages doesn't simply run the numbers once and forget about it. It gives the cell a *formula*, a mathematical expression that tells Pages to do its arithmetic using other cells in your table. If you change a value of any of those cells, Pages automatically updates the formula's result. A formula, in other words, is a smart placeholder that constantly updates its value as you add new data, keeping your tallies up to date so you don't have to. You'll find out much more about working with formulas when you learn about Numbers (see Chapters

19 and 20), and you can use those techniques to build formulas in Pages, too. In the meantime, this section provides a quick intro to help you do basic math in Pages.

Quick Formulas for Common Calculations

Although Pages can perform incredible feats of mathematical gymnastics, most table arithmetic isn't exactly Einstein-level calculus. You usually just want to add up a row or column of values and display the total at the end. Pages' *quick formula* feature offers fast access to the most commonly used math operations, making it easy to run a calculation on a column. To apply a quick formula, select the cell at the bottom of the column of figures that you want to run the calculation on, and then choose an option from the Insert→Function submenu:

- **Sum** adds up the cells.

- **Average** calculates the mean value of the cells.

- **Minimum** displays the lowest value among the cells.

- **Maximum** displays the highest value among the cells.

- **Count** shows the number of numeric or date/time values in the cells (text values aren't included in the tally).

- **Product** multiplies all the cells.

Pages inserts the formula's result into the cell you selected before you chose a formula. In other words, Pages performs the calculation using the values in all the cells *above* the one you selected. So, if you insert a Sum formula in Cell A3, for example, you get the value of cells A1 and A2, added together.

> **NOTE** You can't add formulas to header cells, but you can add them to footer cells.

You remove a formula just as you would any other value: Select the cell and then press the Delete key.

The Formula Editor

Quick formulas are handy for running common calculations involving a range of neighboring cells in a column. For most Pages tables, these prefab formulas provide everything you need. But every so often, you might want to do something a little different: add cells from different parts of the table, or multiply a dollar value in one cell by an exchange rate—if you have a yen for Japanese currency, for example. In that case, you need to create your own custom formula, and that's where the *Functions panel* comes in. Chapter 19 covers all the nitty-gritty details of constructing formulas, but this section presents the basics.

To open the Functions panel for a cell and create a new formula, select the cell and then type an equal sign (=); the Functions panel appears to the right side of the Pages window, and the Formula Editor pops up over the cell itself, as shown in Figure 8-15. If the cell already has a formula, double-click the cell to open both the Functions panel and the Formula Editor. You can also conjure up this duo by choosing Insert→Function→Create Formula.

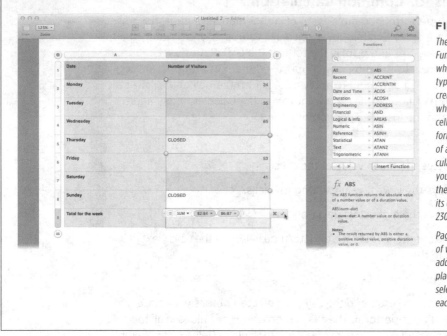

FIGURE 8-15

The Formula Editor and Functions panel appear when you select a cell and type the equal sign (=) to create a new formula, or when you double-click a cell that already contains a formula. To use the value of another cell in your calculation, just click the cell you're interested in, and the Formula Editor inserts its cell reference (page 230) into the formula.

Pages helps you keep track of which cells have been added to your formula by placing differently colored selection handles around each cell (or group of cells).

TIP If the Formula Editor gets in your way, you can move it by putting your cursor over its left side until the cursor turns into a hand, and then dragging the editor to a new spot.

Starting a cell value with an equal sign signals to Pages that you're adding a formula instead of literal text. If you don't start a formula with an equal sign, the cell will just display whatever you type. If you type *=2+2* into the Formula Editor, for example, the cell displays *4*—but when you omit the equal sign and simply type *2+2*, the cell stops doing math for you and simply displays *2+2*.

Just like your math teacher told you in grade school, you do arithmetic with *operators*, a fancy word for the plus, minus, multiplication, and division symbols shown in Table 8-1.

To use another cell's value in your calculation, just click the cell whose value you want to use and the Formula Editor inserts a *cell reference* into the formula. Cell references are coordinates that identify the location of cells in tables, a combination of the column name and the row name. So B2 refers to the cell in column B, row 2. In addition to clicking cells to add their references, you can also simply type their coordinates. To multiply the value in cell B2 by the value in cell C2, for example, the formula is *=B2*C2*.

TABLE 8-1 *Arithmetic operators*

OPERATOR	PURPOSE	EXAMPLE
+	Adds two values	2+2
–	Subtracts one value from another	5–3
*	Multiplies two values	10*10
/	Divides one value by another	20/5

Pages performs math on cells that hold numeric values just as you would expect, but the program chokes on formulas that try to do math on cells with text values. You can, however, do math on dates. A formula that adds 1 to a date, for example, displays the date for the following day, and a formula that subtracts 7 from a date displays the date for the week before. Subtract one date from another to get a duration value (page 219).

In addition to familiar arithmetic, formulas can also include *functions*, predefined shortcuts that do calculations on the cells or values that you give to them. For example, use the SUM function to add several cells: *=SUM(A1,B3,C5)* adds up the values of those three cells. Similarly, *=AVERAGE(D1,D2,D3,D4)* gives you the average value of those four cells. Pages gives you more than 250 functions that perform a wide range of mathematical and financial operations, manipulate strings of text, get the current date and time, and much more.

Although you can type functions directly into the Formula Editor, you can also add them using the Functions panel. This panel gives you access to iWork's entire library of functions, as shown in Figure 8-16. For more info about using functions, see Chapter 20.

When using functions, it's frequently useful to refer to a range of cells or to an entire column or row. When editing a formula, you can add a reference to a set of consecutive cells by dragging across the cells you want to add. Pages inserts a reference in the form of *B1:B5*, for example, which indicates rows one through five in column B (you can also type this reference directly). If you then want to add those cells using the SUM function, for example, the formula is *=SUM(B1:B5)*.

TIP Because adding a range of cells is such a common activity, the Formula Editor offers a shortcut: Type an equal sign to start your formula, and then drag across the cells you want to add up. When you release the mouse, Pages updates the formula to include the SUM function.

To refer to *all* the body cells in a column or row (excluding the header cells), click the column's reference tab (page 210). You can also type the reference by using the column's letter (type *C* or *C:C*) or row number (type *2:2*). For example, the formulas *=SUM(B)* and *=SUM(B:B)* both add all the values in column B, and the formula *=SUM(2:2)* adds all the values in row 2. Just be careful that your range doesn't include the cell where you're adding the formula, because formulas can't include their own cell's value; if they do, Pages displays an error icon in the cell (a red triangle with an exclamation point on it). Putting formulas in a footer row is a good way to help avoid this problem, since row and column references ignore header and footer cells.

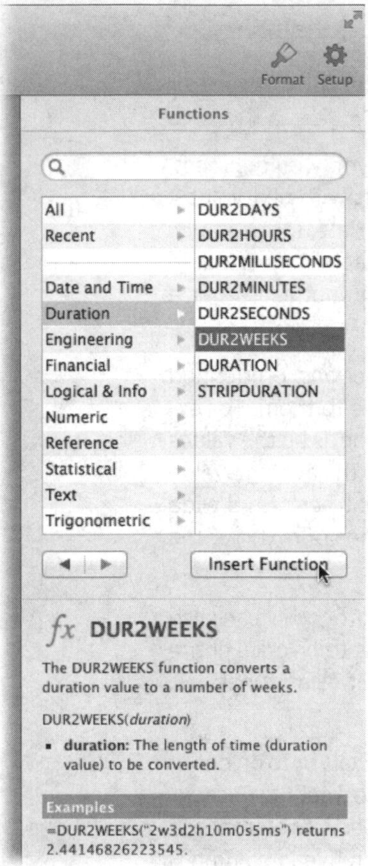

FIGURE 8-16

The Functions panel lets you flip through all of Pages' formula functions.

Select a category in the panel's left column to narrow the selection of functions in the right column. Click a function's name to display a description and examples of it below the table. To add a function to the selected cell, double-click the function's name, or select it and then click the Insert Function button.

NOTE In the example above, *=SUM(2)* always displays "2," since Pages treats "2" as a value instead of a row reference. So always use the 2:2 format when you want a row reference, or use the title in the row's header cell instead. For example *=SUM* (Total Visitors) will show you the total value of all the cells in the column with the Total Visitors header.

When you've finished working on your formula, save it by clicking the Formula Editor's green checkmark or pressing the Return key. To discard your formula without saving, click the red X or press the Esc key.

■ COPING WITH FORMULA ERRORS

When a formula in a table cell is incomplete, contains invalid cell references, or is otherwise incorrect, Pages displays a red triangle icon in the middle of the cell. Click the cell to see a description of the error. To fix the error, double-click the problem cell to open the Formula Editor, and then make your changes.

Moving Formulas

You can move a formula to another cell just as you would any other cell value: Select the cell at the cell level so that it's outlined in blue, and then drag the cell to another spot. You can also copy and paste cells, or copy them by autofilling cells (page 226). For complete details about moving cell content, flip back to page 485.

When you move a formula to a new cell, Pages adjusts the formula's cell references to reflect its new location. For example, if a formula in the footer row of column A adds up all the values in column A, moving that formula to column B changes its cell references to add up the values in column B. References to cells, columns, and rows change relative to the position of the new cell: If you move a formula down two rows, all of its column references move down two rows; if you move it right two columns, all column references shift two columns.

If you want to avoid this cell-shuffling sidestep and use the same cell reference in the new location, you can use an *absolute cell reference*. You do this by adding a dollar sign ($) in front of the column and row identifiers in the cell reference. For example, if you want a formula to refer to cell B5 no matter *where* you copy and paste the formula, use $B5 in the formula instead of B5. For more about absolute and relative cell references, see page 536.

■ Creating Charts

Tables are an efficient way to store and organize large amounts of info in a highly readable format, but charts make your data *dance*. Charts turn numbers into visuals that, when used well, highlight trends at a glance and communicate your data's message far more efficiently than a table of raw numbers. They're certainly less tedious than reading the straight prose: "In 2014, Crazyland Wonderpark's total Squirrel Apocalypse action figure sales rose by a whopping 90% over the sales in 2013's fourth quarter, which is a 99% increase on the sales in the third quarter."

Charts are graphical representations of data that you organize in a table or a spreadsheet. With your numbers in place, the stage is set for a modern miracle: From the stultifying columns of numbers, Pages helps you instantly create a gorgeous chart to reveal the hidden pattern behind the numbers. True, the most revealing charts aren't always gorgeous, and gorgeous charts aren't always revealing. Pages gives you the tools to build and dress your charts, but it's up to you to use them the right way (see "Avoiding Chartjunk" on page 640).

In Pages, you can't build charts *directly* from tables, handy as that would be. But your table data is just a quick two-step away from its chart metamorphosis. As you'll see, you create and edit a chart's data with the aptly named *Chart Data Editor*, which works like a very basic table of numbers—no formulas, no autofilling, and none of the other clever math-minded goodies you'll find in a regular Pages table.

If you're creating a simple chart with a small amount of data, it's quick and easy to enter your data directly into the Editor—just treat it like an ordinary table. For larger and more complicated data sets, however, or when you plan to update chart data frequently, it's much easier to work inside a table. In that case, a better option is to copy and paste the data from a table in Pages or Numbers, or from another spreadsheet program like Microsoft Excel. Copying cells into the Chart Data Editor is a quick maneuver that lets you import large amounts of data into a chart and start shaping its visuals right away.

For all but the simplest charts, copying and pasting from Numbers (or another spreadsheet program) should be your go-to process for banging out charts and graphs, letting Pages present the final polished chart as the result. That's why this book reserves most of the detailed features of working with charts for the Numbers section (specifically Chapter 21). Consider this section an appetizer—an introduction to iWork's chart features and a primer for creating and managing charts in Pages using the Chart Data Editor.

Inserting Charts

Like other objects in Pages, charts are either inline or floating objects (see page 143 for details about these layout styles). To add a chart, click the Chart button in Pages' toolbar and select a chart type from the drop-down menu (Figure 8-17), or choose Insert→Chart and pick a chart type there. The drop-down menu is handy because it shows you previews of the various chart types; the Insert menu simply lists their names. (For a description of all the chart types, see page 601.) When you select a type, a chart containing sample data appears in your document, and Pages opens the Format panel's Chart tab (Figure 8-18).

Resize your chart using one of its active selection handles, just like you would any other object.

■ UNDERSTANDING DATA SERIES AND DATA SETS

Before jumping into editing your chart's data, you'll need to wrap your brain around some of the chart-related lingo iWork uses. In particular, it's important to understand how charts organize data into *data series* and *data sets*. A data series is a group of related data points. In a table, a data series is a row or a column; in a chart, a data series usually has the same color (for example, the blue bars in a bar chart). A data set, on the other hand, is a collection of related data, such as an entire table or a chart, or all the information gathered from survey A across 12 months (where each month is a data series).

The simplest charts have a single data series, but charts like the one in Figure 8-18 compare *two* series. Each region's data tells its own story, which provides just enough info that it could itself be its own chart (Figure 8-19 shows what these two data series would look like in separate charts). But when you combine data series into a single chart, you create a visual comparison between the two stories, providing more context and insight than the two series tell separately.

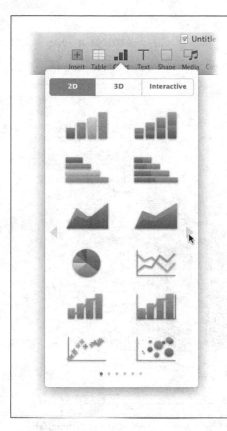

FIGURE 8-17

Add a chart to your document by choosing from this drop-down menu. Click the tabs at the top of the menu to see the options in the various categories (2D, 3D, and Interactive). Pages offers 12 chart types, eight of which come in 3D versions, and four of which offer interactive versions.

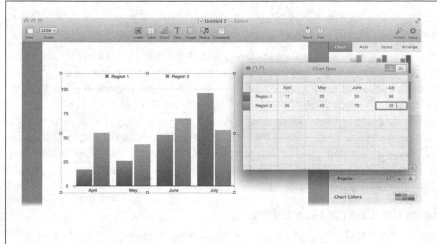

FIGURE 8-18

New charts contain sample data to help you get oriented. For example, the standard bar chart shown here plots two data series (Region 1 and Region 2) over four months.

To see the numbers behind the chart, click the Edit Chart Data button shown in Figure 8-19. Pages displays the Chart Data Editor (the floating window in this screenshot).

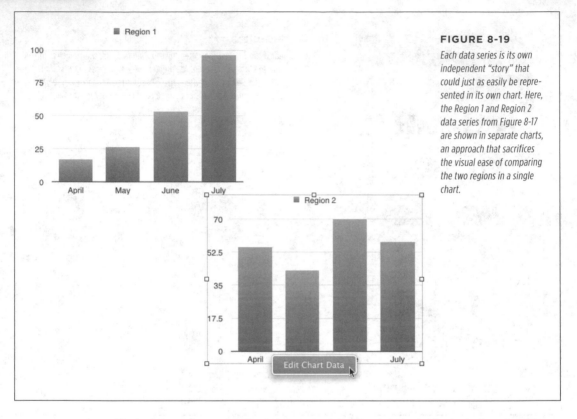

Each data series consists of data values (a.k.a. *data points*) plotted against the x-
and y-axes of the chart. (The x-axis is the chart's horizontal measuring stick, and
its y-axis is the vertical one.) Each of Pages' chart types draws these data points in
different ways (as bars, columns, points on a line, and so on).

In this example, the regions are data series, and the months are data sets. But Pages
lets you flip this around, changing the chart orientation so that the data is grouped
by month instead of by region. Simply open the Chart Data Editor and use the buttons in its upper-right corner to make this change (see Figure 8-20). In other words,
you have a choice of how you want to represent the rows and columns of your data:
When rows are your data series, columns represent the data sets along the x-axis;
when columns are your data series, rows represent the data sets. Either way, data
values in most charts are represented along the y-axis (except bar charts, which
show values along the x-axis).

Using the Chart Data Editor

To open the Chart Data Editor and start entering data for your chart, select your chart
and then click the big blue Edit Chart Data button that appears beneath it. (You can

also open the Editor by selecting the chart and then choosing Format→Chart→Show Chart Data Editor, or by Control-clicking the chart and choosing Show Chart Data Editor from the shortcut menu.) In both Pages and Keynote, you use the Chart Data Editor's lightweight table to add and arrange the data for your charts.

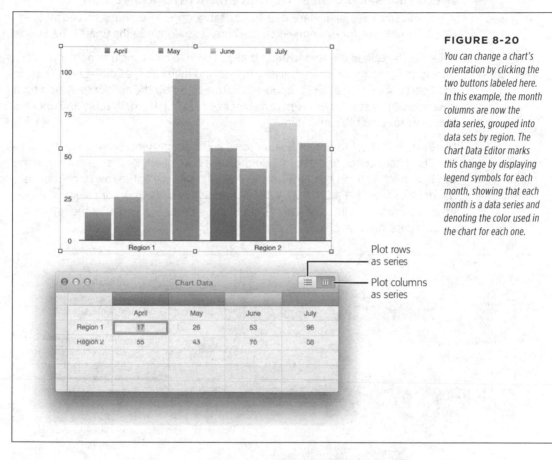

FIGURE 8-20

You can change a chart's orientation by clicking the two buttons labeled here. In this example, the month columns are now the data series, grouped into data sets by region. The Chart Data Editor marks this change by displaying legend symbols for each month, showing that each month is a data series and denoting the color used in the chart for each one.

Plot rows as series

Plot columns as series

Enter your data directly into the Chart Data Editor. Click a data cell and type to replace its contents. Press Tab to move to the next cell to the right, and press Shift-Tab to move to the left (sorry, arrow keys don't work here; you have to tab). Double-click row and column labels to rename them. You can also create new columns and rows by putting the cursor over a reference tab, clicking the tiny triangle that appears, and then choosing Insert Row Above, Insert Row Below, Insert Column Before, or Insert Column After. You can also Control-click a cell and choose these commands from the shortcut menu. (To see the new row or column, you may have to scroll, or expand the Chart Data Editor window by dragging any of its edges.)

You can reorganize the Chart Data Editor's rows and columns by dragging the corresponding reference tabs.

To delete a row or column in the Chart Data Editor, click its reference tab to select the whole shebang, and then press Delete. You can also Shift-click to select several rows or columns and then press Delete to obliterate them all.

■ COPYING SPREADSHEET OR TABLE DATA INTO YOUR CHART

If you already have your data in a Pages table or in a separate spreadsheet—in Numbers or Excel, for example—you can copy it straight into the Chart Data Editor.

Select all the cells in the spreadsheet that you wish to chart, including the cells containing the column and row labels if you like, and then choose Edit→Copy. Then, in the Chart Data Editor, select the top-left data cell (below the header row), and then choose Edit→Paste. Pages inserts the block of cells into the data table and updates the chart to reflect this new data.

Pages does its best to detect header rows and columns when you paste data into the Chart Data Editor, and it uses a simple rule to do this: If the first cell of either the top row or left column contains a letter, Pages treats the entire row or column as a header, as shown in Figure 8-21. When it identifies header rows or columns, Pages inserts those values into the Chart Data Editor's headers and places the remaining cells as data into the table.

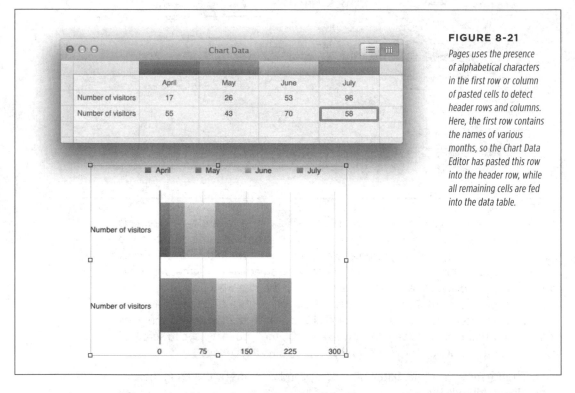

FIGURE 8-21

Pages uses the presence of alphabetical characters in the first row or column of pasted cells to detect header rows and columns. Here, the first row contains the names of various months, so the Chart Data Editor has pasted this row into the header row, while all remaining cells are fed into the data table.

If the pasted block of cells is smaller than the occupied cells in Pages' Chart Data Editor, the occupied cells outside the pasted block remain in the table until you delete them. Select the columns and rows to delete by clicking their header cells, and then press Delete.

Changing the Chart Type

You can change the type of chart at any time by selecting the chart, opening the Format panel's Chart tab, and then choosing an option from the Chart Type drop-down menu (you may have to scroll down to see this menu). Figure 8-22 explains some of the other options in the Chart tab.

> **TIP** Not all charts use the chart data in exactly same way, so when you flip through chart types, your data may not make sense in its new format. Whenever possible, it's a good idea to select your chart type *first* and then load up its data so that it's completely clear to you how Pages will use your data within the chart.

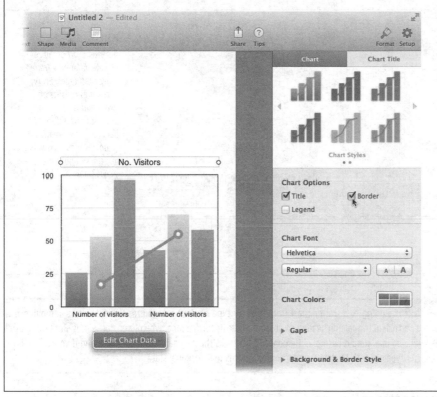

FIGURE 8-22

Switch to a new chart type by selecting the chart you want to change, opening the Chart tab, and then choosing from the Chart Type drop-down menu (at the very bottom of the Chart tab).

The Chart tab also gives you fast access to several other common chart data settings, including hiding or displaying the chart's title and legend. To add a title to your chart, turn on the Title checkbox, and then double-click the word "Title" and type a more appropriate title. You can also add a border by turning on the Chart tab's Border checkbox. In this screenshot, the chart has a title ("No. Visitors") and a border, but no legend.

Most chart types use data in the same format, and flipping back and forth between these styles will generally work as you expect. As described on page 234, these charts use either rows or columns as the data series and the other as data sets along the x-axis, for example. Pie, bubble, and scatter charts, however, have a different view of data than other chart types.

Pie charts illustrate only a single data set, and so they show the percentages for only the first row or column from the Chart Data Editor. If the "Plot rows as series" button is selected in the Chart Data Editor (see Figure 8-20) so that each row is a data series, only the first column's data set is used; if the "Plot columns as series" button is selected instead, the first row's data set is used and the rest of the table is ignored.

Scatter charts work an even bolder change on the data table when flipping between other chart types. This chart type uses pairs of columns as data series, as shown in Figure 8-23. Row headings are removed from the data table, with each row now representing a set of value pairs: The first column is the x-axis value, and the second is the y-axis value, giving the chart the coordinates to plot on the chart.

Finally, bubble charts display *three* data sets. In addition the x and y values, bubble charts plot a third data series: z values. Flip to page 608 for the full scoop on bubble charts.

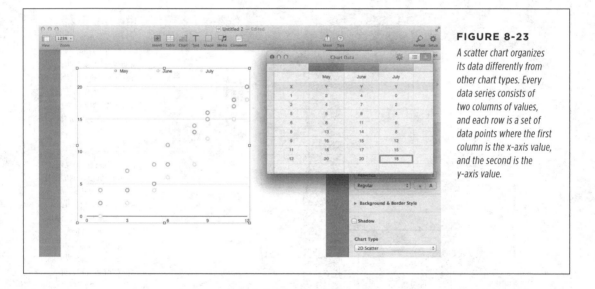

FIGURE 8-23

A scatter chart organizes its data differently from other chart types. Every data series consists of two columns of values, and each row is a set of data points where the first column is the x-axis value, and the second is the y-axis value.

NOTE Changing to a scatter chart from another type of chart reorganizes the data chart, removing row headers and half of the column headers to accommodate its format for a two-column data series. But that doesn't mean your original data is permanently gone; Pages tucks the original data table away, and if you switch back to another type of chart, the header information returns to its original state.

Formatting Charts

Like any other object in a Pages document, you can resize and reposition charts, wrap text around them, and so on—head back to page 191 for a general review of how to modify object styles. Beyond that, though, all the iWork programs provide tools for modifying the appearance of just about every element of your chart. You can make broad changes like painting graph bars with colors or textures, or subtle tweaks like refining the tick marks on the axis lines.

Chapter 21 goes into all the chart-formatting possibilities in detail. That chapter focuses on creating charts in Numbers, but the options and processes of styling charts are nearly exactly the same there as in Pages and Keynote. In all three iWork programs, you use the same settings in the Format panel's various tabs to make your changes. As you'll see, Numbers' Chart tab offers a handful of extra options that are specific to the way its charts interact with tables, but other than that, everything works identically in all three programs. Here's a quick summary:

- **3D effects.** You can convert any chart (except a scatter, bubble, two-axis, or mixed chart) into a three-dimensional model. To convert a chart into its 3D version, select it and then choose one of the 3D chart types by going to the Format panel's Chart tab and opening the Chart Type drop-down menu. When you select a 3D chart, you can change the chart's viewing angle, turn it three dimensionally in space, or add lighting effects and depth. See page 626 for more about working with 3D charts.

- **Chart text and labels.** Each of the tabs in the Format panel offers options for labeling your chart. Add or remove the chart's title or legend by opening the Chart tab and turning the Title and Legend checkboxes on or off (or go to Format→Chart and make your selections from this submenu). Add labels to the x- or y-axis by opening the Format panel's Axis tab and turning on the Axis Name checkboxes (click the buttons at the top of the tab to switch between the settings for the x- and y-axes). This adds placeholders along the different axes: Double-click either placeholder, type your own text, and then save your title by pressing the Return key on your keyboard or clicking anywhere outside of the label-editing box. You can use all of Pages' usual text-formatting tools to style these labels: Click the Format panel's Axis Title tab to take a look. For more about working with chart labels, see page 618.

- **Colors and textures.** Use the Chart Colors setting in the Format panel's Chart tab to change the color scheme of your chart. (These settings aren't available for all chart types.) Flip to page 629 for the full-color version.

- **Slicing pie charts.** Pie charts are completely different animals from the other charts and get a whole new Wedges tab, too. See page 633 for the lowdown on formatting the labels, wedges, and rotation of your pie charts.

- **Formatting the other chart types.** Every chart type offers a slightly different choice of settings in the Format panel's various tabs: Control the gaps between column and bar charts in the Chart tab, for example, or choose the symbols for marking data points in line, area, and scatter charts in the Series tab. See page 635 for details about these options.

- **Trendlines and error bars.** Pages can calculate trendlines and error bars for most 2D charts except for pie charts and stacked charts. These options are available in the Format panel's Series pane. Skip ahead to page 636 for the whole story.

- **Axis and gridlines.** You can add gridlines, tick marks, or axis lines to any chart (except pie charts) using the Format panel's Axis tab. See page 620 to get your charts lined up.

These myriad formatting tools mean that you have a limitless set of possibilities for styling your charts—and in truth, playing with these charts becomes oddly addictive. Don't get carried away, though; your goal is to communicate data, and simplicity and clarity should win out over showy effects. However you ultimately decide to format your information, the next step is to get it out there and share it with others. That's the focus of the next chapter.

Sharing Pages Documents

After you create a Pages document and carefully lay out, tweak, and polish it to perfection, your work is done—if you want to view it only onscreen, that is. More likely, you'll want to print a hard copy, or share it with others via email, AirDrop, Messages, or Apple's shiny new iCloud service, delivering it from your computer into the hands, inboxes, and web browsers of your intended audience. Several new features in iWork make online distribution of your masterpiece especially easy, particularly iCloud, which lets you share your document and gather feedback from invited reviewers in a sleek and simple web interface. You'll also learn how to export files in several formats, ready for other programs like Microsoft Word or Adobe Reader. But first, you'll learn how to require a password so that you can share a document with only certain people who have your stamp of approval.

■ Password-Protecting Documents

Is your document top secret? Classified? For your eyes only? Whether you're working with state secrets or ordering your cat's birthday present, you can slap a padlock on a document so no one can open it unless she knows the password:

1. **Choose File→Set Password to display the dialog box shown in Figure 9-1; in the Password box, type your top-secret password, and then enter it again in the Verify field.**

    Always forgetting things? Give yourself a safety net and add an optional password hint that can help jog your memory if you forget your password.

2. **If you want to add this password to your Keychain, select the "Remember this password in my keychain" checkbox.**

Keychain is Apple's password-management system. If your keychain is just something that you hang your car keys on, then the box on page 245 will get you up to speed on this feature.

3. **When you're happy with what you've entered, click Set Password.**

To let you know that your file is now under lock and key, Pages adds a padlock icon next to your document's title at the top of the Pages window. Now, whenever you try to open this document, Pages asks you to enter the password. If you enter the incorrect password three times in a row, Pages shows you the password hint (if you entered one).

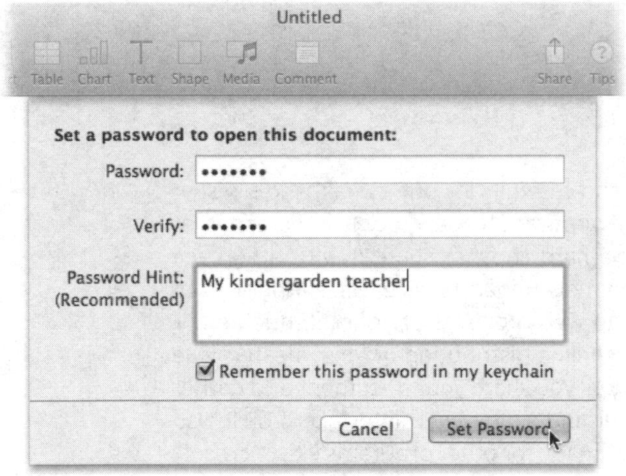

FIGURE 9-1

You can assign a password to your top-secret Pages documents so that only people in the know can open, read, or edit them. When creating your password, you can tell Pages to add this new password to your Keychain (see the box on page 245) by turning on the "Remember this password in my keychain" checkbox before clicking the Set Password button.

If the name of your kindergarten teacher suddenly becomes common knowledge, protect your document by changing your password: Choose File→Change Password, enter your old password, and then type out your new password twice and click Change Password (you may want to create a new password hint and turn on the "Remember this password..." checkbox, too).

When the coast is clear and it's finally safe for the world to read your secret scribblings, remove your password by going to File→Change Password, entering your current password, and then clicking the Remove Password button. The padlock at the top of the Pages window disappears, and anyone can access your document.

NOTE When you export a copy of your document in PDF, Word, or Pages '09 format (you'll learn how later in this chapter starting on page 250) you get the option to keep the current password or to create a new one. However, if you export in plain text or ePub format, your password *won't* apply to the new file.

What's on Your Keychain?

Most of us have multiple passwords for things like Amazon accounts, work email, home email, and that Hotmail address with the embarrassing username you created when you were in high school. If you're security savvy, you should have a different password for each account—but that's a lot of passwords! This is where Keychain comes to the rescue. Keychain is a feature of OS X that stores *all* your passwords for you so you need to remember only one master password: the one that unlocks your Keychain account.

Take a look at Keychain by opening a Finder window on your Mac and choosing Applications→Utilities→Keychain Access, which launches the Keychain Access window. In the Category pane on the left side of the window, select Passwords to view all of your saved passwords; if you're looking for the password for a particular file (or website, program, email account, or whatever) enter a keyword in the Search field at the top of the window. When you find the item you're looking for, double-click it to launch a new window where you can recover the password for that item. To recover the password, turn on the "Show password" checkbox and then enter your Keychain password (if you haven't specified otherwise, this is the password you use to log into your Mac. You can change your Mac password by going to →System Preferences→Security & Privacy, making sure the General tab is selected, and then clicking the Change Password button).

■ Printing Your Documents

For decades, pundits have declared the paperless office to be just around the corner—and now that we've waited long enough, it appears to be slowly coming true. A new generation of worker has become accustomed to reading and archiving documents on the computer instead of squirreling them away into file cabinets.

But we're still a long way from going *completely* paperless, and printing will undoubtedly be one of your preferred methods for liberating Pages documents from your Mac. Printing Pages files is just like printing anything else on your computer, so if you have a handle on how printing works in other programs, feel free to skip this section.

Page Setup

The program's Page Setup options should really be part of the document setup you did when you created your document (see Chapter 5 for details on how to format documents). Still, it's a good idea to double-check them now. Choose File→Page Setup to open the Page Setup dialog box (Figure 9-2), whose main purpose in life is to set the paper size, orientation, and scaling adjustment (if any) for the document.

The Settings drop-down menu is always set to Page Attributes when you open the Page Setup dialog box. Leave it set that way, choose the name of your printer from the Format For drop-down menu, and choose the size of paper you want from the Paper Size drop-down menu. The two Orientation buttons determine whether the paper size you just selected prints out *portrait* (the traditional vertical orientation) or *landscape* (tipped sideways for horizontal orientation). Most documents are portrait style, but if you're printing envelopes, brochures, or panoramas, choose landscape instead.

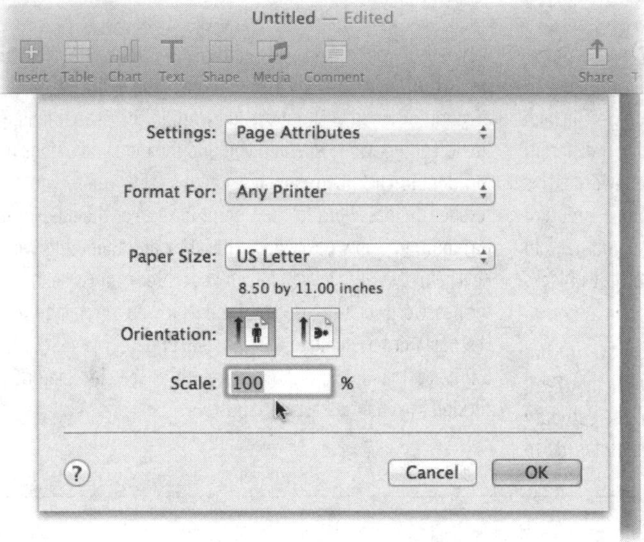

FIGURE 9-2

You set basic document formatting—paper size and portrait or landscape orientation—in the Page Setup dialog box. If you want to print the document at a reduced or enlarged size, adjust the Scale setting to less than or more than 100 percent. The Paper Size options you can choose from may vary depending on the kind of printer you have.

You can get really specific about your Page Setup by opening the Paper Size drop-down menu and selecting Manage Custom Sizes. See page 106 for more information.

When you click OK to close the Page Setup dialog box, Pages takes you right back to your document, where you can continue to work on it or take the plunge and print it out. Pages memorizes these Page Setup settings along with your document, so once you've set it for your document, you don't need to return to Page Setup unless you need to change the settings.

TIP The standard Page Setup settings that you get when you create a new file depend on the template you use. To save your own preferred settings for reuse in other documents, you have to save your document as a template, a topic covered in the next chapter (page 263).

The Print Dialog Box

Although you need to open the Page Setup dialog box only once in the life of a document, you use the Print dialog box every time you need to print it. Press ⌘-P (or choose File→Print) to get started. There are actually two version of the Print dialog box: a simple view, and the expanded view shown in Figure 9-3, which gives you access to more options. If Pages displays the simple view (which it probably will), click the Show Details button to open the full dialog box. From then on, Pages remembers to show you this expanded view when you go to print. To switch back to the simple view, click the Hide Details button.

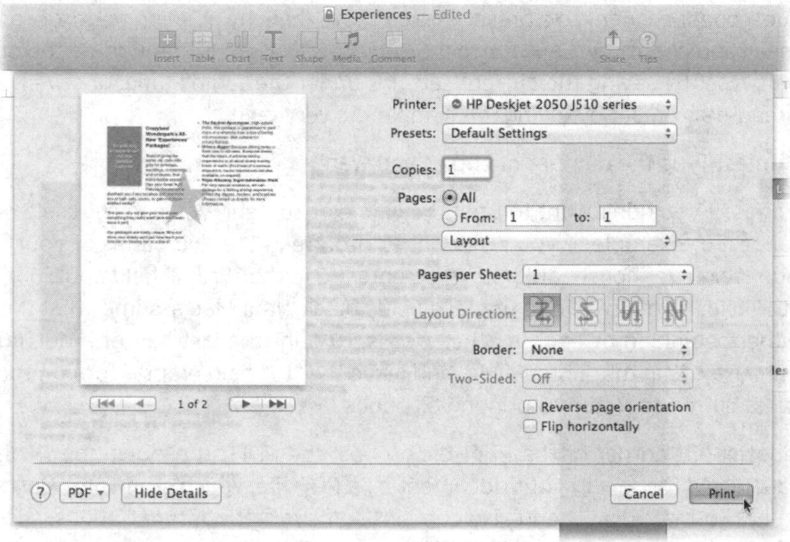

FIGURE 9-3

*Here's the expanded
version of the Print dialog
box (click the Show Details
button to see it).*

*If you have more than one
printer hooked up to your
Mac or network, use the
Printer drop-down menu
to select a printer. (If you
don't see the printer you
want, choose Add Printer
and follow the onscreen
instructions.)*

The expanded Print dialog box gives up half of its real estate for a preview of your document. Use the forward/back buttons to flip through the pages to make sure that it looks like you expect, or to find page numbers if you want to print a limited range of pages.

> **TIP** Any comments you've added to your document (page 103) don't appear in the printed version. This is also true of tracking markup (page 98)—you'll notice that, in the Print dialog box's preview pane, your document is completely free of these extras.

The right side of the dialog box contains the printing controls. The top portion of these settings lets you choose from a fixed set of options, while the options below change according to your selection in the unlabeled drop-down menu that's initially set to Layout. The fixed set of options at the top right prompt you for these basic settings:

- **Printer.** Choose the printer where you want to send your document. If you don't see the printer you want, choose Add Printer from the drop-down menu and follow the instructions that appear.

- **Presets.** Once you have your printing preferences just so, you can take a snapshot of them and save them as a *preset* for future use. If you frequently print two pages per sheet of paper, for example, you might save a preset named Two Per Page where that option is selected. To create a preset, choose "Save Current Settings as Preset" from the Presets drop-down menu, give your preset a name, and then decide whether this preset should be unique to the current printer or shared across all printers. When you click OK, your Mac adds these settings to the Presets menu so that you can access them again from any program. To use a saved preset, choose it from the Presets drop-down menu. If you make subsequent changes to a preset, you can save them by opening this drop-down menu and choosing "Save Current Settings as Preset." Either update the original preset by saving the current settings under the same name, or save it as a brand-new preset by giving it a name of its very own.

- **Copies.** Type the number of copies you want.

- **Pages.** If you don't want to print the whole document, you can choose a page range. For example, if you just want to proofread the five pages of your prenup that cover household pets, then enter *52* in the "From" field and *56* in the "to" field. If you leave one of these fields blank, your Mac assumes that means either beginning or end. In other words, to print the last half of a document enter, say, *12* in the "From" field, and leave the "to" field empty. Turn on the All radio button to return to printing all pages.

In the lower-left corner of the Print dialog box, the PDF drop-down menu offers several options for saving your document as a PDF file, which stands for Portable Document Format. (This menu also contains some rather obscure options, such as "Add PDF to iBooks" and "Send PDF via Messages," which are covered in the box on page 249.) PDFs can be opened with Preview on your Mac or with the free Adobe Reader program on any computer. When you save a document as a PDF, your Mac saves the file on your hard drive instead of printing it. Saving a document as a PDF is handy because you can share your file with others, no matter what programs or fonts they have installed, and they can still see your complete, original layout and formatting.

> **TIP** When you create a PDF using the File→Export option instead of doing it here in the Print dialog box, you have a bit more control over the image resolution in the resulting PDF. See page 253 for details.

The first option in the PDF drop-down menu is "Open PDF in Preview," useful if you're unsure about your document's margin settings or page layout options. Save yourself some time, expensive ink, and deforestation guilt by clicking this option to see exactly what your document is going to look like on the page. Your Mac manages this sneak preview by displaying a PDF version of the document in the Preview program. If you like what you see, click the Print button at the bottom of the Preview window.

Below the Print dialog box's page-range settings is an unlabeled drop-down menu that opens up a slew of other print options. The items in this menu and the controls they provide are different for different printers, but here are a few of the settings you can expect to encounter:

- **Layout.** Choose how many of your document's pages to print per sheet of paper. One is standard, two saves paper, and four or more are best suited for a remake of *The Incredible Shrinking Man*.

- **Paper Handling.** If you're interested in double-sided printing (*duplexing*)—and your printer doesn't offer this feature—choose this option and then use the settings that appear to print only odd or only even pages so you can then flip them over and run them through a second time to print on the back side. Depending on the way your printer shoots out its pages, the Reverse option in the Page Order drop-down menu can make the stack of pages come out with page 1 on top.

- **Collate pages.** When you're printing several copies of a multipage document, turn on this checkbox, and the printer prints the document all the way through before starting on the second copy—all that's left for you to do is staple the pages together. If you turn off this checkbox, then the printer prints, say, five copies of page 1 followed by five copies of page 2, and so on. (This often results in faster printing, especially on laser printers, but of course it also means that you have to go back and organize the pages by hand.)

- **Layout Direction.** When you're printing multiple pages per sheet, use the Layout Direction thumbnails to tell Pages whether page 2 should be to the right of page 1, to the left, below it...and so on.

- **Border.** Open this drop-down and choose a border for your printed page. If you're printing multiple pages on a single sheet, this adds a border around each page, resulting in multiple borders per printed sheet.

UP TO SPEED

Postscript, iBook, Messages, and More

When you open the Print dialog box's PDF drop-down menu, you'll spot some additional options besides PDFs. You won't use these commands often (if you use them at all), but here's the lowdown, just in case:

- **Save as PostScript.** Choose this command to—you guessed it—save your document in PostScript format. What's PostScript? If you're asking that question, then chances are you don't need to use it. If you have a PostScript printer, then you need to save and print your documents in this format.

- **Add PDF to iBooks.** Creates a PDF of your document and adds it to the iBooks app, all in one smooth move. You can learn more about iBooks at *www.apple.com/apps/ibooks*.

- **Mail PDF.** Generate a PDF version of your document and launch the Mail program, where a blank message with your PDF attachment is already waiting for you: Just enter your recipient's email address and click Send.

- **Save PDF to Web Receipts Folder.** OK, so you've put the finishing touches on an invoice, or someone has shared a receipt with you (see page 256 for a master class on sharing Pages documents). You know you should print out a copy for your records, but you're all out of ink, or your printer isn't connected, or you just don't feel like printing anything today. No problem—Pages can create a PDF of any Pages document and stash it away in a special Web Receipts folder inside your Mac's Documents folder. When you're primed for a printing session, just open this folder and print out all the files inside.

- **Send PDF via Messages.** Create a PDF and send it via Messages, Apple's instant-messaging app (formerly known as iChat). You can learn more about sharing PDFs (and other files) via Messages on page 260.

- **Paper Type/Quality.** Choose the type of paper you're printing on and the print quality. When Paper Type/Quality is selected, you can also click the flippy triangle next to the Color Options heading to expand this section and then select grayscale printing to save color ink when you print a draft.

When you're happy with the settings in the Print dialog box, click Print and your print job heads to the printer.

■ Exporting Documents

As you learned way back on page 18, Pages does a great job of opening documents created by other word processors like Microsoft Word. Alas, Word and other programs don't return the favor—while Pages speaks Word, for example, Word doesn't understand Pages at all. So if you want to share a Pages document with Windows users or anyone who doesn't have iWork, you need to *export* the file, telling Pages to save it as a different file type. Other occasions call for exporting, too—you might want to save your file as a PDF to share a read-only version that anyone can open (but not edit), for example.

You work this exporting magic from Pages' Export dialog box. Choose File→Export To, and then choose the format you want to save the file in: PDF, Word, Plain Text, ePub, Pages '09, or Zip Archive. Each of these formats varies in how "true" the result will be to your original document—PDF will be an exact read-only replica, for example, while plain text will keep only the content and strip out all your graphics and formatting. Your results will vary according to your specific document and the export format you choose, but in general, the fewer graphics, columns, tables, headers, footers, and footnotes involved, the more accurate your exported file will be. When Pages runs into problems, it lets you know about translation trouble by opening the Document Warnings window and giving you the details, as shown in Figure 9-4.

When you want to let people edit the document, choose Word, Plain Text, or Pages '09. However, when you distribute a file that's intended only to be read, choose PDF for the most reliable results—the exported document will *always* be a precise match with the original, and PDF documents are readable from any computer. You can also use ePub to export your document in a book format, which can then be opened by apps such as iBooks.

NOTE Exporting a password-protected Pages document (page 252) to ePub or Plain Text will give you an unprotected copy of the file—no password required. Pages warns you about this when you start the export and gives you a chance to cancel if you feel all naked and vulnerable without your password. See page 243 for details about password-protecting your document. If you're exporting your file in Word, Pages '09, or PDF format, you can keep your password, or click Change Password to create a new one.

FIGURE 9-4

When Pages has trouble translating any part of your document into the target file format, it lets you know about it in the Document Warnings window shown here. In this example, after exporting a page-layout document to Microsoft Word, Pages cautions that the exported file doesn't contain form components.

Exporting to Microsoft Word

Microsoft Word (.doc or .docx) files can be opened and edited in Word on either Mac or Windows computers. Because the program is so widespread, pretty much every other word processor can open Word documents, too, making this file format the right choice just about anytime you need to share an editable version of your file with anyone who's not an iWork convert, even if he doesn't use Word himself. (Alternatively, you could share the document online via iCloud. See page 256 for more info.)

To save a copy of your document as a Microsoft Word file, go to File→Export To→ Word, which launches the Export Your Document dialog box. You'll notice that the Word tab is already open (as shown in Figure 9-5).

NOTE Older versions of Word created .doc files, but in Word 2007 for Windows and Word 2008 for Mac, Microsoft introduced the .docx file format. Pages can export in both formats, but you should opt for .doc files if you want to be sure that folks can open your document in older versions of Word. To choose a format for your Word documents, open the Export Your Document dialog box's Advanced Options section, and then choose either .docx or .doc from the drop-down menu.

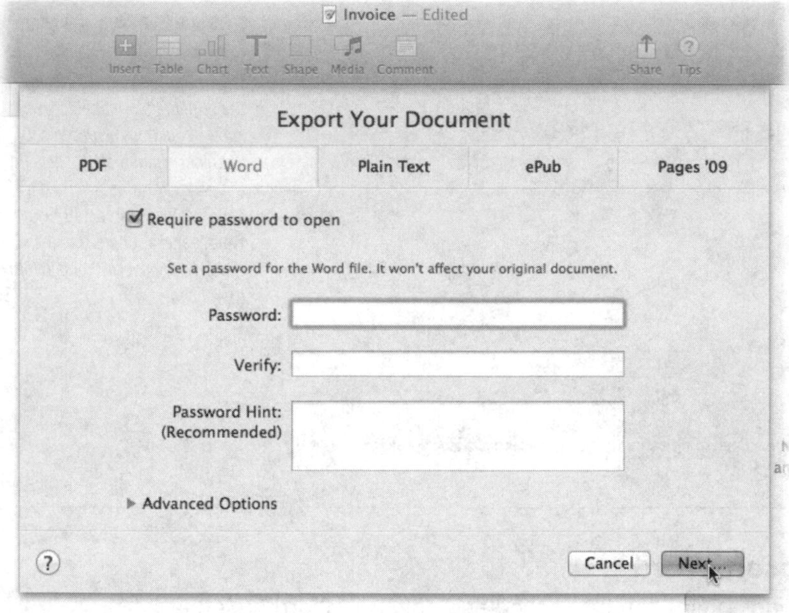

FIGURE 9-5

The Export Your Document dialog box lets you choose a file format. Here, the Word tab is selected, but if you changed your mind and wanted to export a PDF, you could just click the PDF tab instead.

If you want to assign a password to your document, turn on the "Require password to open" checkbox and then fill in the fields shown here.

When you're ready to export, click the Next button, which launches the familiar Save dialog box. Enter a name for your file, specify where Pages should save it, and then click Export.

Don't expect pixel-for-pixel perfection, however. Although Pages does a good job at maintaining your overall formatting and layout in Word, there are usually a few discrepancies. In particular, text spacing differences often give the Word document a different number of pages than your original, and table and column layouts may show some variation, too. Text borders and rules (see page 59) often don't make the transition at all.

The good news is that exported Microsoft Word files maintain all comments and tracked changes from your Pages document—and Pages does the same for imported Word files. So if you're doing some heavy collaboration on a document, flip on change tracking (page 98), and you and your Word-wielding colleagues can track every change throughout the editing process.

Exporting Plain Text

Plain text is the most basic type of word-processing file. The good news is that *any* word processor, regardless of the computer it's running on, can open plain text files and edit the words inside. The bad news is that plain text files don't contain any formatting. Bold, italic, colors, font choices, text alignment, tables, graphs, graphics, backgrounds, and virtually all the other kinds of formatting that make a Pages document so attractive are lost in translation. For most purposes, since you lose even rudimentary text formatting, plain text isn't worth much for creating documents that you exchange with colleagues, but it can be useful in a pinch if you need to save a text file like an HTML page.

To export a plain-text file, choose File→Export To→Plain Text, which opens the Export Your Document dialog box with the Plain Text tab selected. Click Next, type a name for the file in the Save window, and then choose where to save it.

Exporting PDFs

Given the translation hiccups Pages occasionally encounters when exporting to the other formats—especially with complex documents—the only way to export a Pages document and be sure it's going to look *exactly* like you expect is to create a PDF file. This type of file is designed to maintain the *exact* look of a document, no matter what computer it's viewed on. PDF files even include all the fonts inside the file so you don't have to worry about whether your readers have the correct fonts installed.

PDF files are ideal for sharing on websites, since you can open them with most web browsers. You can also open PDF files with the Mac's Preview program or with the free Adobe Reader program that's available for all computer operating systems: Macintosh, Windows, Linux...you name it!

The downside is that you can't edit PDF files without special software. So when you send around a PDF file, consider it read-only. If you think others will need to edit the file, then use one of the other formats instead.

As mentioned on page 248, you can create a PDF file from the Print dialog box, but using File→Export To→PDF instead gives you one advantage that the Print dialog box doesn't: The Export Your Document dialog box that appears includes the Image Quality drop-down menu, which lets you choose from three levels of image quality (see Figure 9-6).

The Best option keeps the original image resolution—but also creates the largest file. Choose Better to reduce the image resolution to 150 dpi (dots per inch), an acceptable quality for inkjet printing, for example. For the smallest file size, choose Good, which reduces images to 72 dpi—a fine resolution for viewing onscreen, but not ideal for printing.

To add a password to the PDF, select the "Require password to open" checkbox to reveal the fields shown in Figure 9-5. If your document already contains a password, you can change it by clicking the Change Password button or remove it by turning off the "Require password to open" checkbox.

When you're ready to export the document, click Next. Choose a file name and location for your new PDF file, and then click Export.

FIGURE 9-6

When you export a PDF file, Pages lets you choose the file's image quality and, optionally, assign a password to the document. To assign a password, click the "Require password to open" checkbox to reveal the password fields shown back in Figure 9-4.

Exporting ePub Docs

ePub is an ebook format (as you probably know, the term "ebook" is shorthand for "electronic book," like the books you can read on a Kindle or a Nook). You can really make a splash with your word-processing document by converting it into an electronic book, complete with stylish front cover. See Figure 9-7 for an example of what a Pages document looks like after it's been given the ePub treatment.

NOTE You can only export word-processing documents to ePub format; this feature isn't available for page-layout documents.

To export in ePub format, choose File→Export To→ePub. In the Export Your Document window, give your ePub file a name and an author. Depending on where your ePub file winds up (the *New York Times* bestseller list, perhaps?), it could be categorized based on its topic, so you can also use the Primary Category drop-down menu to let Pages know whether your file is a biography, a graphic novel, and so on. You can also set the language for your book by clicking the Advanced Options heading and then choosing from the Language drop-down menu. You can also tell Pages to use the first page of your document as the cover image for your book by turning on the "Use the first page as the book cover image" checkbox. (You'll probably want to select this option only if you have a pretty first page, though!)

When you've entered all this info, it's time to export: Click the Next button, tell Pages where to store your ePub document, give the file a name, and then click Export.

Exporting to Pages '09

Pages also lets you save a copy of your document as a Pages '09 file to share with behind-the-times iWork enthusiasts. To export in this format, choose File→Export To→Pages '09, which launches the familiar Export Your Document dialog box. Decide whether you want to assign a password, click Next, choose a destination for the file, and then click Export.

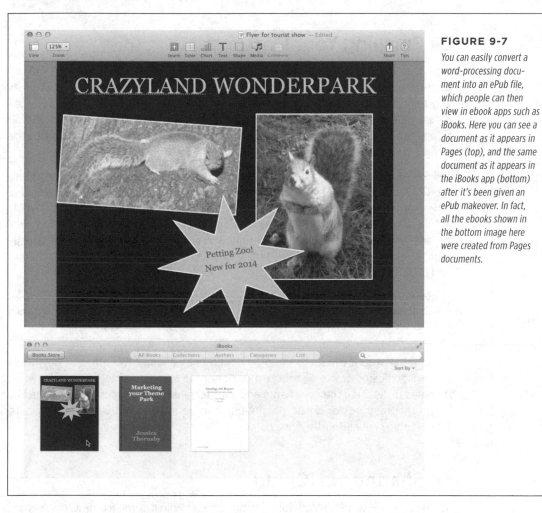

FIGURE 9-7

You can easily convert a word-processing document into an ePub file, which people can then view in ebook apps such as iBooks. Here you can see a document as it appears in Pages (top), and the same document as it appears in the iBooks app (bottom) after it's been given an ePub makeover. In fact, all the ebooks shown in the bottom image here were created from Pages documents.

The hitch, of course, is that any new features of Pages '13 (such as bubble charts and interactive charts) won't translate exactly to the older version's file—but that's the price you pay for not keeping up with the times!

Exporting a Zip Archive

If you plan on posting your Pages document to an online service such as iTunes or Dropbox, you should export it as a Zip archive first to make its file size more manageable. You could find the Pages document in your Finder, Control-click, it and then choose Compress, but some programs won't recognize the resulting file as a valid iWork file.

To be sure that your file is recognized as the snazzy iWork document it is, select File→Export To→ZIP Archive. This launches the Save dialog box; enter a name for your new file, tell Pages where to save it, and then click Export.

■ Emailing Your Document

Now that you know how to export a document, what are you going to do with it? Chances are, you're getting ready to email it to someone. In that case, Pages gives you a shortcut to export your document and automatically attach it to a new email message. Click the Share button in the toolbar, and select "Send a Copy"→Email to open the "Send via Email" dialog box, which turns out to be really similar to the Export Your Document dialog box.

Tell Pages exactly how it should package up your file by clicking the appropriate tab (Pages, PDF, Word, or ePub), setting a password (if you like), and choosing any other settings related to the format you chose (see the appropriate section earlier in this chapter for details). When you're done, click Next, and Pages packs up your file, launches the Mail program, and opens a new message window with your document already attached. All that's left is to address the message, dash off a note, and click Send.

> **TIP** If you're emailing an image-heavy document, you may have a long wait on your hands. To speed things up, before sending the file, try shrinking it down by choosing File→Reduce File Size (see page 167 for details).

As convenient as it can be to fire off a document via email, though, it's not always the most efficient way to distribute a document to lots of people—especially when it comes to catching the comments and suggestions that you receive in return. For that, other methods of online distribution can be more effective, which is where Apple's shiny new iCloud service comes in.

■ Sharing via iCloud

What is this mysterious iWork for iCloud, and where did it come from? iCloud's roots lie in the now-defunct iWork.com, which Apple launched in 2009.

The dearly departed iWork.com was a website that let you upload and share iWork documents. Once you uploaded a document to iWork.com, you could invite friends to take a peek at it. These lucky guests could download a copy of the document onto their computers or post comments on the online version—and that was it. iWork.com didn't let you or your invited guests *edit* the document online, and it didn't display everyone's changes in real time (which would have paved the way for some pretty fun online collaboration). In reality, there wasn't much difference between using iWork. com and sending your buddies a copy of your document via email. Unsurprisingly, iWork.com never caught on, and Apple eventually decommissioned it.

That looked like the end of the road for iWork online, until Apple shook things up by announcing iWork for iCloud at its 2013 Worldwide Developers Conference. Apple calls iWork for iCloud a "web-based office suite" (see the box below for details on what that means). Basically, it's the new-and-improved iWork.com, complete with an online-editing feature all the kids are talking about.

You may already be on first-name terms with Pages, but now it's time to get acquainted with *Pages for iCloud*.

What's a Web-Based Office Suite?

Web-based office suites let you create, edit, share, and store documents online. To use a web-based office suite, you launch a web browser like Safari or Firefox, go to the suite's web address and log into your account (or create an account if this is your first visit), and then you're ready to start creating documents online. One example of a web-based office suite is Google Drive (*http://drive.google.com*), which you might be familiar with if you use Gmail, Google's email service.

Most web-based office suites offer the full range of document types: spreadsheets, word-processing documents, and presentations. Behind the scenes, your documents are saved to the host company's computers rather than *your* computer,

so they're raring to go whenever you log into your account via the suite's website, regardless of what computer you're on. That means you can access your documents from *anywhere*.

The really cool thing about online documents is that you can invite your friends (or enemies, if that's what floats your boat) to work on them with you. Once you invite someone to join in, your document also appears in her account, and she can edit away at it to her heart's content. The next time you log in and open that document, you see all the changes your friend/ enemy has made, or—if you're working on the same document simultaneously—you see her changes *as she's making them*, which is definitely handy when you're trying to collaborate.

What *is* iCloud?

You've probably heard the phrase "cloud computing," which is where the name iCloud comes from. The idea behind cloud computing is that, rather than saving stuff on just one computer (which could get damaged by a thunderstorm, say, or suffer an epic meltdown), it's safer to save multiple versions of your documents on a bunch of different computers in different places. That way, even if one of those computers gets damaged, you can still retrieve your stuff from the other computers via the Internet.

The best thing about cloud computing is that you don't have to buy and maintain a bunch of computers yourself—the company offering the service takes care of that for you. If you use Gmail, for example, rather than storing all your emails on just your home computer, Google stores it on *its* computers. You can then access your Gmail messages from any computer that has an Internet connection. It's the same with iWork for iCloud: Apple stores your documents on its machines so you can access them online.

So, basically, iCloud is a bunch of interconnected computers owned by Apple that store all of your precious documents. And iCloud has enough other talents to reach the finals of one of those cheesy televised talent contests. If you want to know everything that iCloud is capable of, check out *www.apple.com/icloud/features*.

You already have Pages on your Mac, so do you *really* need another incarnation of Pages in your life? Aren't things complicated enough, when you're already struggling to remember whether you created that flyer on your Mac or on your iPhone? Yes, things can get confusing, but that's exactly *why* you need iWork for iCloud: to bring some order to your life.

Given a chance, iWork for iCloud can be your very own ultra-convenient, always-available library containing *all* of your iWork documents—even ones you create on an iPhone, iPod Touch, or iPad! (The iWork apps for these devices are covered in Part Four of this book.)

NOTE This chapter doesn't show you how to create an iCloud account (head over to page 750 for that), or how to create and edit Pages for iCloud documents (that's what Chapter 28 is about). This chapter assumes you already have an iCloud account and shows you how to share your documents via iCloud.

Connecting iWork for Mac to iCloud

After creating your iCloud account (see page 750 for step-by-step instructions), you need to tell your Mac all about this hip new iCloud account it can connect to:

1. **Go to →System Preferences or click the System Preferences icon in the Dock.**

2. **In the System Preferences window, click the iCloud icon; enter your Apple ID and password, and then click Sign In.**

3. **Tell your Mac how it should handle your iCloud account, and then click Next.**

   Choose whether you want to use iCloud to manage your mail, contacts, calendar, and more, and whether you want to use Find My Mac (see *www.apple. com/icloud/find-my-iphone.html*). You can turn off both these checkboxes, if you like. But if you want to use iCloud with iWork, then on the next screen that appears, make sure the Documents and Data checkbox is turned on.

You're now ready to start sharing iWork documents using iCloud.

Sharing via iCloud

You can invite other people to take a look at your document via iCloud by sharing a hyperlink that they can use to view and edit your document in their web browsers. You can send the link directly to someone, or post it somewhere like Facebook or Twitter.

Folks don't even need an iCloud account to view and edit your document—they just click the link and their default web browser launches automatically (if it isn't open already) and displays your document, as shown in Figure 9-8. When you're connected to the web, any changes people make to the iCloud version of your document are beamed into the version you're viewing on your Mac (and vice versa).

To share a document via iCloud, you first need to move it to iCloud. To do that, in Pages, go to File→Move To. Pages opens a familiar Save As dialog box. In the Save As field, give your document a name (if it doesn't already have one). Then open the dialog box's Where drop-down menu, select iCloud, and then click Move.

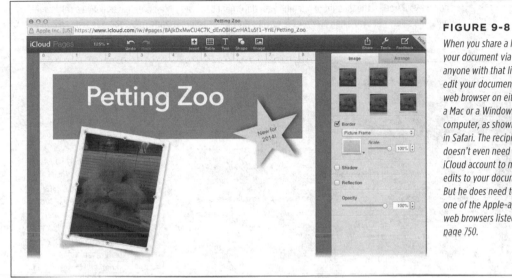

FIGURE 9-8

When you share a link to your document via iCloud, anyone with that link can edit your document in a web browser on either a Mac or a Windows computer, as shown here in Safari. The recipient doesn't even need an iCloud account to make edits to your document. But he does need to have one of the Apple-approved web browsers listed on page 750.

Once you've moved your document to iCloud, you're ready to share it. Click the Share button in Pages' toolbar and choose "Share Link via iCloud." At this point, you have several options:

- **Email.** Selecting this option launches the Mail program, with a new message that's already kitted out with the link that the recipient(s) need to access your document (see Figure 9-9).

- **Messages.** Messages is an instant-messaging app that comes with OS X and iOS. You can use this option to instant message any of your contacts the link to your document.

- **Twitter.** If you're a Twitter fan, you can post the link to your Twitter feed by selecting this option (you'll first need to connect Pages to your Twitter account by entering your Twitter username and password).

- **Facebook.** Select this option to post the link to your Facebook feed. You have some control over who can see the link (for example Friends, Family, Acquaintances, and so on, depending on how you've divided your Facebook contacts), but you can't private-message the link to just one Facebook friend.

- **Copy Link.** Choose this command to copy the link to your document to the Clipboard (page 36). You won't actually see the link onscreen, but you can then paste it anywhere you want.

NOTE Be careful who you share your documents with, and be aware that when you post a link to your document in a public place online (like Twitter or Facebook), you're practically inviting the whole world to come and edit your work. If the thought of opening your document to outside influences leaves you in a cold sweat, give yourself a safety net by making a *duplicate* of your document before sharing it, by going to (File→Duplicate).

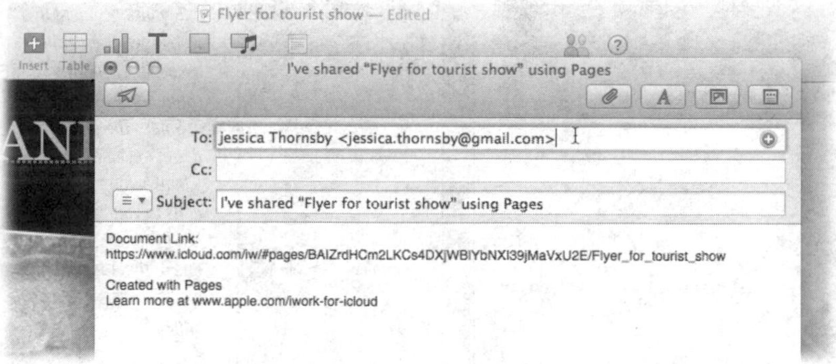

FIGURE 9-9

You can send a link to your document via email (as shown here), Facebook, Twitter, or Messages. When you select Email, Pages launches the Mail application and creates a new message like this one, which contains a subject line and a link to your document. Just enter the recipient's name and an optional message, and then click Send.

You can also send a *copy* of your document via email, Messages, or AirDrop by clicking the Share button in the toolbar, selecting "Send a Copy," and then picking one of these options:

- **Email** sends a copy via email. Selecting this option opens the "Send via Email" dialog box. Choose a format to share your document in by selecting one of the tabs, and then click Next. Pages launches the Mail program, complete with your document attached in your chosen format.

- **Messages** sends a copy of your document via Apple's instant-messaging program. Pick a format to send your document in, and then click Next to create a message with your document attached. Tell Pages who to send the file to, and then click Send.

- **AirDrop** lets you transfer files wirelessly to anyone nearby who's on the same WiFi network. Select this option to open the "Send via AirDrop" dialog box. Choose the format you want to send your document in, and then click Next to send it.

Once you've shared a document, you'll notice that the Share button in the toolbar gets a makeover: It turns from a square-and-arrow icon to a two-silhouette icon. You can now use this button to resend the link to your document or to stop sharing your document. To do either, click the Share button, select View Share Settings, and then choose one of these options:

- **Stop Sharing.** Click this button to make your document private once again. Pages helpfully informs you whether anyone else is currently editing the document, which is handy if you want to avoid rudely pulling the rug from under someone's feet.

- **Send Link.** Has your absentminded colleague misplaced the link you emailed them a whole 55 seconds ago? Resend it by clicking this button and then choosing from the familiar options: Email, Messages, Twitter, and Facebook.

- **Copy Link.** Want to share your document using a method *other* than email, Messages, Twitter, or Facebook? No problem. You can copy the link (and then paste it anywhere you want) by moving your cursor over the white box that contains said link and then clicking Copy Link when it appears (see Figure 9-10).

- **Add Password/Change Password.** Click this button to add a password or edit an existing one.

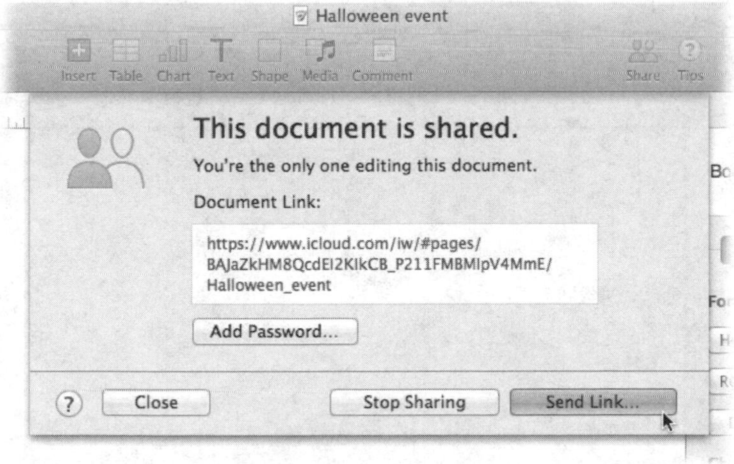

FIGURE 9-10

You can quickly copy the link to your document and paste it anywhere you want, by putting your cursor over the white section of this dialog box and then clicking the Copy Link button when it appears. After that, you can paste the link anywhere you like. You can also add a password to your document at this point. Even if a collaborator has your link, she'll still need to enter the password before she can access your document.

Creating Templates to Streamline Projects

Y ou've undoubtedly used—and come to appreciate—Pages' timesaving templates. They range from the simple, like Classic Letter, to the complex, like multipage newsletter layouts. But whether plain or intricate, they all share the same purpose: to get you started on a document quickly, with a large part of the formatting already in place so you can concentrate on the content instead of the layout. This chapter shows you how to make your *own* templates so you can add them to Pages' Template Chooser, the design roster you learned about way back on page 4.

◼ Template-Building Basics

Don't let templates fool you—they're really just plain old Pages documents. In fact, every custom template you create begins its life as a regular Pages file with text, pictures, tables, and anything else you want. After you get the file just the way you want it, choose File→"Save as Template," confirm that you want to "Add to Template Chooser," give the template a name, and then save the name either by clicking outside of the title-editing box or by pressing Return. From now on, when you open the Template Chooser, this template appears in the My Templates category (Figure 10-1).

When you create a new document based on this template (page 4), the fresh, untitled document looks exactly how your template document looked when you saved it; complete with text, pictures, and so on.

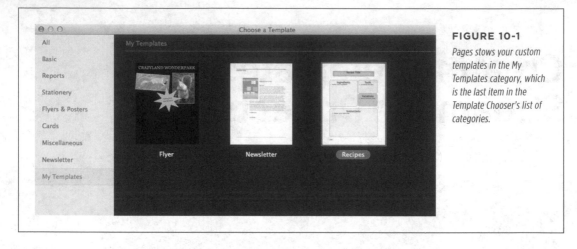

FIGURE 10-1

Pages stows your custom templates in the My Templates category, which is the last item in the Template Chooser's list of categories.

Most of Pages' built-in templates offer sophisticated designs stocked with sample content (and yours certainly can, too). But templates don't have to include any content at all. For example, you might not think of the templates in the Template Chooser's Basic category as "real" templates. While they don't include any content or layout elements, they *do* come loaded with text styles and a slew of settings that define the look of text and objects you add to documents based on them. In fact, creating blank templates like these is the best way to save your preferred settings for fonts, page margins, page numbering, headers and footers—you name it. Simply prep an empty file with all your favorite settings and styles, and then save it as a template. When you choose that template from the Template Chooser, you get a blank, untitled document with the text and object settings as you like them.

Creating and choosing these background settings for your template is very nearly as important as setting up its layout and placeholder text. Specifically, every template—in fact, every Pages document—contains an array of formatting attributes that instruct Pages how to display each and every element of your documents. When designing a template, you can choose to leave these attributes in their standard, or *default*, state or you can modify any or all of them to create your own defaults:

- **Placeholder text and graphics.** Sample text and pictures that can be replaced with a click of the mouse.

- **Document formatting.** The paper size and orientation (vertical or horizontal), page margins, footnote or endnote preferences, and page numbering settings.

- **Text styles.** The collection of paragraph styles in the Format panel's Text tab. (Setting the styles for the Free Form and Body paragraph styles determines your document's default text style.)

- **Headers and footers.** Text or graphics that appear at the top or bottom of all pages, including page numbers, if you like.

- **Background images.** Graphics, watermarks, and other master objects that appear on every page.

The following pages explain how to tweak all these attributes to get your templates looking just the way you want them.

TIP A template can be as many pages long as you need. For example, if you create a 12-page document and save it as a template, then creating a new document from the template starts you off with the same 12-page document. You can also create multiple sections for your template by choosing Insert→Sections and tweaking each section so it looks exactly how you want.

◼ Modifying an Existing Template

Just as you can use Pages' built-in templates as a starting point for your documents, you can also use them as a springboard for your own custom templates. Say that you're a fan of the Business Letter template's basic layout, but you want to update it with your company's logo, change the font, and add a few other tweaks (see Figure 10-2). To do that, you create a new document from the template, make your changes, and then save the updated version as a new template:

1. **Create a new document from the template you want to modify.**

   In this example, you'd choose File→New and choose the Business Letter template (it's in the Stationery category).

2. **If you like, add your logo by clicking the Media button in the toolbar and then choosing your company's logo.**

   You need to add the logo to iCloud, My Photo Stream, or iPhoto first; see page 138 for more info. Adjust your logo's size and placement on the page.

3. **Replace the Company Name and contact details placeholder text with your own information.**

   The Company Name and contact details are in separate text boxes. Click a text box twice to place your cursor inside it. Next, drag across the placeholder text to select it, and then type in your real information.

CRAZYLAND WONDERPARK

123-456-7890
jessica.thornsby@gmail.com

Crazyland Wonderpark
1234 Main Street
Anytown, State

I am sorry to hear that you <ENTER COMPLAIN HERE>, and although I am personally very distressed to hear you did not enjoy your recent visit, at this point I feel I must point out that many visitors enjoy <ENTER ATTRACTION NAME>. Please find below some positive feedback we have received regarding <ENTER ATTRACTION NAME>.

<FEEDBACK. Note: Please try and avoid using the feedback about the cat's birthday party. Although it's positive, I'm not entirely convinced it's sincere.>

<FEEDBACK. Note: Please try and avoid using the feedback about the cat's birthday party. Although it's positive, I'm not entirely convinced it's sincere.>

<FEEDBACK. Note: Please try and avoid using the feedback about the cat's birthday party. Although it's positive, I'm not entirely convinced it's sincere.>

Sincerely,

Jessica Thornsby.

FIGURE 10-2

You can use one of Pages' templates as a foundation to build your own—adding, removing, or changing any of its elements before saving it as a template. Starting with the Business Letter template (left), you can add your own logo, add a background image, change fonts, and more (right).

4. **Update any paragraph styles you want to change.**

   For example, in the Business Letter template, you could change the body text's paragraph style. To do so, place your cursor somewhere within the text you want to change, and then open the Format panel's Text tab so you have access to the Paragraph Styles pane (the white box at the top of the Text tab; if you don't see it, make sure the tab's Style button is selected). Make adjustments so the text looks the way you want (see page 80 for more about modifying styles). When you're done, save your updates by clicking the blue Update button in the Paragraph Styles pane. Repeat this process for any other styles in the template that you want to change.

5. **Lock down the static parts of the letterhead to keep them uniform across all your memos and to protect them from accidental changes.**

   In this example, you probably want to lock the logo, company name, and contact details. Select an object that you want to keep as is, and then choose Arrange→Lock. You can also select the object, open the Format panel's Arrange tab, and then click the Lock button.

6. **Add a background image, if you like.**

   If you want to add a bit more style to your letterhead, you can use your logo as a background image. Select the logo in your document (if you haven't added your logo yet, do so as described in step 2, and make sure it's a floating object as described on page 145), and then open the Format panel's Arrange tab. Open the Text Wrap drop-down menu and choose None so your text doesn't wrap around the image as you position it (see page 181 for more about text wrapping). Drag the logo's selection handles to increase its size and adjust its position (see Chapter 7 for details), and then turn down its opacity using the Style tab's Opacity slider. When you've got the image just right, choose Arrange→Section Masters→"Move Objects to Section Master." (Flip back to page 132 if you need a refresher on background objects.)

7. **Save your document as a new template.**

    Choose File→"Save as Template." Next, click the "Add to Template Chooser" button, give the new template a name, and then press the Return key or click anywhere outside the title editing box to save your template with its new title.

TIP If you choose File→"Save as Template" and decide that, whoops, you just wanted to save your document, not save it as a template, click the Save button in the "Create a custom Pages template?" dialog box to save your masterpiece as a plain old Pages document.

After you save the template, the letterhead document you've been working on remains open. So if you want to keep working on it, click the Cancel button to give the Template Chooser the old heave-ho, and then you're free to continue working on your document. You can save your document as a regular document at any time by going to File→Save. When you do that, you basically have two versions of the file: one that's a regular document and one that's a template available from the Template Chooser. You can make changes to the regular-document version just like any other Pages document. But, if you want to start a brand-new document that uses the template's formatting, simply create a new document based on the custom template you created.

Creating Templates from Scratch

If you're a real do-it-yourselfer, you can create templates from scratch by starting with the Blank template and building a sample document. Even though you're starting with a "blank" template, your new document still contains a complete set of standard settings for text and object styles, and document formatting. You can accept these factory settings or change some or all of them for your custom template.

Start by creating a new document based on one of the Blank templates in the Template Chooser's Basic category. This empty canvas will become the *model document* that you use to create your template. Choose File→Save right off the bat to save the file as a regular Pages document (don't choose "Save as Template" just yet), and give it a title. As you work on your document, Pages periodically saves your work, but why run the risk of losing your work if a power outage or a computer malfunction strikes between these auto-saves? Get into the habit of pressing ⌘-S to save your work every so often. (You'll save it as a template file only after you've finished creating the model document.)

After you've created and saved your new document, choose File→Page Setup and select the paper size and orientation you want. Now you're ready to choose the standard settings and create new styles for the document's various elements: text styles, text box styles, shape styles, table styles, image styles, and movie styles. You can add as few or as many of these elements as you like. The following sections explain the details.

Defining Text Styles

First, you need some text to style. If your document is currently text-free, add a blank text box (Insert→Text Box) and then place your cursor inside it; if your document already contains body text, click to place your cursor in it. Then open the Format panel's Text tab and, in the Paragraph Styles pane at the top of the tab, click the little triangle, select Body from the drop-down menu (if it's not already selected), and then type some text into the document so you have something to work with. You can then modify the text's appearance by adjusting the settings in the Format panel's Text tab (click the Style button to see your options). You can also open the Fonts window (page 42) by pressing ⌘-T.

Once your text looks the way you want it to, save your changes by clicking the blue Update button that has appeared next to the style's name in the Paragraph Styles pane (see Figure 10-3). Pages replaces the stock style with the one you just created.

Work your way down the list of paragraph styles in the Paragraph Styles pane's drop-down list, clicking a style's name, modifying its formatting, and then saving the results with the Update button. Create a new style by adding some dummy text and then updating it so that it's formatted the way you want. Then click the little triangle in the Paragraph Styles pane and click the + in the drop-down menu's top-right corner. This creates a new style with a boring placeholder name; type out your new title and then save it either by pressing the Return key or clicking anywhere outside the title-editing box.

Remove any unwanted styles by opening the Paragraph Styles drop-down menu, putting your cursor over the style's name, and then clicking the > that appears to the right of the style's name and choosing Delete Style.

This section was just a quick rundown of modifying styles. You can find all the details about creating and editing styles in Chapter 3, starting on page 75.

Setting Document Formatting

Set the standard document styles for files using your template by clicking Setup in Pages' toolbar, and then, in the Setup panel that appears, opening the Document tab. For example, use the Printer & Paper Size drop-down menus to change the page size, or choose a Page Orientation option (portrait or landscape). You can also set the document's margins and choose your header/footer preferences in this tab.

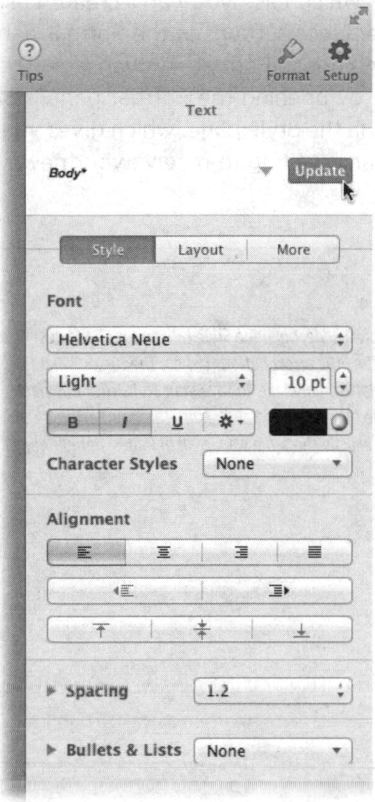

FIGURE 10-3

Update the text styles in the Blank template with your own preferences. Choose a style from the Paragraph Styles drop-down menu, update its formatting using the settings shown here, and then save your changes by clicking the blue Update button (where the cursor is here).

To set your preferences for handling page numbering, headers, and footers, switch to the Setup panel's Section tab. To use different headers or footers on the first page of your document than on other pages, for instance, turn on the "Hide on first page of section" option.

For complete details about document formatting, see Chapter 5.

Creating New Object Styles

Every type of object in Pages has a selection of styles that you can apply to give the object an instant makeover—just select the object, open the Format panel's Style tab, and then choose a style from the Styles pane at the top of the tab (the white box containing six thumbnails). However, as you learned in Chapter 7, you're not restricted to the six default styles that Pages provides for each object. If your color taste wanders toward eyeball-scorching yellow with a bile-green border, you can create this (dubious) style, and then save it for easy access later. When you save the document as a template, this new style comes along for the ride and appears in the Styles pane whenever you create a new document based on this template.

Exactly how you create a new style depends on the type of object you're dealing with (unless you're working with a table, in which case you can't create custom styles at all). Essentially, you'll insert an object, use settings in the Format panel's Style tab to adjust it to your liking, and then choose Format→Advanced→Create [Object] Style. You can also save your style by opening the Format panel's Style tab and then clicking the little arrow buttons in the Style pane, which gives you access to six blank thumbnails that are ready and waiting to receive your new style (as shown in Figure 10-4).

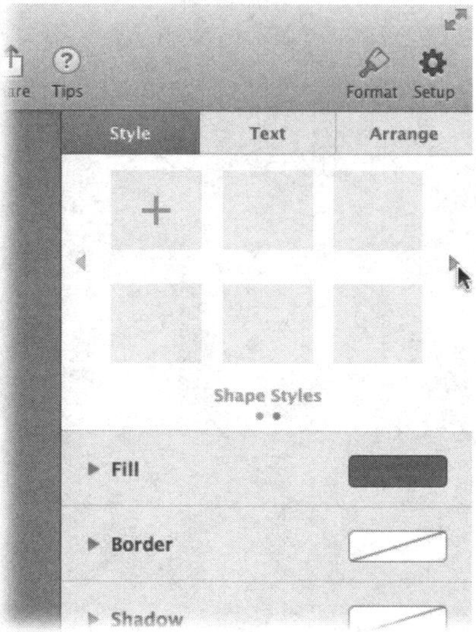

FIGURE 10-4

To create a new object style, open the Style tab, and in the Styles pane click one of the little arrow buttons (where the cursor is here) to get access to six blank thumbnails. To save your style, click the blank thumbnail with the big + plastered on it. From this point on, you can apply this style in exactly the same way as all of Pages' default object styles.

When you create object styles in a regular document, they apply to that document only. But when you save the document as a template, any new documents created from that template will include your new object style.

■ TEXT BOXES

Add a floating text box to your document (Insert→Text Box), and type some text into it. Then use the Format panel's text Tab and/or the Fonts window to set the font, style, color, alignment, column layout, paragraph spacing, and so on—or even better, simply select a paragraph style to use. (See page 39 for details on text formatting.)

When you're done editing and formatting the text, press ⌘-Return to select the text box at the object level. Then use the Format panel's Style tab to set all its object attributes: fill, border, shadow, reflection, and opacity. Use the Arrange tab to set the wrapping style (page 181). Don't bother adjusting the text box's size or rotation—Pages doesn't save these attributes when you create a new style.

When you're pleased with the appearance of the text and the text box, select the text box at the object level (if the insertion point is still inside the text, press ⌘-Return). Then choose Format→Advanced→Create Text Box Style. Pages stashes away all the adjustments you've made as a new style. Take your new style out for a spin by adding another text box, selecting the new style by opening the Format panel's Style tab, and then using the arrow buttons at the top of the tab to find your newly created, custom style. Click the style's thumbnail to apply it to the text box—the second text box should now match your model text box in all respects. Start typing and you see the text displayed in your style's chosen font. Now that you've created your text box style, you can delete these sample text boxes to get them out of the way, if necessary.

■ SHAPES

Since they can also contain text, shapes are very similar to text boxes. Insert a shape in the document and repeat the steps you used for formatting your text box's text and object attributes. When you're happy with the effect, choose Format→Advanced→Create Shape Style to add this new style to the Styles tab. Insert another shape to test it out, and then delete the shapes to get them out of your hair.

■ CONNECTION LINES

Add a connection line to your document by clicking the Shape button in the toolbar and choosing the curvy line in the drop-down menu's top-right corner. Use the Format panel's Style tab to choose its stroke style, weight, color, and endpoints—you can even add a shadow or reflection if you like.

NOTE Don't bother dragging the connection line's handles to adjust its curvature and length, because Pages doesn't save these changes as part of your style. In other words, applying a style to a connection line doesn't change its shape, angle, or size.

When you're done styling your connection line, choose Format→Advanced→Create Line Style.

■ CHARTS

Defining chart styles for your template is a bit different from other objects because there are 24 varieties of charts to choose from, including all the 3D and interactive charts. In theory, you can create custom styles for each type of chart—or at least the ones that you plan to use in your template. (You can find complete details on formatting charts starting on page 626.) Unfortunately, this feature works only partially as advertised. Here's how it's supposed to go: Insert a chart, adjust the chart's attributes (size, gridlines, tick marks, axis labels, text wrapping, and so on), and then choose Format→Advanced→Create Chart Style. Test your style by adding a new chart of the same type (a pie chart, for example), opening the Format panel's Style tab, and scrolling through the Styles pane to find the style you just created. Click the style to apply it to your chart—up to this point everything works fine.

However, if you add a different chart type to your document and then take a scroll through the available styles, something weird happens: The style you just created for the totally different chart type makes an appearance, but when you apply it to your current chart, it rarely works as expected (if at all). If you're lucky, some of the common elements like borders make it through to the new chart style, but sometimes even these elements can get lost in translation.

If you're planning to use a mix of chart types, it's best to decide the elements that all of your charts will have in common, such as a color scheme or a border effect, and then create a style that has all of those elements. You can then apply this style to all of your charts, regardless of type, and make tweaks as necessary.

■ IMAGES

Insert an image into your document by clicking the Media button in the toolbar or by going to Insert→Choose. After that, use the Format panel's Style tab to gussy up the image by adding a stroke, reflection, shadow, or picture frame, or adjust the image's opacity. Set the text-wrapping style in the Format panel's Arrange tab, too. (You can't set a standard image size or rotation, and any image masks are likewise ignored, so don't bother with those settings.) When you're done, choose Format→Advanced→Create Image Style. See page 191 for more about modifying object styles.

■ MOVIES

Insert a movie into your document, and then make any of the adjustments you'd apply to a picture (as with images, size and rotation are ignored). When you're ready to commit your movie style to Pages' memory, choose Format→Advanced→Create Movie Style.

■ CHANGING YOUR MIND

As you build your document, you may change your mind about some of the styles you've created. Pages helps you out here, letting you modify a style and then update all the objects that use that style, all in one smooth move.

To update a style, add an object and then apply the style that's due for an update. Make all the formatting changes you want to apply to the style, and then open the Format panel's Style tab. Scroll through the Styles pane until you find the style in question, Control-click its thumbnail, and then select "Redefine Style from Selection" from the shortcut menu. A window appears asking whether you want to do either of the following:

- **Update all objects that use the current style.** This applies your updates to all the objects in your document that use this style.

- **Don't update objects, and disconnect them from the style.** Updates the style with your changes, but rather than updating the objects that use this style, these objects retain their formatting and are no longer classed as part of this style.

Creating Placeholders

Now that you've created new styles for every possible element that you can add to a document (with the exception of tables), you're ready to format your model document with placeholder images and text. Approach your model document as if you were building a complete prototype of your final design—mock up the entire catalog, brochure, newsletter, letterhead, or whatever it is you're designing.

If you've already published a full newsletter, for example, you could use a previous edition as the basis of the model document for your newsletter template. Or you can build the model from scratch by placing sample text and graphics, adding layout and section breaks, columns, headers and footers—all the elements you might include in your final newsletter, formatted just the way you want them.

When you have all your design elements in place, you're ready to mark your sample text and graphics as *placeholders*, a special category of temporary content that's easy to replace when you use your custom template to create new documents.

■ REGULAR TEXT VS. PLACEHOLDER TEXT

You can add two different kinds of text elements to a template: regular, editable text and *placeholder text*. When you click some regular text, you can place your insertion point within it and add or delete characters—there's nothing unusual about it. When you click some placeholder text, however, Pages highlights the entire placeholder, which can be a word, a line, a paragraph, several paragraphs, or even the whole document. Then, when you type even one character, Pages replaces the whole placeholder with what you've typed.

Use regular text for content that you don't plan to change from document to document, or that you might need to modify only occasionally. This choice is good for the salutation on a letter, or a story that's repeated in your newsletter every month with small changes, such as, "Congratulations to Employee of the Month Jennifer Ball of the Beans from Around the World exhibit! She's now automatically entered in our Employee of the Year competition and could be the lucky winner of a gift basket full of beans!"

Use placeholder text when you just want to demonstrate how and where text should appear, but you don't actually want to use the example text in the final document. Placeholders are just that—disposable text that fills in for the real text that will be provided later. Because it's throwaway copy, you can use any text you want for a placeholder: Copy some random text from another document, from a web page, or use so-called "Greek" text like you find in Apple's templates (see "Lorem Ipsum Dolor?" on page 132 and the Tip below). If you're building a template that will be used by someone else, placeholder text is also a good place to add instructions about how to use the template, such as "Type Headline Here."

TIP There are plenty of sources of "Lorem ipsum" text on the Internet. A good one is *www.lorem2.com*, where you can copy the text from your web browser and then paste it into Pages. Or, if you prefer placeholder text that's a bit less stuffy, try *www.malevole.com/mv/misc/text* which generates text using the lyrics of TV theme songs from the 1970s.

Placeholders begin life as regular text. So to add some placeholder text, simply type or paste your text in just like you would with any other kind of text. Then, to convert it to placeholder text, choose View→Show Invisibles, and then select the text you want to turn into a placeholder—but if there's a paragraph break at the end of it (¶), make sure you *don't* select it (see Figure 10-5). Then choose Format→Advanced→"Define as Placeholder Text."

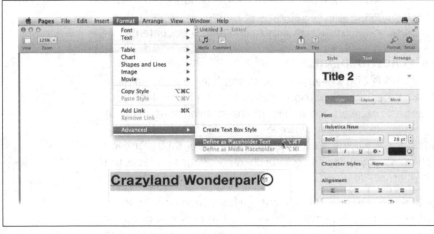

FIGURE 10-5

After creating your model document, you can change blocks of text into placeholder text for your template. Choose View→Show Invisibles, and select all the text you want to convert except the final paragraph break (circled). Then choose Format →Advanced→ "Define as Placeholder Text."

NOTE If you *do* select that final paragraph break, when you try to replace the placeholder text, your words take on the format of the *following* paragraph instead of the placeholder paragraph. (This is typically an issue only when you're adding a placeholder into an area of text where there's more than one paragraph.)

Once you've turned text into a placeholder, clicking anywhere within it selects the whole block, ready to be replaced with "real" text. This means, though, that you can't edit the placeholder text—any change you make will replace the whole thing. So if you need to modify placeholder text—perhaps you want to update the template instructions you've included in it—you first have to select the placeholder text and choose Format→Advanced→"Define as Placeholder Text" once more, which turns the selected placeholder text back into regular *editable* text. Make your changes, and then select the text and choose Format→Advanced→"Define as Placeholder Text" once again.

■ PLACEHOLDERS FOR PICTURES, MOVIES, AND SOUND

Pages can create placeholders for your graphics, too. Use *media placeholders* for any pictures, movies, or audio you'll want to replace when you create a new document:

a video interview with the employee of the year (and her new luxury, bean-tastic gift basket), and so on. You don't have to make *every* graphic a placeholder, though. Leave regular pictures in your document when you always want to use them in the finished product—background images, logos, or your author portrait, for example.

To turn any media object into a placeholder, select it and then choose Format→ Advanced→"Define as Media Placeholder." Now, when you drop a picture onto the placeholder, it replaces the placeholder graphic and inherits its picture frame, masking, size, rotation, shadow, reflection—all the formatting you applied to it (see Figure 10-6). Likewise, when you drop a movie or sound onto the placeholder, it replaces the placeholder and fits snugly into your layout with all the placeholder's original settings.

FIGURE 10-6

Once you've defined a photo as a media place-holder, the familiar gray icon appears in its bottom-right corner. Click this button to launch the Media Browser, and then choose an image to replace it with. You can also drag a photo from your desktop or a Finder window onto the placeholder (as shown here); when you drop the photo, Pages replaces the placeholder with your new image.

You can reposition, resize, rotate, and adjust any of a media placeholder's attributes. To remove the placeholder, select it and then press Delete. Turn a media placeholder back into a regular object using the same command: Choose Format→ Advanced→"Define as Media Placeholder" to remove the checkmark from this setting and return the object to regular duty.

Deleting Templates

If your innocent penchant for creating custom templates turns into a raging addiction, you'll need to start deleting the templates you no longer need. To delete any of your custom templates, open the Template Chooser by choosing File→New, select the My Templates category, and then Control-click the template you want to remove. Select Delete, and Pages asks you whether you really, truly want to obliterate that poor, defenseless template. To remove the template forever, click Delete, or give it a reprieve by clicking Cancel.

NOTE You can't delete any of the templates that Pages provides out of the box—you can only delete templates in the My Templates category.

You can also rename templates (handy if you created your templates in a rush, and now keep getting the Untitled 1 template mixed up with Untitled 2). To rename a template, in the Template Chooser's My Templates category, Control-click the template, and then select Rename. Enter your new title, and then save it by pressing Return or clicking anywhere outside the title-editing field.

■ Sharing, Exchanging, and Buying Templates

You can't share templates directly, but a simple workaround is to create a new document based on the template you want to share and then sharing that document via iCloud, email, Facebook, or any of the methods described on pages 258–261. Once your buddy has the document safely downloaded onto his Mac, he can open the document and then go to File→"Save as Template" and, hey, presto, the template appears in his Template Chooser.

Templates Online

If you've created a fabulous template, consider sharing it with the world by submitting it to *www.iworkcommunity.com*. This website offers an ever-expanding collection of templates created by Pages aficionados around the world—all free for the downloading.

If you don't mind spending a little coin, you can also buy templates. Bundles of professionally designed Pages templates are available for sale online from commercial design outfits including *www.jumsoft.com* and *www.stocklayouts.com*. Once you've downloaded a template, unzip it if necessary (by finding the file in your Downloads folder and double-clicking it). You can then open the newly unzipped file or folder, and Pages will pop up and ask whether you want to add this template to the Template Chooser.

Keynote for Mac

Creating a Keynote Slideshow

Right from their invention, slideshows have been a mixed blessing. Old-timers will recall painfully long evenings enduring carrousels of family vacation slides inflicted upon unwitting guests by an enthusiastic host. As a kid, you might've been subjected to educational filmstrips about igneous rock or isosceles triangles. Slide projectors, filmstrips, overhead transparencies—ever since we figured out how to project images, we've used these projections to try to connect with audiences, with uneven results. Since the mid-1990s, those technologies have given way to the computer slideshow, which all too often drowns audiences in bullet points and clunky clip art.

But it doesn't have to be that way. On the contrary, well-designed slideshows can bring a presentation to life, helping a speaker engage and educate her audience with stimulating visuals. Keynote can help you do just that.

Keynote is a *presentation program* for making slideshows, usually to accompany a talk or other live presentation. In fact, the program was originally designed specifically for Apple founder Steve Jobs, a design stickler who was well known for his entertaining and effective presentations. Like its Microsoft counterpart PowerPoint, Keynote lets you build screens of text and graphics to illustrate important points. But Keynote does Microsoft one better with an emphasis on polished visuals and a light, streamlined interface that never gets in your way. With its cinematic transitions and stunning effects, Keynote makes your slides sparkle (literally, if you like).

Keynote lets you create everything from simple slides that contain words on a plain background or a single picture, for example, to carefully designed slides containing photographs, animation, and even movies and sound. Whether you opt for simple or fancy, the basic process is the same: Pick a *theme*, a predesigned template that gives your slideshow a cohesive style or look; create the individual slides; and then arrange them in the proper order.

This chapter takes you through the basics of these steps, giving you an overview of all of Keynote's main features before diving into them in more detail in the following chapters.

> **TIP** If you've got pre-presentation jitters, go to this book's Missing CD page at *www.missingmanuals.com/ cds* and download *Great_presentations.pdf*, which contains lots of advice on preparing and delivering the perfect presentation.

◼ Themes = Templates

If you've made your way through the Pages section of this book or peeked ahead at Numbers, you already know that those programs come with a whole arsenal of killer design templates that you can adopt or adapt for your own documents. Keynote does the same but, in a gotta-be-me moment, refers to its templates as *themes*. Don't let the vocabulary shift throw you; whatever you choose to call them, themes work exactly the same way as templates in Pages and Numbers.

The very first time you launch Keynote, you're presented with the friendly "Welcome to Keynote" window. When you click Continue, the "New in Keynote" screen gives you a rundown of some of the program's new features. You have two options for how to continue: "View My Presentations" or "Create a Presentation." Since you probably haven't created any presentations yet, you'll probably want to click the "Create a Presentation" button, which opens the Theme Chooser window (described in a sec). If you do have existing presentations (ones you created in iWork '09, say), feel free to click "View My Presentations" to do just that.

Every *other* time you launch Keynote, the Open dialog box greets you. This handy dialog box lets you open both Keynote documents *and* PowerPoint documents, which are compatible with Keynote.

> **NOTE** If you've created an iCloud account and connected it to your Mac as described on page 752, then your Open dialog box is split into two tabs: iCloud and On My Mac (they're in the dialog box's upper-left corner). iCloud contains any Keynote presentations you've saved (or moved) to your iCloud account. You can launch any document stored in iCloud by selecting it in this window and then either clicking Open or double-clicking the file itself. Once you open your presentation, you can edit it exactly the same as any presentation stored on your Mac—the only difference is that all your edits are saved online as part of your iCloud account, rather than locally on your computer. Select the On My Mac tab to explore and open files stored on your computer.

To create a new presentation, click the New Document button. This launches the Theme Chooser window, complete with Keynote's 30 built-in themes (Figure 11-1). Just like the Template Chooser in the other iWork programs, this window shows miniature previews of the available slide designs.

FIGURE 11-1

The look and feel of your presentation depends on which theme you choose. Keynote comes with 30 Apple-designed themes, and you can also create your own or purchase themes from third-party designers. When you spot a theme you want to use, click it and then click Choose, or simply double-click the theme's thumbnail.

TIP If at any point you want to open a slideshow you created earlier, go to File→Open and choose the file from the Open dialog box. If you opened the file recently, you can also go to File→Open Recent and select it from this submenu.

Unlike templates in Pages and Numbers, Keynote's themes aren't divided into categories. The Theme Chooser displays them all in one big bucket.

TIP As you'll learn in more detail on page 284, you can choose different sizes for your slides. However, if you know in advance that you want 16:9, widescreen-size slides, you can create your presentation so that 16:9 is the default—just click the Wide button at the top of the Theme Chooser before picking your theme. If you're not sure what size you need, just leave the Standard button selected (you can change the slide size after you've created your presentation).

When you find the theme you want, double-click it, or click it once and then press Return or click Choose. Whichever method you use, a new, untitled document window zooms out from the Theme Chooser, and you're on your way.

TIP If you find yourself using that same theme all the time, you can tell Keynote to use it *automatically* for new documents instead of pestering you with the Theme Chooser every time. Choose Keynote→Preferences, and then click the General button. In the For New Documents section, click the "Use theme" radio button, click Change Theme, and then make your selection in the Theme Chooser.

■ Your First Keynote Slideshow

As word of Crazyland Wonderpark's Beans from Around the World attraction spreads, you're invited to "How've You Bean?" the world's leading summit on all things beany. The plan is to give an introductory talk on some criminally overlooked and undervalued species of bean and how more can be done to draw attention to these unsung heroes of the bean world. To build your slideshow, you turn to Keynote.

For this project, open the Theme Chooser by going to File→New or pressing ⌘-N, and then choose the Gradient theme—a simple theme for a look as bold, dramatic, and practical as a haricot bean (canned or dried, they're both show-stoppers!). A new document window appears, filled with the title slide for your presentation (Figure 11-2). You're now ready to explore your workspace and start designing your slides.

> **TIP** Although you haven't done a thing yet, it's a great idea to save the project right at the start. Choose File→Save (or ⌘-S), name your presentation, select a destination folder, and then click Save. From then on, periodically press ⌘-S as you work to save your changes on your hard drive or in iCloud, protecting you from power outages, software glitches, and the like. Keynote helps you out by auto-saving your document from time to time, but this should be used as a worst-case-scenario safety net: Get into the habit of regularly saving your document.

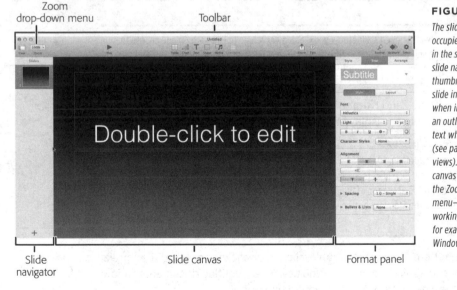

FIGURE 11-2

The slide you're editing occupies center stage in the slide canvas. The slide navigator displays thumbnail images of each slide in the presentation when in Navigator view, or an outline of your slides' text when in Outline view (see page 296 for more on views). Adjust the slide canvas' display size using the Zoom drop-down menu—when you're working on a small screen, for example, choose "Fit in Window."

TIP To adjust the size of the slide navigator, put your cursor over the border where navigator meets slide canvas (where the cursor is positioned in Figure 11-2); when the cursor turns into a double-headed arrow, drag to make the slide navigator wider or narrower, and the thumbnails resize accordingly. (If the slide navigator is already as thin as it's going to get, your pointer turns into a line with a *single* arrow—if you continue to drag, the slide navigator disappears completely.)

One of the things that makes using iWork so comfortable is that all its programs share a similar look and feel. The strong family resemblance between Keynote and its siblings starts with the controls in the document window. If you're familiar with Pages from the preceding chapters, you'll feel right at home with your old friends the toolbar, and the Format panel's familiar collection of tabs.

At the top of the window, Keynote's toolbar displays its standard collection of buttons, which provide quick access to frequently used commands. You'll learn more about each of these buttons in the coming chapters, but here's a quick tour:

- **View** offers options for changing the document window display.

- **Zoom** lets you change how closely you're zoomed in on the current slide.

- **Play** plays a full-screen slideshow starting with the current slide.

- The various object buttons—**Table**, **Chart**, **Text**, **Shape**, **Media**, and **Comment**—insert that type of object into your document.

- **Share** lets you share your presentation via iCloud or send a copy via channels such as email, Facebook, and AirDrop (page 408 has more on sharing your iWork documents).

- Click the **Tips** button to get info on how to use Keynote. Tips appear as little yellow notes scattered around your screen. Click the Tips button again to send them packing.

- **Format** opens and closes that all-important Format panel.

- Click **Animate** to add Transition effects to your presentation (see page 351).

- The **Setup** button replaces the Format panel with the Setup panel, which contains two tabs: Presentation and Audio.

TIP You can hide and reveal the toolbar by choosing View→Hide Toolbar (or →Show Toolbar), although in most cases you'll want to keep the toolbar onscreen.

The Format panel runs down the right-hand side of your screen. As in the other iWork programs, the contents of Keynote's Format panel morph depending on what you select in the current slide: Click a chart, for example, and you get access to the Chart tab, which is full of settings for editing your chart; select an image, and the Format panel gains an Image tab. This transforming panel stays on the move, adapting to your needs as you progress through the design process. If you prefer to give up this convenience in favor of a few pixels of additional real estate, you can tuck the

Format panel away by clicking the Format button in the toolbar, and get it back by clicking this button a second time.

Slide Size and Slide View

Before diving into your slides, you should decide just how much slide you want. The *slide size* setting determines the number of pixels in each screen of your presentation. You can choose the size by clicking the Setup button in the toolbar, and then, in the Setup panel that appears, opening the Presentation tab. There, open the Slide Size drop-down menu and choose a size (as shown in Figure 11-3).

FIGURE 11-3

Choose a size for your slides by going to the Setup panel's Presentation tab and opening the Slide Size drop-down menu (where the cursor is here). You can choose from Standard, Widescreen, or Custom Slide Size to open the "Set a custom slide size..." window (as shown here).

Keynote's Slide Size drop-down menus offers two default slide sizes: Standard (4:3), Widescreen (16:9), and Custom Slide Size. If you choose the final option, Keynote opens the "Set a custom slide size" dialog box shown in Figure 11-3 so you can type an exact size.

What size should you choose? That depends on the projector you'll use to give your presentations. Ideally, your slide size should match the resolution of the projector that you'll use. So try to track down the projector and find out its resolution.

When entering a custom slide size, don't enter a giant size in the hope of fitting more stuff onscreen. While that's technically what will happen, keep in mind that the screen itself doesn't change dimensions; increasing the slide size only packs more pixels into the same space. So as you add more pixels, everything in the slide gets smaller on your projected screen, making it that much more difficult for your audience to see. Using a very large slide size *does* increase the sharpness of the image on projectors that can handle it—just be sure to increase the size of your text and images to maintain the same proportion in your slides.

Whatever slide size you choose, it's a good idea to adjust the *slide view* of your Keynote window so that you can see an entire slide at once. Keynote opens new slideshows at full size: 100 percent. Trouble is, depending on your slide size, this may be more slide than you can fit into your window, particularly on smaller laptops. Save yourself some scrolling hassle by adjusting the Zoom drop-down menu (Figure 11-2) so that you can see the slide's edges. You can also choose "Fit in Window" so that the current slide always fills up the window. (These options are also available from the View→Zoom submenu.)

Adding Text

When you open a new slideshow, Keynote gets you started by displaying the *title slide* for your selected theme (officially, it's called the Title & Subtitle slide). The exact layout varies from theme to theme, but the title slide typically consists of a title, subtitle, and some simple decoration. You're not obliged to use this layout—you can rearrange it, add new elements, or choose an entirely new slide design from the theme's collection of master slides (more on all that in a bit). For now, go with what Keynote gives you, which is shown in Figure 11-2.

Most new slides, including title slides, have *placeholders* that show where to add your text, pictures, or other objects to the layout. The placeholders for text aren't shy about telling you what to do: "Double-click to edit," they command. It really is that simple: Double-click the large title text, and then type your title. Next, double-click the placeholder text below, and then type your subtitle. Presto! You've already finished your first slide: "Beans: Being All They Can Bean?"

You can format text just like you do in Pages, using the Format panel's Text tab (or the Fonts window). For more on working with Keynote's text boxes, see page 321. Don't worry about these finer formatting points just yet, though. You can make all those changes later. The easiest way to get started with a slideshow is to get the first pass of all your text into the document—enter it all at once and then organize it. You can worry about designing your slides *after* you have all your ideas lined up.

You've already got the first slide in place, so keep on going with the rest. Click the + button in the bottom-left corner of the Keynote window, and the "Add a slide" menu shown in Figure 11-4 opens so you can choose the style of your new slide. Don't worry about this too much for now—just click the first thumbnail in the menu to create a second slide that looks exactly like your first.

When you add a new slide, Keynote also adds its thumbnail to the *slide navigator*, the left pane of your slideshow window. This gives you an easy way to navigate your slides—just click a slide's thumbnail to work on it in the slide canvas. For more on the slide navigator, see page 298.

At this point, you *could* continue typing the rest of your text, clicking the + button to add a new slide for each topic or idea in your talk, but let's be honest: Visually, that's a bit dull—no one wants a text-only presentation! Time to spice things up a bit.

Changing the Slide Layout with Master Slides

Every theme comes with a collection of slide layouts called *master slides*. These prefab designs consist of some combination of title, body text, and picture. The title slide that appears whenever you create a new presentation is actually one of many master slides. You can switch up a slide's design anytime by choosing a new master slide from the "Add a slide" menu.

Try it now by adding a third slide to your presentation: Click the + button in the Keynote window's bottom-left corner, and then choose a new master slide, as shown in Figure 11-4. This time, pick a master slide that contains both text *and* a picture.

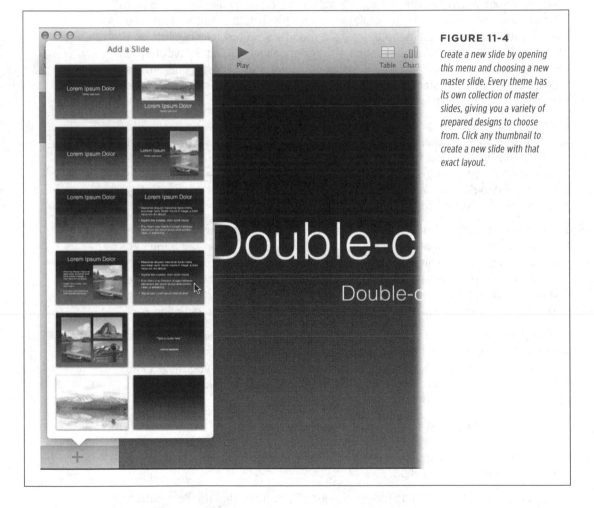

FIGURE 11-4

Create a new slide by opening this menu and choosing a new master slide. Every theme has its own collection of master slides, giving you a variety of prepared designs to choose from. Click any thumbnail to create a new slide with that exact layout.

Adding an Image

The image in the new master slide makes things prettier, sure, but that landscape image doesn't exactly relate to the topic at hand. It's not supposed to, though—it's just a *media placeholder* waiting for you to drop in your own picture. You add pictures to Keynote just like you do in Pages and Numbers: via the Media Browser. Click the icon button in the bottom-right corner of any media placeholder to launch the Media Browser. Next, click the Photos tab to browse available photos, and then click any photo to replace the media placeholder, as shown in Figure 11-5. If you prefer, you can also add images by dragging them from your desktop or a Finder window and dropping them onto your media placeholder.

FIGURE 11-5

Replace a media placeholder by dragging a picture from your desktop and dropping it onto the placeholder picture, as shown here. When you do that, Keynote automatically resizes and crops the picture to fit the placeholder's dimensions.

You can also replace a media placeholder by clicking the icon in the placeholder's bottom-right corner, which launches the familiar Media Browser.

Just like Pages' placeholders, Keynote automatically sizes the picture to fit the placeholder's dimensions, cropping some of the photo, if necessary. When you drag a horizontal picture onto a vertical placeholder, for example, Keynote lops off its sides to keep the vertical layout. If that's not quite what you had in mind, you can change the way the image is cropped by editing its image mask. See page 158 for details.

In fact, you can change just about anything you want about your picture—and the surrounding text, too. Move it, resize it, rotate it, whatever. You're not locked into any of the prefab layouts of your theme's master slides. That's because...

Slide Design Works Just Like Page Layout

Designing and editing slides in Keynote is nearly identical to creating a page-layout document in Pages. You add and arrange the same set of *objects*—text boxes, pictures, shapes, tables, charts, movies and sounds—on the slide canvas just as you would compose them in a Pages document. Click an object to select it; drag it to a new location on the slide; resize it by dragging one of the selection handles along its border; and use the Format panel's Style tab to add effects, borders, picture frames, and color fills. Chapter 12 gives all the details about how to work with objects in Keynote, but if you're a Pages aficionado, you already have the know-how to understand exactly how it works.

For example, say you want to add a new title slide that includes some images. Since your talk is all about putting some underappreciated beans firmly in the spotlight, a shot of some colorful jelly beans might get your audience in the right mood to think out of the box.

First, click the + button and choose a new master slide. Any slide with a media place-holder and a title will do, so click the thumbnail of a suitable slide. Keynote provides a placeholder image and title just as before. Double-click the placeholder title and type your own: "Meant to Bean, or a Has-Bean? Introducing Some Commonly-Overlooked Beans." When you do that, something strange happens: Once the title box is full of text, your text automatically shrinks so it can all fit. Continue typing, and your text gets smaller and smaller.

Why? Turns out Keynote handles placeholder title boxes and body text boxes a bit differently.

■ WORKING WITH TITLE BOXES

Many master slides contain *title boxes*, text boxes that are given special treatment in Keynote.

Click a title box once to uncover eight selection handles around its edges, and then resize it by dragging these handles. If you make a title box *smaller*, Keynote auto-matically shrinks the text inside it and does its best to keep all your words visible. Keynote admits defeat only when it becomes impossible to display all the text—only then do you see the *clipping indicator,* a white + sign at the bottom of the text box that indicates that there's more text than Keynote can display.

> **NOTE** Selection handles are a good way to identify title boxes and body text boxes (another special form of text box, covered on page 322): They both have eight selection handles, whereas all *other* text boxes in Keynote have only two selection handles.

If you instead make a title box *larger,* the text inside it expands to fill the extra space. But if you increase the text's font size using the Format panel's Text tab, this has no impact on the size of the title box: As you increase the font size, the text expands until it completely fills the box, and then it stops growing.

Keynote's special treatment of title boxes is due to *auto-shrink,* a feature that reduces a title box's font size just enough to squeeze in all its text (see Figure 11-6).

You can delete a title box in a couple of different ways. The easiest is to select it and then press the Delete key. Or make sure that you don't have any objects selected (press the Esc key or click a blank area of your slide), and then turn off the Title checkbox in the Slide Layout tab (the Slide Layout tab is covered in more detail later on—see page 322). If you choose a master slide that doesn't include a title box, you can add one by opening the Slide Layout tab and then turning on the Title checkbox.

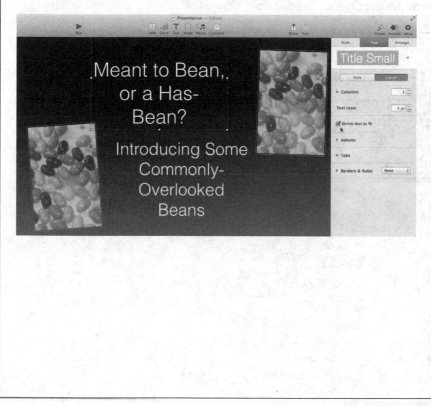

FIGURE 11-6

When entering text in a slide's title box, Keynote's auto-shrink feature makes your text smaller so that it fits within the box. Auto-shrink applies only to title boxes, and all title boxes arrive with this feature turned on. To turn auto-shrink off for a particular title box, select the box, and then open the Format panel's Text tab, click the Layout button, and then turn off the "Shrink text to fit" checkbox. That way, the text remains the same size no matter how much you type, meaning that some of your text will be clipped (hidden) when it gets too long for the title box to handle. If auto-shrink is turned on, the text shrinks so that everything you type remains visible.

■ WORKING WITH TEXT BOXES

The rules are completely different for "standard" text boxes. Click any text box that *isn't* a title box or a body text box (see page 321 for more details) to uncover a measly two selection handles. (If you see eight selection handles, you've got a title box or body text box instead.) These handles let you adjust only the width of the text box, not its height. As you add text, Keynote handles the vertical resizing, and the text box grows and shrinks vertically to accommodate your text. Unlike with title and body text boxes, Keynote doesn't automatically change the text's font size as you resize the box, although the box *will* grow or shrink as you change the text's font size (see page 39 for info on formatting text).

■ ADDING IMAGES

As you learned on page 8, it's easy to replace a media placeholder with your own image, either by clicking the icon in the placeholder's bottom-right corner and then using the Media Browser or by dragging an image from a Finder window or the desktop and dropping it onto the placeholder. If you like, you can tip the photo askew to give it a more casual feel: ⌘-drag one of the picture's selection handles to rotate the picture. Then make it look more like a scrapbook photo by adding a picture frame: Click the picture once to select it, and then choose a frame from the Format panel's Style tab, as shown in Figure 11-7.

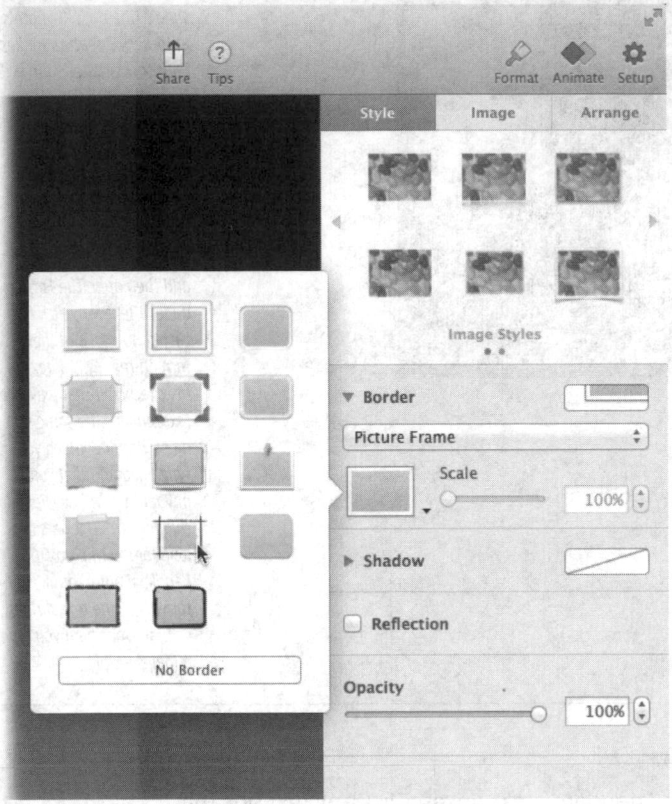

FIGURE 11-7

Keynote makes it easy to add a picture frame to a photo, text box, shape, or movie. Click the object once to reveal its selection handles, and then open the Format panel's Style tab. Click the Border heading to expand that section, open the drop-down menu, and then select Picture Frame. You can then click the Border section's thumbnail to open the menu shown here, where you can choose a frame style. (See page 166 for more info about creating border effects.)

Add a second image by clicking the Media button in the toolbar and making your selection from the Media Browser, or by dragging an image from a Finder window or the desktop and dropping it onto a blank portion of the slide. Either way, Keynote adds your picture as a new image object. You can then resize it by dragging its selection handles. Rotate the image and add a picture frame just like the first picture. Drag the two pictures on the slide to arrange them into just the right composition, and you've got a sweet little vignette of beany goodness for your title slide, as shown back in Figure 11-6. Figure 11-8 explains how to change the layering order of objects.

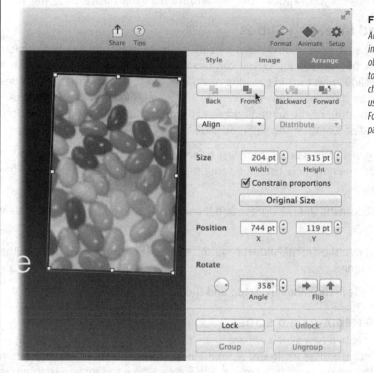

FIGURE 11-8

Arrange objects on a slide by dragging them into position. Because Keynote puts each object on its own layer, the objects stack on top of each other like a scrapbook. You can change the stacking order of these layers using the buttons at the top of Arrange tab. For more on organizing object layers, see page 187.

■ ADDING OTHER OBJECTS

Of course, you're not limited to adding images to slides. You can use the toolbar buttons to add iWork's whole range of objects:

- **Table.** Click this button to insert—you guessed it—a table (see page 205).

- **Chart.** Bring numbers to life with a colorful graph (see page 233).

- **Text.** Add more text boxes to your slides by clicking this button (see page 323).

- **Shapes.** Click this button and then choose a shape—or draw your own (see page 168 for more info).

- **Media.** You can grab audio and video clips from the Media Browser, too, or drag them into your document. See page 336 for more about audio and page 339 for video.

■ GOING BACK TO THE MASTER SLIDE LAYOUT

If you've made some changes to your slides that you now regret—what were you thinking with that fuchsia/chartreuse color scheme?—you can always revert to the original master layout. Control-click an empty part of the slide canvas so that no objects are selected, and then choose "Reapply Master to Slide" from the shortcut menu that appears. Your slide elements snap back to their original positions and formatting. (Any objects you've added that weren't in the original master slide stay put.)

Adding and Inserting Slides

You've already seen how to add slides by clicking the + button at the bottom left of your screen, but did you know you can use this button to insert slides into the middle of the slideshow, too? In the slide navigator, select the slide that comes immediately *before* the spot where you want to add a new slide, and then click the + button at the bottom of the screen and select a master slide thumbnail. Keynote adds the new slide just after the selected slide.

Keynote also gives you several other ways to add new slides. When you use any of these methods, the new slide uses the same theme and master slide layout as the selected slide:

- Select a slide in the slide navigator, and then press Return or choose Slide→New Slide.

- Control-click a slide in the slide navigator, and then choose New Slide from the shortcut menu.

- Select a slide in the slide navigator, and then press Shift-⌘-N.

■ CREATING MEDIA-BASED SLIDES

You can also create a new slide containing an image, movie, or sound file by dragging the file into the slide navigator from a Finder window or the desktop. When you do that, the cursor sprouts a green circle with a + on it to indicate that you're going to add a new slide. When you drop the file, Keynote creates a new slide containing only the picture, video, or audio you dropped—as usual, the new slide uses the same theme and master layout as the preceding slide. This works when you drag *multiple* media objects, too, giving you a quick and easy way to build a complete photo slideshow in one fell swoop. For example, select multiple pictures on your desktop by dragging across them or by ⌘-clicking each picture, and then drag them into the slide navigator—and just like that Keynote gives you a slew of new slides, one for each picture.

■ A BLANK SLATE

Sometimes you want to start with an empty slide—no text boxes, pictures, nothing—so that you can build your own slide design completely from scratch. For example, maybe you want to build a slide with only a table or a chart and you want a clean canvas to start from. One way to go is to create a new slide and delete all its elements by choosing Edit→Select All (⌘-A) and then pressing Delete. But a less destructive approach is to choose a blank master slide layout for your new slide. All of Apple's built-in themes have one—just open the + drop-down menu in the bottom-left corner of the Keynote window, click the empty thumbnail, and Keynote gives you a master slide devoid of any text or pictures.

Adding Transitions

Most of your Keynote work focuses on creating a presentation with amazing content. But Keynote also makes it easy to control what happens *between* your slides. Just like you aim for clever transitions between ideas and topics in your talk, Keynote lets you make correspondingly crafty visual transitions. Bold or subtle, ridiculous or sublime, Keynote gives you a range of cinematic effects to shift from one slide to another.

You add transitions by clicking the Animate button in the toolbar to open the Transitions tab on the right side of your screen (Figure 11-9). Click the big blue "Add an Effect" button to open a drop-down menu that includes all of Keynote's transition styles. Keynote applies whatever transition you select *after* the currently selected slide—when you play your slideshow, your new special effect moves that slide out of the way and introduces the next one. When you select an effect, Keynote shows you a preview of how the transition will look when you play the slideshow. Click the new Preview button that appears in the Transitions tab to play the transition again. Figure 11-9 explains how to use the other settings that appear.

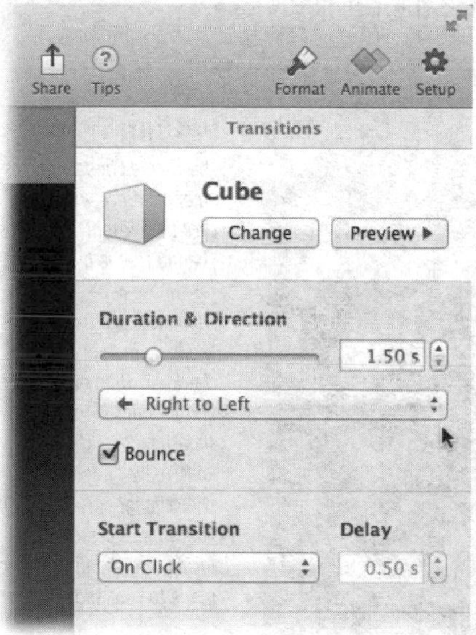

FIGURE 11-9

The Transitions tab lets you add a visual transition from the selected slide to the next one. Click the "Add an Effect" button (not shown) and choose an effect from the drop-down menu, and Keynote shows a preview of the transition (here, the Cube effect creates an illusion that your slides are mounted on a spinning cube).

You can adjust the length of the transition using the slider below the Duration & Direction heading or the text box to its right. Change the direction of your transition using the Duration & Direction section's drop-down menu (where the cursor is here), and then choose when the transition triggers using the Start Transition drop-down menu.

NOTE You'll learn how to play the slideshow in just a couple of pages (and then in lots more detail in Chapter 14). Champing at the bit to play the slideshow right now? Just click the Play button on the toolbar!

Keynote offers lots of different transitions, from old-school movie tricks like wipes, dissolves, and fades to newer stunts like 3D effects and fancy acrobatics that make objects fly and shimmer across the screen. Browse through the Effects drop-down menu to find the transition that suits the content and tone of this part of your talk (once you've added an effect, you can change it at any time by clicking the Change button in the Transitions tab). Find out more about these effects and other animations by flipping to Chapter 13.

Changing the Theme

You chose a theme when you first created your presentation, but don't sweat the choice too much—Keynote doesn't hold you to your decision. You can select a new theme for all the slides within your presentation anytime you like. This is handy when you discover midway through the project that the theme you chose clashes with the images you want to include.

To change the theme for all slides in your presentation, click the Setup button in the toolbar, open the Presentation tab, and then click the Change Theme button (or choose File→Change Theme). Keynote unfurls a slightly modified version of the Theme Chooser (see Figure 11-10). If you've made some formatting changes to your slide that you want to keep, leave the "Keep your style changes" checkbox turned on. (Turn this setting off to start from scratch and completely reset the look of your slides to the new theme.) Either double-click a new theme's thumbnail to switch to that theme, or click the thumbnail once and then click Choose.

FIGURE 11-10

The Theme Chooser makes an appearance when you click the Presentation tab's Change Theme button (or choose File→Change Theme). If you turn off the "Keep your style changes" checkbox, then everything on the slides in your slideshow gets the new look. Leave "Keep your style changes" turned on if you want to preserve any formatting changes you've made to your slides.

NOTE Each presentation can have only one theme. Although you can customize every part of a slide, you can't mix and match multiple themes within a single presentation (although it is possible to sneak around this restriction by copying and pasting a slide with a different theme into your document; page 417 has the details of this cheat).

Using the Presenter Notes Pane

As you work through your presentation, you'll almost certainly develop detailed ideas for your talk—ideas that are too detailed to include on the slides themselves but too important to risk forgetting. For just that reason, Keynote gives you a space to jot down notes, a for-your-eyes-only cheat sheet for stashing info about each slide.

To display the Presenter Notes pane, choose View→Show Presenter Notes or click the View button in the toolbar and then select Show Presenter Notes. Either way, a new pane appears beneath the slide canvas (see Figure 11-11). You can use this area to keep anything from a detailed speaking script to brief reminders of what to say during the slide. When you present the slideshow, Keynote can display your notes on your own screen, while the audience sees only the slides on the projector's screen. See page 379 for more about using this presenter display feature.

Presenter notes are a good place to stow "notes to self" about the slides you're creating. Use this pane as a temporary notepad for chunks of text that may or may not make it into a slide, or as a memo pad where you can keep track of work to do on a slide: facts to check, pictures to update, unhinged allegations to run past the legal department, and so on.

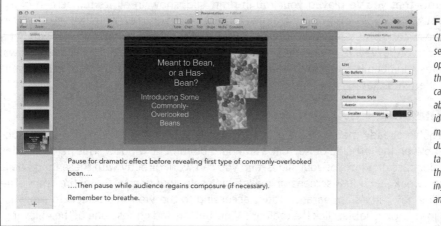

FIGURE 11-11

Choose View→Show Presenter Notes, and Keynote opens a receptacle below the slide canvas where you can stow notes to yourself about the slide. This is an ideal place to keep reminders about what to say during each part of your talk—much, much better than keeping your speaking notes on the slide itself and reading them aloud.

Every slide has its own Presenter Notes pane, and you can type or paste as much text as you want into it—a scroll bar appears when your text is taller than the pane. (You can make the notes pane larger or smaller by putting your cursor over the border where it meets the slide canvas and then dragging to resize them.) Use the Format panel's Text tab and/or the Fonts window to format the note text as you would any other text in your slides. If you're using the field for reminders while speaking, for example, you might find it helpful to use a large, bold font that you can easily read at a glance.

TIP If you print out your slideshow, you can print your presenter notes, too, although you see only as much of the note as can fit on the page beneath the image of the slide—longer notes get clipped. Choose File→Print, and then click the Show Details button. You can then turn on the "Include presenter notes" checkbox. For more about printing slideshows, see page 399.

Playing the Slideshow

When you've got a draft of your slideshow ready, give yourself a preview screening. In the slide navigator, select the slide where you want to start viewing (the first slide, if you want to start at the beginning) and then click the toolbar's Play button. Keynote takes over your computer's screen, displaying the first slide on a black background. Advance through the slides by clicking the mouse button or by pressing the space bar, Return, or the arrow keys on your keyboard. To return to the editing window, press the Esc key. (If you'd rather your presentation finished by fading to black, see the box on page 297.)

There's lots more you can do while playing a slideshow during a presentation—and Keynote even gives you a special view for rehearsing. For all the details, see page 379.

■ Browsing and Organizing Your Slides

Now that you've played your rough-draft slideshow in all its full-screen glory, you've no doubt discovered that you have some work to do to reveal the stunning presentation hidden within. Keynote offers several display modes to help you get a big-picture view of your slideshow—or more accurately, lots of little-picture views: slide thumbnails that you can select, shuffle, copy, and delete to whip your presentation into shape.

The Slide Navigator

You've already met the slide navigator, which displays a visual map of your slideshow on the left side of Keynote's standard document window. This pane includes miniature previews of your slides, and you can work directly with these thumbnails to tweak individual screens or make wholesale changes to the entire show. The slide navigator's appearance varies according to the *view* you select. To see what views are available, click the toolbar's View button and choose one of the following:

- **Navigator.** This is Keynote's standard view: The slide navigator displays a vertical strip of thumbnails, miniaturized replicas of your slides.

PRESENTATION STATION

Fade to Black

If you've ever given slideshow presentations with a slide projector, you've probably used a solid cardboard "black slide" as the final slide in the tray. This opaque slide prevents a white screen from appearing when you advance to the final slide—and prevents your audience from screaming in surprised agony from this nuclear flash.

In Keynote, the view of your desktop that appears at the end of a slideshow doesn't sear any retinas, but its appearance is at best unprofessional and at worst embarrassing. (Ahem, shouldn't you have tucked away that *Geeks Gone Wild* folder before the presentation?)

To avoid this awkward situation, create a black slide at the end of your presentation by adding a slide and choosing the empty master slide. Then open the Format panel, and the Slide Layout tab opens automatically (if it doesn't, you may have accidentally selected an object on your slide; press Esc to deselect it).

Click the empty box to the right of the Background heading to open a menu that includes a smorgasbord of colors, and then click the pure black swatch, and Keynote makes your slide black, too. Finally, Control-click this black slide in the slide navigator and select Duplicate from the shortcut menu to create a *second* black slide.

Now, when you reach the end of your presentation, the screen goes black—and stays black even if you accidentally give the mouse an extra click.

- **Slide Only.** Bye-bye, slide navigator. This view excuses the navigator from the table to make more room for the slide canvas.

- **Light Table.** The slide navigator takes over, replacing the slide canvas and showing your slides in one big grid for an all-at-once view of your presentation.

- **Outline.** The slide navigator changes to a text-only view with the titles and text of all your slides. You can edit the text directly in the slide navigator, a fast way to belt out the initial outline of your text. See page 302 for the rest of the story on Outline view.

NOTE All of these views are also available via the View menu at the top of your screen.

In Navigator and Outline views, you can adjust the width of the navigator pane by putting your cursor over the line where the navigator meets the slide canvas. When your cursor turns into a funky double-headed arrow, drag to the left to reduce the navigator's width, or drag to the right to increase it (see Figure 11-12). Hide the slide navigator completely by clicking the View button and then choosing Slide Only; restore the slide organizer view by clicking the same button and selecting Navigator.

The following sections have more info about each of these views and what they're useful for.

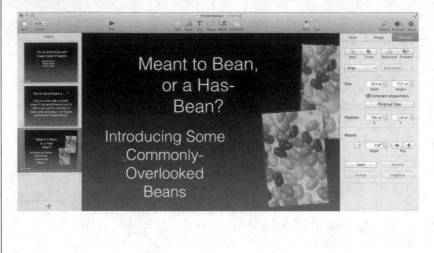

FIGURE 11-12

Navigator view displays thumbnail images of your slides. Make the slide navigator wider or narrower by placing your cursor over the navigator's right edge, and when your pointer turns into a double-headed arrow, drag to resize. In this screenshot, the slide navigator has been scaled up so it's easier to read the text on the slide thumbnails. (Compare this setup with Keynote's default setup shown in Figure 11-2.)

Navigator View

Navigator view is the view you see when you open a new Keynote document. In this view, the slide navigator displays thumbnail versions of each slide along with its slide number, and indicates whether slides have been grouped (page 299). When your slides differ visually, Navigator view makes it easy to find your way around your presentation using these thumbnails. Click a slide's thumbnail to select it, and Keynote loads it into the slide canvas so that you can see it up close and make changes.

In this view you can reorder, delete, and duplicate your virtual slides. You can also lump them into groups to make a long slideshow more manageable, or designate slides for Keynote to skip during the presentation. The following sections explain how.

■ DUPLICATING SLIDES

You can duplicate a slide—including its contents—so that you can use it in another part of your presentation or use it as the basis for a new slide. To do so, press Option while dragging a slide's thumbnail in the slide navigator pane; a green ball bearing a + sign appears next to your cursor to let you know that Keynote is about to duplicate the slide. You can then drag your cursor up or down the column of thumbnails, and a blue line appears as you drag to show where the new slide will appear when you release the mouse button.

You can also duplicate a slide by Control-clicking it in the slide navigator and choosing Duplicate, or selecting the slide in the navigator and then pressing ⌘-D. Either way, Keynote creates a duplicate immediately below the selected slide.

> **TIP** You can access most of the navigator's commands through Keynote's shortcut menus. Control-click (or right-click) within the slide navigator pane to summon this mini-menu containing commands such as New Slide, Cut, Copy, Paste, and Duplicate.

Finally, you can use the Copy and Paste commands to duplicate slides. Select a slide in the navigator pane and then choose Edit→Copy (or press ⌘-C). Then select the slide directly above where you want the duplicate to appear, and then choose Edit→Paste (or press ⌘-V).

You can also select two or more slides and then duplicate them all at once. Here's how to select multiple slides (selected slides have a yellow border):

- Drag up or down on the right or left edge of the slide navigator (in the empty space on either side of your slides) to select a continuous group of slides.

- Click one slide in the navigator to select it, press and hold the Shift key, and then click another slide to select all the slides between the two you clicked.

- Click one slide to select it, and then hold the ⌘ key while you click the other slides.

- Click one slide to select it, and then choose Edit→Select All (⌘-A) to select *all* the slides in your presentation.

Once you've selected the slides you're interested in, use any of the techniques described above to duplicate them.

> **TIP** You can use the keyboard to move around in the slide navigator or select multiple slides. With a slide selected in the navigator pane, use the up and down arrow keys to select the slide above or below it. Select multiple slides by holding the Shift key while pressing the up and down arrow keys to select slides above or below the current one.

■ ORGANIZING AND GROUPING SLIDES

The slide navigator makes it easy to shuffle the deck and reorder your slides: Drag a slide up or down in the navigator and drop it into a new spot. Move a bunch of slides at once by selecting the whole crowd of them and then dragging them to a new location.

As you drag, a blue line indicates where the slide (or slides) will land when you release the mouse button. If you drag the slide directly up or down, the blue line stays lined up with the left edge of the slide directly above it. But, if you drag the slide to the right, the blue line jumps a little to the right, indicating that Keynote will indent the slide if you drop it there. By indenting a group of related slides, you create a *group*—which is really useful for organizing your slides (see Figure 11-13). You can choose to hide or show a group of indented slides (known as the *children*) by clicking the flippy triangle next to their *parent slide* (the one they're indented beneath) or by double-clicking that parent slide.

NOTE   Indenting slides and showing or hiding groups is only for your convenience while editing—this organization has absolutely no effect on your final presentation.

FIGURE 11-13

You can divide your presentation into groups of slides to help bring some order to proceedings—especially useful in longer presentations. When you indent a slide, it becomes a child of the parent slide. You can add grandchildren (and great-grandchildren, and so on) to this family tree by dragging slides to the right. As you drag, the blue line indicates the indent position for your slides. Here, slide 2 is a child of slide 1, and slide 3 is a child of slide 2 (and therefore a grandchild of slide 1).

If you click a parent slide's flippy triangle (like the one circled here), Keynote hides all that slide's descendants.

Slide grouping is especially handy when your presentation includes lots of slides. If you create groups of slides for each section of your presentation, you can keep the sections you're not working on hidden—making it much easier to find your place or to move from one section of the slideshow to another.

You can make as many indent levels as you need to organize your slides. Use the following techniques on one slide or on a group of selected slides:

- Drag a slide to the right to *indent* it one level, to turn it into a "child" and group it under the slide above.

- Drag a slide to the left to *promote* it, or move it to a higher level, removing it from a group—and making it a "parent" of any slides indented beneath it.

- Press Tab to indent the selected slide to the right; press Shift-Tab to promote a slide to the left.

NOTE If you indent a slide that has children, they move along with their parent slide, retaining their indents beneath it.

■ DELETING SLIDES

When you're ready to delete a selected slide (or several) from your presentation, press Delete or choose Edit→Delete.

If you delete a parent slide—a slide above an indented slide or group of slides—Keynote keeps the child slides and promotes them to the level of the deleted parent.

You can delete an entire indented group of slides by clicking the flippy triangle next to the parent slide to hide the group and then deleting the parent slide. Keynote removes the parent *and* all its children (and its children's children) from the presentation. If you remove such a family by mistake, press ⌘-Z (or choose Edit→Undo) to restore it to the slideshow.

■ SKIPPING SLIDES

Keynote can *skip* slides you want to remove from the presentation without actually deleting them. You can use this trick to try out two different versions of a particular slide or section you're working on, or to modify a presentation for a certain audience. You can skip a slide or a whole section of the presentation for one audience and then turn it back on for another. For example, your travelogue on Amsterdam could feature the beautiful flower markets and your canal cruise for one audience, and its famous herb-loving coffee shops and red-light district for another.

Control-click a slide in the slide navigator (or select a group of slides and then Control-click one of them), and then choose Skip Slide from the shortcut menu (alternatively, you can select the slides[s] and then choose Slide→Skip Slide). Keynote collapses the slide's thumbnail into a line in the navigator. You can still select, edit, move, or delete a skipped slide—it just doesn't play in the presentation (see Figure 11-14). Bring skipped slides back into the show by Control-clicking them in the slide navigator and then choosing Don't Skip Slide (or by selecting them and then choosing Slide→Don't Skip Slide).

TIP If you have to deliver similar presentations to two or more groups repeatedly, save yourself the trouble of remembering to reconfigure the presentation; duplicate the entire Keynote file (choose File→Duplicate). Then either delete slides or skip slides to tailor each presentation to its specific audience.

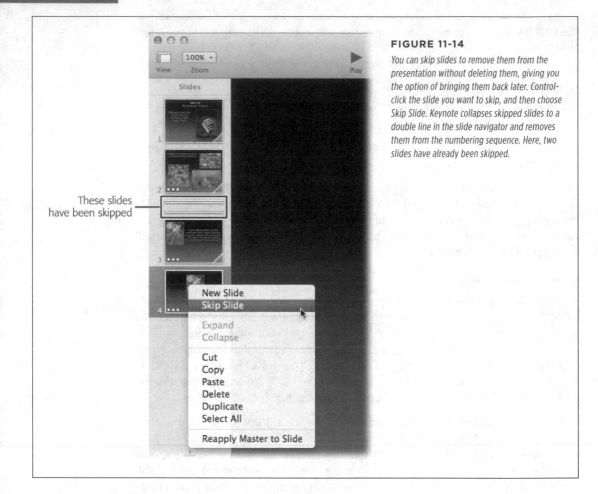

FIGURE 11-14

You can skip slides to remove them from the presentation without deleting them, giving you the option of bringing them back later. Control-click the slide you want to skip, and then choose Skip Slide. Keynote collapses skipped slides to a double line in the slide navigator and removes them from the numbering sequence. Here, two slides have already been skipped.

These slides have been skipped

Outline View

When you get right down to it, a slideshow is really just a fancy outline in disguise, a presentation tool that visually organizes your talk into topics (slides) and subtopics (bullet points). Outline view makes this structure especially clear, so it's a handy way to marshal your ideas, particularly when you first start organizing your presentation. This lets you shift your attention from the layout of your slides to the text and logic of your talk.

To switch to this view, click the View button in the toolbar and select Outline, or go to View→Outline. In the slide navigator, Keynote displays each slide's number next to a tiny slide icon and the slide's text, if any (see Figure 11-15). The outline includes two kinds of text: slide titles and bullet points. Some slide designs have a subtitle instead of bullet points—but from Outline view's perspective, a subtitle is equivalent to a bullet point.

> **TIP** The following few sections help you get a handle on Outline view. You can create a Keynote document to try the following techniques for yourself—or you can download *outline_view.keynote*, which already has all the bullet points and headings you need for an exciting Outline-view experience. Head to *www.missingmanuals. com/cds*, download the document, and then open it and switch to Outline view so you can see exactly what this view is capable of.

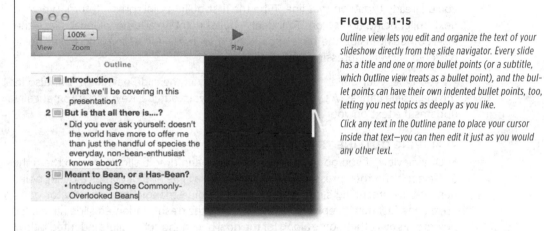

FIGURE 11-15

Outline view lets you edit and organize the text of your slideshow directly from the slide navigator. Every slide has a title and one or more bullet points (or a subtitle, which Outline view treats as a bullet point), and the bullet points can have their own indented bullet points, too, letting you nest topics as deeply as you like.

Click any text in the Outline pane to place your cursor inside that text—you can then edit it just as you would any other text.

In Outline view, you can type directly in the slide navigator to add or edit text in your slides. You can add text formatting, too—changing font, size, color, and so on—and the changes are reflected in the slide canvas. However, those formatting changes don't show up in the slide navigator itself, which always uses the same display font no matter what crazy formatting you apply. In other words, Outline view is all about content, not design.

> **TIP** You can change the font size that Keynote uses for its outline. Choose Keynote→Preferences and then click the General button. Use the Outline View Font drop-down menu to make the text larger or smaller.

Outline view lets you add, delete, move, and duplicate slides just as you can in Navigator view. For example, grab a slide's icon and drag it to move it to a new location. This type of slide organizing isn't Outline view's strong point, though; it's most useful when you want to add, organize, or delete text, or move text between slides.

> **TIP** If your lines of text are more than a few words long, widen the slide navigator by putting your cursor over the border between the navigator and the main slide canvas. When the cursor turns into a double-headed arrow, you can drag to resize both panes.

■ ENTERING OUTLINE TEXT

When you add a new slide in Outline view, whatever you type first becomes the slide's title. Press Return to add a new slide below the first.

> **TIP** If you press Return while your cursor is inside a slide's bulleted list, you'll create a new bullet point instead of a new slide. To escape the list, double-click the slide's icon to temporarily hide the bullet points. You can then hit Return, and Keynote creates a new slide using the selected slide's layout.

If you want to create a bulleted list rather than a new slide, press Tab, and Keynote turns the current line into the first bullet point of a new list—including any text that you'd already typed on that line. Type the first bullet point, press Return, type the next bullet point, and so on. To indent a bullet point an additional level, place the insertion point inside the bullet point and then press Tab. Bump the bullet point back out a level by pressing Shift-Tab.

As you type, your bullet points appear not only in the slide navigator, but also in the main slide canvas. As you make changes to your outline, Keynote automatically updates the text on your slides.

■ MOVING OUTLINE TEXT AND BULLETS

In Outline view, if you go to the slide navigator and drag a slide's icon to the right (or select it and then press Tab), it ceases to be a slide and becomes a bullet point beneath the preceding slide. As you drag, the blue-triangle indent indicator pops up to show just how deeply you're indenting. If the freshly indented slide has bullet points of its own, they come along for the ride, becoming sub-bullets indented below the slide-turned-bullet. You've just moved the slide's content, title and all, into the body text of the previous slide. Figure 11-16 shows an example.

Going back the other way, when you drag a bullet point all the way to the left (or select it and then press Shift-Tab) it becomes a slide; its bullet point text becomes the slide's title, and any bullet points below it become bullet points on the new slide.

If your slide has more than one level of bullet points, you can drag them left (or select them and then press Shift-Tab) to *promote* them, or drag them right (or select them and then press Tab) to *demote* them in the hierarchy.

Move bullet points to a new location in your slideshow by treating their bullets like handles: Select the text of one or more bullet points, grab a bullet (the dot itself, not the bullet point's text), and then drag it to another position in the presentation—or even to an entirely different slide. As you drag, the blue-line-and-triangle guideline appears and helpfully shows where your bullet points will land when you drop them. (If you Option-drag a bullet point, you *copy* it to its new location, leaving the original unscathed.)

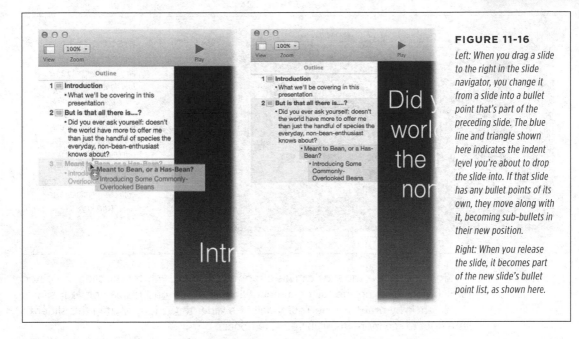

FIGURE 11-16

Left: When you drag a slide to the right in the slide navigator, you change it from a slide into a bullet point that's part of the preceding slide. The blue line and triangle shown here indicates the indent level you're about to drop the slide into. If that slide has any bullet points of its own, they move along with it, becoming sub-bullets in their new position.

Right: When you release the slide, it becomes part of the new slide's bullet point list, as shown here.

■ SELECTING MULTIPLE BULLET POINTS

In Outline view, you can select multiple bullet points, multiple slides, or a combination of both, by dragging your cursor up or down across those items in the slide navigator. As you drag, Keynote highlights the selected items. You can select multiple bullet points or slides that aren't all in a row by selecting one, holding ⌘, and then clicking the additional bullets or slides. Once selected, you can move the group left or right or drag them to a new location in the slideshow.

■ PRINTING THE OUTLINE

If having a hard copy of the outline would help you organize your slides more easily, Keynote lets you print your outline exactly as it appears in the slide navigator in Outline view. The outline doesn't have to be showing onscreen when you choose File→Print (or press ⌘-P). In the Print dialog box, click the Show Details button, click the Outline thumbnail, and then click the Print button or press Return. (For more about printing Keynote slideshows, see page 399.)

Light Table View

Back in the day, slideshow presenters had to don white gloves to sort actual 35 mm slides by hand and load them into projector trays. This process was impossible without a light table to lay the slides on, shuffle them around into a different order, and decide which ones to cut from the show or send to the lab for duplication.

Keynote's Light Table view (Figure 11-17) lets you do that same organization with your onscreen slides—white gloves required only if you want to make a fashion statement.

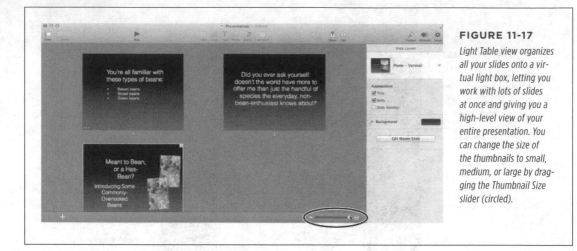

FIGURE 11-17

Light Table view organizes all your slides onto a virtual light box, letting you work with lots of slides at once and giving you a high-level view of your entire presentation. You can change the size of the thumbnails to small, medium, or large by dragging the Thumbnail Size slider (circled).

In Light Table view, the slide canvas disappears to make way for the slide navigator, which now takes up the full document window with a grid display of your slides. Pack 'em in by dragging the Thumbnail Size slider to the left, or drag this slider to the right to see more detail in your thumbnails.

Apart from the expansive real estate enjoyed by the slide navigator, Light Table view is otherwise similar to Navigator view. You can move, duplicate, or delete slides in this jumbo-sized slide navigator just as you do in Navigator view's skinny version (page 298). To return to the slide canvas and the view you were using previously (Navigator, Outline, or Slide Only), double-click a slide.

■ Saving Your Slideshow

Hopefully you've been saving your slideshow right from the moment you first created it by tapping ⌘-S every few minutes. If not, take care of that crucial bit of business right now. Choose File→Save or press ⌘-S to save your file. The first time you save a Keynote document, the Save dialog box drops into view, letting you choose a name and location to use when saving your new slideshow. Keynote also saves your presentation periodically (if you haven't yet saved your presentation, Keynote gives it a placeholder title until you manually save it), but it's still a good idea to get into the habit of manually saving, just to be safe.

If you're not familiar with the Mac's standard Save window, refer to page 12 for a primer.

■ Opening an Existing Slideshow

Go ahead, take a break—you deserve a little reward after creating your first Keynote slideshow. No really, go have a cupcake and treat yourself to a trashy sitcom. When you come back, though, you'll need to know how to get back to your slideshow masterpiece.

Keynote makes it easy to fetch an existing slideshow, regardless of where you are in Keynote. Even if you've just launched the program and are looking at the Open dialog box, you can still go to the File→Open Recent submenu and choose from your latest projects.

To open a slideshow that's *not* listed in the Open Recent submenu, go to File→Open to reveal the standard OS X file browser, where you can choose a file. If you're not familiar with how to use this dialog box to browse for your file, head over to page 17 for a brief tour. You can also use the Finder to locate a slideshow file on your computer, and then double-click the file to launch Keynote and open the slideshow.

Importing Files from Another Program

Keynote can open slideshows created in Microsoft PowerPoint. When you import these files, Keynote creates a brand-new Keynote slideshow based on the original file. That means that any changes you make apply to this new copy only; you're not changing the original PowerPoint document.

NOTE Keynote lets you *save* presentations as PowerPoint documents and a host of other formats, too. See page 401 for the details.

Keynote does its best to maintain the look of the original PowerPoint slideshow, along with all its text, colors, layout, and so on—but you may notice occasional differences. As you might expect, the more advanced features and formatting included in the original slideshow, the more likely it is that Keynote may have trouble duplicating the slides exactly.

NOTE If Keynote runs into trouble during an import, it speaks up, letting you know there was a problem and offering to show you a rundown of the details.

Now that you're fortified with that cupcake and you've got your Keynote slideshow open again, you're ready to tackle the nuts-and-bolts details of the program's presentation magic. The next chapter takes you through all Keynote's nooks and crannies to give you detailed control over every slide's layout.

Laying Out Slides

The toughest part of preparing a presentation is figuring out what you're going to say. Once you've got *that* behind you and have poured a rough text outline into Keynote, everything that follows is the fun part, the visual candy. This is the design phase, where you craft eye-catching slides to illuminate your presentation's key points. You'll compose your slideshow masterpiece with iWork's colorful palette of objects: pictures, shapes, text boxes, tables, charts, and movies—all the same elements that you use in Pages for page layout and in Numbers for designing multimedia reports.

In fact, designing slides in Keynote is practically identical to designing documents in the other iWork programs. You use the very same tools, techniques, toolbar buttons, and panels to create and manipulate your design elements. This tight integration of tools is good news, since it means that you don't really have to learn three different programs: Once you've mastered formatting layouts in one iWork application, you've mastered it in all of them. There are minor changes from program to program, but the fundamentals remain the same.

This chapter spares your patience (and quite a few trees) by not rehashing every last detail already explained in Chapter 6's exploration of the layout tools in Pages. You'll still learn how to fill your Keynote slides with text boxes, pictures, tables, charts, and the rest, but in cases of overlap, the chapter frequently points you back to the details provided earlier in the book.

Before getting into all that good stuff, though, you'll take a quick diversion into the details of a good hygiene regimen when creating a new slideshow.

■ Setting Up the Keynote Document

Before you can start creating slides, you first have to create a Keynote document: the container that becomes the virtual slide tray for your presentation. To do so, launch Keynote (if it's not already running) and then choose File→New to open the Theme Chooser. Select a theme, and then click Choose (see page 280).

From there, it's a good idea to do some initial housekeeping to establish exactly how you'd like Keynote to present your slideshow, setting the ground rules for how you and your audience will interact with it. The Presentation tab is where you take care of these preliminaries. Click the Setup button in the toolbar, and open the Presentation tab, as shown in Figure 12-1. The following sections explain some of the settings on this tab.

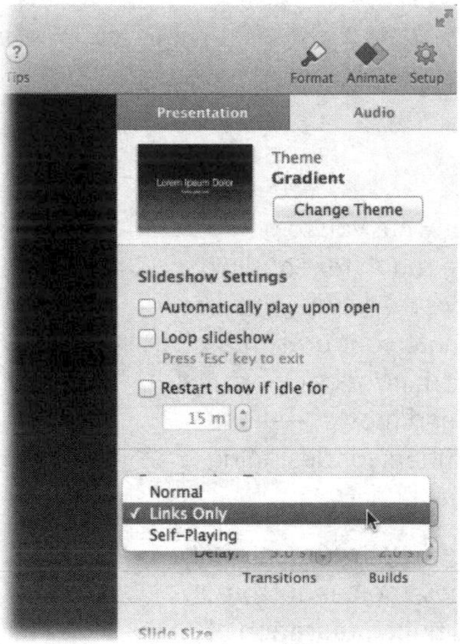

FIGURE 12-1

Use the Presentation tab to control how Keynote plays your slideshow. Choose the type of presentation you'll create by opening the Presentation Type drop-down menu shown here and then selecting Normal, Links Only, Recorded (not shown here), or Self-Playing.

Choosing a Presentation Type

Before you start plugging in your content, you need to think about how you're going to deliver this presentation. Will you be in control, advancing the slides manually? Will it play automatically, all by itself? Will the viewer control the show, by clicking buttons onscreen? Keynote can create four varieties of slideshow to satisfy each of these scenarios. Choose one of these presentation styles by clicking the Setup icon in the toolbar and then selecting the Presentation tab. Open the Presentation Type drop-down menu (Figure 12-1), and then choose from the following:

- **Normal.** This choice gives you a presentation that you control yourself by click- ing the mouse, using the keyboard, or using a remote control (see page 385). Keynote automatically creates this type of show unless you tell it otherwise.

- **Links Only.** Create this kind of presentation if you want viewers to interact with your show by doing things like navigating from slide to slide, choosing to view different parts of the slideshow, visiting a web page, or creating an email message. Also known as an Interactive slideshow, this style of presentation is ideal for self-paced training or lessons. See page 343 for more information about using hyperlinks to create this kind of show.

- **Recorded.** This option is available from the Presentation Type drop-down menu only *after* you've made a recording in the Audio tab. (See page 395 for the lowdown on recording slideshows.) Playing a Recorded presentation is the next best thing to being there. In a recorded presentation, your slideshow plays like a movie, with a prerecorded narration soundtrack. You prepare the show by recording yourself as you go through each slide; Keynote saves the audio along with your timing for advancing through each slide. When you play the slideshow, Keynote plays back your voiceover and moves through the presentation just as you recorded it.

- **Self-Playing.** Like the Recorded style, this option is also for a presentation that plays all by itself, without human intervention. But instead of saving a recorded presentation, the slides change automatically after a fixed length of time. You can set the slide interval for the whole show or on a slide-by-slide basis. See page 393 for details on setting up self-playing shows.

Password-Protecting Your Slideshow

God forbid that anyone get a sneak peek at the marketing presentation for the all-new snack food that'll be launched at Crazyland Wonderpark's on-site café this fall: Mints and Olives (Now in a Can!). Better set a password! To protect your top-secret presentation, open the Presentation tab and turn on the "Require password to open" checkbox. Keynote asks you to provide and verify your password. You can also provide an optional password hint, which Keynote displays after you try to open a presentation three times with the wrong password. (You can also set a password by choosing File→Set Password.)

You can also save this password to your *Keychain* (see page 245 for details about Keychain).

> **NOTE** If you plan to share your document with others (page 408), don't forget to send along the password, too, or the recipients won't be able to open it!

If you need to change the password at any point, go to File→Change Password. You'll need to enter your old password before creating the new one. To remove the password altogether, go to File→Change Password, enter your old password, and then click Remove Password.

A wholly different way to password-protect your slideshow is to require a password to stop it when it's already playing. This is particularly useful for slideshows that are destined to entertain the general public in a kiosk setting, for example. That way, your kiosk visitors can't turn off the presentation.

To secure your presentation against the public, go to Keynote→Preferences, click the Slideshow tab, and then turn on the "Require password to exit slideshows" checkbox. You can then create and verify your password, and then click Set Password. If you need to change the password at any point, go to Keynote→Preferences, click the Slideshow tab, and then select Change Password. To remove the password, go to Keynote→Preferences, click the Slideshow tab, and then click the "Require password to exit slideshows" checkbox once more to remove its checkmark.

■ Working with Objects

Keynote, Pages, and Numbers have so much in common that, if they were people, they'd definitely be BFFs. They share a common collection of *objects*—the pictures, charts, tables, shapes, text boxes, movies, and sounds that combine to create a great document. Designing a Keynote slideshow is very much like designing a page-layout document in Pages. Both programs give you a canvas on which you organize and layer individual objects to create the finished composition.

A fundamental difference in Keynote, however, is that there's no such thing as an inline object (as there is in Pages). All objects in Keynote are effectively *floating objects* whose locations are independent of every other object on the slide. (If you're curious, see page 143 for a review of how inline and floating objects work in Pages.)

Apart from that, objects in Keynote follow essentially the same laws of physics as they do in Pages. The rest of this chapter reviews how to work with those objects. Before getting into the specifics of each object type, though, here's a quick review of what they all have in common—how to select, move, and manipulate objects on a Keynote slide.

Selecting Objects

Every object on the page is contained in its own invisible box, and you have to grab this box anytime you want to do something with the object. To select an object and its containing box, click it once so that its selection handles appear, as shown in Figure 12-2. These handles indicate that you've selected the object at the *object level*. Now you can move the object, rotate it, and apply other effects to it.

> **NOTE** All objects have eight selection handles, apart from text boxes, which have two. More on this on page 323.

FIGURE 12-2

Top: Click an object once to select it at the object level, and Keynote displays selection handles along the object's border (the two white squares shown here). Now you can move, rotate, or add effects to the overall object.

Bottom: Clicking an object more than once typically selects content inside the object. Here, the word "canned" is selected, and the text box's selection handles are no longer visible. Now you can edit the text, but you can't move the text box or make changes to the overall object. Press ⌘-Return to pull back and select the text box at the object level.

By contrast, clicking objects additional times selects the content *inside* them—the text of a text box or a shape, a cell inside a table, the bars of a bar chart, and so on. At that point, you're no longer working with the object as a whole but rather the stuff inside it; that means you can no longer move the object or change most of its object properties. To do those things, you have to take a step back and select the object at the object level (so that you can see its selection handles). If you're working with content inside an object and you want to pull back and work with the object as a whole, press ⌘-Return—just like clicking drills into an object, ⌘-Return pulls you back out.

TIP If you're struggling to remember all these keyboard shortcuts, you can simply click outside the object to deselect it and then click it once to select it at the object level.

To select multiple objects at once, Shift-click each object, or drag across them: Click an empty area of the canvas, and then drag to draw a selection box. Keynote selects all objects inside or touching the selection box.

> **TIP** To select all objects in a slide, choose Edit→Select All or press ⌘-A.

Moving and Copying Objects

When you boil it down to the basics, designing a Keynote slide is simply about arranging objects on a slide canvas. Move an object to its proper place by selecting it at the object level and then dragging it into position. To limit an object's movement to horizontal, vertical, or 45-degree angles, press the Shift key while you drag.

> **TIP** As you drag, a little box appears next to your cursor that shows the X (horizontal) and Y (vertical) position of the object's top-left corner relative to the ruler. (Choose View→Show Rulers or press ⌘-R to show the ruler.) You can turn this informational feature on or off by choosing Keynote→Preferences, opening the Rulers tab, and then turning off "Show size and position when moving objects."

For pixel-perfect control, select the object at the object level, and then use the arrow keys on your keyboard to move the object a point at a time, or hold down the Shift key while you press an arrow key to bump it over *10* points.

To duplicate an object, press Option while you drag, and a clone of the object springs out of the original. You can also select an object and then choose Edit→Duplicate (⌘-D), and Keynote likewise gives you a copy of the object. This is a nifty trick for adding a duplicate to the same slide. When you want to put a copy on a *different* slide, it's Copy and Paste to the rescue: Select the object at the object level, choose Edit→Copy, and then go to the other slide and choose Edit→Paste. Keynote deposits your freshly minted copy onto the second slide.

Resizing, Rotating, and Flipping Objects

Selection handles do more than simply advertise that you've selected an object; they also let you change an object's dimensions or rotate it.

To resize an object, drag one of its selection handles. Hold down the Shift key as you drag to preserve the object's proportions. Hold down the Option key to resize an object from its center, so that the object stays centered on the same point on the slide as you grow or shrink it. You can also specify the exact size of an object using the Format panel's Arrange tab, shown in Figure 12-3, where you can change the size of the object using the Width and Height boxes. (To display the Format panel, click the toolbar's Format button.)

Pictures normally keep their original proportions when you resize them—no need to hold down the Shift key as described above. If you *do* want to squish and stretch an image into new proportions, select it and then turn off the "Constrain proportions" checkbox in the Arrange tab.

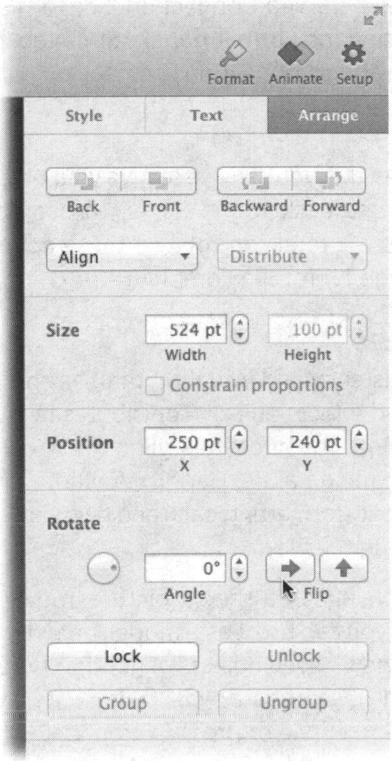

FIGURE 12-3

The Arrange tab lets you specify the exact size, position, and rotation angle of the selected object. Click one of the Flip buttons (where the cursor is positioned here) to turn the object on its ear.

When you flip or rotate a shape that contains text, the text goes along with it. When you're suddenly unable to read your mirror-image text, you can put it back to its original left-to-right position by choosing Format→"Shape and Lines"→"Reset Text and Object Handles."

Give an object a jaunty tilt by rotating it: Hold down the ⌘ key while dragging a selection handle. Hold down Shift-⌘ while you drag to limit the rotation to 45-degree increments, or hold down Option-⌘ to rotate the selection around the handle opposite the one you're dragging (instead of rotating the object around its center).

You can also rotate using the Arrange tab: Select the object, and then spin the Rotate dial or type a number into the Angle field. The Arrange tab also lets you turn an object on its head or convert it into a mirror image by using the Flip buttons. Click one of these buttons, and your object performs a little somersault.

Connecting Objects

Keynote can yoke two objects to each other with a *connection line*, a special variation on the program's line shape, which makes it easy to manage flow charts or organizational diagrams. Like a regular line, you can style a connection line's color, style, thickness, and endpoints (adding arrows to one or both ends, for example). The difference is that the ends of the line are always anchored to the connected objects. No matter how you might move the objects on your slide, the line bends, stretches, and shrinks to maintain this visual link.

To add a connection line between two objects, Shift-click those objects, and then choose Insert→Line→Straight Connection Line, Curved Connection Line, or Right Angle Connection Line. Then style the line using the Format panel's Style tab, just like you would with a regular object. For more about connection lines, see page 184.

Styling Objects

Keynote has a variety of effects, or *object styles*, that you can use to give your objects a graphic makeover: shadows, reflections, borders, background colors, transparency, and more. The Format panel's Style tab gives you total control over these options. See "Modifying Object Styles" starting on page 191 for the complete story.

■ COPYING AND REUSING OBJECT STYLES

Behind every great design is a focus on consistency and visual rhythm; having too many variations of fonts, colors, text sizes, and effects quickly contributes to a distracting, crazy-quilt slideshow design. But here's the hitch: Restyling every object just the way you want it can be a time-consuming hassle. Happily, Keynote gives you a few techniques to let you sidestep manually formatting each and every object, keeping your design clean and consistent along the way:

- **Copy Style and Paste Style.** After you've styled a shape, picture, movie, or other object exactly the way you want it, you can use it as a model, applying its formatting to other objects in your slideshow—even objects of another type, in many cases. Select the object (or table cell or chart data series) whose style you want to use, and then choose Format→Copy Style or press Option-⌘-C. Then select another object, choose Format→Paste Style (Option-⌘-V), and presto! Keynote transforms the selected object, replacing all its styles and formatting with the style of the original object.

- **Reapply Master.** To strip a slide of all its unique style changes so that it uses the theme's standard look for the current master slide, choose Format→"Reapply Master to Slide." If you've moved the title, body text, or any other standard elements from the original slide, this command also restores the original layout.

- **Paste and Match Style.** When you paste an object or text into your slideshow, Keynote normally does its best to match the formatting of the original. So, when you paste in a table from Numbers or a text box from Pages, for example, it gets the same styling as it had in the original document. Keynote is just trying to be helpful, but when the result doesn't match the style of your slideshow, or when you inadvertently paste tiny text into your Big Headline, that means more work for you, reformatting the material to match its new context. Save yourself the trouble by choosing Edit→"Paste and Match Style." When you paste an object with this command, Keynote automatically applies the master slide's default colors and styles to the pasted object. When you paste text, it uses the same text formatting as the surrounding text.

- **Create Object Style.** Pages provides a handful of default styles that you can apply to each object. To see what styles are available for the selected object, open the Format panel's Style tab, and then click any of the thumbnails at the top of the tab to try them on for size. You can also create and save your own object styles by formatting an object so that it looks exactly how you want it, and then going to the top of the Styles tab and clicking the left or right arrow to bring up six blank thumbnails. Click the thumbnail with the + on it to save your style. From this point onward, you can use this style in exactly the same way as Keynote's standard object styles. (Alternatively, save your style by selecting the object and then choosing Format→Advanced→Create [Object] Style.) You can learn more about creating object styles on page 269.

> **NOTE** You can create new styles for all object types *except* tables.

Layering Objects

When objects overlap, one covers the other. You can control where objects sit in this stack of layers using the Format panel's Arrange tab. Select an object and click the Forward or Backward button to nudge the object higher or lower in the stack, or click Front or Back to move it to the very top or bottom. For details about working with object layers, see page 187.

Aligning Objects

It sounds mundane, but a big part of elegant design is simply keeping things lined up so that objects adhere to an overall pattern—centered on the page, for example, or with their left edges all lined up. Like Pages and Numbers, Keynote offers *guides* to help you keep things straight. But it also has a few tricks of its very own to help you size and space objects precisely.

■ AUTOMATIC ALIGNMENT GUIDES

As you drag an object across a slide, Keynote keeps an eye on its position relative to all the other objects on the slide. When the object you're dragging is close to lining up with another object, an alignment guide appears, drawing a line between the two objects, as shown in Figure 12-4. The alignment guide vanishes when you move past the object or drop what you're dragging.

These guidelines vary the way they work their magic depending on your preference settings. With Keynote's standard settings, the program displays alignment guides when the object you're dragging lines up with the *center* of another object. If you prefer, you can set it up so that the alignment guides appear when objects line up with the *edges* of other objects, too. This is helpful, for example, if you want to arrange objects so that their left or right edges are perfectly aligned. Keynote offers two preference settings to change when alignment guides are shown. You'll find these settings in the Rulers tab of Keynote→Preferences (see Figure 12-6): "Show guides at object center" and "Show guides at object edges." You can select either, both, or neither. If you turn off both options, Keynote won't display alignment guides at all.

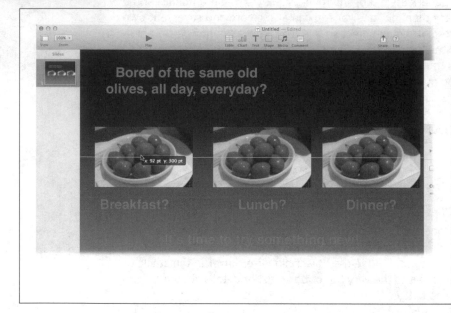

FIGURE 12-4

When you're moving an object that's lined up (or nearly lined up) with another object, Keynote draws an alignment guide through both objects to show you that they're lined up. As shown here, Keynote's standard settings line up objects through their center. You can also choose to line them up along their edges by going to Keynote→Preferences and adjusting the Alignment Guides settings on the Rulers tab.

TIP You can *temporarily* disable alignment guides by pressing ⌘ while you drag an object.

■ USING RELATIVE SIZING AND SPACING GUIDES

A pair of Keynote-only features help you space and size objects equally, too. *Relative spacing guides* pop up when you're moving an object and it becomes evenly spaced with two or more other objects. *Relative sizing guides* appear when you're resizing an object and the object approaches the same height or width as another object. The whole drama unfolds in Figure 12-5.

To switch the relative guides off, go to Keynote→Preferences, click Rulers, and then turn off "Show guides for relative spacing" and "Show guides for relative sizing." As with the alignment guides, you can *temporarily* disable the relative guides by pressing ⌘ key while you move or resize an object.

■ DRAWING YOUR OWN ALIGNMENT GUIDES

Keynote's automatic alignment guides remain invisible most of the time, showing up only temporarily while you're moving objects. However, you can draw your *own* alignment guides that stick around and remain visible as long as you like. To add an alignment guide to a slide, chose View→Show Rulers (or press ⌘-R) to reveal Keynote's measuring sticks. Click either ruler and drag into the canvas, and the cursor tows an alignment guide behind it. Drop the alignment guide when you have it where you want it.

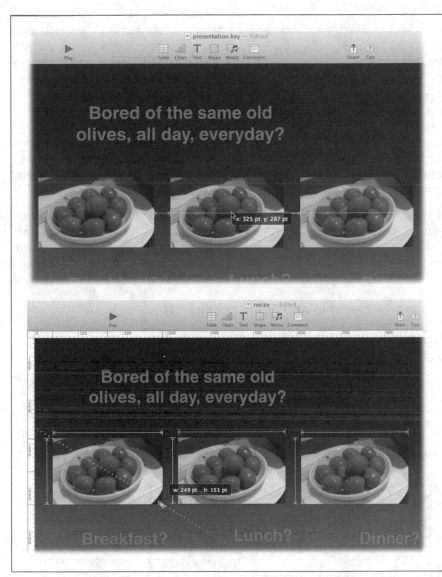

FIGURE 12-5

Top: When you're moving an object and it becomes evenly spaced with two or more other objects, Keynote's guides light up to let you know. Here, the guides flash on to show that the image in the middle (which is being dragged) is lined up with the other two images in the series.

Bottom: As you resize an object, the relative sizing guides spring into action when the object approaches the same height or width as another object on the slide. Here, the guides indicate that the picture on the left is the same height and width as the other two pictures.

NOTE These guides are for your eyes only. They don't show up when you play the slideshow or when you print the slides—only when you're editing slides.

You create vertical alignment guides from the vertical ruler and horizontal alignment guides from the horizontal ruler. You can move an alignment guide anytime you like by dragging it to its new location; drag it back onto the ruler to send it up in a puff of smoke. To hide these guides temporarily, choose View→Guides→Hide Guides; get them back by choosing View→Guides→Show Guides or by dragging a new alignment guide into the slide.

The techniques described above add guides only to the currently selected slide and don't affect other slides. To add alignment guides to many slides at once, add them to the *master* slide instead; the guides then become instantly available to any slide that's based on that master slide. (For details on editing master slides, check out page 416.)

■ SWITCHING ON THE MASTER GRID

Keynote's *master grid* gives you a bit more order and precision for keeping your objects on the straight and narrow. Like a sheet of graph paper, this grid scores your slide with regularly spaced lines—except that this grid is invisible in your final presentation.

The master grid is turned off under Keynote's standard settings. To switch it on and make those lines visible, go to View→Guides→Show Master Guides. The exact number and position of the gridlines you see depends on the slide's layout; each layout has its own master grid (some slides don't display any gridlines). You can hide the grid again by going to View→Guides→Hide Master Guides.

■ CHANGING THE GRID AND GUIDE COLORS

Unless you tell it otherwise, Keynote's alignment guides and master gridlines are yellow. You can change the color of any of these lines in Keynote's Ruler preferences. Choose Keynote→Preferences, and then click the Rulers tab. Click the color well in the Master Guides or Alignment Guides sections (see Figure 12-6) to call up the Color Picker, where you can choose your preferred color (see page 192 for more on the Color Picker).

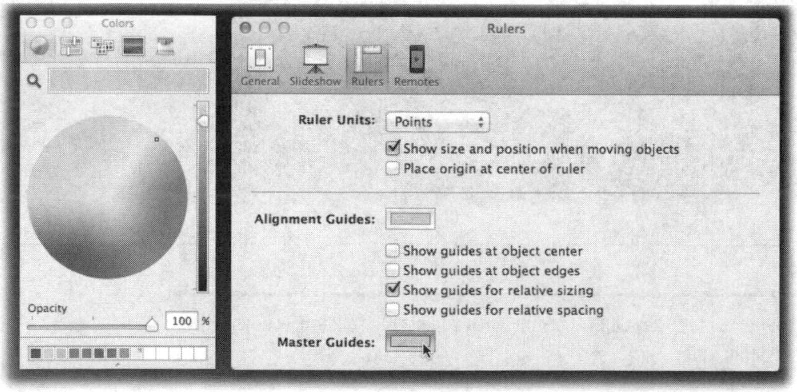

FIGURE 12-6

Keynote's Ruler preferences let you control the color of alignment guides and master gridlines. Simply click the relevant color well and pluck a new color from the Color Picker, as shown here.

■ ONE-CLICK OBJECT ALIGNMENT

When you're in a hurry and don't want to mess around with grids and guides, hand the whole thing over to Keynote and let it align and space a set of objects for you automatically. You do this via the Arrange→Align Objects and Arrange→Distribute Objects submenus. See page 186 for the skinny.

Grouping and Locking Objects

Once you have objects placed, sized, and lined up exactly where you want them, you can *group* or *lock* them to make sure they stay in the same position relative to each other (grouped) or in the same spot on the slide (locked).

When you group a set of objects, they always travel as a pack. You can move, rotate, and resize them all at once or animate the entire group so that they appear or disappear from the slide all at once (see page 190 for details). Select the objects to include in a group by Shift-clicking each one and then either choosing Arrange→Group, or opening the Format panel's Arrange tab and clicking the Group button. To disband a group, select it and choose Arrange→Ungroup, or go to the Arrange tab and click Ungroup. See page 190 for more info about grouping.

> **NOTE** You cannot group objects that arrive as part of your theme—you can group only objects that you've added to a slide yourself.

In Pages and Numbers, you can't edit grouped objects individually, but Keynote doesn't have this restriction, so you can get at any member of a group with an extra click. Click the object you want to edit once to select the whole group and then click again to select the individual object. You can now make changes to that object's size, format, rotation, or anything you like without affecting the rest of the group.

> **WARNING** If you apply a build effect (page 358) to a group and then later ungroup the objects, Keynote tosses out the build effect. So if you just want to make a quick change to the formatting of one or more of the objects but want to keep the group's build effect, don't ungroup the objects. Instead, use the technique described above to edit an individual object in the group.

When you lock an object, Keynote glues it down on the slide so that you can no longer move it (or make any other changes to it, for that matter). Select the object and choose Arrange→Lock or click the Lock button in the Format panel's Arrange tab. See page 191 for the details.

■ Adding and Formatting Text Boxes

Any text on a slide has to live within a text box or a shape. Keynote provides three kinds of text boxes:

- **Title text boxes.** Most Keynote themes contain a number of master slides (page 286) that contain title text boxes. There can be only one title text box per slide.

Text you enter in one of these text boxes appears as the slide's title in Outline view (page 302). Although they're usually designed to hold a relatively short title, you can actually add as much text as you care to squeeze in.

- **Body text boxes.** You often see body text boxes featured in Keynote master slides under their alternative moniker, bullet text boxes. Like title text boxes, Keynote permits only one body text box per slide. Text you enter in this kind of text box shows up in Outline view as bullet points, with a bullet for each paragraph. In the slide itself, you can change the bullet style or remove bullets from the slide completely by going to the Format panel's Text tab, clicking the Style button, and then using the Bullets & Lists drop-down menu (see page 68).

- **Free text boxes.** These text boxes take their name from their freedom from the outline (text in a free text box doesn't appear in Outline view) *and* their freedom from Keynote's master slides—you typically use free text boxes on an individual slide to supplement a master slide's basic design. Use text boxes to add image captions, callouts, or any text that you want to treat differently from a slide's title or body text.

- **Shapes.** These are free text boxes' shapely cousins. You can use any shape (except for lines) as a text container. Insert a shape by clicking the Shapes button in the toolbar and picking an option from the drop-down menu, or by choosing Insert→Shape and selecting a shape by name. Double-click inside a shape to begin entering text. Like free text boxes, Keynote doesn't display text within shapes in Outline view.

Inserting Title and Body Text Boxes

Many master slides contain a title text box, a body text box—or both. If the slide you're working on doesn't have one of these text boxes and you want to add one, you need to use the Slide Layout tab. To open this tab, make sure the Format panel is open (if it's not, click the Format button in the toolbar), and then click any blank area within your slide so that no object is selected; Keynote opens the Slide Layout tab. In this tab, turn on the Title or Body checkbox, depending on what you want to add to your slide.

You can likewise remove one of these text boxes from a slide by turning off its checkbox in the Slide Layout tab—although you can remove it more directly by selecting the text box on the slide and then pressing Delete.

When you remove a slide's title or body text box, you don't *really* delete its contents. A slide's title and body text have special standing in Keynote, which considers these fields to be the slide's essential content. So even if you remove the title or body text from the displayed slide, Keynote still includes that info in Outline view, for example, stashing it away for safekeeping. If you later decide to restore the title or body text back into your slide—switching to a new master slide that has those fields, for example—Keynote plugs in the original content for you. This also means that you can change master slides as many times as you like, and the title and body text make the jump right along with you, automatically finding their new position in the layout.

Inserting Free Text Boxes

Unlike every other object in iWork, Keynote's free text boxes have only two selection handles, one on each side. That means you can adjust their width but not their height—at least not with selection handles. Keynote manages the height of free text boxes automatically: As you enter text, these text boxes grow vertically to accommodate your words. Likewise, when you delete text, the text box shrinks back down to size.

You have two ways to insert free text boxes in your slides: Click the Text button in the toolbar and then choose a formatting option from the drop-down menu, or choose Insert→Text Box, and Keynote adds a small text box to the middle of the slide with the word "Text" inside it. Now you can reposition the box, adjust its width, and add your own text.

> **NOTE** If you add a free text box to a master slide, it normally becomes part of the slide's background. In other words, you've chained it to a spot on the master slide and it appears on every slide created from that master as uneditable text. This type of unchangeable text is useful to display, for example, a company name, copyright information, or a teaching module's title. See Chapter 15 for details about editing themes and master slides.

Editing Text in Keynote

Tap out your text in Keynote by double-clicking the text you want to edit (clicking a text box just once selects it at the object level; clicking again lets you edit the text itself). From there, the basics of text editing are the same in Keynote as they are in the other iWork programs—and in other Mac programs, for that matter. For a review, head back to "Basic Text Editing in iWork" starting on page 32.

■ WORKING WITH LISTS AND BULLETS

For better or worse, bullet points are a fact of life for many slideshow presentations, and that means that much of your job editing text in Keynote is really about editing *lists*. Bullet points, nested outlines, and numbered lists—they might take different forms, but they're all lists, and Keynote gives you a few special shortcuts to make quick work of organizing and rearranging them.

You can nest bullet points below other bullet points as outline subtopics. To indent a bullet point to the right, place the insertion point anywhere in its text in the slide canvas, and then press Tab. "Outdent" the bullet point to the left by pressing Shift-Tab.

Select an entire list item by clicking its bullet symbol (or number, letter, or other label). From there, you can drag the list item by the bullet to a new location:

- Drag up or down to move it to a new location in the same list.

- Drag left or right to indent or outdent it.

- Drag to another text box to move it to another list.

- Drag it to an empty location on the slide canvas to create a new free text box.

- In Outline view, drag it onto another slide to move it to that slide.

TIP Free text boxes always start out as regular text, with no bullets or numbering. Convert a text box from regular text to a bullet list (or vice versa) by heading to the Format panel's Text tab, clicking the Style button, and then using the Bullets & Lists drop-down menu. That's also where you can change the appearance, spacing, and labeling of your bullet points. For more, skip back to page 68.

■ CLIPPED TEXT AND AUTO-SHRINK

Keynote manages overstuffed text boxes differently from Pages, which clips text that won't fit (see page 7). In fact, Keynote's free text boxes don't know the meaning of too much text: The text box keeps growing and growing as you add more content, expanding right off the slide if you keep pouring prose into it. The only way to manage runaway text in free text boxes is to delete some of the text or to reduce its font size to make it fit.

Shapes behave more like they do in Pages: When the shape isn't big enough to display all the text, it adds a +-shaped clipping indicator to the bottom selection handle to show that some text is hidden (see Figure 12-7). Keynote hides these clipping indicators during the slideshow—their purpose is only to give you feedback while editing.

Where title boxes and body text boxes are concerned, Keynote's *auto-shrink* feature looms large, as you saw in Chapter 11 (page 288). When auto-shrink is turned on, Keynote adjusts your font size to make sure all the text fits. You can tell Keynote to keep its mitts off the size lever by selecting the title or body text box, going to the Format panel's Text tab, clicking the Layout button, and then turning off "Shrink text to fit."

FIGURE 12-7

When a title box can't contain any more text, Keynote adds a clipping indicator to the bottom of the box (circled). To uncover the hidden text, drag the selection handles to make the box bigger so that all your text is visible.

NOTE The auto-shrink option is available for title text boxes and body text boxes only—not for shapes or free text boxes.

■ CHECK YOUR SPELLING

Keynote normally has its automatic spell checking turned on, flagging misspelled words—or words not in its dictionary—with a red underline. Choose Edit→Spelling and Grammar→Check Spelling While Typing to turn this feature on or off.

To display the Spelling window for manual spell checking, choose Edit→Spelling and Grammar→Show Spelling and Grammar. Keynote shares many elements, including its spell checker, with Pages. See page 89 for the rest of the story on spell checking.

■ SMART QUOTES AND AUTO-CORRECTION

Keynote can monitor what you type, automatically correcting errors or inserting *smart quotes*, which curve into a different shape for opening quotes or closing quotes, like so: '' "". You can also use Keynote's auto-correction tools to give you quick shortcuts for commonly typed words and phrases. See page 97 for all the details.

Formatting Text

Once you've got your text into Keynote, you can dress it up by formatting it however you like. Choose a new font, splash your text with some color, make it larger or smaller—whatever you want to do, Keynote provides plenty of formatting tools to give you control over the look of your words. When you select a text box, the Format panel's Text tab gives you fast access to the most popular text formatting options (see Figure 2-3 on page 40). Keynote applies any formatting changes you make to the selected text or paragraph (if any), or to whatever you type next after adjusting the formatting settings.

When you need more control over your text's formatting, click the Text tab's Layout button, or open the program's Fonts window or ruler. With only a few exceptions, formatting your text with these tools is identical to formatting text in Pages. You'll find those details described in the Pages chapters (especially Chapter 2), but here's an overview of text formatting in Keynote.

■ THE FONTS WINDOW

Choose Format→Font→Show Fonts or press ⌘-T to open the Fonts window (shown in Figure 2-5 on page 42). Page 42 has the full story about the Fonts window, but the settings in this window let you do the following:

- Choose a font and see font samples.

- Set the font size.

- Set the font color.

- Set the document color, which is actually the paragraph background color—not to be confused with the text-box fill color setting in the Format panel's Style tab. The document color overrides the text box fill color and is also constrained by your document's inset margin setting. In other words, you see the text-box fill color in the text box's margin, and the document color behind the block of text.

- Choose the text underlining or strikethrough style and color.

■ THE LAYOUT TAB

Select the text you wish to format, open the Format panel's Text tab, and then click the Layout button to see this tab. Keynote's Layout tab is divided into five sections (see Figure 12-8):

- **Columns.** Lets you change the number of columns of text to display in the text box, including the width of the columns and gutters (the gaps between columns). Working with columns in Keynote works just like it does in Pages; see page 116 for more info.

- **Text Inset.** Sets the amount of padding between the boundary of the text box and its content (see page 150).

- **Indents.** Here, you can change the left or right indentation of the selected paragraph. You can also use the First setting to control how indented the first line of the paragraph is (see page 57 for the lowdown on indenting text).

- **Tabs.** Lets you perfect existing tabs and create new ones. You can also remove tabs and add leader lines in this section (page 52 has the skinny).

- **Borders & Rules.** A border is a box that surrounds the selected text, while a rule is a line that appears between paragraphs. See page 59 for more info on adding these kinds of lines to your text.

■ THE FORMAT MENU

Open the Format→Font submenu to do any of the following:

- Show or hide the Fonts window by choosing Show/Hide Fonts.

- Change the font style (bold, italic, underline, strikethrough, or outline).

- Increase or decrease the font size (choose Bigger or Smaller).

- Adjust *tracking*, the space between two characters (see page 44).

- Turn ligatures on or off (see page 47).

- Adjust the font's baseline (see page 46).

- Adjust the text's capitalization.

You can also choose Format→Text and select one of the paragraph alignment settings: Align Left, Align Center, Align Right, or Justify.

■ SETTING MARGINS, INDENTS, AND TABS WITH THE RULER

Choose View→Show Rulers to reveal Keynote's vertical and horizontal scales on the top and left sides of the slide canvas. The top ruler displays the bullet alignment, margin settings, and tabs for the selected paragraph. You can use this ruler to adjust the text margins and the first-line indent, and set tabs for each paragraph in a text box. So far this system is pretty much the same as ruler usage in Pages (for a refresher, see "Setting Tabs" and "Indenting Text" on pages 52–58), except that you get double the amount of ruler real estate, in the form of the additional, vertical ruler. Keynote also adds a new wrinkle—and a new icon—to its rulers: the *bullet alignment mark* (see Figure 12-8).

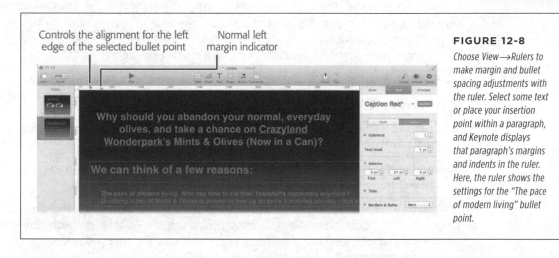

Controls the alignment for the left edge of the selected bullet point

Normal left margin indicator

FIGURE 12-8

Choose View→Rulers to make margin and bullet spacing adjustments with the ruler. Select some text or place your insertion point within a paragraph, and Keynote displays that paragraph's margins and indents in the ruler. Here, the ruler shows the settings for the "The pace of modern living" bullet point.

> **TIP** The left margin indicator in Figure 12-8 shows the left edge of the text area, where non-bullet text lines up. The bullet marker indicates where the left edge of the bullet lines up for the selected text.

To make any ruler adjustments, place your insertion point within the paragraph you want to adjust or select text that spans two or more paragraphs. (Since text boxes can have more than one paragraph, each text box can have more than one ruler format.) Drag the bullet, margin, or tab indicators and watch the effect on the selected text. If you've set an inset margin (by opening the Format panel's Text tab, clicking the Layout button, and adjusting the Text Inset setting), the inset margin controls the outer limits for the margin settings.

There's a hitch to using tabs in text boxes that feature bullet points: When your insertion point is within a bullet point, Keynote reserves Tab and Shift-Tab for indenting and outdenting that bullet point. That means that, when your insertion point is in a bullet point, the Tab key is useless for creating actual tabs. Keynote sidesteps the problem with Option-Tab, which works the way you would normally expect the Tab key to behave, advancing the text to the next tab stop.

◼ Inserting Photos and Other Graphics

You can add just about any kind of graphic file into a Keynote slide. JPEG, PDF, GIF, PNG, PSD, PICT, and TIF are just a few of the formats that Keynote accepts. Simply drag them onto the slide canvas from your desktop or a Finder window, grab them via the Media Browser, or go to Insert→Choose.

Replacing Media Placeholders

Many Keynote master slides contain *media placeholders* where you can drop pictures, movies, or audio clips. These placeholders provide consistent size and placement from slide to slide and also do some behind-the-scenes magic to automatically size and crop—or *mask*—your pictures to fit. You already got a taste of this in Chapter 11, but here's the drill on how to quickly update a media placeholder:

1. **Click the + button at the bottom of the slide navigator to add a new slide.**

2. **Choose a master slide containing a media placeholder.**

3. **Click the icon in the media placeholder's bottom-right corner to open the Media Browser.**

4. **Use the Media Browser to find the picture you want to use, and then click the picture to replace the media placeholder with it (Figure 12-9).**

   You could also drag an image file from a folder on your hard drive, and drop it onto the media placeholder to instantly replace the placeholder with your chosen image. (Need help finding the perfect image for your slideshow? See the box on page 331 for some suggestions of where to look.)

Either way, Keynote replaces the placeholder with your image, keeping the same size, effects, and dimensions as the original placeholder. Want to try a different picture instead? You can repeat this step as many times as you like, dropping new pictures onto the placeholder until you find the look you want.

> **NOTE** When Keynote makes images larger or smaller to fit a media placeholder, the result typically looks sharp and tidy. The exception is when you drag a small, low-resolution picture into a placeholder; if Keynote has to enlarge the picture to fit, the blown-up version will be fuzzy or pixelated. Whenever possible, try to work with original images that are at least as large as the slide's display size (page 284); this gives you the flexibility to enlarge the pictures to fill whole slides, if you like.

If you're not thrilled by the way that Keynote shrinks and crops your image to fit the placeholder, you're not stuck with it. You can move, resize, rotate, or style your image however you like, just like any other object. You can also change the way the image is cropped by editing its image mask, which you'll learn about in a sec.

> **TIP** Another way to keep Keynote from cropping images is to use object placeholders rather than media placeholders. See the box on page 330 for the lowdown.

If you switch to a new master slide after adding a picture to a media placeholder, Keynote keeps your picture and plugs it into the new slide layout, just like it does with the slide's title and body text—but only if the new master slide also has a media placeholder. If you switch to a new master slide without a picture, Keynote tosses your picture out of the slideshow (as always, though, you can get it back by choosing Edit→Undo or pressing ⌘-Z).

FIGURE 12-9

Top: Replace a media placeholder with your own picture by dragging the replacement image from your desktop or a Finder window and then dropping it onto the placeholder image.

Bottom: When Keynote replaces the placeholder, it keeps the same size, dimensions, and effects as the original placeholder. Here, this horizontal image is cropped so that its sides are lopped off to fit the placeholder's vertical layout.

Object vs. Media Placeholders

Although it's distinctly unpopular with Apple's theme designers, who correctly prefer to use media placeholders for pictures, you can also add a picture to an *object placeholder* in a slide. Object placeholders are a feature leftover from previous generations of Keynote and, in general, don't have many practical applications. But if you stumble into one or feel the urge to experiment, here's the scoop:

As you'll learn on page 330, object placeholders are intended for tables and charts, but they can also hold media objects like pictures and movies, albeit with somewhat lame results. To add an object placeholder, click the View button in the toolbar and select Edit Master Slides (or choose View→Edit Master Slides). All of your master slides now appear in the slide navigator. Select the one you want to add the object placeholder to, and that master slide appears in the slide canvas. You can then add an object using one of the buttons in the toolbar (Table, Chart, and so on). Once you've done that, you can turn it into an object placeholder by opening the Format panel's Style tab and turning on the "Define as [Object] Placeholder" checkbox (where [Object] is the type of object you added).

The difference between the two kinds of placeholders is that media placeholders crop and resize pictures so they fill every pixel of the placeholder. By contrast, when you drag a picture to an object placeholder, Keynote resizes the picture but never crops it—the whole picture, in its original dimensions, appears within the object placeholder without any cropping, often leaving empty space inside the placeholder box.

Also, once you drag a picture or movie to an object placeholder, it loses its placeholder powers—unlike media placeholders, you can't audition new images until you find the one you want. After you use an object placeholder for an image or a movie, it turns that image or video into a regular object. The lesson here: Just because you *can* use object placeholders for pictures doesn't mean you *should*. Media placeholders work much better. For more on creating both types of placeholders in themes and master slides of your own, check out Chapter 15.

NOTE More specifically, Keynote remembers placeholder pictures only when you switch to a master slide with a placeholder that has the same name, or *tag*, as the placeholder on the first master slide. You set placeholder tags by choosing View→Edit Master Slides, selecting the placeholder you want to tag, opening the Format panel's Style tab, and then entering a tag in the Tag field. (When you're done, choose View→Exit Master Slides or click Done at the bottom of the Keynote window.) See page 418 for more details.

By contrast, Keynote never throws out "regular" pictures. In other words, any pictures that you add to your slides outside of the master's placeholders always stick around in exactly the same location when you switch from master slide to master slide. (The same goes for any object that you add to a slide outside of its title, body text, or placeholders.)

DESIGN TIME

Finding the Perfect Photo

Images can have a big influence on your presentation, lending drama or humor to your talk and giving your audience visual "hooks" to help them remember your main points. Like all the iWork programs, Keynote makes it easy to grab pictures from iPhoto or other nooks and crannies of your Mac. But if you're not the world's greatest photographer or don't have a collection of pictures for the topic at hand, the Internet is a great resource for picture-hungry presenters.

The golden rule is that you need to be respectful of the talented folks who created the pictures you find on the Web. Just because you stumble across a photo online doesn't necessarily mean you can use it free and clear in your presentation or project. Every photo belongs to its photographer, and you should get her permission before using it, as well as the OK of anyone pictured in photos. It's common courtesy—and the law.

Happily, many photographers have donated their work to the public, sharing their photos under *Creative Commons licenses,* which allow free use of images under specific conditions. These conditions vary according to the work and might, for example, limit use to non-commercial projects, or simply require a photo credit. When in doubt, check with the photographer.

There are a slew of sites where photographers share their work. Here's a handful of the best:

- **Flickr** (*www.flickr.com*) is the mother of all photo-sharing sites. It hosts an endless, ever-growing stream of photos from a huge community of photographers, both amateur and professional. Many (but not all!) of these photographers share their pictures under Creative Commons licenses. Thankfully, the site's Advanced Search page makes it easy to filter out images that *aren't* released under Creative Commons.

- **MorgueFile** (*www.morguefile.com*) is a library of free, high-resolution photos for both commercial and personal projects. All images are free and may be used without additional permission from, or credit for, the photographer.

- **Stock.xchng** (*www.sxc.hu*) hosts over 40,000 photos and counting, all offered free of charge.

- **Wikimedia Commons** (*http://commons.wikimedia.org*) is operated by the same folks who run Wikipedia. The site contains photos, videos, and sound files—the terms of use vary among images, so be sure to read the Licensing and Permissions section for each photo.

- **FreeDigitalPhotos.net** (*www.freedigitalphotos.net/*) contains photographs and a wide selection of original illustrations.

- **OpenPhoto** (*www.openphoto.net*) includes photographs, image mosaics, and a small selection of digital art.

- **Pixel Perfect Digital** (*www.pixelperfectdigital.com*). In addition to photos, Pixel Perfect Digital offers a small selection of abstract images and textures, released under a Creative Commons Attribution license.

- **FreePhotosBank.com** (*www.freephotosbank.com*) offers the usual photos of animals, landscapes, and food. But it's also worth taking a look at the site's "abstract" category, which contains lots of digital artwork, backgrounds, and patterns.

If none of these websites meet your needs, there are a couple of search engines that scour the web for freely licensed images, which can be a life-saver when you're looking for something obscure. Check out Google's Advanced Image Search (*www.google.com/advanced_image_search*) and set the Usage Rights drop-down menu to one of the "free to use" options.

If there's a downside to the sprawling amateur photography sites mentioned above, it's that they're sprawling and amateur. While they're full of remarkable photos, it can sometimes take time to find them. Commercial stock-photo companies save you time by featuring carefully selected images from professional photographers. Getty Images (*www.gettyimages.com*), Jupiter Images (*www.jupiterimages.com*), and Corbis (*www.corbis.com*) are the big, big players in this field. But there are lots of smaller stock-photo houses with correspondingly smaller fees and, often, quirkier collections. These include *www.veer.com*, *www.crestock.com*, *www.dreamstime.com*, *www.istockphoto.com*, and *www.shutterstock.com*.

Adding and Editing Pictures

Don't feel limited to the paint-by-numbers layouts of Keynote's master slides. You can add as many "regular" pictures as you like to any slide—not just slides based on masters with media placeholders. (Struggling to find suitable images for your slideshow? See the box on page 331 for some ideas of where to go for great images.)

As you saw in Chapter 11, adding an image to a slide works just like replacing a placeholder except that you drop the image on an empty part of the slide canvas instead of on a media placeholder. You can also select Insert→Choose, or click the toolbar's Media button, and then find the image file you want to add to your slideshow. Drag one of the picture's selection handles to resize it, or drag the picture itself to reposition it.

In addition to the usual assortment of formatting, shadows, reflections, and picture frames that you can add to any object via the Format panel (see pages 191–203), Keynote gives you some simple editing tools to transform images:

- **Masks.** Add a mask to an image to crop it, specifying exactly what portion you want to show in your slide (page 158 reveals the details behind the mask).

- **Instant Alpha.** Remove background colors with iWork's Instant Alpha feature, which turns portions of your picture transparent, handy for creating cutout effects, as shown in Figure 12-10. Page 162 makes it all clear.

- **The Adjust Image window.** Fine-tune your picture's color, contrast, and levels with the Adjust Image window, which gives you sliders to calibrate every aspect of your picture. Turn to page 164 for the color commentary.

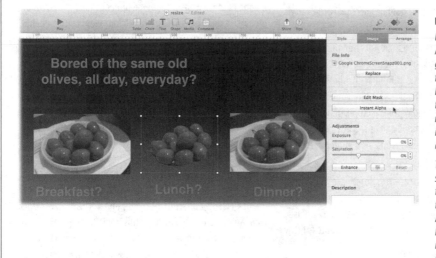

FIGURE 12-10

Use Keynote's Instant Alpha tool to make background colors see-through for a cutout effect. Here, Instant Alpha has removed the napkin and bowl in the middle photo, firmly placing those all-important olives in the spotlight.

To use Instant Alpha, select the picture, open the Format panel's Image tab, and then click Instant Alpha. Next, click and hold the color you want to remove, and then drag to include neighboring colors. See page 162 for more info.

◼ CREATING NEW SLIDES FROM PICTURES

When you want to fill one or more slides with a picture, drag and drop the picture (or group of pictures) directly onto the slide navigator. Keynote gives each picture a slide of its own using the master directly above your insertion point. If you're building a photo slideshow, for example, start with a blank master slide and then drag your pictures into position beneath it in the slide navigator. If you're using pictures that are at least the resolution of your slides (usually 800 × 600 or 1024 × 768 pixels), Keynote inserts them full-frame—no resizing required.

TIP Keynote places pictures added in this manner on the top layer. If the photo gets in the way of your text boxes, use the Arrange menu to send it to the back of your slide (see page 187).

Managing File Sizes for Image-Heavy Slideshows

Go ahead and fill your slideshows with lush visuals—rich imagery provides your audience with memory cues for recalling your points later. The one downside to packing your slideshow with pictures is that it can pack your hard drive, too. Pictures can be big, which in turn makes for big files. When size matters—if you're emailing your slideshow to someone, for example—Keynote offers some ways to keep a lid on your image-heavy documents.

◼ UP WITH DOWNSAMPLING: SHRINKING BIG IMAGES

Under the program's standard settings, when you insert an image, Keynote shrinks large pictures so that their width fits on the slide (for vertically oriented images, this means that the top and bottom may still spill outside the slide). This process, called *downsampling*, has two advantages: It's easier to work with images at this scale, and they take up less space on your hard drive.

NOTE This process doesn't affect the original image file from your iPhoto collection or hard drive; it just applies to the copy of the image that Keynote imports into your slideshow.

Keynote ships with downsampling turned on, but every once in a while, this normally helpful feature might get in your way. Downsampling reduces the overall size of the image, which means removing pixels and, with them, some of the finer details of your picture. If you want to use a tiny detail of a large picture, for example, your downsampled image may not look so good when you mask it and then try to blow up the detail. In this case, even clicking the Original Size button in the Format panel's Arrange tab won't help; Keynote considers the downsampled version that it imported to be your original image.

If you prefer to maintain a picture's original size when you add it to a slide, no matter how large the image might be, choose Keynote→Preferences, click the General tab, and then turn off "Scale placed images to fit on slide." From then on, Keynote inserts images at their full size.

■ REDUCING FILE SIZE

Are you actually using every pixel of those images you added? If you've shrunk or masked images in your slideshow (almost certainly the case if you've added any pictures by way of a media placeholder), you can tell Keynote to toss those unused pixels. The program will then save only the smaller version of the picture, shrinking your file size in the process.

To reduce the size of *all* images in your presentation (along with any shortened video or audio clips), choose File→Reduce File Size. Keynote asks if you really want to go through with this and provides a size savings estimate, as shown in Figure 12-11. (If Keynote can't reduce the file size of the media files any further, it lets you know that they're already at their optimal size.)

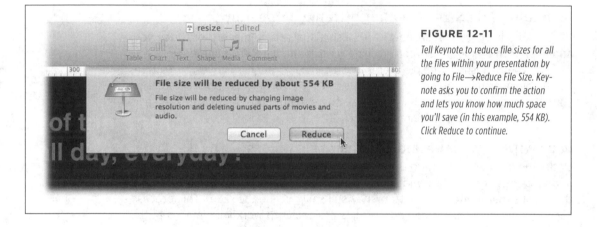

FIGURE 12-11

Tell Keynote to reduce file sizes for all the files within your presentation by going to File→Reduce File Size. Keynote asks you to confirm the action and lets you know how much space you'll save (in this example, 554 KB). Click Reduce to continue.

NOTE You can't pick and choose which images, audio clips, or video clips you reduce. When you run the Reduce File Size command, Keynote reduces *all* the media files throughout your document.

The one snag is that, after running this command, you no longer have the rest of the image to work with; as far as Keynote is concerned, the way the picture looks in your slideshow is now the original image. Any bits that you cropped out are no longer available, and enlarging the picture will look clunky at best. That means that it's a good idea to save this command until you've completed your slideshow and you're fairly sure that you're done working with its images (and audio and video clips). The *real* original image, however, remains untouched on your hard drive or iPhoto library, so if you need to go back to it, you can simply add the picture to the slideshow again.

NOTE Keynote can't shrink *all* images. Images used in image fills (page 196) or with action builds (page 371) are impervious to this weight-loss technique.

Adding Shapes

You can add simple geometric shapes, lines, and arrows to your slideshow by clicking the Shape button in the toolbar and then choosing from the drop-down menu. You can also insert shapes by choosing Insert→Shape and selecting a shape's name from this submenu.

You can adjust shapes' borders and fills, giving them colored, gradient, or image fills. And like all other objects, you can adjust their size, opacity, rotation, and so on. Shapes can also serve as creatively shaped text boxes: Double-click inside a shape and the blinking insertion point appears, ready for you to type or paste in text. (Head back to page 32 for a review of text editing in Pages.)

For the full story on working with shapes, see page 168.

Building Tables and Charts

When you need to present complex information or large amounts of data clearly, tables and charts can help you organize that info in an attractive and understandable way. Get started by clicking the toolbar's Table or Chart button to add the object to your slide, and then stroll back to Chapter 7 for a review.

When designing tables and charts for Keynote, be careful to keep them relatively simple and uncluttered so that they come through clearly on the screen. If you have a detailed table or chart where it's important that you get across every morsel of deliciously dense data, consider sharing it in a separate handout instead; paper does a much better job than a projected screen at presenting high-resolution info.

If you have more than a handful of data points or want to highlight anything more than big-picture trends, it's best to do your crunching in Numbers, and then print the results as your handout. In fact, because Numbers is specifically tuned to deal with data, it's almost always a good idea to run your numbers there and then paste them into Keynote, rather than working with them directly in your slideshow. That's particularly true when it comes to charts, as you'll learn in a moment. The bottom line: If you're just working with a handful of rows and columns, it's fine to do it in Keynote; when you're charting more complicated data or using tables with complex formulas, do your data work in Numbers.

Whatever method you use to get your tables or charts into Keynote, the program has a benefit not available in Pages or Numbers: You can build them gradually on the screen, disclosing a little bit of information at a time until you've revealed the entire table or chart. For example, a table could appear on the screen row by row, column by column, or even cell by cell. Likewise, chart data can appear one data series at a time, one data set at a time, or by individual data points. See pages 362–366 for details on creating builds for tables and charts.

Using Numbers Charts in Slideshows

The Chart Data Editor for Pages and Keynote (page 233) is simple but clunky, and it doesn't let you add formulas for automatic calculations like you can in Numbers charts. That's fine for simple data sets, but it's not ideal for larger collections of numbers. In those cases, save yourself time and frustration by creating your charts in Numbers and then pasting them into Keynote.

After you paste a Numbers chart into Keynote, you can update its data as usual from the Chart Data Editor.

■ Adding Movies

Add a little motion to your presentation by including a video. If you're feeling avant-garde, you can even add several movies per slide (though the performance you get with multiple movies depends on your computer's processing power).

To add a touch of the silver screen to your computer screen, click the toolbar's Media button to open the Media Browser, and then click the Movies tab. Select a video file to add it to the slide canvas. In the slide navigator, you'll notice that the slide's thumbnail now displays three white circles in its bottom-left corner. These circles also appear when you add an audio file to a slide, letting you see at a glance which slides contain media clips.

NOTE The Media Browser includes only movies stored in iPhoto, iMovie, and your Movies folder. Add other movies by dragging their icons from a folder on your hard drive onto the slide canvas, or by selecting Insert→Choose to find the file on your computer.

Keynote's media placeholders (page 286) welcome movies as well as images. When you drop a movie onto a placeholder, Keynote sizes and positions the movie to fit into the placeholder's border as closely as possible, adding picture frames, shadows, reflections, and any other effects the placeholder might carry with it. However, Keynote doesn't crop and squeeze movies to make them fill the whole placeholder as it does with pictures; the movie always keeps its proportions.

When you add a movie to a slide, the movie becomes a regular object—just like a picture or shape—and you can resize, rotate, add a shadow, or change its opacity just like any other object. Resize the movie by dragging one of its selection handles, and reposition it by dragging the movie itself.

NOTE If your video clip starts with a black screen and then fades in, it shows up on your slide as a black rectangle unless you use the Format panel's Movie tab to tell Keynote to display a different *poster frame* (click the Movie tab's Edit Movie heading to expand that section and display the Poster Frame slider—see Figure 12-12). Think of the poster frame as the movie poster that advertises your video; it's the frame of video that Keynote displays before you tell it to start playing the video. Keep in mind that, unless you tell it otherwise, Keynote doesn't play the video until you click the slide or press the space bar. If you tell Keynote to play your video as soon as you arrive at the slide, it's best to leave the poster frame set to the first frame in the movie. Otherwise, when the slide appears, the poster frame appears briefly onscreen before the movie begins playing—making a jumpy beginning to your video. See the list below for more about setting a poster frame.

Playing Movies

The Format panel's Movie tab is your virtual editing studio for preparing your movie screening. Here you control the length, volume, and playback preferences for the selected video. Click the Edit Movie heading to expand that section (as shown in Figure 12-12), and then set your preferences for the following:

- **Volume.** Use this slider to hush the movie from its full recorded volume; dragging it all the way to the left mutes the sound.

- **Trim.** This slider controls where your movie begins and ends. Drag the left handle to the frame where you want your video clip to start, and drag the right handle to where it should end. As you drag, Keynote updates your video.

- **Poster Frame.** Drag this slider to the frame of the video that you want to display before the movie starts playing.

- **Repeat.** This option is initially set to None, which means the movie plays through to the end and stops. Set this option to Loop instead, and the movie plays to the end and immediately starts again at the beginning—over and over. If you choose Loop Back and Forth, the movie plays to the end, switches into reverse, plays backward to the beginning, and then plays forward again—over and over. You might find this setting useful for a time-lapse movie of a rosebud opening or the clip of your kid in a high-dive competition.

- **Start movie on click.** Keynote's standard setting is to have this checkbox turned on, which means the movie waits for your signal (a click of the mouse or a press of the space bar) before it starts to play. Turn this setting off to make Keynote play your video as soon as the slide opens.

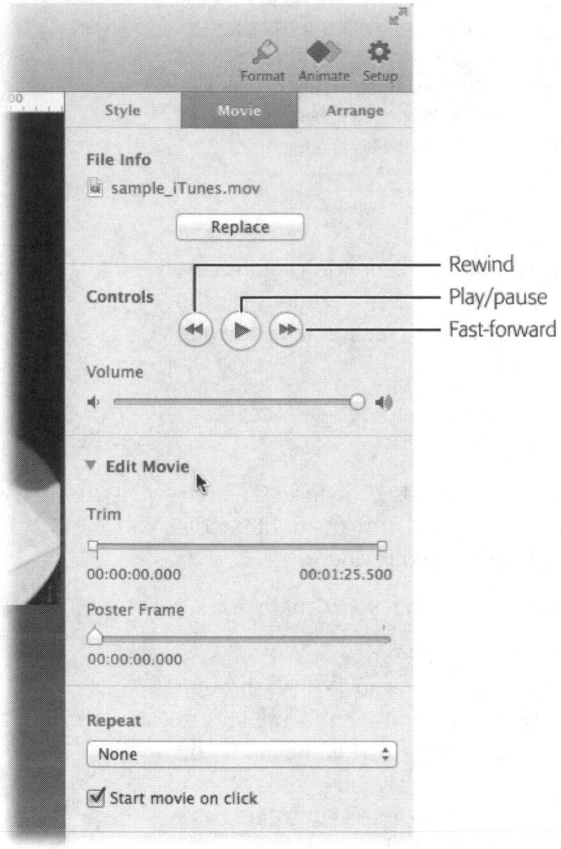

FIGURE 12-12

The Movie tab is your master projectionist, controlling all the technical details of your video's playback—from where it starts and stops to whether it loops. You can use the buttons labeled here to play, rewind, or fast-forward through the movie while you're editing.

Use the buttons in the Controls section to preview the movie while you're editing it. You can also play the movie on the slide canvas by clicking it once and then pause it by clicking again.

However, the Movie tab doesn't do you much good while you're actually presenting. Instead, Keynote gives you a set of video controls that appear when you point to the movie on the slide during your presentation. Under Keynote's standard settings, these controls are always available, but you can turn them on or off in the program's preferences: Choose Keynote→Preferences, click the Slideshow tab, and turn "Show playback controls when pointer is over a movie" on or off.

If you prefer not to sully your pristine slideshow with mouse pointers and video controls, you can instead use the keyboard to drive your movie during the presentation. Press or hold the keys listed in Table 12-1 to shuttle through the video. These key assignments may seem random when you read them on the page, but they make more sense when you rest your fingers on the J, K, and L keys. (No need to press ⌘ or any other key while using these keys; just press 'em solo to control your video.)

TABLE 12-1 *Keyboard controls for movie playback*

KEY	ACTION
J	Hold down to rewind
K	Press to pause; press again to continue playing
L	Hold down for fast-forward
I	Press to jump to the start of the movie
O	Press to jump to the end

Managing Multimedia Files

Under its standard settings, Keynote copies any audio or video files you include in your presentation into the Keynote document. This is exactly what you want if there's any chance that you might show your presentation on another computer (a possibility you should always plan for, in case your laptop gives up the ghost just as you step up to the podium).

The downside to this behavior is that these audio and movie files can turn your Keynote slideshow into a huge file. If you prefer to save disk space and don't want Keynote to import these files into your document file every time, you can tell it not to: Choose Keynote→Preferences, click the General tab, and then turn off the "Copy audio and movies into document" option. When this setting is turned off, Keynote doesn't copy audio and movies when you save your presentation.

If you opt to copy the audio and video files into your slideshow, you can take some steps to reduce the presentation's file size. When you shorten the length of a video clip by changing its start and stop endpoints, you can tell Keynote to leave the unused portion on the cutting room floor, discarding it from your file. To do this, go to Format→Reduce File Size (see page 334 for details).

NOTE The Reduce File Size command applies to *all* the files throughout your slideshow, including images and audio clips.

■ Making Noise: Sounds and Soundtracks

You can add sound—music, narration, or sound effects—to a Keynote presentation in three different ways: as a soundtrack for the entire show, as a song or sound effect for a single slide, or as voiceover narration for an auto-playing slideshow. This section focuses on the first two methods. For details about recording voiceovers for *recorded slideshows*, see page 395.

The sound files you add to your slides can be single iTunes songs (which don't have to be actual songs—they can be just sounds), a whole playlist, or one or more audio files you have in a folder on your hard drive. Keynote understands a wide range of sound files, including MP3, AIFF, AAC, and more.

Adding a Soundtrack

A Keynote *soundtrack* starts playing right from the first slide, and plays through all the slides for as long as the song or playlist lasts. Since a soundtrack affects the whole presentation, it doesn't matter which slide you choose when you set it up.

Start by preparing the soundtrack. If you're using more than one song or sound file, assemble them in an iTunes playlist. If your soundtrack consists of a single song or sound file, it doesn't *have* to be in iTunes—but having it there does make it easier to insert. Once you've got your files in order, follow these steps:

1. **Click the Setup icon at the right end of Keynote's toolbar to open the Setup panel, and then click its Audio tab, which is shown in Figure 12-13.**

FIGURE 12-13

The Setup panel's Audio tab (not to be confused with the Format panel's Audio tab, which is discussed in the next section) is soundtrack central. Drag files into the Add Audio Files box, or click the icon circled here to choose your favorite track(s). (Page 395 explains how to use this tab to record a voiceover for your presentation.)

If you change your mind about one of the tracks you've added, select it in the Audio tab's list of tracks and then press Delete.

2. **Add a song or playlist to your presentation.**

Keynote gives you a couple of ways to do this. You can drag files from your desktop or a Finder window into the box in the Audio panel labeled "Add Audio Files." Or you can click the icon circled in Figure 12-13 to open a trimmed-down version of the Media Browser that includes only sound files. Click the song or playlist you're interested in to add it to your presentation.

3. **If you've added more than one audio file and they're not in the right order for your presentation, drag them up or down in the Audio tab until they're in the order you want.**

4. **Use the Audio tab's Soundtrack drop-down menu to tell Keynote how to play your audio file(s).**

If you want your soundtrack to play through once, choose Play Once. Choose Loop instead if you want it to play over and over again. Or, if you want to present your slideshow without a soundtrack, you can choose Off to mute the soundtrack without deleting it from your presentation (so you can turn it back on later).

5. **Select a track in the Audio tab and then click the tab's Play button to preview your audio and set its volume level.**

Use the unlabeled volume slider to reduce your soundtrack's volume. (You can set only one volume level for the whole soundtrack; you can't set different tracks in your soundtrack to different volumes.) You should reduce the volume of your overall soundtrack, for example, when you want to add voiceover narration or sound effects for individual slides—which just happens to be the topic of the next section.

Adding Sound to a Single Slide

Sound files that you add to an individual slide play only while that slide is onscreen. You can use slide-specific sounds to layer sounds in your presentation. For example, you might want to add sound effects or narration over a background music track.

Keynote normally waits until you click or press the space bar before playing a slide's sound file, and then it continues playing it until the clip ends or you advance to the next slide. However, you can adjust this behavior by turning off the Audio tab's "Start audio on click" setting.

TIP Keynote can't play audio for just a selected set of slides. You can use a soundtrack to play audio through all slides, or you can play audio on a single slide, but you can't create audio for a limited selection. If that's something you really want to do, the only workaround is to add audio to a single slide and then use builds to change the content on that slide, faking the look of multiple slides. For more on builds, see page 358.

To add a sound file to a slide:

1. **Click the Media button in the toolbar to open the Media Browser, and then click the Music tab.**

2. **Click a song to add it to your presentation.**

If your song or sound file isn't available in the Media Browser, drag it onto the slide canvas from your desktop or a Finder window instead. Or click Insert→Choose, and then find the file you're after.

3. **In the slide canvas, click the new audio object to select it (see Figure 12-14).**

To signal that your slide has audio, Keynote represents the sound file with a loudspeaker icon on the slide canvas. You can move the sound icon anywhere on the slide—it's visible only when you're editing; Keynote doesn't show it when you play the slideshow. To play the sound when you're editing the slide, click the icon's Play button, and click the Pause button to, well, pause.

4. **In the Format panel, open the Audio tab—shown in Figure 12-14—if it doesn't open automatically.**

If you want your sound file to play through once, choose None from the Repeat drop-down menu. Choose Loop instead if you want it to play over and over again, or choose Loop Back and Forth to play the sound through forward and then play it backward—over and over until you advance the slide (but frankly, that's a little creepy).

FIGURE 12-14

When you add audio to your slide, it appears as a loudspeaker icon that you can select just like any other object. Click it and then open the Format panel's Audio tab to get access to Keynote's audio-editing controls (which are almost identical to its video-editing controls). You can play, pause, rewind, and fast-forward the audio clip using the buttons in the Controls section; change its volume using the Volume slider; decide whether the soundtrack should play through once or multiple times; and tell Keynote whether to start the audio as soon as you open the slide.

5. **If necessary, use the controls in the Audio tab's Edit Audio section to trim your sound file.**

Click the Edit Audio heading to expand that section. You can then use the two handles on the Trim slider to shave off the beginning or end of your sound file, if necessary.

6. **In the Audio tab's Controls section, click the Play button to preview your audio and set its volume level.**

Use the Volume slider to adjust your sound file's volume. The playback controls in the tab's Control section let you preview the sound while you set the volume.

NOTE Keynote can't add playback controls to slides.

When you're done fiddling with your new sound file, click the Play button in Keynote's toolbar to preview your audio-enhanced presentation.

■ Working with Hyperlinks

Keynote can turn almost any object on a slide—a text box, image, shape, table cell, or movie—into a *hyperlink*. You can even turn individual words into hyperlinks. A hyperlink is like a teleporter built right into your slideshow: Clicking one beams you away to a new onscreen location. You can tell Keynote to take you to any of these places when you click a hyperlinked object:

- A specific slide in the presentation

- A web page in your web browser

- A new, preaddressed email message in your email program

- The end of the slideshow, returning you to Keynote's edit mode

Among other things, hyperlinks provide the navigation when you're building a kiosk presentation or any slideshow where your viewers click buttons to steer through the slides on their own (such as a self-paced lesson or a product catalog). If you're creating a hyperlink-only presentation (see page 398), you *have* to create hyperlinks to move from one slide to the next—clicking the mouse button or using the space bar doesn't work. You can create a menu or table of contents, for example, so the viewer can navigate to different parts of the slideshow and add Forward and Back buttons to each slide.

To create a hyperlink, select some text or an entire text box, image, shape, or movie, and then choose Format→Add Link or press ⌘-K. This opens a window where you can make several decisions regarding said hyperlink (see Figure 12-15). Select the type of link from the "Link to" drop-down menu (the following sections describe your options). The settings in the hyperlink window change depending on the type of link you select. If you choose Exit Slideshow, for example, Keynote shows you no additional options; clicking the hyperlinked object simply ends the slideshow, depositing you back in edit mode. The other options, however, require more info, as described in the next few sections.

Keynote displays a hyperlink icon—a blue ball, bearing a white arrow (it's visible in Figure 12-15)—on any object you've added a hyperlink to. (This icon appears only while you're editing the slideshow, not during the presentation.) If you want to adjust a hyperlink's settings—to change it from a Slide link to a Webpage link, say—click this icon to reopen the hyperlink settings.

Linking to Slides

You can use hyperlinks to create doors between slides in your presentation, letting you skip from slide to slide by clicking the linked objects. To create this kind of link, select Slide from the "Link to" drop-down menu. When you do that, Keynote lets you choose which slide you want to link to (see Figure 12-15): Next slide, Previous slide, First slide, Last slide, Last slide viewed, or Slide [number].

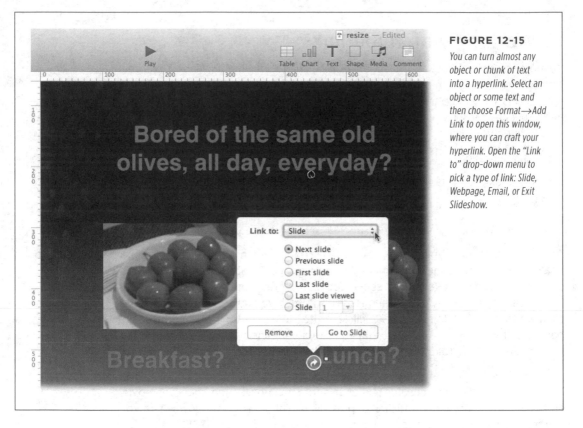

FIGURE 12-15

You can turn almost any object or chunk of text into a hyperlink. Select an object or some text and then choose Format→Add Link to open this window, where you can craft your hyperlink. Open the "Link to" drop-down menu to pick a type of link: Slide, Webpage, Email, or Exit Slideshow.

The "Last slide viewed" option can be useful for a button on a menu slide, for example, to return the viewer to the slide she was viewing before she came back to the menu—like the beloved Back button in your web browser.

The "Slide [number]" choice can jump to any slide in the slideshow. Simply enter the number of the slide you want to link to. If you later change the order of the slides in your presentation, Keynote keeps up with you by changing the hyperlink's slide number so that it continues to point to the same slide. For example, if you choose slide 15, but you later shuffle your slides so that it's now slide 12, Keynote updates the hyperlink to point to slide 12.

If you've selected a word or phrase for your slide hyperlink, the hyperlink settings window includes a Display field that contains the text you selected. Changing the text in this field updates the text in your slide and vice versa. Keynote underlines any text you've turned into a hyperlink on the slide canvas while you edit.

Linking to Web Pages

Let your slideshow travel the Web with this most familiar brand of hyperlink, a web link. To create this kind of link, in the "Link to" drop-down menu (Figure 12-15), choose Webpage. Then enter the web address in the Link field. (Feel free to skip the *http://* part—just start with *www.* and Keynote fills in the rest.)

When you click a web page link during your presentation, you step out of Keynote. Your web browser fires up and takes you to the selected web address. This means that your desktop is visible (so keep it tidy!), but Keynote hides so that your presentation isn't visible during your Internet session. After your jaunt around the Web, click the Keynote icon in the Dock to resume your presentation where you left off. (If you want your presentation to include an *image* of a web page rather than the actual page in your browser, the box on page 346 explains how to do that.)

NOTE   Under its standard settings, Keynote detects email and web addresses and turns them into hyperlinks *automatically*. So when you type an email or web address, Keynote underlines it and turns it into a hyperlink. To turn off this feature, choose Edit→Substitutions and then click the Smart Links option to remove the checkmark next to it.

Sending Email

Choose Email from the "Link to" drop-down menu (Figure 12-15) to create a link that opens a new message in your email program—preaddressed, with the subject line filled in, ready for you to write your message. This can be a handy way to get instant feedback from viewers of a self-paced lesson, or to collect contact info from potential customers at a tradeshow. In the hyperlink settings window, enter the email address for the message in the To field, and enter a subject line for the message in the Subject field.

When you turn a word or phrase into an email hyperlink, the Display field works the same way it does for a web page link (described above).

■ Note to Self: Adding Comments

Keynote doesn't offer the same kind of detailed change tracking as Pages, but it does let you add sticky-note comments to your slides—a quick way to leave yourself reminders or to let colleagues suggest changes for your presentation. One useful way to use comments, for example, is to slap them on your slides after doing a first-pass run-through of your presentation (see page 379)—quick, casual notes to capture your first impressions of where you need to tweak things: "Needs better transition," "Got lost here," "Where are the stats?" and so on.

Web Page Snapshots

Sometimes you don't want to actually open a web browser during your presentation—you simply want to show your audience a picture of a web page. Early versions of Keynote offered a feature called *web view*, which let you embed a screenshot of a web page in your slideshow; Keynote could reach out to the Web to update this snapshot on demand. Alas, this feature was removed in iWork '09, which means that when you want to include screenshots of web pages, you have to take them yourself.

Fortunately, OS X includes a program called Grab, which makes it easy to take *screen grabs*, a picture of your entire screen, a single window, or a specific portion of your screen. Here's how to use it to take a snapshot of a web page:

1. **In your web browser, open the page you want to include in your slideshow.**

2. **Open your Finder and launch Grab from your Mac's Applications→Utilities folder.**

3. **In Grab, choose Capture→Window.** Then take a moment to get your browser window sized and prepped just the way you want it.

4. **Click Grab's Choose Window button, and then click the browser window.** Grab snaps a picture of the web page and opens the resulting image in a new window.

5. **Choose File→Save and tell Grab where to save your image.** Grab saves your image as a TIFF file.

6. **In Keynote, select Insert→Choose, browse to the picture you just saved, and then click Insert.**

To make your screenshot clickable so that it also takes you to the actual web page, select the image in Keynote, and then add a Webpage hyperlink by going to Format→Add Link.

To add a comment to a slide, click the toolbar's Comment button or choose Insert→Comment. The first time you add a comment, Keynote asks permission to access your contacts. If you're fine with that, click OK; otherwise, click Don't Allow. After that, Keynote asks for a name to use for your comments; enter whatever you like in this field. (To change this name later, go to Keynote→Preferences, click the General tab, and edit the Author field.) Happily, you have to perform these setup steps only once. Keynote then adds a sticky note to your slide (see Figure 12-16). Type your suggestion, reminder, or hare-brained idea, and Keynote records it in the sticky note.

TIP If you select an object before adding a comment, Keynote links the two, so there's no doubt *which* text box you're complaining about.

Delete the comment by clicking Delete in the sticky note's bottom-left corner, or by selecting the comment and then pressing the Delete key. You can also hide comments without deleting them by choosing View→Comments→Hide Comments; bring them back with View→Comments→Show Comments.

FIGURE 12-16

Add a comment to a slide, and Keynote slaps on a sticky note—perfect for quick reminders or suggested changes. Drag the note to position it anywhere on the slide canvas, and resize it by putting your cursor over any of the note's four corners and then dragging when the cursor turns into a double-headed arrow. (If you selected an object before adding your comment, the comment is linked to that object, so you can't reposition the sticky note.)

Comments never appear in the slideshow you show to your audience, but if you have a presenter display set up while making a presentation (page 379), you can make the comments appear there. Be careful, though; you can't move the comments during the presentation, so they may hide parts of your slide that you'd like to be able to see during your talk. In general, you're better off using presenter notes instead of comments for reminders you want to keep handy during your talk. For the details, head back to page 295.

■ Changing Slide Backgrounds

Every master slide has a background that matches the other slides in its theme. It's usually a good idea to stick with these matching slide backgrounds for the sake of maintaining a consistent appearance throughout your slideshow. However, you may want to set off different segments of a presentation with different themes, or create a slide that diverges completely from the status quo (you rebel, you).

To change a slide's background, click any blank spot on the slide to open the Format panel's Slide Layout tab (if it doesn't appear, click the Format button in the toolbar and then press Esc to make sure you haven't accidentally selected any objects). On the tab, click the Background heading to expand that section. You can then open the first drop-down menu in that section to choose one of the following background fill types:

- **No Fill.** As you might expect, this choice removes the background entirely, rendering the background white. This is as close as you can get to the retina-burning white screen of a jammed slide projector. Unless you're going to be filling this white space with a lot of text or objects, it's probably not a very good choice. Unlike on the printed page, in the projection business, white space is *not* your friend.

- **Color Fill.** If you choose this option, a color well appears in the Slide Layout tab. Click it to choose from Keynote's default colors, or click the color wheel icon to launch the Color Picker (page 192).

- **Gradient Fill.** Choose this style to create a gradient—a gradual blending from one color into another. When you go this route, Keynote displays two color wells so you can choose your colors. In addition, you can control the angle of the color shift with the Angle knob, the arrow buttons, or by typing an angle directly into the angle measurement box. See page 194 for details on gradients.

- **Advanced Gradient Fill.** This option lets you add more colors to your gradient. Add colors, change where each color takes hold, and control how quickly the colors blend. You can also switch from a *linear gradient* to a *radial gradient*. Page 195 explains all of these advanced gradient settings.

- **Image Fill.** Choose this option if you want to use a photograph or other image as your slide background. This option is probably already selected if you're working on a slide that's part of a theme, since the theme's background is an image. With this setting selected, Keynote displays an image well in the blank space next to the Background heading. To use your own image, drag an image file from your hard drive into this image well, or click the Choose button and then select an image file in the dialog box that appears.

  When Image Fill is selected, the second drop-down menu in the Background section determines how Keynote displays your chosen image in the background. The menu's various options let you display the picture at its original size, stretched to fill the slide's background, tiled over the background (handy if you're working with a particularly small image), scaled and cropped to fill the whole background ("Scale to Fill"), or scaled to just fit the background ("Scale to Fit"). See page 196 for more details on how image fills work.

- **Advanced Image Fill.** This option is a variation on Image Fill. It lets you blend a color with an image in order to, for example, make a rosy sunrise picture even rosier. This is also a great way to dim a background image by tinting it black or white. You'll find details on page 198.

■ Adding Slide Numbers

You can add the Keynote equivalent of a page number—a slide number—to any slide. Click any blank spot on a slide to open the Format panel's Slide Layout tab, and then turn on the Slide Number checkbox. Keynote inserts the slide number, centered at the bottom of the slide, as a free text box (page 323). You can reformat the number or reposition this text box just like any other free text box. But unlike other text boxes, you can't add text or replace the number in it, since Keynote updates this number if you move the slide to a different position in the show. If you want your slide number to read, "Slide number 5," for example, you have to add *another* free text box to hold the words "Slide number."

If you want to use slide numbers throughout your presentation, you probably want to add the slide number to your master slides, as described on page 418.

Animating Slides

O ver the course of the last couple of chapters, you've written, organized, and designed your slides into the perfect presentation. Congratulations—you've no doubt got an elegant and insightful slideshow on your hands. But even after all your care and attention, your presentation still isn't all that different from an old-fashioned slideshow: a collection of static slides that march past your audience one after the other. Now it's time to make some waves in your slides' still waters by adding motion to your presentation, animating your slides with *transitions* and *builds*.

Transitions work their magic *between* slides, moving you from one slide to the next with effects that range from subtle dissolves to bombastic explosions that send objects flying on and off the screen. Builds, on the other hand, happen *within* individual slides, letting you pull the strings of objects and bullet points to make them appear, disappear, move, grow, shrink, and generally dance on your slides.

Besides adding some visual excitement to your slideshow, transitions and builds can help you present information more clearly, add drama, signal changes in topic, and—if you use them wisely—give your slideshow a professional polish. This chapter takes you through Keynote's special-effects laboratory to show you how to add slide transitions and object builds.

■ Adding Transitions

Until you add a transition between slides, Keynote switches instantly from one slide to another—a quick change that film editors call a *hard cut*. Transitions soften things up, easing from one slide to another with a visual effect. Be adventurous in your experimentation with transitions but judicious in what you actually choose for your final presentation. Go easy on the flash and sparkle—you're building a presentation, after all, not a pinball machine. You don't want your audience to walk away impressed by your fancy transitions but unable to remember your message.

Transitions can serve two very different purposes in a slideshow: They can create smooth and subtle segues from one slide to another, or they can provide dramatic punctuations that highlight the break between slides. So when you choose transitions, think about whether your goal is to move smoothly to the next slide, to provide a noticeable break between topics, or to startle the audience with your visual derring-do.

Also, consider your message and your audience as you choose transitions. If your presentation is a morale booster for the cheerleading team, you can probably get away with anything. But if you own a funeral home and your presentation to the bereaved describes the various services you offer, you'll want to opt for a more reserved set of transitions. If you have any doubt about which transition to use, err on the side of simplicity.

To insert a transition between two slides, you add it to the *first* slide in the pair. It can help to think of transitions as graceful exits—you apply a transition to a slide to determine exactly how it passes the torch to the next slide. In the slide navigator, Keynote indicates transitions by adding a small blue triangle to the bottom-right corner of the thumbnails (Figure 13-1).

FIGURE 13-1

Keynote reminds you that you've added a transition to a slide by adding a tiny blue triangle to its thumbnail in the slide navigator. When you play the slideshow, the transition appears between that slide and the one that follows it.

Because transitions control the flow to the next slide only, you can't create a transition into the first slide of the presentation. If you want to start with a transition, you need to create a blank slide for the beginning of the show and transition from that to your "real" first slide.

To add a transition, in the slide navigator, select the slide(s) you want to apply it to, and then click the Animate button in the toolbar to open the Animate panel's Transitions tab. (When you add a transition to several slides at once, it becomes the exit transition for each of the selected slides.) To choose a transition style, click the "Add an Effect" button at the top of the tab, which opens the gigantic Effects drop-down menu shown in Figure 13-2.

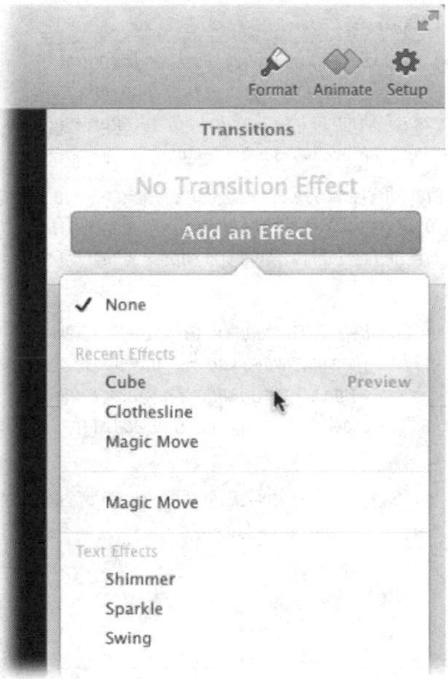

FIGURE 13-2

You control and preview slide transitions from the Transitions tab's Effects drop-down menu (click the "Add an Effect" button to open it). Keynote includes a lot of transitions, so be sure to scroll through the whole menu.

To add an effect to your selected slide(s), click its name. To preview a transition, click the word "Preview" next to its name.

TIP If you add a transition and then change your mind, you can get the Effects drop-down menu back by clicking the Transitions tab's Change button.

The Effects drop-down menu divides transitions into several categories. Choose None at the very top of the menu to strip the slide(s) of any transition, reverting to Keynote's standard hard cut. Below that, the Recent Effects section shows the last few transitions you used in your recent Keynote slideshows (you don't see this section if you're adding your first transition). Consider this Keynote's subtle way of encouraging you to reuse the same transitions rather than cramming as many variations as possible into your slideshow. Transitions are like fonts: You usually need only one or two styles in a single presentation.

After those options, the Effects drop-down menu lists all of Keynote's transition effects. To preview each one, click the word "Preview" next to the effect's name in the menu (see Figure 13-2). When you find an effect you like, click its name to add it to your selected slides(s). Keynote previews the effect and updates the Transitions tab to include various settings for that transition. The exact settings you see depend on which effect you choose; Figure 13-3 shows the settings for the Flip effect.

FIGURE 13-3

Use the slider in the Duration & Direction section to control how long the transition lasts. You can set transition durations anywhere from a fraction of a second up to 60 seconds—but most of them look best in the 1- to 2-second range.

Many transition effects move from one side of the screen to the other, move in or out, and so on. The drop-down menu in the Duration & Direction section is where you choose which way the effect moves.

The Start Transition drop-down menu controls whether Keynote switches to the next slide only when you click the mouse or press the space bar (choose On Click) or automatically after a specified amount of time (choose Automatically and then adjust the Delay field).

To preview your transition after tweaking these settings, click the Preview button near the top of the tab.

TIP If you find that you nearly always use the same transition between slides, save yourself some time by adding that transition to your master slides. This makes your selected transition the standard offering for all slides based on the masters you select. For more on editing master slides, see page 418.

The following sections describe some of Keynote's specialized transition effects.

Adding Object Effects

Object effects (which are listed in their own section of the Effects drop-down menu; see Figure 13-2) move every object on your slide—sometimes separately, sometimes individually. Every screen element—even individual bullet points, in some cases—moves as you switch to a new slide. Object effects are at their most dramatic for transitions between slides that each include several images or other objects and when both slides have the same background.

Object effects are often best used when you're continuing on the same or similar topic as the previous slide. That's because they make it *look* as if you remain on a single slide while words and pictures move on and off. Keynote swaps individual objects out for other objects, creating the illusion that you're not changing slides so much as changing specific elements—introducing new points rather than an entirely new topic.

Here are the object effects you can choose from:

- **Object Cube.** The screen appears to turn as if the two slides were pasted onto neighboring sides of a cube.

- **Object Flip.** The objects flip like a postcard, revealing the second slide on the reverse. You can flip them from the right, the left, randomly, or make them all revolve simultaneously.

- **Object Pop.** The objects on the first slide shrink and disappear, and then the objects on the second slide appear tiny and grow to full size.

- **Object Push.** The first screen slides out of the way to make room for the second. Here, however, the objects on the slide move in a staggered sequence, so that every bullet point, image, chart, and table moves on and off the screen at its own pace.

- **Object Zoom.** Every object from the first slide zooms out toward the viewer and gets replaced by the objects from the second slide, which zip into place from the far distance.

- **Perspective.** This one scatters slide elements to the wind: The first slide tilts into the distance and its objects fly in all four directions while the second slide's objects scramble to assemble.

Wordplay with Text Effects

Like object effects, *text effects* create slide transitions by transforming individual objects—but these effects focus only on the slides' text, right down to animating individual letters. Other objects dissolve in and out to complete the transition. The result is a clever replacement of one word or phrase with another.

These effects are perfect for slides with large, prominent text, like two title-only slides where you want to show movement from one concept to another: "Consumption" transforms to "Conservation," for example. For best results, make sure that the text on both slides is in the same font and size; it's also a good idea to make sure the text is in the same spot on both slides.

Like object effects, text effects have their own section in the Effects drop-down menu (see Figure 13-2). These are your options:

- **Shimmer.** This effect lights up the words on the first slide in magic pixie dust, making them transform dazzlingly into the words on the second slide.

- **Sparkle.** This transition lights a fuse under your slideshow, sending a field of sparks running across the text on the first slide, changing it to the text on the next slide as it goes.

- **Swing.** Text boxes on the first slide swing as if hanging from their top edges, spinning up and around and transforming into the words on the second slide, which swing for a moment before coming to a halt.

Magic Move Transitions

Keynote's object and text effects are useful when you're replacing the objects on one slide with completely new ones. But what about when you have the same object on both slides? That's where *Magic Move* comes in, gracefully animating a graphic from slide to slide. While an object effect would sling all of one slide's objects offscreen to make room for the next slide, the Magic Move transition is more discriminating. The "magic" kicks in when Keynote identifies images, shapes, or text boxes that appear on both slides and glides them—voilá!—to their new locations on the second slide. Meanwhile, other objects from the old slide dissolve away as new ones fade in.

Say that your title slide features the enormous and impressive logo of Crazyland Wonderpark, and the second slide also includes the logo, but this time tucked away in the bottom-right corner. With the Magic Move transition, the logo coasts smoothly down into the corner, shrinking as it goes, as the rest of the slide's new content fades in. That's right—Keynote not only *moved* the logo, but it shrank it, too. Magic Move lets you move, resize, rotate, and fade objects from slide to slide. Flip them, add shadows, change color fill, add reflections—Magic Move "tweens" all these changes, morphing an object to its new appearance. Figure 13-4 shows an example.

The secret behind Keynote's magic trick is that the transition works only when you start with the *same* image, movie, or shape on both slides. Keynote is pretty clever about figuring out which objects are the "same," but for the most foolproof results, it's a good idea to copy the object from one slide to the next. You can do this by pasting an object from the first slide to the second slide, or by duplicating the *entire* first slide and then modifying its contents to make the second. As far as Keynote is concerned, the clones on the two slides are now linked. No matter how you bump them around and change their object properties on either slide, the Magic Move transition keeps up, gliding the object from one slide to the next.

> **NOTE** Magic Move doesn't work with tables, charts, text boxes, or grouped objects. Also, it doesn't work on shapes if you change the text they contain.

For best results with Magic Move, follow these steps:

1. **Create your first slide with all the elements that you want to use.**

2. **Select the slide in the slide navigator, and then duplicate it by choosing Edit→Duplicate Selection.**

3. **In the duplicate slide, change one (or more) of the objects on the page by repositioning, resizing, rotating, or changing its opacity, color, reflection, or shadow.**

   You can change the object's *properties*, but not its *content*. Magic Move works only on objects that have the exact same text (for shapes) or picture on both slides. Other objects simply dissolve in and out during the transition.

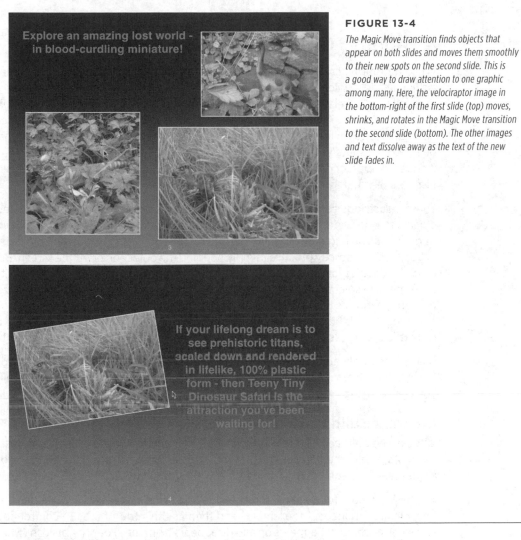

FIGURE 13-4

The Magic Move transition finds objects that appear on both slides and moves them smoothly to their new spots on the second slide. This is a good way to draw attention to one graphic among many. Here, the velociraptor image in the bottom-right of the first slide (top) moves, shrinks, and rotates in the Magic Move transition to the second slide (bottom). The other images and text dissolve away as the text of the new slide fades in.

4. **Add any other objects you want on your new slide, and delete any objects you don't.**

5. **Select the first slide in the slide navigator, and then, in the Animate panel's Transitions tab, choose Magic Move from the Effects drop-down menu (see Figure 13-2).**

   When you play the slideshow, the shared objects morph to their new locations and sizes on the second slide.

TIP To see some examples Magic Move in action, go to *www.missingmanuals.com/cds* and download the sample presentation *magic_move.keynote*. Every slide in that slideshow uses Magic Move.

■ Adding Object Builds

While transitions create animations between slides, *object builds* add animations *within* a slide. Builds got their name because they originally did just one thing: gradually added elements to a slide, *building* it up block by block until the whole slide was in place. Although each generation of presentation software has added new features to builds, this building function is still very much at the center of what builds do. This lets you do things like make bullet points appear one by one; bring pictures, shapes, or other objects onto the slide individually or in groups; or gradually display a pie chart slice by slice as you talk through each of its elements.

These industrious construction workers are called *build ins* because they add new objects to your slide. Their counterparts—the demolition workers—are called *build outs* and, as you might guess, their role is to remove objects from a slide. Both types of builds can be strictly practical, simply popping the object on or off the screen. But Keynote provides lots of eye candy you can use to introduce objects into slides, with an impressive selection of animation styles that make your graphics plunge, blaze, pop, and sparkle as they materialize. (As with transitions, use discretion when adding object builds. It's nice to have all these options available, but not every slide needs its text to appear as if it's been shot from a machine gun or whirled in a Cuisinart.)

Builds aren't only about grand entrances and exits, however. *Action builds* let you move objects from place to place on a slide—and shrink, grow, or rotate them while you're at it. The following sections explain how to use all three kinds of object builds.

Creating Build Ins and Build Outs

If you haven't already, click the Animate button in the toolbar to open the Animate panel. As you learned earlier, the first tab you see there is Transitions. But as soon as you select any object, you get three new tabs: Build In, Action, and Build Out.

The basic process for creating object builds on a slide is to select an object—a text box, picture, or shape, for example—and then use this trio of tabs to control how and when each object appears on and disappears from the slide. The build in (when objects appear on the slide) and the build out (when objects disappear from the slide) are completely separate operations. You can have either one without the other, or you can have both (or none at all).

TIP Want to edit a slide transition but don't see the Transitions tab? Simply deselect all objects on your slide (either by clicking an empty area or by pressing the Esc key), and the Transitions tab reappears.

The basics of setting up a build are a lot like adding a transition, except that you apply the effect to an object rather than to a whole slide:

1. **Make sure the Animate panel is open (click the Animate button in the tool-bar, if necessary).**

2. **Select the object that you want to build.**

   The object you pick can be any kind of text box, a single bulleted item, a picture, chart, table, movie, or sound file. When you select an object, the Animate panel changes to display three tabs: Build In, Action, and Build Out.

3. **To determine how this object *appears* on the slide, click the Build In tab.**

   To determine how it *disappears* from the slide, click the Build Out tab instead.

4. **Click the tab's "Add an Effect" button to open the Effects drop-down menu (shown back in Figure 13-2), and choose an animation style for your build.**

   See page 293 for a reminder of how to choose an animation effect from this menu. When you apply an effect, Keynote plays it once, and updates the Build In tab to include settings related to the effect you chose (see Figure 13-5). You can see the effect again by clicking the tab's Preview button.

5. **If applicable, choose a direction for your effect from the drop-down menu in the Duration & Direction section.**

   Like transitions, many build effects let you choose whether an object makes its entrance from the left or the right, by plunging down from above, and so on.

6. **Use the slider and/or text field in the Duration & Direction section to tell Keynote how much time you want it to spend performing the effect.**

7. **If applicable, use the settings in the Delivery section to control how text within your selected object appears or disappears.**

   The next section (page 360) has info on using these settings to control how Keynote animates text.

That's it—you've just added a basic build to your slide! Enjoy its full onscreen effect by playing the slideshow. If you created a build *in*, the slide first appears without the object you added the build to. Trigger the build by clicking your mouse or pressing the space bar; instead of advancing to the next slide, Keynote makes your object materialize onscreen. Likewise, when a slide contains a build *out*, the object is initially included onscreen, and clicking the mouse or pressing the space bar sends the object on its way.

When you add several builds to a single slide, Keynote normally marches through them one at a time; each time you click during your presentation, you trigger the next build. After all the builds are complete, clicking advances to the following slide.

You can control the order in which these builds happen by clicking the Build Order button at the bottom of the Animate panel (see Figure 13-5), and then dragging and

CHAPTER 13: ANIMATING SLIDES   359

dropping builds to reorder them. You can also make builds happen simultaneously or trigger them automatically after a specific amount of time. For the full story on controlling build order, see page 367.

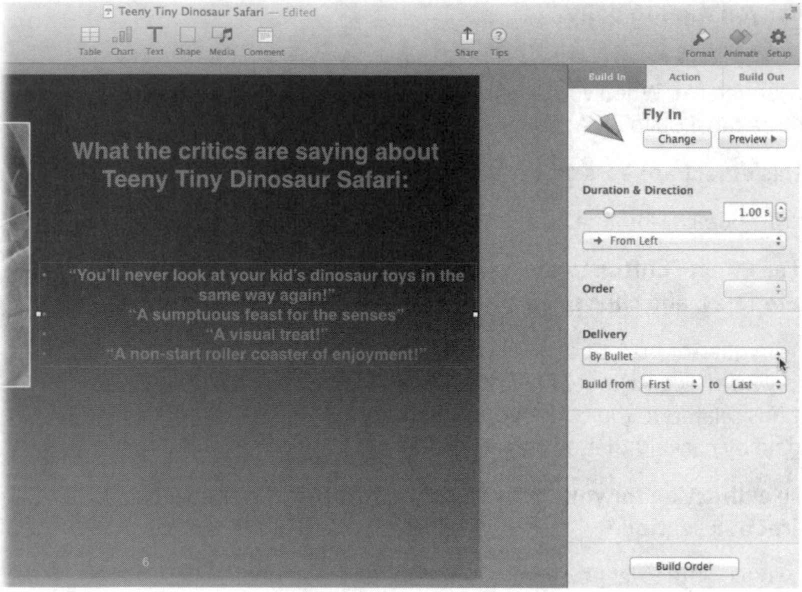

FIGURE 13-5

When you add a build to a text box, you can make Keynote show or hide its bullet points one at a time. The settings in the Build In tab in this screenshot mean that the bullet points fly onscreen from the left, one bullet point at a time.

Choose an option from the Delivery drop-down menu to give each bullet point its own moment to shine.

TIP You can add a build to a set of grouped objects (see page 321 for details on Keynote's Group command). When you do this, the entire group builds in or out as if it were a single object. Be careful, though: If you ungroup the objects, then Keynote tosses out the build; even if you regroup the objects later, you have to add the effect all over again. One workaround for this is to copy the group's build settings before you ungroup the objects: Select the group, choose Format→Copy Animation. Then ungroup the objects and make whatever changes you want to make. Finally, regroup the objects, and then choose Format→Paste Animation to restore the group's build settings. See page 376 for more about copying builds.

When you first create your build, the animation applies to the entire object (or group). The whole text box, for example, materializes or vanishes at once when you play the slideshow. With the exception of pictures, however, all objects contain additional content elements—bullet points, graph bars, table rows, and so on—and you can make Keynote reveal these elements individually instead of all at once. As the following sections explain, the specific options you have vary according to the type of object you're working with.

■ BUILDING TEXT

Body text boxes, free text boxes, and shapes offer options that let you build the text bullet by bullet or paragraph by paragraph. When you're giving your presentation, that means you can reveal each bullet point or paragraph as you discuss it (so your audience doesn't read ahead), or get rid of each bullet or paragraph when you're done talking about it. To achieve that effect, each bit of text gets its very own build—which means that clicking the mouse or pressing the space bar steps through the build for each bit of text.

Start by adding your text—either a bulleted list or multiple paragraphs—to a shape or text box. Then select the shape or text box at the object level (page 149) and add a build in or build out as described in the previous section. You can then control how Keynote reveals the text of the selected text box or shape by choosing an option from the Delivery drop-down menu shown in Figure 13-5. "All at Once" is the standard setting and applies the build to the entire text box at once, with no individual treatment of the content inside. Depending on the text you've added to your object and the type of effect you're applying, you'll see some of the following options:

- **By Bullet.** Choose this option to build one bullet at a time.

- **By Bullet Group.** For nested bulleted lists, this option steps through each top-level bullet one at a time, simultaneously building any bullets indented below it.

- **By Highlighted Bullet.** Like the By Bullet option, this method steps through the bullets one at a time, but it also dims preceding bullets so that only the current bullet is highlighted, as shown in Figure 13-6.

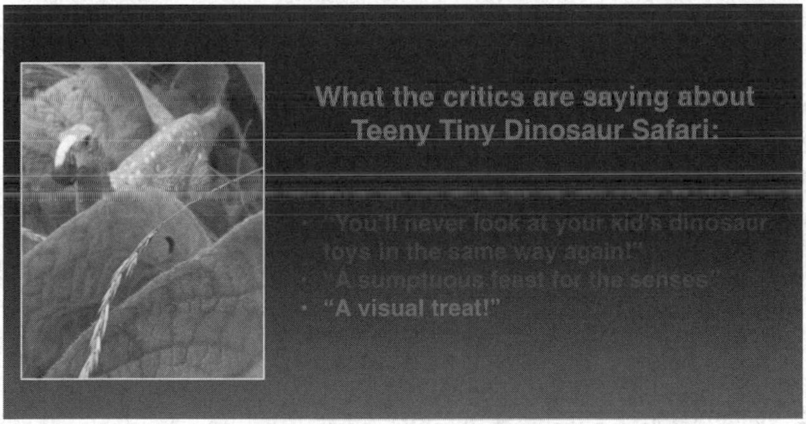

FIGURE 13-6

As you build a bulleted list with the By Highlighted Bullet option selected, Keynote fades previous bullet points and highlights the most recent one.

- **By Paragraph.** Like the By Bullet option described above, this setting applies a separate build to each paragraph.

- **By Paragraph Group.** Stagger the animation based on each *block* of text (a block can be a paragraph or a bullet point).

- **By Highlighted Paragraph.** When you select this option for a build-in effect, Keynote highlights each block of text as it appears. When you use this option for a build-out effect, each paragraph is highlighted briefly before it disappears.

TIP Some text effects (page 360) let you further choose how to apply the effect—making it happen letter by letter, word by word, or all at once. Dissolve, Flip, Move In, and Move Out all let you make the choice; just open the Text Delivery drop-down menu and choose from By Object, By Word, or By Character.

When you choose one of these bullet- or paragraph-delivery options, the "Build from" settings appear below the Delivery drop-down menu (you can see them in Figure 13-5). The standard setting is First to Last, which means Keynote builds every item in the text box. If you want to apply the effect to only *some* of the items in the text box, choose the beginning and ending bullet or paragraph numbers from the two drop-down menus.

Keynote normally treats all the builds for the bullets or paragraphs within a shape or text box as a single group, building the items one after the other as you click through them in your presentation. However, you may want to blend in other builds as you step through your list. Say you want to reveal a new picture every time you move to a new item in a product list. To do that, click the Build Order button at the bottom of the Animate panel, and Keynote shows every bullet point as its own item in the Build Order window, so you can reorder each one individually. For details on ordering builds, see page 367.

NOTE While you can change the order of builds for individual bullets to interweave them with other object builds, text builds can happen only from the top down. In other words, you can't make the last bullet build before the first, for example.

■ BUILDING TABLES

Tables are chock-full of content bits and pieces: rows, columns, cells, and the text inside them. Keynote gives you a variety of ways to gradually show or hide these elements, letting your content take its place at the table little by little. With the following techniques, you can build dramatic tension as you reveal your table data and build up to the final column, for example, to show this year's dismal sales figures for mints and olives as entirely separate foodstuffs, and then the sky-high projected sales for—*wait for it!*—"Mints & Olives (Now in a Can!)"

To begin, select a table, and then open the Animate panel's Build In or Build Out tab, depending on the effect you want to create. Select a build effect, direction, and duration as described on page 359, and then choose one of the following table build options from the tab's Delivery drop-down menu:

- **All at Once.** This is the standard delivery option; Keynote treats the whole table as a single object.

- **By Row.** Choose this option to build *in* the table one row at a time, starting at the top, or build *out* the table one row at a time, starting at the bottom.

- **By Column.** This option builds in the table one column at a time, starting at the left, or builds out the table one column at a time, starting at the right.

- **By Cell.** Select this option to build in the table one cell at a time, left to right and top to bottom. When building out, this option removes cells one at a time beginning at the bottom right.

- **By Row Content.** This option first builds in the entire table, but with all of its cells empty, and then fills in the cells' contents row by row. When building out, Keynote reverses the process, removing the contents of each row from the bottom up and finally removing the entire, now-empty table.

- **By Column Content.** Like By Row Content, this option first builds in the empty table and then fills in each column's content. When building out, Keynote removes the contents of each column before deleting the table's framework.

- **By Cell Content.** Choose this option to build in the table's structure followed by the cells' contents, one cell at a time starting at the top left. When building out, Keynote removes the contents of each cell starting at the lower right before finally removing the table's framework.

- **By...Reverse.** You can also use any of the above effects in reverse by choosing the menu item with "Reverse" at the end of it (for example, By Row Content Reverse or By Cell Reverse). As the name suggests, this is the standard effect—but back-to-front. For example, By Cell Content builds in from the bottom up and builds out from the top down.

TIP With all the build effects that tables has to offer, things can get a little complicated. Should you use Row Content build in, or By Row Content Reverse build out? And what's the difference, anyway? If you're getting in a tangle, you can always apply the effect, preview it (click the Preview button at the top of the tab), and then change your mind and press ⌘-Z to undo the effect, or choose a new effect from the Effects drop-down menu.

No matter which delivery option you choose, all the table's elements share the same build effect. Building in and building out, however, are separate actions, so you can make a table leave the slide in a different way than it arrived. You could, for example, build in the table by row content with the Move In effect and then build it out by column with the Dissolve effect.

To coordinate or interweave the builds for your table with those of other objects, open the Build In or Build Out tab, and then click the Build Order button. As with bullets or paragraphs in text builds, this option lets you change the build order of each table element or specify its own build timing. For details on controlling build order, see page 367.

■ BUILDING CHARTS

Like tables, you can build in or build out a chart all at once—like any other object—or gradually, to dramatically assemble or disassemble it from its various elements. Send the wedges of a pie chart flying, or make the columns of your bar chart stand up one at a time. The order is determined by the order your data appears in the Chart Data Editor (page 236).

To apply a build to a chart, select the chart, and then open the Animate panel's Build In or Build Out tab. Then click the "Add an Effect" button and select your build effect. Once you use the tab's settings to pick direction and duration options, you're ready to choose an option from the Delivery drop-down menu. Your exact options depend on the type of chart you're building. For 2D charts, your options may include these:

- **All at Once.** This is the standard delivery option; Keynote treats the chart as a single object.

- **Background First.** Choose this option and Keynote builds in the chart in two steps: first the background, axes, and gridlines, then the chart's data. For a build out, Keynote performs these steps in reverse.

- **By Series.** Select this option for a build-in effect, and Keynote first adds the chart's background and then adds its data, one data series at a time. For a build out, the effect is the opposite.

- **By Set.** When you choose this option for a build in, Keynote first adds the chart's background and then adds its data, one data set at a time. You guessed it: It works the opposite way for a build out.

> **TIP** Need to brush up on the difference between data series and data sets? See page 234.

- **By Element in Series.** With this option, Keynote builds in the chart by first adding the chart's background and then adds each data point, one data series at a time. Building out works the opposite way.

- **By Element in Set.** You guessed it—Keynote first builds in the chart's background and then adds each individual data point, one data set at a time. For a build out, it performs these steps in reverse order.

- **By Wedge.** This option is available only for pie charts. Choose it, and Keynote builds the chart in or out one slice at a time.

> **NOTE** Keynote gives you only three options for area charts: All at Once, Background First, and By Series. When you build a pie chart, you get only two choices: All at Once and By Wedge.

For 3D charts, the Delivery menu offers the same set of options listed above. However, the Effects drop-down menu for this type of chart offers several remarkable 3D effects that provide a dramatic drumroll for your three-dimensional data, letting viewers seemingly swoop and swirl around the chart as it comes into view. These effects are listed under the 3D Chart Effects category in the Effects drop-down menu (Figure 13-7):

- **3D Crane.** Swoops into the chart as it spins and grows, like a Hollywood crane shot. Build outs do the same thing, but while pulling *back*.

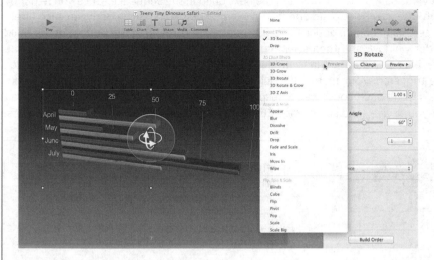

FIGURE 13-7

3D charts get special treatment in the Effects drop-down menu, with a special category of 3D effects for build ins and build outs. (For 3D pie charts, the menu includes one additional option not shown here: 3D Radial.)

- **3D Grow.** The bars, lines, or wedges of your chart sprout into view for build ins and shrink away for build outs.

- **3D Radial.** For pie charts only: The wedges fly into the center for build ins and explode out for build outs.

- **3D Rotate.** The chart builds in by spinning horizontally into place or builds out by spinning away.

- **3D Rotate & Grow.** Two great tastes that go great together: This one combines the Grow and Rotate effects into a single, simultaneous show-stopper.

- **3D Z Axis.** The chart pushes into the slide as if nudged in from the audience's side of the screen. For build outs, the chart zooms toward the viewers and out of the screen.

With 3D effects, Keynote giveth, and Keynote taketh away; except for the Grow effect, these 3D builds have fewer delivery options than their 2D cousins. Most of the 3D effects have just two: All at Once and Cascade, which gradually reveals (or hides) all the data points in a wave.

No matter what build effect you choose when you build a chart, the chart's background and data elements all use that same effect. But you can choose different build effects for building in and building out.

When you add builds for charts, as with tables and text, you can reorder and set timings for the individual elements in your object. Just click the Build Order button to open the Build Order window, which lists all the builds on the current slide (see

Figure 13-8). You can reorder them by dragging them into new positions in the list. By default, Keynote plays each of your builds when you click your mouse, but you can automate them by telling Keynote to wait a specific period of time after the previous build before triggering the next build in the sequence. Once you're happy with the order your build effects run in, you can set the delay between each effect by selecting a build, opening the Start drop-down menu at the bottom of the Build Order window, and then selecting the After Build option. You can then type the specific delay duration in the Delay field. You can also mix and match how builds are triggered: Your first build could trigger when you click the mouse (On Click), the second build could wait 5 seconds and then trigger, the third build could wait for you to click, and so on. Page 367 has more details about adjusting build orders.

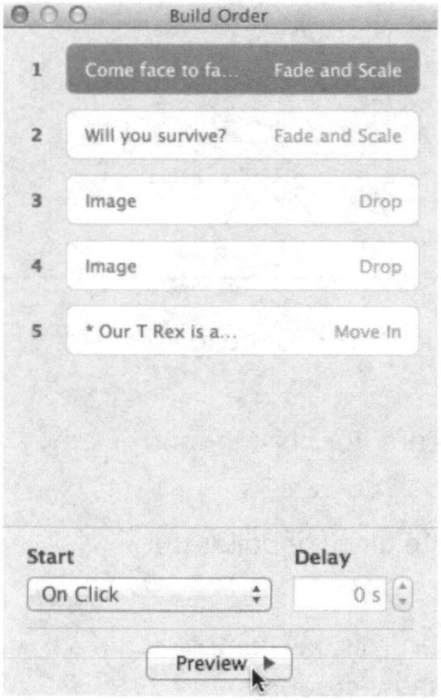

FIGURE 13-8

The Build Order window lists all of a slide's builds in the order that Keynote will play them during your presentation. Each item in this list includes the object's name and the build effect you've applied to it.

Drag builds up or down in this list to change their order. To preview a build, select it in this list, and then click the Preview button.

Controlling Movies and Sounds with Builds

When a slide includes a sound or a video clip, Keynote doesn't start playing this media clip automatically when you open the slide during your presentation; you need to press the space bar or click the screen again to get it to start playing. However, by using builds, you can automate when audio or video starts playing on your slide. When you add a build into a movie or sound, the clip automatically starts playing when the build occurs. Likewise, a build out makes the clip *stop* playing.

TIP You can also tell Keynote to start playing a media clip automatically by selecting the audio or video object, opening the Format panel's Audio/Movie tab (the name of the tab depends on which type of clip you're working with), and then turning off the "Start [audio/movie] on click" checkbox. After that, Keynote will start playing the clip as soon as the slide opens.

Movies have the usual assortment of visual effects that you can add to their builds, so you can add the Dissolve effect, for example, to make a movie materialize onscreen as it starts to play. Movies also have a pair of effects that are unique to them: Start Movie (for build ins) and Stop Movie (for build outs). Unlike build ins and build outs for other objects, these start-and-stop effects don't move the movie on or off the screen. Choosing Start Movie for a build in means the movie still takes its place on the slide as soon as the slide appears—the build in simply makes the clip start playing. Similarly, choosing Stop Movie for a build out doesn't remove the movie from the slide; it just stops the action.

Meanwhile, the *only* effects available for sound objects are Start Audio and Stop Audio, since sounds—as you know—don't appear onscreen.

■ Ordering and Automating Builds

As you gradually turn a once-quiet slide into a symphony of elaborate builds, you'll need to play conductor to keep your animations in organized harmony. The Build Order window is where you coordinate the order and timing of the current slide's builds. You can tell Keynote to play certain builds automatically, wait for your click, or launch several builds at once.

Open the Build Order window by clicking the Build Order button at the bottom of the Animate panel's Build In, Action, or Build Out tabs. No matter which tab you launch the Build Order window from, it always lists all the current slide's build effects (see Figure 13-8). Every time you add a new build to any object on the slide, Keynote adds it to this master list, which acts as the playlist for your slide's performance; when you play the slideshow, Keynote steps through the builds in the order shown here. New builds get added to the end of this list, but you can change this order by dragging the build to a new spot in the list.

Click an item in the Build Order window, and then click Preview to see that build effect in action. You can click through the effects one at a time to see how the slide will behave during your presentation. Selecting a build in this window makes Keynote display its settings in the Animate panel, ready for you to edit (if the Build Order window is getting in the way, you can drag it to one side). To delete a build, select it in the Build Order window, and then press Delete.

TIP Want to get some practice changing the running order of builds? Go to this book's Missing CD page at *www.missingmanuals.com/cds* and download *build_order.keynote*. This sample presentation is full of build-in and build-out effects; it's currently a bit of a mess, but you can neaten it up by opening the Build Order window and making some adjustments.

Playing Builds Automatically or Simultaneously

Keynote's standard behavior is for a build to play only after you click the mouse or press the space bar during your presentation. In other words, Keynote waits for your signal before continuing to the next build in the list. However, you can give Keynote the go-ahead to play builds on its own, or to trigger multiple builds at the same time, by using the Start drop-down menu at the bottom of the Build Order window. To do this, select the build you want to edit, open the Start drop-down menu, and then choose from the following:

- **On Click** starts the build when you click the mouse or press the space bar—Keynote's standard behavior.

- **After Transition** starts the first build as soon as the previous slide's transition animation has ended, regardless of whether you've applied a transition animation to the previous slide. (If you don't apply a custom transition animation, Keynote deems the standard hard cut effect a transition and still gives you this menu option.)

- **With Build** starts the build at the same time as the previous build in the list. (You don't see this menu option if you select the first build on the slide, or if the slide has just one build effect applied to it.) To trigger two builds at the same time, they have to be next to each other in the Build Order list. When you choose this option, Keynote updates the Build Order list by removing the space between the two builds' list entries, so that they're touching in the list (see Figure 13-9). This lets you see, at a glance, which "groups" of builds will happen together and which trigger separately. You can stagger the start of each build effect within the group by setting a time in the Delay field.

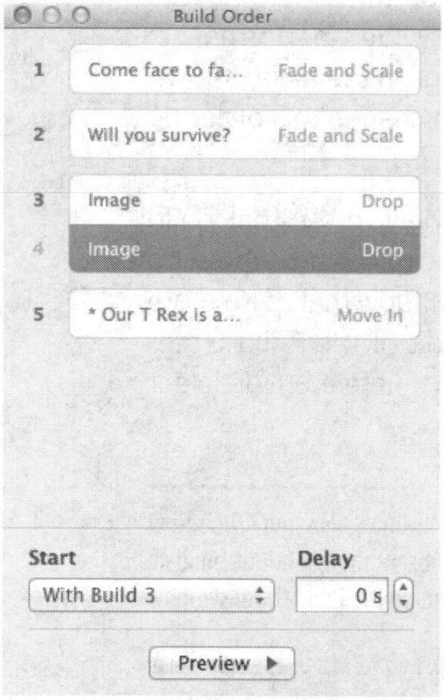

FIGURE 13-9

When you open the Start drop-down menu and choose With Build, Keynote squishes these simultaneous builds together in the list so you can see which builds trigger simultaneously, and which builds are all lonely and happen on their own. Here, build 4 is set to run simultaneously with build 3, so they're grouped together.

- **After Build** starts the build as soon as the previous build finishes (or, for the first build on a slide, immediately after the slide appears). You can add a pause between the two builds by typing a number of seconds in the Delay box. (You see this menu item only if your slide has more than one build applied to it; also, you won't see this item if you select the first build on the slide.)

> **TIP** You can also make several objects build as one object by grouping them: Select all the objects, choose Arrange→Group, and then create a build for the entire group.

Mingling Builds of Text, Tables, and Charts

As you've seen, many objects give you the option to build their content gradually, revealing each bullet of a text box individually, for example. Similarly, you can create separate build ins and build outs for individual table elements and chart parts. To use this feature, select the object, open the Animate panel's Build In or Build Out tab, and then choose any option *other* than "All at Once" from the Delivery drop-down menu.

When you choose one of these gradual delivery methods, Keynote's standard behavior is to group all of these "mini-builds" together. In the Build Order window, these builds appear as separate entries, as shown in Figure 13-10. When you play the slideshow, you march through all of these mini-builds before moving along to any other builds. For example, if you've chosen the By Bullet delivery method for a text box's build in, you click the mouse to reveal each bullet one at a time during your presentation; only after all the bullets are revealed will Keynote move on to the next build.

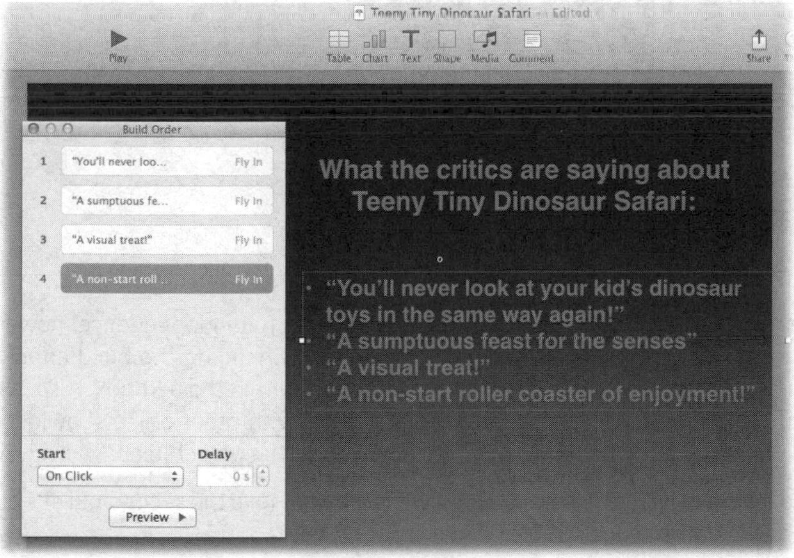

FIGURE 13-10

When you select By Bullet as the delivery method for a text box's build in, as shown here, Keynote reveals each bullet one by one. You have to reveal all the bullets before you can progress to any other builds.

In this case, the build in appears as four items in the Build Order window's list. The first one controls the appearance of the first bullet, the second one represents the second bullet, and so on.

Treating all of an object's gradual builds as a single, unbreakable block isn't always convenient. For example, say you want to interweave a text box's build in with a pie chart's build in, so you can show a new wedge of the chart as you reveal a corresponding bullet point. No problem. Simply open the Build Order window and drag the builds around in the list, exactly the same way as you'd reorder separate builds (just because they're applied to the same object doesn't mean other objects can't appear onscreen in between the mini-builds). This freedom allows you to sprinkle other builds in between, like mingling text-box and pie-chart builds (see Figure 13-11).

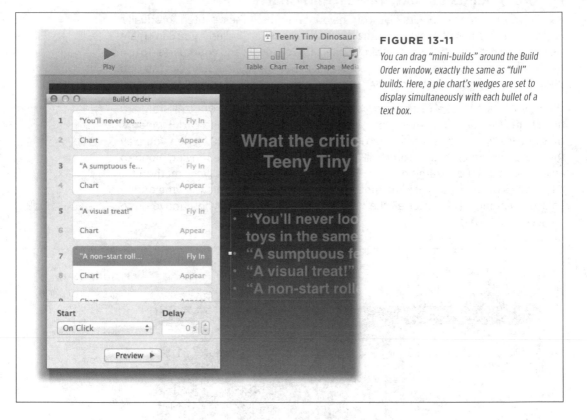

FIGURE 13-11

You can drag "mini-builds" around the Build Order window, exactly the same as "full" builds. Here, a pie chart's wedges are set to display simultaneously with each bullet of a text box.

These freshly liberated builds don't *quite* have their full independence, however. First, they all have to use the same effect settings: Changing the build effect for one bullet, for example, changes it for *all* the bullets within the text box. Also, while Keynote lets you reorder these builds to mix them with other objects' builds, the content always has to build in the same order within the object itself:

- Text boxes always build top to bottom; you can't move the second bullet's build above the first, for example.

- Charts always build in the order they were entered in the Chart Data Editor (page 236).

- Tables always build in the order determined by the Delivery drop-down menu, so you can't scramble the order in which rows, columns, or cells appear.

Adding Animations with Action Builds

So far, the builds you've seen have been one-way trips on or off the slide, but Keynote also lets you create your own custom builds called *action builds* to move, rotate, fade, and resize pictures without making them wander on or off the slide. With a click of the mouse, Keynote turns you into a skilled animator, making your objects skitter and whirl to any spot on the slide. You can make an object perform multiple actions simultaneously or one at a time to create elaborate effects and trajectories. Make an object move to the corner of your slide, for example, as it also spins and grows; or make the object travel to one side of the slide, pause, and then move along to its next station when you're ready.

> **TIP** Action builds are a lot like the Magic Move transition (page 356). If you find yourself confusing the two, remember: Action builds are for moving an object within the *same* slide, whereas Magic Move is for transitioning to a *new* slide. Action builds also let you create more elaborate animations than Magic Move.

To add an action build, select the object you want to animate and then open the Animate panel's Action tab. Open the Effects drop-down menu by clicking the "Add an Effect" button, and choose from the following effects: Move, Opacity, Rotate, or Scale. Once you choose an effect, Keynote adds a second, transparent version of the object to your slide. This see-through clone is the Ghost of Object Future, showing you a preview of how and where the object will wind up when the action is over (see Figure 13-12). The Action tab also sprouts controls related to the effect you selected. You can use those controls if you like, but it's actually much easier just to work with the ghost object directly.

If you want to move the object to a new location, for example, just drag the ghost where you want it to go. Rotate it by ⌘-clicking one of the ghost's selection handles, or drag its selection handles to resize. Adjust the ghost object until you've arranged it on the slide the way you want it to look when it finishes its action animation. After each change you make, click the Action panel's Preview button to take a peek at how your action build is shaping up.

> **NOTE** If you choose Opacity as your action build, you can dictate how your object's opacity will change by dragging the Action tab's Opacity slider.

No matter which type of action build you choose initially, you can still pile all the other effect types onto the same animation so they all happen simultaneously. Behind the scenes, Keynote actually adds a separate build action for each effect, but it's clever enough to schedule them to happen at the same time. Look in the Build Order window and you'll see that it lists separate builds for the move, rotate, scale, and opacity builds, all set to happen simultaneously. You'll learn more about setting up multiple action builds in a moment.

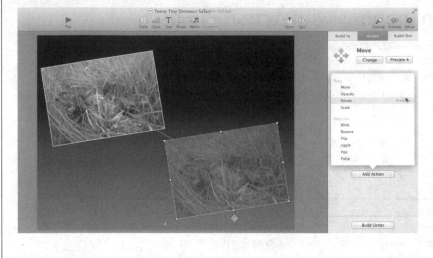

FIGURE 13-12

When you add an action build to an object, Keynote shows you a ghost version of the object to indicate its future position. Here, the picture is set to move down and to the right when Keynote plays this build. The red line connecting the two versions of the image shows the path the object will follow to its new location. You can add more actions to this build by clicking the Add Action button in the Action panel.

As with any other type of build, you can remove an action build by selecting it in the Build Order window and pressing Delete. If you decide, for example, that you don't want to rotate the object while you're moving and scaling it, click the Rotate item in the list and then press Delete. Check what effect this has on your slide by clicking the window's Preview button—you'll see that the object no longer rotates during its animation. You can also select the ghost object in the slide canvas and press Delete; Keynote removes the action build and any other builds set to appear simultaneously with it.

After you're done constructing your action build and you deselect the object, it looks just like any other object; Keynote doesn't show its ghost version, only its initial position on the slide. The only indication that the object is special is the red diamond that appears just beneath the object when you select it. Click this diamond and Keynote once again reveals the object's ghost image (or several of them, if the object has more than one build action). Click the ghost object again to work on it, or press Tab to toggle from the ghost image to the original object.

Moving Objects Along a Path

Keynote plays a game of connect the dots when you use a Move action build to nudge an object across a slide. When you first add the action, you're just working with two objects—the start position and the destination, which is represented by a ghosted version of the object. Keynote draws a red line between the two points to show you the *path* it will follow, a straight line from start to finish. If you prefer to take the scenic route, however, you're not locked into the straight and narrow. You can make an object zig-zag or follow a curved path, too.

To make the object zig-zag, add additional *nodes* to the path—the "dashes" that Keynote connects as it moves the object. Add a node by putting your cursor over the path until you see a white dot. Click this dot to turn it red—it's now an active node. Drag the node to a new spot on the slide canvas, and Keynote updates the red trail to show you the object's new course. This new point on the itinerary adds a smooth (rounded) corner to the path, but you can switch it for a sharp angle by Control-clicking the point and selecting Make Sharp Point, as shown in Figure 13-13. If you want to turn a sharp point curvy, Control-click it once more and select Make Smooth Point. You can also change a node from straight to curved, or vice versa, by double-clicking it.

> **TIP** You can move the entire motion path by putting your cursor over the path and then, when the cursor turns into a hand, dragging the path.

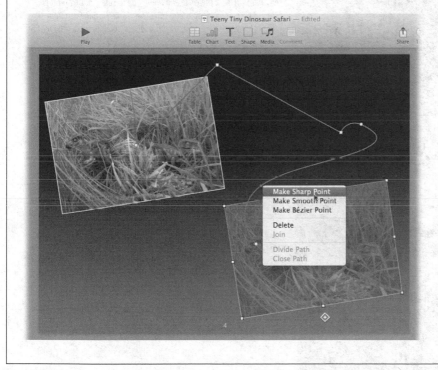

FIGURE 13-13

Change the shape of an object's path by placing your cursor over the path until a white dot appears. Add this dot as a new point on your object's journey by clicking the dot to turn it red (it's now a node). You can then change the object's course by dragging this node anywhere on the slide canvas.

Double-click a node to switch it from a straight point to a curved point or vice versa. You can also make a path curved or straight by Control-clicking a node and then choosing Sharp or Smooth from the shortcut menu shown here.

If editing a motion path sounds suspiciously like editing the points of a shape (page 173), that's because motion paths and shapes are close cousins. In fact, you can use a shape to define your path instead of drawing it by hand—a huge timesaver when you want an object to trace a circle or an ellipse. To do that, insert the shape you want your object to follow, Shift-click the shape and then the object to select them both, and then choose Format→"Shapes and Lines"→"Make Motion Path from Shape." Next, click the shape again, and Keynote turns it into the motion path for the object *and* adds a move action build to the object. The original shape will still be visible, but you can turn down its opacity to make it invisible, if you like. Figure 13-14 tells the whole story.

If you want the object to pause its motion at some point in its journey, you can add additional move actions, each one a separate action build. In your presentation, for example, you would click the mouse once to move the object to its first location and then click again to move it to the next. Doing this means that you string multiple action builds together—which just happens to be the next topic.

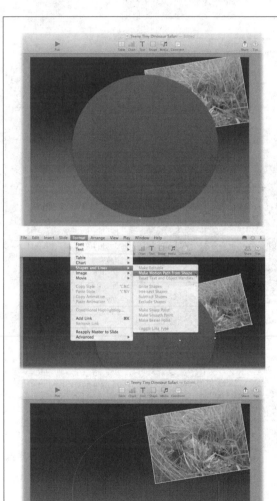

FIGURE 13-14

You can use a shape to set an object's course in an action build. For example, say you want an image to spin around the outline of a circle.

Top: Start by adding both objects to your slide.

Middle: Shift-click the circle and the image to select both, and then choose Format→"Shapes and Lines"→"Make Motion Path from Shape." Keynote asks you to confirm which shape to use as the motion path, so give the circle a click.

Bottom: Keynote adds a move action build to the image, tracing the outline of the original circle, but the circle is still in the way (it covers part of the image). You can make this pesky shape as good as gone by clicking the Format button in the toolbar, opening the Style tab, and then setting the circle's Opacity to zero. The result is a transparent circle, as shown here.

Multiple Action Builds

Keynote lets you add as many action builds to an object as you can muster. You've already seen that you can apply multiple effects to an object at once, making it move, resize, rotate, and fade all at the same time, for example. You can also create actions that happen as separate events, stringing them together back to back or weaving them with other objects' builds. During your presentation, for example, you could move an object to one place on the slide, and then click the mouse to trigger other builds, click the mouse again to move the object to a second location, and so on.

To add an additional action build to an object, click the Add Action button in the Action tab, or click the red-diamond + icon beneath the ghost image. Either way, you can then choose the effect you want, and Keynote adds *another* ghost to the slide to show that you're working with a new action. Make your changes to this ghost image to tell Keynote how the object should wind up at the end of its new action. Figure 13-15 shows an object with several move actions—and if you like the look of this presentation, you can download it (complete with action builds) by going to this book's Missing CD page at *www.missingmanuals.com/cds*. Look for the file *action_builds.keynote*.

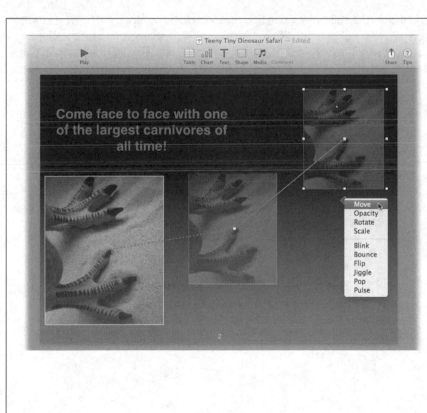

FIGURE 13-15

When you add multiple action builds to an object, Keynote represents each one with its own ghost image. Here, the T. Rex moves from the bottom-left corner to the middle of the slide and then to the upper right. When you play the presentation, the image pauses at each spot until you trigger the next move.

When you're editing the slide, select a ghost image to edit its path; Keynote displays the selected path segment as a solid red line and the others as dashed red lines. To add still more actions, click the red-diamond + icon below the last ghost image (here, that's the one in the top right), and choose from the available effects.

Your new actions show up in the Build Order window with the rest of the slide's builds, and they work the same way, too. Drag and drop them in the list to change their order, and use the window's Start drop-down menu to tell Keynote how you want to trigger each stage of the object's actions.

Copying Builds to Other Objects

Once you've got an object trained to behave just the way you want it with a build in, build out, or series of action builds, you can copy *all* those builds to another object in your slideshow, making it behave exactly the same way as the original object. Simply select the object that you've already added builds to, and then choose Format→Copy Animation; then select the other object and choose Format→Paste Animation. And with that, your objects' mind-meld is complete: The second object takes on all of the build know-how of the original, absorbing even lengthy strings of action builds. (Note that, if the target object already has any builds applied to it, this technique replaces those builds with the pasted ones.) Use the Build Order window to fine-tune when and how those copied builds should take place.

Now hold onto the spirit of sharing and move generously along to the next chapter, where you'll learn about the different ways you can share your presentation with others. From playing the slideshow in front of an audience to distributing it on paper or over the Internet, the next chapter is all about getting the word out.

Sharing Your Slideshows

y now, you've discovered the dirty secret of Keynote presenters everywhere:
Building a Keynote slideshow turns out to be more fun than work. Tinkering
with visual effects as you combine your own content with Apple's elegant
themes is so addictively creative that it sometimes seems as if simply *making* a
slideshow is reason enough to use Keynote. Chances are, though, you're not building
a slideshow just for kicks. The whole goal of a slideshow is to *share it* with others,
screening it on a computer monitor or projection screen—for an audience of one
or a teeming multitude. It's presentation time, and this chapter plumbs every detail
of running your slideshow for a live audience, as well as setting it up to play on its
own in full, automated glory.

Keynote provides several other ways of getting the word out, too, including printing
your slides, exporting your presentation in various file formats that can be opened
by other programs, and sharing online using Apple's shiny new iCloud service. Fire
up the projector, warm up that printer, and ready your Internet connection—this
chapter gives you the lowdown on sharing your gorgeous slides onscreen, on paper,
and online.

■ Setting Up the Presentation

First things first: You have to get both Keynote and your computer ready for the big
show. The specific backstage preparations depend on exactly how and where you'll
display the slideshow. For most presentations, you're the one in the spotlight, driving
the slideshow as you speak in person to your audience—a class, a board of directors,
or a room of fez-topped conventioneers, for example. Preparing and playing a live

slideshow is where this chapter begins, but starting on page 393, you'll also learn how to set up your slideshow to play on autopilot or let your viewers navigate it themselves by clicking onscreen buttons. No matter which of these methods you use, however, your first stop should be Keynote's display settings to choose your slideshow preferences and set up the presenter display.

NOTE See page 390 for details on configuring your slideshow to play in normal, self-playing, recorded, or hyperlinks-only mode.

Setting Slideshow Preferences

Some of Keynote's preferences apply only when you play the slideshow, so be sure to review them before showtime. Choose Keynote→Preferences, and then click the Slideshow tab. Keynote presents you with a hodgepodge menu of options that affect various aspects of your presentations, from how and where your slides should be projected, to when your pointer should be allowed onscreen. Figure 14-1 shows a reliable, standard selection for live presentations. Here are your options:

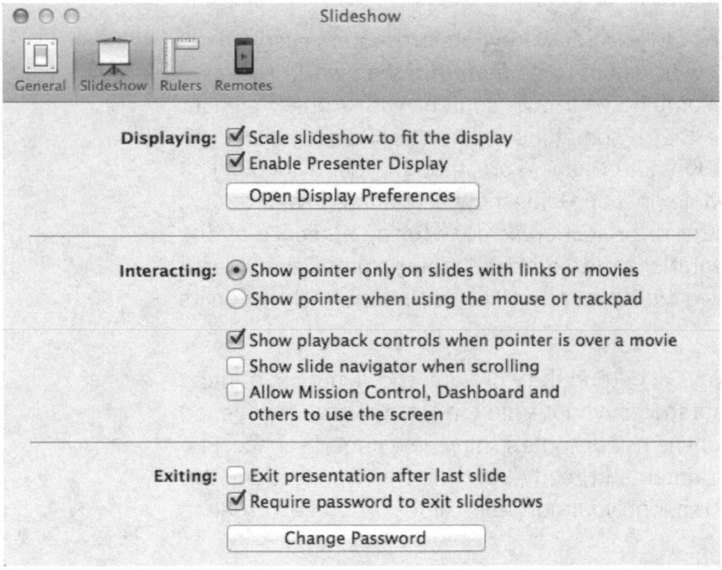

FIGURE 14-1

The preferences shown here are a good configuration for live presentations.

The "Scale slideshow to fit the display" option makes your slides show full screen, without a black border around their edges. Turning off "Exit presentation after last slide" keeps the last slide in your presentation onscreen even if you accidentally click the mouse or press the space bar after you're done.

- **Scale slideshow to fit the display.** Turn on this checkbox to make your slides as large as possible, filling the available height without leaving any black border. You usually want this checkbox turned on, although it means that your slides may lose some of their image quality. An even better option is to make sure that your display's resolution matches the size of your slideshow. See page 284 for details about setting and choosing a slide size.

- **Enable Presenter Display.** As you'll learn in the next section (page 380), presenter display can be extremely handy.

- **Open Display Preferences.** Click this button to open your Mac's System Preferences Display pane, where you can set your display resolution, color depth, and—if you're using two displays—screen arrangement (see page 382).

- **Show pointer.** Keynote gives you two pointer options: "Show pointer only on slides with links or movies" and "Show pointer when using the mouse or trackpad." Choose the former (which is the standard setting) to keep the pointer hidden from view except when you actually need it—to click a hyperlink or to control a movie's display, say. If you choose the latter option instead, the cursor is visible only when you move the mouse, which is useful if you want to point things out on your slides during the show. But since the merest touch of the mouse makes the pointer appear, this also means that clicking your mouse to advance slides will often make the pointer appear. So if you go with this second option, use the space bar, the right arrow key, or a remote control to advance slides instead of clicking the mouse.

- **Show playback controls when pointer is over a movie.** Turn this option on to get complete access to a movie's playback controls. See page 337 for more info about playing movies during your presentation.

- **Allow Mission Control, Dashboard and others to use the screen.** When you're giving a Keynote presentation, you may find yourself accidentally launching applications such as Mission Control and Dashboard. To prevent any other applications from launching while you're giving your talk, keep this checkbox turned off.

- **Exit presentation after last slide.** When you turn on this checkbox, Keynote returns to its editing mode when you advance past the last slide in your slideshow. For a live presentation, it's a good idea to turn this checkbox off to keep the last slide in your presentation onscreen even if you accidentally click the mouse or press the space bar. This is like putting a padlock on your slideshow so that you don't accidentally slip out to your desktop. This prevents the dramatic finale of your presentation from being ruined by a view of the Keynote editing window, your cluttered icons, or the desktop picture of the outfit your cat wore last Halloween (really, you're the only one who finds it funny). When you're ready to exit the slideshow, just press the Esc key.

- **Require password to exit slideshows.** If you plan on leaving your presentation running somewhere public (a kiosk in your local library, for example), you'll probably want to add a password so the general public can't exit your carefully prepared slideshow and hop on Facebook instead. Adding a password to your presentation is covered in detail on page 311.

Setting Up the Presenter Display

When you want your presentation to look effortless—when you want to be sure you hit every point and anticipate every transition—Keynote has a solution: Cheat. Your favorite presentation software gives you a crib sheet called the *presenter display*, where you can sneak a look at your notes, monitor how much time you have left, and preview upcoming slides. To use this for-your-eyes-only control panel during your presentation, you need to display your presentation on two screens—a big screen for your audience and another screen (often your laptop) for your cheat-sheet presenter display. But even when you don't have a second screen for the presentation itself, the presenter display can be useful when you're rehearsing *before* you give your talk.

Choose Play→Rehearse Slideshow, and Keynote reveals the presenter display, shown in Figure 14-2. When you're simply rehearsing, you can use this screen to practice and time your presentation, and to make sure that your presenter notes (page 295) have all the info you'll need. The following sections describe all the nifty features of Keynote's presenter display.

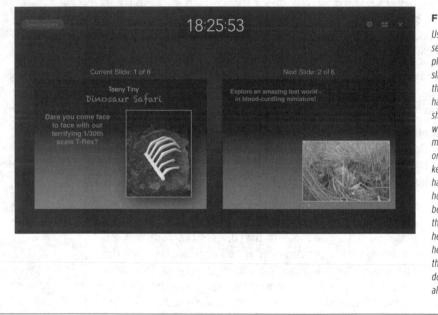

FIGURE 14-2

Using Keynote's standard settings, the presenter display shows you the current slide and the next slide (or the next build, if your slide has builds); basically, it shows you what to expect when you next click the mouse, hit the space bar, or tap one of the arrow keys. If the current slide has builds, Keynote lists how many builds are left before you advance to the next slide (not shown here). The clock at the top helps you keep track of the current time so you don't waffle on past your allocated time slot!

■ PLAYING A SLIDESHOW FROM THE PRESENTER DISPLAY

From the presenter display, you can play and control the slideshow just as you would when you view the normal slideshow. You'll learn all the down-and-dirty details about playing slideshows on page 390, but here's the gist to get you started:

- Advance to the next slide (or build) by clicking the mouse or pressing any of these keys: the space bar, Return, right arrow, or down arrow.

- Go back to the previous slide by pressing the left arrow or up arrow.

- Exit the slideshow and return to edit mode by pressing Esc.

- Press R to reset the timer (if shown).

To jump to a different part of your slideshow, use the presenter display's slide navigator, which you open by clicking the Show Navigator button in the upper-left corner. Keynote reveals a strip of slide thumbnails along the left side of the screen, as shown in Figure 14-7. You can scroll through the slides here and click a thumbnail to make it the current slide.

> **TIP** For the fastest trip to and through the slide navigator, use the keyboard. Press the equal key (=) or the hyphen (-) key to bring up the slide navigator. Then press the up or down arrow key to move to the previous or next slide. When the slide you want is highlighted, press Return to make it the current slide.

■ CUSTOMIZING THE PRESENTER DISPLAY

Figure 14-2 shows Keynote's standard view of the presenter display, featuring the current slide, the next slide, and the current time. To customize the presenter display, head to the upper-right part of the screen and click the icon shown in Figure 14-3. The drop-down menu that opens lets you turn the following options on and off:

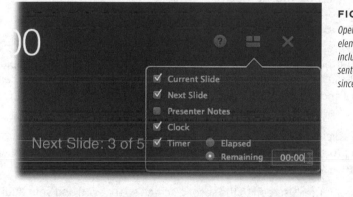

FIGURE 14-3

Open this drop-down menu to add and remove elements from the presenter display. These elements include the current slide and next slide, the presenter notes, the current time, and the time elapsed since you launched your presentation.

- **Current Slide** is the slide your audience sees. If the slide has builds, this is the current state of its builds.

- **Next Slide** shows a preview of either the next slide or the next build (whatever the audience will see when you next hit the space bar, the arrow button, and so on).

- **Presenter Notes** shows the presenter notes for each slide. To scroll through these notes, press the U (up) or D (down) key, or use the scroll bar on the right side of the Presenter Notes pane.

- **Clock** shows the current time.

- **Timer** gives you two options: Choose Elapsed, and Keynote shows the time elapsed since you started your presentation; choose Remaining, and Keynote shows the time remaining. (How does Keynote know how long you've got for your presentation? You tell it by entering a duration in the field to the right of the Remaining button.)

■ USING THE PRESENTER DISPLAY DURING THE PRESENTATION

Now that you've got your presenter display just so, all that remains is to tell Keynote how you actually want to use it during your presentation. If you want to show your presentation on an external screen, then connect your computer to a display, projector, or Apple TV via AirPlay or a video adapter. (See the next section for more info.)

NOTE AirPlay lets you stream audio, video, and photos from your iDevice to your Apple TV. This means you can do all sorts of funky things, like use your iDevice as a controller for your TV, showing off your holiday snaps on the big screen, and, of course, beaming your Keynote presentation to your Apple TV. You can learn more about AirPlay at *www.apple.com/airplay*.

Once you've got everything hooked up properly, click the Play button in Keynote's toolbar; the presentation plays on the connected screen, and Keynote switches your Mac to the presenter display. To switch between the slideshow display and presenter display, press the X key on your keyboard.

Connecting a Second Display

The easiest way to present a Keynote slideshow is right on your computer's screen, by clicking the Play button in the toolbar. If your audience is small (two or three people, say), this method can work well. If you have your presentation on a laptop, you can take it to your audience and be ready to present at a moment's notice—perfect for the road-warrior salesman or college recruiter.

But when your audience is larger, it's time to connect your computer to a large monitor or video projector. The first thing you need to decide is what you'd like to show on each screen. You've got two options:

- **Mirror** your computer's screen to the second screen so that you and your audience see exactly the same thing.

- Set up a **dual display** so that you can show your audience the slideshow on the big screen while you use the presenter display on your computer. This is how the pros roll. (Apple calls this setup "extended desktop.")

Once you know how you'd like to set things up, follow these steps:

1. **Attach the second monitor or projector to your computer using the necessary cable and cable adapter—nicknamed a *dongle* (page 384)—if you need it.**

2. **Choose Keynote→Preferences, click the Slideshow tab, and then click Open Display Preferences (or choose ⌘→System Preferences, and then click Displays).**

3. **In the preferences window, click the Arrangement tab.**

   If you don't see an Arrangement tab, that means that your Mac hasn't detected the external monitor. Double-check that the monitor is turned on and plugged into your Mac.

4. **If you're setting up your slideshow for mirroring, turn on the Mirror Displays option (your Mac typically switches to this mode automatically when you plug in an external display), and then skip to step 6.**

5. **If you're setting up your slideshow for dual display, position the screen images to control how your computer's desktop spans the two displays.**

   Setting the arrangement of the two displays isn't too important for Keynote presentations. This option is mainly for people who are lucky enough to have two monitors that they can use to create a larger desktop. When you're setting up the typical Keynote dual-display arrangement, it's most important to set the *primary display* (the one showing the presenter display) and the *secondary display* (the one your audience views). Drag the menu bar from one screen image to the other to make either display primary—usually, you'll want to make your computer screen the primary screen.

6. **Click the Display tab.**

   Two Display windows appear, one on each of your displays. If you have the Mirror Displays setting turned on, you can select a display resolution for each monitor from the Resolution list. If necessary, click the Color tab and choose a color depth for each display.

   If you have Mirror Displays turned off, you can choose from "Best for display" or Scaled (in most situations, you'll want to select "Best for display").

   If you're using mirroring—either because your computer doesn't support dual-display mode or because you prefer to see exactly the same thing your audience sees—use the same resolution and color depth for each display. For best results when you're in extended-desktop mode, your Keynote slide size should be the same as the screen resolution for the display you'll be using for the slideshow presentation.

   Most video projectors use either 800 × 600 or 1024 × 768 pixel resolution, which match the standard sizes for most Keynote themes. Set your display resolution to match your projector's resolution. If you created your Keynote slideshow at a lower or higher resolution, Keynote can scale the slideshow up or down to fill the screen. The program scales slides down *automatically* if they're larger than the screen. Use Keynote's Slideshow Preferences (page 378) to scale up to fill the screen if the slides are smaller than the screen.

NOTE If you don't get an image on your second display when you plug it in—or if the image is squashed, stretched, or unstable—first try turning the display off and then on again. If that doesn't work, leave the display connected and restart your Mac, which should bring your screens into synchronization.

When you're set up for dual display, Keynote gives you a quick way to swap displays when you're presenting: Press the X key, and the two displays switch roles—the one showing your slides now gets the presenter display and vice versa. (For more on the presenter display, see page 379.)

Connecting Your Audio Output

If your slideshow includes sound and you're presenting to a group of people instead of just a single viewer, you need some kind of amplifier. Many video projectors have a built-in amplifier and speaker that can work in a pinch for a small group. But in most cases, you need something with a little more oomph and a lot more fidelity. Depending on the size of your presentation space, your sound system could be a set of tiny external computer speakers, a public address system capable of filling Yankee Stadium, or anything in between.

Connect your computer's audio output jack to the amplifier's input. The type of cable you need to link the two depends on the input connections on the speakers, amplifier, or PA system. The computer's end of the cable requires a 1/8-inch stereo miniplug (the kind on your iPod headphones, for example). The amplifier end probably requires the same miniplug or a pair of RCA plugs (those are the red and white plugs you often find on the backs of stereos). It's good to have one of each of these cables in your bag.

Choose →System Preferences, click Sound, and then click the Output tab. Adjust the Output volume slider to about 80 percent and play part of your slideshow that contains audio. Use the volume control on the amplifier or PA system to adjust the sound to a comfortable level.

If you're lucky enough to have pros in charge of your audio setup, they'll take care of the connections and be able to adjust the volume during the presentation. If you're on your own, then either you or a helper should be able to adjust the volume during the show, in case people in the back can't hear or you notice those in the front stuffing Kleenex in their ears.

The Mighty Dongle

When you're giving a presentation from your laptop, be sure that *someone* has the right *dongle*, the adapter cable that connects your Mac to the projector. There's nothing worse than discovering that your presentation is locked inside your computer with no way of getting onto the big screen. The dongle is your slideshow's only means of escape.

Finding the right dongle can get confusing because there are several possible combinations of plugs—you need just the right one to fit both your Mac and the projector.

Even if you bring a dongle with you, in other words, there's no guarantee that it'll fit the projector. Apple currently offers five types of "current" adapters:

- Apple Thunderbolt cable
- Apple Mini DisplayPort to Dual-Link DVI Adapter
- Apple Mini DisplayPort to DVI Adapter
- Apple Mini DisplayPort to VGA Adapter
- Apple HDMI to DVI Adapter

But in addition to these, there's a range of "legacy" adapters for older models of Macs and projectors, so your best bet is to head over to Apple's website and find the adapter(s) that were designed to work specifically with your model of Mac: *http://support.apple.com/kb/ht3235*. If you're *really* confused, bring your Mac into your local Apple Store or electronics store so they can help you figure out what type of connector you need.

Remote Controls

The trouble with running a presentation from your laptop is that you have to run the presentation, well, from your laptop. Your computer tethers you to the podium, tying you to a fixed spot on the stage. Fortunately, several remote-control options let you escape the lectern and roam the stage, flipping through your slides with a flick of your hand.

■ USING YOUR IDEVICE AS A REMOTE

The good news is that if you already own an iPad, iPhone, or iPod Touch (collectively referred to in this book as *iDevices*) and have Keynote for iOS installed, then you can use your iDevice as a remote control. That's right: In addition to letting you create and edit presentations on your iDevice, Keynote for iOS also lets you control your Keynote presentations without being glued to your laptop.

> **NOTE**   If you're not familiar with Keynote for iOS, Chapter 25 has all the info you need.

Just like Keynote for Mac's presenter display (page 379), Keynote for iOS's Remote mode shows you the current slide or, depending on your settings, it can show you the next slide or the presenter notes for your current slide (see Figure 14-6). You move forward and backward by swiping the screen, which also swipes your slides back and forth. Easy.

Before you dive in and set up Remote, there are a few minor caveats to get out of the way. First, if you're using your iPhone as a remote control, it doesn't stop being a phone. So if someone calls in the middle of your talk, even if you have your ringer off, you still have to accept or decline the call before you can continue driving your slideshow. Because of that, it's a good idea to forward your calls to another number before you start presenting. At the very least, set the phone to vibrate rather than having it play a ringtone.

Also, Keynote for iOS's Remote feature works by connecting to your computer over a WiFi network. So if either your iDevice or computer has a spotty connection to the network, you may get stranded mid-stage without a working remote. This can be remedied, though, with a bit of advance planning; see the "Wimpy WiFi?" box below.

Wimpy WiFi?

Keynote for iOS's remote feature whispers its instructions to your computer over a WiFi wireless network—in order to work, your iDevice has to be connected to the same WiFi network as your computer. But what happens when you don't have WiFi access, or there's only a weak signal, or enthusiastic conference-goers are soaking up all the bandwidth, leaving none for you? If the network's not sturdy, all you've got in your hand is a good-looking iDevice; your iDevice as a remote is kaput.

Don't despair. When you don't have a reliable WiFi network to count on, you can make your own using your Mac's built-in *computer-to-computer network* feature:

1. On your Mac, click the WiFi icon in the menu bar (🛜) at the top of your screen, and then choose Create Network.

2. If you don't see a WiFi icon in the menu bar, choose →System Preferences, and then click Network. Select the current network in the left-hand pane (it should have a green dot next to it and say "Connected"), and then, in the right-hand pane, turn on "Show WiFi status in menu bar."

3. In the window that appears, give your new network a name—Remote Possibility, perhaps—and, if you want,

pick a channel from the drop-down menu (Keynote automatically chooses channel 11, which usually works fine).

4. Open the Security drop-down menu and choose one of the available settings.

5. If a WPA setting is available, that's usually the best (and safest!) option. WEP settings are older and generally much less secure, so you should use them only if they're the only option.

6. Type a password for your network, type the password again to confirm it, and then click Create.

7. Your Mac creates its own private WiFi network; now you just need to connect your iPhone, iPad, or iPod Touch to it.

Tap the Settings icon on your iDevice and choose Wi-Fi. Select your new network, type the password, and then tap Join. You've now got a private, reliable wireless connection directly to your computer.

Finally, as svelte as these handheld devices might be, iDevices (especially iPads) are still fairly hefty relative to the standard presentation remote. So if you like to travel light when you're onstage, you might prefer to use a standard remote control instead of an iDevice (see page 388 for a rundown of remote-control options). That said, if you'd like to have your presentation notes with you without being chained to your computer, iDevices are pretty much as small as they could be for that use, and you'll probably find it worth toting around.

Keynote for iOS's remote feature puts a miniature view of your slideshow's presenter display on your iDevice. But Keynote won't let just any old iDevice start pushing its buttons. It insists on a formal introduction first, a process called *linking*. Here's how to link Keynote on your Mac to Keynote on your iDevice:

1. **On your Mac, make sure that Keynote is accepting remote connections.**

   Go to Keynote→Preferences, click the Remotes tab, and turn on the Enable checkbox (as shown in Figure 14-4). Leave the Preferences window open—you'll need it again in step 4.

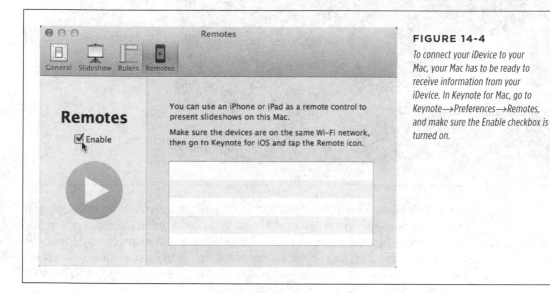

FIGURE 14-4

To connect your iDevice to your Mac, your Mac has to be ready to receive information from your iDevice. In Keynote for Mac, go to Keynote→Preferences→Remotes, and make sure the Enable checkbox is turned on.

2. **Make sure that your iPhone, iPad, or iPod Touch is connected to the same WiFi network as your computer.**

   On your iDevice, tap the Settings icon and then choose Wi-Fi to select the network.

3. **On your iDevice, tap the Keynote icon to launch the app. In Documents view (basically, the first screen that appears—see page 709 for details), tap the Keynote Remote icon indicated in Figure 14-5. (If this is your first time using the app's remote feature, you'll need to tap Continue, too.)**

   Keynote for iOS now tries to connect to your Mac.

4. **On your Mac, in Keynote's Preferences window, you'll see your iDevice listed on the Remotes tab; click Link.**

   Both Keynote for Mac and Keynote for iOS display a four-digit passcode. Check that the passcode is appearing correctly on both devices, and then, on your Mac, click Confirm. On your iDevice, the Keynote Remote drop-down menu updates to show a big, green Play button to let you know you're connected and can now use your iDevice as a remote control.

   You can add more iDevices by tapping the remote icon in the Keynote for iOS toolbar again, selecting Devices in the drop-down menu that appears, and then giving "Add a Device" a tap.

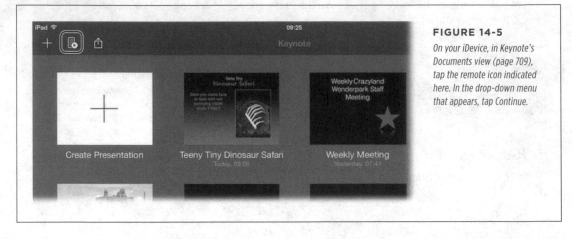

FIGURE 14-5

On your iDevice, in Keynote's Documents view (page 709), tap the remote icon indicated here. In the drop-down menu that appears, tap Continue.

Once you've linked Keynote on your iDevice to Keynote on your Mac, whenever you tap the Remote icon in the iOS app's toolbar, you see a green Play button. Tap this button, and your Mac starts playing the Keynote presentation you have open. (If you've got more than one slideshow open, the one in the top window starts playing.) On the Mac's screen and to your audience, the slideshow looks just as it would if you'd started playing it from your Mac.

On your iDevice, tap the Options button indicated in Figure 14-6 to choose from several views:

- **Current.** Displays the current slide only.

- **Next.** Displays either the next slide or how the current slide will look after the next build animation.

- **Current and Next.** Displays the current slide and the next slide or build.

- **Current and Notes.** Displays the current slide and your presenter notes.

To exit the remote view completely, tap the X in the top-right corner of your iDevice, or press Esc on your Mac.

■ OTHER REMOTE CONTROLS

Don't feel left out if you don't have an iDevice. Apple and other manufacturers also sell other remote-control devices—many of them simple clickers that are much smaller than any iDevice.

Apple's slender wisp of a remote control is marketed for controlling movies and music in iTunes, iPods, and even your home stereo, but it works for Keynote presentations, too. These little wonders used to come with every MacBook laptop, but you now have to order them separately. For details, head to *http://store.apple.com*.

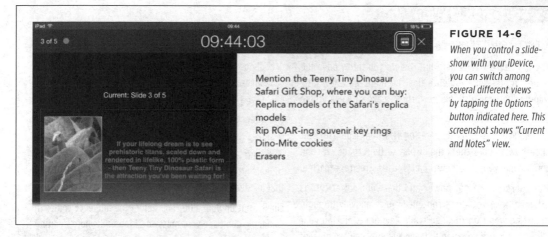

FIGURE 14-6

When you control a slide-show with your iDevice, you can switch among several different views by tapping the Options button indicated here. This screenshot shows "Current and Notes" view.

Most remote controls (although not the Apple Remote) use RF radio waves to communicate with a receiver plugged into your laptop's USB port. That means there's no need to point the remote at your laptop (as you would with a TV remote that communicates using infrared beams). But pointing still comes in handy: When you want to point something out on one of your slides, some remotes have a built-in laser pointer, so you don't have to fumble with more than one device.

Some remotes can also function as a mouse, or control your iTunes and DVD playback. However, when you're in the midst of the presentation, you may find that simpler is better—and the only buttons you really need are forward and backward. One good option is the Laser Presentation Remote by Targus (*www.targus.com*).

■ SETTING UP THE REMOTE

If you plan on using an iDevice as a remote, you first need to link your iDevice to the computer that's running Keynote (see page 387). Take a minute to do that in advance of your talk, and make sure it actually *works* before your audience begins arriving. Likewise, make sure you have the iDevice display set the way you want it; if you plan to refer to presenter notes during your talk, set it to portrait display mode; otherwise, use landscape. Finally, be sure that your iDevice is charged so that it doesn't wink out in the middle of your presentation.

If you're using a different remote control, the same idea holds: Make sure the thing works. Turn it on and click through a few slides just to be sure.

Your presentation should now be in pretty good shape, but there are a few extra steps you can take before hitting that Play button to make sure the big day goes off without a hitch. The box on page 390 has some last-minute tips.

PRESENTATION STATION

Prep Your Mac

The big day is finally here but, before you throw open the doors and let your audience flock in, there are a few last-minute checks you should perform to make sure everything goes smoothly.

Assuming you're using Keynote and a MacBook laptop for your slideshow, double-check the display settings (page 378) and confirm that your slideshow projects on the screen as expected.

Make sure you've got power and that your power cord is plugged in so you don't run out of juice midway through. Your Mac won't go to sleep while Keynote is playing your slideshow, but if you plan to leave Keynote, you can prevent your Mac from drifting off to sleep by updating your system preferences. Here's how:

1. Choose →System Preferences, and then click Energy Saver.

2. Click the Battery tab and set the "Turn display off after" slider to Never.

If you're using Keynote for iOS to control your slideshow with your iPhone, iPad, or iPod Touch, it can take a while to connect it to your computer (see page 385). So be sure to do that in advance.

Finally, put up your title slide before the audience comes in so people don't see your messy desktop or Keynote's editing screen.

■ Playing Keynote Slideshows

Dim the house lights, raise the curtains, and cue the applause sign: It's showtime at last. With the spotlight on you and your pitch, the last thing you need is a complicated set of controls for moving through your slides. Happily, Keynote makes it dead easy to advance through your slides using the keyboard or a remote control.

To get started, open the Keynote document and select the first slide in the show using the slide navigator or by choosing Slide→Go To→First Slide. (You can also select a different slide if you'd like to start somewhere in the middle of your presentation.) Now start the show by clicking the toolbar's Play button, choosing Play→Play Slideshow, or pressing Option-⌘-P. Your first slide flickers onto the screen, and you're on.

TIP You can set up your slideshow to begin playing automatically as soon as you open the document, not a bad idea for slideshows you've finished editing. Click the Setup button in the toolbar, open the Presentation tab, and then turn on "Automatically play upon open." That way, Keynote opens directly to the first slide and launches into your slideshow, completely bypassing the editing screen—the "man behind the curtain" whom it's best to keep tucked away from your audience. To stop the show and bring up Keynote's editing screen, press the Esc key, Q (for "quit"), or period [.].

Controlling the Presentation

The basics are easy, and the controls work exactly the same whether you're using the presenter display or normal slideshow mode. Keynote gives you lots of different ways to handle the most common actions—moving forward and backward—so that you don't have to hunt around the keyboard guessing. It doesn't matter which method you use for this basic navigation, just go with whatever feels comfortable:

- **Advance** through your slideshow by clicking the mouse, clicking your remote control, or by pressing the space bar, Return, the right arrow key, the down arrow key, or N (for "next").

- **Go back** by pressing the left arrow key, the up arrow key, Delete, or P (for "previous").

- **Exit** the slideshow by pressing the Esc key, Q (for "quit"), or period [.] (as in "the end, period").

TIP If you're using an extended keyboard (one with a number pad), pressing Home always takes you back to the very first slide, and pressing End zips you to the last slide.

When you've set up slides with builds that are set to build On Click, then advancing as described above steps through each of these builds before moving on to the next slide.

■ HOPPING AROUND THE SLIDESHOW

While you were building your slideshow, you no doubt grew fond of the slide navigator, which helps you quickly move around your slideshow. When you're making your way through your full-screen slideshow, you can bring your old pal with you: Press the – or + key on your keyboard to display the slide navigator, as shown in Figure 14-7. (If you open the navigator by pressing +, then the next slide in your presentation is already selected; if you open it by pressing –, then the previous slide is selected instead.) You can then use the slide navigator to jump to another slide anywhere in the presentation.

You can also open the slide navigator by typing a slide's number. When you do that, Keynote opens the slide navigator with that slide already selected; simply press Return to hop to that slide and close the slide navigator.

When the slide navigator is open, use the up and down arrow keys or the + or – keys to move forward or backward through your slides, and then press Return to actually *open* that slide. Alternatively, use the slide navigator's scroll bar or type a slide number and then click Go (or press the Return key) to jump to that slide.

As you move through the thumbnails in the slide navigator, Keynote puts a yellow outline around each one but keeps the main slide unchanged. When you've found the slide you need, hop to it by pressing Return or clicking its thumbnail. Keynote closes the slide navigator and changes the main view to the new slide.

FIGURE 14-7

Press the + or – key to open Keynote's slide navigator during a presentation. Then, select a slide using the + or – keys, the up and down arrow keys on your keyboard, or by typing a slide number. When the slide you're after has a yellow outline around it, press Return to jump to that slide (and hide the slide navigator).

If you decide you don't want to switch to another slide after all, click outside the slide navigator or press the Esc key to close it.

■ **PLAYING MOVIES**

Play a movie by clicking it once, and pause it by clicking it once more. If you've turned on movie-playback controls in Keynote's Slideshow Preferences (page 385), you can put your cursor over the movie and use the controls that appear at the bottom of the video object. See page 337 for more details about playing movies during your presentation.

■ **OPENING LINKS AND OTHER PROGRAMS**

Use your cursor to click hyperlinks, just as you do on web pages. If the hyperlink opens an email message or a web page, Keynote pauses, hides the slideshow, and switches to your email program or web browser. When it's time to switch back to the slideshow, press ⌘-Tab or click Keynote's Dock icon (which now sports a green Play button).

You can also break out of your slideshow to use another program by pressing H (for "hide"), which hides the slideshow and takes you back to the last program you were using. From there, you can use your computer normally to open files or run other programs, without ever revealing your Keynote editing screen. To head back to the slideshow, which is waiting for you where you stopped it, press ⌘-Tab or click the Keynote icon in the Dock.

■ PAUSING THE SHOW

You can freeze a slideshow—even midway through a build—by pressing F. To pause the slideshow and dim the screen to black, press B. To make the screen white instead, press W.

Thaw out your frozen show and resume playing by pressing any key.

■ CALLING UP THE KEYBOARD CHEAT SHEET

If all of these keyboard shortcuts are making your head hurt, you don't need to memorize them. Just be sure you know the basics: how to go forward, backward, and exit your slideshow. From there, if you get stuck during your presentation, call up the keyboard commands by pressing the question mark [?] key. Keynote reveals a window listing all the keyboard commands available while you're playing a slideshow. (It's not exactly the classiest thing to do during a talk, but hey, if you're stuck, you're stuck.) In presenter mode (page 725), you can also call up this cheat sheet by clicking the question mark icon at the top of the screen.

This detailed window lists all the keyboard commands described in this chapter, plus a few extras for power presenters. Often, though, true power presenters aren't anywhere near their keyboard—they're roaming the stage to engage more directly with their audience, flipping through slides with the help of a remote control. If you happen to have an iPhone, iPad, or iPod Touch, then you've got the best of both worlds—a remote with a miniature presenter display built in.

■ Creating Self-Playing Slideshows

If using your iDevice to run your slideshow isn't enough automation for you, Keynote is ready. Self-playing (a.k.a. kiosk) slideshows put your Keynote presentation on autopilot. They play automatically, advancing each slide and build according to the timings you set. Kiosk presentations are usually set to loop over and over again to promote your latest product, explain a museum exhibit, or embarrass attendees at your 20th high school reunion.

> **TIP** Even though these kinds of slideshows are completely automatic, Keynote still responds to certain keyboard commands during the presentation. You can keep viewers from stopping the presentation by requiring a password (see page 311), but even then they'll *still* be able to pause it using the F, B, or W keyboard shortcuts. The only foolproof way to prevent viewers from meddling with the slideshow is to remove the keyboard—or, in the case of a laptop, cover it.

Keynote has two flavors of self-playing slideshow:

- **Timed slideshows** advance automatically based on timings that you set either for individual slides or slideshow-wide.

- **Recorded slideshows** let you record a voiceover while you advance through your slides; Keynote saves your entire performance and plays back your slides *and* your silver-voiced narration exactly as you recorded them. Once you've recorded a voiceover, you can play it alongside your slideshow by choosing Play→Play Recorded Slideshow.

As you learned way back on page 310, you select a presentation type in the Setup panel's Presentation tab.

Timed Slideshows

When you turn your presentation into a timed slideshow by setting the Presentation Type drop-down menu to Self-Playing (see Figure 14-8), Keynote plays all transitions and builds automatically according to the timetable you set. When you select this option, the Transitions field below the menu lets you tell Keynote the number of seconds it should wait before transitioning to the next slide (for slides with builds, this countdown starts after the last build is complete). In the Builds field, tell Keynote how long to wait before starting each *build* on each slide.

These document-wide settings apply to transitions and builds that are set to begin On Click. If you have transitions and builds set to happen automatically after a certain amount of time has elapsed, Keynote respects these custom settings. This means that you can use the Presentation tab to set standard timings, but also create special timings for individual slides. To customize the timings of individual slides, click the Animate button in the toolbar, and then enter specific settings for the following:

- **Transitions.** Open the Animate panel's Transitions tab by clicking either a blank area of your slide or by pressing the Esc key (If the Transitions tab doesn't appear, click the Animate button in the toolbar). Set the Start Transition drop-down menu to Automatically, and then, in the Delay box, enter the number of seconds you want Keynote to display the current slide.

- **Builds.** Select any object that has a build effect or action build applied to it, and then click the Build Order button that appears in any of the Animate panel's three tabs (Build In, Build Out, or Action). Then, in the Build Order window, select the build effect whose timing you want to change. Finally, open the Start drop-down menu, choose With Build or After Build, and then enter the time delay in the Delay box.

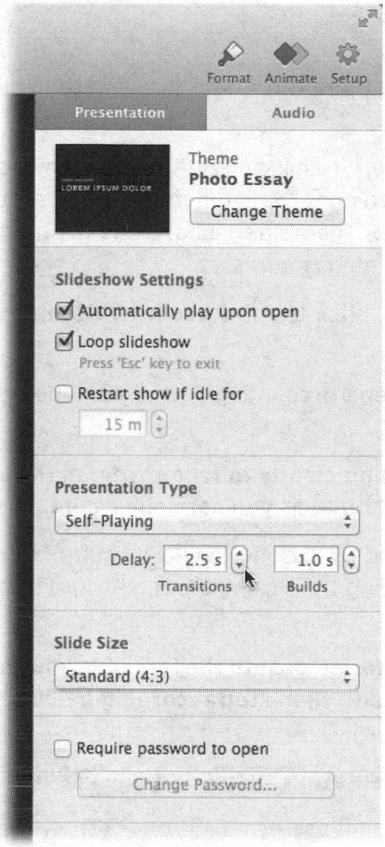

FIGURE 14-8

In the Setup panel's Presentation tab, open the Presentation Type drop-down menu and pick Self-Playing to turn your presentation into a timed slideshow. Set how long Keynote should wait between transitions and builds using the aptly named Transitions and Builds fields.

You can override these settings for individual slides using the Animate panel's various tabs.

Recorded Slideshows

Recorded slideshows capture your voice and presentation for posterity, playing it back exactly as you saved it. Before you can turn a normal presentation into a recorded slideshow, you first have to record the narration, where you do your patter as you advance through the slideshow. Keynote records both the audio and your slideshow timing, tying the two together to play them back like a movie. This is a good way to distribute a polished view-only presentation, or to capture a live presentation to share later on YouTube, for example. (See page 411 for more about exporting slideshows to YouTube.) To make sure your voiceover is clear, see the box on page 398 for advice on finding a good mic.

Here's how to record a voiceover:

1. **Click the Setup button in the toolbar, open the Audio tab, and then click Record.**

   Keynote switches you to recording mode, which includes the current time, current slide, and next slide. (Keynote recordings always run from the first slide in your presentation through the last slide.) There's also a bar along the bottom of the screen that includes voiceover-related controls.

2. **To start recording your presentation, click the red Record button at the bottom of the screen.**

   Keynote gives you a few seconds to prepare, counting down from 3 before it begins recording.

3. **Start giving your presentation, speaking clearly to record your narration, and advancing through each slide and build as you normally would.**

   You can pause the recording at any time by clicking the Pause button (it has two vertical lines on it). Resume recording by clicking the red Record button once more.

4. **Continue to the end of the slideshow (or at least to the last slide you want to include in the self-playing show), and then stop recording by clicking the Record button.**

5. **Save your recording and exit the presentation by pressing the Esc key.**

   Keynote takes you back to the main editing screen. Figure 14-9 shows what the Audio tab looks like now. You can tell there's an existing recording because Keynote lists the date and time you made your recording at the top of the tab (before you record anything, you see the words "No Recording" in this spot instead).

Now, when you select Play→Play Recorded Slideshow, your presentation plays and the audio runs along with it.

NOTE While it's still possible to change the delay between your transitions and builds, this has absolutely no effect on the speed of your presentation.

FIGURE 14-9

After you create the narration for a recorded slideshow, the Audio tab shows that there's a saved recording.

If you're not pleased with how the narration turned out, you can delete your recording by clicking Clear. If you click Record, Keynote launches into record mode with your current recording already loaded up. If you hit the Record button in record mode, Keynote records over your current audio track.

If you don't like part of your recorded slideshow, you have two options:

- **Rerecord it.** This means you're starting from scratch, throwing out the original recording. Simply make sure you're at the start of your presentation, and then head to the Setup panel's Audio tab and click Record. In record mode, click the Record button, and start giving your presentation.

- **Replace a portion of it.** You can also replace part of your original recording. Keynote will keep all the narration for the slides before the selected slide and then tack your new narration onto the audio afterward. This is the way to go when you want to pick up your narration in the middle of the slideshow. Go to the Setup panel's Audio tab, click Record, pinpoint where you want to begin recording from using the slider at the bottom of the screen, and then click the Record button.

If you add, remove, or edit any slides after recording your audio, you'll see a warning that asks, "Are you sure you want to make this edit?" Keynote warns you that such changes could make it so that your recording no longer matches your edited presentation. If you want to create a copy of your presentation and edit that rather than the original, click Duplicate. If you decide not to make the change, click Cancel. And if you want to go through with the change despite Keynote's warning, click Edit. If you make such an edit, then you'll see a "Recording out of sync" warning at the top of the Setup panel's Audio tab. Keynote tries to make the best of this situation and plays your presentation as it was when you recorded it (meaning it displays the *unedited* slides and leaves out any slides you created after recording your audio): The version of the slides shown may be old, but at least the audio makes sense. In this situation, all you can really do is to give your out-of-date audio the heave-ho by clicking the Clear button at the top of the Audio tab, and then record a new voiceover that matches your updated presentation.

Is This Thing On?

To get your voice into your Mac, you need a microphone. Most Macs have built-in mics—but don't be tempted to use them to record narration. The quality of these mics is poor, plus they pick up a lot of noise from the computer. Instead, consider using an external microphone to give your slideshow the audio it deserves; consumer-level microphones are inexpensive ($100 or less) and deliver much better results. If your Mac has an analog audio input jack and you've already got a microphone, you can plug it right into your computer (although you might need an adapter cable to plug into the Mac's 1/8-inch stereo miniplug).

If your Mac doesn't have an audio input jack, you'll need a USB microphone like the Go Mic from Samson (*www.samsontech.*

com) or the Snowball from Blue (*www.bluemic.com*). You can also use a telephone operator–style headset that plugs into your Mac's USB port, like the Rig by Plantronics (*www.plantronics.com*). Bonus: You can also use the headset for online game-playing or making calls over the Internet with programs like Skype or Apple's Messages.

Once you've plugged in your mic, you can set input levels in your Mac's System Preferences. Choose →System Preferences and click the Sound button. In the Sound window, click the Input tab and select your microphone. Adjust the input volume, and when you're happy with the silky sounds of your own voice, close the window.

■ Setting Up Hyperlinks-Only Slideshows

Instead of feeding your presentation to your viewers as an automated slideshow, you can make the whole thing self-serve. In a hyperlinks-only slideshow, people help themselves to your presentation's buffet, navigating through the slides at their own pace by clicking onscreen buttons.

You can't simply turn a normal presentation into a hyperlinks-only presentation the way you can with a self-playing presentation. You have to plan ahead for this kind of slideshow when you design and create your slides, because hyperlinks-only presentations require you to include one or more hyperlinks on every slide (see page 343). Once you've created your hyperlink-packed slideshow, you can then turn it into a hyperlinks-only presentation. In the Setup panel, click the Presentation tab, open the Presentation Type drop-down menu, and then select Links Only.

TIP If you're creating a slideshow with Forward and Back buttons on every slide, give yourself a shortcut by adding those buttons to your master slides (you'll learn about editing master slides on page 418). Use arrow shapes for your buttons, for example, and then add hyperlinks to each: Select the object, go to Format→Add Link, choose Slide from the "Link To" menu, and then pick "Next slide" or "Previous slide."

In this kind of presentation, Keynote expects viewers to navigate with hyperlinks, so the normal slide-advancing techniques and keyboard shortcuts don't work. The only keys the program responds to are Esc and period (.), which stop the slideshow; and the question mark (?), which summons the now-useless Presenter Keyboard Shortcuts window that lists all the commands you *can't* use in a hyperlinks-only presentation. Now that's just mean.

■ Printing Slides and Handouts

Printing isn't the first thing that pops into your mind when you think of presentation software, but printing your slideshow is extremely helpful—or even essential—in certain circumstances. Doing so lets you do the following:

- Provide a printed handout of some or all of the slides so your audience members can make notes during the presentation without being distracted by mindlessly copying everything on the screen.

- Print your slideshow-in-progress, along with your draft presenter notes, for review by your team members, or for your own use so you can study it on the subway before the big event.

- Print your slideshow's outline so you can run your text by the legal department.

Choose File→Print, and Keynote unfurls the Print dialog box. If it's just a tiny window with three measly drop-down menus, click the Show Details button to reveal Keynote's print options in their full glory (Figure 14-10). Choose your printer in the Printer drop-down menu, and if you want to print more than one copy, enter a number in the Copies box. To print less than the whole slideshow, enter a slide range in the From and To boxes; to print just one slide, enter its number in both boxes, or choose the "Selection" option to print the currently selected slide.

Leaving Keynote selected in the drop-down menu circled in Figure 14-10 reveals all of Keynote's printing options. The settings right below the drop-down menu let you choose the big-picture layout for your printout:

- **Slide** prints one slide on each page at maximum size.

- **Grid** lets you squeeze between 2 and 16 onto a single printed page in a grid-style layout.

- **Handout** makes Keynote print between one to six slides on a page. Keynote arranges the slides from top to bottom on the left side of the page, in a layout that's intended for taking notes next to each slide.

- **Outline** prints only the outline, just as it appears in the slide navigator (sorry, free text boxes don't make the cut).

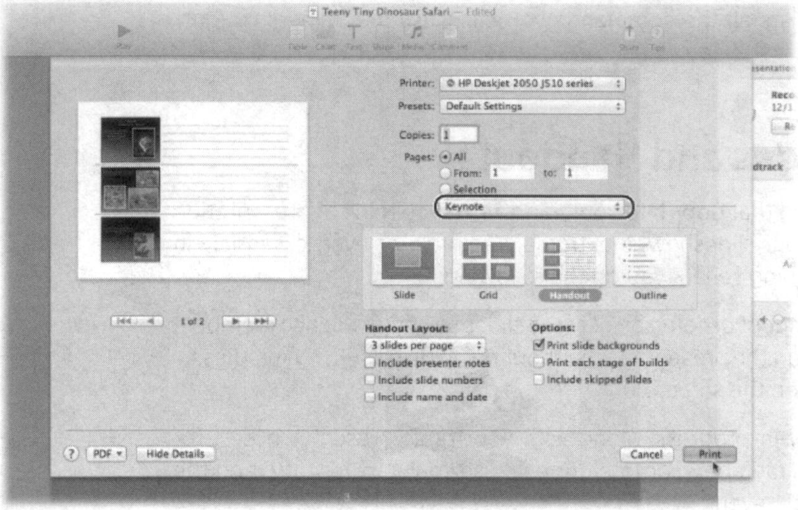

FIGURE 14-10

The Print dialog box looks different depending on which version of OS X you're running. Here, OS X Mavericks' Print window shows a preview of your printed document on the left. Click the arrow buttons below the preview to flip through all the pages that Keynote will print. On the right are the Keynote-specific printing options. To switch to other printer options, make another selection from the unlabeled drop-down menu that's set to Keynote here (circled).

Use the various checkboxes that appear under these settings to determine how Keynote prints the slides. You see slightly different options depending on which style you chose above, but these options are available for all the printing styles except Outline, which doesn't print slide images:

- **Include slide numbers.** Turn on this option to print the slide number next to each slide image.

- **Include name and date.** Makes Keynote print the title of your presentation and today's date at the bottom of each page.

- **Print slide backgrounds.** To save ink, turn this checkbox off unless you absolutely need to see backgrounds and fills in your printout. Telling Keynote not to bother printing slide backgrounds can also make your text legible at smaller sizes.

- **Print each stage of builds.** When you turn on this checkbox, Keynote prints each slide build as a separate slide. You can leave this option turned off if you use builds only to gradually add bullet points to a slide. However, you might turn on this option when you build slide elements in and out repeatedly, which would leave you—if you turned this checkbox off—with a printout showing a confused pile of elements in the slide.

- **Include skipped slides.** If you've removed any of your slides from the presentation by skipping them (page 301), turn on this checkbox and Keynote includes them in the printout.

There are also a couple of settings that are available only when you select certain print styles:

- **Use page margins.** This option, which is available only when you select the Slide print style, makes sure the slides' borders stay within the printer's print area.

- **Include presenter notes.** This option is available only if you choose the Slide or Handout print style. It prints out your slides complete with any presenter notes you've added.

> **NOTE** Unlike most programs, Keynote doesn't include a File→Page Setup option that lets you select your paper size and orientation. Instead, these options are tucked away in the Print dialog box. To change these settings, open the Print dialog box, open the drop-down menu that's circled in Figure 14-10, and then choose Page Attributes. Keynote's standard page orientation is landscape (horizontal), which is the way to go if you're printing full slides. However, for notes, handouts, and outlines, vertical orientation is probably better.

Got it? Click Print, and you're done.

Exporting to Other Formats

Keynote lets you export your slideshow to a variety of file formats, making your presentation accessible on computers that don't have Keynote installed—or to heathens who don't own Macs. You can save your presentation for editing and viewing in PowerPoint or Keynote '09, or export it for browsing as a PDF, a collection of HTML files, a QuickTime movie, or as a thicket of JPEG, PNG, or TIFF image files. The following sections explain how.

Saving as PowerPoint

The 800-pound gorilla of presentation software is, of course, Microsoft PowerPoint. Keynote can save slideshows in PowerPoint format, which people can view and edit on any computer—Mac or Windows—that has PowerPoint. Although PowerPoint uses the same file format on Macs and Windows machines, these two operating systems handle fonts and graphics in completely different ways, which you'll surely notice when viewing your presentation on a Windows computer.

Equally frustrating are the inconsistencies when you export from Keynote to Power-Point on the Mac. Many of Keynote's transitions and builds don't display properly—or at all—because PowerPoint doesn't know the corresponding effect. Keynote does the best with what's available, mapping effects to similar effects when it can; otherwise, it replaces transitions with a standard dissolve. Some bulleted text may disappear, the appearance of fonts and graphics can change, and movies and sounds may not display as you intended. In other words, nearly all of Keynote's panache is vulnerable to mistranslation because PowerPoint doesn't know all of Keynote's tricks. So if you need to play your presentation on a computer that doesn't have Keynote installed and you want to preserve Keynote's visual splendor, export it as a QuickTime movie (see page 403), which you can play and control just like the original Keynote slideshow.

Still, there are times you want to—or have to—save your slideshow in PowerPoint format. Unlike a QuickTime file, you can edit a Keynote slideshow you've exported to PowerPoint like any other PowerPoint presentation. Just limit yourself to simple transitions and build effects—in other words, avoid all the cool stuff that Keynote does so well. That way, your slideshow can make the transition from Keynote to PowerPoint with little change.

To save your presentation in PowerPoint format, go to File→Export To→PowerPoint, and Keynote unrolls the Export Your Presentation dialog box (Figure 14-11).

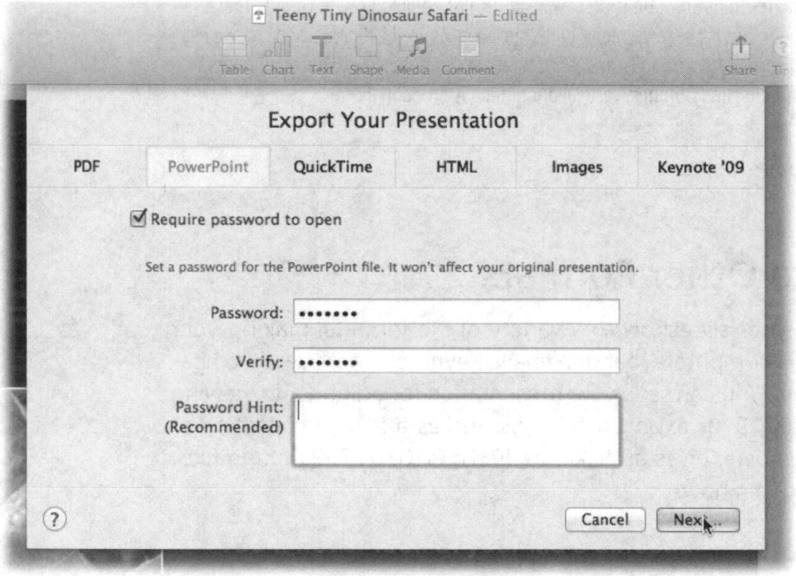

FIGURE 14-11

When you choose File→Export To→PowerPoint, Keynote automatically selects the PowerPoint tab here. Decide whether you want to protect your presentation with a password, and then click Next. This opens the familiar Save As dialog box, where you can give your new PowerPoint file a name and choose where to store it on your computer.

TIP You can leave the name of the document the same as the Keynote file's name. Keynote appends the .ppt extension to the name so that you—and your Mac—can tell the different versions apart.

Saving as Keynote '09

If your friends are doing a poor job keeping up with the Joneses—that would be you—when it comes to upgrading to the latest version of iWork, you can save your slideshow as a Keynote '09-friendly file. Choose File→Export To→Keynote '09 to open the Export Your Presentation dialog box with the Keynote '09 tab selected. Protect your file with a password, if necessary, and then click Next. This opens the Save As dialog box, where you can name your file and pick where to save it. (New features introduced in the latest version of iWork, such as new transitions and build effects, won't make the leap to this older format, so your slideshow may lose a bit of visual flair.)

Sorry, your pals are out of luck if they're using an even older version of Keynote. Your best option is to export the presentation as a PowerPoint file and then let the laggards import that into their version of Keynote.

Creating a QuickTime Movie

By exporting a Keynote slideshow as a QuickTime movie, you preserve all your transitions and builds, since QuickTime actually creates a movie while Keynote plays your slideshow. Unlike a traditional movie, though, you can control this kind of movie like your original slideshow. A QuickTime movie gives you the same presentation options as you have for your regular Keynote slideshow—you can click to advance slide by slide and build by build, or save it as a self-playing, recorded, or hyperlinks-only slideshow. (In QuickTime Player, choose View→Enter Full Screen to show your slideshow at full strength.)

Better yet, when you save a presentation as a QuickTime movie, you can play it on any computer that has QuickTime Player installed. QuickTime Player is Apple's media-authoring and -viewing program, so it comes preinstalled on all Macs—and on any Windows PC with iTunes installed. You can also download it free from *www. quicktime.com*.

QuickTime lets you save your presentation in various sizes and qualities, ranging from large files with full-quality video down to small files more suitable for a web page. To get started choose File→Export To→QuickTime to open the Export Your Presentation dialog box. You'll notice that the QuickTime tab has a few more options than you've seen before (Figure 14-12). Begin by picking a presentation style from the Playback drop-down menu:

- **Self-Playing.** When you view this kind of QuickTime slideshow, you can't manually control it—every slide and build advances automatically. This kind of movie is like Keynote's self-playing presentation (page 393), except the build durations and slide durations are the same for the entire slideshow—you can't vary the timing of individual slides.

  When you choose this option, Keynote displays additional settings. In the "Go to next slide after" field, enter the number of seconds each slide should remain onscreen after all its builds are complete; in the "Go to next build after" field, enter the number of seconds that should separate each build on each slide.

- **Slideshow Recording.** This is the same as Keynote's recorded presentation style; to use this option, you first have to record a voiceover (page 395).

Select a size and quality for the movie from the Format drop-down menu: 1024 × 768, 720p, or 1080p. If you prefer to choose your own settings to produce some other blend of size and frame rate, use a different video compressor, or alter the movie's audio quality, choose Custom and see Figure 14-13.

If your slideshow includes any sound, it will be included when you export your project as a QuickTime movie. If you want a silent presentation, then remove any sound effects or audio soundtrack before exporting.

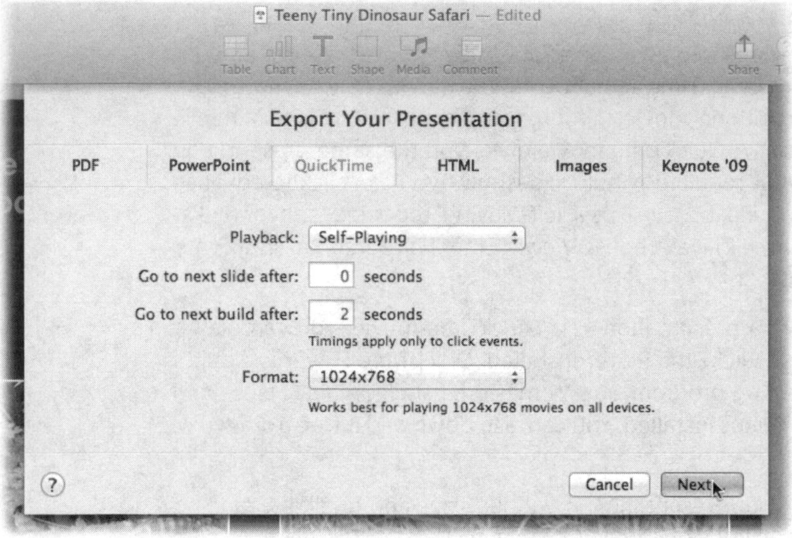

FIGURE 14-12

Select an option from the Playback drop-down menu to determine what kind of movie QuickTime creates. If you choose Self-Playing, then you can then set the slide and build duration. These settings override any you may have set in the Animate panel's various tabs.

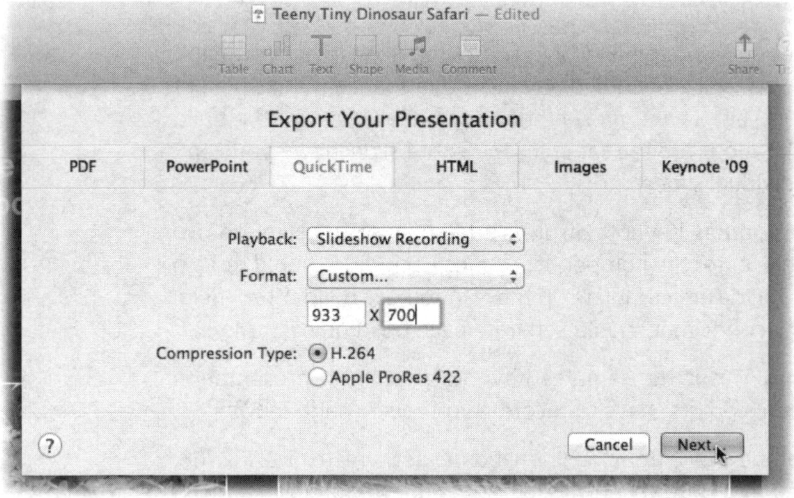

FIGURE 14-13

If Keynote's three off-the-rack QuickTime formats don't provide the fit you desire, choose Custom to create the perfect export. The settings that appear let you choose a custom movie size, and you can use the Compression Type setting to tweak your video's behavior. Choose from H.264 (one of the most widely used formats for distributing video content) or Apple ProRes 422 (which is generally used for video editing and not viewing).

TIP If the slideshow includes an audio soundtrack, the QuickTime movie will keep playing until the audio finishes. So if your slideshow is a lot shorter than the audio, consider using a shorter audio file for your soundtrack.

When you've set all the QuickTime options, click Next to open the Save As dialog box. Then name the movie, select a destination folder, and click Export. The Creating Movie window appears while Keynote is generating your slideshow and disappears when your file is created. Use your Finder window to navigate to where you saved your QuickTime presentation, and double-click to play it.

TIP You can learn more about QuickTime at *www.apple.com/quicktime*.

Saving as PDF

If you want to share your slideshow with people who don't have Keynote *and* you'd like to use a format that's more universal than PowerPoint or QuickTime, Keynote lets you export your slides as a PDF document, which pretty much any computer can open. Every Mac can read PDF files with OS X's Preview program, and Adobe makes free versions of its Adobe Reader program for virtually any computer operating system (it's available from *www.adobe.com/reader*)—making PDF the best bet for a universally readable file.

Alas, all of your soaring transitions and builds are brought to a standstill in a PDF file, which reduces your slideshow to a collection of static images. That means your viewers don't see any transitions, builds, or movies, or hear any sounds. But they can see all your text and images, making PDFs a useful way to solicit comments from your coworkers before the presentation or to distribute the slides to your workshop attendees afterward. Exporting to a PDF also preserves any hyperlinks in your slideshow, so you can still navigate a PDF of a hyperlinks-only slideshow, for example.

To create a PDF document from your slideshow, choose File→Export To→PDF to open the Export Your Presentation dialog box's PDF tab (Figure 14-14). Select your settings, and then click Next. Give your file a name, pick a destination in the Save As dialog box, and then click Export.

Exporting Slides as Image Files

Keynote can turn your slideshow into a collection of individual image files—one for each slide or build. You'll find this ability handy when someone asks you to email a copy of just one or two of your slides, or if you want to include a few of your slides in a Pages document as part of a handout or on your website. Keynote can create three different kinds of image files:

- **JPEG** is the most popular compressed image format. JPEG compression can yield files that are a fraction of the original file size, although at some sacrifice of image quality. Keynote lets you adjust the quality (and file size) of JPEG images—the higher the quality, the larger the file.

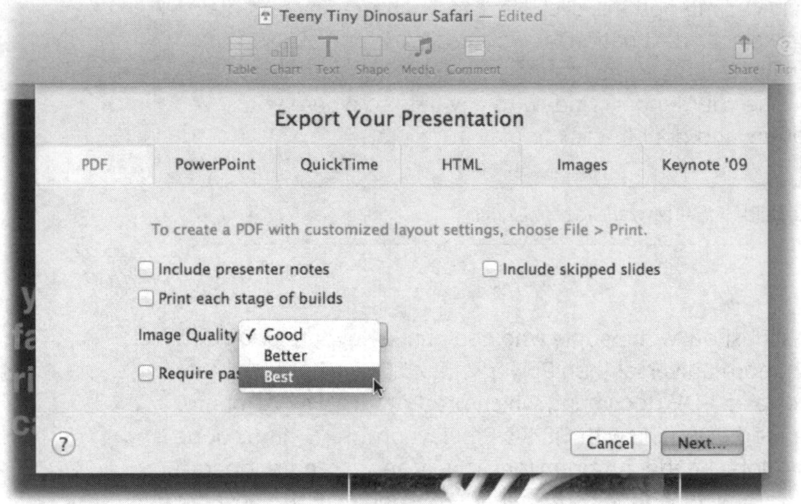

FIGURE 14-14

The PDF export settings provide many of the same options as Keynote's Print window (page 399). In addition, you can choose an image quality; select a lower quality to reduce the file size. The lowest option, Good, is fine for viewing onscreen; Better works well for basic printing; and Best is ideal for final-draft, high-quality printing.

- **PNG,** pronounced "ping," is designed for use on web pages. Like JPEG, PNG also compresses the image file, but it produces a higher-quality image.

- **TIFF** image files aren't compressed—and therefore have the highest possible image quality, but also the largest file size.

To export images, choose File→Export To→Images, and the Export Your Presentation dialog box appears with the Images tab open (Figure 14-15). To create an image from each slide in the slideshow, select All. If you want to create images from just some of the slides, click the From option and enter a range of slide numbers in the two boxes (to create an image of just one slide, enter that slide number in both boxes).

Turn on the "Create an image for each stage of builds" checkbox if you need individual image files for each of your slide builds. Use the Format drop-down menu to select the type of image file—JPEG, PNG, or TIFF—and then click Next to bring up Keynote's Save As dialog box.

Enter a name for your images in the Save As box. (As Keynote saves each of your slide images, it appends a number to the name you enter here—resulting in, for example, mints-and-olives-are-great001, mints-and-olives-are-great002, and so on.) Then tell Keynote where to save your slide images. If you want to keep the images together in their own folder, click the triangle to the right of the Save As field, and then click the New Folder button that appears; give the new folder a name, and then click Create. Finally, click Export, and a progress bar appears to show you that Keynote is toiling away, converting your slides to images.

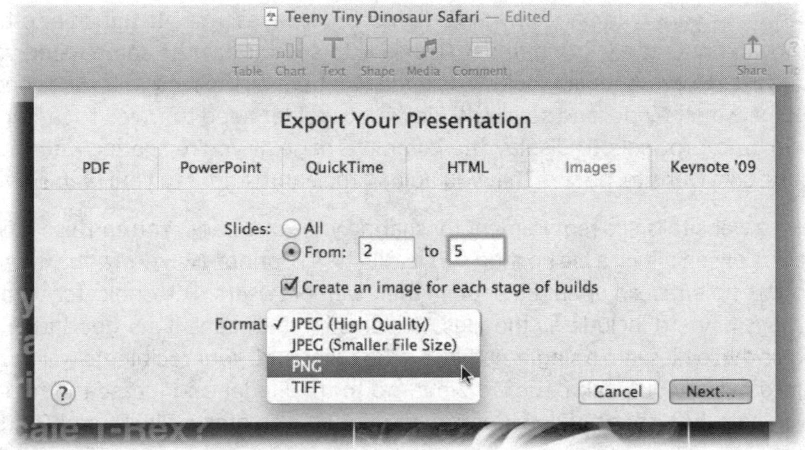

FIGURE 14-15

Set the slide range and image format, and tell Keynote whether to make individual images from each build. It's often a good idea to make a sample export of one slide in each format and compare their quality, so you can pick the format that suits your needs.

Exporting a Slideshow as a Web Page

Everybody's got a web browser, which means that everyone can view your slideshow when you export it as a web page. Right up there with saving your presentation as a PDF file, HTML (the format used for web pages) is ideal for distributing your slideshow far and wide without running into software compatibility trouble. You can view the slideshow right in your browser, and click the mouse to advance or use the optional navigation buttons to move back and forth.

Like exporting a PDF file, though, the resulting web page is stripped of your slideshow's transitions, build effects, movies, and music. In this format, your slideshow becomes a collection of still pictures—the same pictures, in fact, that you would get from exporting the slides as images, only presented together on a web page. Also—and this might seem strange for a web page—any hyperlinks in your slideshow *don't* make it through the export process.

> **TIP** Saving a slideshow as a web page isn't the only way to share it on the Web. You can display an exported QuickTime movie on a web page, for example, and Keynote also offers several easy options tailored for sharing the presentation online, such as Vimeo, YouTube, and iCloud. See pages 409–413 for details.

The size of the resulting web page matches the slide size in the Setup panel's Presentation tab (page 284). To make sure that the slideshow can fit in a browser window, open the Setup panel's Presentation tab, click the Slide Size drop-down menu, select Custom Slide Size, and then choose 800 × 600 before doing the export. With that done, you're ready to go: Choose File→Export To→HTML, and the Export Your Presentation dialog box appears with the HTML tab selected; click Next to launch the oh-so-familiar Save As dialog box. You know the drill: Enter a file name, specify where Keynote should save the file, and then click Export.

■ SHARING YOUR EXPORTED WEB PAGE

Keynote saves your web page as an HTML file, but it saves a whole bunch of other stuff too, and puts them into a folder (it's easy to spot: It has the same name you provided in the Save As dialog box). This folder contains all the files your slides need to look the way they do, and so all the files in this folder need to travel together in order for web browsers to display the complete page. If you're sharing your new web page on a website, be sure that you upload the entire folder to your web server.

Actually, a website isn't a requirement for sharing your web page. You can also email it to others or send it via a file hosting service such as Dropbox (*www.dropbox.com*), and your recipients can open the page in their web browsers. The one catch is that you always have to include *all* the files. For email, that means it's a good idea to compress these files into a single zip file; on the other end, your recipients will unzip the file to get at your web page. To zip it, go to the Finder and locate the folder. Select it, and then choose File→Compress; your Mac creates a file named [folder name].zip, which you can then send via email.

■ Emailing Slideshows

Sending your Keynote documents via email is probably the most common way to share slideshows—possibly even more than presenting them to crowds of adoring fans. Keynote makes emailing an easy process: With just one click, you can export the file and open an email message with the file already attached. Click the Share button in the toolbar, select "Send a Copy," and then choose Email. Keynote launches the "Send via Email" dialog box, where you can choose a file type for your attachment: Keynote, PDF, PowerPoint or QuickTime. Depending on the file type you choose, you can make some extra decisions about the format of your exported document. When you're ready, click Next to open Mail, your Mac's email program. A new message pops up with your file already attached, ready to be addressed and sent to the lucky recipient.

> **NOTE** This command is tuned to use Mail. If you use another email program, you'll have to go the long way 'round: Export the file (if you plan to send it in a non-Keynote format), create a new mail message in your favorite email program, and then attach the file to it manually.

■ Sharing Your Slides Online

From collaborating with team members before your presentation to sharing your brilliance with the world after the fact, posting your slideshow online makes it easy for others to find your work. Keynote offers built-in tools to fast-track your presentation to the Web: Share and collect feedback using iCloud; post a movie version of your slideshow on YouTube or Vimeo; or share it via Facebook and Twitter. The following sections provide the details.

Using iCloud with Keynote

Whether you want to share a slideshow with coworkers, distribute lecture notes to your class, or run a presentation by your team, iCloud is a nifty way to do it. The Web-based service is specifically designed to help you share a document with a small group of viewers and collect their feedback. Many people do that by circulating a document via email, but feedback can be difficult to track that way. And with Keynote's media-heavy files, you're often working with files big enough to make email servers choke. Distributing your slideshow via iCloud solves both problems, providing easy file viewing and a single location for gathering comments.

For detailed info about using iCloud, head back to page 284. Meanwhile, here's the quick version, with a few notes specific to using iCloud with Keynote slideshows:

Before you can share anything via iCloud, you first need to create an iCloud account and tell your Mac about said account (page 750). Once you've done all that, you can share your document via iCloud in several ways. Click the Share button in the toolbar, select "Share Link via iCloud," and then choose from the following:

- **Email.** When you select this option, your Mac boots up the Mail program and creates a new message, already filled out with a link the receiver can use to view and edit your document. Just enter the recipient's address and click Send.

- **Messages.** Instant-message the document's link to an iPhone, iPad, iPod Touch, or Mac via Message (see *http://support.apple.com/kb/HT5395* for more about Messages). Enter a recipient or click the blue + to pluck a name out of your Address Book, and then click Send.

- **Twitter.** Post the link to your document to your Twitter account. Just keep in mind that Twitter is public by default, so unless you've protected your tweets, everyone in the *world* can see the link, meaning that you're potentially inviting anyone and everyone to change your document. Proceed with caution!

- **Facebook.** Post a link to your Facebook wall. The link is still pretty public (especially if your Facebook profile is visible to lots of people) so, again, be cautious about using this option.

- **Copy link.** Copy the link and then paste it wherever you want.

> **NOTE** If you haven't saved your presentation to iCloud, when you click any of these options, Keynote displays a dialog box asking whether you want to move your document to iCloud. Click the "Move to iCloud" button, and Keynote handles the rest.

Viewing and editing a document in iCloud is almost identical to working on it on your Mac (Keynote for iCloud is covered in detail in Chapter 29). After you share a document via iCloud, Keynote's Share button changes to let you know the presentation is no longer your private property: It turns into two head-and-shoulders silhouettes. If you want to stop sharing your document at any point, choose Share→View Share Settings→Stop Sharing (Figure 14-16).

FIGURE 14-16

After you've shared a presentation, the Share button undergoes a bit of a makeover to let you know that other people have access to it. If you want to stop sharing your presentation, click this new Share button, select View Share Settings, and then click the Stop Sharing button. In this window, you can also share the link to your document with more people (or resend the link, if an absent-minded colleague has misplaced it): Click the Send Link button and choose one of the options from the drop-down menu that's open in this screenshot.

When you're editing a presentation that has been shared with you via iCloud, the experience is very similar to editing a presentation in the privacy of your Mac (see Figure 14-17).

Send a Copy

When you share via iCloud, you invite other people to collaborate on your document with you. That means there's just *one* copy of your document, and while you're editing it on your Mac, your collaborators are editing it via the magic of the World Wide Web. If the thought of someone else getting her grubby little paws on your presentation gets you all in a tizzy, you can give your untrustworthy collaborators their own version of your document. That way, they can edit the copy to their hearts content, and then send it back to you—all without them ever laying a finger on your original document. Sending a copy is also a good way to distribute a document that you want others to *read* but not edit.

To send a copy of your presentation, click Share→"Send a Copy," and then choose from the following options:

- **Email.** Send a copy of your document via email. Selecting this option opens a "Send via Email" dialog box, where you can choose the format of your copy (Keynote, PDF, PowerPoint, or QuickTime). Click Next to launch Mail, which pops up with a new message already filled out with some basic text and your document already attached.

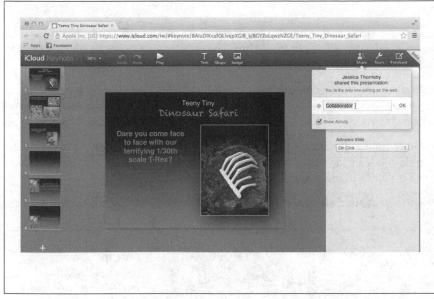

FIGURE 14-17

When you're editing a presentation that's been shared with you via iCloud, you can work on it in pretty much the same way you edit a slideshow on your Mac: The toolbar, Format panel, and slide navigator are all present and accounted for. You can review who else is editing it by clicking the Share button. In the Share drop-down menu shown here, you can change your user-name from Collaborator to something that better reflects your personality.

- **Messages.** Send a copy of your document via Messages. Choose a format for your copy, click Next, and Keynote presents you with a message with your document attached, ready for you to send.

- **AirDrop.** Send a copy via AirDrop, a service that lets you beam files to other Macs and iOS devices that understand AirDrop (most do). Choose whether to send your presentation as a PDF file, PowerPoint, QuickTime video, and so on, and then click Next. The recipient then has to accept your AirDrop before the presentation can be beamed to his computer or iDevice. You can learn more about Airdrop at *http://support.apple.com/kb/HT4783*.

- **Facebook.** Send your presentation to Facebook as a movie. Choose your Self-Playing settings, or opt for a Slideshow Recording (of course, you need to have created a recording first), and then click Next. Keynote transforms your presentation into a video; click Post to send it to Facebook.

The YouTube and Vimeo options are a little more in-depth and therefore deserve sections of their very own.

YouTube and Vimeo

If iCloud documents are aimed at small groups of friends and coworkers, YouTube and Vimeo movies are just the opposite—they're aimed at getting the attention of the whole world. You can add your Keynote slideshows to YouTube and Vimeo's ever-growing collection of online movies—an easy way to share your slideshow and to let others embed it in their blogs and websites.

■ SHARE A VIDEO ON YOUTUBE

Before you can add your own motion-picture masterpiece to YouTube, you have to create a YouTube account. If you don't have one yet, visit *www.youtube.com* for more info.

To post your video to YouTube, choose Share→"Send a Copy"→YouTube. Keynote then asks you a few questions about how you'd like to format your slideshow movie (Figure 14-18). When you're happy with the settings you've chosen, click Next.

YouTube movies can be of two presentation styles: Self-Playing and Slideshow Recording. (Slideshow Recording is grayed out until you record a voiceover for the slideshow; see page 395.) For Self-Playing movies, you can adjust these two settings:

- **Go to next slide after.** The number of seconds you want the movie to pause before advancing to the next slide (this countdown starts after the last build on the slide, if it has any builds).

- **Go to next build after.** The number of seconds the movie pauses between builds.

FIGURE 14-18

Choose Share→"Send a Copy"→YouTube to share your slideshow as a movie on the super-popular video-sharing website. To get started, tell Keynote whether you're creating a self-playing presentation or whether you want to use the Slideshow Recording option (which is available only if you've actually created a recording!). If you select Self-Playing, you can choose how long each slide and build should hang around before Keynote advances to the next slide/build. Click Next, enter your account details as shown here, and then click Send to post to YouTube.

Click Next, log into your YouTube account, and then give your soon-to-be-viral YouTube video a name, a description, and a category (see Figure 14-18). In the Tags field, type keywords that describe your slideshow's topics; these will help people find your video when they search YouTube. If you don't want your movie to be seen by anyone but you and your designated viewers, turn on "Make this movie personal." Finally, click Send, and Keynote churns out the movie and uploads it to YouTube.

■ SHARE A VIDEO ON VIMEO

To post a video to Vimeo, you first have to create a Vimeo account; go to *www.vimeo. com* if you don't already have one. Once you're all signed up with the website, you can publish your Keynote presentation:

1. **Go to Share→"Send a Copy"→Vimeo.**

2. **Open the Playback drop-down menu and choose between Self-Playing and Slideshow Recording.**

   If you choose Self-Playing, tell Keynote how long it should wait before advancing to the next slide ("Go to next slide after") and the next build ("Go to next build after").

3. **Click Next.**

   If this is the first time you're posting a video to Vimeo, you may need to enter your account details by clicking Add Account and following the onscreen instructions.

4. **Enter a title, description, and tags for your movie. You can also make your movie private by turning on the "Make this movie personal" checkbox.**

   Tags help viewers find your video, so it's worth putting some thought into these.

5. **When you're ready to send your video out into the big wide world of Vimeo, click the Publish button.**

Customizing Keynote Themes

D on't be fooled by the good looks of Keynote's theme library—it's a lot more than a pretty face. Sure, Apple's elegant themes look great (and they make you look great, too), but deep down, they're all about productivity and efficiency. Using one of these themes lets you skip the big-picture design phase and get right to work on your material. And when you use a theme, each of your slides is based on a master slide, which means that you can instantly apply changes to a whole batch of slides by updating that master layout—or by changing the standard look of the theme's text, charts, and other objects. Customizing themes, in other words, lets you work smarter and faster, sidestepping the need to make changes to individual slides, object by object, over and over again.

When you customize a theme—or build one from scratch—you only have to do it once. You can save your creation as its own theme to use it again for other documents, and Keynote adds it to the Theme Chooser, giving you yet another starting point for building your slideshows: a standard theme for your company's marketing presentations, your school's slideshows, or just a blank slideshow with the standard settings configured the way you like. Share your theme with others or, if you suffer from a debilitating fear of document design, install a theme created by someone else. You can find lots of additional themes online, for free and for sale (see page 426).

This chapter tours Keynote's theme machinery, showing you how to create and modify themes and install new ones.

■ Keynote Theme Basics

Whether your design is baroque or basic, every slideshow is based on a theme, which boils down to a collection of prefab slide designs called *master slides*, each with its own layout and standard settings (slide background, fonts, object fills, and so on). Master slides lay the foundation for the overall layout and look of each slide in your presentation; you can change the layout of an individual slide by choosing a different master slide (click the + button in the bottom-left corner of the Keynote window, and then choose a master slide from the drop-down menu). If you later edit a master slide's layout or settings, Keynote automatically makes your changes to *all* the slides based on that master.

When you edit a theme, you're really just editing its master slides—updating the layout or background, adding a logo or a copyright notice, switching the standard colors of its charts, and so on. You can also build a theme from the ground up, creating new master slides from scratch.

To work with a theme's master slides, you first have to open the *master slide navigator*. In the toolbar, click the View button and then select Edit Master Slides. The navigator responds by displaying thumbnails of all the master slides for your slideshow's theme, as shown in Figure 15-1. These are the same thumbnails that show up when you click the + button in the screen's bottom-left corner.

Master slides have a few special features, but for the most part, they look and work just like regular slides when you edit them. Select a master slide in the navigator, and Keynote displays it on the slide canvas, ready for you to edit.

■ Modifying a Theme

Keynote comes with 30 themes. For any given project, chances are that at least one or two of these themes will come mighty close to the design you'd like to use. When a theme is close but not quite, you can change it by editing its collection of master slides as explained in the following sections.

> **NOTE** When you edit the master slides in a slideshow, you're not making changes to the original theme, only to the way it looks in *this* slideshow. Other slideshows that use this theme remain unchanged. You can, however, save your changes as a custom theme, as explained on page 425.

Importing Master Slides

You can modify or add master slides to a theme, as you'll soon see, but don't overlook the lazy route: swiping the work of others (or at least of other slideshows). Keynote makes it easy to borrow master slides from other Keynote themes and documents. In fact, Keynote does this every time you apply a new theme to your slideshow: When you change a slide's theme (by clicking the Setup button in the toolbar, opening the Presentation tab, and then clicking the Change Theme button), Keynote pours all the master slides from the new theme into the master slide navigator.

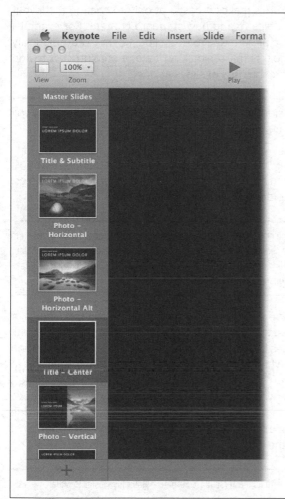

FIGURE 15-1

*Select View→Edit Master Slides, and the slide navigator displays all
the master slides for your current theme. Click one of the master slides
to modify it, duplicate it (press Return or choose Edit→Duplicate), or
delete it (press Delete). Choose View→Exit Master Slides to get back
to the regular slide navigator.*

But switching your presentation's theme is a bit drastic if you just want to get your
hands on a master slide or two. To import a single master slide from another theme,
create a second presentation based on that theme, and then create a slide that uses
the master slide you're after. You can then drag this slide from the second presentation's slide navigator and drop it into the current presentation's slide navigator.
You can now use this interloping slide as the basis for a new slide, or use it as a sort
of temporary master slide, creating copies whenever you need a different theme
to spice up your presentation. Once this temporary master slide has outstayed its
welcome, getting rid of it is as easy as selecting its thumbnail in the slide navigator
and then hitting the Delete key.

Modifying Master Slides

When you make a change to a master slide, the change cascades through every slide that uses that master slide. This makes it easy not only to change the layout and styles of all these slides, but also to add new standard content. For example, when you add a free text box or a picture to a master slide, Keynote automatically adds it to the other slides that use that master, making it a one-step process to add a slide number, a logo, or footer text to lots of slides at once.

NOTE If you want to create a new master slide without modifying the layout of any slides already in your slideshow, see "Adding New Master Slides" (page 419).

Each master slide includes some combination of elements and standard settings, such as the position of the title and body text boxes, background text and graphics, media placeholders, and placeholder text.

NOTE Unlike regular slides (where you can select several in the slide navigator to apply changes to them all at once), you can select only one master slide at a time. So if you want to change the background of all your slides, for example, you need to do it one slide at a time, stepping your way through the whole collection. Take a deep breath and prepare to apply the same background again and again.

Changing any of those attributes on a master slide instantly affects the appearance of the slides generated from it. Move the title text box to a new location and change its color, and the titles of all the slides based on that master switch to the new position and color, too. The exception is when you've already applied custom formatting to an individual, non-master slide. In this example, if you've already moved one slide's title to a new location, that slide *won't* get updated automatically when you move the master slide's title. Local changes on individual slides, in other words, override changes made at the master-slide level, while objects still in the master's original location get updated to reflect the change.

TIP To make a slide come back in line with its master, choose Format→"Reapply Master to Slide."

In addition to simply changing what's already on the master slide, you can add new objects, too. Add an image object for your logo, a free text box for your copyright footer, or a shape as a decorative container around the whole slide. Think of your new objects like wallpaper; these elements appear on your slides as uneditable background objects—you can change their content only from the master slide, not from the regular slide.

The exceptions are the small handful of special objects controlled by the Slide Layout tab: the title text box; the body text box; and media, text, or object placeholders. These portions of the slide are *designed* to be edited, so they don't simply sink into the background like other objects you add to a master slide. You turn them on and

off from the Format panel's Slide Layout tab, which gets a new name and a slightly
different look when you're editing master slides, which brings us to...

■ THE MASTER SLIDE LAYOUT TAB

When you select a master slide in the master slide navigator (choose View→Edit
Master Slides to display it), the Format panel's Slide Layout tab bows out and gets
replaced by the Master Slide Layout tab (Figure 15-2). This tab determines whether
the slide displays the title and body text box, as well as object placeholders (see page
330) and the slide number. Use the checkboxes to turn these elements on or off.

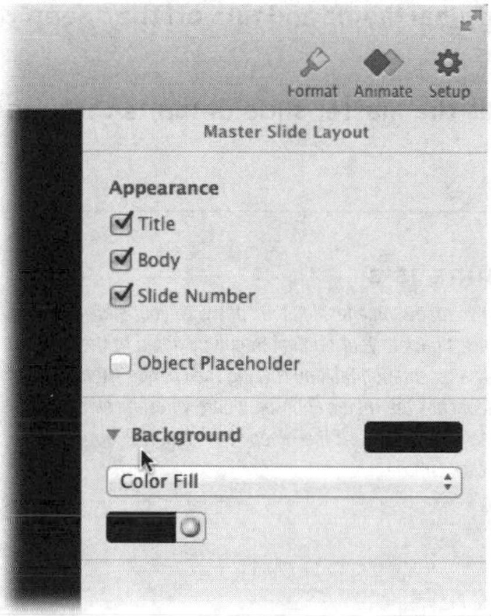

FIGURE 15-2

*When you're editing a master slide, the Master Slide Layout tab
replaces the Slide Layout tab. Click the Background heading to expand
that section (as shown here), and then choose whether to include a
background fill, and, Voilà if so, what kind. You can also tell Keynote
whether the slide should feature a title, body text, or a slide number
by turning the checkboxes on and off.*

*Most of the time, when you're editing master slides, the Master Slide
Layout tab pops up automatically. If it's nowhere to be seen, click
the Format button in the toolbar and then make sure no objects are
selected, either by clicking on a blank portion of the slide or pressing
the Esc key. Voilà: The Master Slide Layout tab appears.*

Adding New Master Slides

The easiest way to create your own master slide is to find one that's similar to what
you'd like to create and use it as a starting point. If you prefer to start from an empty
slide, choose a blank master slide as your model.

In the master slide navigator, select the master slide you want to use as the basis
for your new slide, and then duplicate it using any of these methods:

- Choose Edit→Duplicate Selection.

- Press Return.

- Control-click it and then choose New Master Slide.

No matter which way you duplicate the original master slide, Keynote makes a carbon
copy of it and displays its thumbnail in the master slide navigator. Double-click the
new master slide's name—it's currently called "[Original's name] copy"—and give it

a more descriptive label. Then make changes to your new master slide as described in the previous section.

Reverting to the Original Theme

Who'd have thought that mustard yellow, hot fuchsia, and mud brown would make such an ugly combination? If your attempts to embroider your theme with a few elegant touches have instead butchered it beyond recognition, Keynote lets you head back to square one and restore the original theme settings:

1. **Choose File→Change Theme, or click the Setup button in the toolbar, open the Presentation tab, and then click Change Theme, as shown in Figure 15-3.**

2. **In the Theme Chooser, select the original theme and turn off the "Keep your style changes" checkbox.**

3. **Click Choose, and Keynote restores the master slide defaults throughout your presentation.**

FIGURE 15-3

If you've made some fashion faux pas with your slides, you can revert back to your original theme by going to the Setup panel's Presentation tab and clicking the Change Theme button. This launches the Theme Chooser, where you can select your original theme, turn off the "Keep style changes" option, and then click Choose.

TIP If you want to strip away all those bad formatting decisions from just a single slide, select that slide in the slide navigator, and then choose Format→"Reapply Master to Slide."

Building Themes from Scratch

Creating a brand-new theme is really the same as modifying an existing theme, but with a bit of initial pruning and planning. Here's how to get started:

1. **Create a new Keynote document using the theme of your choice.**

   Keynote creates a presentation containing a single Title & Subtitle slide.

2. **Choose View→Edit Master Slides.**

   This opens the master slide navigator shown back in Figure 15-1.

3. **Delete all the master slides *except* the Blank one.**

   You have to delete each master slide individually, since Keynote doesn't let you select more than one master at a time. Simply select each one in the master slide navigator and then press Delete. However, you'll eventually hit a snag: When you try to delete the Title & Subtitle master slide, you see a dialog box that says, "1 slide currently uses this master slide. Choose a different master slide." That's because your presentation contains that Title & Subtitle slide Keynote created back in step 1. Before you can delete this master slide, you need to switch the automatically created Title & Subtitle slide to use a new master slide. Conveniently, there is one master slide that you want to stick around: the Blank slide. So, in the dialog box, click the Blank thumbnail, and then click Choose. You can now delete the Title & Subtitle master slide.

The master slide navigator should now contain only one master slide: Blank. The next section explains how to proceed.

Create a "Master" Master Slide

To make sure that you keep your background and text styles consistent from slide to slide, it's a good idea to create a *master* master slide—a model that you'll use as the basis for each of the master slides you create. That way you can duplicate this master slide to make new masters, and those slides will automatically inherit this slide's text and background settings. Get these settings right on this first master slide and you won't have to change them for subsequent slides.

To get started, select the Blank master slide in the master slide navigator. Then, in the Format panel's Master Slide Layout tab do the following:

1. **Click the Background heading to expand this section, and then use the various settings to select a color, gradient, or image fill for your slide backgrounds.**

2. **Turn on the Title, Body, and Slide Number checkboxes to add those text boxes to the master slide.**

With the title, body text, and slide number options turned on, you now have those three main text boxes on your slide. Set the size and position of these text boxes and—more importantly—format the font, text, and bullet styles for each text box the way you want them to appear throughout your theme. If you're feeling thorough, you can format each of the body text box's five indent levels differently so you can highlight their different levels of importance (see page 39 for more info on formatting text).

TIP When setting a master slide's text formatting, it's particularly useful to have some sample text to work with. Create a regular slide in the slideshow, apply your master-in-progress to this sample slide, and then add text and images to this regular slide. Then, as you make changes to the master, periodically switch to your sample slide to see the results.

Even if you don't plan to have all of these text boxes on every master slide you build (and you almost certainly won't), place these boxes in spots where you think most slides will use them. This is particularly important for the title text box; you don't want the title hopping around when you switch master layouts in your slideshow.

Finally, use the Insert menu or Keynote's toolbar buttons to add any other background elements that you want to appear on every slide. Add these as regular image objects, text boxes, or shapes—for example, your company logo, a photograph, copyright text, or a company tagline. Turn down the opacity of these objects to fade them if you plan to put text and other content on top of them in your slides. When you have your background objects in place, *lock* them so you don't accidentally select or move them: Select the objects and then choose Arrange→Lock.

With your "master of masters" complete, you're ready to start building your various master slides. Simply duplicate this original master slide for each new master you want to create, modifying each one to give it a unique layout.

Adding Text and Media Placeholders

When you first add objects to a master slide, Keynote creates them as background objects: Images, free text boxes, and other objects show up as fixed and uneditable on your regular slides. That's great for logos, watermarks, and other permanent fixtures, but not so wonderful if you're looking for variety. That's where *placeholders* come in. As their name suggests, these stand-ins simply show where text, images, audio, and movies should go—you replace them with your real content when you edit the slide.

Text boxes and shapes set to be *text placeholders* show up on your slides as regular objects, ready for you to edit their text. *Media placeholders*, on the other hand, have the extra smarts to know how to squeeze and stretch pictures and movies: When you drop a picture or a movie onto a media placeholder, Keynote automatically replaces the placeholder with your selection, sized and positioned to fit the placeholder's dimensions.

You can add as many placeholders as you like to a master slide. To create one, add an object to the master slide and then select the object. In the Format panel's Style tab, turn on the "Define as Media Placeholder" checkbox for a picture or a movie, or the "Define as [Text/Shape] Placeholder" checkbox for a shape or a text box (as shown in Figure 15-4).

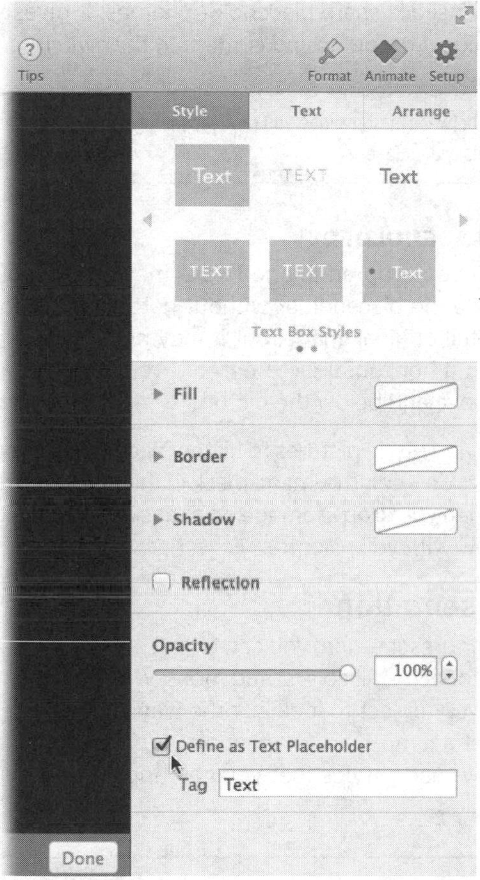

FIGURE 15-4

To turn an object into a placeholder, select the object, open the Format panel (if it isn't already open), and then select the Styles tab. Near the bottom of this tab, you'll find a "Define as Placeholder" setting (where the cursor is positioned here). Turn on this checkbox to turn the object into a placeholder, or turn it off to turn the object back into an ordinary object.

You can also add tags in this tab, which are described in the next section.

■ NAMING PLACEHOLDERS WITH TAGS

The Tag field immediately below the "Define as [Media/Text/Shape] Placeholder" checkbox is optional, but it plays an important role. A *tag* gives your placeholder a name that tells Keynote how to translate placeholder content across different master slides. When placeholder objects have the same name, this tells Keynote that these placeholders should share content when you switch master-slide layouts.

For example, when you edit your slideshow and switch a slide's layout by choosing a new master slide, Keynote automatically transfers your title and body text to the new layout. But it transfers placeholder content only if both master slides contain text or media placeholders with the same tag. If each master slide has a media placeholder tagged "Illustration," for example, then a picture in the placeholder will make the transition when you switch a slide's master. If the two master slides have different tags for their placeholders (or if the new master slide doesn't have a placeholder at all), then Keynote tosses out the picture and it doesn't show up in the new layout.

Because of this, it's a good strategy to be consistent and descriptive in the way you tag your placeholders. When master slides share placeholder names, it gives you more flexibility to change master slides without losing content in the switch.

NOTE Because tags identify placeholders between master slides, you can't repeat tags on the same master slide. Every placeholder on a slide has to have its own unique tag.

■ ADDING MASKS TO MEDIA PLACEHOLDERS

Keynote's standard behavior when you drop an image into a media placeholder is to resize the image so it fits inside the placeholder without getting cropped. In other words, you'll always see the full original image, but it may not fill the whole placeholder. For example, dragging a horizontal picture into a vertically oriented placeholder leaves empty space above and below the picture.

To have Keynote automatically crop and resize pictures to fill the placeholder's exact dimensions—like Pages' placeholders do—edit the image mask in the master slide as explained on page 158. That way, when you drop an image on a masked placeholder, Keynote fills the *entire* mask window with your picture.

Adding Styles to Your Presentation

Whenever you add an object to your presentation, you can tweak every element of its appearance—borders, shadows, opacity, fill colors, and more. While it's great to have this level of control, getting every object to look just the way you want it can be time consuming. To help you get a jump-start on creating your perfect object, Keynote offers a collection of ready-made styles that you can apply to an object with the click of a button.

NOTE You can apply and create custom styles regardless of whether you're editing master slides or normal slides: They work exactly the same either way.

To take a look at these styles, select any object and then click the Format button in the toolbar to open the Format panel (if it's not already open). Open the Style tab and you'll find six default styles at the top of the tab; click any of these styles to apply it to the selected object.

While these default styles are a good starting point, they're not the most adventurous effects that Keynote has to offer. Thankfully, it's quick and easy to create your own styles. To do so, add an object and then format it until it looks just the way you want. For example:

- **Free text box.** Enter some text in the box and then select and format that text. Set the background fill, the border, shadow, and opacity for the text box.

- **Shape.** Insert a shape, enter some text, and then select and format the text. Then set the shape's background fill, border, shadow, and opacity.

- **Image.** Insert an image and adjust its border, shadow, opacity, and reflection.

- **Chart.** Go through each of the chart types, styling each the way you want it to appear. See page 271 for some caveats about defining standard chart styles.

> **NOTE** You can't create custom styles for tables.

You can then save all of this formatting as a custom style by going to Format→Advanced→Create [Object] Style. Alternatively, you can save the style by heading to the Format panel's Style tab and clicking the right or left arrow near the top of the tab to make Keynote scroll to a set of empty thumbnails. Simply click the thumbnail with the + on it, and Keynote saves your style as a new thumbnail.

However you create object styles, you apply them in exactly the same way as you apply Keynote's default styles: Go to the Format panel's Style tab, click the right and left arrows to scroll through the various styles until you find the one you want, and then click the style's thumbnail to apply it to your selected object. When you save your slideshow as a theme, all the styles you create come along for the ride. (Page 269 offers a more in-depth look at object styles.)

Saving Custom Themes

After you've gone to all the trouble of modifying or creating your own master slides, they still exist only within that one Keynote document. But if you save them as a theme, they're available whenever you want them, right in the Theme Chooser.

When you're ready to go, choose File→Save Theme, click "Add to Theme Chooser," and then give your new theme a name. Keynote saves your custom themes in a separate section of the Theme Chooser: Click the My Themes button at the top of the window to take a look at all of your themes. From this point on, your custom theme works exactly the same as Keynote's default themes.

You can also save your theme as a file. Themes that are saved in this way don't show up in the Theme Chooser, but you can share them with others: Go to File→Save Theme, click Save, and then choose a location on your hard drive or iCloud.

NOTE If you save your theme to iCloud, the next time you open Keynote on your iDevice, the theme appears as a downloadable file.

Even though a theme saved as a file doesn't automatically show up in the Theme Chooser, you can still add it to the Theme Chooser by double-clicking the file in your Finder, and then clicking "Add to Theme Chooser" when prompted.

Sharing and Buying Themes

Now that you've created your own eye-popping Keynote theme, it's time to share it with your friends and coworkers. The easiest way to share a theme is to save it to an easily accessible location on your computer (as shown in Figure 15-5), and then send the file as an email attachment.

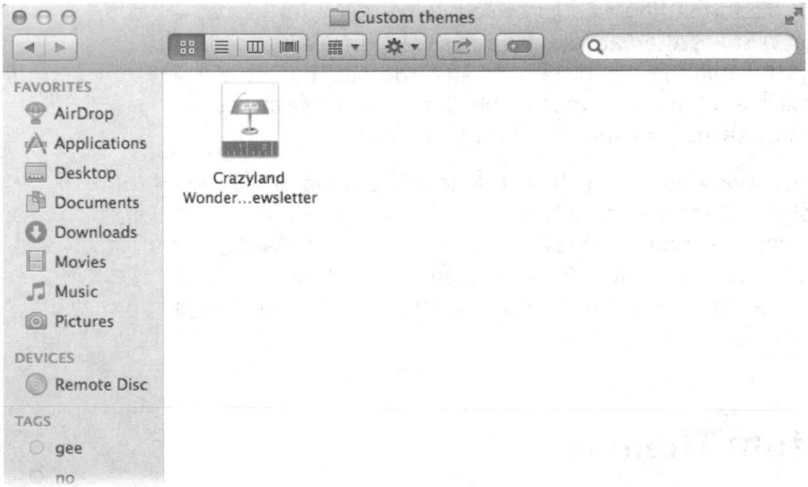

FIGURE 15-5

When you're saving a theme that's ready to share, it's a good idea to give it a memorable title and to save it somewhere that's easy to find, such as your Documents folder, desktop, or even inside its own folder. Keynote saves themes as files with a .kth extension.

If you added your theme to the Theme Chooser instead of saving it, don't worry: Just create a new presentation based on your theme, and then go to File→Save Theme, but this time click Save and then stash your theme somewhere you can easily find it. You can then send this file as an email attachment or post it online so that everyone can enjoy your work.

When someone sends you a Keynote theme, double-click the file and a box appears asking if you want to add this file to your Template Chooser.

Whether or not *you* decide to share your creations, lots of other people are doing it. Apple's built-in Keynote themes includes a wide variety of designs, but there are hundreds, maybe thousands of other professionally designed templates for you to discover. Type *Keynote themes* into Google to find an ever-growing collection of theme developers. You'll find some of the best from the following companies:

- **Jumsoft.** *www.jumsoft.com*

- **Keynote Theme Park.** *www.keynotethemepark.com*

- **Keynote Pro.** *www.keynotepro.com*

Numbers for Mac

Creating a Numbers Spreadsheet

Don't be fooled by its name: Numbers has a mind for math, sure, but the iWork spreadsheet program does much more than just crunch digits. If you've always thought of spreadsheets as the exclusive and arcane domain of the accounting department, think again. Numbers can juggle figures for the most demanding spreadsheet jockeys, but you can also use it to store and organize just about any kind of information.

A spreadsheet is a list machine: Use it for to-do lists, contact lists, event planning, team rosters, product inventories, invoices—anything you might put into a list or a table, you can put in a spreadsheet. And then Numbers can make your list dance. Once you've plugged in your data, Numbers can sort it, filter it, categorize it, or combine it with data from other lists. In other words, Numbers isn't just a fancy calculator; you can use it as your own private *database*—a place to store, manipulate, and view data from all kinds of different angles.

Of course, Numbers can do math, too. When your data happens to take the form of digits—class grades, your check register, a valuation of assets minus depreciation—Numbers churns through your calculations, updating your totals as you add and edit data. The program knows more than 250 *functions,* feats of mathematical gymnastics that range from simple addition to complex accounting algorithms.

But all that is standard stuff, the basic work of spreadsheet programs for the last three decades. What's novel about Numbers is its attention to visual design; your spreadsheets have never had such great-looking figures. Just like the other iWork programs, Apple gave considerable care to making it easy—even fun—to design stunning spreadsheet documents. Mix your data tables with colorful charts, photos, and graphics, and they're suddenly multimedia presentations (see Figure 16-1). You even know how to do it already: Laying out a Numbers document is just like creating a page-layout document in Pages, or a slideshow presentation in Keynote. Drop design elements onto the spreadsheet canvas as *objects,* nudge them into place, and style them with colors, picture frames, reflections, shadows—you name it.

Budget Planning

KAREN'S BIRTHDAY

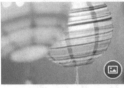

FIGURE 16-1

In Numbers, you're not limited to gray columns of figures. You can add photos, charts, and text to create slick multimedia presentations. Apple's built-in templates offer stylish examples: Here, the Party Planner and Recipe templates show off some of the possibilities.

Number of Guests
18

BUDGET

Description	Per Person Cost	Fixed Costs	Total Costs
Site Rental		$300.00	$300.00
Decorations		$200.00	$200.00
Music		$150.00	$150.00
Food	$30.00		$540.00
Drinks	$20.00		$360.00
Other	$10.00		$180.00
Budget Total			$1,730.00

BUDGET OVERVIEW

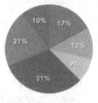

10% 17%
21% 12%
9%
31%

● Site Rental ● Decorations ● Music
● Food ● Drinks ● Other

Recipe

HOW TO USE: Enter the number of people the recipe serves and how many you plan to prepare for. Then, enter your ingredients and amounts needed in the first two columns, using the pull-down menus for measurement types (for example, oz or cup). Finally, replace the sample instructions with your own recipe instructions.

The formula will scale the recipe for you. Match the measurement units for the scaled amount to get the proper conversion.

Sample Recipe

	Recipe serves	Prepared for
	4	8

Ingredient	Amount		Scaled amount	
Penne pasta	8	oz	1	lb
Olive oil	1	tbsp	2	tbsp
Sliced zucchini	1/2	cup	1	cup
Cooked, shredded chicken	1/2	cup	1	cup
Garlic cloves	4	----	8	----
Tomatoes	1/2	cup	1	cup
Fresh basil	1	tbsp	2	tbsp
Parmesan cheese	3	tbsp	6	tbsp

Shopping List

Ingredients	Have it	Quantity
Penne Pasta	☐	1 lb
	☐	
	☐	
	☐	
	☐	
	☐	
	☐	
	☐	
	☐	
	☐	

In this ballet of objects, *tables* are always the star in a Numbers spreadsheet. You already met these data grids in Pages (Chapter 8) and Keynote (Chapter 12), where they played only supporting roles. In Numbers, tables take the spotlight as the organizing elements for your data. The program's interface is designed for working efficiently with table cells, adding a few tricks that you won't find in Numbers' iWork cousins.

This chapter gets you started with a high-level introduction to Numbers' features, showing you how to create, save, and print a basic spreadsheet, followed by a tour of a more complex and graphical report.

Picking a Numbers Template

As with the other iWork programs, your Numbers journey starts with the Template Chooser. When you launch Numbers or choose File→New to create a new document, the Template Chooser appears and tempts you with a selection of 31 spreadsheet templates (Figure 16-2).

> **NOTE** To open a file you've already created, pick a file on your hard drive by clicking File→Open or make a selection from the File→Open Recent submenu.

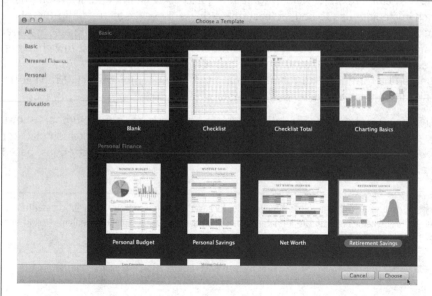

FIGURE 16-2

When you launch Numbers or create a new spreadsheet, the Template Chooser prompts you to select a template for the new file.

When you spot a template you like, double-click it or select it and then click the Choose button to open a new, untitled document based on that template.

TIP If you find yourself turning to the same template again and again, you can cut out the Template Chooser by picking a standard template to use every time you open a new document. Go to Numbers→Preferences, click the General tab, and then turn on the "Use template" option in the For New Documents section. Click the Change Template button and select your standard template from the Template Chooser. After you do this, you can get the Template Chooser back at any time by going to Numbers→Preferences→General and selecting Show Template Chooser.

Numbers templates play a different role from templates in the other iWork programs. In Pages and Keynote, templates define only the *look* of your document. While some Pages templates are designed for newsletters or reports, for example, you can fill them with any type of text or images. Numbers templates provide a similarly colorful and elegant selection of templates, but nearly all of them are intended for very specific purposes.

If you want to build an invoice, a workout tracker, or a plan for an upcoming party, Numbers has a template for each use. Those templates are preloaded not only with a layout of page elements, like all iWork templates, but also with calculations designed to achieve the specified task. As you'd expect, the Running Log template can chart your running pace and calculate your average run time and distance, but it can't help much with collecting your accounts receivable—that's an entirely different kind of legwork.

Unless a template specifically targets the goal you have in mind, it doesn't have much immediate use to you, at least not in the same sense as the fill-in-the-blank templates in Pages and Keynote. But even in such cases, Numbers templates are ideal demonstration documents. As you make your way through the next few chapters, be sure to browse the Template Chooser's offerings to explore how Apple pieced together the formulas and functions that make these templates tick. (You'll learn all about formulas and functions in Chapters 19 and 20.)

When you select a category in the Template Chooser's left pane, Numbers shows you a preview of related templates in the main window. Double-click a template (or click it once and then click Choose) and a fresh, untitled document opens, based on the template you chose.

TIP Even if you don't plan to use a template for its advertised purpose, you still might choose it for its style—its color scheme and standard formatting. You can always wipe out a template's contents to start from scratch but still get the benefit of its good taste.

◼ Your First Spreadsheet

Following the storming success of Mints & Olives (Now in a Can!), your mind is racing with other food products the cafes, restaurants, and snack machines of Crazyland Wonderpark can churn out to peckish visitors. You already have a couple of ideas, but are they any good? There's only one way to find out: Invite some lucky guests to sample these gastronomic delights, and then get them to rate each product on factors such as taste, smell, value, and edibility.

Your first task is to create a form the taste-testers can fill out as they're chowing down. There should be rows for each product, columns for each criteria, and cells where the taste-testers can write their scores. That kinda sounds like a spreadsheet, right?

To get started with your new spreadsheet, double-click the Blank template in the Template Chooser. Numbers opens a wide window containing a single *table*—an empty grid constructed from rows and columns that chop the table up into blocks called *cells* (Figure 16-3). Numbers labels its *columns* with letters (A, B, C...) and *rows* with numbers (1, 2, 3...). Columns and rows intersect in cells, giving each cell an address. Combine the column letter and row number to make a cell coordinate: For example, D4 is the cell in column D, row 4.

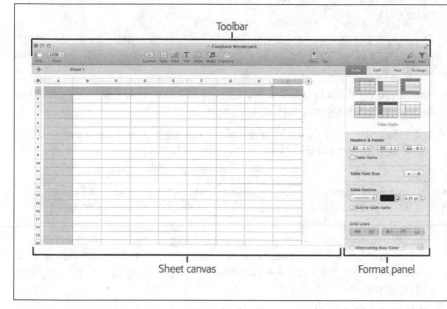

Toolbar

Sheet canvas

Format panel

FIGURE 16-3

Here's what you see when you create a new spreadsheet from the Blank template. The table is inside the sheet canvas, the big workspace that fills most of the window. Topping off your document window is the toolbar, featuring buttons for commonly used commands. The Format panel changes depending on your current selection in the sheet canvas. Here, a table cell is selected, so the Format panel shows options for formatting that cell and its table.

This table is where you'll list all the foodstuffs you'll be testing. Each row will hold the name of one product, with the cells of each column left empty for the taste-tester to fill in her comments: A score out of 10 for how tasty the snack is, for example. You'll create and label up all these rows and columns in just a moment, but first take a moment to get acquainted with your Numbers workspace.

If you want to take a really close look at your data, you can zoom in. Choose a magnification level from the Zoom drop-down menu in the toolbar, or head to the view View→Zoom submenu and choose Zoom In (⌘->) or Zoom Out (⌘-<). You can also choose Actual Size (discussed in detail in the box on page 25).

The Toolbar and Format Panel

If you've already explored Pages and Keynote, then Numbers puts you in familiar surroundings. The layout, icons, and controls of the spreadsheet document window share lots of features with your word-processing and slideshow documents, so you'll be up to speed in no time.

At the top of the window, the Numbers toolbar offers quick access to the commonly used commands. You'll learn more about each of these buttons in the coming chapters, but here's a quick tour.

- The **View** button offers options for opening the Find & Replace window, adding rulers to your sheet canvas, and hiding comments.

- As you just learned, the **Zoom** button lets you, well, zoom.

- The **Function** drop-down menu adds a calculation to the selected cell (see page 442).

- The object buttons—Table, Chart, Text, Shape, Media, and Comment—insert a new chart (Chapter 21), text box (page 148), shape (page 168), media item (page 156), or comment (page 469).

- The **Share** button lets you share your spreadsheets via all sorts of channels: Facebook, Twitter, email, iCloud, and more.

- The **Tips** button covers your screen in sticky notes, giving you hints and tips about how to get the most out of Keynote. Whenever you see a sticky note with a > symbol on it, click it to launch a window with even *more* information.

- Click the **Format** button to open and close the Format panel. The Format panel is a shape-shifter, constantly updating and changing depending on what you're doing in Numbers. For example, if you select an image in a spreadsheet, the Format panel pops up with the Image tab open; if you're editing a movie, it offers you the Movie tab. It also includes some tabs that apply no matter what object you select, such as the Arrange tab, which lets you control the positioning, rotation, and more.

- Click the **Sort & Filter** button to create filtering rules that determine which rows in a table are visible (page 502) and to sort your data (page 500).

- Directly underneath the toolbar is a **+** button that adds a new sheet to your spreadsheet. See page 446 for an intro to working with sheets.

Like the other iWork programs, Numbers lets you customize the toolbar by adding, deleting, and reorganizing its buttons. To set the toolbar up just the way you want, select View→Customize Toolbar (page 21 has more details about this important bit of interior decorating).

> **TIP** You can hide and reveal the toolbar by choosing View→Hide Toolbar (or Show Toolbar).

The Format panel is your sidekick, displaying an ever-changing array of tools depending on your current selection in the sheet canvas. In Numbers, you spend most of your time working on tables and table cells, so the Format panel typically displays options for styling the text, data, colors, and borders of table data. But when you select another object type—a chart, text box, shape, movie, sound, or picture—the Format panel shows options that are specific to that object. If you prefer to give up this convenient strip of tools to save a little room, you can send it on its way by clicking the Format button in the toolbar (get it back by clicking this button again).

Working with Table Rows, Columns, and Cells

When you add data to your spreadsheet, you stow every piece of data in a table cell. Cells are formed by the intersections of rows and columns, which are the main organizing elements of your tables. Cell data can be just about anything: words, numbers, dates, time durations—whatever.

> **TIP** Before you even get started entering info, it's a good idea to save your file right away. Choose File→Save and choose a name and location for your file. Although Keynote does auto-save your file, tapping ⌘-S to save the file every few minutes is still a good habit to get into…just in case. For more info on saving your spreadsheets, see page 448.

■ LABELING YOUR DATA IN HEADER ROWS AND COLUMNS

The first thing you need to do is to figure out what data will go where. Start by naming your table's columns and rows. When you create a new spreadsheet using the Blank template, Numbers gives you a table with a *header row* and a *header column*, which you use to label your table. The program shades each of these to set them apart from the rest of your table, where you'll store the actual info (the *body rows* and *columns*). You'll learn all about the special role of header rows and columns on page 492. For now, just think of them as the places where you label your data.

Don't confuse the header row and header column with the table's *reference tabs*, the lettered and numbered labels at the top and left sides of the table (Figure 16-4). As you'll learn, those tabs let you select and edit an entire row or column at a time, and each one also acts as a handle that you can grab to move its corresponding row or column. You'll get a glimpse of reference tabs in action in a few pages, and you'll learn much more about them in the coming chapters.

In your header column, you'll want to enter all your criteria so your lucky taste-testers know what they're judging each product on. Click each cell—the first cell you'll want to fill out in this example is A1—and type *Product Name*. Hop to the next column by pressing the right arrow or Tab key, and then type the label for that column (Description), and so on. Repeat these steps until you've labeled all the columns and rows you plan to use.

> **NOTE** Don't confuse header cells with the table's reference tabs, which label the rows and columns with numbers and letters, respectively. As you'll see, reference tabs help you to work with whole rows and columns at once.

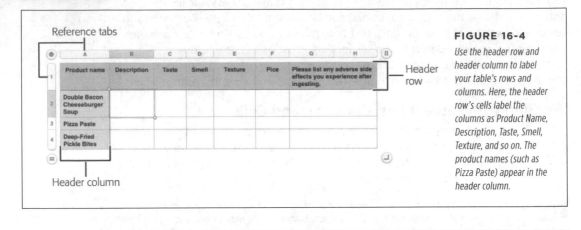

FIGURE 16-4

Use the header row and header column to label your table's rows and columns. Here, the header row's cells label the columns as Product Name, Description, Taste, Smell, Texture, and so on. The product names (such as Pizza Paste) appear in the header column.

NOTE You don't *have* to set up your table data in tidy rows and columns. If you're feeling ornery, you can take a scattershot approach and add info to cells willy-nilly. But creating an orderly, tabular structure as shown in Figure 16-4 keeps your data organized and, as you'll see in the following chapters, infinitely malleable. Oddly enough, creating a rigid structure actually makes the info *more* flexible.

■ SELECTING AND EDITING CELLS

The next chapter goes into all the down-and-dirty details of navigating and editing tables in Numbers, but the basics are straightforward: When you're working in a table, skip ahead to the next cell by pressing Tab or the right arrow key. Press Shift-Tab or the left arrow key to throw the machinery in reverse and jump one cell *back* (to the left). Use the up or down arrow keys to move—you guessed it—up or down. You can also click a cell to select it. (See page 461 for a roundup of other ways of selecting cells and moving around in tables.)

TIP In many cases, you can use Return to move down to the cell below the selected cell and Shift-Return to move to the cell above. There are a few special considerations for the Return key, though; page 461 has the details.

Once you've selected a cell, just start typing to fill it in. That's fine when you're filling in a cell for the first time, but when a cell already contains data, you wipe it out as soon as you start typing, replacing it with your new info. To *edit* a cell's contents instead of replacing it outright, double-click the cell or select it and then press Option-Return.

That's all you need to know to start entering data; now you're ready to add your first foodstuff, Double Bacon Cheeseburger Soup. This label goes in the first header column cell below the header row (that's A2); select the cell and get typing. You'll notice that as you type, your cells expand as necessary, but if you ever need to tweak and change the size of your cells, you can—Figure 16-5 shows how.

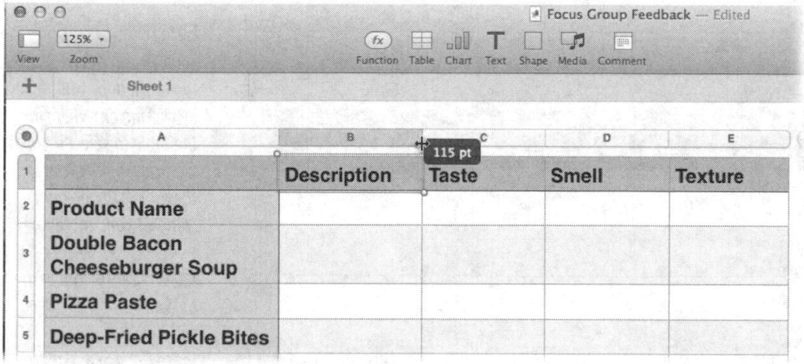

FIGURE 16-5

The cells in Numbers' standard table shift as you type, but you can also fine-tune them yourself. To make a column wider or narrower, point your cursor at the right border of its reference tab until the cursor turns into a bar with two arrows. Then drag the border to the right to make the column wider, or to the left to make it narrower.

> **TIP** If you find yourself squinting to see the text in your spreadsheet's tiny boxes, you can adjust the magnification level via the Zoom drop-down menu in the toolbar.

Congratulations—you've got a bona fide spreadsheet on your hands! You can't start a snack food revolution with just one product, though. Go ahead and add the rest: Jump down to the next row and add the name of the next tasty morsel (Pizza Paste), and then continue along through your list until your spreadsheet is a smorgasbord of unusual goodies.

■ ADDING AND REMOVING COLUMNS AND ROWS

If your table is getting full and your data needs more space to stretch out, you can add columns to the far right of your table by clicking anywhere in the table and then clicking the icon that appears in the table's upper-right corner (see Figure 16-6). Keep clicking this icon (or drag it to the right) to add more columns.

To add more rows to the bottom of your table, select your table and then click the icon that appears in the table's bottom-left corner. Keep clicking this icon (or drag it downward) to add more rows.

You can also get particular about where your new column or row should appear. To add a row at a specific point in your table, put your cursor over the reference tab for the row that's either directly above or directly below where your new row should go. When the arrow button appears in the reference tab, click it, and then select either Add Row Above or Add Row Below (see Figure 16-7). Likewise, you can add a column in a specific location by placing your cursor over the reference tab of the column directly to the left or to the right of your desired location, clicking the arrow when it appears on the tab, and then selecting either Add Column Before or Add Column After.

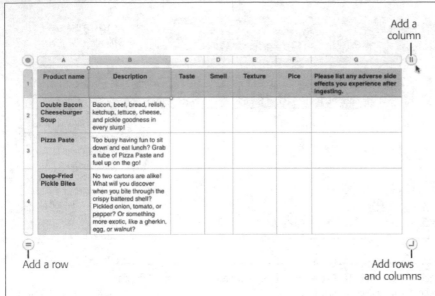

Add a
column

Add a row

Add rows
and columns

FIGURE 16-6

You can add columns to the far right of your table by clicking anywhere in the table to select it and then clicking the icon in the table's upper-right corner. To add more rows to the bottom of your table, click the icon in the bottom-left corner. Keep clicking (or dragging) these icons to add more rows and columns to your table. To add rows and columns simultaneously, drag the icon in the bottom-right corner.

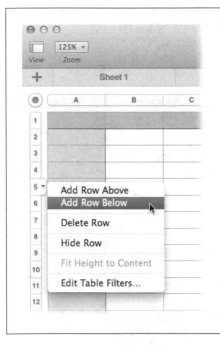

FIGURE 16-7

You can add a row in a specific spot by putting your cursor over a reference tab (make sure it's the reference tab that's directly above or directly below where you want to put your new row). When the arrow symbol appears, click it to open this drop-down menu, and then select Add Row Above or Add Row Below. In this screenshot, a row is about to be inserted after row 5.

TIP You can also insert columns and rows by selecting a cell, and then going to the Table menu and choosing Add Row Above, Add Row Below, Add Column Before, or Add Column After.

These methods of adding columns and rows are pretty long-winded. So do yourself a favor and learn these keyboard shortcuts (these work only when you've selected a cell, not when you're actually editing its text):

- Press **Option-right arrow** to add a new column to the right of the selected cell.
- **Option-left arrow** adds a new column to the left.
- **Option-up arrow** adds a new row above.
- **Option-down arrow** adds a new row below.

At some point you'll want to delete rows and columns, too. Select your table, and then put your cursor over the column or row's reference tab until the arrow symbol appears. Click this arrow to open the drop-down menu shown in Figure 16-7, and then select Delete Row or Delete Column to banish those unwanted cells from your table (the command you see depends on whether you've clicked the reference tab for a row or a column). Be warned, though: Any data in those cells disappears along with them!

TIP You can also delete rows and columns by dragging the same icons you use to add them (all these icons are labeled in Figure 16-6). For example, drag the top-right icon leftward to delete columns. However, you *can't* use this technique to delete cells that contain data; if you run into occupied cells, Numbers prevents you from dragging any farther.

There's plenty more to learn about adding, deleting, rearranging, and resizing rows and columns—you'll find complete info starting on page 489.

■ SORTING YOUR SPREADSHEET

Now that you've packed your spreadsheet full of up-and-coming snack food sensations, it's a snap to get them in order. To arrange your data in alphabetical order, put your cursor over the reference tab of the column in question, click the arrow when it appears, and then choose Sort Ascending. Numbers instantly shuffles your snacks into alphabetical order. Repeat for as many columns as you want. You can also opt to Sort Descending, which arranges your data in reverse order (Z–A or 99–1).

NOTE Numbers doesn't sort the header row when it reorders your table, only the rows below it. The header row always stays fixed at the top of your table.

You can create more detailed sorting rules, even telling Numbers to filter out some rows as it goes. Numbers calls this process *reorganizing,* and you'll learn all about it on page 500.

YOUR FIRST
SPREADSHEET

Fast Math: Quick Formulas and Instant Calculations

As you know, spreadsheets are good at math. Numbers can manage incredibly complex *formulas* to display calculated values in any cell of your spreadsheet. You'll see a whiz-bang example of formulas in action later in this chapter, and you'll get the full story in Chapters 19 and 20. But before you go all Einstein on your spreadsheet, the simple truth is that most spreadsheet formulas aren't exactly rocket science. Most folks put spreadsheets to work by adding columns of figures or doing other basic math. Numbers makes it especially easy to do these common calculations with its *quick formulas*, six predefined operations that you can apply to any column.

NOTE Before you can start using formulas, you'll need some data to run those formulas *on*. You can download the sample file *data.numbers*, a spreadsheet that contains lots of data for you to play with, from this book's Missing CD page at *www.missingmanuals.com/cds*.

Add a quick formula to your table by selecting the cell where your results will appear. When choosing your cell, bear in mind that, in its simplest form, a quick formula can only perform calculations on the entire column of cells directly above it (excluding the data in the header row).

TIP You can apply quick formulas to rows and groups of selected cells too, but that involves an extra step and a bit of dragging and dropping; it's covered on page 515.

For example, imagine you've finished the taste-testing, have entered all of the ratings into a spreadsheet, and now want to work out each product's average score. In this scenario, you'd select the cell where you want the result to appear, click the Function button in the toolbar, and then choose Average (see Figure 16-8). Numbers displays the average rating in the selected cell. Want to cheer yourself up and display the highest rating each product achieved instead? Click the Function button again, and then choose Maximum. Numbers crunches the values of all the cells directly above the selected cell and shows you the highest score.

NOTE Based on these examples, it may seem like formulas aren't very flexible, since Numbers can only perform these calculations on an entire column. Don't worry—you can actually get Numbers to crunch data across *any* group of cells, columns, rows, and even across different tables entirely. Stay tuned for more info!

After you add a quick formula to your table, Numbers doesn't just forget about it. A formula is a smart placeholder that updates whenever relevant cells change (in this example, values in the Pizza Paste column). If you add a new row or change any of the rating values, the formula updates the cell showing the average rating to reflect this change. Using quick formulas in footers (as shown in Figure 16-8) is an easy way to tally whole columns, but you can also use them to tally *any* selection of cells. To learn more about putting formulas to use, see page 515.

What's that? *Quick* isn't fast enough for you? In that case, check out Numbers' *instant calculations,* a constantly updating pane of tallies based on the currently selected cells. The Instant Calculation bar appears at the bottom of your screen when you highlight values in more than one cell, showing you the sum, average, minimum, maximum, and count (the *number* of values) of your selection. (The bar vanishes when you have only one cell selected.) Figure 16-9 shows an example, and page 517 lets you in on some nifty tricks you can do with instant calculations.

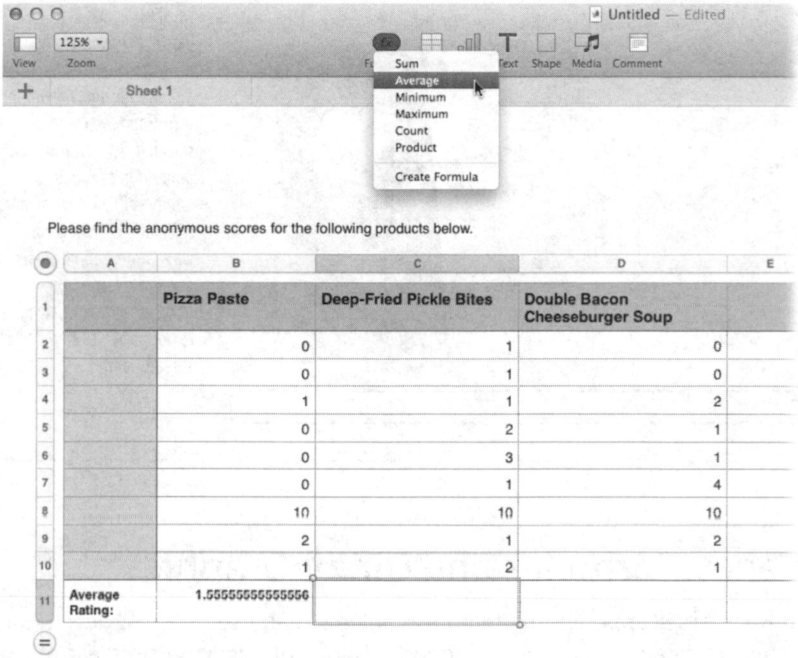

FIGURE 16-8

Apply a quick formula to an entire column by selecting the last cell in that column, clicking the Function button in the toolbar, and then selecting one of the options from the drop-down menu. When you apply the Average function to a rating column for example, Numbers displays the average value for that column, as shown here.

Changing the Table Style

When you create a spreadsheet using the Blank template, Numbers starts you off with a simple grid, its header row and column displayed in gray. As you'll learn in Chapter 18, there are lots of ways you can dress up a table—styling its text, colors, and borders, and even adding shadows or pictures. Numbers tries to anticipate your style needs, however, so that you don't have to trouble yourself with the window dressing.

Every template, including the Blank one, comes loaded with several prefab *table styles.* To change the table style, click anywhere in the table and then head to the Format panel's Table tab (if necessary, click the Format button to open the Format panel). There click one of the thumbnails in the Table Styles pane at the top of the tab. Presto! Your table now has alternating row colors, or blue headers, or no grid, or shaded cells. Anything in this menu of style options is yours to command.

TIP You can choose from lots of different styles when you first add a table object: Click the Table button in the toolbar, and then use the left and right arrows in the drop-down menu to see what's available.

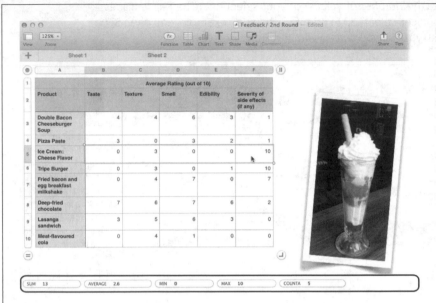

FIGURE 16-9

When you select more than one cell, the Instant Calculation bar (circled) shows stats for that group. From left to right, it lists the sum, average, minimum value, maximum value, and the count of selected cells. (These tallies don't include empty cells.) These instant calculations are a great way to see common stats about a select group of numbers without having to add formulas to the spreadsheet.

Fancy Formulas and Glitzy Graphics

Even if Numbers stopped at the features you've already seen, you'd have a ton of great stuff. You can squeeze lots of good info out of even the simplest of grids, especially with formulas in your corner. But Numbers lets you create more than just simple grids: When you add more sophisticated formulas and mix in some high-octane graphics, your workhorse columns of numbers turn into a multimedia report or an interactive cockpit that lets you monitor your stats.

You'll learn about these advanced techniques later in the book—formulas in Chapter 19, charts in Chapter 21, and other multimedia layout fun in Chapter 22. But just to see what's possible, take a quick spin through Apple's Grade Book template. Choose File→New, click the Education category, and then double-click the Grade Book template. Numbers creates a new, untitled document based on the template (Figure 16-10).

The top of the spreadsheet looks familiar enough: a simple-looking grid. It's a table of grades with one student's grades on each row, lined up in a column of assignments. The header row shows the "weight" of each assignment (how much the assignment's score counts toward the final grade). The Total column uses those weights to calculate the final score, and the Final Grade column shows the corresponding letter grade.

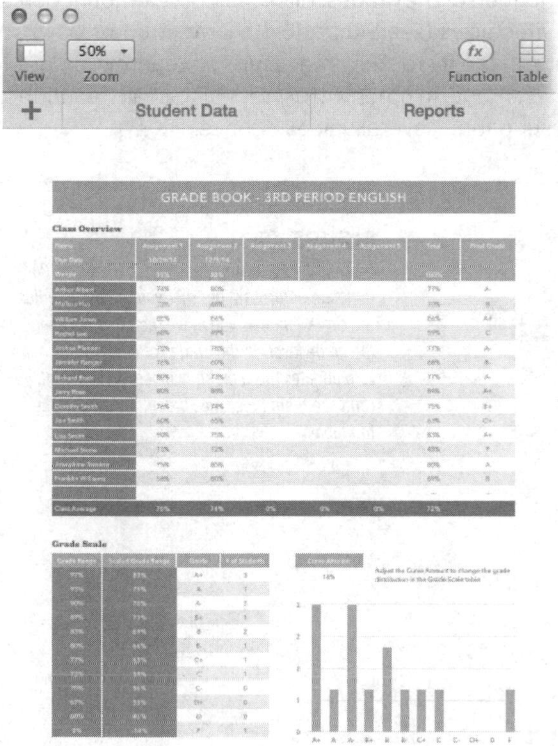

FIGURE 16-10

The Grade Book template features three tables and a chart on its first sheet. Through the magic of formulas, the tables all share information. The top table displays the students' grades using the grade-range scale in the Grade Scale table, which also counts the number of A's, B's, C's and so on in the top table. The Grade Scale table adjusts the grade levels based on the amount in the tiny Curve Amount table. The chart, meanwhile, displays the grade curve, a visual graphic of the counts shown in the Grade Scale chart.

Things get more interesting when you look at the bottom of the sheet, which features two *more* tables and a chart. See what's happening here? The sheet canvas holds more than one table, effectively letting you put lots of mini-spreadsheets onto a single sheet. The sheet works just like a page-layout document or a Keynote slide: You can drop pictures, charts, shapes, text boxes, and of course tables onto the sheet—as many as you like wherever you want.

TIP To add an additional table to your sheet, click the toolbar's Table button and choose a table template; Numbers drops a new table at the bottom of the sheet. For more about adding tables, see page 205.

When you add multiple tables to a sheet, the tables can stand alone, showing their own info independent of the rest, or they can talk to one another and swap data. In the Grade Book template, for example, the top table includes formulas that pluck information from the Grade Scale table to determine each student's letter grade in the last column. The Grade Scale table gets something in return, fetching info from the top table to count the number of students with each letter grade. The chart in the lower right, meanwhile, displays the same info graphically.

Curve Amount is the last table on the sheet, a little two-cell organism that indicates the amount to adjust the distribution of the grades. Click the Curve Amount percentage to edit it, and a slider materializes (see Figure 16-11). Drag it up or down, and the tables and chart all update on the fly to show the results of your revised grading curve. Changing the curve percentage, in other words, sets off a chain reaction that ricochets through the tables, updating several values at once.

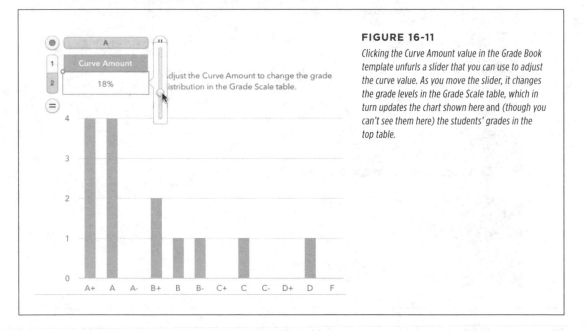

FIGURE 16-11

Clicking the Curve Amount value in the Grade Book template unfurls a slider that you can use to adjust the curve value. As you move the slider, it changes the grade levels in the Grade Scale table, which in turn updates the chart shown here and (though you can't see them here) the students' grades in the top table.

This sounds complicated and looks impressive, but don't be daunted. It's really just a handful of well-placed formulas in table cells that monitor values in other tables and update when information changes. Moving the slider up and down turns the whole thing into a machine for visualizing classroom grades on a curve. In Chapter 20, you'll explore how to craft formulas like this to make one table process or summarize the data of another. For now, just consider this template a demonstration of what's possible with Numbers—spreadsheets can be *much* more than simple grids.

■ Organizing Data with Sheets

Once you start adding more tables to your spreadsheet, the sheet canvas can get crowded fast. To keep things clear and your message focused, you can organize your tables, charts, and other data into multiple sheets within the same Numbers document. Like adding a new slide to a Keynote slideshow, a new sheet gives you a fresh slate to display and work with your data. From its name, you might think that a sheet is a single page, but that's not the case; when you print it, a sheet can span several pages. A sheet is more like a chapter than a page, a way to organize your data around distinct themes for your spreadsheet's presentation. For example:

- A company's financial statement might have separate sheets for the balance sheet, income statement, and cash flow.

- A lab report might have a summary sheet graphing the results of an experiment, with subsequent sheets displaying the raw data.

- Your personal spreadsheet for contact info might divide contacts into separate sheets for business associates, friends, and family members.

To add a new sheet, click the + button in the upper-left part of the Numbers window or choose Insert→Sheet, and Numbers gives you a clean sheet with a single table. The sheets are lined up as tabs in the Sheets bar, as shown in Figure 16-12. When you add a new sheet, Numbers automatically assigns it a name; if you're happy with such lyrical names as Sheet 1, Sheet 2, and Sheet 3, then you're all set. If you prefer something more descriptive, you can change the name by double-clicking its tab and typing out a new name.

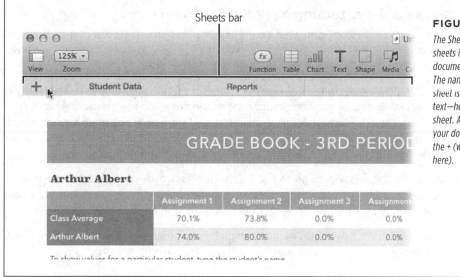

FIGURE 16-12

The Sheets bar shows the sheets in your Numbers document, lined up as tabs. The name of the current sheet is displayed in blue text—here, it's the Reports sheet. Add more sheets to your document by clicking the + (where the cursor is here).

Shuffling Sheets

Use the Sheets bar to move through your sheets: Click a sheet's tab, and Numbers loads it in the sheet canvas. To change the order of your sheets, simply drag a sheet's tab to a new position. You can also use the Sheets bar to copy a sheet, including all of its data and objects, by putting your cursor over a sheet's tab, clicking the arrow that appears, and then choosing Copy Sheet. Then put your cursor over another sheet's tab, click the arrow that appears, and click Paste Sheet to insert your copy immediately *after* this sheet.

If you have several sheets, each with several tables or charts, the Sheets bar can spill offscreen. To scroll the Sheets bar, click the arrow buttons that appear on its right edge.

To delete a sheet and its contents, put your cursor over its tab in the Sheets bar, click the arrow when it appears, and then select Delete. Tread carefully: This command deletes the sheet's tables *and* all of its data.

■ Saving Your Spreadsheet

Choose File→Save or press ⌘-S to save your spreadsheet. The first time you save a Numbers document, the Save As dialog box drops into view, letting you choose a name and location for your new file. If you're not familiar with the Mac's standard Save As dialog box, flip back to page 12 for a review.

Numbers, along with the other iWork programs, keeps earlier versions of your document stashed away for safekeeping. If you make a mistake and want to roll back time to an earlier version of your document, go to File→Revert To (to get a reminder on your Mac's time machine, travel back to page 39).

Password-Protecting Your Spreadsheet

One shudders to consider what could happen if your half-baked plans for future foodstuffs fell into the wrong hands. When your spreadsheet contains sensitive information, Numbers lets you lock it up with a password.

To add a password, go to File→Set Password. Then type in your password, verify it in the second field, and enter an optional hint in case you have a mental block (see Figure 16-13). Click the Set Password button, and from now on, when anyone opens the spreadsheet, Numbers asks for the password. If you enter the wrong password three times in a row, Numbers displays the password hint you supplied.

To update the password, go to File→Change Password. You'll need to enter your old password before you can create a new one. Once you've typed out your new password twice, enter an optional password hint, and click Change Password.

You can lift the password protection completely by going to File→Change Password, entering your old password, and then clicking Remove Password.

■ Opening an Existing Spreadsheet

When you're ready to return to a saved document, choose File→Open to reveal the standard OS X file browser, and then select a file. If you're not familiar with using the Open dialog box to find files, jump back to page 17 for a quick tour.

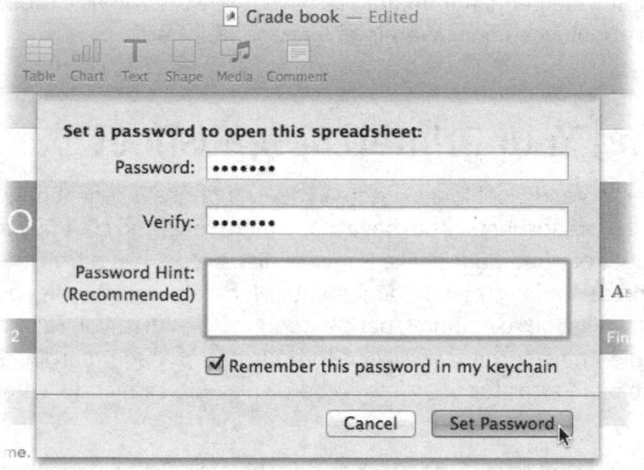

FIGURE 16-13

When you go to File→Set Password, Numbers asks you to enter and confirm the password. You can also add a hint that Numbers can display in case you forget the pass phrase.

Once you've set a password, a padlock icon appears next to the document's title at the top of your screen (not shown here).

To fire up a document you were working on just recently, open the File→Open Recent submenu and choose one of your latest projects. You can also double-click the spreadsheet's icon on your desktop or in the Finder, or drag it onto the Numbers icon in the Dock to launch Numbers and open the file.

Importing Files from Another Program

Alas, most of the world doesn't use Numbers as its everyday spreadsheet program. Microsoft Excel is far and away the world's most popular spreadsheet program, and sooner or later someone will ask for your spreadsheet as an Excel file. Fortunately, all the iWork programs speak Microsoft, and Numbers can open Excel files and translate them into Numbers spreadsheets. Ditto for CSV (comma-separated values) and Numbers '09 files.

Importing one of these files works very much like opening a regular Numbers document: Choose File→Open and select the file. Numbers imports the file and opens it as a new Numbers document. When you save the file, that means you save it as a *Numbers* document unless you specifically save a copy of the file in another format (see page 663).

Numbers does a good job of importing Excel files, especially when the spreadsheets are reasonably straightforward. But if you're importing complex spreadsheets with sophisticated formulas, Numbers may run into trouble. Numbers can't display formula calculations for functions it doesn't know, of course, and although Apple has been adding functions to Numbers at an impressive pace, Excel still has far more tricks in its function library than Numbers does. So if you use an Excel spreadsheet that relies on those features or certain arcane functions, you may be disappointed when you open it in Numbers.

When Numbers realizes it's struggling to import certain elements of a file, it lets you know, offering to list any elements that might not have made the trip as expected. (You can learn more about Document Warnings on page 18).

◼ Previewing Your Printed Spreadsheet

The way your Numbers spreadsheet looks onscreen doesn't typically reflect how it'll look when you print it. Spreadsheets often have many more rows and columns than can fit on a single sheet of paper. But unlike Pages, which shows you a true-to-life view of every page break for lengthy text documents, Numbers normally keeps its page breaks to itself while you're editing. That's a good thing—when you're updating a data-dense table, the last thing you want to do is dodge page margins and leap across page breaks. Better for your info to be displayed seamlessly, without interruption.

Eventually, though, you'll want to see what your document looks like on paper before you send it to the printer. Numbers gives you a separate view—*Print Preview*—that lets you control how your document will look on the printed page (or when you export your spreadsheet to a PDF file, for example), and lets you scale your content up or down so that page breaks occur exactly where you want them—or don't occur at all.

Before jumping into Print Preview, make sure you've got your document and sheet layout set up the way you want them.

Unlike most Mac programs, Numbers doesn't offer the tried-and-true Page Setup option in its File menu, the place where you normally set your paper size, preferred printer, and page orientation. Instead, those details are handled in Print Preview, which you open by choosing File→Print (see Figure 16-14).

TIP You can get back to your normal Numbers view at any time by pressing the Esc key.

When you switch to Print Preview, Numbers chops up the sheet into page "tiles," showing you exactly how it will look when you print it or export it to a PDF file (page 667). If your sheet is wider or longer than a single page, Numbers tries to shrink it to fit onto a single page (and is usually successful, unless you're working with a huge table). Sometimes this is a handy feature, but for larger tables, you end up squinting to see what you've written. In that case, you'll need to crank up the Content Scale slider in the Print Preview tab. When you increase the scale, the content may spill into one or more additional pages. When a table spans more than one page, Numbers repeats its header rows or columns to help you keep your place. Figure 16-15 shows what all of this looks like.

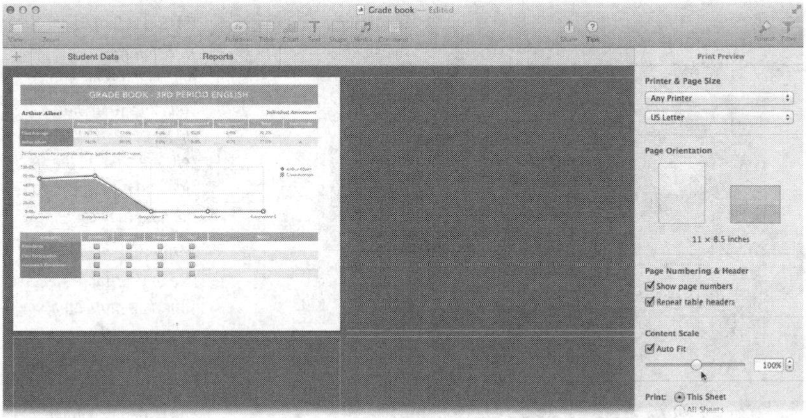

FIGURE 16-14

Print Preview view shows you exactly how each of your sheets will appear on the printed page. You can flick between them using the tabs in the Sheets bar (here, the Reports sheet is selected). The print settings for the currently selected sheet are shown in the Print Preview tab.

The Content Scale slider (where the cursor is here) lets you make the sheet's contents larger or smaller to fit the printed page.

In the Print Preview tab, you can also change the following print settings:

- **Printer.** Use this unlabeled drop-down menu to choose which printer you want to send your spreadsheet to.

- **Page size.** Choose how big, or small, your printed spreadsheets will be (see page 268 for more info on page size).

- **Page Orientation.** Print your spreadsheet in portrait or landscape orientation.

- **Show page numbers.** Add page numbers to all of your pages.

- **Repeat table headers.** Turn off this checkbox if you don't want to repeat header rows or columns when you print the sheet.

- **Print.** Choose whether to print only the currently selected sheet (This Sheet) or *all* the sheets in your document (All Sheets).

- **Done.** Exit Print Preview and return to Numbers' normal document-editing mode.

When you've arranged your pages just the way you want them and sprinkled them with headers and footers, it's time to do some actual printing: Click the Print button at the bottom of the Print Preview tab. You'll find more info about printing in Chapter 23 (page 661).

With a clean, sorted, printed spreadsheet on your desk, your mission to launch the world's latest snack sensation is well under way. But new challenges await, dear reader. Make sure you're prepared for them by learning everything there is to know about editing and formatting your tables; it all starts in the next chapter.

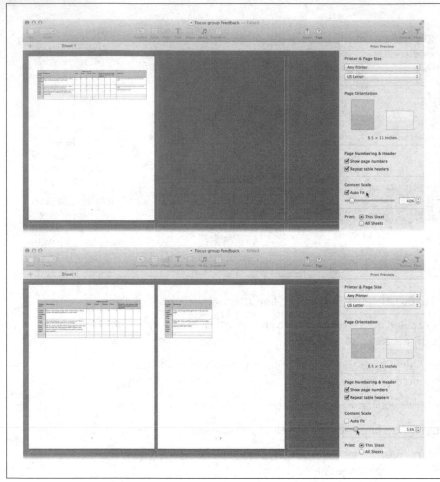

FIGURE 16-15

Top: Numbers is trying to help you out by shrinking your cells to fit onto a single page. However, the cells are a bit on the small side and it's difficult to see the data they contain.

Bottom: To increase the size of your table and give your data more breathing space, grab the Print Preview panel's Content Scale slider and drag it until you're happy with how your table is displayed. When you increase the scale enough, your content spills onto additional pages. Here, Numbers repeats the header column on the second page so readers can keep track of the data you're showing. If you change your mind and want to constrain your table to a single page again, turn the Auto Fit checkbox back on, and Numbers smooshes all your cells onto a single page.

Editing Tables in Numbers

I f spreadsheets are all about efficiency, then the tables they contain are the key to number-crunching nirvana. Tables help you plow through calculations in a snap; they organize and reorganize your info quickly; and they squeeze your data into a compact display. For all that Numbers can do for you, though, much of the spreadsheet work boils down to data entry and table formatting, and that part's up to you. Now it's *your* turn to be efficient: To get the most out of your spreadsheet, you need to be nimble as you edit your data. This chapter shows you how.

The last chapter gave you a quick intro to entering data into tables and working with rows and columns. Now you'll take a deeper look at wrangling table objects, editing table cells, working with Numbers' data formats, and using a bevy of shortcuts to enter data quickly. By the time you're done, you'll be spinning around your table faster than a game of musical chairs. Let's get to it.

■ Working with Table Objects

In Numbers, tables are *objects*, just as they are in Pages and Keynote. If you've already made your way through the rest of this book, objects are already old friends. They're the building blocks of every iWork document, the design elements that you slide across the page—or in this case, the sheet canvas—to create your layout. In Numbers, tables are the main focus, and you may frequently have spreadsheets where a single table is your one and only object. But no matter how many or how few objects you pile into your document, you have to know how to select and edit these guys in order to work on your spreadsheet.

NOTE You'll learn more about working with other types of Numbers objects—pictures, text boxes, shapes, movies, and sounds—in Chapter 22, hot on the heels of a whole chapter on chart objects in Chapter 21.

Selecting a table object tells Numbers that you're ready to edit it, but what part exactly? Tables have many different elements (rows, columns, cells, and the data inside them), and you can select any of them individually. Selecting the table at these different levels lets you edit it in different ways but blocks you from editing it in others. Understanding how to select a table and its parts—and move quickly among them—is the first step to becoming a fleet-footed spreadsheet jockey. But first, you need to add a table.

Adding a Table

Whenever you create a new spreadsheet document, Numbers includes a table on the sheet canvas—sometimes several, depending on the template you use (page 433). If you start from the Blank template, for example, Numbers gives you a single table grid, selected and ready to go. When you add a new sheet (page 446), Numbers likewise gives you a fresh table to get you started.

To add a new table to the current sheet, click the toolbar's Table button, and Numbers shows you a drop-down menu of predefined tables (Figure 17-1). (You can also add a table by choosing Insert→Table, but with that method you just get a list of table types rather than a visual preview of your options.) Your choices vary according to the template you used to create your document, but each option comes stocked with its own visual style and structure. Choose a table, and Numbers deposits it in your document (if your document has multiple sheets, it appears in the current sheet).

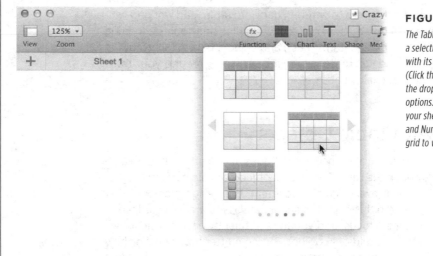

FIGURE 17-1

The Tables drop-down menu holds a selection of prefab tables, each with its own style and layout. (Click the arrows on the sides of the drop-down menu to see more options.) To add a new table to your sheet, click it in this menu, and Numbers gives you a fresh grid to work with.

TIP You can also create a brand-new table by dragging cells, rows, or columns out of another table and dropping them in a blank section of your sheet: In the original table, select the elements you want to use, and then drag them to a blank part of the canvas. (Note that doing this removes the cells' data from the original table, so the result is the same as performing a *cut*, as opposed to a *copy*). You'll learn more about this technique on page 485 (for copying and moving cells) and page 498 (for rearranging rows and columns). The box below explains one reason you might want to split a big table in two.

PAIN POINT

Big Tables Bog You Down

The latest version of Numbers is much speedier than its predecessors, but it still gets winded when it comes to very large tables. If you work with tables containing tens of thousands of rows, for example, Numbers shows the strain. Opening such files requires long waits; also, scroll bars may lag and stutter, and recalculation of formulas can take several seconds.

When you're feeling weighed down by a single big table, try adding a new one. Numbers often speeds up quite a bit when

you split large data sets into multiple sheets or tables. By doing that, you give the program less to lift at once—fewer rows to process, fewer figures to juggle. Not all data can be broken up easily into slices like this, and it's certainly not the most convenient way to manage your info, but managing multiple tables is often less of a headache than wading through a sluggish interface.

Selecting Table Elements

You can work with a table at several different *selection levels*, each of which lets you edit or format the table in different ways. At each level, Numbers gives you visual cues to let you know what part of the table you're working with. Although you'll spend most of your time at the cell level (since that's where you add data), selecting the table at other levels has its uses, too. Here's a quick tour.

◼ SELECTING THE WHOLE TABLE

When you select a table at the table or *object level*, you're working with the entire table. You can't edit the table's content at this level, but you can move the grid across the canvas, resize it, or apply formatting changes to the whole shebang—to change the font, for example, or to add borders or backgrounds to the entire table. (You'll learn more about all the various options for styling your table on page 506.)

To select a table at the object level, click it once to select it at the cell level, and then do the following:

- Press ⌘-Return.

- Click the icon in the table's upper-left corner (see Figure 17-2).

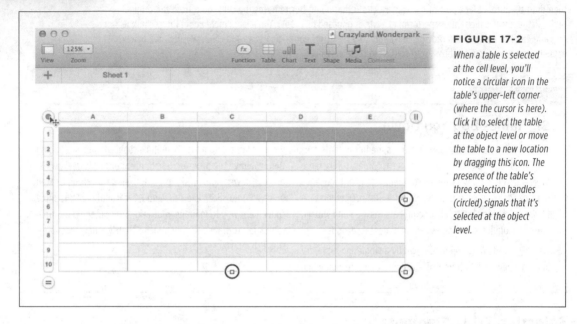

FIGURE 17-2

When a table is selected at the cell level, you'll notice a circular icon in the table's upper-left corner (where the cursor is here). Click it to select the table at the object level or move the table to a new location by dragging this icon. The presence of the table's three selection handles (circled) signals that it's selected at the object level.

When a table is selected at the object level, the three selection handles sprinkled along the table's bottom-right corner (Figure 17-2) show that you've selected the table—in fact, they're the only indication. If you drag any of these selection handles, you'll resize the table, although probably not in the way you'd like. The most common way to change a table's size is by adding or deleting rows and columns (see page 490). Dragging the selection handles, however, changes the table's overall size without changing the number of rows and columns. The height and width of those rows and columns shrink and grow as you change the table's shape and size. You can similarly change the table's size by selecting it and then setting its overall height and width in the Format panel's Table tab (see page 496 for more details).

To delete a table—*along with all its data*—select it at the object level and then press Delete.

■ SELECTING CELLS AND THEIR CONTENTS

Click any cell to select it, and Numbers outlines the cell to let you know that it's active and adds two selection handles to it. When you select a cell, the cell's reference tabs also light up to help you pinpoint the active cell. Figure 17-3 gives you the picture.

NOTE You don't have to select Numbers tables at the object level before you can select a cell; just click anywhere inside a table to select one of its cells.

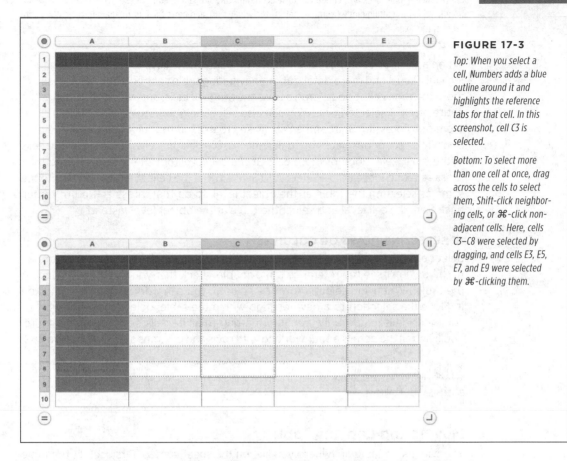

FIGURE 17-3

Top: When you select a cell, Numbers adds a blue outline around it and highlights the reference tabs for that cell. In this screenshot, cell C3 is selected.

Bottom: To select more than one cell at once, drag across the cells to select them, Shift-click neighboring cells, or ⌘-click non-adjacent cells. Here, cells C3–C8 were selected by dragging, and cells E3, E5, E7, and E9 were selected by ⌘-clicking them.

From here, any changes you make apply only to the selected cells and the text within them. At the cell level, you can set the background and borders of individual cells, for example. Be careful, though: Numbers implicitly selects the full text of the selected cell—so if you start typing as soon as you first select it, you'll replace any data inside. If that's not your plan, click inside a selected cell (or press Option-Return), and Numbers places the insertion point inside the cell, letting you add or edit the existing cell content. Now you're no longer at the cell level but at the *text level*, and you can apply text formatting to individual words or characters within the cell. You can tell that you've selected a cell at the text level when you see the blinking insertion point in the cell, or if text is highlighted inside the cell. You'll learn more about editing and formatting cell data starting on page 473.

TIP The simple way to think about selecting tables, cells, and content is that clicking drills deeper into a table, and ⌘-Return pulls back out. Click a cell to select it, and click it again to edit the text inside. Press ⌘-Return to pull out of this editing mode (Numbers selects the whole cell), and press ⌘-Return again to select the entire table at the object level.

When a cell is selected, use the Tab, Return, and arrow keys to jump to a neighboring cell. (You'll find more details about navigating table cells on page 461.) To select more than one cell at once, drag across the range of cells, and Numbers outlines the entire block of selected cells. You can also select neighboring cells by Shift-clicking them or by pressing Shift and an arrow key to expand the selection to the cell next door. To select or deselect nonadjacent cells, ⌘-click the cells. To select all the cells in the table, select one or more cells *at the cell level* (not the text level), and then press ⌘-A or choose Edit→Select All. (Selecting all the cells in a table isn't quite the same as selecting the table at the object level; to do that, press ⌘-Return to pull back from the cell level and select the table at the object level instead.)

■ SELECTING ROWS OR COLUMNS

Select an entire row or column by clicking its reference tab, as shown in Figure 17-4. (If you don't see the reference tabs, double-check that you've actually selected the table!) When you select a row or a column, you can work a range of magic on it: Move the selection to a new location within the table, delete the whole row or column, hide it temporarily, apply formatting to all its cells or borders, and more. You'll find all the details about working with rows and columns starting on page 489.

TIP Shift-click reference tabs to select multiple neighboring rows or columns; ⌘-click them to select non-adjacent rows or columns.

Moving and Copying Tables

You can drag a table anywhere you like on the sheet canvas. First, select the table (at either the object, cell, or text level), and then put the cursor over the round icon in the table's upper-left corner. The cursor sprouts a four-headed arrow (as shown in Figure 17-2) to signal that it's ready for heavy lifting: Click the icon and drag the table to its new location.

TIP If nothing happens when you try to drag the table's upper-left icon, you're probably not clicking the actual handle but instead clicking a *frozen header row:* a floating set of column labels. Turn to page 494 for more about these cool numbers, and in the meantime try scrolling back up to the top of the table and trying again.

Hold down the Shift key while you drag to limit the move to a straight horizontal, vertical or 45-degree route. Hold down the Option key while you drag to create a new copy of the table; the clone leaps out of the original table and lands wherever you drop it.

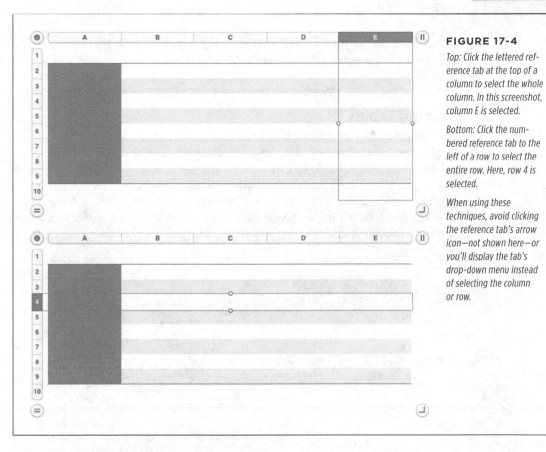

FIGURE 17-4

Top: Click the lettered reference tab at the top of a column to select the whole column. In this screenshot, column E is selected.

Bottom: Click the numbered reference tab to the left of a row to select the entire row. Here, row 4 is selected.

When using these techniques, avoid clicking the reference tab's arrow icon—not shown here—or you'll display the tab's drop-down menu instead of selecting the column or row.

To nudge a table ever so slightly, select it at the object level, and then press an arrow key on your keyboard to move the table just one point in that direction. Hold down the Shift key while you press the arrow to bump the table 10 points per key press.

To move the table to a precise location, select the table, click the Format button in the toolbar to open the Format panel (if it isn't open already), and then open the Arrange tab. In the Position section, use the X and Y Position fields to precisely position the table's top-left corner horizontally and vertically. (You may notice that the Arrange tab's Rotate, Angle, and Flip settings are grayed out; that's because, in Numbers, tables are immune to such antics.)

TIP If you need help figuring out where to place your table, choose View→Show Rulers or press ⌘-R to see the rulers. You can change the units used in the rulers by going to Numbers→Preferences, opening the Rulers tab, and then picking an option from the Ruler Units drop-down menu.

To move a table to a different sheet, select the table and then choose Edit→Copy (or press ⌘-C) or Edit→Cut (⌘-X), switch to the new sheet, and then choose Edit→Paste (⌘-V).

NOTE If you move a table to a new sheet and other tables contain formulas that refer to the moved table, those formulas keep up automatically, following the table to its new address. You'll learn more about formulas in Chapter 19.

Naming Tables

Every table has a name, though table names aren't visible unless you specifically display them. Numbers' default table names aren't exactly full of personality (it calls them Table 1, Table 2, and so on), but you can change them so they're more descriptive. If the table's name isn't visible, coax it out of hiding by selecting the table and then heading to the Format panel's Table tab and turning on the Table Name checkbox. The table's name then appears above it in your document. To change this name, double-click anywhere on the title, and then get typing (see Figure 17-5).

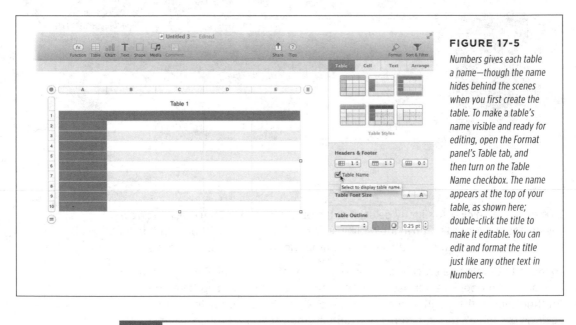

FIGURE 17-5

Numbers gives each table a name—though the name hides behind the scenes when you first create the table. To make a table's name visible and ready for editing, open the Format panel's Table tab, and then turn on the Table Name checkbox. The name appears at the top of your table, as shown here; double-click the title to make it editable. You can edit and format the title just like any other text in Numbers.

NOTE On any sheet, no two tables can share the same name. That's because table names aren't just decorative labels, they're unique identifiers that you can use to refer to tables in formulas, as you'll discover in Chapter 19.

You can change the font and text style of a table's title exactly the same way you edit normal text. Use the Format panel's various tabs and/or the Fonts window to style the text as you wish (see page 39 for more info).

■ Navigating Table Cells

Like pretty much everything on your Mac, you can select table cells by pointing and clicking with your mouse. But when you start dealing with hundreds or thousands of cells, clicking to edit each one turns into serious exercise. Rather than developing an over-muscled mouse arm, put your energy into committing some crucial keyboard shortcuts to memory. Once you've selected a table cell, you can move all over your table without lifting a finger off your keyboard.

The Tab and arrow keys are your greatest allies, letting you hop to the cell next door. Press Tab to select the cell to the right of the current one; press Shift-Tab to move to the left. You can also use the arrow keys to select the cell in the corresponding direction—up, down, left, or right. (See the box "Where Does the Arrow Point?" below to sharpen your arrow skills.)

UP TO SPEED

Where Does the Arrow Point?

The range of your keyboard's arrow keys changes depending on your current selection level. When you have a cell selected at the cell level, the arrow keys bump you over and select the next cell (left, right, up, or down). When the cell is selected at the text level, however, the arrows instead move you around *inside* the cell.

When you're motoring through your cells for the first time, for example, you can use the Tab and arrow keys to move to each one, type your data, and then Tab or arrow to the next cell. Even though you're typing text into the cell, it's still selected at the cell level, not the text level, and your arrows take you

to the next cell. That's because text-level editing is triggered only when you click inside a selected cell or press Option-Return to edit the cell's existing text. In that case, the arrow keys no longer target neighboring cells. Instead, they shuttle you around the text *inside* the cell.

To make the arrow keys move you outside the cell again, press ⌘-Return to leave text-level editing behind, selecting the cell at the cell level. Or press Tab or Shift-Tab to move to the next cell to the right or left; Numbers selects the new cell at the cell level, and your arrow keys get their cell-leaping powers back.

Hopping Rows with the Return Key

You can also use the Return key to move to a new cell. Pressing Return moves you *somewhere* in the row below. Exactly where Return lands you, however, depends on what you've been up to. Normally, the Return key takes you down to the cell directly below your current selection. But when you've been using the Tab key to navigate between cells and editing content anywhere along the way, pressing Return selects the cell below the one where you *started* tabbing. This behavior sounds confusing, but it's really helpful if you're in a marathon data-entry session, adding many rows of content: When you tab through the columns of cells in each row, *enter data in at least one of the cells*, and then press Return, Numbers jumps you down to the first column of the next row, ready for your next entry. (If you press Return when you're in the table's last row, Numbers adds a new row for you automatically.) Pressing Shift-Return moves you to the cell above the one that's currently selected.

NOTE The Return key's column-tracking behavior works only when you use the Tab key to move between columns. If you use the mouse or arrow keys to move from cell to cell, the Return key simply moves you down to the cell below the current one.

◼ Editing Table Cells

Now that you've got the hang of moving around your table's cells, it's time to fill them up with data. As you learned in the last few pages, typing into a cell works slightly differently when you have the cell selected at the cell level versus the text level. When you select the cell at the cell level (by clicking it once or moving to it with the Tab or arrow keys), what you type replaces any data already in the cell. If you instead want to *edit* existing data, then select the cell at the text level—by clicking inside the selected cell or pressing Option-Return—before you start typing.

When you select the cell at the text level, Numbers places the insertion point inside the cell and lets you edit whatever text is there. Editing data inside a cell works just like text editing everywhere in iWork—and in most Mac programs, for that matter. For pointers, head back to page 32 for a review of basic text editing. When you're done typing the cell data, press ⌘-Return to pull back to the cell level, or press Tab to continue on to the next cell.

To delete a cell's contents, select it at the cell level and then press Delete. This clears the value in the cell but leaves its formatting behind—any borders or fill color sticks around. To strip out all the formatting, too, choose Edit→Clear All, or cut the cell to the Clipboard by pressing ⌘-X or choosing Edit→Cut. (See page 506 for details about adding borders and backgrounds to cells.)

TIP As usual, you can use the Edit→Undo (⌘-Z) command to take back any changes you make (see page 38 for a review of the Undo and Redo commands).

Handling Data That Doesn't Fit

When you want to squeeze a large amount of data into a single cell, you have three options:

- **Adjust text wrapping.** When text wrapping is turned on (as it is initially), Numbers automatically enlarges cells to accommodate your data. When you turn text wrapping *off*, the data can spill into neighboring cells.

- **Resize.** You can make columns and rows wider to contain more data.

- **Merge.** You can merge cells so that data can span several cells.

The following sections explain these options in detail.

■ LETTING CONTENT SPILL INTO NEIGHBORING CELLS

When a table's "Wrap text in cell" checkbox is turned on in the Format panel's Text tab (as it is initially), text never spills out of a cell. Instead, the text wraps to a new line when it hits the cell boundary, and Numbers increases the height of the row as you type additional lines of text (unless the row has been set to a fixed height as explained on page 212, in which case the text gets clipped at that height).

You can turn this setting off for individual cells (or whole tables) to allow text and numbers to spill over into cells next door, but this works only when the neighboring cell is empty. If the neighbor contains data, Numbers hides any data that stretches past the cell boundary. Figure 17-6 shows all this in action.

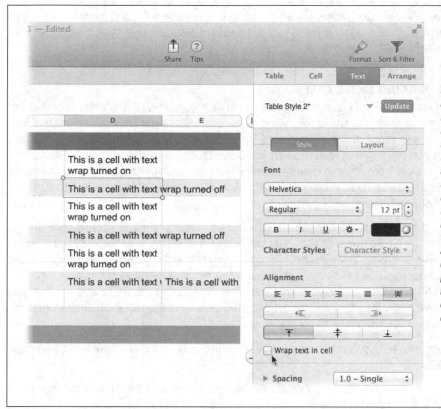

FIGURE 17-6

Turn off a cell's "Wrap text in cell" checkbox to allow text to spill into neighboring cells when those cells are empty. When the cell next door contains data, however, text doesn't spill; instead, it gets clipped to remain inside its cell boundaries (as shown in the last filled-in cell in column D here). Fortunately, the data remains intact behind the scenes. When you select a clipped cell at the text level (either by double-clicking the cell or pressing Option-Return), Numbers displays the entire contents of the cell—even the hidden part.

■ SIZING ROWS AND COLUMNS TO FIT YOUR VALUES

As you just learned, if you leave text wrapping turned on, Numbers automatically resizes your rows to fit your content (the cell with the most content dictates the width of each row). However, as soon as you manually change the size of a row (page 496) or turn text wrapping off, that row no longer grows to accommodate your data. To tell Numbers to resume automatically resizing your row(s), you need to use the Fit button.

Select a cell in the row where you want to resume automatic resizing, go to the Format panel's Table tab, and then click the Row & Column Size heading to expand that section. Click the Fit button next to the Row field, and Numbers resumes automatically adjusting that row's height to fit its contents. (You can also choose Table→"Resize Row to Fit Content" to do the same thing.)

To adjust the width of the current column to fit all the content its cells contain, click the Fit button next to the Column field, or choose Table→"Resize Column to Fit Content." Unlike resizing rows, resizing a column is a one-time-only deal: Your columns won't automatically resize if you add and remove content (although your rows may still expand vertically).

NOTE If Numbers is already automatically resizing your cells to fit your content, then the row Fit button is grayed out. If you've already clicked the column Fit button and haven't manually resized the column since, the column Fit button is also grayed out.

■ MERGING TABLE CELLS

When content spills out of its cell as shown in Figure 17-6, it might *look* like you can edit it by selecting any of the cells it crosses, but that's not the case. No matter how Numbers might display a cell's data, it still "lives" only in the original cell, and that's the cell you have to select to edit it. So even if some of the content in Figure 17-6 spills over from column D into column E, you have to select the cell in column D to edit it; clicking a cell in column E just selects that blank cell, not the text that begins in column D (remember, text can spill over only into blank cells).

But that's not always convenient. When you know that the cell's content will always span a specific range of cells, you can *merge* those cells into one big mega cell, as shown in Figure 17-7. Numbers knocks down the walls between the merged cells, and now you can click anywhere inside the newly expanded cell to edit it. This is useful for giving several columns the same title, for example. To add a single title above three columns, you'd merge the top cells of those three columns so that the merged cell spans the three columns.

To merge cells, select two or more neighboring cells, and then choose Table→Merge Cells.

You can merge both rows and columns at once—to make a 2 × 2 block, for example—but the selected cells have to form a rectangle. The cells also have to be the same type: all body cells, all header cells (page 492), or all footer cells (page 495).

Paragraphs, Line Breaks, and Tabs

Because the Return and Tab keys have special roles in navigating among cells, you can't use them add a new line or tab stop to a table cell. In most cases, you'll just include brief snippets of data in your cells—numbers, short text labels, names—but occasionally you may want to include longer text (a column of important comments left by your taste-testers, for example).

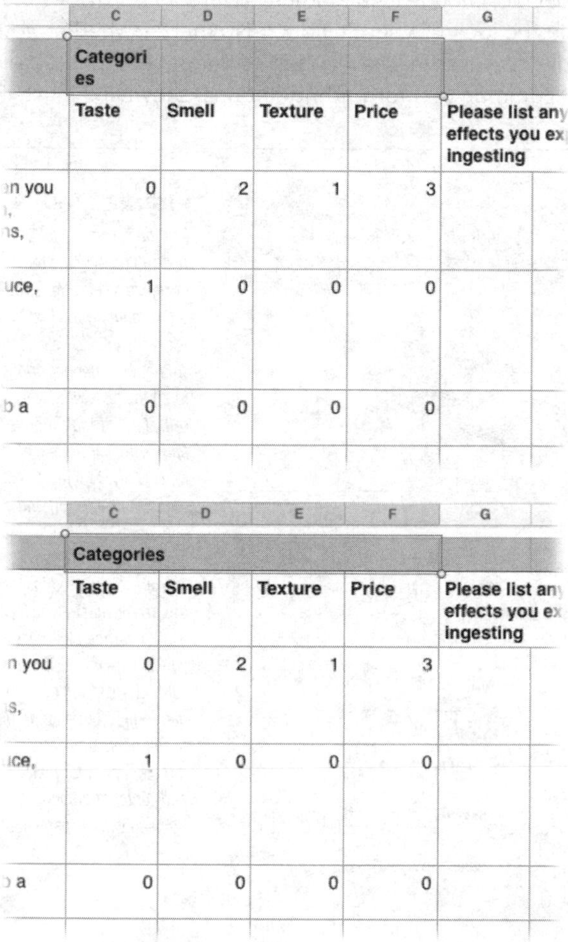

	C	D	E	F	G
	Categori es				
	Taste	Smell	Texture	Price	Please list any effects you ex ingesting
n you ı, ıs,	0	2	1	3	
uce,	1	0	0	0	
b a	0	0	0	0	

	C	D	E	F	G
	Categories				
	Taste	Smell	Texture	Price	Please list any effects you ex ingesting
n you ıs,	0	2	1	3	
ıce,	1	0	0	0	
ɔ a	0	0	0	0	

FIGURE 17-7

Top: Here, the Categories heading is supposed to apply to four cells below it (Taste, Smell, Texture, and Price)—something that isn't immediately obvious. To merge the selected cells (C1–F1) into a single-cell organism, choose the Table→Merge Cells command.

Bottom: This screenshot shows the four cells after they've been merged. Now it's clearer that "Categories" is the title for these four cells. Centering the word "Categories" within the merged cell would help make that relationship even clearer; pages 48–50 have more information about aligning text.

To add a new line to a cell, select it at the text level and then press Option-Return. (If the cell is selected at the cell level, pressing Option-Return selects it at the text level; pressing Option-Return again inserts a paragraph break.) To add a tab stop to a cell, press Option-Tab.

TIP If you're after a line break instead of a paragraph break, press Option-Shift-Return. Page 52 explains the difference between the two. (Alas, unlike Pages, Numbers doesn't have a Show Invisibles command to show you where you've used a line break or a paragraph break.)

Formatting Text

You can format the text within table cells using all the font styles you've already seen in Pages and Keynote. Choose a new font, shade it in a new color, make it larger or smaller, add extra line spacing, change its alignment—Numbers provides plenty of formatting tools to shape the look of your cell data. No matter whether you've got a cell selected at the object, cell, or text level, the Format panel's text tab gives you fast access to the most common text formatting options, shown in Figure 17-8.

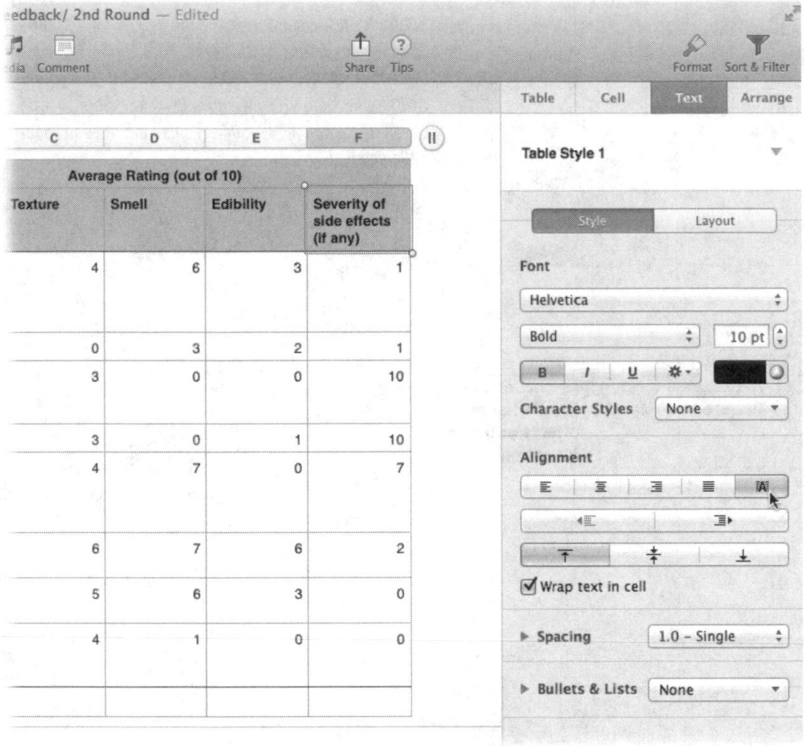

FIGURE 17-8

Use the Format panel's Text tab to style the text of selected cells. Here, the cell containing the text "Severity of..." is selected so that any changes apply to all the text within this cell. The Text tab's menus and buttons include font family; typeface; font size; font color; and alignment. Automatic alignment (where the cursor is positioned in this screenshot)—which is usually turned on unless you change it—positions content according to its data type: right alignment for numbers and dates, left alignment for text, and center alignment for Boolean values (page 479).

Numbers applies your formatting changes to all the cells included in the selection: When you have the table selected at the object level, all text in *all* cells updates to reflect your changes. Select a row or column, and your changes hit the text in all its cells. When you select just a portion of a single cell's text, you focus the change only on that selected text—to make a single word **bold** or *italic*, for example, or to increase the line spacing of the current paragraph.

With only a few exceptions, formatting your text with these tools is identical to formatting text in Pages. You'll find those details described in the Pages chapters (especially Chapter 2). Here's an abbreviated tour of text formatting in Numbers.

■ THE TEXT TAB

Click the Format panel's Text tab (and make sure the Style button is selected) to display most of Numbers' text formatting options. As you saw back in Figure 17-8, the settings are divided into four sections: Font, Alignment, Spacing, and Bullets & Lists. To change the color of the text in the selected cells, click the rainbow-colored color wheel icon in the Font section, and Numbers rolls out the Color Picker for you to make your choice (page 192). Click the Spacing heading to adjust the spacing between lines and paragraphs.

You can control the look of paragraph bullets or numbers by clicking the Bullets & Lists heading. Then use the settings that appear to swap out traditional bullet dots for numbers, letters, or spiffy images, and fine-tune the amount of indent. See page 68 for details on using bullet points and bullet styles.

You can access some additional text formatting options by clicking the Text tab's Layout button (see Figure 17-9).

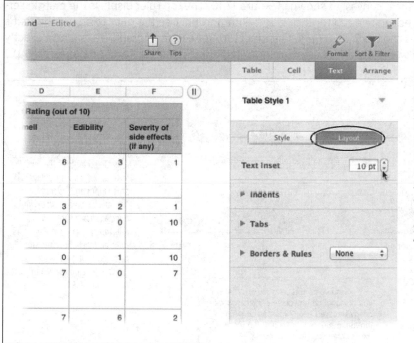

FIGURE 17-9

You can access additional text formatting options by clicking the Text tab's Layout button (circled). The Layout settings let you fine-tune your text's indent, as well as add borders, rules, and change the background color of your text.

The Text Inset setting is especially useful in tables, adding space between cell boundaries and data to make text-heavy tables a bit more readable. Here, cells include 10-point padding around the content within.

■ THE FORMAT MENU

Choose Format→Font to do any of the following:

• Show or hide the Fonts window.

• Change the font style (bold, italic, underline, or outline).

• Increase or decrease the font size.

- Adjust the spacing between characters (see page 44).

- Turn ligatures on or off (see page 47).

- Adjust the font's baseline (see page 46).

- Adjust the text's capitalization.

Choose Format→Text and select one of the paragraph alignment settings: Align Left, Align Center, Align Right, Justify, or Auto-Align Table Cell. This last option aligns text based on its data type: Text aligns left, numbers and dates align right, and Boolean values (page 479) align center.

■ SETTING MARGINS, INDENTS, AND TABS WITH THE RULER

You can set margins, indents, and tabs for individual paragraphs of a table cell using the ruler. To do this, select the cell at the text level by double-clicking it or selecting it and pressing Option-Return. Then choose View→Show Rulers (or press ⌘-R) to reveal Numbers' vertical and horizontal measuring sticks on the top and left sides of the sheet canvas, as shown in Figure 17-10. The top ruler displays the margin settings, indent, and tab for the selected paragraph. Use the ruler to adjust the text's margins and the first-line indent, and set tabs for each paragraph in a text box, exactly as you would in Pages (see "Setting Tabs" and "Indenting Text" on pages 52–58).

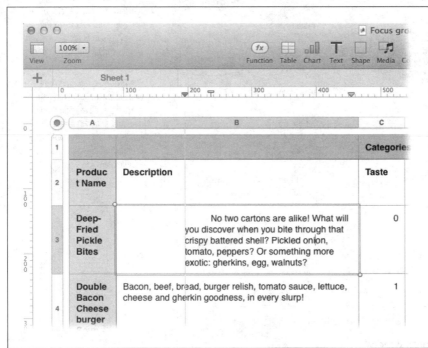

FIGURE 17-10

Choose View→Show Rulers in order to make margin and tab adjustments with the ruler. Select a cell at the text level, and Numbers displays the margins and indents for the selected paragraph in the ruler, as shown here. Add a tab stop by clicking in the ruler, and then move the stop by dragging it. Here, a new tab stop is being applied to the text in cell B3.

Create new tabs by clicking once on the ruler and then dragging the tab into position. Control-click a tab marker and choose one of the four tab styles from the drop-down menu: left, center, right, or decimal (see page 55). Or you can just double-click the tab marker repeatedly to cycle through the various styles.

You can fine-tune your tab settings by going to the Format panel's Text tab, clicking the Layout button (if it's not already selected), and then clicking the Tabs heading to expand that section (see page 56 for more info).

Adding Comments

You can flag a table cell with a comment to leave yourself a reminder, to give someone else feedback, or to offer others instructions on how to use the spreadsheet. To add a comment to a cell, select the cell at either the cell or text level, and then click the Comment button in the toolbar or choose Insert→Comment.

The first time you add a comment, Numbers may ask whether it can access your contacts; click OK to give it permission or Don't Allow to keep its mitts off your address book. After that, you see a dialog box that says "Type a name to use in comments"; type the name you want displayed on each of your comments. (You can change this name later by choosing Numbers→Preferences, clicking the General tab, and editing the Author field.) After that setup work, a *comment balloon* materializes, floating above the table like a speech bubble that's anchored to the cell, as shown in Figure 17-11. The cell now sports a *comment indicator*, a colored triangle in the cell's top-right corner. You're ready to type your comment.

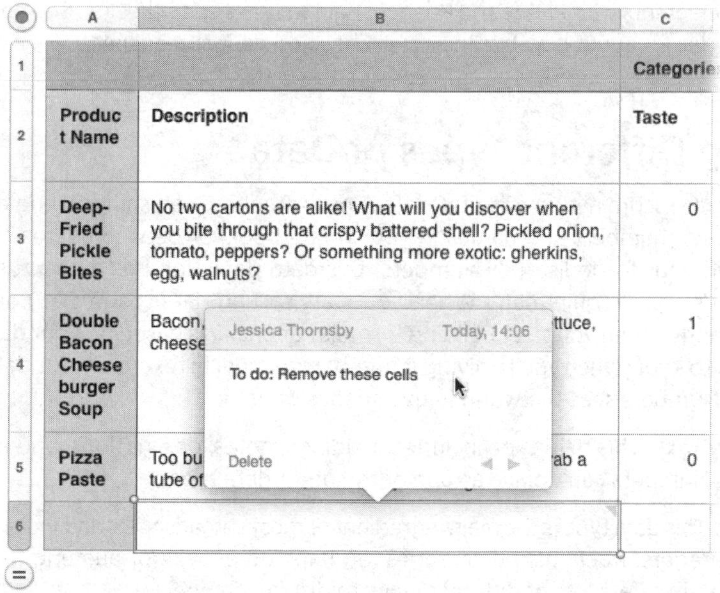

FIGURE 17-11

When you add a comment to a table cell, Numbers ties a comment balloon to the cell. To hide all comments, go to View→Comments→Hide Comments, or use the View button in the toolbar. To get your comments back, repeat the process, but choose Show Comments instead.

To display a comment that's collapsed (so its comment indicator is visible, but not its balloon), click its indicator. To hide all comments, click the View button in the toolbar and choose Hide Comments; bring them back by choosing View→Comments→Show Comments. To remove the comment permanently, click the Delete link in the comment balloon's bottom-left corner. If you delete the text or object the comment is attached to, the comment disappears, too. You can find out more about comments on page 469.

■ ADDING STICKY NOTES OUTSIDE OF TABLES

You can also add general comments to the current sheet, rather than to a specific table cell. To do so, deselect all tables by clicking a blank part of the sheet canvas, and then click the Comment button in the toolbar (or choose Insert→Comment). Numbers adds a big sticky note on top of your sheet, but the note doesn't point to a specific object or cell. Drag the note to position it wherever you'd like, or delete it by clicking the Delete link in its bottom-left corner.

Unlike the cell-specific comment bubbles, you can position a sticky note anywhere you want by clicking its heading bar and then dragging it to a new location.

Checking Your Spelling

Numbers normally has its automatic spell checking turned on, flagging misspelled words—or words not in its dictionary—with a red underline. Choose Edit→Spelling and Grammar→Check Spelling While Typing to turn this feature on or off.

Choose Edit→Spelling and Grammar→Show Spelling and Grammar to display the Spelling window so you can do manual spell checking by clicking Find Next. Numbers shares many elements with Pages and Keynote, including its spell checker. See page 89 for all the details about how to run a spell check on your spreadsheet.

■ Using Different Types of Data

Numbers has a discriminating nose for data. For example, it can sniff out the difference between numbers and names in your grade book, or between dates and checkboxes in your to-do list. For Numbers, this data detection isn't just a fussy party trick—it's a job requirement. When you start sorting data (page 500) and, more importantly, when you start building formulas and charts based on your data, Numbers has to know when you're giving it numbers to crunch, text to sort, or dates to schedule. Numbers sees the world in five shades of data:

- **Ordinary text.** This data type includes headings, notes, descriptions, and any text that Numbers can't place as one of the other data types.

- **Number.** This data type is the main ingredient of most spreadsheets and includes prices, integers, fractions, percentages, and any other type of numeric data. The program offers lots of different ways to display numbers.

- **Dates and times.** This data type includes calendar dates (like December 6, 2015), time of day (like 12:26 p.m.), and the combination of both (December 6, 2015, 12:26 p.m.). You can enter and display this info in a variety of formats.

- **Durations.** A length of time, like weeks, hours, or even milliseconds.

- **True or false values.** This on-or-off data type is also known in nerd circles by its chirpier name, *Boolean* values. Behind the scenes, these values are either TRUE or FALSE (in all caps), but you'll typically see them in Numbers spreadsheets as a simple checkbox (see page 479). You might use these values in to-do lists to mark items completed, in grade books to mark pass/fail, or in complex formulas that evaluate conditions. See Chapter 20 for more info.

> **TIP** Get your hands on a table that contains examples of all five of these data types by going to this book's Missing CD page at *www.missingmanuals.com/cds* and *downloading data_types.numbers.*

Most of the time, you don't have to give these data types a second thought, since Numbers is good at automatically figuring out the *data type* of each cell just by looking at its information and formatting. As Numbers does this, it displays your data in subtly different ways. You can get a hint of how the program has interpreted your data by looking at its cell alignment, as shown in Figure 17-12.

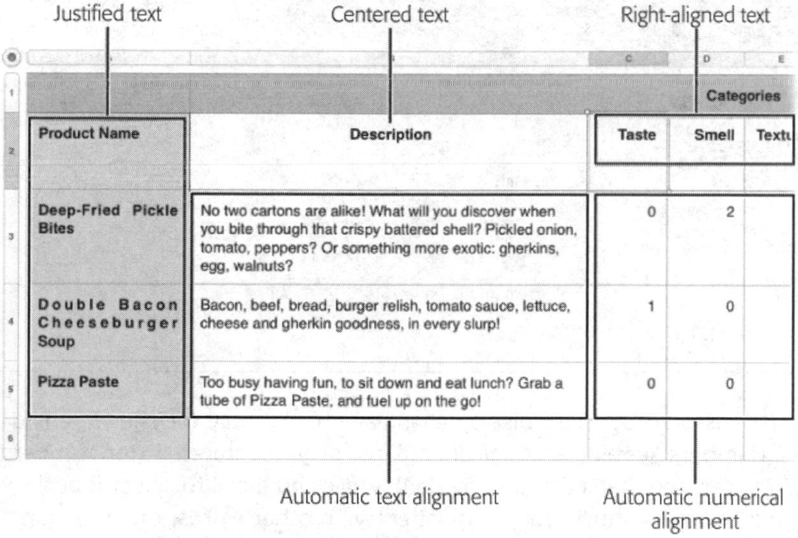

FIGURE 17-12

Numbers changes the text alignment of your cells (left, right, or centered) based on the type of data you enter. It aligns text to the left, numbers and dates to the right, and Boolean values stay centered. That's just the standard treatment, however, and you can change this formatting however you like (see page 48).

This image shows a mix of auto-aligned data and data that's been manually aligned using the the Text tab's settings.

The program can display numbers and dates in several different forms. For example, numbers can include a comma (or not) to mark off thousands; a percentage sign; or a currency symbol. Dates are equally flexible, showing the same moment in time in a variety of different formats.

You can explicitly control how Numbers displays your data by setting cells' data format, as you'll learn on page 473. Until you do that, though, the program makes its own call about how to format the data. Numerical data is generally displayed as you enter it, but sometimes with minor differences. If you enter an amount with a dollar sign, for example, Numbers displays it with two decimal places, even if you add more decimal places (see Figure 17-13).

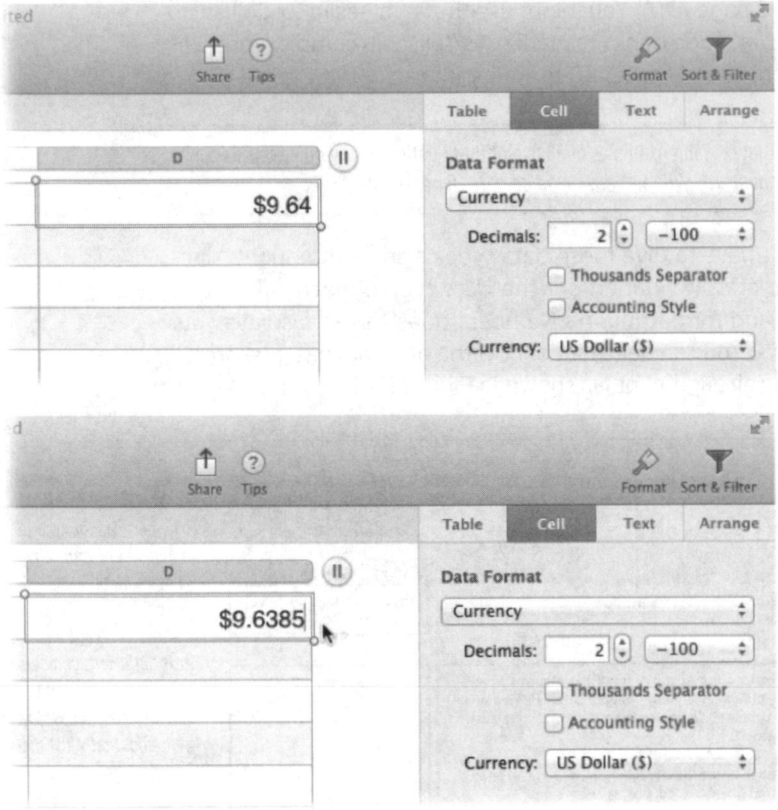

FIGURE 17-13

Top: Because the person entering this data included a dollar sign when entering this value, Numbers assumes that this value is a currency. Because of that, Numbers displays only two decimal places—.64—since that's standard practice for most currencies, even though the original value was $9.6385.

Bottom: Double-clicking the cell to select it at the text level displays the actual value, as shown here. When you go back to selecting the value at the cell level (or no longer have the cell selected at all), the value reverts to the rounded value, $9.64.

Don't get flustered by these display changes—they're only for show. Behind the scenes, Numbers keeps your original data just as you entered it (for numbers, at least). You can see that's the case by double-clicking a cell to select it at the text level; and Numbers shows your original entry. In other words, the way Numbers *displays* your data isn't necessarily the same as the way it *stores* it. No matter how it displays your data, the important thing to know is that Numbers treats all numbers, dates, and times the same when it comes to calculations. When you enter a currency as $9.6385, it may show up in the table as $9.64, but it will still count as $9.6385 when Numbers does any math that includes that value.

Choosing a Data Format

The way your cell displays its data is called the *data format*. Most cells start life using Numbers' *Automatic* data format, which detects the data format to display as described above, but you can tell Numbers to use a specific data format for any or all of your cells.

To change the data format, select the cells you want to update; if you select one or more rows, columns, or tables, you can choose the data format for all the cells within them in one swoop. Then select the Format panel's Cell tab and open the Data Format drop-down menu (shown in Figure 17-14).

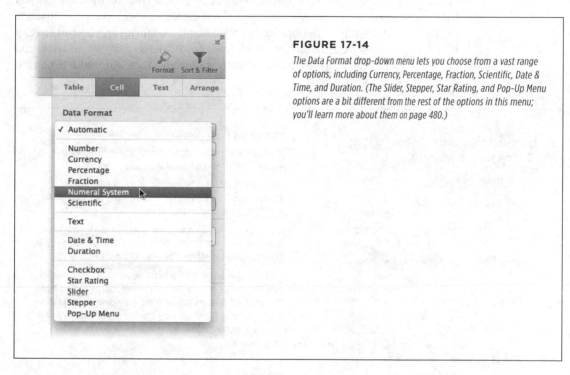

FIGURE 17-14

The Data Format drop-down menu lets you choose from a vast range of options, including Currency, Percentage, Fraction, Scientific, Date & Time, and Duration. (The Slider, Stepper, Star Rating, and Pop-Up Menu options are a bit different from the rest of the options in this menu; you'll learn more about them on page 480.)

It's OK if you add data to a cell that doesn't match your selected data format. Nothing breaks or explodes—Numbers just treats the data like ordinary text. So, if you have a column set to display data as currency and you enter a date into a cell there, Numbers can tell it's not currency and won't treat it as such. Instead, Numbers displays the date exactly as you enter it and won't do the magic formatting tricks that it would normally do when you enter a date into a cell with the Automatic or Date & Time data format applied.

> **TIP** You can explicitly tell Numbers to treat a cell's value as ordinary text—and display it exactly as you type it—by setting it to use the Text data format. You'll learn more about that on page 476.

When you make your selection from the Data Format drop-down menu, most of the time the Cell tab will display additional settings related to that format. If you decide to wing it and use the Automatic data format, these options likewise change depending on the data type Numbers detects. When Numbers thinks you're dealing with a date, for example, it offers you the date-formatting options.

What follows is a tour of the most commonly used of Numbers' many data format options.

■ THE NUMBER FORMAT

When you select Number from the Data Format drop-down menu, Numbers formats the selected cell(s) to display as many decimal places as you type, no thousands separator, and a – minus symbol for negative numbers. However, you can specify how many decimal places Numbers should display, as well as whether and how you want it to format the thousands separator and negative values. Figure 17-15 has the whole story.

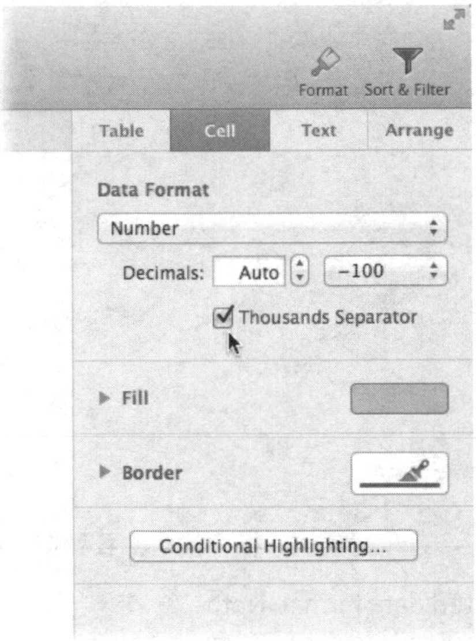

FIGURE 17-15

When you select the Number data format, you can fine-tune how Numbers displays your numerical info.

Use the Decimals field to tell Numbers to display more or fewer decimal places. If a data value has more decimal places than you set here, Numbers rounds the value for you.

To dictate the way negative values are displayed, use the unlabeled drop-down menu that's set to –100 here. And the Thousands Separator checkbox makes the difference between 1000 and 1,000.

Don't be thrown by the fact that this is the only data format with the word "number" in its name. Most of the other data formats are meant to be used with numbers, too, but Number is a good format for values that don't fit any of the other, more specific numeric options (such as Currency, Percentage, and so on).

■ THE CURRENCY FORMAT

When you've got your mind on your money and your money on your mind, the Currency format is the one for you, so select it from the Data Format menu. This format works similarly to the Number format except that Currency always displays two decimal places and adds a currency symbol (such as $, €, or £) that coincides with whatever is selected in the Currency drop-down menu (it's initially set to US Dollar). To use a currency other than US Dollar, open the Currency drop-down menu and choose anything from the Brazilian Real to the Thai Baht.

When you select Currency, you can also change the number of decimal places Numbers displays, turn the thousands separator on or off, and tell the program how to display negative numbers. Turn on the Accounting Style checkbox to display the currency symbol at the left edge of the cell instead of right next to the value.

THE PERCENTAGE FORMAT

To display numbers followed by a percent symbol, select Percentage from the Data Format drop-down menu. This is more than a simple cosmetic change: Numbers treats values formatted this way as percentages—25% is counted as 0.25, for example. Numbers also takes this into account when you apply this format to cells that already contain data; for example, a cell with the value of 5 in Automatic format becomes 500% when you switch to the Percentage format. The value makes the transition unchanged, however. But when you add a new value to a cell that *already* has the Percentage format applied, Numbers treats the value as a percentage (for example, entering *5* displays 5% and, behind the scenes, Numbers treats the value as 0.05).

Like the Number and Currency formats, when you choose the Percentage format, you can also tell Numbers to display a certain number of decimal places, whether to include a thousands separator, and how to display negative numbers.

THE FRACTION FORMAT

Use this format to replace the decimal portion of a number with a fraction. You can then select an accuracy level from the Accuracy drop-down menu that appears. This setting determines how detailed a fraction Numbers displays, from one digit in the denominator (1/8) to two digits (1/24) to three digits (1/553). You can also choose to have the fractions displayed with a fixed denominator (halves, quarters, eights, sixteenths, tenths, or hundredths), and Numbers rounds your value to the nearest fraction using that denominator. For example, 10.5 displays as 10 1/2 when the format is halves, 10 2/4 when the format is fourths, and 10 4/8 when the format is eighths. If you don't pick an Accuracy setting, then Numbers picks the fraction closest to the actual decimal value.

NOTE As with rounding in other number formats, fractional rounding is just for display purposes—Numbers always remembers the "real" value for you.

THE NUMERAL SYSTEM FORMAT

When counting in multiples of 10 just won't cut it, you can switch to a whole different numbering system. The Numeral System format displays numbers in binary, hexadecimal, or any other counting system from base 2 to base 36.

If you have no idea what binary or hexadecimal numeral systems are, then chances are you'll never need this data format, but here's the gist: The base of a counting system determines how many digits you use; our familiar decimal system uses base 10, for example, and each digit's "place" represents units of 10 raised to the power of 1, 2, 3, and so on—that means units of 10, 100, 1,000, 10,000. Other numeral systems work the same way, but with a different number of digits. In the base 2 (a.k.a.

binary) system, there are only two digits: 0 and 1. No matter what numeral system you use, however, the actual *value* of the number is the same, it's just *displayed* in a different counting system.

To switch the selected cells to a different numeral system, choose Numeral System from the Data Format drop-down menu. In the Base field, choose the base value of the system you want to use. Use the Places field to tell Numbers how many digits to display, including leading zeroes. The Minus Sign option gives you the traditional minus sign (–), and the Two's-Complement checkbox gives you the two's complement system of encoding negative numbers, which is mainly used when dealing with computing and binary numbers.

■ THE SCIENTIFIC FORMAT

Use the Scientific format to display very large or very small numbers in compact form. Numbers uses this format when it needs to squeeze a value into a narrow column.

Once you choose this format from the Data Format drop-down menu, you can use the Decimals field to change the number of decimal places Numbers displays. Numbers rounds the value to fit the specified number of decimal places, but only for display purposes; the actual value remains safely stowed away for use in formulas, or if you change the display format at a later date.

■ THE TEXT FORMAT

This format tells Numbers to treat a value like ordinary text and display your data exactly as you enter it. This is convenient when your data contains values that Numbers would otherwise interpret as another data type. For example, if you enter the product number 1883-12-13 into a cell that's set to the Automatic data format, Numbers assumes that you're entering a date: December 13, 1883. Setting the cell's data format to Text tells Numbers not to treat it as one of its special data types.

> **TIP** Even when a cell is set to another format—Automatic, Number, or whatever—you can still tell Numbers to treat the cell's value as ordinary text. Start the cell's value with an apostrophe ('1883-12-13), and Numbers treats the value as text (and doesn't display the apostrophe itself).

■ THE DATE & TIME FORMAT

Set selected cells to display dates and/or times by opening the Data Format drop-down menu and choosing Date & Time.

> **TIP** Numbers takes its standard date and time formats from OS X's System Preferences. See the box on page 478 for more info.

Human beings have lots of different ways to represent dates and times, and Numbers does its best to be flexible. You can type a full date (like January 6, 2015), for example, or you can type an abbreviated date using dashes or slashes (01-06-2015 or 1/6/15). Whichever way you do it, Numbers recognizes your value as a date and displays it according to the settings you select in the Cell tab. You can tell Numbers exactly how to format the value using the Date drop-down menu; you can do the same with any time data by making a selection from the Time drop-down menu.

If you don't provide a year (you type *Jan 6* or *1/6*, for example), Numbers assumes you mean the current year. If you provide a year but only two digits, Numbers assumes you're talking about the new millennium when the year is less than 50 (1/6/15 is 2015), but otherwise you slip back to the last century (1/6/51 is 1951). Entering the year with four digits, of course, clears up any ambiguity.

> **NOTE** If you enter a date that doesn't exist (June 31, 2015, for example), Numbers treats it as ordinary text instead of a date.

Times are a bit more straightforward: You simply type numbers separated by a colon. If you enter two numbers in this format (8:45), Numbers treats them as hours and minutes. Add a third number, and Numbers treats it as seconds (8:45:35). This format works as is for 24-hour times (14:23, for example), but be sure to add "pm" to the time if you're using a 12-hour clock and working past noon (2:23 pm, for instance). Numbers is lenient about how you add am and pm; you can leave out the space (2:23pm) or enter it in capital letters (2:23 PM), or both.

To enter *both* a date and a time, separate the two pieces of info with a space, and Numbers swallows both at once, happily digesting a combination like 1/6/15 2:23 pm. In fact, Numbers *always* stores both a date and a time for your Date & Time values, even if you enter just one or the other. When you enter only a date, for example, Numbers sets the time to midnight; when you enter only a time, Numbers assumes you mean today.

However you type your dates and times, the settings in the Cell tab determine how Numbers displays them. If the Time drop-down menu is set to None, it won't display a time value even if you enter one; the same goes for the Date drop-down menu. As usual, Numbers doesn't *forget* the date or time that you enter, even if it doesn't show it. If you later change the format to display the missing info, Numbers still has the complete date and time stowed away and displays it according to your preferences.

■ THE DURATION FORMAT

Select Duration from the Data Format drop-down menu when you want to display a period of time in any unit from weeks to milliseconds. For example, you can format the duration field to display 3 hours, 9 minutes, and 15 seconds as 3:09:15, 3h 9m 15s, or 3 hours, 9 minutes, 15 seconds. You can choose exactly what units to display by clicking the Custom Units button and then selecting any of the buttons that appear below it (see Figure 17-16). If you don't opt for Custom Units, Numbers looks at the data you've entered and does its best to turn it into a duration, though you may get unpredictable results, especially when large numbers are involved.

FIGURE 17-16

You can change how Numbers displays durations by clicking the Custom Units button and then selecting the units you want to display. Left to right, you can choose from weeks, days, hours, minutes, seconds, and milliseconds. (You have to select neighboring units; for example, you can display a duration as weeks, days, and hours, but not weeks and hours, or hours and seconds). You can also choose a format for the selected duration from the Style drop-down menu.

You can use durations in formulas to add and subtract amounts of time, for example. Especially handy: When you subtract one Date & Time value from another, you get a Duration value. For more on doing math with dates, times, and durations, see page 539.

UP TO SPEED

Regional Rules

Your Mac knows where you live and how folks there do things. All the iWork programs, including Numbers, take cues from your OS X System Preferences to manage things like date and time formats, currency, and whether or not you're a fan of the metric system.

When Numbers is working with dates, for example, it knows that Americans think of the third day of May as 5/3, while Brits prefer 3/5, and it interprets your entry accordingly. In the same way, Numbers assumes that you prefer to work with dollars as a standard currency when you're in the US, but switches over to the dinar when you happen to be in Tunisia.

The Language & Region pane of your Mac's system preferences controls all these formatting decisions, not only for iWork but for every other well-behaved program on your computer. To open this pane, go to →System Preferences and click Language & Region. The settings you choose there don't have to correspond to where you actually live—you can set them to anything you like. Use the Region drop-down menu to choose any region to switch to its local date, time, number, currency, and measurement conventions. You can also choose which calendar your Mac uses and whether it favors the 24-hour clock or not.

Adding Special Controls to Cells

One pitfall of working with large amounts of data is the inevitable typos. Fortunately, Numbers gives you a few controls that can help reduce fat-finger keyboard errors, keeping your data tidy and making the data-entry process a bit easier. These options add checkboxes, sliders, steppers, star ratings, and pop-up menus—familiar visual devices that provide an alternative to typing values manually. To add one of these controls to the selected cell(s), open the Format panel's Cell tab and choose from the Data Format drop-down menu. The following sections explain each control.

■ CHECKBOXES FOR BOOLEAN VALUES

Everybody knows what a checkbox means: yes or no, complete or incomplete, on or off. Don't look now, but that checkbox is what your neighborhood geek calls a Boolean indicator. Checkboxes are so familiar that it might seem a little overwrought to apply such a fancy term to them, but a Boolean value's simple choice of TRUE or FALSE is really just an on/off switch, like a checkbox. Numbers lets you use checkboxes as a friendly way to flip that Boolean switch. Turn a checkbox on to set the cell's value to TRUE, or turn it off to set it to FALSE.

But really, Boolean shmoolean. Although you can indeed put these TRUE/FALSE values to use in formulas and to filter your content—as explained in Chapter 20—you'll usually just appreciate the visual utility of having checkboxes in your spreadsheet. Figure 17-17 shows a simple example of checkboxes in a to-do list. Click a checkbox to toggle it on or off.

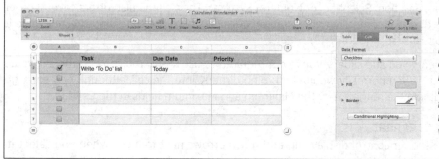

FIGURE 17-17

This spreadsheet uses checkboxes to indicate completed items in a to-do list. Behind the scenes, turning on a checkbox sets the cell's value to TRUE; turning it off sets the value to FALSE.

To add a checkbox to the selected cell(s), select Checkbox from the Cell tab's Data Format drop-down menu. (To quickly turn an entire row or column into a list of checkboxes, click that row or column's reference tab before choosing the Checkbox data format.) If any cells already contain a TRUE Boolean value, Numbers automatically turns on their checkboxes. Otherwise, any existing values are replaced with FALSE, meaning that their checkboxes are switched off.

■ STAR RATINGS

Star ratings can be found in anything from music magazines to theater and book reviews to feedback forms for Double Bacon Cheeseburger Soup. Star ratings let your readers see, at a glance, what's hot and what's not. The maximum number of stars you can award any item is five, and the minimum is a mean-spirited zero (sorry, no half-stars or negative numbers here!). To apply the Star Rating formatting to the selected cell(s), open the Data Format drop-down and choose Star Rating, which adds five dots to your cell(s). To rank the item higher than zero, click the dots to turn them into stars—or downgrade an item by clicking the stars to turn them back into dots.

> **TIP** If the cells already contain data before you apply this data format, Numbers does its best to translate the numerical data into star ratings (any number higher than 5 becomes a 5-star rating). So if you're dealing with large amounts of ratings, adding this data first may be quicker than going through each cell and manually turning stars off and on.

■ SLIDERS FOR NUMBERS

Add a slider to a number cell and Numbers lets you change the cell's value with a flip of the wrist. Sliders are particularly valuable when you have a cell hooked up as part of a formula and want to test "what if?" scenarios to see how the rest of your spreadsheet's values change as you gradually change one cell's value. The Grade Book template that you saw on page 445 is a good example of this.

To add a slider to the selected cell(s), choose Slider from the Data Format drop-down menu. Sliders work with any type of number format (Number, Currency, Percentage, Fraction, Scientific, or Numeral System). The Cell tab also offers several other settings for controlling how Numbers displays both the slider and the cell value it controls (see Figure 17-18).

Even if you add sliders, you're not required to use them. You can edit the cell value just as you normally would, by typing directly into the cell, although you can't go outside the range set by the Minimum and Maximum fields in the Cell tab.

■ STEPPERS

A stepper control displays up and down arrows next to a cell when you select it. Like sliders, steppers let you set a range and a fixed increment for number values. While a slider is useful for moving quickly through a range of values, a stepper is better for carefully nudging values by specific increments. To add a stepper to the selected cell(s), open the Data Format drop-down menu and choose Stepper. Figure 17-19 shows what the Grade Book template looks like when its slider is replaced by a stepper.

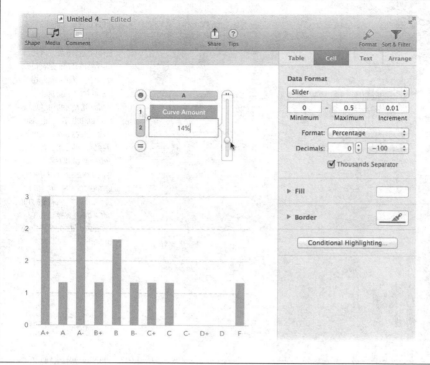

FIGURE 17-18

Sliders make their presence known only when you click a cell with the Slider format. In this example, the Curve Amount slider lets you set the number of points to adjust grades.

The Cell tab's settings let you control the behavior and appearance of the slider, including the minimum and maximum values of its range. The Increment field sets the amount the cell value increases or decreases as you nudge the slider up or down. The Format setting determines the cell's number format (number, currency, percentage, and so on).

■ POP-UP MENUS FOR PREDEFINED VALUES

The Pop-Up Menu data format lets you offer a fixed selection of values for a cell. When you select a cell with this data format, like the one shown in Figure 17-20, a flippy triangle appears to its right; click the triangle to reveal the available options.

Wherever possible, you should assign the Pop-Up Menu data format to cells *before* entering their data. When you add a pop-up menu to a cell that already has data, all of that data gets bundled into the first option in the pop-up menu—regardless of whether you separated the values with commas or put each one on a new line.

> **NOTE** To change the order of values in a pop-up menu, grab a value in the Cell tab's table (shown in Figure 17-20) and drag it to a new position. And you can control whether the cell is initially blank or displays the first item in your list by choosing a value from the Cell tab's drop-down menu: "Start with First Item" or "Start with Blank."

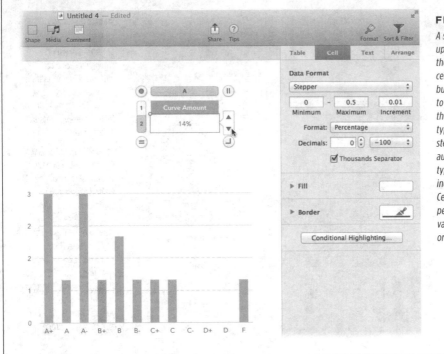

FIGURE 17-19

A stepper control puts up and down arrows to the right of the selected cell. Click the arrows to bump the value according to the increment set in the Cell tab. You can also type values directly into stepper cells, but Numbers automatically corrects any typed values to fit the increment specified in the Cell tab. This makes a stepper a good way to force values to fit specific steps or units.

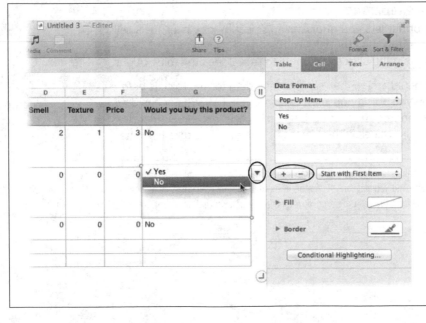

FIGURE 17-20

Cells with pop-up menus sprout a flippy triangle when you select them (circled, left). Click the triangle to reveal a pop-up menu of the allowed values for that field.

In the Cell tab, you add and remove items from the pop-up menu by clicking the + and – buttons (circled, right). To rename a menu item, double-click it in the Cell tab's table.

■ Add It Quick: Data-Entry Shortcuts

Let's face it, typing row upon row of data into a spreadsheet can be dreary, time-consuming work. To ease the pain, Numbers includes several features that help fill your grid quickly, even suggesting entries when the program thinks it knows where you're headed with a cell value. This section surveys those speedy shortcuts.

Auto-Correction and Smart Quotes

Numbers can monitor what you type, automatically correcting errors or inserting *smart quotes*, or curly quotes, which curve into a different shape for opening quotes or closing quotes. You can also use Numbers' auto-correction tools to give you quick shortcuts for commonly typed words and phrases. Turn these features on or off in the Substitutions window (open it by choosing Edit→Substitutions→Show Substitutions). See page 97 for all the details.

Autofilling Cells

Numbers is clever at spotting patterns, and you can use that talent to fill a run of neighboring cells with sequential numbers, days, or months. The program's *autofill* feature uses the content in one or more cells to add values to the cells around it. You can use autofill to simply copy the value and formatting of a single cell, but the feature is especially useful for adding a series of values that increment from cell to cell.

Whenever you select one or more cells and then put your cursor over them (without clicking), Numbers displays a *fill handle*—a little yellow circle like the one shown in Figure 17-21. Drag the fill handle over the cells you want to fill, and Numbers pastes any data, data format, formula, or background fill associated with the selected cell(s) into the new cells, replacing any previous values they contained. You can autofill up or down along the same column, or left or right along the same row, but you can't drag diagonally to autofill a block of cells.

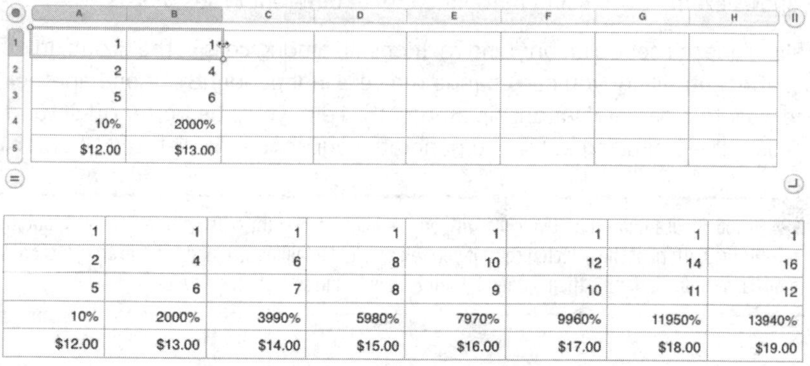

FIGURE 17-21

Top: Put your cursor over the selected cell(s), and a fill handle appears on the border closest to your cursor.

Bottom: Dragging the fill handle along a row or column autofills neighboring cells with the value and formatting of the original cell. All the rows shown here have been completed using autofill.

Top table:

	A	B	C	D	E	F	G	H
1	1	1						
2	2	4						
3	5	6						
4	10%	2000%						
5	$12.00	$13.00						

Bottom table:

1	1	1	1	1	1	1	1
2	4	6	8	10	12	14	16
5	6	7	8	9	10	11	12
10%	2000%	3990%	5980%	7970%	9960%	11950%	13940%
$12.00	$13.00	$14.00	$15.00	$16.00	$17.00	$18.00	$19.00

NOTE When you copy a formula into a new cell—whether by moving, pasting, or autofilling—Numbers updates the formula's cell references to reflect the new location. You'll learn all about formulas in Chapter 19; for details, see "Copying or Moving Formulas" on page 534.

You can also autofill several cells with the same value by selecting a range of neighboring cells and choosing Table→Autofill Cells→Autofill Right; Numbers replaces all the cells' existing values (if any) with the leftmost value in the selection. Similarly, choose Autofill Left to fill the selected cells with the rightmost value, Autofill Down to use the top value, or Autofill Up to use the bottom value.

NOTE When the cell you're autofilling from contains a comment (page 469), the comment doesn't get copied into the other cells. However, comments do get deleted when a cell's content is replaced via autofill.

Cloning individual cells like this is useful when you're setting up a table and want to copy cell formatting or initial cell values. But autofilling really earns its supper by saving you time building simple lists with regular increments: 1, 2, 3...; 5, 10, 15...; A, B, C...; Jan, Feb, Mar, ...—you get the idea.

To do this, select two cells before dragging. For example, if your selected cells contain 1 and 2, Numbers adds the values 3 and 4 when you drag the fill handle through the two adjacent cells. And if two selected cells contain 5 and 10, Numbers adds the values 15 and 20 when you drag through the adjacent two cells. Likewise, if two selected cells contain A and B, Numbers adds the values C, D, E, and so on when you drag the fill handle into new cells.

This works with days, months, and dates, too: Select just one date cell, and then drag the fill handle into neighboring cells to increment the date day by day. When you select two cells and drag the fill handle, Numbers increments the value by the interval between the two initial dates. If seven days separate the dates in the selected range, for example, then Numbers bumps each autofilled value up by a week. Figure 17-22 shows examples of using autofill to create different types of lists.

Autofilling doesn't set up an ongoing relationship among cells in the group. In other words, after autofilling, you can change the cells independently of one another. (If you *do* want to create a relationship among the cells, you'll be better off setting up a formula instead of using autofill to generate your sequential list; see Chapter 19.)

NOTE If you choose more than two cells with an irregular interval (or cells with text values), autofilling simply repeats the pattern of the selected cells: If you select cells containing 1, 2, and 5, for example, then dragging the fill handle adds 1, then 2, then 5, then 1, then 2, then 5, and so on to the new cells.

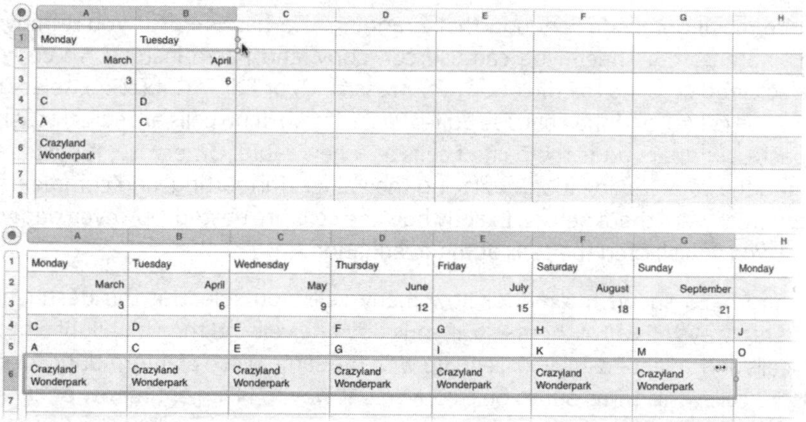

FIGURE 17-22

This before-and-after snapshot shows the effects of using autofill on different types of values and patterns. Autofilling each row in the top table gives the results shown in the bottom table.

Moving and Copying Cells

While you can use autofill to copy a single cell's content into adjacent cells, it doesn't help when you want to copy a cell's content further afield, or work with a whole block of cells. For that, Numbers provides a few different methods for copying and moving cells.

You can move cells within a table, to another table, or to another spot on the canvas to create a whole new table of their own. To start, select the cell(s) you want to move, put your cursor over the cells, and then click and hold your mouse button until the selected cells turn gray and appear "lifted" off the screen. You can then drag the selection to its new location in any table; the ghostly image of the original cells follows the cursor as you drag, and Numbers highlights the cells where the selection will land if you release the mouse button.

When you've dragged the cells to the desired position, drop them. Numbers replaces any existing content with the moved cells' content, formatting, comments—everything; meanwhile, Numbers empties out the original cells, stripping them bare not only of their values but also of all formatting. If you drag the selection to the canvas instead of onto a table, Numbers adds the cells to the canvas as a brand-new table. You can also move entire rows or columns by clicking the reference tab once to select it, and then clicking again and holding down your mouse button for a second so that the column or row appears to "lift" off the page; then drag it to its new location.

To *copy* cells instead of move them, hold down the Option key while you drag. The cursor sprouts a + sign in a green bubble to let you know that Numbers is duplicating rather than moving the selection. As before, Numbers replaces the values and formatting of the destination cells, but this time the original cells remain intact.

If you're moving cells far enough that dragging is a hassle—or if you're moving them to a different sheet—you can use cut, copy, and paste instead. To copy or move selected cells, go to Edit→Copy (or press ⌘-C) or Edit→Cut (⌘-X), select the destination cell(s), and then choose Edit→Paste (⌘-V). If no cells are selected when you paste, Numbers adds the pasted cells as a new table. Otherwise, it pastes the cells into the selected location, replacing the values, formatting, and comments of any cells that were there before. Exactly how the cells are pasted, however, depends on how you've selected the cells at the destination.

As Figure 17-23 shows, no matter how many cells you select at the destination, Numbers always fills *all* of them—so, if you copy one cell and then highlight a group of 50 cells and select Paste, you'll end up with the same piece of information in each of the 50 cells. This turns out to be a convenient way to fill an entire row or column with a single value, formula, or display format: Copy a single cell to the Clipboard with the value and formatting you'd like to apply. Then click the reference tab for the destination row or column to select it, and then choose Edit→Paste. Numbers fills in *all* the cells with clones of the original.

> **TIP** The same trick works if you just want to paste cells' *formatting* but not their content. Instead of using the regular Copy and Paste commands, however, Choose Format→Copy Style and Format→Paste Style. If you want to paste only values without changing the underlying style and format of the destinations cells, choose Edit→"Paste and Match Style."

Numbers also lets you paste cells so that they nudge other cells out of the way instead of replacing them. Choose Insert→Copied Rows or Insert→Copied Columns, and Numbers moves existing cells aside before pasting in the cells. (This works best when you've copied an entire row or column.)

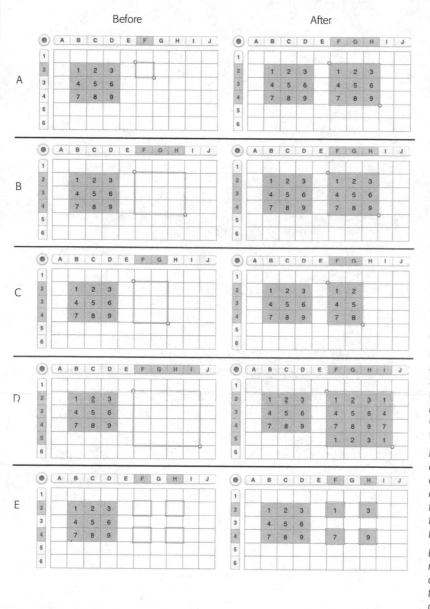

FIGURE 17-23

This series of screenshots shows what happens when you paste the nine shaded cells on the left into different combinations of target cells.

A. When you select just one cell at the destination, Numbers pastes the whole Clipboard selection, and the selected cell becomes the top-left corner of the pasted cells.

B. When you select the exact same pattern of destination cells as the Clipboard's cell selection, Numbers pastes the entire collection as is into the destination cells. (Here, you get the same result as example A.)

C. When you select a collection of destination cells smaller than the group on the Clipboard, Numbers pastes only a subset of the Clipboard cells, starting with the top-left corner.

D. When you select a collection of destination cells larger than the group on the Clipboard, Numbers tiles the Clipboard selection into the selected cells to repeat them.

E. When you select non-neighboring destination cells, Numbers pastes them into the table in the corresponding checkerboard pattern.

Organizing Tables in Numbers

Now that you can spin your way across tables faster than a can-can dancer, you've got all the know-how you need to fill up your grids with data. But all that info is useful only if you can pluck it back out again, and that's where a little organization goes a long way. Once you've got your data loaded into a table, it's time to massage it into shape—structuring it, sorting it, searching it, and filtering it. This chapter shows you all the ways that Numbers can help you tidy your tables and find the right info at the right time.

This organizational effort is about more than shuffling data, though: A pristine table also *looks* clean, and this chapter shows you how to make your data more accessible (and your tables prettier) with the judicious application of borders and background fills. Once you've transformed your gray numbers into shapely figures, Numbers makes it easy to perform the same makeover miracle again and again by storing styles. Before you dig into this interior decoration, though, you'll learn about organizing the structure of your table, starting with rows and columns.

■ Working with Rows and Columns

Filling table cells quickly is all well and good—after all, that's how you'll spend most of your time as you work with your spreadsheet. But while cells may be where you actually sling your data, it's the rows and columns that hold the whole thing together and keep your info organized. Good row and column management makes for good table manners. It's also efficient. This section shows you the fastest ways to add, insert, delete, resize, and hide rows or columns, letting you grow or prune your table quickly as the need arises.

NOTE As you squeeze and stretch a table's rows and columns, its overall size naturally changes, too. When you have other tables or objects on the sheet, Numbers nudges the positions of those objects relative to your growing or shrinking table. This prevents the table from running over other objects when it gets larger, or from creating too much space between objects when it gets smaller.

Adding and Deleting Rows or Columns

When you've selected one or more of a table's cells, the table sprouts icons at each of its four corners. You can use three of these icons to add or remove cells at the edges of the table. With the exception of the top-left icon—which you can drag to move the table to a new position—the icons resize the table, adding new rows and columns, and removing empty rows or columns as you drag (using these handles to remove rows/columns that contain data is covered in a moment). Figure 18-1 gives you the lay of the land.

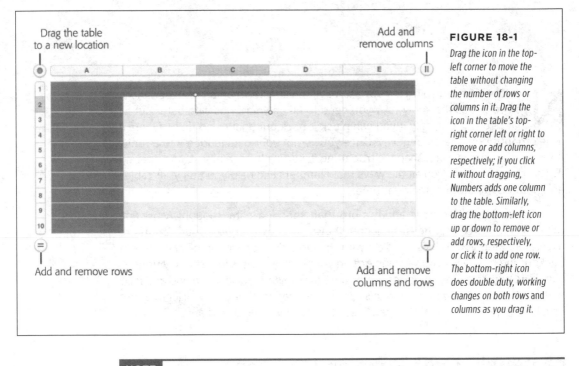

Drag the table
to a new location

Add and
remove columns

Add and remove rows

Add and remove
columns and rows

FIGURE 18-1

Drag the icon in the top-left corner to move the table without changing the number of rows or columns in it. Drag the icon in the table's top-right corner left or right to remove or add columns, respectively; if you click it without dragging, Numbers adds one column to the table. Similarly, drag the bottom-left icon up or down to remove or add rows, respectively, or click it to add one row. The bottom-right icon does double duty, working changes on both rows and columns as you drag it.

NOTE Numbers won't let you add rows when you're filtering table content (see page 502). To start adding rows again, remove the filtering criteria or turn off filtering completely.

Numbers also adds new rows and columns as you edit your table, giving you new cells as you bump up against the table's boundaries by pressing Tab or Return.

■ DELETING ROWS OR COLUMNS THAT CONTAIN DATA

You can use the icons described above to remove only *empty* rows or columns. If you try to drag one of the icons through a row or column that contains data, Numbers throws on the brakes and will go no farther. That's a good policy, since it prevents you from carelessly chucking entire swaths of data with an ill-considered flick of the wrist.

To remove a row or column that contains data, you have to be more explicit about it. To flip off the safety, hold down the Option key while dragging the appropriate icon, and Numbers deletes rows or columns regardless of whether they contain content.

You can also delete rows or columns with menu commands. Select an empty cell (or a series of neighboring cells, at least one of which is empty) in the row(s) or column(s) you want to delete, and then choose Table→Delete Rows or Table→Delete Columns. Numbers throws out the offending rows or columns and cinches up the table around them. (You can also select entire rows or columns before choosing these commands, but it's not necessary; selecting a single cell within a row or column is enough to tell Numbers which one you want to delete.)

The Delete command is also available in the reference tab drop-down menu for each row and column (see Figure 18-2). These menus hold a handy collection of tools for working with rows and columns. When a single cell is selected, the menus offer the Delete Column or Delete Row command. When you select more than one cell in neighboring rows or columns, the options change to Delete Selected Columns or Delete Selected Rows.

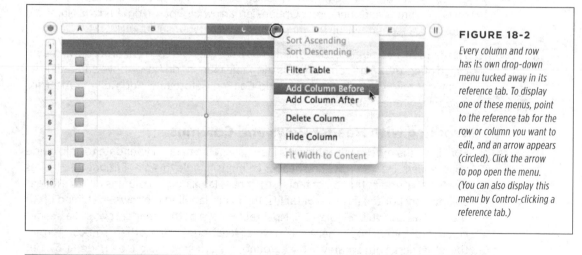

FIGURE 18-2

Every column and row has its own drop-down menu tucked away in its reference tab. To display one of these menus, point to the reference tab for the row or column you want to edit, and an arrow appears (circled). Click the arrow to pop open the menu. (You can also display this menu by Control-clicking a reference tab.)

NOTE Pressing the Delete key deletes only the data *inside* selected cells, not the cells themselves.

■ **INSERTING ROWS OR COLUMNS**

A table's icons let you add rows and columns at the edges of the table, but that doesn't help you when you want to insert rows or columns in the *middle* of the table. You'll find yourself doing that frequently, especially for rows, so it's a good idea to get familiar with the Option–arrow key shortcuts for inserting new rows and columns:

- Add a row above the selected cell by pressing **Option–up arrow** or by choosing Table→Add Row Above.

- Add a row below the selected cell by pressing **Option–down arrow** or by choosing Table→Add Row Below.

- Add a column to the left of the selected cell by pressing **Option–left arrow** or by choosing Table→Add Column Before.

- Add a column to the right of the selected cell by pressing **Option–right arrow** or by choosing Table→Add Column After.

> **TIP** You can also access these commands by Control-clicking a cell.

When you select cells in *multiple* rows or columns, these commands add the same number of rows or columns as your selection. For example, if you want to add three rows to your table, select cells in three neighboring rows, and then press Option–up arrow or choose Table→Add Rows Above; Numbers adds three rows above your current selection. The same works for columns: When you have cells selected in several columns and then press Option–left arrow or Option–right arrow, Numbers adds the same number of columns before or after your selection.

You can also add multiple rows or columns from the reference tab drop-down menu, which offers the same commands as the Table menu: Add Row Above and Add Row Below for *row* reference tabs, and Add Column Before and Add Column After for *column* reference tabs.

Working with Header Rows and Columns

For all but the most basic tables, it's just plain polite to label your data to help guide your readers. Header rows and header columns handle this bit of etiquette. Header rows always ride at the top of tables, their cells labeling the columns below. Header columns anchor the left side of tables, their cells labeling the rows stretching off to the right, as shown in Figure 18-3. Most tables have both a header row and a header column, but you should generally have at least one or the other. You can format these headers with whatever background or border you like (see page 506), but Numbers typically starts you out by shading them to stand out from the other rows and columns, which are known as the *table body*.

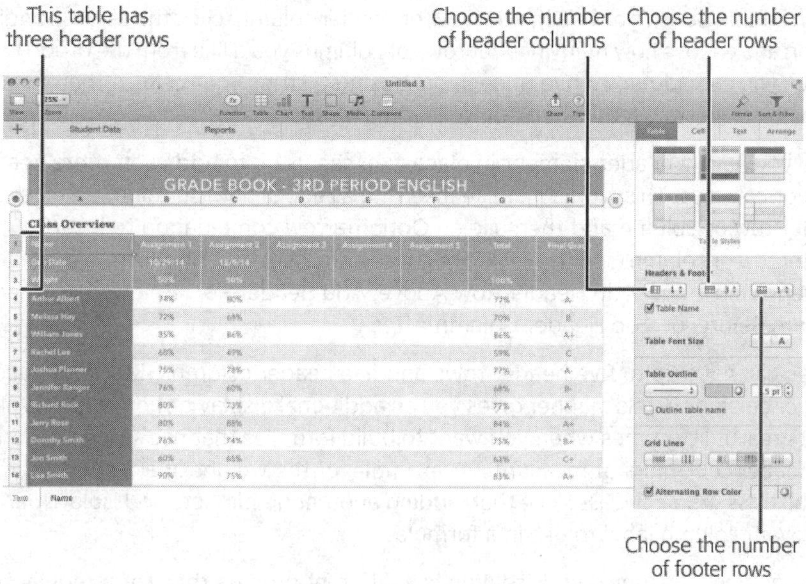

This table has
three header rows

Choose the number
of header columns

Choose the number
of header rows

FIGURE 18-3

This grade book table has three header rows and a single header column that lists student names. Choose how many header rows and columns to display (or remove them entirely) by opening the Format panel's Table tab and using the two header drop-down menus labeled here. (You can add up to five header rows or columns.) This tab is also where you control the number of footer rows, which you'll learn about in the next section.

Choose the number
of footer rows

NOTE When a table contains both header rows and header columns, they have some shared real estate where their cells intersect in the top left of the table. Such cells are considered to be part of the header *row*. Header columns appear below any header rows.

Header rows and columns not only help readers understand your data—they help Numbers figure it out, too. By labeling your data with these header elements, you give Numbers a *name* for your rows and columns, and the program uses these names in a variety of ways.

When you learn about formulas in the next chapter, you'll see that Numbers uses these row and column names to refer to specific cells when it works its mathematical magic. Header cells also provide shortcuts for applying a quick formula to an entire row or column. There's more on all this in Chapter 19.

Finally, header rows and columns are also persistent: When a table spans more than one page, Numbers repeats its header rows and columns on each of those pages when you print the sheet. This helps you and your readers keep your bearings as you flip from page to page. You can preview this effect (or turn it off) in Print Preview (page 450).

Because of the special status of header rows and columns, you add them to tables in a different way than you add normal rows and columns. The Format pane's Table tab provides buttons that let you add and remove a table's header elements (they're in the aptly named Headers & Footer section, and they're labeled in Figure 18-3). When a table doesn't have a header row or header column, click the corresponding button and choose how many header rows or columns you'd like from the drop-down menu (you can add up to five of each); choosing 0 strips your cells of their header or column row status, but their contents remain.

Once you have a header element in place, you can use it to add even *more* header rows or columns. This works just like inserting a regular row or column: Select the header row or column and then use an Option-arrow combination to insert a new header row or column (see page 441); or choose one of these options from a header's reference tab menu: Add Header Row Above, Add Header Row Below, Add Header Column Before, or Add Header Column After.

Tables can have up to five header rows and five header columns. Stacking header rows or columns in this manner gives you an additional display option, which is nice, but its real utility comes when you want to build formulas that use some portion of the header cell—units of measure, for example, or the weight of a test score in an overall class grade. In cases like that, adding another header lets you isolate part of the row or column label to use in a formula.

While *adding* a header row or column is a different process than for a regular row or column, you *delete* them the same way: Choose Delete Row or Delete Column from the header's reference tab drop-down menu. You can also select a cell in the column/row, and choose Table→Delete Row or Table→Delete Column.

NOTE Be careful when you delete header rows or columns. Although you can always add header elements back to the table, any content that was in the original header row or column won't come back with it. Deleting a header element sends its contents to the data boneyard; if this isn't what you had in mind, you can turn a header element back into ordinary cells without deleting any of its contents (see page 496).

■ FREEZING HEADER ROWS AND COLUMNS

As soon as you start working with more than a casual sprinkling of data, it doesn't take long before your tables extend well beyond the height or width of a single screen. As usual, you can use Numbers' scroll bars to shuttle around your sheet. But since the header row and header column are tied firmly to the top and left edges of the table, scrolling away from the first row or column means that your data labels slip out of view, too. And, right on cue, you immediately forget what the heck all those columns of numbers represent.

Happily, Numbers can put that forgetful scenario on ice by *freezing* your header rows and columns. With this cool feature turned on for a table, when you scroll its header row or column off the screen, Numbers freezes the header element in its tracks, stopping it at the edge of the visible sheet canvas to float above the rest of the table below. This keeps your data labels in view even when the "real" header is hundreds of rows offscreen. Figure 18-4 shows a frozen header row.

To make your life easier, most of Numbers' built-in templates come with their header rows and columns already frozen. To see whether your document has frozen header rows and columns, open the Table menu; if you see checkmarks next to the Freeze Header Rows and Freeze Header Columns entries, then you're all set. But if either one of these settings lacks a checkmark, simply select it to turn it on and freeze your header row(s) or column(s). These options are also available in the Format panel's Table tab. Click the appropriate button in the Headers & Footer section, and then select the Freeze option at the very bottom of the drop-down menu, as shown in Figure 18-4.

NOTE You can't freeze footer rows (which are the subject of the next section).

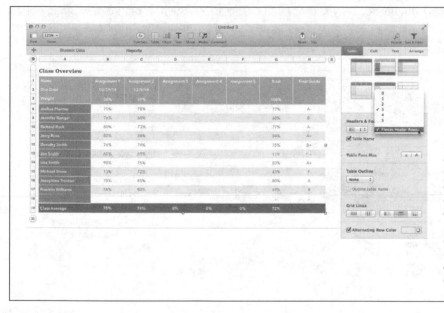

FIGURE 18-4

With the Freeze Header Row option turned on, the first row of this table floats above the other rows, keeping the column labels in view. (The effect is subtle, but notice that the table's first few rows are numbered 1, 2, 3, 8. That's because rows 1–3 are frozen header rows, and rows 4–7—which are regular rows—aren't visible because someone has scrolled down in the table.) The table's top-left and top-right icons also come along for the ride.

Adding Footer Rows

As you might guess, the footer row is the header row's opposite, staking out the bottom row of the table. Although footer rows don't quite have the same heady importance as their column-labeling counterparts, they're often deployed to display column sums or other calculations involving the cells above. In fact, as you'll learn in the next chapter, that role is where the footer row's one and only superpower comes in: It can "catch" quick formulas that you add to header cells, automatically calculating the rows above. See page 521 for the details.

Apart from that, adding a footer row to a table is simply a way to draw attention to the bottom row(s). You can add up to five footer rows to a table, and Numbers typically shades them to set them apart from the body rows. Add one or more footer rows by choosing a number from the Table tab's drop-down menu labeled back in Figure 18-3. Alternatively, choose Table→Footer Rows.

If you choose zero from either of these menus, you strip the footer row of its special status, turning it into an ordinary row (its data remains, though). To actually delete a footer row along with all of its data, open its reference tab drop-down menu and choose Delete Row, or select the row and then choose Table→Delete Row.

Resizing Rows and Columns

You adjust the size of rows and columns by dragging the boundaries between reference tabs. When you point the cursor between two reference tabs, it turns into a double-headed arrow, signaling that it's ready to push the boundary for you. To resize a row, drag the bottom border of its reference tab; to resize a column, drag its tab's right border. As you drag, Numbers displays the new height or width in points (or whatever unit you've selected in the Ruler tab of the Numbers→Preferences window). Figure 18-5 shows an example.

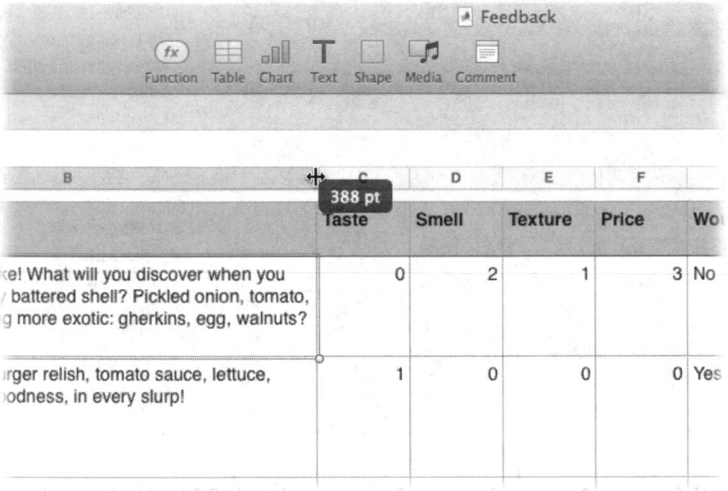

FIGURE 18-5

Change the width of a column by dragging the right border of its reference tab left or right. Here, the double-arrow cursor indicates that Numbers is ready and raring to resize; dragging left makes the column narrower, and dragging right makes it wider. All the while, a black tooltip shows the new width of the column (here that's 388 points).

■ MAKING ROWS OR COLUMNS THE SAME SIZE

You can also use the same method to resize *several* rows or columns at once: Select all the rows or columns you'd like to squeeze or stretch by Shift-clicking or ⌘-clicking their reference tabs. Then resize *one* of the selected rows or columns (drag the right border of a column's reference tab, or the bottom border of a row's reference tab) and all the selected rows and columns change size simultaneously.

If you're not a precision mouse jockey but still want to fix the size of rows or columns to a very precise height or width, the Format panel's Table tab lets you specify an exact size. Select the rows or columns you want to adjust, click the Table tab's Row & Column Size heading to expand that section, and then use the Row and Column fields to adjust the size.

All the methods mentioned so far change the overall size of the table, too: Making rows and columns larger makes your table swell; making them smaller makes your table shrink. When you want to resize rows or columns *without* changing the table's overall size, Numbers offers two commands that spread out row and column sizes evenly. Choose Table→Distribute Rows Evenly or Table→Distribute Columns Evenly, and Numbers makes all the selected rows or columns the same size within the available space, without changing the size of the table. If you apply these egalitarian commands when you have an entire table selected at the object level (page 455), Numbers makes *all* the rows or columns in the table the same size.

> **NOTE** The Distribute Evenly commands aren't grayed out when you have just one cell, row, or column selected, but in such situations, clicking these commands is pointless.

■ TAILORING ROW AND COLUMN SIZE TO YOUR CONTENT

When you want to tighten rows or columns as much as possible while still showing all your content, Numbers can resize them automatically to fit the exact size of your content. This is handy for revealing clipped content (page 324) or eliminating unused white space. The exact technique for doing this depends on whether you're resizing columns or rows.

To resize a column to fit its content, put your cursor over the column's reference tab, click the arrow that appears, and then select "Fit Width to Content." You can resize multiple columns at a time by Shift-clicking their reference tabs and then selecting "Fit Width to Content" from any of the selected reference tabs' drop-down menus. You can also select any cell within a column (or cells spanning multiple columns), and then choose Table→"Resize Column(s) to Fit Content." Finally, you can go to the Format panel's Table tab, click the Row & Column Size heading to expand that section, and then click the Fit button next to the Column field.

Whichever route you opt for, Numbers adjusts the width of the selected column to precisely fit its widest content. This is a one-time thing; if you edit your data, Numbers won't continue to update the column's width to fit your content, at least not until you again choose Table→"Resize Column to Fit Content" (or use one of the other options).

Automatic resizing works differently for rows. Unless you set rows to be a specific height, Numbers always adjusts row height to fit your content. In other words, rows grow as you add new lines (at least, they do when text wrapping is on—see page 463) or make the font size larger, and they shrink when your content shrinks. They're always a flexible height until you explicitly drag them to a new size or set their height in the Table tab's Row & Column Size section. After you do that, your rows cease to be flexible and, as a result, their fixed height can clip cell contents or leave unused white space. To make the height of selected rows flexible again, do one of the following:

- Open the reference tab drop-down menu for the row in question, and then select "Fit Height to Content." You can apply this setting to multiple rows at a time by Shift-clicking their reference tabs to select them all and then choosing this command from one of their reference tabs' drop-down menus.

- Choose Table→"Resize Row to Fit Content." Apply this setting to multiple rows simultaneously by first selecting cells that span multiple rows.

- Open the Format panel's Table tab, click the Row & Column Size heading to expand that section, and then click the Fit button next to the Row field.

NOTE For pointers on handling content that's too big for a cell, head back to page 462.

Moving Rows and Columns

To move a row or column to a new location, simply drag its reference tab. The tricky part is that you have to click the reference tab once to select it *before* you start dragging. If you drag an unselected reference tab, you'll select neighboring rows and columns instead of moving the row or column you targeted. So click the reference tab, release the mouse button, and *then* click again and drag. As you drag, Numbers displays a blue guideline to show you where the row or column will land. When it's in the right spot, release the mouse button, and Numbers inserts the row or column in its new home, closing up its old position. This trick also works for moving several neighboring rows or columns, as shown in Figure 18-6.

NOTE You can't move non-neighboring rows or columns simultaneously. If you Shift-click the reference tabs of rows or columns that aren't right next to each other, Numbers selects those rows or columns *and* all the ones in between.

Numbers doesn't limit you to moving rows and column only within the same table. You can drag them by their reference tabs to other tables, too. Or drop them into a blank location on the canvas to create a whole new table.

NOTE You can't move header rows, header columns, or footer rows. Their special status means that they're always anchored in place. You can, however, move or copy their contents outside of the headers and footers. See page 485 for a roundup of techniques for moving and copying cells.

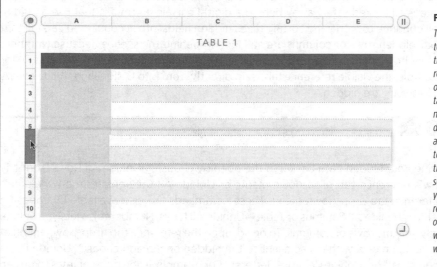

FIGURE 18-6

To move one or more rows to a new spot, first select the rows by clicking their reference tabs. (Shift-click or Shift-drag the reference tabs to select multiple neighboring rows.) Then drag the reference tab of a selected row up or down to move it to a new location, as shown here with a selection of two rows. As you drag, the heavy blue rectangle on the left edge of the table shows you where the rows will land when you drop them.

To *copy* the column or row instead of moving it, hold down the Option key while you drag, or use the Clipboard:

1. **Select the row or column by clicking its reference tab.**

   You can select multiple rows or columns by Shift-clicking or Shift-dragging their reference tabs.

2. **Choose Edit→Copy or press ⌘-C.**

3. **Select the row or column immediately *after* the spot where you want to insert the copied row or column.**

4. **Choose Insert→Copied Rows or Insert→Copied Columns, and Numbers inserts the row or column into its new location.**

   In contrast to Edit→Paste, these Insert menu commands wedge a new column or row into the table before the selected cells; the Paste command *replaces* the selected cells instead.

Hiding Rows and Columns

Information can enlighten, but *too* much info can overwhelm or make it difficult to focus. When you're working with a sprawling set of data, Numbers lets you temporarily sweep parts of it away so that you can work with just the relevant info for the task at hand. You do this by *hiding* rows or columns. This trick is invaluable when, for example, you have a wide table with lots of columns, but you care about only a few of them right now and want them all to fit on your screen without scrolling.

To hide a row or column, open its reference tab drop-down menu and choose Hide Row or Hide Column. When you have cells selected in multiple rows or columns, the command changes to Hide Selected Rows or Hide Selected Columns, which makes all those rows or columns vanish. This disappearing trick is only an act; the data is all tucked safely away behind a digital curtain. Formulas that use a hidden cell continue to work, and sorting takes hidden fields into account. You can tell that your hidden rows or columns are still lurking behind the scenes because Numbers safely holds their reference tabs in reserve: When you hide columns C and D, for example, the visible reference tabs skip directly from B to E, signaling that the rows in between are hidden.

NOTE You can't hide rows or columns that contain merged cells.

Bring your hidden data back into the open by choosing Unhide All Rows from any row's reference tab drop-down menu, or Unhide All Columns from any column's reference tab drop-down menu. These commands are also available by choosing Table→Unhide All Columns or Table→Unhide All Rows. Numbers also lets you unhide only specific rows or columns. To do so, open the reference tab drop-down menu of the column or row that's adjacent to the hidden one(s) and choose "Unhide Rows [numbers]" or "Unhide Columns [letters]." For example, if you hide column B, you can restore it by opening the reference tab drop-down menu for either column A or C.

NOTE If you copy a Numbers spreadsheet into Pages or Keynote, any hidden rows or columns don't make the trip. So be sure to unhide all data that you want to include *before* sending the table on its way.

■ Sorting and Filtering Data

No matter how tangled, disordered, or generally cluttered your spreadsheet data might be, Numbers can give it an instant makeover. On your command, Numbers sweeps in to *sort* your table's rows into any order you like, *filtering* out irrelevant data along the way.

This luxury means that you don't have to give any particular thought to the specific order of your data as you enter it. Just get your info into the table willy-nilly and then let Numbers sift and sort it for you. Not only is Numbers an adept organizer, but it's also a great reorganizer. You're not stuck with any single view of your data; you can sort it this way and then that way, or filter out certain data and then bring it back to focus on a new area. This section gives you a rundown of all your options.

Sorting Rows

Here are a few things to know about how Numbers sorts data: In Numbers' sorting scheme, numbers come before letters. So when you sort in ascending order, numbers come before text; the reverse is true when you sort in descending order. Also, if you're sorting dates or times, Numbers pays attention only to their *chronological* order. In other words, dates don't get sorted alphabetically by month name; instead, January is always before February if you sort in ascending order. Finally, empty cells always wind up at the bottom of the sort order, no matter whether you're sorting in ascending or descending order.

> **NOTE** Numbers doesn't include header and footer rows when it sorts a table. These special rows always stay glued to the top and bottom of the table.

You can pick a column and use it to sort the table's rows in ascending order (A, B, C or 1, 2, 3) or descending order (Z, Y, X or 3, 2, 1) according to the values in that column. To sort your data, open the reference tab drop-down menu for the column in question, and then choose Sort Ascending or Sort Descending. Numbers obeys by sorting *all* the rows in your spreadsheet according to the data in the column you chose.

You can sort *multiple* columns in one fell swoop by Shift-clicking their reference tabs, and then opening one of the selected reference tab's drop-down menus and choosing Sort Ascending or Sort Descending.

You can also create *sorting rules*, which are a little more time consuming, but are useful if you want to sort an entire table in one go, or if you have a multi-stage plan for sorting your table. To create a sorting rule for a table:

1. **Select the cell(s) you want to sort.**

   You can apply a sorting rule to an entire table or just to certain rows. If you want to sort the entire table, it doesn't matter what part of the table you select—just select any cell, or even select the table at the object level. To sort specific rows, select at least one cell in each row.

2. **Click the Sort & Filter button in the toolbar, and then make sure the Sort & Filter panel's Sort tab is open.**

3. **In the Sort tab's unlabeled drop-down menu, tell Numbers whether you want to sort the entire table or just selected rows.**

4. **Click "Add a Column," and then choose a column to sort by.**

   Numbers creates a new rule in the Sort & Filter panel.

5. **Open the rule's Ascending/Descending drop-down menu, and choose whether your rule should sort the rows in ascending order or descending order.**

6. **If necessary, add more sorting rules.**

   Numbers applies your sorting rules in the order they're listed in the Sort tab. To move a rule higher or lower in the running order, put your cursor over the rule until a lined icon appears in its upper-left corner, and then grab this icon and drag it to a new position. To delete a rule, place your cursor over it and then click the trash can icon that appears in the rule's upper-right corner.

7. **When you're ready to sort your data, click the Sort Now button.**

Filtering Rows

You already know that you can manually hide a table's columns and rows by making a selection and telling Numbers to tuck them out of view (page 499). The Filter panel puts a new spin on this by letting you create *filtering rules*. These rules tell Numbers which rows it should show, and which rows it shouldn't, based on the values they contain (or don't contain). For example, you could tell Numbers to display only rows that contain values higher than 5, or values that are less than the average. This is handy when you're dealing with large tables and want to see only a specific set of data, such as students who are achieving passing marks, or incomplete items on your to-do list.

When you want to strip away unwanted noise in a table, the Filter panel has you covered: Click the toolbar's Sort & Filter button (circled in Figure 18-7) and click the Filter tab (or choose Table→Sort & Filter Options). Then, click the "Add a Filter" button and choose the column you want to filter, as shown in Figure 18-7.

NOTE Although you apply filtering to columns, it's actually the rows that end up disappearing.

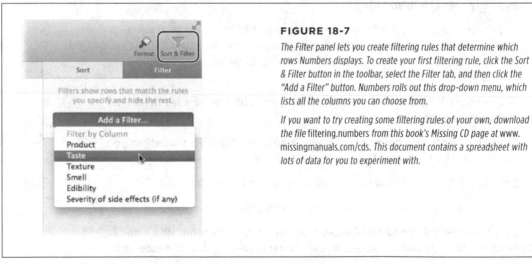

FIGURE 18-7

The Filter panel lets you create filtering rules that determine which rows Numbers displays. To create your first filtering rule, click the Sort & Filter button in the toolbar, select the Filter tab, and then click the "Add a Filter" button. Numbers rolls out this drop-down menu, which lists all the columns you can choose from.

If you want to try creating some filtering rules of your own, download the file filtering.numbers *from this book's Missing CD page at www. missingmanuals.com/cds. This document contains a spreadsheet with lots of data for you to experiment with.*

When you select the column to filter, Numbers opens the "Choose a Filtering Rule" menu, as shown in Figure 18-8. Your options are divided into five categories:

- **Numbers.** Filters in this category are based on whether the row is equal to a certain value, is above average, is in the top 10%, and other numerical goodness.

- **Text.** Filter rows based on the text they contain, or don't contain. For example, you can tell Numbers to display a cell only if its content starts or ends with a certain word or letter, contains a certain word, or doesn't contain a certain word.

- **Dates.** These filters let you do things like display a row only if its value equates to yesterday, today, or tomorrow; if its data occurs within the next month; and so on.

- **Durations.** For example, display the row only if its duration value is greater or less than a certain value, or falls into (or outside) a set time frame.

- **Blank.** This category contains two settings: Show only cells that are blank, and show only cells that aren't blank.

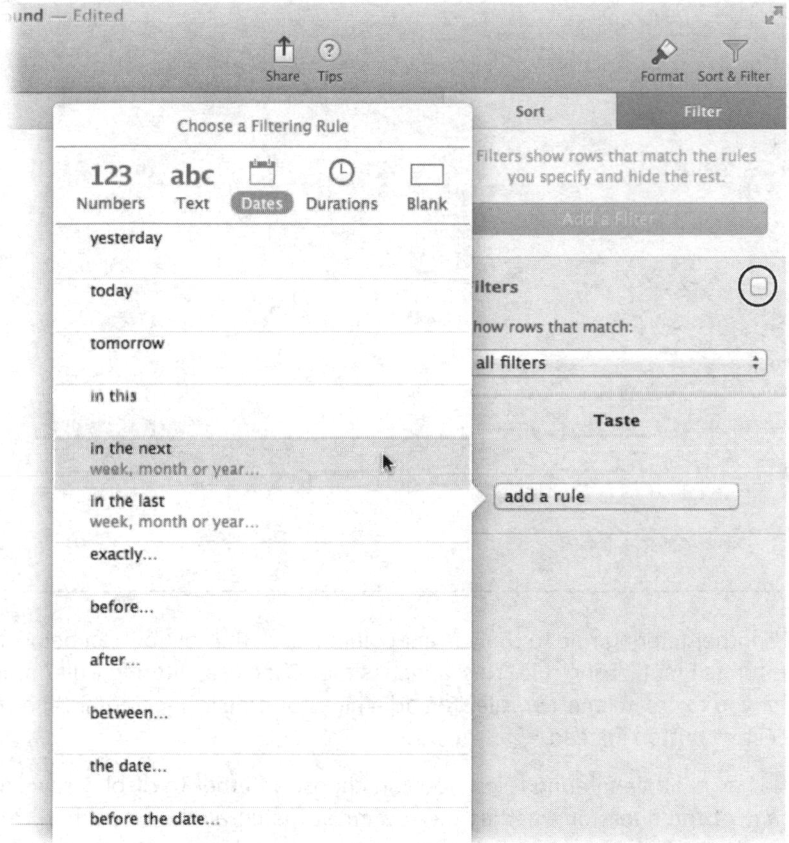

FIGURE 18-8

The "Choose a Filtering Rule" menu is divided into five categories. Click any of the buttons along the top of this menu to view the rules that fall within that category. Here you can see the rules in the Dates category. Click any rule to add it to the Filters panel, ready for you to customize and use. You can remove a rule by deleting it, or you can suspend all the rules for the selected table by turning off the Filters checkbox (circled).

Select your category and browse the available rules. When you see one you want to use, click it to add it to the Filter panel. Depending on the rule you select, you'll see several options for customizing it. For example, if you select the "equal to" rule, you can enter the number the row must correspond to. If you select the "must not contain" button, you'll see a field where you can type the text the row must *not* contain. Figure 18-9 shows some examples of customized filtering rules.

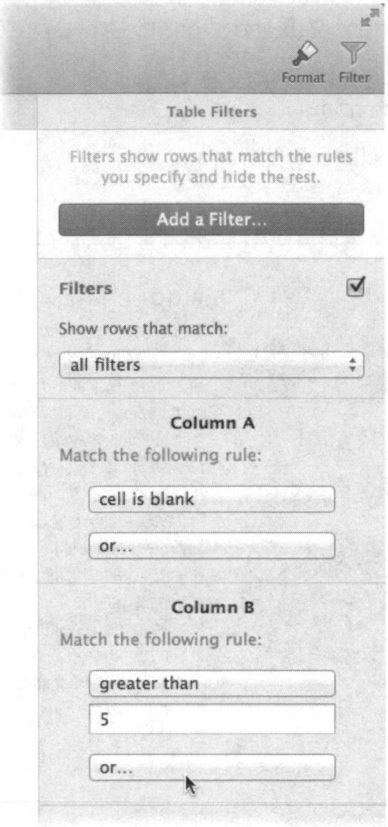

FIGURE 18-9

Numbers has a rule for every occasion. This example shows two different rules: one that applies to column A and one that applies to column B. A row will be displayed only if it has no value in column A and a value higher than 5 in column B.

To add another rule for column B, click the "or" button where the cursor is positioned in this screenshot. To add a rule for a different column, click the "Add a Filter" button instead.

To add another filtering rule to the current column, click the "or" button below the settings for its first filtering rule. This launches the "Choose a Filtering Rule" menu, ready for you to create another rule. To add a filter to some other column, click the "Add a Filter" button instead.

If a table has multiple filtering rules, you can choose whether to display rows that match *any* of the filters or whether the row must match *all* the filters before it's displayed. In the Filters section of the Filters panel, click the drop-down menu and choose "all filters" or "any filter."

As soon as you hit the Return key on your keyboard or click anywhere outside of the Filters panel, Numbers applies your rule. Check to see whether the table now shows the information you want to see. If not, tweak your filtering rules and then press Return or click outside the Filters panel, and Numbers automatically updates the table to reflect your changes.

Unlike sorting, which reorders the table only when you tell it to, filtering updates the table anytime you make any changes to your data. So if you edit a value so that a row no longer matches the filter rules, Numbers whisks the row out of sight. Alas, the always-on nature of filtering rules means that Numbers doesn't let you add any new rows to the table when filters are turned on. To suspend filtering rules, open the Filter panel and turn off the Filters checkbox. To permanently delete a filtering rule, move your cursor over the rule's name in the Filter panel, and then click the trash-can icon when it appears. To delete all the filtering rules for a given column, in the Filter panel, move your cursor over the name of the column and then click the trash-can icon that appears next to it.

You can also filter tables quickly based on the particular values within a column. To see these quick filtering options, open the column's reference tab drop-down menu, select Filter Table, and then click any of the options that appear in this submenu. For example, if the column lists the star ratings of your product, you can choose to display only rows that contain the value 5 stars (or 4, or 3, and so on). Or if you have a spreadsheet of student grades, you can display only rows that contain an A grade.

◼ Find & Replace

Even after you've sorted and filtered your spreadsheet into a set of perfectly groomed and organized tables, it's not always easy to put your hands on the exact piece of data you're looking for. As you plump your data into a giant haystack, the individual needles get harder and harder to find. Happily, Numbers' Find feature makes quick work of hunting down wayward data, and the Find & Replace feature lets you change these results to transform found words and phrases into something else.

If you want to pinpoint (and maybe even replace) a particular piece of text or data, press ⌘-F or click the View button in the toolbar, and then select Show Find & Replace. Either way, Numbers reveals the Find & Replace window. Despite its name, you don't *have* to replace text that you find with this window—you can use it simply to *find* text. Most of the time, though, you'll probably use the Find & Replace window to put both parts of its name to use, morphing matching text into a new word or phrase. Figure 18-10 shows you how to fill out the Find & Replace window's fields.

> **NOTE** When you first open the Find & Replace window, you may see only one text field, not two as shown in Figure 18-10. The number of fields depends on whether you're using just the window's find capability, or both its find *and* replace features. To switch between the two, click the gear icon (circled in Figure 18-10) and choose an option from the drop-down menu.

FIGURE 18-10

To find text in your spreadsheet, enter the word or phrase you're looking for into the Find field (the upper one). If you want to find and replace data, type the replacement text in the Replace field (the lower one), and then click the appropriate button at the bottom of the window. Click the gear icon to refine your search. (If the Replace field isn't visible, click the gear icon and choose Find & Replace).

NOTE Find & Replace searches only within the current sheet. To search a different sheet, click its name in the Sheet bar.

If you're sure that you want to replace all instances of the Find text with the Replace text, click Replace All, and Numbers rockets through your spreadsheet, making the changes. To review individual instances of the search text before replacing them, click the right-facing arrow button, and Numbers takes you to the first match. (If you can't see the match, it could be hidden behind the Find & Replace window; that's why it's a good idea to move the window out of the way when you're running a search.) If you don't want to replace the text, click the right-arrow button again to hop to the next match. Otherwise, click Replace or, even better, click Replace & Find to make the replacement and then jump to the next match.

■ Make It Pretty: Borders and Backgrounds

Like other objects in iWork, you can add borders, fills, and other effects to tables to make them colorful or subdued, flashy or conservative. More than just pizzazz, well-placed background fills and borderlines also make tables more readable, guiding the readers' eyes through the data and demarcating header rows and columns.

When you apply color fills or borders to other types of objects, Numbers colors or adds lines around the *entire* object. You can do that with tables, too, but you can also add these styles to individual rows, cells, or columns. In this respect, every cell acts like a separate object that you can style however you want. But before you start styling each and every one of your cells individually, it's a good idea to start at the object level, applying a uniform background and border format to the entire table. This gives your table a design foundation and establishes consistency. From there, you can make formatting changes to individual rows, columns, and cells. Whatever level of the table you're working with, this section explores how to fine-tune its lines and colors.

> **TIP** Once you have the text, color, and borders of a table or cell formatted just the way you want, you can use it as a model for others. Select the table or cell, and then choose Format→Copy Style. Then select one or more other cells or tables, choose Format→Paste Style, and Numbers applies the formatting.

Styling Outlines and Gridlines

Every table has two types of borders that you can use. The first is the table's *outline*, which is the border that goes around the four sides of the table's exterior. The second are the smaller *gridlines* that divide up the table body, the header rows and columns, and the footer rows.

To change the appearance of a table's outline, open the Format panel's Table tab. The Table Outline section has everything you need to customize the outline (see Figure 18-11):

- **Line style.** Use this drop-down menu to choose a line style. If you've already styled your outline and realize that you've made some questionable style choices, you can undo all your table outline formatting by selecting Default Table Style from this menu. To remove the outline completely, choose None.

- **Color.** Give the border a splash of color, either by clicking the color well and choosing one of the default colors or by clicking the color wheel icon to launch the Color Picker (page 44).

- **Line thickness.** Use this field to adjust the thickness of the outline.

You can add or remove gridlines from the table body, from header rows and columns, and from footer rows using the five buttons in the Table tab's Grid Lines section (see Figure 18-11). From left to right, click these buttons to:

- Show or hide horizontal gridlines in body columns.

- Show or hide vertical gridlines in body rows.

- Show or hide horizontal gridlines in header columns.

- Show or hide vertical gridlines in header rows.

- Show or hide vertical gridlines in footer rows.

Figure 18-12 shows various gridline configurations.

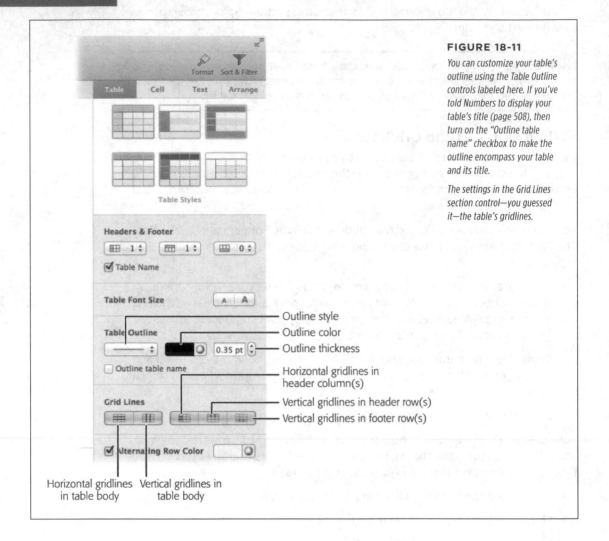

FIGURE 18-11

You can customize your table's outline using the Table Outline controls labeled here. If you've told Numbers to display your table's title (page 508), then turn on the "Outline table name" checkbox to make the outline encompass your table and its title.

The settings in the Grid Lines section control—you guessed it—the table's gridlines.

Background Colors and Images

Add a background fill to an entire table, or to individual rows, columns, or cells to set them apart from the rest of the table (think header and footer rows) or to create a visual rhythm with alternating rows. Just like any other object in iWork, tables and their elements can accept solid colors, gradients, or images as their backgrounds.

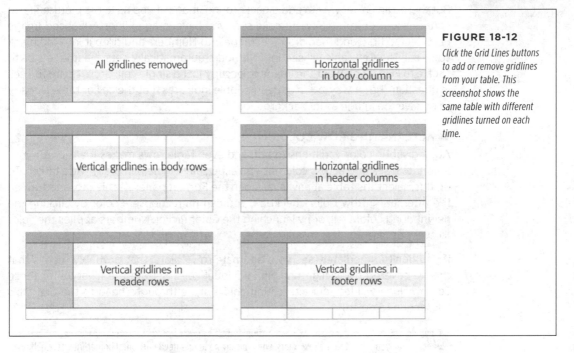

FIGURE 18-12

Click the Grid Lines buttons to add or remove gridlines from your table. This screenshot shows the same table with different gridlines turned on each time.

To choose a background style for a *whole table*, select the table at the object level (page 209), open the Format panel's Cell tab, and then use the settings in the Fill section. For all your filling possibilities, see page 192.

To add a background to *one or more cells*, select them, and then head to the Format panel's Cell tab and adjust the settings in the Fill section. You can also apply background colors to selected cells using drag and drop:

1. **Select the cells you want to color (you can skip this step if you want to color just a single cell).**

2. **Choose View→Show Colors to display the Color Picker (page 44).**

3. **Select a color, adjust its opacity, and drag it from the Color Picker's color well into the selected cells.**

   As you drag, Numbers outlines the table cell(s) beneath your cursor in blue to indicate that you can drop the color anywhere to recolor a cell.

■ ADDING IMAGES TO TABLE CELLS

The only way Numbers lets you add an image to a table cell is as a background image. You can do this by opening the Format panel's Cell tab and clicking the Fill heading to expand that section. In the section's first drop-down menu, select

Image Fill or Advanced Image Fill. You can then click the Choose button and pluck an image from your hard drive.

But there's an easier way to add a background image: If you have the picture file on your desktop or in the Finder, make sure you have Image Fill or Advanced Image Fill selected first, and then drag the image into Numbers and drop it into the blank square in the Cell tab's Fill section. Numbers automatically sets the image size to "Scale to Fit." If you want the image to occupy just a single cell, drop it onto the cell in question. Either way, a + in a green bubble indicates that the cell or table is ready to receive the image as its background.

■ ALTERNATING ROW COLORS

Adding subtle color variations to odd and even table rows makes it easier for your reader to track info across columns—an especially big help in really wide tables. To do this, select the table at any level, open the Format panel's Table tab, and turn on the Alternating Row Color checkbox. You can then choose a color by clicking the neighboring color well, or by launching the Color Picker. Numbers applies the color to every other row of your table.

If you don't immediately see your alternate row colors, that probably means that they're covered by backgrounds in individual cells. Setting the fill style for those cells to None will let your alternating colors shine through (head to the Cell tab's Fill section to do so).

> **TIP** When you add alternate row colors, you typically no longer need horizontal borderlines between rows; having both only adds visual noise. Turn off horizontal borders using the Grid Lines buttons in the Table tab (see page 507 for details).

■ Conditional Formatting

Cell formatting isn't only about aesthetics; it can also be part of a data surveillance system. Numbers lets you add tripwires to cells to trigger formatting changes when the cell's value meets certain conditions. In a budget spreadsheet, for example, you could make the cell with your bank balance turn bright red when your funds get dangerously low (an event that might make *you* turn a sickly green). Or you could highlight to-do items whose due dates are closing in, or revenue figures for sales reps who've met their monthly quotas.

To apply conditional formatting, you select one or more cells and then define rules to trigger new formatting. Each rule specifies the visual effect to associate with cells when they meet the rule's conditions. You might make your checking account balance turn amber when it dips under $250 and bright red with bold letters when it goes under $50, for example. When the cell doesn't meet any of the conditions you add, nothing happens, and the cell simply displays as it normally would. Here's how to set it up:

1. **Select one or more cells.**

2. **In the Format panel, click the Cell tab, and then click the Conditional Highlighting button.**

   Numbers opens the Conditional Highlighting panel.

3. **To create a new rule, click the "Add a Rule" button.**

   Numbers displays the "Choose a Highlighting Rule" menu, which is divided into five categories: Numbers, Text, Dates, Durations, and Blank. The categories and rules are exactly the same as Numbers' filtering rules (see page 502).

4. **Explore the various categories and rules, and when you find one that fits the bill, click it.**

5. **If the rule you selected needs to know what value should trigger the new cell formatting, enter that value in the Conditional Highlighting panel.**

   You can also use the value of another table cell as a test value for the rule; in that case, Numbers monitors the values of both cells and triggers the conditional formatting when the condition is satisfied. To choose another table cell, in the Conditional Highlighting panel, click the blue oval on the right side of the value field; the cell reference field appears. Click the table cell whose value you'd like to use, or type a cell reference (the cell's coordinates—C3, D5, G9, and so on), and then press Return.

6. **Choose how you want the cells formatted by clicking the last drop-down menu in the Conditional Highlighting panel and then selecting one of the available styles.**

   If none of these styles suits you, create your own style by selecting Custom Style from this drop-down menu. Then use the familiar text-formatting controls that appear in the Conditional Highlighting panel to create the formatting you're after.

7. **Once you've built your rule and chosen your formatting, click Done to save it.**

   To add additional rules, click the "Add a Rule" button. Rinse and repeat.

> **NOTE** When you apply more than one conditional formatting rule to a cell, it's possible that the cell's value could meet more than one of these conditions. In that case, Numbers manages the overlap by applying only the formatting of the topmost matching rule in the Conditional Highlighting panel. To reorder rules in this panel, put your cursor over a rule and then click and drag the three-line icon that appears to the left of the rule's title.

To remove a rule for a selected cell, move your cursor over the rule in the Conditional Highlighting panel, and then click the trash-can icon when it appears. To remove all the rules for the selected cell, click the gear icon in the bottom left of this panel, and then select Clear All Rules.

You can review your conditional formatting rules for a cell at any time by selecting that cell, opening the Format panel's Cell tab, and then clicking the Show Highlighting Rules button.

Working with Table Styles

As you settle into a groove with your spreadsheets, you'll likely develop a set of consistent formatting habits, using the same color schemes, border styles, and font choices over and over again. That steady consistency is a good thing: It not only reinforces the professional brand or personal style of your documents, but it also gives regular readers of your documents (including you) subtle cues for understanding different parts of your data. It's a good practice, for example, to craft a visual system that distinguishes different kinds of tables. Tables that contain only summary calculations from other tables' data might use a gray background to indicate that they shouldn't be edited. Tables for income might use pale green headers, and tables for expenses pale red. You get the idea.

The last few pages have shown you how to do exactly that type of table formatting, styling the colors, borders, and text of individual tables and cells. But as you add more tables to your spreadsheet and more documents to your collection, you'll find that meticulously reformatting every single table to match your personal preferences quickly becomes a dreary chore.

Numbers anticipates this problem by giving you a handful of *table styles*, predefined collections of formatting rules that you can apply to any table with the click of a mouse. Table styles, in short, make quick work of formatting (and reformatting) the common visual characteristics of your tables, ensuring that your tables maintain a consistent look.

Every Numbers template comes with its own collection of table styles, and you can put them to use right away. Just select a table, open the Format panel's Table tab, and then click a style in the Table Styles pane at the top of the tab. Figure 18-13 shows an example.

Applying a table style changes the table's font, color, and border formatting *without* touching its content or data formats. Specifically, table styles dress up the following attributes:

- The table's background color or background image

- The background and text formatting of body cells

- The line style, color, and opacity of the table's inner borders and outside edges

- The background, text formatting, and borders of header rows, header columns, and footer rows

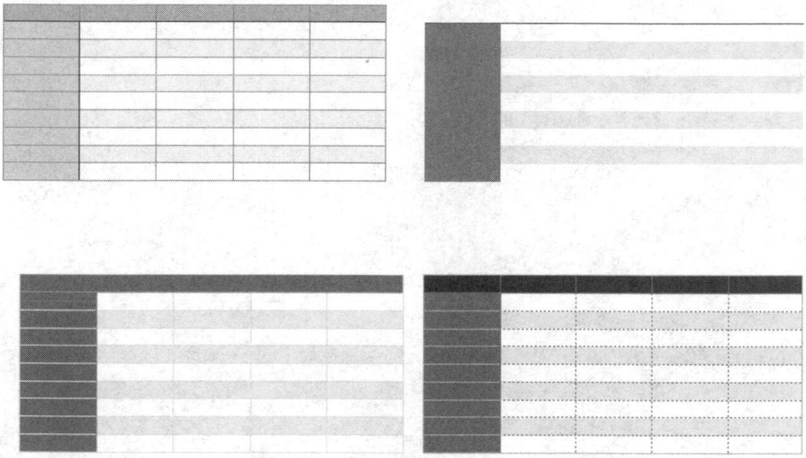

FIGURE 18-13

Click a predefined style in the Table Styles pane to change the look of the selected table. Here, four versions of the same table show various table styles.

Using Formulas

Just on its own, a table is good. It gets your data organized and sorted, all in one place. And now that you know how to build and style this baby, you can show it off with panache. But your table doesn't *do* much yet. Isn't a spreadsheet supposed to balance your checkbook, manage your company's budget, and find you true love? Although Numbers might not offer any love potions, it does have all kinds of other *formulas* to set your grid in motion.

In Numbers, formulas are responsible for the fundamental magic behind your spreadsheet, mixing and mashing your raw data into facts, figures, and bottom-line tallies. Formulas are equations that you add to cells to make them calculate: add up columns, find average grades, or figure the net present value of an investment. A formula's calculations can range anywhere from simple math (1+1) to complex constructions that gather values from other tables or apply sophisticated financial algorithms. This chapter starts you at the shallow end of that pool, getting you acquainted with Numbers' basic arithmetic before you move on to the gee-whiz functions magic in the next chapter.

Whether your table's math is simple or sophisticated, Numbers makes the *process* of adding and editing formulas easy, giving you lots of ways to build and insert these number-crunching gizmos into your table's cells. You can compose an elaborate formula by hand, sure, but you can also drag and drop common calculations into a table or add up a column with just a click. This chapter tours all these techniques.

Formula Basics

On the surface, a formula cell looks just like any other. It displays the results of its calculation, and this result looks just like the values typed directly into the table. But under the hood, the actual value of the cell is an equation—the formula—that tells Numbers how to generate that cell's value. To see the formula, select the cell, and Numbers displays its formula in the *Formula bar* at the bottom of the screen, as shown in Figure 19-1.

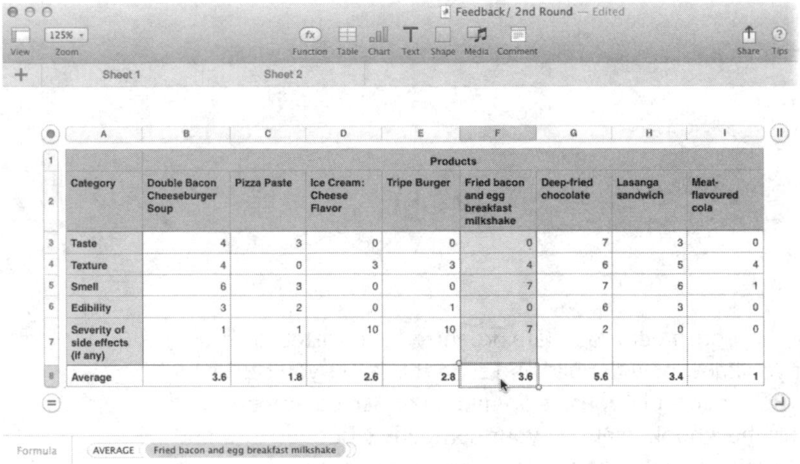

	Products							
Category	Double Bacon Cheeseburger Soup	Pizza Paste	Ice Cream: Cheese Flavor	Tripe Burger	Fried bacon and egg breakfast milkshake	Deep-fried chocolate	Lasanga sandwich	Meat-flavoured cola
Taste	4	3	0	0	0	7	3	0
Texture	4	0	3	3	4	6	5	4
Smell	6	3	0	0	7	7	6	1
Edibility	3	2	0	1	0	6	3	0
Severity of side effects (if any)	1	1	10	10	7	2	0	0
Average	3.6	1.8	2.6	2.8	3.6	5.6	3.4	1

FIGURE 19-1

Inspiration has struck again and you've cooked up a second round of potential snack foods for the lucky visitors of Crazyland Wonderpark. This table shows the scores each product achieved in the latest round of taste testing. The selected cell shows the average score for the Fried Bacon and Egg Milkshake. Although its displayed value looks mild-mannered enough, the Formula bar reveals its secret identity as a formula.

Don't worry just yet about the structure and vocabulary of the formula in Figure 19-1; you'll learn about the construction and building materials of formulas later in this chapter. For the moment, it's important to understand only a few basics about the way formulas work:

- **A formula lives in a single cell.** Even when a formula uses the values of other cells—to add up a column of numbers, for example—the formula always sits in the cell where the result is displayed.
- **Formulas always stay up to date.** Numbers constantly monitors your spreadsheet for changes. Whenever you edit your table, the program hustles to update the results of any affected formulas. Editing a number in a column of cells, for example, instantly changes the value of the cell showing that column's total.
- **You can use formulas with any data type.** Although you'll typically use formulas for numbers, they aren't strictly limited to math. Formulas can work their magic on dates, text, and durations, and they can even take direction from TRUE/FALSE Boolean values.

- **The Formula bar lets you view and edit a cell's formula.** As you'll soon see, Numbers offers many ways to add a formula to a cell. But once you've placed a formula, viewing the guts of said formula always works the same way: Select the cell to display the formula in the Formula bar. To edit your formula, double-click the formula to launch a little dialog box called the Formula Editor. You'll learn more about editing formulas starting on page 522.

Instant Calculations

Before you add a single formula to your table, Numbers is already spoilin' to do its math, running numbers even when you don't ask for them. The action happens in the Instant Calculation bar at the bottom of the document window, where Numbers offers constant commentary on your current selection of cells. When you select two or more cells containing numeric values, the Instant Calculation bar displays a set of tallies for the selected cells (see Figure 19-2).

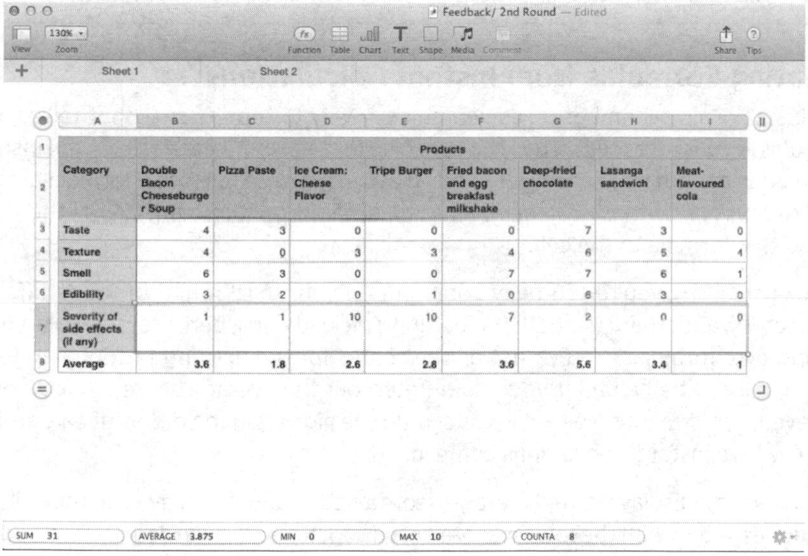

FIGURE 19-2

When you select two or more cells that contain numeric values, the Instant Calculation bar shows the sum and average of those values, the minimum value, the maximum value, and the overall count (the number of values in the selection). Empty cells and cells with non-numeric values are ignored by all the calculations except Count.

TIP Select multiple cells by ⌘-clicking, Shift-clicking, or dragging across the cells. You can also select an entire row or column by clicking its reference tab. For more on selecting table elements, see page 455.

You can select any combination of cells to make the Instant Calculation bar do its thing. Choose multiple columns or rows, for example, or select a block of cells several columns wide and several rows deep. The cells don't have to be next to each other, either; select any cells in the table by ⌘-clicking them, and Numbers still pours their values into its instant-calculation mill.

Having an always-on calculator in plain view is handy for doing a quick check on the status of any group of cells you might fancy, but its display is fleeting. As soon as you click away to another cell or otherwise change your selection, the Instant Calculation bar changes to display the tallies for the new group of cells. That's fine when you're after a one-time check, but it's less convenient when you frequently want to see a calculation for a specific set of cells. In that case, it makes sense to give the calculation a permanent home in your table. As it turns out, that's exactly what formulas do.

> **TIP** The rest of this chapter assumes you're using the Instant Calculation bar's standard setup, but if you find yourself frequently using functions besides SUM, AVERAGE, MIN, MAX, and COUNTA, you can add them to the Instant Calculation bar. To do so, select multiple cells to open the Instant Calculation bar, and then click the gear icon at the right end of the bar to open a drop-down menu of additional functions. Add any of these functions to the Instant Calculation bar by clicking them. If the bar starts to get crowded, Numbers adds scrolling arrows. Or you can remove a function (including the five default ones) by opening the gear menu and clicking the offending function, which removes the checkmark next to its name *and* removes it from the Instant Calculation bar.

Creating Formulas from Instant Calculations

The Instant Calculation bar gives you an easy way to turn its snapshot tallies into formulas in your table cells. The little capsules that surround each tally in the Instant Calculation bar are more than just handy containers; each one has a formula hidden inside. Drag one of these *calculation capsules* and drop it into any cell of the table to add that formula to the cell.

For example, say you're too busy conjuring up your third round of foodstuffs for Crazyland Wonderpark (something featuring pickled eggs, perhaps?) to waste time fussing over formulas. You've got all the scores for the existing products in front of you, but it'd be helpful if you could figure out the average score each product achieved, not to mention which items scored the highest in the different categories. This is where instant calculations come in.

You'd start by displaying the average score each product achieved across all the categories, along with the lowest score each foodstuff was awarded. Before adding your formulas, you need somewhere for them to live, so add three footer rows to the bottom of the table by opening the Format panel's Table tab, clicking the footer button (the rightmost button in the Headers & Footer section), and then choosing 2 from the drop-down menu (see page 215 for more info on footer rows). Label these rows Average and Minimum, as shown in Figure 19-3. Then make the Instant Calculation bar show the tallies for the first culinary delight by selecting all the cells that contain its scores, and then drag the calculation capsule for the average and minimum into the corresponding cells in the footer rows.

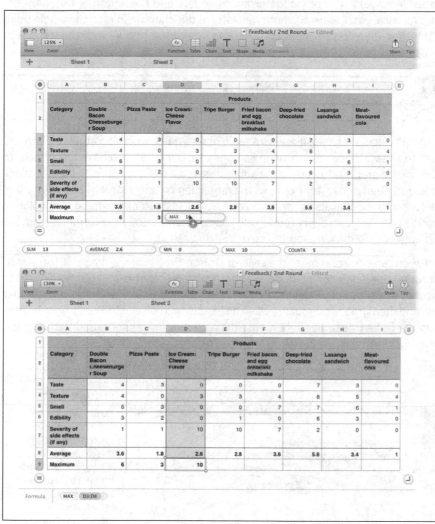

FIGURE 19-3

Top: Grab an instant calculation by its capsule, and drag it into a table cell. The cursor sprouts a green + bubble to show that it's about to add the calculation to the cell. Release the mouse button, and Numbers adds a formula to the cell, replacing any previous value it might have contained.

Bottom: After you drop a calculation capsule into a cell, Numbers switches focus and selects the target cell where you dropped the capsule. The Formula bar now shows the formula that's been added to the cell, and Numbers highlights the cells included in the formula.

You can take a closer look at this document (complete with calculations) by downloading the file calculation.numbers from this book's Missing CD page at www.missingmanuals.com/cds.

TIP The cell where you drag the capsule doesn't have to be in the same table as the selected cells; you can add the formula to any table you like.

As you can see in Figure 19-3, bottom, the cell where you drop the calculation capsule gets more than just a simple numeric value. Numbers doesn't just copy the *result* from the Instant Calculation bar; it adds a corresponding *formula* to the cell so that it always shows an accurate tally of the scores in that column. Change any of the scores above, and the tallies update to reflect the change.

The formula, in other words, plants the instant calculation inside your table, linking it to the specific cells you selected before you dragged the calculation capsule into place. Here again, it's not yet important to understand the jargon or format of the cell's formula; you'll learn all about that later in this chapter. In fact, the whole point of this drag-and-drop maneuver is that you don't *have to* deal with the formula at all; Numbers builds it for you automatically.

> **TIP** You can delete a formula from a cell in the same way you'd delete any other value: Select the cell and then press the Delete key.

Dragging calculation capsules into a table makes quick work of formulas when you want to show a calculated result in just one cell. But when you have *lots* of cells to fill in, all this drag-and-drop mousework turns into a tedious chore. In the Feedback table described above, for example, the remaining columns still have empty cells in the footer rows, all waiting for formulas. Luckily, instead of dragging a calculation capsule into each and every footer cell, you can instead copy the formulas from the first column into the neighboring columns.

Sure, you can copy and paste the cells, or Option-drag them, but autofill is the fastest route. You'll find complete details about autofill on page 483, but here's how to use it in this situation: Select the cells that already contain formulas in the footer row, and then grab the circular, yellow fill handle on the selected cell's right border. Drag the fill handle to the right across the neighboring columns, and Numbers fills them with formulas. Figure 19-4 shows the result.

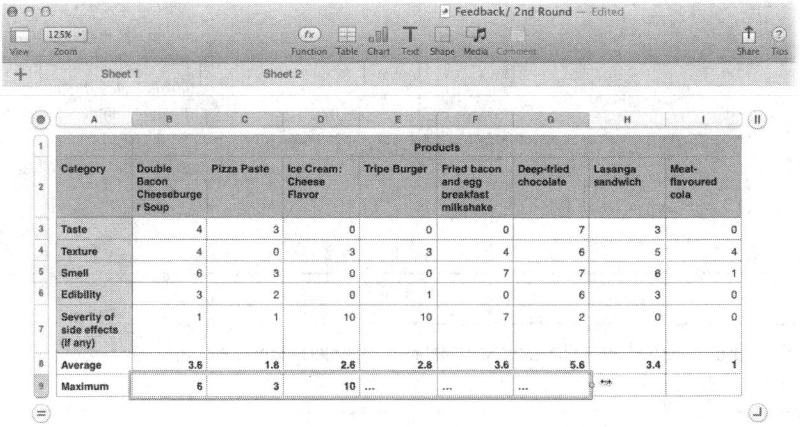

FIGURE 19-4

You can use autofill to copy formulas from one column to another. As you drag across the columns, Numbers inserts formulas into the cells but customizes them for each column so the formulas work with the scores in the cells directly above. In this example, the formulas in cells B9, C9, and D9 are being dragged across the rest of this row to give you a nice collection of cells showing the maximum score each product achieved.

Category	Double Bacon Cheeseburger Soup	Pizza Paste	Ice Cream: Cheese Flavor	Tripe Burger	Fried bacon and egg breakfast milkshake	Deep-fried chocolate	Lasanga sandwich	Meat-flavoured cola
Taste	4	3	0	0	0	7	3	0
Texture	4	0	3	3	4	6	5	4
Smell	6	3	0	0	7	7	8	1
Edibility	3	2	0	1	0	6	3	0
Severity of side effects (if any)	1	1	10	10	7	2	0	0
Average	3.6	1.8	2.6	2.8	3.6	5.6	3.4	1
Maximum	6	3	10	...	...	...		

See what happened there? Numbers was clever enough to guess that you didn't want to repeat the same calculation over and over for the cells in the first column.

Instead, it updated the formulas in each of the columns to run their numbers on the column above. Now you've got a tidy set of calculations at the bottom of each column to summarize what's going on with the scores above. When Numbers copies formulas that work with other cells in the table, it automatically updates your cell references. You'll find out more about copying formulas, as well as this theory of relativity, on page 534.

Adding Quick Formulas

Plunking a formula into a cell and then copying it into neighboring cells works just fine, but because repeating a formula is such a common activity, Numbers provides a shortcut in the form of *quick formulas*. Like instant calculations, quick formulas offer fast access to common actions, but they're specifically tuned for inserting formulas into your table—and best of all, they can add formulas to lots of cells in one swoop. You can use these one-click wonders on any selection of neighboring cells in the same row or column, but they're especially clever when applied to header or footer cells, instantly adding row or column tallies to your table.

When you add a quick formula (you'll learn how in a sec), Numbers inserts your formula into the selected cell and applies the formula's calculations to all of the body cells that are directly *above* the selected cell. If you add the Sum quick function, for example, the selected cell displays the result of adding up the values of all body cells above it.

You can apply a quick formula by selecting a cell and then choosing a *function* by clicking the Function button the toolbar or going to Insert→Function. Functions are the predefined calculations that Numbers knows how to do. As you'll learn in the next chapter, Numbers knows over *250* functions, many of which manage complex algorithms appropriate to the financial or engineering worlds. Quick formulas, however, stick to the basics, giving you easy access to six of the most commonly used functions:

- **Sum** adds the values of all the cells in the column directly above it.

- **Average** calculates the mean value of the cells.

- **Minimum** displays the lowest value among the cells.

- **Maximum** displays the highest value among the cells.

- **Count** shows the number of values in your selection.

- **Product** multiplies the values in all the cells.

NOTE Like instant calculations, quick formulas ignore empty cells and non-numeric values (except Count, which tallies date, time, and text values).

As mentioned above, when you insert a quick formula into a cell, Numbers runs the selected calculation on all the body cells that are directly above that cell. This is useful for tallying up the total of a column and is found in many spreadsheets, including some of Numbers' templates (see Figure 19-5).

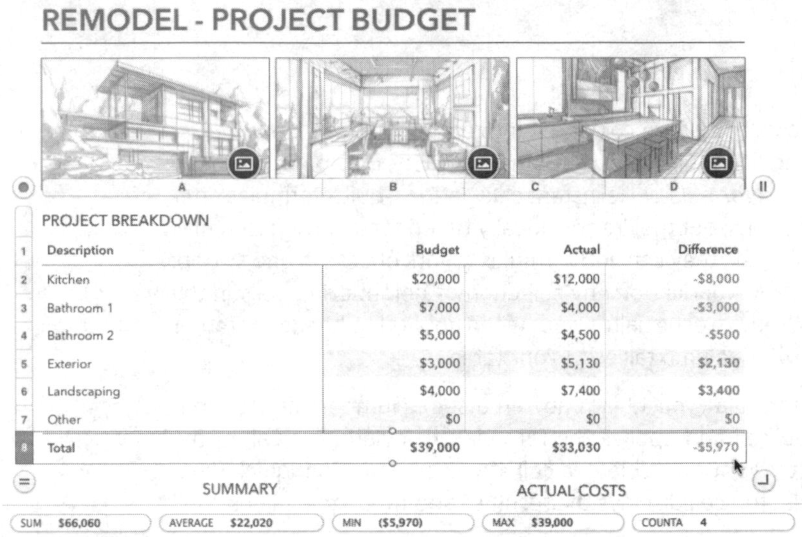

FIGURE 19-5

It's common practice to add formulas to the last row in a table or to the footer row. This allows readers to get a feel for your entire table by scanning just one line. Many of Numbers' templates follow this practice, including the Home Improvement template shown here.

REMODEL - PROJECT BUDGET

PROJECT BREAKDOWN

	Description	Budget	Actual	Difference
1				
2	Kitchen	$20,000	$12,000	-$8,000
3	Bathroom 1	$7,000	$4,000	-$3,000
4	Bathroom 2	$5,000	$4,500	-$500
5	Exterior	$3,000	$5,130	$2,130
6	Landscaping	$4,000	$7,400	$3,400
7	Other	$0	$0	$0
8	Total	$39,000	$33,030	-$5,970

SUMMARY — ACTUAL COSTS

| SUM | $66,060 | AVERAGE | $22,020 | MIN | ($5,970) | MAX | $39,000 | COUNTA | 4 |

■ Editing Formulas

When you're doing simple math on neighboring cells—adding up a row or a column, for example—quick formulas are all you need. However, as helpful as this feature might be, Numbers' quick formulas and instant calculations can handle only very simple equations. When you require something slightly more sophisticated—another type of calculation or working with nonadjacent cells, for example—it's time to build your own formula. This section introduces you to the basics of editing formulas, along with the tools that Numbers offers for making the job easier.

Anatomy of a Formula

A formula is an *equation*, a statement that says, "This cell's value is equal to this calculation." To signal its status as an equation, every formula starts with the = sign. Numbers figures out the value of whatever follows that = sign and presents it to you in the cell containing the formula, which is called the *formula cell*. The simplest possible formula is:

=1

As soon as you select a cell and then press the = key, the *Formula Editor* pops up, with your cursor already positioned inside, awaiting further instructions. (The Formula Editor is the tiny toolbar shown in Figure 19-6; you'll get an in-depth introduction to it starting on page 526.) Continue typing the rest of your formula, and then either hit the Return key on your keyboard or click the Formula Editor's green checkmark.

TIP Don't try to exit the Formula Editor by clicking outside of it. When you click any cells while the Formula Editor is open, Numbers adds the values of those cells to your formula—whoops!

Numbers strains its mighty math muscles to evaluate the right side of the = sign and arrives at the startling conclusion that the value is in fact one. The cell's value is thus treated and displayed as 1.

NOTE Technically, the cell's "real" value is the formula itself. But for display purposes and when the cell is used in other cell's formulas, Numbers considers its value to be the calculated value.

Setting a cell's value to a specific number by using a formula isn't especially exciting or even terribly helpful (it's easier to type the value directly into the cell and dispense with the = sign entirely). Things start to get more interesting when you give Numbers some math to work with. Again, let's keep it simple:

    =1+1

Once again, Numbers puts its genius for figures to work, this time deciding that the calculated value of the cell is 2, as shown in Figure 19-6.

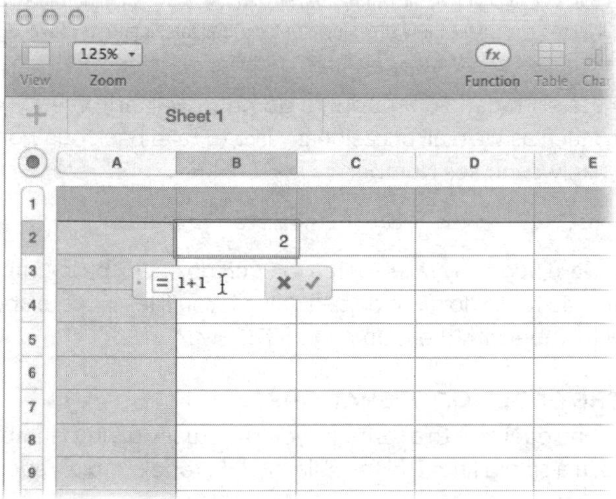

FIGURE 19-6

Double-click a formula cell to reveal its underlying equation in the Formula Editor. Here, a cell with the formula =1+1 shows its calculated value: 2.

Normally, the Formula Editor appears directly on top of its formula cell. But you can move it around (as was done here) by dragging the faint gray dot on its left side. Doing so lets you see both the cell's formula and its result (though the formula is also displayed in the Formula bar).

You get the idea: Whatever value is created by the equation on the right side of the = sign becomes the displayed value for the cell. It's worth underlining, though, that a formula *must* start with an = sign in order to open the Formula Editor and get treated as a formula. If you enter simply *1+1* into a cell (with no = sign), Numbers treats the entry as text. So instead of calculating its value, the cell simply displays 1+1.

■ NUMBERS' ARITHMETIC OPERATORS

Way back in grade school, at least one of your beloved math teachers tried to teach you the word *operator*, the technical term for the + sign, – sign, and all the other symbols that tell you to make one number perform some mathematical transformation on another. Just like the equations you recall so fondly from your school days, Numbers relies on operators to understand how you'd like it to do math. Table 19-1 lists the operators that Numbers understands, along with examples of how to use them.

TABLE 19-1 *Numbers' arithmetic operators*

OPERATOR	DESCRIPTION	EXAMPLE	RESULT
+ (plus sign)	Add two values	=2+2	4
– (minus sign)	Subtract one value from another	=4–1	3
* (asterisk)	Multiply two values	=2*3	6
/ (forward slash)	Divide one value by another	=10/2	5
^ (caret)	Raise one value to the power of another value	=10^2	100
% (percent symbol)	Divide value by 100	=5%	0.05

NOTE   Numbers also has another kind of operator, the *comparison operator*, which lets your formulas make some simple logic decisions. You'll learn more about these tiny morsels of artificial intelligence on page 570.

Numbers lets you use these arithmetic operators to do only, well, arithmetic. You can't use them with text. Much as we'd all occasionally like to take back our words, for example, this formula only confuses Numbers:

```
="conversation with boss" - "comment about hideous tie"
```

You might wish the result were *huge pay raise* (or maybe *get job back*), but Numbers returns only an error when you try to do math on text values. You'll learn more about error messages and how to cope with them on page 537.

■ UNDERSTANDING THE ORDER OF OPERATIONS

When you add more than one operator to a formula, you're actually giving Numbers several calculations to do in a single line. The formula =1+2+5, for example, requires two calculations:

1. **Add 1 and 2 to get 3.**

2. **Add 5 to get 8.**

That's a straightforward example, and it's easy to understand the result. But when you start adding ever more operators to a formula—subtracting, dividing, multiplying, and exponentiating all at once—it's important to understand the *order of operations*. That's the set of rules that Numbers follows to figure out the order in which it will tackle the various calculations in your formula. For example, what's the value of this formula?

```
=25 - 5 * 2
```

The answer is 15, although you might have thought the answer was 40 if you didn't follow the tried-and-true order of operations that your algebra teacher taught in high school. In case your memories of algebra class are vanishingly distant, here's a quick review. Numbers attacks every formula in this order:

1. **Calculations inside parentheses**

2. **Percents, from left to right**

3. **Exponents, from left to right**

4. **Division and multiplication, from left to right**

5. **Addition and subtraction, from left to right**

Let's walk through an example to see how this works in practice. Consider this formula:

```
=1 + 16 / 2 ^ 3 * 4 - 2
```

There are no parentheses or percentages here, so Numbers skips to the third item in its list, calculating exponents. Numbers does its magic on 2^3 to get 8, so the next phase of calculating looks like this:

```
=1 + 16 / 8 * 4 - 2
```

Division and multiplication from left to right are up next. First up it's 16/8 to get 2:

```
=1 + 2 * 4 - 2
```

...followed by 2*4 to get 8:

```
=1 + 8 - 2
```

Finally, Numbers is down to addition and subtraction from left to right: 1 plus 8 is 9. Subtract 2, and Numbers arrives at its final result:

```
=7
```

You can control the order of operations (or simply make it easier to read and organize your formula) by adding parentheses, which group calculations together so that Numbers figures the value inside them before running through its regular order of operations. Take a look at how a single pair of parentheses can affect the value of the sample equation above:

$$1 + (16 / 2) \wedge 3 * 4 - 2 = 2,047$$

$$1 + 16 / 2 \wedge (3 * 4) - 2 = -0.996$$

$$1 + 16 / 2 \wedge 3 * (4 - 2) = 5$$

In formulas, parentheses always travel in pairs. If you include just one parenthesis without its companion to "open" or "close" the pair, Numbers will complain with an error message.

Meet the Formula Editor

Numbers shows its affection for formulas by wrapping them in their own sleek editing field. Numbers admits you to this luxury suite when you select a cell and type the = sign as the first character, signaling that you're creating a formula. This triggers the appearance of the almighty Formula Editor (Figure 19-7), a wide text field that hovers above the selected cell, expanding as necessary to contain your formula. The Formula Editor also pops up when you select a formula cell at the text level by double-clicking it or by pressing Option-Return.

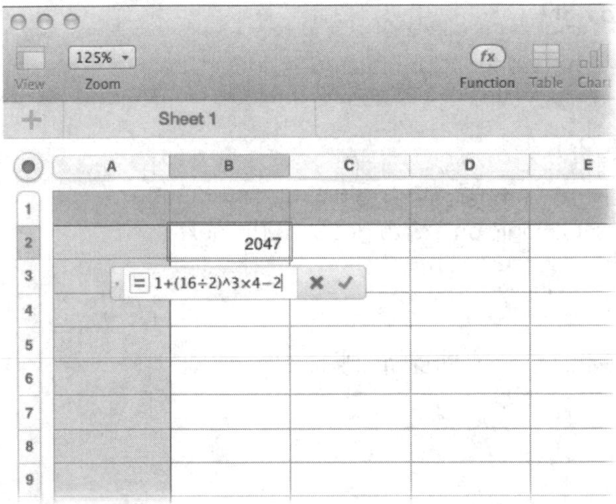

FIGURE 19-7

The Formula Editor appears when you start editing a formula inside a table cell, floating above the cell itself. As you type, the Editor expands to the right, giving you room for lengthy formulas. Here, the Formula Editor has been dragged down so that it doesn't cover up the selected cell. To move the Formula Editor, put your cursor over the gray dot on its left side and then drag.

Type your formula into the Formula Editor's text field and then press Return or click the Formula Editor's green checkmark; either way, Numbers saves your formula and you're free to continue editing your table. You can also press Tab or Shift-Tab to commit your changes and move to the next cell. But what you *shouldn't* do to save your formula is click another cell. Normally, when you're editing a cell, clicking any other cell stores your changes and selects the clicked cell. However, when you're editing a formula in the Formula Editor, clicking another cell *includes* that cell in the formula itself. (You'll learn more about cell references in the next section).

If you change your mind midway through adding or editing a formula, just close the Formula Editor and reset the cell to its original value by pressing Esc or clicking the Formula Editor's red X.

Using Cell References

Now that you've got formulas doing a bit of math, you can see that any table cell can operate as a high-falutin' calculator. But even with all the fancy operators you explored a few pages back, if your calculations use only constant numbers (1, 2, 3, and so on), the results aren't really all that different from the very first =1 formula you saw a few pages ago. Because you're using plain old constant numbers in these calculations, the "answer" to your equation is always the same no matter how you might change the table around that formula cell. It's a calculation, sure, but it doesn't respond to the spreadsheet environment around it.

By contrast, formulas become much more flexible and useful once you start to fold in the data you've entered elsewhere in your spreadsheet. You already saw Numbers doing this with instant calculations and quick formulas earlier in this chapter. Naturally, you can do the same with your own formulas, too. To do that, you use *cell references*, placeholders in formulas that point to values in other cells in your spreadsheet.

Think of cell references as coordinates that combine the name of the cell's column with the name of its row. Remember the game Battleship? In the game, your hidden playing board is a grid where you lay out your ships—just like the data in your table. Players call out coordinates, trying to hit each other's ships: *A9! C12! F4!* It works the same way with your table: The letter of a column's reference tab combines with the number of a row's reference tab to give you the location of a cell. Plug in the right coordinates, and you hit the bull's-eye ("You sank my subtotal!").

When you include a cell reference in a formula, you tell Numbers to fetch that cell's value and use it in the formula's calculation. The simplest example is =A1, which tells Numbers to set the value of the formula cell to the value found in cell A1. More often, though, you'll use cell references in various math equations, adding them as value placeholders where you would traditionally use constant values. Instead of =2+2, for example, you might have the formula =B2+C5, which tells Numbers to add the values of those two cells and display the result. If the values of those cells change, Numbers automatically recalculates the formula, so your formula cell always reflects the current data in your spreadsheet.

Say you're working on getting a handle on exactly how much each of your up-and-coming culinary wonders will cost you. You've started to build a basic grid to figure the cost of each ingredient, as shown in Figure 19-8.

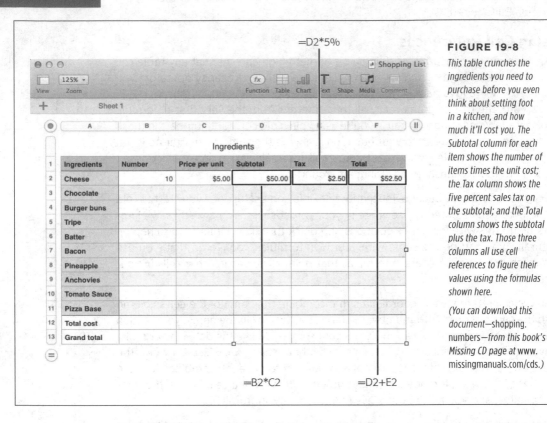

FIGURE 19-8

This table crunches the ingredients you need to purchase before you even think about setting foot in a kitchen, and how much it'll cost you. The Subtotal column for each item shows the number of items times the unit cost; the Tax column shows the five percent sales tax on the subtotal; and the Total column shows the subtotal plus the tax. Those three columns all use cell references to figure their values using the formulas shown here.

(You can download this document—shopping. numbers—from this book's Missing CD page at www. missingmanuals.com/cds.)

Figure 19-8 shows the formulas for the three columns that require calculations; they're really just plain old formulas that use cell references instead of constant values. There's something else interesting going on here, too. Take a close look at the formulas in the Tax and Total columns; their formulas reference cells that in turn contain formulas referencing *other* cells—a chain reaction. So if you change the value in the Number column, for example, the Subtotal column updates to reflect the new value. That triggers a change in the Tax column, and *that* change updates the value in the Total column.

■ ADDING CELL REFERENCES TO FORMULAS

When you're editing a formula, you can add cell references by typing their coordinates, just like the formulas shown in Figure 19-8. But really: A1, B5, G3, R2D2, C3PO? Huh? While coordinates are an efficient way to pinpoint the locations of cells, they're not especially meaningful as *names*. This makes them hard to remember and, as a result, you might be prone to make mistakes when working with them directly. Fortunately, Numbers lets you sidestep these dreary coordinates and identify cells in a few different ways when editing formulas.

The most direct route is to click the cell you want. When you're working in the Formula Editor, clicking any cell inserts its cell reference into the formula.

TIP If you're in a hurry to add up the values in several cells, see the box on page 530 for some handy shortcuts.

Alternatively, if you prefer to keep your fingers on the keyboard, you can use the arrow keys to find the cell you want to include: While you're editing a formula, hold down the Option key and use the arrow keys to navigate the table. As you pass through cells, their cell references appear in the formula at the insertion point. When you land on the cell you want, release the Option key, and Numbers adds the cell's cell reference to your formula.

You can also add a cell reference by typing the cell's plain-language name, constructed from your header labels. When your table has a header row and/or header column, you can combine those header values to build coordinates instead of using the reference-tab letters and numbers. The result is a friendlier version of the cell's letter-number coordinates. In the table shown in Figure 19-8, for example, the plain-language name of cell D5 is "Subtotal Tripe" (that's its column header followed by its row header). In fact, these are the names that Numbers prefers to work with in its formulas, too; if you click a column's reference tab to add that entire column to your formula, Numbers uses the plain-English column header in its formula, rather than its alphabetic reference (A, B, C, or whatever). This is a helpful convention since these long-form names tend to be more descriptive of the cell's *content* than just its *location*.

TIP Prefer short nicknames to long ones? Babs over Barbara? B2 instead of "Q1 2009 Revenue"? Tell Numbers to keep it short and use the letter-number coordinates instead of header cells: Go to Numbers→Preferences, click the General tab, and then turn off the "Use header names as labels" option.

These header names aren't just for display; you can use them when you're entering a formula. Because these names can run long, Numbers gives you some editing help by offering to auto-complete cell names as you type. When you start typing, a bar of suggestions appears just beneath the Formula Editor and suggests a header name, the name of a sheet or a table, and so on. Figure 19-9 shows this feature in action.

NOTE Numbers doesn't offer auto-completion suggestions when you turn off the "Use header names as labels" checkbox in Numbers→Preferences.

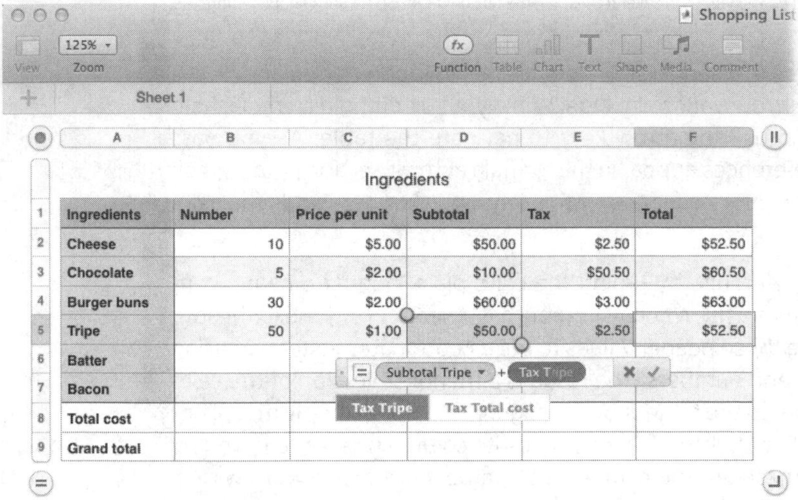

FIGURE 19-9

When you're typing a cell reference, Numbers tries to auto-complete it. Here, Numbers offers to complete "Tax T" as either "Tax Tripe" or "Tax Total cost." To accept the highlighted suggestion (here, that's "Tax Tripe"), press Return or click the suggestion. You can move between suggestions using the Tab key. To ignore the suggestion, just keep typing.

> **TIP** You can download the sample document shown in Figure 19-9 (*ingredients.numbers*) from this book's Missing CD page at *www.missingmanuals.com/cds*.

UP TO SPEED

The Plus Side of References

You can use cell references however you like in any formula or function—they're interchangeable with the constant values you used to plug into equations in your high-school math class. But Numbers makes it especially easy to use cell references to *add* cell values. In fact, unless you give the program a hint that you're not doing addition, it assumes that's exactly what you're up to.

To create a formula that adds any group of cells in your table, just select the formula cell, type the = sign, and then start clicking table cells. As you go, Numbers inserts the cell references into your formula, automatically wedging the + sign between them, giving you an instant sum.

If the values you want to add are all neatly organized in neighboring cells, it's even easier: Select the formula cell, type the = sign, and drag from one end or corner of the group of cells to the opposite end or corner. When you let go of your mouse, Numbers adds up the values in your selection, but this time it dispenses with the + sign and instead uses the SUM function with a *range reference* to describe your cell selection. You'll learn more about functions in Chapter 20 and range references on page 545, but for now all you need to know is that the formula adds up all of your selected cells.

■ VIEWING AND EDITING CELL REFERENCES

However you add a cell reference to your formula, it shows up in the Formula bar and Formula Editor as a colored *reference capsule* with the cell's name or reference-tab coordinates inside. Each reference capsule gets its own color, and when the formula cell is selected, Numbers color-coordinates them with the corresponding cells in the table, highlighting those cells in matching colors. This color-by-numbers trick makes it instantly clear which cells you're using in the formula. To make sure a formula is operating on the cells you expect, just click the formula cell, and the cells it references light up.

The highlighted cells are more than just a visual reference, though. You can also drag them to change the cell reference in your formula. When you're working in the Formula Editor, Numbers dresses up each referenced cell with a selection box, complete with circular handles in its upper-left and lower-right corners (see Figure 19-10). When you move your cursor over one of these handles, the cursor turns into a double-headed arrow to indicate that you can drag to add or remove cells from the referenced range. To change a cell reference to point to a different cell altogether, put the cursor over the cell you want to change. When you see a *four*-headed arrow trailing behind your cursor, you can drag the selection box to a new cell, and Numbers updates the formula with the revised cell reference, as shown in Figure 19-10.

> **TIP** Selection boxes appear around a formula's referenced cells only when you're *editing* the formula; simply selecting the formula cell isn't enough. To trigger this feature, open the Formula Editor by double-clicking the formula cell or by selecting the cell and then pressing Option-Return.

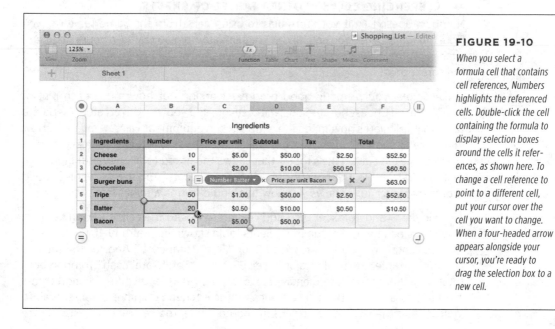

FIGURE 19-10

When you select a formula cell that contains cell references, Numbers highlights the referenced cells. Double-click the cell containing the formula to display selection boxes around the cells it references, as shown here. To change a cell reference to point to a different cell, put your cursor over the cell you want to change. When a four-headed arrow appears alongside your cursor, you're ready to drag the selection box to a new cell.

This drag-and-drop method is the very same technique that you'd normally use to move a cell's contents to a new spot. But when you're editing a formula, the cell's contents stay put; the only thing that moves is the cell-reference selection box. Similarly, dragging either circular handle on a cell-reference selection box doesn't replace the contents of the cell's neighbors as it would when you use the fill handle in normal editing mode (page 483). Instead, dragging the handle expands the cell-reference selection to include the cell's neighbors. This creates a *range reference*, which you'll learn about on page 545.

You can also change a cell reference directly in the Formula Editor. Click a reference capsule to select it, and Numbers highlights the selection box around the corresponding table cell. Double-click a capsule to edit its cell-reference address. To remove a cell reference from your formula, select its capsule and then press Delete.

If you click the flippy triangle on the right side of each reference capsule, a dropdown menu appears, giving you access to settings that let you preserve certain cell references. You'll learn more about preserving cell references on page 536.

NOTE You can drag a cell reference out of the Formula Editor by double-clicking it to make it editable and then dragging it to a new location. However, you won't get much mileage from these reference capsules: When you double-click a reference capsule to make it editable, it loses its magical abilities and turns into plain text. Dragging a reference capsule into a table cell, for example, replaces that cell's value with the capsule's cell-reference name only. Dragging the cell reference into a blank part of the sheet canvas instead creates a text box containing the cell-reference name. In both cases, the cell reference remains intact in the formula.

■ REFERENCING CELLS IN OTHER TABLES OR SHEETS

Numbers doesn't limit your formulas to using cells from the same table or even from the same sheet. You can mix and match data from any table in your document, which is especially handy for displaying summaries of data calculated elsewhere in the spreadsheet.

For example, you've made good progress working out how much each pint of Double Bacon Cheeseburger Soup will cost you, and you've even created a separate table that calculates how much the extra kitchen equipment will set you back. Now you'd like to show all of those table tallies in a single executive summary. You've created a cell in each table's footer that shows the grand total of everything within that individual table, but how do you see the total costs from the two tables added together? Figure 19-11 shows you how this kind of formula might look.

To fill in the Grand Total cell, you add cell references to the cells showing the final tally from each table. For the Ingredients table shown in Figure 19-11, for example, the cell containing the final total is F8, or "Total Total cost." And for the Kitchen Equipment table, the final total is in cell F5, a.k.a. "Total Total cost." To bring both totals together in the Ingredients table, enter the cell reference for the Ingredients table's total, and then the cell reference for the Kitchen Equipment table's total. To indicate that the second value is from another table, the cell reference starts with the table's name (Kitchen Equipment), followed by two colons and then the cell's coordinates. Either of these cell reference styles does the trick:

```
= F8 + Kitchen Equipment::F5
= Total Total cost + Kitchen Equipment::Total Total cost
```

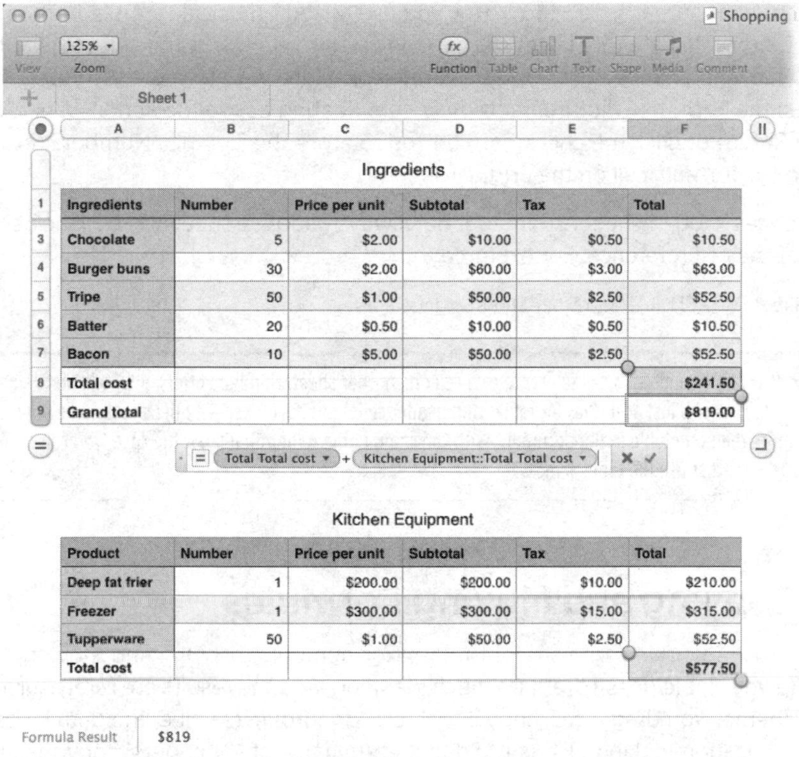

FIGURE 19-11

Adding a table name to a cell reference lets you point to a cell in a separate table. Here, the Grand Total cell in the Ingredients table adds the total value of that table to the grand total of the Kitchen Equipment table.

The table name is optional if there's only one cell in the spreadsheet with that name. For example, if the Kitchen Equipment table were the only one with a cell named "Total Total cost," then you could drop the table's name from the cell reference, and Numbers would still find it. But in the spreadsheet shown in Figure 19-11, both tables have a cell named "Total Total cost," so you need to include the table name.

You can type these foreign-table cell references manually into your formula, but that can require a lot of typing. Numbers eases the effort by offering the same kind of auto-completion suggestions that it does for header cells: After you type the first letter of a table's name, Numbers displays suggestions to complete the entry for you.

As usual, though, the most direct way to add a cell reference is simply to click the cell. When you're working in the Formula Editor, clicking a cell *anywhere* in the spreadsheet adds that cell reference to your formula. If you need to scroll to get to the reference cell, the Formula Editor stays put, floating above as you scroll the sheet below. This lets you continue editing the formula even if the formula cell itself is no longer in view. After you press Return or click the Formula Editor's checkmark button to store the formula, Numbers springs you back to the formula cell's location in the spreadsheet.

This applies to adding cell references for tables that live on an entirely different sheet of your spreadsheet, too. After you've started editing a formula in the Formula Editor, click another sheet's tab in the Sheets bar, select the cell you want to reference, and Numbers inserts its cell reference into your formula. As you switch sheets, the Formula Editor remains onscreen, floating above the action. When you press Return or click the checkmark button to store the formula, Numbers returns you to the formula cell on the original sheet.

References to other sheets often—but not always—add the sheet name to the beginning of the cell reference. For example:

```
Sheet Name::Table Name::Cell Reference
```

> **TIP** If you're typing out a cell reference to a cell on another sheet, Numbers offers auto-complete suggestions for sheet names just as it does for tables and header cells. You have to specify the sheet name only when there's more than one table in the document with the same name. When that's not the case, you can drop the sheet name and just use the table name.

■ Copying and Moving Formulas

When you're working with straight-up text or numbers, copying and moving data around your table doesn't require much planning, and the results are rarely surprising. Whether you drag a cell, copy it, paste it, or autofill its value, the data lands in its new location looking just as it did in its original spot—Numbers' copy machine always makes a perfect duplicate. With formulas, however, it's not always clear what "perfect duplicate" means, especially when cell references are involved. When you plunk a formula into a new location, Numbers sometimes makes changes to the formula's cell references in an effort to anticipate your needs. As you shuffle formulas around your spreadsheet, it's important to understand how and when Numbers modifies your formula to blend in with its new surroundings—and how you can control those changes.

When you *copy* a cell by pasting, autofilling, or Option-dragging, Numbers updates the formula's cell references so that they point to different cells relative to the formula's new location. Say that you have a formula in cell A1 that contains a reference to the cell next door at B1. When you copy the formula down to the next row (cell A2), Numbers updates the formula's cell reference to point to cell B2. Numbers assumes that the *relative position* of the referenced cell is more important than the actual original address. So even though the copied formula is in a new spot, it still points to the cell next door.

This turns out to be a huge timesaver when you want to repeat a formula in many cells—to tally all the cells in each row or column, for example. The Ingredients table from earlier in the chapter offers an example, as shown in Figure 19-12. Instead of updating each of the formula cells for every row, you can copy them quickly using autofill (page 483), and Numbers updates the cell references for you.

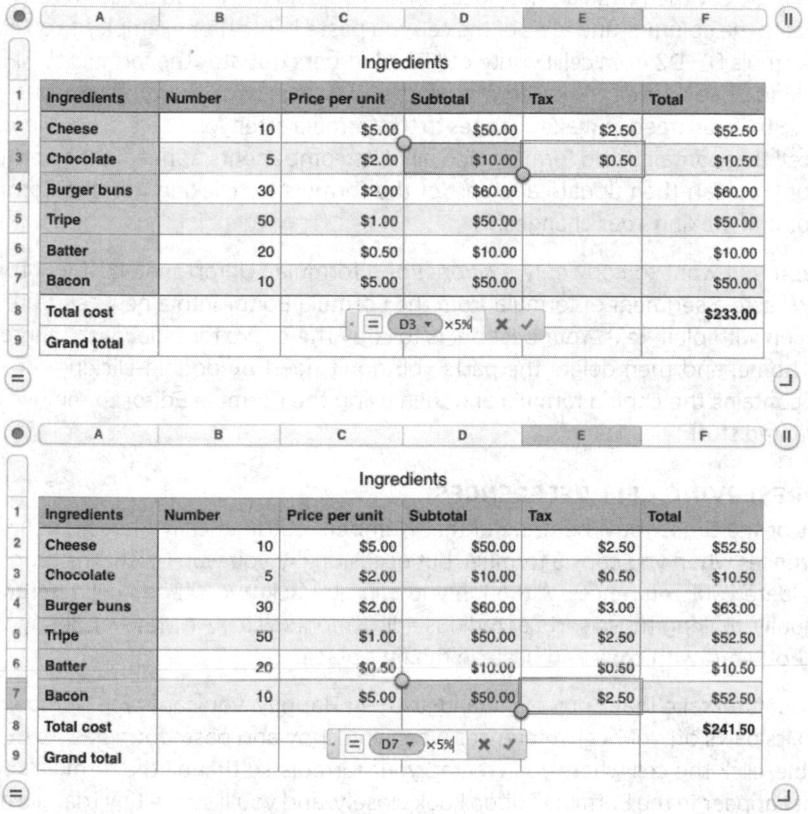

FIGURE 19-12

Top: The amount of tax you can expect to shell out for each ingredient is calculated by taking the value in the Subtotal cell and multiplying it by 5%. When you copy this formula to the rows below, Numbers automatically updates the cell references to reflect the change in row.

Bottom: In row 7 (selected in this screenshot), Numbers has automatically updated the formula's cell reference to D7.

Reusing Formulas

Unless you get a kick out of operators, parentheses, and cell references, you won't be jumping up and down at the prospect of typing out the same formula time and time again. Thankfully, Numbers lets you quickly copy and paste an existing formula into a new cell. To copy a formula, simply click the cell that contains the original formula, and then copy and paste the formula into a new cell.

TIP If you just want to copy the computed *result* of a cell's formula instead of the formula itself, you can sidestep all this fuss about cell references. Select the cell, choose Edit→Copy, and then select Edit→Paste Formula Results. The displayed result of the original cell shows up in the new cell without its formula—a mild-mannered value without the formula cell's special abilities.

You'll notice that the copied formula isn't an *exact* replica of the original, as Numbers takes a look at the formula's new location and adjusts the formula's cell references to match the columns and rows of the cell you paste it into. For example, if you copy the formula D1+D2 from cell D3 into cell F3, Numbers updates the formula to F1+F2. This kind of adjustment is called *mapping,* and it usually gives you the results you want. But if you need to make changes to the formula after you paste it, double-click the cell that contains said formula, and all of its components appear in the Formula Editor. You can then update any part of the formula by clicking it in the Formula Editor and making your changes.

What if you want to copy only a *snippet* of a formula? Unfortunately, if you try to copy/paste a segment of formula from the Formula Editor into a new cell, you just wind up with plain text. Your best bet is to copy the *entire* formula, paste it into its new home, and then delete the parts you don't need by double-clicking the cell that contains the copied formula and then using the Formula Editor to remove the unwanted stuff.

■ PRESERVING CELL REFERENCES

Most of the time, you'll be grateful that Numbers automatically updates your cell references when you copy a formula, but occasionally you won't want the program to update your references. Although you *can* go back and change cell references manually, making those sorts of tedious adjustments will have you wondering why you bothered with copy and paste in the first place.

But don't forsake that Copy command just yet! Happily, you can *force* Numbers to keep its paws off your cell references when you copy and paste formulas. To do so, double-click the cell where you created your formula so that all the formula's segments appear in the Formula Editor. Look closely, and you'll spot a tiny triangle next to each cell reference. Click this triangle to open a drop-down menu that contains checkboxes that you can adjust to tell Numbers which cell references to preserve and which ones are fair game.

The drop-down menu includes two checkboxes: Preserve Row and Preserve Column. In the cell reference E7, E is the column, and 7 is the row, so you can preserve the 7 by turning on Preserve Row, and preserve the E by turning on Preserve Column. Numbers places a $ in front of any reference that it'll preserve. For example, $C4 means that the C part of the reference will be preserved, but the 4 is fair game; C$4 means the 4 is preserved but the C isn't; and C4 means both parts are preserved.

■ Coping with Formula Errors

As clever as Numbers can be, it's not hard to confuse it when you don't follow its rules or speak Its language correctly. The program expects your formulas to be formatted correctly, to use cell references for cells that actually exist, and to provide values that let it complete the actions you request. When that's not the case or when Numbers otherwise can't make sense of your formula, it complains by putting a red triangle with an exclamation point on it—the error icon—in the middle of the formula cell.

Click the icon to make Numbers display the error message in a pop-up; the message provides a brief description of what got Numbers mixed up. Often the message gives you enough information so you can quickly find and fix the error. When you get the vaguely worded message "The formula contains a syntax error," that usually means that you've got something out of order in your formula. Check to make sure that all of your parentheses match up, that you've got arithmetic operators where they should be, and that all of your function arguments are properly separated by commas (page 541).

Advanced Data Crunching with Functions

You can get lots done in your spreadsheets simply by mixing formulas with the ingredients you've seen so far: cell references, operators, and constant values. You could put down this book right now and be wildly productive with Numbers—the whole world of basic algebra is your oyster. But the great thing is that you don't *have* to do the algebra (or eat the oyster, for that matter). Numbers gives you more than 250 predefined calculations called *functions* that juggle figures so you don't have to construct the equations yourself. They can even perform a few tasks that are flat-out impossible to do with straight-up arithmetic.

Functions can handle a range of jobs including simple addition, converting teaspoons to tablespoons, and figuring out an asset's depreciation. They're not limited to working with numbers, either. Functions can transform text, traverse the calendar, construct sentences, make logical decisions, and sift through tables to find certain values. This chapter shows you how to put this remarkable collection of timesavers to use in your formulas. You'll start with the most common tasks and move on to sophisticated strategies for wrangling data across multiple tables.

■ How Functions Work

Think of Numbers' built-in function library as an army of math-minded elves waiting to do your bidding. Each elf has a specific job it knows how to do; you give it the raw materials it needs to do that job—a set of numbers to average, for example—and it comes back with the answer. You don't have to understand *how* it gets the answer or what equations and incantations it performs behind the scenes; just give it your figures, and it hands you the result. Every one of your little minions has a name and even brings along its own basket to hold the raw materials you provide.

Without a doubt, the busiest and most popular of all spreadsheet functions is SUM. (Yup, functions' names are always in caps, to make them easy to spot; even if you type them lowercase, Numbers capitalizes them automatically.) You've already seen this little guy in action several times in the previous chapter. SUM's job is simple: It adds the numbers you put in its metaphorical basket, a pair of parentheses that you add immediately after the function's name. For example, this formula adds the numbers inside the parentheses and returns the value 10:

```
=SUM(4, 2, 3, 1)
```

Every function name has to be followed by a pair of parentheses in order for you to give it your data. Inside the parentheses is the place where you ask the question you want answered. The raw materials you pour into a function's parentheses are known as its *arguments*. They get along better than their confrontational name suggests, even lining up in a specific order to feed the function the info it needs. Some functions, for example, require a specific set of arguments in a defined order; you have to ask your question in precise terms. The CONVERT function, for instance, converts a number from one unit to another. To make a cell display the number of miles in five kilometers, for example, you put the question to CONVERT with a specific series of three arguments, like so:

```
=CONVERT(5, "km", "mi")
```

In this example, the arguments are the number that you want to convert (5), the current units of that number (km), and the units in which you would like the answer (mi). CONVERT obligingly lets you know that the answer is 3.107 (and many decimal places more, too). You can type arguments directly into the Formula Editor or, more commonly, represent some or all arguments with cell references. Figure 20-1, for example, shows a table that lets you perform any unit conversion you'd like by editing the values in the table's cells.

> **NOTE** Don't worry, you don't have to memorize all the function names and the arguments they require. Numbers makes it easy to put your hands on that info when you need it, as you'll learn when you meet the Functions tab on page 542.

Whether you type your arguments in manually or use cell references, there are a few rules to keep in mind as you build your argument list:

- **Arguments go inside parentheses.** Every function name should be followed by a pair of parentheses containing the function's arguments. Sometimes, Numbers can take a formula without parentheses and add them for you, but this isn't an exact science: Play it safe and get into the habit of adding them yourself.

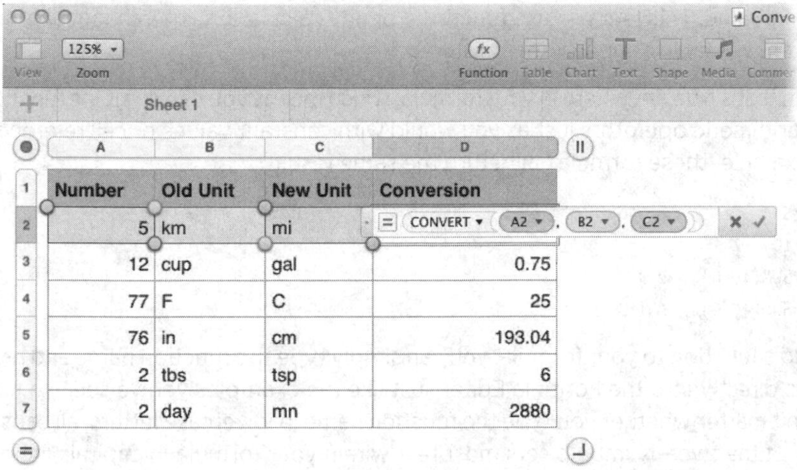

FIGURE 20-1

The CONVERT functions in the last column of this table pluck their arguments from the first three columns using cell references. Changing a value in column A, B, or C changes the result in the last column. Instead of converting from tablespoons to teaspoons in row 6, for example, you could change the units in columns B and C to pints and quarts (pt and qt), and Numbers updates the conversion's result accordingly.

- **Arguments are separated by commas.** It's just like your English teacher taught you: Separate items in a list with commas. (As you'll learn on page 545, however, a special kind of cell reference called a *range reference* can represent several cell references at once, sidestepping the need for a long list of comma-separated values.)

- **Text arguments go inside quotes.** As demonstrated in the CONVERT example above, any text value has to go inside quotation marks. (Cell references *aren't* considered text, even though their values might contain text. So don't put cell references inside quotation marks or they'll stop working as references.)

- **White space is your friend.** Functions can get complex, but you can at least make them easier to read and edit by giving them a little space to breathe. Feel free to sprinkle spaces into your formulas to create visual breaks between arguments, operators, and functions. Numbers ignores extra spaces except inside quotation marks or cell references, so the only effect spaces have is to make your life easier.

Arguments can even include other functions or calculations. The formula to display the mile equivalent of five kilometers could also be written like any of the following alternatives, where the first argument always calculates to 5:

```
=CONVERT( SUM(2, 3), "km", "mi" )
=CONVERT( (10 / 2), "km", "mi" )
=CONVERT( AVERAGE(4, 6), "km", "mi" )
```

Remember the order of operations from the last chapter (page 524)? Numbers always does calculations inside parentheses first, and that includes the parentheses that hold function arguments. In the examples above, this means that Numbers figures the value of the first argument (5) before it sends the function on its way to fetch the final value. This lets you use functions, or any calculation, interchangeably with constant values in your argument list.

In fact, that's true anywhere in your formula, which means you can combine functions with arithmetic operators just as you would with constant values or cell references. For example, these formulas all return the same result:

```
=5
=10 / 2
=SUM(4, 6) / 2
=SUM(4, 6) / AVERAGE(1, 3)
```

To add a function to your formula, you can simply type the function name and arguments directly into the Formula Editor, just like the examples you've seen so far. It doesn't matter whether you type the function name in lowercase letters, all caps, or a mix of the two—Numbers sets most text within your formula in capitals, helping to make the whole thing easier to read.

As you type in the Formula Editor, you'll notice that Numbers helps you out by suggesting functions that match what you've typed so far. For example, if you type *su* Numbers displays several suggested functions beneath the Formula Editor: SUBSTITUE, SUM, SUMIF, and so on. You can click one of these suggestions to add it to your formula, or scroll through the list using the arrow keys on your keyboard or the Tab key. When you find the suggestion you want to add, make sure it's highlighted, and then press Return. Or just keep typing, and Numbers narrows its suggestions. If you've filled in your header rows and/or columns, Numbers also suggests headers that match what you're typing.

If you're not a fan of Numbers putting words in your mouth, you can type your functions and headers in full, and then press Return to add what you've just typed to your formula.

TIP If you need to type something that *isn't* a function or a header, eventually Numbers will run out of suggestions, and you won't be able to type another letter. To get around this problem, simply put quotation marks around what you're typing.

■ Adding Functions with the Functions Tab

Typing functions into the Formula Editor by hand works well enough for common, easy-to-remember functions like SUM. But when you cobble together more complex functions—or when you're not sure of the function name or even if such a function exists—a little help is in order. The Format panel's *Functions tab* lets you thumb through Numbers' entire library of functions, where each one is listed with a complete description of its arguments and what it does, as well as examples. When you find the function you want, Numbers inserts it into your formula with labeled placeholders for the function's arguments.

You can open the Functions tab in two ways:

- Type = in the cell where you want to create your formula.

- Select your cell, and then choose Insert→Function→Create Formula.

Either way, Numbers opens the Functions tab in the Format panel, as shown in Figure 20-2. (If you don't see the panel, click the Format button in the toolbar.) The Functions tab organizes your view of the function library. In the table at the top of the tab, the left column groups functions into categories, including the All category, for when you want to drink from the fire hose, and Recent, which helps you focus on your commonly used functions (or at least the last 10 of them). When you choose a category in the left column, the right column lists the functions in that category alphabetically by name. Click a function, and the bottom of the tab offers a detailed description of it, including tips and examples.

Formula Editor

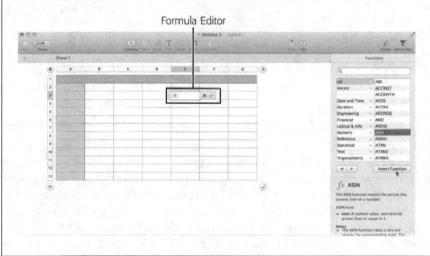

FIGURE 20-2

When you're working in the Formula Editor, Numbers automatically opens the Functions tab. Browse the functions using the table at the top of the tab, and read the description of a function at the bottom by clicking its name in the table's right-hand column. To insert a function into your formula, double-click its name or select it and then click Insert Function (where the cursor is here).

Browsing function categories is a good way to get acquainted with the many possibilities that functions offer, but don't take the category names too literally. The Engineering category, for example, might seem daunting, but that category includes the CONVERT function—as useful to home cooks counting the number of tablespoons in a quarter cup as it is to physicists converting joules to ergs. Similarly, the serious-sounding Statistical category includes the commonly used AVERAGE function.

Because these category names are a bit loose, the Functions tab's search bar is often the most efficient way to find the function you're looking for. This miniature search engine scours functions' description text, so even if you don't know a function's name, searching for a word related to what you want it to *do* can help you find what you need. Type your search term into the field at the top of the tab, and the Functions tab's table displays functions that match what you've typed; click a function's name to see its description. To return to the regular category display, clear the search field.

When you find your function, double-click it or select the formula and then click Insert Function; either way, Numbers adds it to the formula for the selected cell. Handily, the Functions tab inserts more than just the function's name into your formula; it also gives you *argument placeholders* to remind you what info the function needs and, where applicable, in what order. As you can see in Figure 20-3, these placeholders show up as gray capsules (dark gray ones are required, light gray ones are optional); click any of them to see a brief description of its purpose in the Formula bar. You can get more info on the arguments by reading about the function in the Functions tab.

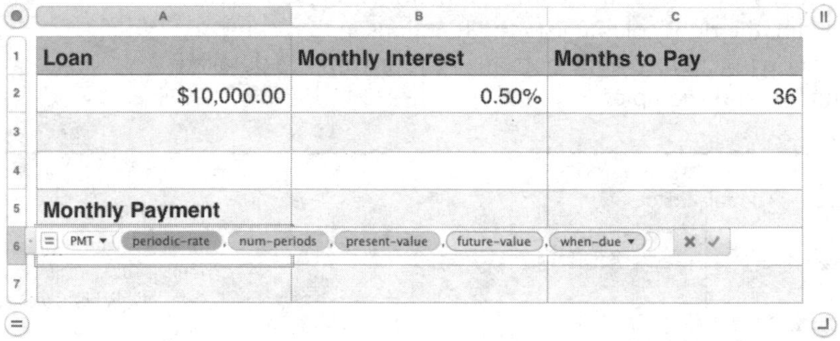

FIGURE 20-3

In this example, the PMT function will calculate the monthly payment for a loan when you provide the periodic interest rate ("periodic-rate"), the number of periods to pay ("num-periods"), and the present value of the loan ("present-value"); the other two arguments are optional.

To fill in an argument placeholder, double-click it, and then type a value. You can also use a cell reference: Click a capsule to select it and then either click the cell whose value you want to use for that argument or hold down Option and use the arrow keys to navigate to the cell. In the PMT function in Figure 20-3, for example, you would use cell B2 for the periodic rate, cell C2 for the number of periods, and cell A2 for the present value of the loan. The resulting formula will tell you what your monthly payment would be to pay off your $10,000 loan in three years. (For another example of the PMT function at work, check out Numbers' built-in Mortgage Calculator template, which shows you monthly payments under a variety of interest rates and payment schedules.)

Some argument placeholders (like "when-due" in Figure 20-3) contain drop-down menus that list all the argument's allowed values; click the capsule's menu arrow to see your choices.

■ Using Cell Ranges in Functions

All the function examples you've seen so far have used cell references with the same comma-separated format as any other argument. That works fine when you have just a small handful of arguments—to add the values of four cells, for example:

```
=SUM(B1, B2, B3, B4)
```

But that's actually longer than just doing it directly with the plus sign:

```
=B1 + B2 + B3 + B4
```

And either method becomes hideously long when you decide to add a column of 10,000 values. In the time it would take to type or click all the cells, you may as well just add up the values yourself. Happily, Numbers provides a shorthand called a *range reference* that lets you point to any collection of neighboring cells (a *range*). Many functions accept range references as arguments, including SUM, which adds up all the cells described by the range. To provide a range reference, you give Numbers the cell reference for the top-left and bottom-right cells in the range, separated by a colon. (If it's a single-column range, then your job is to name the top and bottom cells.) B1:B4, for example, describes adjacent cells in a column: cells B1 and B4 *and* the cells in between (B2 and B3). For example, these two formulas return the same result:

```
=SUM(B1, B2, B3, B4)
=SUM(B1:B4)
```

In other words, even though a range reference is just a single argument, it actually "unpacks" into several values. You can even string multiple ranges together by separating them with commas just as you would with any other argument. For example, these two formulas give you the same result:

```
=SUM(B1, B2, B3, C10, C11, C12)
=SUM(B1:B3, C10:C12)
```

A reference to adjacent cells in a row works the same way. B2:E2 refers to cells B2, C2, D2, and E2. Cell references can similarly describe a block of cells: D6:E10 gives you rows six through 10 in columns D and E—10 cells in all. Figure 20-4 gives some examples.

TIP   Be careful that you don't accidentally include the formula cell in one of its range references, or Numbers will choke and display an error message. You're not allowed to refer to the formula cell itself in its own formula. (You also can't refer to another cell that depends on that formula cell for its value.)

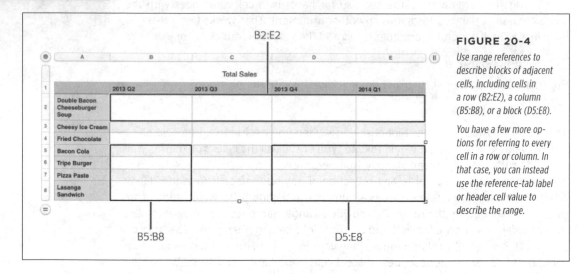

FIGURE 20-4

Use range references to describe blocks of adjacent cells, including cells in a row (B2:E2), a column (B5:B8), or a block (D5:E8).

You have a few more options for referring to every cell in a row or column. In that case, you can instead use the reference-tab label or header cell value to describe the range.

Unlike working with individual cells, Numbers doesn't give you the option of using header names when you refer to cells in reference ranges—you have to use the letter-number coordinate format instead. But Numbers lifts that restriction when you want to create a reference to *every* cell in a row or column. In that case, you can just refer to the row or column by its header value alone to create a *row reference* or *column reference*. If column H of your table is labeled "2014 Q3," for example, either of these formulas adds up every cell in that column:

```
=SUM(H)
=SUM(2014 Q3)
```

When you leave off the row coordinate of a cell reference, in other words, it turns into a range reference for the entire column. You can do the same thing to add up rows, too. If the second row of your table is labeled "Feedback," you can add up all its values like so:

```
=SUM(Feedback)
```

It doesn't work quite the same way as columns, however, when you want to refer to rows by their reference-tab numbers instead of their header names. That's because Numbers reads the 2 in =SUM(2) as the *number* 2 instead of the sum of all cells in *row* 2. To clear up the confusion, you use a *row range*, which indicates all cells in the specified range of rows; since you just want one row, the start and end row are the same. Here's how you tell Numbers to add all the cells in row 2:

```
=SUM(2:2)
```

If you want to add all the cells in *multiple* rows or columns, you simply indicate the first and last ones to include, using the reference-tab letters and numbers for your row and column references, like so:

```
=SUM(B:D)
=SUM(2:4)
```

NOTE   When you point to entire rows or columns of cells using row and column references, the range typically includes the header and footer cells, too. This is no problem for the SUM function, which simply ignores text values, but it could cause confusion (or at least an error or warning message) for functions that expect only numbers. So when you want to exclude header and footer cells, use a specific cell range instead of a row or column reference.

Adding Cell Ranges to Formulas

You can type range references directly into your formula, just as you can with cell references. As usual, the most direct (if not necessarily the fastest) way to indicate a range of cells is to point them out with your mouse. With the insertion point inside the Formula Editor, drag your cursor across a range of cells from one end to the other, and Numbers inserts the appropriate range reference into your formula.

You can also trace out a cell range without lifting your hands from the keyboard. Press and hold Option, and then use the arrow keys to move to one end of the range. Then, while still holding down the Option key, press and hold Shift while you use the arrow keys to expand the selection. When you've selected the range you want, release both keys, and Numbers adds the range reference to your formula. Or release only the Shift key and, while still holding the Option key, use the arrows to reposition the entire cell range on the table.

When you're working in the Formula Editor, Numbers highlights the referenced cell ranges in the table, using the same color as their reference capsules in the formula—just as it does for single-cell references. These cell ranges are bordered by a selection box that you can drag to a new spot in the table, as shown in Figure 20-5. (Dragging a range's box updates only the range reference's address in the formula; it doesn't affect the *data* in the selected range of cells.) To shrink or expand the area included in the range reference, drag the circular handle at the top left or bottom right of the selection box.

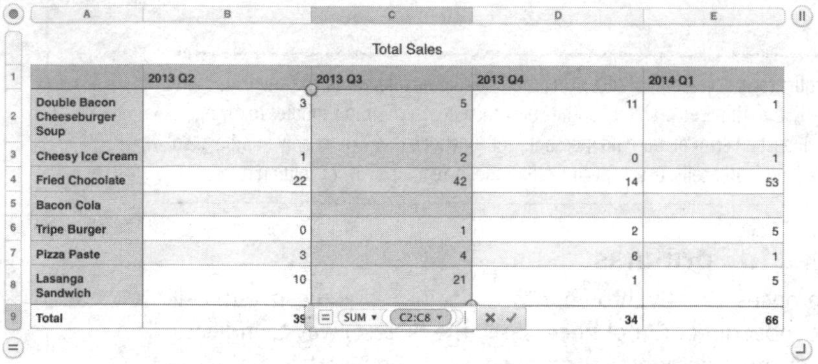

FIGURE 20-5

When the Formula Editor is open, you can adjust the location and size of the formula's cell range by dragging the selection box that surrounds the cell ranges used in your formula, or by dragging the selection box's circular handles to resize it.

■ Common Math Functions

Numbers offers a wide range of functions for managing your adventures in arithmetic, including lots of advanced functions tailored for accountants, statisticians, and rocket scientists. Although these brainy functions are often crucial to folks working in a specific field, they're too esoteric for the general public, often requiring specialized knowledge even to understand *why* you might use them. Some of these topics would require a whole other book (and possibly a graduate degree) to explain. If you wouldn't know a multinomial coefficient from a multinational coffeehouse, then chances are you'll never come close to using *all* the functions iWork offers. As a result, this book doesn't delve into these deep, dark nooks and crannies.

Instead, this section provides a review of commonly used math functions. Although this treatment only scratches the surface of the function library's numerical know-how, you can, as always, find a complete list of all iWork formula functions in the Functions tab.

> **TIP** Numbers' Help menu also includes a handy overview of functions, including introductory material for working with financial and accounting functions. To check it out, choose Help→Numbers Help, or go to *http://help.apple.com/functions/mac/4.0.*

Quick-Formula Functions and Basic Math

In the last chapter's review of instant calculations and quick formulas, you met the most popular functions in Spreadsheet Land. SUM, AVERAGE, MIN, MAX, COUNTA, and PRODUCT are the most commonly used math functions, which explains their privileged status in the toolbar's Function drop-down menu and (except for

PRODUCT) in the Instant Calculation bar. In addition to using these functions in quick formulas, you can also include them in your own custom formulas, and many of them have other closely related functions that you might consider as alternatives (MEDIAN instead of AVERAGE, for example). This section provides a quick tour of these basic functions.

■ SUM: ADDING NUMBERS

The SUM function will almost certainly be in the heaviest rotation in your function playlist. This function's one and only job is to add up what you hand to it. As discussed earlier in the chapter, its arguments are simply the set of values to add, which you can enter directly or represent with functions, cell references, or cell ranges. Here are some examples:

```
=SUM(A1, D4)
=SUM(A1:D4)
=SUM(A1, B1:D4, 200, 15.1, 35%)
```

> **TIP** Because Numbers uses commas to separate arguments, *don't* use commas in your numbers when writing functions. If you do, Numbers reads a number like 1,200 as two separate arguments. For example, =SUM(1,200, 3) gives you 204, not 1,203. In other words, you need to write =SUM(1200, 3) instead.

SUM ignores text values and empty cells, but it *can* work with dates and durations. You can even use SUM to add durations to a date to get a whole new date. With this and one or two other date-specific exceptions, however, you can't mix and match data types. You should generally work with either numbers or durations, but not both at once. To find out more about doing math with dates and times, see page 564.

> **NOTE** SUM also has a discerning cousin, SUMIF, which adds values in cell ranges only when they meet certain conditions. You'll learn more about conditional functions starting on page 569.

■ COUNT, COUNTA, AND COUNTBLANK: HOW MANY?

The COUNT function, of course, counts the number of values you give to it, but only if those values are numbers or dates. For example:

```
=COUNT(1, 2, 3)
```

When you include one or more range references as arguments for COUNT, the function counts all of the cell values within that range. For example, assuming that all six cells in the range A1:B3 contain numeric values, this formula returns 6:

```
=COUNT(A1:B3)
```

If you want to count cells that contain *any* type of value, including text and Boolean values, then use COUNTA instead ("A" stands for "all"). This function works the same way as COUNT but is far better at including every value and non-empty cell that you give it.

When you find yourself in the throes of nihilism, COUNTBLANK lets you focus on the emptiness, returning the number of *empty* cells in a range. Unlike the other counting functions, COUNTBLANK accepts just one argument—a range reference:

```
=COUNTBLANK(A1:B3)
=COUNTBLANK(C)
=COUNTBLANK(4:4)
```

NOTE Like SUM, COUNT also has a COUNTIF counterpart that lets you add conditions about which values it should count.

MAX AND MIN: FINDING THE BIGGEST AND SMALLEST

The MAX and MIN functions bust out the record books to award the honor for biggest or smallest value in a collection. Like COUNT, these functions accept a list of values, cell references, and cell ranges and then go to work—but only on numbers, dates, and durations (they ignore text and Boolean values). MAX returns the largest number or latest date in the collection, and MIN returns the smallest number or earliest date. For example, this formula examines eight cells and hands back the largest value:

```
=MAX(B2:D3, E4, F5)
```

NOTE MAX and MIN don't let you mix data types in a single operation. You can compare numbers, dates, or durations, but don't combine them into one calculation.

If you want to include text and Boolean values in the mix, use MAXA or MINA instead. (As with COUNTA, the "A" is for "all.") However, MAXA and MINA still dispense only numeric values, so don't think that you can use them to find the lowest and highest text values, alphabetically speaking. Instead, text values are assigned the value 0, which may be useful if you want to treat the word "None" as 0 instead of ignoring it, for example. In MAXA and MINA calculations, the Boolean value TRUE counts as 1 and FALSE counts as 0. Empty cells, however, get ignored.

LARGE, SMALL, AND RANK: RANKING VALUES

These three functions let you work with cell values based on their rank in a collection of values. While MAX and MIN let you find only the bookend values for a range of cells, LARGE and SMALL let you find the value that's a specified number of steps from the largest and smallest.

LARGE and SMALL both require two arguments: the range of cells to work with and the ranking of the value to fetch. In the LARGE function, the ranking refers to the number's position when the collection is ordered from large to small. For SMALL, it's the reverse. This formula, for example, finds the second-largest value in a range of cells:

```
=LARGE(B2:B15, 2)
```

LARGE and SMALL can look up the rankings for numbers, dates, and durations, but you can't mix those data types. All cells in the range must have the same data type, or Numbers complains with an error.

While those two functions look up a value based on its rank, RANK does the opposite: It looks up the rank of a value in a range of cells. This formula finds the rank of cell B3 (from highest to lowest) in the range B2:B15:

```
=RANK(B3, B2:B15)
```

TIP You can also rank values in reverse order, so that rank 1 has the lowest value in the list—when you're ranking golf scores, for example. To do this, add a third argument to the RANK function, setting it to FALSE or 0.

Figure 20-6 shows both the RANK and LARGE functions at work. Say you're pulling together some data about the total sales made by burger vans and cafes across Crazyland Wonderpark and want to work out the ranking of each new product based on how many units they've sold. For example, cell E2 shows the total sales of Bacon Cola in 2014 Q1, so you can discover that this tasty treat ranked fourth in sales for that quarter using this formula:

```
=RANK(E2, 2014 Q1)
```

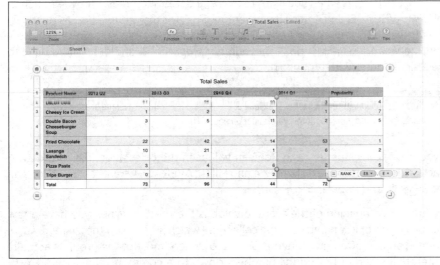

FIGURE 20-6

The Popularity column uses the RANK function to find the ranking of the cell next door according to the values in the 2014 Q1 column. Although this is information that you could find by sorting the table by its 2014 Q1 column, showing the rank is useful when you want to sort your table some other way. Here, for example, the table is sorted alphabetically by product name.

Copy that formula down the Popularity column to fill in the rest of the rankings, as shown in Figure 20-6. To call out the top three a bit more, you decide to display the top three products in a separate table. Those values use the LARGE function to display the first-, second-, and third-highest amounts (for the highest amount, the result is the same as using the MAX function):

```
=LARGE(2014 Q1, 1)
=LARGE(2014 Q1, 2)
=LARGE(2014 Q1, 3)
```

> **TIP** It would be more enlightening to have Numbers fetch the names of the highest-ranking products, too, showing that Cheesy Ice Cream is Crazyland Wonderpark's latest culinary hit. You can do that by using lookups, a topic you'll discover on page 582.

■ AVERAGE AND MEDIAN: FINDING THE MIDDLE VALUE

The average value of a set of numbers is, of course, the sum of the values divided by their count (how many there are). This is something you could easily do with =SUM()/COUNT(), but Numbers is all about saving you time, so it provides the AVERAGE function to return the mean value (another name for "average") of a collection. AVERAGE accepts a bunch of arguments for processing, and these values can be constants, cell references, range references, or other functions. For example:

```
=AVERAGE(A1, B2:B9, 39.4)
=AVERAGE(C3, SUM(A2:A6))
```

AVERAGE ignores text and Boolean values, working only with numbers, durations, and dates. In fact, one area where AVERAGE outdoes what you might do with =SUM()/COUNT() is when you want to average dates and times. Throw a bunch of dates at AVERAGE, and it finds the "average date" for the group. This has relatively dubious value for more than two dates or times, but it's handy to find the middle point between a pair. Just don't mix numbers, durations, and dates—you have to use a single data type throughout.

> **NOTE** The AVERAGEIF function lets you include or exclude values from the average based on a condition of your choice. You'll learn more about this gatekeeper on page 574.

If you want to include text and Boolean values in the calculation, the AVERAGEA function does just that. Just like MAXA and MINA, AVERAGEA treats text and Boolean FALSE as 0, and Boolean TRUE as 1.

A common companion of the average value is the *median*. When you have a few unusually high or low numbers in the collection, which might skew the average value, the median can often give a better picture of where most of the group is actually centered. Instead of boiling the numbers down to a common value as AVERAGE does, MEDIAN finds the middle number in the group. If you ordered the numbers in the collection from lowest to highest, the median would be the number in the center, so that half the numbers in the group are less than the median and half are greater. If there's an even number of values in the collection, MEDIAN averages the two middle numbers to get its result. Here are some examples:

The median of 1, 2, 3, 4, and 5 is 3:

```
=MEDIAN(1, 2, 3, 4, 5)
```

The median of 1, 2, 3, 4, 5, and 6 is 3.5:

```
=MEDIAN(1, 2, 3, 4, 5, 6)
```

The median of 7, 7, 7, 7, and 999 is 7:

```
=MEDIAN(7, 7, 7, 7, 999)
```

Like AVERAGE, the MEDIAN function can work with dates and times, too, but ignores text and Boolean values (and there's no MEDIANA alternative).

■ MULTIPLYING WITH PRODUCT

The PRODUCT function is a simple replacement for the * multiplication operator (page 524) in the same way that SUM replaces the + operator. Give PRODUCT a collection of values, and it multiplies them together—as long as they're numbers. PRODUCT ignores *all* non-numeric values. This formula multiplies 3, 5, and 10 and hands back the value 150:

```
=PRODUCT(3, 5, 10)
```

Just like the other functions reviewed in this section, PRODUCT can also accept cell references and range references, which let you multiply lots of values in a hurry:

```
=PRODUCT(B1:B15)
```

■ QUOTIENT AND MOD: DIVIDE AND CONQUER

While PRODUCT is more or less a shorthand for the * operator, QUOTIENT does something more than simply act as a substitute for the / division operator. In fact, it often returns an entirely different result than the division operator would. QUOTIENT does *integer division*, which means it lops off the result's decimal value and returns only whole numbers. While 13/5 gets you 2.6, QUOTIENT's answer is 2:

```
=QUOTIENT(13, 5)
```

This is the kind of division that you learned in grade school where your answer to 13 divided by 5 would be "two with a remainder of three." If you also want to get at that remainder number, you'll have to remember that the high-falutin' name for the remainder is the *modulus*. That's where the MOD function gets its name, and it works just like the QUOTIENT operator except that it returns the remainder. This formula confirms that the remainder of 13/5 is in fact 3:

```
=MOD(13, 5)
```

Rounding Numbers

Many numbers are unmanageably long thanks to the digits that stretch off to the right of the decimal point. When it comes to *displaying* this fractional portion of a number, Numbers bends to the space available, rounding numbers to fit their enclosing cells (page 474) or letting you set a cell's data format (page 473) to give you control over where to plant a number's decimal point. If you adjust a cell's data format to display its value with three decimal places, for example, then it rounds 3.14159 to 3.142. But as you've learned, the rounding is only for show; under the hood,

Numbers retains the original value, and you can use the cell's value in calculations without losing any precision.

In most cases, that's what you want. But sometimes you *want* to change the underlying value so that the rounded value gets used in calculations. Likewise, if you're doing a calculation inside a formula and need to use a rounded result for another calculation in the same formula, Numbers' display settings won't help you.

Finally, Numbers' standard rounding method rounds numbers up if the next digit is 5 or greater, but what if you want to use a different method? Rounding to the nearest multiple of 5, for example? Or always rounding down instead of up? It turns out that there are *lots* of ways to round numbers, and your trusty spreadsheet program gives you no fewer than 10 functions to bump numbers up or down to the value or decimal accuracy you want. This section takes you through the options.

■ SIMPLE ROUNDING WITH ROUND, ROUNDDOWN, AND ROUNDUP

The ROUND function applies the traditional rounding method, just like your grade-school math teacher taught you: ROUND bumps numbers up when the next digit is 5 or greater and down when the next digit is less than 5. For example, it rounds the number 1.5 up to 2, and the number 1.4 down to 1. ROUND accepts two arguments: the number to round and the number of decimal digits to keep. For example, this formula returns the number 8.46:

```
=ROUND(8.4579341, 2)
```

If you set the number of decimal digits to a *negative* number, the function rounds numbers to the left of the decimal point—rounding to the nearest 10, 100, 1,000, and so on. Another way to think of it is that a negative number in this argument determines how many zeroes appear at the end of the rounded whole number. For example, setting the number of digits to –2 rounds to the nearest hundred; the result has two zeroes to the left of the decimal point. This formula returns 2500:

```
=ROUND(2463.3, -2)
```

As their names suggest, the ROUNDDOWN and ROUNDUP functions always round numbers up or down (respectively), no matter what the next digit is. These alternatives take the same arguments as ROUND, letting you choose how many decimal digits to keep. For example, =ROUNDDOWN(1.99, 0) returns 1, and =ROUNDUP(1.01, 0) returns 2.

As far as these three ROUND functions are concerned, rounding up really means moving the number away from zero, and rounding down means moving it closer to zero. Because of that, when you work with negative numbers, rounding up actually makes the number *smaller*: –1.5 rounds to –2.

NOTE   A quirky pair of functions named EVEN and ODD offer a variation on ROUNDUP, rounding a number up to the nearest even or odd number. For example, =EVEN(2.1) gives you 4, and =ODD(2.1) gives you 3.

■ LOPPING OFF DECIMAL DIGITS WITH INT AND TRUNC

The INT (integer) and TRUNC (truncate) functions don't bother with rounding at all. They simply snip off a number's digits at a specified point, ignoring the pruned portion completely.

INT's job is to take a single value and lop off all numbers to the right of the decimal point: 5.954 becomes 5. TRUNC, on the other hand, lets you specify the number of decimal places to keep when you bring out the carving knife. That means these two formulas deliver the same result (5):

```
=INT(5.954)
=TRUNC(5.954, 0)
```

If you instead wanted to shorten the number to one decimal point, this formula would give you 5.9:

```
=TRUNC(5.954, 1)
```

These functions are useful when you're dealing with units that always travel in whole numbers. For example, if your calculations tell you that the average classroom can accommodate 20.5 students, INT turns that into 20 so your space planning doesn't include splitting hapless pupils down the middle.

> **NOTE** At first glance, these functions look like they do the same thing as ROUNDDOWN, and that's true for positive numbers. When you work with negative numbers, though, the behavior is different. While ROUNDDOWN turns –1.5 into –2, INT simply ignores the decimal place and returns –1.

■ MROUND, CEILING, AND FLOOR

The ROUND family of functions is handy for rounding numbers to the nearest decimal or whole number, but what if you want to round a number to some other unit? When you want to round values to the nearest multiple of 5 or prices to 50-cent increments, MROUND does the trick. MROUND takes two arguments: the number you want to round and the increment (a.k.a. *factor*) you want to use. When you're rounding 128 to the nearest multiple of 5, for example, this formula tells you the value is 130:

```
=MROUND(128, 5)
```

The CEILING and FLOOR functions play the ROUNDUP and ROUNDDOWN roles for MROUND, always rounding either up or down to the increment you specify. For instance, using FLOOR for the previous example rounds 128 *down* to 125:

```
=FLOOR(128, 5)
```

One place where these three functions are useful is for calculating prices at round-ish numbers like increments of 25 cents. This formula, for example, rounds the price in cell B2 to the nearest 25-cent value:

```
=MROUND(B2, 0.25)
```

Totally Random

How do I generate random numbers?

When you need a quick collection of random numbers for your spreadsheet, turn to the RAND and RANDBETWEEN functions, which pluck numbers from thin air. You might put the resulting numbers to use to build a pop quiz for your math students or to sort a table in random order, for example.

RAND takes *no* arguments and gives you a random number between 0 and 1 (but never equal to either). For example, this formula returns results like 0.3682823833:

```
=RAND()
```

More often, though, you'll want a number within some range other than 0 and 1. You can get that by multiplying times the range of numbers you want. To get a random number between 0 and 25, for example, use:

```
=RAND() * 25
```

When you want integers between and *including* 1 and 25, you need to do an additional sleight of hand, using INT (page 555) to chop off the decimals and then add 1:

```
=INT( RAND() * 25 ) + 1
```

Because that starts to get messy, Numbers gives you the RAND-BETWEEN function, which returns a random number between (and including) its two arguments. This lets you reduce that last noisy example to this:

```
=RANDBETWEEN(1, 25)
```

Whichever method you use, you'll soon see that Numbers has a thing for generating random numbers. Every time you add or change *any* formula in your document, Numbers recalculates each and every random number in your spreadsheet, plugging in a new value. The randomness just keeps on coming. To avoid this, you can copy and paste the random numbers back into your document as regular values so that they stop recalculating. To do that, select the cells, choose Edit→Copy and then, with the cells still selected, choose Edit→Paste Formula Results.

Did that earlier mention of shuffling a table's entries in random order pique your interest? To do that, fill a column with random numbers and then sort the table using that column (see page 500 for details about sorting).

■ Transforming Text in Formulas

Numbers has a mind for math, but it's also got a talent for juggling words and rearranging letters. The program's many text functions let you work with your cells' text entries to clean up your data, combine prose into new constructions, or pluck a snippet of text from the middle of a longer passage.

The way you'll most commonly work with your text values is to combine them into entirely new values. In the same way that you add numbers with the + operator, you combine text with the & operator, which glues two bits of text together. In Numbers, text snippets are called *strings*, and combining them is called something only a geek could love: *concatenation*. It works just like addition, only with strings instead of numbers. This formula, for example, concatenates a first name and a last name into a full name, putting a space in between for good measure (as you learned on page 541, you need to put quotes around text arguments in formulas):

```
="Walter" & " " & "Kovacs"
```

That's a bit odd on its own; normally, you'd just type *Walter Kovacs* directly into the cell. But this method becomes much more useful when those first and last name values are replaced with cell references:

```
=B2 & " " & C2
```

Figure 20-7 shows how you can use that recipe to create a new column of product names and their ingredients, when your table contains separate columns for product names and ingredients.

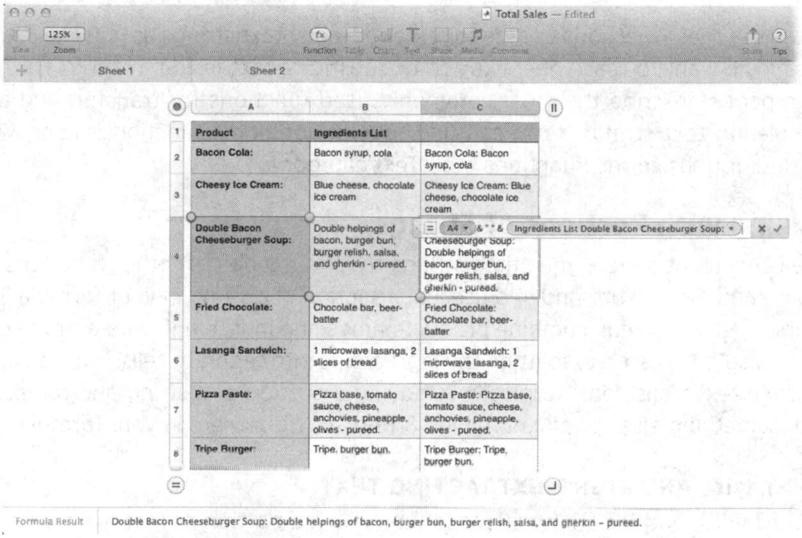

FIGURE 20-7

You can use a formula to combine the text values of various cells into a single value, like a product's name and its list of ingredients. In this screenshot, the formulas in column C combine the values in the previous two cells.

You can mix and match both cell values and "literal" text strings in your formulas. The important thing to remember when you type strings directly into a formula is that they need to be contained in quotation marks.

When you combine cell values into a text string, they can contain any type of data—numbers, dates, durations, whatever. When you do that, Numbers converts the value to text, using the same display format as the original cell, even when that's not necessarily that cell's complete underlying value. For example, say the value of cell B2 is 35.4325, but it displays as $35.43 because it's set to the currency format. In that case, the following formula returns "Price: $35.43":

```
="Price: " & B2
```

TIP If you want to use a different format from the one imposed by the cell's data format, then you can use the FIXED or DOLLAR formats to do exactly that. See page 562.

Whatever data types you pour into a concatenation, they always come out as text on the other side. For instance, to Numbers, the *numeric* value of "Price: $35.43" is zero.

When you're feeling especially wordy, you can use the CONCATENATE function, which does the same thing as the & operator, combining the arguments into a single string in the order listed:

```
=CONCATENATE(B2, " ", C2)
```

NOTE Sorry, no range references allowed in the CONCATENATE function, only single-cell references.

You can use these methods to glue together as many text strings as you like. Other times, you'll want to rearrange, extract, or substitute text inside a string. The following pages describe the most commonly used functions for transforming and manipulating text strings. (You can find several additional functions, along with their descriptions, in the Functions tab's Text category.)

Working with Portions of Strings

While concatenation lets you stitch strings together, a host of other functions let you slice and dice text to find and use just a section of a string in your formula. For example, just as you can combine product names and ingredients into a single cell, you can also go in reverse, splitting the ingredients into separate cells. You can even perform a text transplant, surgically removing a portion of a string and replacing it with something else—a miniature Find & Replace right there in your formula cell.

■ LEFT, MID, AND RIGHT: EXTRACTING TEXT

The LEFT, MID, and RIGHT functions let you pluck a portion of text from a string. You choose the number of characters to use from the beginning, middle, or end of the string, and the function returns that slice of text. (These functions leave the original string or cell value untouched and intact.)

When you give LEFT a string and a number of characters, for example, it returns that number of characters from the very beginning (or "left") of the string, leaving aside any text that follows. One use of this is to display a brief excerpt from a lengthy string. If cell B2 contains the entire text of the Gettysburg Address, for example, the following formula displays only the first 30 characters, including spaces ("Four score and seven years ago"):

```
=LEFT(B2, 30)
```

RIGHT works exactly the same way but returns the text from the end of the original string. When used on the Gettysburg Address cell, this formula returns "shall not perish from the earth.":

```
=RIGHT(B2, 32)
```

NOTE If the string length that you give LEFT or RIGHT is the same as or longer than the length of the original string, then the functions return the entire original string.

Unlike the other two functions, MID isn't tethered to either end of the string. The MID function fetches a run of text from anywhere within the original text. To do this, though, you have to tell MID where you want to start your new string and where you want to end it. You do that by supplying three arguments: the source string, the start position, and the string length. The start-position argument is the number of characters (including spaces, line breaks, tabs, and so on) from the start of the original text. Numbers counts the first character of the string as 1 and moves along from there. The string-length argument is the number of characters you want to extract. For example, this formula returns *b*:

```
=MID("abc", 2, 1)
```

■ LEN, FIND, AND SEARCH: COUNTING CHARACTERS

The only hitch with the LEFT, RIGHT, and MID functions is that you need to know the precise location and length of the text that you want to grab. Splitting a column of full names into first and last names, for example, is tricky because all the names start and stop at different places in each string. Happily, Numbers gives you three functions that can help you do your letter-counting research to pass the appropriate numbers along to your text-extracting function.

The LEN function (short for LENgth) tells you how many characters are in a string. This formula, for example, returns *3*:

```
=LEN("abc")
```

Say you want to trim very long cell entries using the LEFT function and add an ellipsis (...) afterward to show that the entry has been clipped. But you *don't* want to add an ellipsis if the original string is so short that it doesn't *need* to be reduced. The solution is to check the string's length before you clip it, using LEN in combination with the IF function to make the call. You'll learn all about IF starting on page 569, but for now here's a quick example:

```
=IF( LEN(B2)>30, LEFT(B2,30) & "...", B2 )
```

This tells Numbers to check to see if the text in cell B2 is longer than 30 characters and, if so, display the first 30 characters followed by an ellipsis. If the text is shorter than 30 characters, Numbers displays the original value of cell B2.

Where LEN is a one-trick pony, always counting to the end of the string, FIND and SEARCH are more flexible. Their job is to find a snippet of text within a string and tell you its position. These functions accept three arguments:

```
=SEARCH(search-for, source-string, start-pos)
```

The first argument is the text you want to find in the original string: the source string that you provide in the second argument. The third argument—the position where you want to start your search—is optional; if you leave this argument out, Numbers uses the value 1 to start at the beginning of the string. This formula, for example, helps you discover that the word "shall" starts at character 16 of the string:

```
=SEARCH("shall", "Search and you shall find")
```

NOTE If the original string contains more than one instance of the text you're searching for, SEARCH and FIND both return the position of the *first* match, counting from the left.

SEARCH and FIND work exactly the same way, except that FIND is more of a stickler. FIND requires *exact*, case-sensitive matches and doesn't allow wildcards (see the box on page 579). SEARCH, on the other hand, ignores the difference between upper- and lowercase letters and lets you include wildcards for more flexible searching. So unless it's important to match the case of the text you're hunting for, SEARCH provides a more hassle-free experience.

The project of splitting your ingredients gives you a chance to see several of these functions working together. Figure 20-8 shows the final result, using the values in the Ingredients List column to create separate values in the final column. There are a few steps involved in arriving at the formulas that extract these ingredients. The ingredients split on spaces, of course, so to find the end of the first ingredient, you start by finding the position of the first space in the string. For the Tripe Burger, that search looks like this:

```
=SEARCH(" ", Ingredients List Tripe Burger:)
```

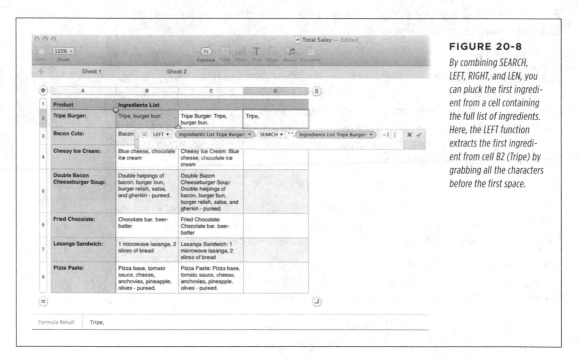

FIGURE 20-8

By combining SEARCH, LEFT, RIGHT, and LEN, you can pluck the first ingredient from a cell containing the full list of ingredients. Here, the LEFT function extracts the first ingredient from cell B2 (Tripe) by grabbing all the characters before the first space.

This formula returns 7, the position of the space immediately after the first ingredient in this list. If you subtract one from that value, you have the length of the first ingredient, enough information to use LEFT to grab it. This formula returns the first ingredient, Tripe:

```
=LEFT(Ingredients List Tripe Burger:, SEARCH(" ", Ingredients List Tripe
Burger:,start-pos) - 1 )
```

The last ingredient starts one character after the space you found in the first step, so you know its position from the start of the string. To use RIGHT to retrieve that last ingredient, however, you need to know its position relative to the *end* of the string. To find the number of spaces to count back from the end of the string to the beginning of the ingredient's name, you subtract the space's position from the length of the string:

```
=LEN(Ingredients List Tripe Burger:) - SEARCH(" ", Ingredients List Tripe
Burger:,start-pos)
```

That formula gives you the length of the last ingredient's name. Giving that length to RIGHT extracts the name:

```
=RIGHT(Ingredients List Tripe Burger:, LEN(Ingredients List Tripe Burger:) -
SEARCH(" ", Ingredients List Tripe Burger:,start-pos) )
```

After you've plugged those formulas into the new column for the Tripe Burger, you can copy them into all of the other products' rows, too, for a tidy collection of individual ingredients.

■ SUBSTITUTE: REPLACING TEXT

The SUBSTITUTE function finds and replaces text in a string, returning the new-and-improved value. The function takes three arguments and an optional fourth:

```
=SUBSTITUTE(source-string, existing-string, new-string, occurrence)
```

The first argument is the original string, the second is the string you want to find, and the third is the replacement text to add to the string. This formula, for example, displays "Larry, Moe, and Shemp":

```
=SUBSTITUTE("Larry, Moe, and Curly", "Curly", "Shemp")
```

> **NOTE** The fourth argument in this formula (occurrence) is optional and tells Numbers to replace only a specific instance of the text when there are multiple matches. For example, if there are three occurrences of the existing-string text in the original string, setting the occurrence argument to 2 tells Numbers only to replace the second one. If you leave out the occurrence argument, Numbers replaces *all* instances of the text.

The function is *case sensitive*, so the existing-string text has to match the upper-case and lowercase letters of the original text in order to trigger the substitution. If Numbers doesn't find the existing-string text anywhere, then the function returns the original string untouched.

> **NOTE** The replacement text in a substitution doesn't have to be the same length as the text it replaces: All strings can be whatever size you like.

Cleaning Up Text

Data entry is, alas, a human endeavor, and so it's prone to lots of odd little mistakes—extra spaces, mistyped characters, inconsistent capitalization. Numbers' functions can help you tidy up these typos or otherwise help transform the format of text to meet your specific needs.

Numbers gives you three functions to nudge the case of your characters up, down, or a combination of the two. All three functions take a single argument—the value of the original string—and return the text with its new capitalization. Here are your capitalization options:

- **UPPER** returns an all-caps version of the original string. For example, =UPPER(B2)

- **LOWER** returns a lowercase version of the original string.

- **PROPER** returns a string with the first letter of every word capitalized and the rest lowercase.

However, just a single extra space in your data can gum up formatting, choke data lookups (page 582), and foil text substitutions. The TRIM function cleans your data up around the ears, getting rid of extra spaces. Specifically, it removes all spaces before the first character, all spaces after the last, and any double-spaces anywhere in the middle. The result is a spick-and-span text string where every word is separated by only a single space.

TRIM accepts a single argument—the text you want it to tidy up—and returns the trimmed string. This formula, for example, returns "Space: the final frontier":

```
=TRIM( "   Space:   the final frontier   ")
```

Formatting Numbers in Text

When you treat a number as text, Numbers has to decide how to format it in your string. As you've seen, the way a number is displayed in a cell is often different than the actual number that's stored away. The real number is always a plain, unadorned figure with no formatting. Even when a currency cell displays $1,250.05, for example, the number's actual value may be something like 1250.04934—no dollar sign, no thousands separator, and lots more decimal digits. Right there, Numbers already has two choices about how it should include the number in a string when you call on it: Does it use the formatted currency value or the actual value?

Numbers always guesses that you want the formatted value. If the currency amount mentioned above is in cell B2, then this concatenation results in "Only $1,250.05":

```
="Only " & B2
```

That's a pretty good guess, but it's not *always* what you'll want. Maybe you'd like to round the number to the nearest dollar, leave off the thousands separator, or eliminate the currency symbol. Numbers gives you two functions—FIXED and DOLLAR—that set the formatting of your number when you use it in a text string.

NOTE Even though text and numbers are different data types behind the scenes, Numbers is clever about switching a value's type when it sees that's what you want to do. As described above, when you use the & operator on two numbers to combine them as text, Numbers knows that they should be treated as text strings and does just that. Likewise, you can add two text strings when they look like numbers. When you have a string like "42" or "$9.99," for example, Numbers is smart enough to know that it should treat it as a number if you try to use it in math. In other words, the program figures out that "42" + "$9.99" = 51.99. You never have to explicitly change a number into text or vice versa unless you want to format a number a certain way (the topic of this section).

The FIXED function takes a number and turns it into a string based on the specific formatting rules you supply. The function lets you specify the number of decimal places to include and whether to include a comma thousands separator in the string. FIXED takes three arguments:

```
=FIXED(num, places, no-commas)
```

The first argument is the number you want to format; the second is the number of decimal places you want to round the number to (this works just like ROUND on page 554); and the third option excludes a comma thousands separator when you set it to TRUE or 1. (The comma is included if you set the third argument to FALSE or 0.) Only the first argument is required. If you leave out the places value, Numbers rounds to two decimal places. If you leave out the no-commas argument, Numbers includes a comma thousands separator in the string.

To return to the previous example, where cell B2 is formatted as currency and contains the value 1250.04934, using FIXED on that cell ignores the cell's currency formatting and instead uses the formatting you choose. The following use of FIXED returns a string with the full value and no comma separator so that the result is "Only 1250.04934":

```
="Only " & FIXED(B2, 5, TRUE)
```

This version rounds to the nearest whole number and adds the thousands separator to get "Only 1,250":

```
="Only " & FIXED(B2, 0)
```

The DOLLAR function works the same way but adds the $ sign to the value and offers no third argument to include or exclude the thousands separator. For example, using DOLLAR on the B2 cell containing 1250.04934, this formula returns the string $1,250.05:

```
=DOLLAR(B2)
```

■ Working with Dates and Times

Calendars and datebooks are grids of days, blocks of time that you can add and subtract. You probably do this math all the time: 3 days from now; a week from tomorrow; a year ago Tuesday; 15 shopping days until Christmas. This kind of "date math" is crucial to planning projects and coordinating with others. Turns out that Numbers is great at date math, making it easy to, for example, fetch a date that's a certain number of days (even specifically *business days*) from another date.

Numbers is particularly good at this because it understands calendars differently from us humans. While we think of a date as a day and a time as a specific moment on the clock, Numbers doesn't distinguish between the two: A date is a time is a date. When you enter a date into Numbers, you're entering a time, too; you might not do it explicitly—the time may not even be visible in your spreadsheet—but it's there. If you don't enter a specific time, then Numbers assumes you mean 12:00 a.m. (midnight) on the date you entered. Likewise, when you enter a time, there's a date attached to it. If you don't specify the date, then Numbers assumes you mean today. In other words, every date in Numbers is actually a precise moment in time.

For Numbers, the calendar is just one big rolling conveyor belt, measured in milliseconds. This makes it easy for Numbers to move back and forth in time—whether you want to leap ahead a few years or jump back a few seconds, Numbers just rolls the conveyor belt back or forth and spits out the new time in any format you want: as a date, a time, the day of the week—whatever.

This section introduces you to doing calculations with dates, times, and durations, and explains functions you can use to get information about any moment in time that you care to zoom in on. Fire up the time machine—it's time to explore Numbers' date functions.

> **NOTE** This section covers most of Numbers' date and time functions—certainly the most common ones. To learn about the stragglers not included here, check out the "Date and Time" category in the Functions tab.

Doing Math with Dates and Times

Numbers provides several functions for working with dates and times, and you'll learn all about them in the next few pages. First, though, there's a lot you can do with the arithmetic operators and math functions you've already seen. This section explores how to add, subtract, average, and order dates, times, and durations. This section uses the term *date value*, but that's simply shorthand for "date-and-time value." Any math that you can do with a calendar date you can also do with a time of day. (As explained earlier, Numbers doesn't see the difference.)

> **TIP** Don't forget that when your formula returns a date, time, or duration value, you can adjust that value's formatting by editing the cell's data format in the Format panel's Cell tab. See page 473 for more info.

■ ADDING OR SUBTRACTING DURATIONS FROM A DATE VALUE

When a formula adds a duration value to a date value, Numbers returns a brand-new date value equal to the original date moved into the future by the amount of time in the duration. Add a day to January 8, and Numbers returns January 9. Add an hour to 3:00 p.m., and Numbers returns 4:00 p.m. This is a convenient way to set the due date on an invoice, for example. If you put today's date in cell B3, this formula returns the date 30 days in the future:

```
=B3 + "30 days"
```

As the example above shows, you can type a duration and its units directly into the formula, but *you have to put it in quotes*. You can type the duration's units in any of the formats shown in Table 20-1—they're the same units you can use to type a value into a cell using the Duration data format (page 477).

TABLE 20-1 *Duration units*

DURATION	ACCEPTED UNITS
Week	week, weeks, wk, wks, w
Day	day, days, d
Hour	hour, hours, hr, hrs, h
Minute	minute, minutes, min, mins, m
Second	second, seconds, sec, secs, s
Milliseconds	millisecond, milliseconds, ms

TIP Numbers lets you use a shorthand for working with durations in days. When you add a regular number to a date, Numbers interprets the number as days. For example, ="1/8/2015" + 2 gives you the date January 10, 2015.

You can mix and match the durations that you add, either in the same text string or in several text strings. If you want to find a time a certain number of days, hours, minutes, and seconds later than the time shown in cell B4, for example, either of these formulas will do it:

```
=B4 + "1d 1h 2m 30s"
=B4 + "1 day" + "1 hour" + "2 minutes" + "30 seconds"
```

Of course, you can also use a duration value from a cell reference, too:

```
=B4 + B5
```

Subtraction works the same way to move back in time from a fixed date:

```
=B4 - "3 days"
```

NOTE Numbers doesn't let you add two dates together (although you *can* subtract one date from another, as you'll see shortly). This means that you can't include more than one date when adding durations.

Adding durations to a date to get a new date makes it convenient to rough out a timeline for project planning, as Figure 20-9 demonstrates.

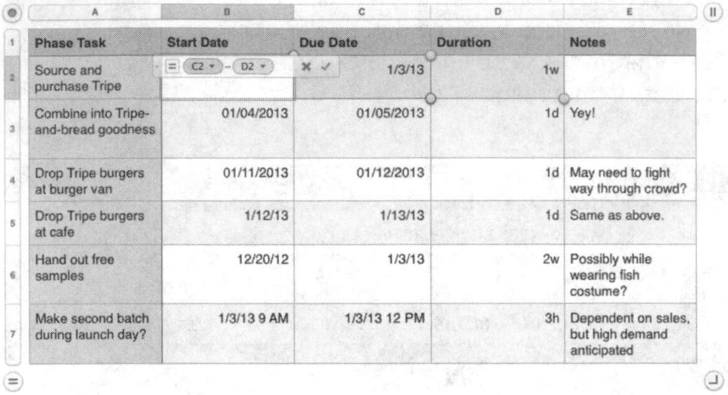

	A	B	C	D	E
1	Phase Task	Start Date	Due Date	Duration	Notes
2	Source and purchase Tripe	= C2 - D2	1/3/13	1w	
3	Combine into Tripe-and-bread goodness	01/04/2013	01/05/2013	1d	Yey!
4	Drop Tripe burgers at burger van	01/11/2013	01/12/2013	1d	May need to fight way through crowd?
5	Drop Tripe burgers at cafe	1/12/13	1/13/13	1d	Same as above.
6	Hand out free samples	12/20/12	1/3/13	2w	Possibly while wearing fish costume?
7	Make second batch during launch day?	1/3/13 9 AM	1/3/13 12 PM	3h	Dependent on sales, but high demand anticipated

FIGURE 20-9

You're sketching out a timeline for the launch of your all-new Tripe Burger. You enter a date when each task needs to be completed by in the Due Date column, and how long each task should take in the Duration column. In the Start Date column, you subtract the duration from the due date. Copying the formula down the Start Date column gives the estimated start dates of each phase of the launch. Adjusting the duration of any of the phases automatically updates every date that follows.

WORKDAY: LEAVE YOUR WEEKENDS OUT OF IT

For project plans like the launch of your tripe-based treat, it's often more accurate to count only *business* days so the project plan doesn't include weekends. (Even theme park owners deserve a day off!) That's where the WORKDAY function comes in, ready to monitor your office hours and protect your weekends.

The WORKDAY function accepts three arguments: the date you're counting from, the number of workdays you want to add or subtract, and an optional argument of excluded dates. The second argument can be either a regular number (the number of days) or a duration value. A number of days is straightforward and easy to understand: 2 means two workdays, period. When you use a duration value, however, things get trickier. No matter what time unit the duration value is displayed in—days, weeks, or milliseconds—Numbers first translates the value into days and then plugs that value in as the number of *workdays*. If your duration is displayed in hours, for example, you might be tempted to think those are work hours—making 24 hours the same as three business days, for example. But that's *not* how it works. In that case, Numbers translates 24 hours into 1 day, which tells WORKDAY to count one workday from the start date.

In the Tripe Project table, you can replace the formula that subtracts the duration from the due date with the WORKDAY function. Here, the Duration field is set to display the number of weeks, hours, and days, so the hours-days confusion described above isn't an issue. For example, here's how to work out when you should start your fortnight-long task of handing out free samples in order to finish by the due date (taking into account the fact that you don't plan on working seven days a week):

```
=WORKDAY(C7, D7)
```

The WORKDAY function's optional exclude-dates argument is useful for indicating holidays or other days when working is so out of the question. This argument can be a cell or range reference to one or more date values, or you can type it as an *array* of dates, like so:

```
=WORKDAY( A2, C2, {"4/12/2014", "5/1/2014"} )
```

TIP To find the number of workdays between two dates, use the NETWORKDAYS function: NETWORKDAYS(*start-date, end-date, exclude-dates*). This puppy returns the net number of days between the start and end dates (excluding any dates you specify).

■ SUBTRACTING ONE DATE VALUE FROM ANOTHER

When you subtract one date or time value from another, the result is a duration value, a useful way to quickly see the elapsed time between two dates or times, like the time it takes you to whip up a batch of deep-fried chocolate treats, or the billable hours you worked for a client before lunchtime.

■ USING MATH FUNCTIONS WITH DATE VALUES

As mentioned earlier in this chapter, the SUM, MAX, MIN, and AVERAGE functions all work with dates and durations, too. You can use MAX or MIN to find the latest or earliest date or time in a series, or use AVERAGE to find the midpoint between two dates. The SUM function adds dates, durations, and numbers, with the same result you've just seen for using the + operator with those values. Whether you use SUM or + with dates and durations, a few caveats apply:

- You *can't* sum date values with other date values.

- You *can* sum a date value with durations, as long as only one date value is involved.

- You *can* sum a date value with regular numbers as long as only one date value is involved (numbers get treated like durations in days).

- You *can't* sum regular numbers with durations unless one of the values is also a date. (In that case, the numbers are treated like days.)

Building Dates and Times in Formulas

As you've seen, you can use cell references in formulas to refer to date values, but you can also add date values directly to formulas. The most direct way to do this is to add a date or time (or both) as a text string. You can type this string in any of the formats that you'd use to type a date or time into a table cell (see page 476). For example, any of these formulas return the date value January 9, 2015:

```
="1/8/2015" + 1
="January 8, 2015" + 1
="01-08-2015" + 1
="1-8-15" + 1
```

Numbers also provides four functions for inserting date values into formulas. TO-DAY and NOW both insert the current date. TODAY sets the time to 12:00 a.m., and NOW sets the time to—you guessed it—the current time. The values inserted by these functions update each time you open the spreadsheet or add or update a new function. For example, this formula shows you the amount of time that's elapsed since today began at midnight:

```
=NOW - TODAY
```

You could insert these functions into a formula cell to display today's date on an invoice or other correspondence, or use a Date & Time formatted text field to do the same job (see page 476).

Building a date using the string formats shown above is almost always the easiest way to go, but Numbers also gives you the DATE and TIME functions, which you can use to construct date values:

```
=DATE(year, month, day)
=TIME(hours, minutes, seconds)
```

For the DATE function, the year value has to be the *full* year. If you enter *15* thinking you're going to get 2015, you'll be 2000 years off—Numbers sets your date to the year 15; enter *2015* instead.

Extracting Date and Time Info

Numbers provides a slew of functions to give you lots of details about any individual date, time, or duration. Here are some of the most common:

- **YEAR(date).** The date's four-digit year.
- **MONTH(date).** The number of the date's month. For example, MONTH("April 15, 2015") returns 4.
- **MONTHNAME(date).** The name of the date's month.
- **WEEKNUM(date, first-day).** The number of the week within the date's year.
- **DAY(date).** The date's numeric day of the month.
- **DAYNAME(day-num).** The name of the date's day of the week. You can also use a number from 1 to 7 as the argument: DAYNAME(1) is Sunday, for example, and DAYNAME(7) is Saturday.
- **WEEKDAY(date, first-day).** Returns a number from 1 to 7 corresponding to the day of the week for that date. The standard setting sets Sunday to 1, but you can use an optional second argument to set Monday to 1 and Sunday to 7—WEEKDAY (date, 2)—or set Monday to 0 and Sunday to 6—WEEKDAY(date, 3).

- **HOUR(time).** Returns the time's hour as a number from 0 to 23.

- **MINUTE(time).** Returns the time's minute.

- **SECOND(time).** Returns the time's second.

- **DUR2DAYS(duration).** Converts a duration value to a number of days.

- **DUR2WEEKS(duration).** Converts a duration value to a number of weeks.

- **DUR2HOURS(duration).** Converts a duration value to a number of hours.

- **DUR2MINUTES(duration).** Converts a duration value to a number of minutes.

- **DUR2SECONDS(duration).** Converts a duration value to a number of seconds.

- **DUR2MILLISECONDS(duration).** Converts a duration value to a number of milliseconds.

What IF: Adding Logic to Formulas

All the functions you've met so far have performed straight-up calculations. They've taken a set of values, worked a predefined transformation on them, and returned a value, no questions asked. For the functions in the Functions tab's "Logical & Info" category, however, asking questions is the whole point. These discriminating functions sit your data down for an interview, ask probing questions, and then decide what to do based on what they discover:

- "Is your grade higher than 93 percent? Yes? Congratulations, you get an A."

- "Have you paid your January bill? No? The amount goes into accounts receivable."

- "Has this check cleared? Yes? Add it to the reconciled balance in the check register."

This category of functions imposes true-or-false conditions on your data: If yes, do this; if no, do that. It's like the game Twenty Questions: The "questions" these functions ask can be complex, but the answers are always simple: yes or no. It sounds basic, but the result can be quite powerful, letting you sift through mountains of data to pluck out summaries of what's found within. Before tackling the mountains, though, you'll start with a molehill, learning how to set a single cell's value based on one or more conditions.

Setting Conditions with the IF Function

The IF function is Numbers' general-purpose decision-maker. It checks to see if some condition is true and, based on the outcome, it does either one thing or the other. You make this kind of decision every morning: If it's raining, you take an umbrella on the way out the door; otherwise, you leave it at home. The IF function makes that decision look like this:

```
=IF(Is it raining?, Take umbrella, Leave umbrella at home)
```

The IF function takes three arguments: the condition to be examined, the "yes" value, and the "no" value. If the condition is true, the function hands back the "yes" value; otherwise, it returns the "no" value. The decision path is simple—just two options; the trick is knowing how to set the right condition.

■ USING COMPARISON OPERATORS

A *condition* is a statement that is either true or false. Two is less than one: FALSE. Two plus two is four: TRUE. These are examples of Boolean values: TRUE.

Remember Boolean values? You learned about this data type way back in Chapter 17 when you read about data formats. As you discovered then, you can use a checkbox to set a Boolean TRUE/FALSE value in a spreadsheet cell. The other way to create a Boolean value is to build a condition using Numbers' *comparison operators*. Table 20-2 lists all these operators, which you can use to build conditions for your IF functions (and a few others, too).

TABLE 20-2 *Numbers' comparison operators*

OPERATOR	WHEN YOU'RE ASKING WHETHER...	EXAMPLE	RESULT
=	Two values are equal	1=2	FALSE
< >	Two values are not equal	1< >2	TRUE
>	The first value is greater than the second	1>2	FALSE
<	The first value is less than the second	1<2	TRUE
>=	The first value is greater than or equal to the second	1>=2	FALSE
<=	The first value is less than or equal to the second	1<=2	TRUE

The Example column in Table 20-2 shows a range of simple conditions using numbers, but conditions can use a wide range of values on either side of the operator: cell references, functions, strings, dates, a calculation—anything that returns a value that can be compared. A condition that asks whether cell A2 is equal to B2, for example, looks like this:

```
=A2 = B2
```

To ask whether A2 is more than double the sum of column B, you'd do this:

```
=A2 > SUM(B) * 2
```

TIP You might recognize these comparison operators as symbols from math class, but Numbers puts them to work with text, dates, and times, too. The greater-than and less-than operators compare text alphabetically (a is less than b), and compare dates and times chronologically (yesterday is less than tomorrow).

You can put these conditions into the IF function's argument list just as you see them here. For example, this formula tells you whether cells A2 and B2 contain the same value. If so, it displays the word "Equal"; if not, it displays the word "Unequal":

```
=IF(A2=B2, "Equal", "Unequal")
```

The condition in the function's first argument can be anything you like as long as it results in a TRUE or FALSE Boolean value. Since checkboxes set Boolean values, for example, that means you can use a cell reference as your condition argument when the cell contains a checkbox. Figure 20-10 shows a very simple example of this.

The example in Figure 20-10 isn't exactly the most practical use for deploying a checkbox to control calculations. A check register offers a slightly more sophisticated example. Say that you're keeping all your checking-account transactions in a table. As usual, when it's time to balance your checkbook by comparing your Numbers check register with your bank statement, your outstanding checks prevent your balance from matching up. Adding a column to store the running balance of cleared transactions will help make sure that you're in sync with the bank. You can use a checkbox and an IF function to automatically update that balance, as shown in Figure 20-11.

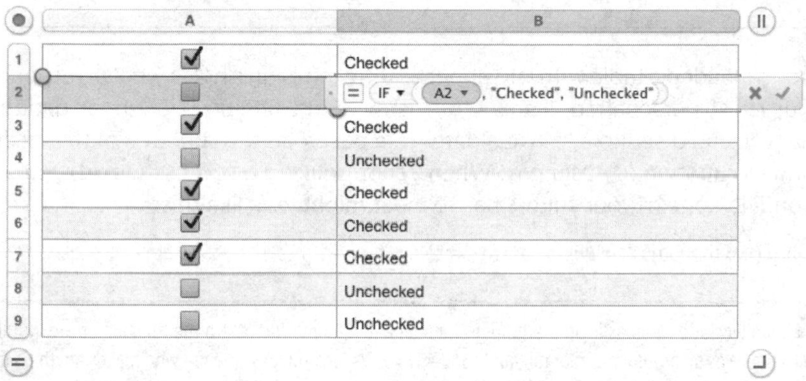

FIGURE 20-10

You can use any Boolean value as a condition in the IF function, including the values of checkbox cells. The second column of this table displays "Checked" or "Unchecked" depending on whether the checkbox next door is turned on or off.

■ **TESTING MULTIPLE CONDITIONS WITH AND AND OR**

A handful of Numbers' functions are specifically designed to be used as conditions in IF functions and always return Boolean values. You can use these functions to build more complex conditions than you can with a single comparison operator. The AND and OR functions are particularly helpful here, letting you combine several comparisons at once to see if any or all of them are true:

- **AND** accepts two or more conditions as its arguments and returns TRUE if *all* the conditions are true. If even one of the conditions is false, then the function returns FALSE.

- **OR** also accepts two or more conditions but returns TRUE if *any* of the conditions are true. A single yes vote carries the day.

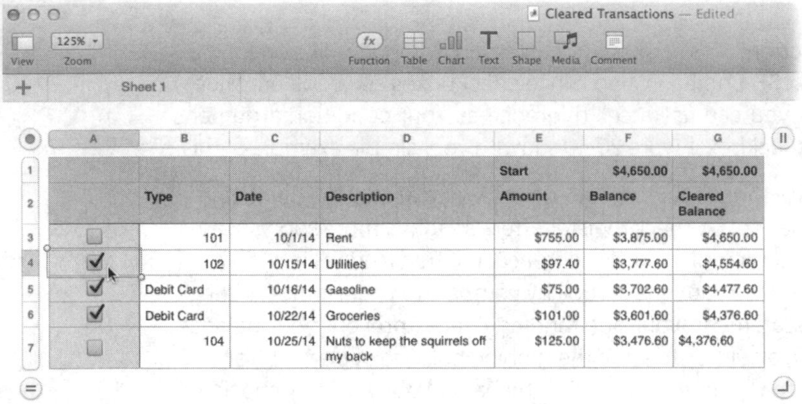

FIGURE 20-11

Click the checkbox in the left column to indicate that a transaction has cleared the bank. The formula in the Cleared Balance column adds the transaction's value to the column's running balance only if the checkbox is turned on; otherwise, it keeps the previous row's balance. Since the column tallies only cleared transactions, the balance at the bottom of that column should be the same as the balance at the bank.

Say you've loaded a table with info about all the promising singles who've responded to your latest personal ad. If this effort is all about finding your sugar daddy or mama, you could set up a "Make a date" rule based on the contents of the Income (B) and Occupation (C) columns. When you're seeking a successful rock guitarist, the condition one of your suitors has to meet might look like this:

```
=AND(B2>100000, C2="Rock Guitarist")
```

TIP Don't include commas in your argument numbers. If you type *100,000* in the function above, Numbers sees the comma as an argument separator, and suddenly you're looking for someone who makes anything more than $100 per year. And, baby, you're too good for that riff-raff.

If an astronaut would also suit your profile, you could change the second argument to an OR function:

```
=AND(B2>100000, OR(C2="Rock Guitarist", C2="Astronaut"))
```

As you see here, you can combine AND and OR functions to build fairly complex conditions. In this example, the function returns TRUE only for an income of more than $100,000 *and* an occupation of either guitarist *or* astronaut (no wonder you're still single). Because the whole shebang returns a TRUE or FALSE value (the result of the AND function), it qualifies as a condition that you can include in your IF function.

```
=IF(
    AND(
        B2>100000,
        OR(C2="Rock Guitarist", C2="Astronaut")
    ),
    "Make a date!",
    "Keep looking"
)
```

TIP   As you start building even mildly complex IF functions, they quickly devolve into lengthy tangles of parentheses, commas and operators. To keep yourself sane and to have a chance at making sense of your own formulas, it's a good idea to apply some extra formatting as shown in the example above.

Numbers ignores any white space that you add between the elements of your functions—including spaces, returns, line breaks, and tabs. Press Option-Return or Option-Tab to insert line breaks and tab stops in the Formula Editor.

▪ OTHER CONDITION FUNCTIONS

In addition to AND and OR, Numbers provides a handful of other TRUE/FALSE functions that you can use as conditions in your IF functions:

- **ISBLANK** returns TRUE if the cell-reference argument is empty; otherwise, it returns FALSE. For example, ISBLANK(A1).

- **ISERROR** returns TRUE if the argument results in an error; otherwise, it returns FALSE. It could help you see whether you're going to hit a "division by zero" error, for example: ISERROR(A1/B1).

- **ISEVEN** returns TRUE if the argument is an even number, and FALSE if it's not.

- **ISODD** returns—you guessed it—TRUE if the argument is an odd number, and FALSE if it's not.

- **NOT** flips the value of a Boolean value. NOT(TRUE) returns FALSE, and NOT(FALSE) returns TRUE.

The IFERROR function is typically handier than ISERROR because it handles cases where you'd normally use ISERROR, but uses less space. IFERROR takes two arguments, testing the first to see if it returns an error. If you're error-free, the function returns the value of that first argument; otherwise, it returns the value of the second argument. For example, say you want to dodge the dreaded "division by zero" error that so often finds its way into table cells. Here are two examples of how you could use the two functions to avoid that error by inserting 0 into the cell when division isn't possible:

```
=IFERROR(A1/B1, 0)
=IF(ISERROR(A1/B1), 0, A1/B1)
```

■ NESTING IF FUNCTIONS TO GIVE MULTIPLE INSTRUCTIONS

So far, you've seen how an IF function can choose between two options. That might be useful in a grade-book scenario if you want to show whether a student has passed or failed. But it would be even better if you could figure out the actual letter grade based on his final percentage score. You can do just that by *nesting* IF functions, fitting one into another like a series of Russian dolls. For example, you already know how to find out whether a grade is an A (in this example, the student's score is stored in cell F3):

```
=IF( F3 >= 90%, "A", "Not an A" )
```

When you replace the no value "Not an A" with another IF function, you can give Numbers additional conditions to try:

```
=IF( F3 >= 90%, "A", IF(F3 >= 80%, "B", "Lower than B") )
```

Numbers tries that second IF function only when the first condition is false: It's not an A; is it a B? As soon as it hits a true condition, the function returns the true-value argument for the corresponding IF function. If none of the conditions are true, it returns the false-value argument of the final IF function (in the above example, that's "Lower than B"). You can keep on nesting values to get all your grades. With a little extra formatting, that looks like so:

```
=IF(    F3 >= 90%, "A",
    IF( F3 >= 80%, "B",
    IF( F3 >= 70%, "C",
    IF( F3 >= 60%, "D",
    "F" ) ) )
  )
```

As you start stacking up parentheses with formulas like this one, it's important to make sure that every opening parenthesis is matched by a closing parenthesis and vice versa!

TIP As you might guess, things can get pretty hairy when you add more than just a few nested IF functions. When you have *lots* of conditions you want to test, it's probably better to create a separate table that maps one value to another (the minimum grades for each grade level, in this example) and then do *lookups* against that table. That's the approach the Numbers' Grade Book template uses; you'll learn about lookups starting on page 582.

Smart Summaries: COUNTIF, SUMIF, and AVERAGEIF

For such a simple concept, the IF function is extraordinarily flexible—but it still has its drawbacks. Most notably, it's lousy at trying to process lots of values in a *range* of cells. Even if you just want to do something simple like show a count of how many A grades your class achieved, IF can't manage the job. It doesn't know how to sift through the Grade column to test each individual cell value and then add up the matching values. For that type of job, you need to turn to IF's bean-counting cousins COUNTIF, SUMIF, and AVERAGEIF.

These functions do the same basic job as COUNTA, SUM, and AVERAGEA, except that those sans-if functions blithely include each and every value in the specified range. By contrast, the COUNTIF, SUMIF, and AVERAGEIF functions let you set a condition that each value has to satisfy in order to be included in the calculation. When you're counting the Grade column, for example, COUNTIF lets you limit the count to values that match the letter A.

All of these functions require two arguments: the range of cells to work on and a condition to use to test each of those cells. This formula, for example, counts all A values in the range F3:F28:

```
=COUNTIF(F3:F28, "=A")
```

The condition in the second argument looks different than the ones you've seen so far—not only is it in quotes, but it's missing the left side of the = comparison operator. That's because Numbers treats each value in the first argument's range *as* the left side of that condition. It steps through each value individually and plugs it into the comparison. If the value is A, it's counted; otherwise, Numbers moves on to the next value.

If you don't include a comparison operator in the second argument, then Numbers treats the whole argument as a value to match, just as if you had included the = comparison operator. That means that you could drop the = sign and write your A-counting formula like this:

```
=COUNTIF(F3:F28, "A")
```

Now that you're just dealing with plain values in that second operator, you can put anything you like in there—a cell reference, a function, a number, text. When that comparison value matches a value in the specified range, Numbers adds it to the tally. For example, to count all cells in the range that match the value of a specific cell (C2, say), you'd do this:

```
=COUNTIF(F3:F28, C2)
```

You can also construct a condition by building a text string that looks like a condition. If you decide you want to count values that are greater than the value in cell C2, for example, you can't just use ">C2" as the condition because Numbers thinks you're talking about the *text* C2, not the cell. Instead, you can build the condition text by combining ">" with the value of the C2 cell, like so:

```
=COUNTIF(F3:F28, ">" & C2 )
```

■ ADDING AND AVERAGING A ROW OR COLUMN BASED ON VALUES OF ANOTHER

You can use SUMIF and AVERAGEIF to do the same kind of thing as the COUNTIF examples shown above, tallying the values of a range when those values meet a certain condition. For example, you might use AVERAGEIF to find the average of only passing scores in a Grades column:

```
=AVERAGEIF(Grades, ">60%")
```

Often, though, it's more useful to add or average a row or column when *another* column or row meets a condition. Say you have a table containing a list of customers' unpaid invoices. With hundreds of outstanding bills, it would be handy to have a way to look up the total owed by an individual customer.

To allow exactly this kind of calculation, SUMIF and AVERAGEIF take a third optional argument. When you provide it, you tell Numbers that you want to set your "if" condition on a different range of cells (the *test values*) than the ones you're actually adding up (the *sum values or avg values*). When you use this format, the cell range in the first argument is the collection of test values that determine whether to add individual cells in the third argument, which is also a cell range:

```
=SUMIF(test-values, condition, sum-values)
```

This might sound complicated, but it's easy to understand when you see it in action. In the invoice example, you want to see the Amount Due value for the product entered in the Product Ordered cell. But why edit the formula every time you want to see the amount for a different product? Better to simply type any product name into the Product Ordered cell and make the formula look up the amount, as shown in Figure 20-12:

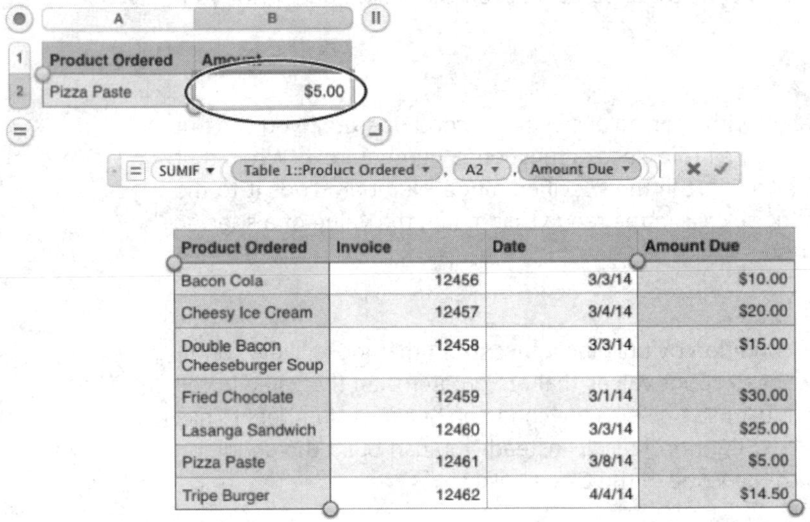

FIGURE 20-12

When you type a product name into cell A2 of the top table, the formula in the Amount cell (circled) fetches the Amount Due from the bottom table.

You can download this sample document (products.numbers) from this book's Missing CD page at www.missingmanuals.com/cds.

> **NOTE** The two cell-range arguments in a given SUMIF or AVERAGEIF function have to be the same height and width. For example, using A1:A8 and B2:B9 works just fine (both are a column of eight cells), but combining A1:A3 and B1:B2 results in an error because they're different heights.

An especially common use of SUMIF works in combination with checkboxes—adding a column of numbers, for example, when their values are either checked or unchecked.

This lets you add a running tally to checklists, or work through "what if?" scenarios: What's the outstanding balance of your unpaid expenses this month? How much will it cost to do your selected home improvements this year? What are the expenses for the wedding guests who have RSVP'd? This is a common enough scenario that Numbers provides a template that does just this very task. In the Template Chooser, pick the Checklist Total template (it's in the Basic category), and Numbers creates a new document with a table that adds up the column of figures for checked rows only. Behind the scenes, the SUMIF function makes that table tick.

■ ADDING MORE CONDITIONS: COUNTIFS, SUMIFS, AND AVERAGEIFS

COUNTIF, SUMIF, and AVERAGEIF are great at zeroing in on a slice of your data, but they're limited by their ability to apply only one "filter." In the invoice example you just saw, SUMIF can winnow the invoices based on one condition: the product's name. But what if you *also* want to limit the results to invoices more than 30 days old to show the total that's past due? In that case, you need to add a second condition, which you can do by adding an "S" to your trusty COUNTIF, SUMIF, and AVERAGEIF functions.

In SUMIFS and AVERAGEIFS, the first argument is the range of cells you want to tally, followed by two or more arguments that describe the test values and conditions. In an invoice, for example, the sum-values argument is the Amount Due column, and you want to set conditions on the Customer and Date columns. A first pass looks something like this:

```
=SUMIFS(Amount Due, Customer, A2, Date, "<1/6/15")
```

That does the job, adding up amounts only for invoices with the matching product name and dates before January 6, 2015. But that means you have to edit the formula *every* time you want to refresh the past-due amount. Yuck. Better to have the formula figure out the 30-day date for you. You can build the condition text within the function itself, but you'll need to rely on a little bit of the date math you learned back on page 564, subtracting 30 days from NOW:

```
"<" & ( NOW - "30d" )
```

Plugging that condition into the function, you get:

```
=SUMIFS(Amount Due, Product Name, A2, Date, "<" & ( NOW - "30d" ))
```

You could keep on adding additional pairs of test values and conditions, too, to winnow down the conditions even further. But you could also have fewer—all of these IFS functions work just fine with only one condition. When you do that, the result is the same as doing a SUMIF with its single condition, although the order of the arguments is different:

```
=SUMIFS(Amount Due, Product Name, A2)
```

It's worth noting, too, that the test-value ranges don't have to be different from the range of cells you want to add up. This is useful, for example, if you want to do your math on values in a specific range. To add up the amount due on invoices billing between $50 and $100, for example, you could do this:

```
=SUMIFS(Amount Due, Amount Due, ">50", Amount Due, "<100")
```

This tells Numbers to do both its addition *and* tests on the same column, adding only values that are more than $50 but less than $100.

The AVERAGEIFS function works the same way, averaging the values in the first argument based on the test values and conditions that follow. The COUNTIFS function, however, follows a different pattern, completely tossing out the first argument you use in SUMIFS and AVERAGEIFS, so that the arguments contain only test values and conditions:

```
=COUNTIFS(test-values1, condition1, test-values2, condition2, ...)
```

With its marching orders in hand, COUNTIFS steps through the test-value cell ranges and increments its counter every time all the conditions are true. This is especially useful for setting conditions in columns; COUNTIFS delivers the count for all rows where the value is true. To show the count of outstanding invoices relating to the private birthday bash Crazyland Wonderpark hosted for your best customer's pet cat (specifically, invoices for the event that are more than 30 days overdue), run this formula:

```
=COUNTIFS(Customer, "Mister Snuggle Bear Birthday", Date, "<" & (NOW-"30d"))
```

Wildcards can make these functions even more useful. The box on page 579 has the lowdown.

■ PULLING IT ALL TOGETHER: USING IF MATH TO SUMMARIZE DATA

Say that the baseball season is in full swing for the Theme Park Staff & Supporters league, and the good folk at Crazyland Wonderpark are having a great season (they even won their last game against archnemesis SuperHappyFamilyFuntime Park Gardens). The coach has asked you to help track a few of the team's basic batting statistics. He has diligently recorded each and every batting appearance of every Crazyland Wonderpark player into a simple table with hundreds of entries (see Figure 20-13), but he needs help plucking out the stats for individual players.

Create a separate table to hold your summary stats. The table will show at bats; hits; batting averages; and tallies for singles, doubles, triples, home runs, walks, strikeouts, and RBIs, as shown in Figure 20-14. When you're done, the table will consist almost entirely of COUNTIF, SUMIF, and COUNTIFS functions to gather the statistics for each individual player.

NOTE Baseball statistics sticklers will no doubt be pained by the inclusion of walks in the at-bats tally, but we're keeping things simple here.

GEM IN THE ROUGH

Something Wild for Searching Text

The COUNTIF, SUMIF, and AVERAGEIF functions (as well as their "IFS" siblings) know a special trick for matching text values: They let you use *wildcards* to find loose matches. Just like wildcards in a card game can represent any card you want, these little jokers are stand-ins for any text character. Numbers has two wildcards:

- **? (question mark) matches any single character.** For example, "?uper" refers to any value that begins with a single character followed by "uper." *Super* and *duper* match, but *pauper* doesn't because it has *two* characters before "uper" (you'd need "??uper" or "p?uper" to match *pauper*).
- *** (asterisk) matches any number of characters, or none at all.** For example, "astro*" refers to any value that begins with "astro," including *astro* itself. *Astronomy, astroturf,* and *astronaut* all match, but *gastronomy* doesn't. To match all these options, including *gastronomy*, "*astro*" does the trick, matching any value that contains "astro" anywhere in the word.

To generate a count of competing establishments who offer *gastronomy* or *gastronomic* delights, for example, you'd use COUNTIF on a column of rival theme parks. If the column was named Rivals, the formula would look like this:

```
=COUNTIF(Rivals, "gastronom*")
```

(In Numbers, wildcard text matches aren't case-sensitive. So "Gastronom*" matches *gastronomy* and *GASTRONOMIC*.)

This turns into a bit of a headache when you want to search for text that includes a question mark or an asterisk, because Numbers treats your ? and * as wildcards. To signal that you want to treat these characters as actual text, add a ~ (tilde) in front of them. For example, to count the number of instances of "Question?" in cells A2–A9, you could use this formula:

```
=COUNTIF(A2:A9, "Question~?")
```

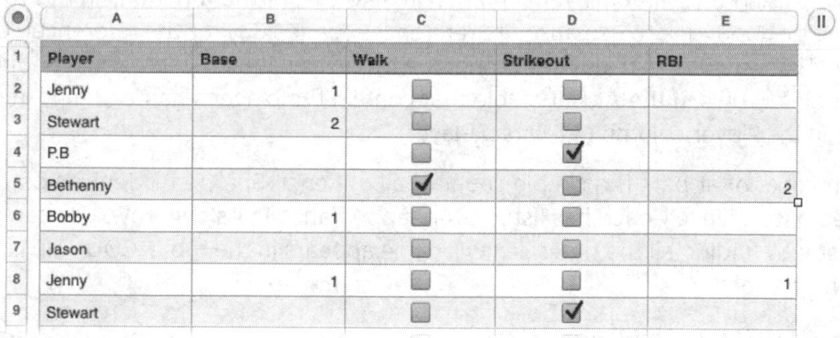

	A	B	C	D	E
1	Player	Base	Walk	Strikeout	RBI
2	Jenny	1	☐	☐	
3	Stewart	2	☐	☐	
4	P.B		☐	☑	
5	Bethenny		☑	☐	2
6	Bobby	1	☐	☐	
7	Jason		☐	☐	
8	Jenny	1	☐	☐	1
9	Stewart		☐	☑	

FIGURE 20-13

Coach's simple table shows every batting appearance for the season. If a player gets a hit, the base number is entered in the Base column (4 is a home run). Walks and strikeouts are indicated with checkboxes, and if a hit drives any runners home, the number is noted in the RBI (runs batted in) column.

NOTE It's typically a good strategy to put the table with the raw data (in this example, that's the At Bats table) on a separate sheet for your polished report, letting you tuck all the raw data out of sight in the back. In Figure 20-14, though, both tables are on the same sheet so they're easy to see.

Player Stats

Player	At Bat	Hits	AVG	1B	2B	2B	HR	Walk	SO	RBI
Jenny										
Stewart										
P.B										
Bethenny										
Bobby										
Jason										
Gretchan										
Jill										
Josh										

FIGURE 20-14

The Player Stats table will hold the individual stats culled from the At Bats table below it. In each row, formulas will use the players' names to boil down the individual stats with the help of the COUNTIF, SUMIF, and COUNTIFS functions.

At Bats

Player	Base	Walk	Strikeout	RBI
Jenny	1	☐	☐	
Stewart	2	☐	☐	

Start by building the statistics for a single player: Jenny from the Amazing Pencil Sharpeners exhibit. Add her name to the leftmost column of the Player Stats table, and you'll use that cell to gather and tally her info from Coach's At Bats table. Since you'll be using this same player condition in nearly all of the functions in this row's cells, it's a good idea to use absolute references (page 233) for the referenced columns. That way, you can reuse the condition text in all your columns. Your condition will look for rows in the At Bats table that contain the player's name (Jenny in cell $A2) in the Player column (At Bats::$Player).

The number of at bats is a simple count of all of Pencil-Sharpener Jenny's batting appearances. Since Coach has listed every appearance in its own row, you can get that stat by finding all the times Jenny's name appears in the table. COUNTIF is the tool for the job:

```
=COUNTIF(At Bats::$Player, $A2)
```

Hits are a count of all values in the Base column that are higher than zero. That means you're counting rows that match two conditions—one in the Player column and one in the Base column. Time to call COUNTIFS from the bullpen:

```
=COUNTIFS(At Bats::$Player, $A2, At Bats::$Base, ">0")
```

The 1B (single), 2B (double), 3B (triple), and HR (home run) columns are also counts of the Base column but require matches for specific values—the number of bases in the hit. Here are the formulas for these four columns:

```
=COUNTIFS(At Bats::$Player, $A2, At Bats::$Base, 1)
=COUNTIFS(At Bats::$Player, $A2, At Bats::$Base, 2)
=COUNTIFS(At Bats::$Player, $A2, At Bats::$Base, 3)
=COUNTIFS(At Bats::$Player, $A2, At Bats::$Base, 4)
```

AVG is the batting average—nothing fancy here, just the Hits cell divided by the At Bats cell (C2/B2). But it's a good idea to make sure you avoid a division by zero error, which would happen for players who haven't yet stepped up to the plate:

```
=IFERROR(C2/B2, 0)
```

The Walks and SO (strikeouts) columns are counts of checked (TRUE) values in the corresponding columns of the At Bats table:

```
=COUNTIFS(At Bats::$Player, $A2, At Bats::Walk, TRUE)
=COUNTIFS(At Bats::$Player, $A2, At Bats::Strikeout, TRUE)
```

The RBI value is the sum of the player's runs batted in from the At Bats table:

```
=SUMIF(At Bats::$Player, $A2, At Bats::RBI)
```

You've now got an entire row of Jenny's personal batting stats. To get the rest of the team, fill in the left column with player names, and then copy the cells from Jenny's row: Select the row's body cells, and then drag the fill handle down to the bottom of the table. The result is shown in Figure 20-15.

Player Stats

	A	B	C	D	E	F	G	H	I	J
	Player	At Bat	Hits	AVG	1B	2B	3B	Walk	SO	RBI
2	Jenny	47	20	0.4255319148	10	5	2	8	7	9
3	Stewart	25	7	0.28	5	2	0	2	9	3
4	P.B	18	3	0.1666666666	2	1	0	5	5	3
5	Bethenny	38	15	0.3947368421	5	4	2	7	9	9
6	Bobby	14	3	0.2142857142	3	0	0	2	4	4
7	Jason	18	3	0.1666666666	2	1	0	2	4	4
8	Gretchan	38	15	0.3947368421	5	4	2	7	9	9
9	Jill	14	3	0.2142857142	3	0	0	2	9	3
10	Josh	47	20	0.4255319148	10	5	2	7	9	3

At Bats

Player	Base	Walk	Strikeout	RBI
Jenny		1		

FIGURE 20-15

When you use autofill (page 483) to copy the body cells from Jenny's row, Numbers brings the formulas along with them, calculating each player's individual stats. Each row uses the player name in the left column to look up all the player's numbers.

From a giant mess of unordered data, you've plucked out every player's batting stats in a matter of minutes. Now that you've got it all in a tidy summary table, you can further sort and filter the table to see which players have the most home runs, top batting average, and so on. Even better, the stats stay up to date: As Coach continues to add batting appearances to his At Bats table, the Player Stats table reflects every hit and homer. Count that as a home run for IF functions!

■ Looking Up and Fetching Cell Data

The data-matching functions you saw in the last section—COUNTIF, SUMIF, AVERAGEIF, and their variations—are terrific at working with data in groups and tallying up matches in the aggregate. But because their job is to find a match, work it into a calculation, and then zip along to the next match, they're all about the bottom line. They can't share the content or location of individual cell values. That's perfect for summarizing many matching items, but when you want to fetch information related to a single unique table entry (a product, a student, an interest rate, a tripe burger), you have to look elsewhere.

Lookup functions retrieve data from a specific cell in a spreadsheet based on its content. From there, you can branch out to pluck content from nearby cells. This means you can do the following:

- Look up a product by its part number and have Numbers automatically plug the product's name and price into a packing list.

- Fetch the letter grade that corresponds to a student's percentage score and add it to your grade book.

- Type a company name into an invoice and have Numbers retrieve its address from a table of contact info, plugging it into the invoice for you.

The common feature among these examples is that all involve a prestocked table of reference data (a product catalog, a grade scale, a table of companies' contact info) where every item, grade level, or company is listed just once. You can then use that storehouse as a kind of card catalog, letting Numbers' lookup functions retrieve info on your behalf about any item inside. The Functions tab groups the lookup functions in the Reference category, and that's the right way to think of them—a collection of fleet-footed reference librarians ready to look up any cataloged snippet of information.

Although you can use lookups on *any* table cell, retrieving organized reference data is certainly their most common and powerful use. By letting Numbers find and fill in reference data on your behalf, you save yourself the time and potential errors of entering the data manually. Your spreadsheet could even have *several* reference tables; in that case, lookup functions can mix and match their data in various and useful ways across your document's sheets. This section shows you how to use lookup functions and work around some of their foibles.

Using VLOOKUP and HLOOKUP

The two most commonly used lookup functions are VLOOKUP and HLOOKUP which, despite a few quirks, offer the best balance between ease of use and flexibility for this category of functions. These two guys work the same way but see the world from different directions: VLOOKUP and HLOOKUP perform vertical and horizontal lookups, respectively. VLOOKUP lets you find a specific *row* in a large table of data, and HLOOKUP seeks out a specific *column*. Once these functions find the row or column you're looking for, you tell them to hand you the value of any specific cell inside.

Because most tables organize individual entries by row, you'll likely use VLOOKUP far more frequently than its column counterpart, so this section focuses on VLOOKUP. But both functions work with a similar set of arguments, three of them required and the last one optional:

```
=VLOOKUP(search-for, columns-range, return-column, close-match)
=HLOOKUP(search-for, rows-range, return-row, close-match)
```

Let's tackle the initial two arguments first, because there's something a little tricky going on here. The *search-for* argument is the value you're trying to find; when you're looking up a product by its part number, for example, this argument is the part number you're trying to locate. The second argument is the overall range of cells you're interested in working with. This range has to embrace not only the cells you're searching (the Part Number column, for example) but also the cells whose values you ultimately want to retrieve (the Price column, perhaps). This range, then, is always a block of cells—it has to be at least two columns wide for VLOOKUP or two rows high for HLOOKUP.

An example helps. Say you've closed a lucrative deal to sell some of your snack foods to your local late-night takeout restaurant. You have a list of product IDs, and you're using VLOOKUP to find the corresponding prices in your product table, shown in Figure 20-16. So the columns-range argument for this lookup should stretch from the ID column to the Price column; that way, it includes both the *search-for column* (ID) and the *return column* (Price). If you wanted to retrieve the product name instead of the price, then the range could include just the ID and Product Name columns.

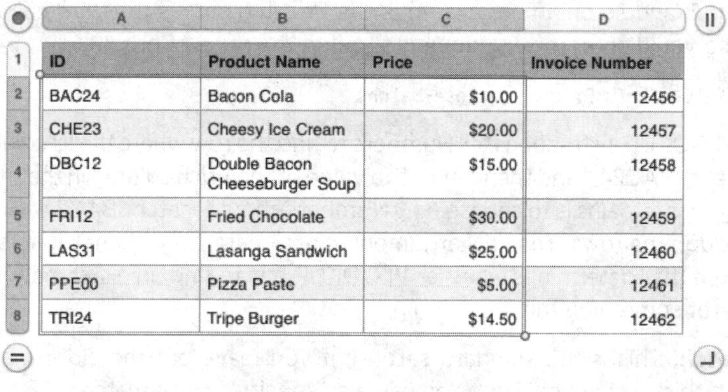

	A	B	C	D
1	ID	Product Name	Price	Invoice Number
2	BAC24	Bacon Cola	$10.00	12456
3	CHE23	Cheesy Ice Cream	$20.00	12457
4	DBC12	Double Bacon Cheeseburger Soup	$15.00	12458
5	FRI12	Fried Chocolate	$30.00	12459
6	LAS31	Lasanga Sandwich	$25.00	12460
7	PPE00	Pizza Paste	$5.00	12461
8	TRI24	Tripe Burger	$14.50	12462

FIGURE 20-16

The range for a VLOOKUP has to start with the column you're searching (the ID column, in this example) and include the column whose value you want to retrieve (here that's Price). This means a VLOOKUP function's columns-range argument must always be at least two columns wide. The rows described by the range also define the portion of the table that VLOOKUP will search.

You can express this using a column range (ID:Price, in this example) or a specific block of cells (A2:C8). Whichever format you choose, understand that this also describes the *rows* that VLOOKUP will search within. You could limit the search to only a specific portion of the table by targeting a set of rows. This range, in other words, describes the canvas your lookup works on, including the search column, the results column, and the rows to search.

One other wrinkle: For VLOOKUP, the *left* column in the range *has to* be the column you want it to search. (For HLOOKUP, the *top* row of the range has to be the row you want it to search). In this example, the search column is the ID column, and the range ID:Price tells VLOOKUP that's the case. If you instead wanted to look up a price using the product name, then the Product Name column would have to be the leftmost column in the range: Product Name:Price. This has an important consequence: Because the range has to include both the search and result columns, and because the search column is always the leftmost column of the range, the result column can't be located to the left of the search column. In other words, VLOOKUP can fetch the values of cells *only* when they're to the right of the column you're searching. Likewise, HLOOKUP can retrieve cell values only when they're below the search row; no upward lookups. That's not always convenient, and in a few pages you'll learn some alternative strategies for finding values outside the lookup range.

That shortcoming doesn't affect the product ID lookup example, however. You've got the ID column pegged for the left column of the range, and you're ready to search for your first product ID, BAC24. That means that you've got the first two arguments of your VLOOKUP function defined. Just two to go—the *return-column* and *close-match* arguments:

```
=VLOOKUP("BAC24", ID:Price, return-column, close-match)
```

The return-column argument determines which cell value you get back after VLOOKUP finds the row you're looking for—in other words, the thing you're really and truly in search of. This value is also called an *offset*, a numeric value that instructs Numbers how many columns to move over to find the data you're looking for. This number is relative to your selected range: The leftmost column in the range is column 1, the next is column 2, and so on. In our example, the Price column is the third column in the range, so you'd enter these arguments to find the price of product BAC24:

```
=VLOOKUP("BAC24", ID:Price, 3, close-match)
```

So far, these VLOOKUP instructions tell Numbers to find the row where the ID column matches the text "BAC24," and then return the value of the Price column in that row. The only thing that remains is to choose *how* Numbers should match "BAC24" when searching through the rows. The final argument, close-match, is optional; it acts as an on-off switch that determines whether VLOOKUP has to find an exact match or if you'll settle for something that's close:

- **Close Match.** This is the standard setting; if you leave out the close-match argument, this is what you'll get. You can also specify a close match by setting this argument to either TRUE or 1.

  When you go with a close match, you tell Numbers that, if it doesn't find any exact matches, it should give you the value from the row that most closely matches your search value. This means that the matching row is the closest value in the search column that is also *less than* the value you're searching for. Think of this as the *Price Is Right* rule: The winner is the bidder with the closest value without going over. (For text, this less-than comparison works alphabetically; for dates and types, chronologically.) This is particularly useful when you're searching a reference table that's organized by ranges of values, as you'll see in the grade-book example on page 588.

- **Exact Match.** Choose this option by setting the close-match argument to FALSE or 0. This option returns a value only when there's an *exact* match for your search value; otherwise, the function returns an error. (Text matches aren't case-sensitive, however, so you don't have to type the right mix of uppercase and lowercase letters to get a match.)

This is typically the option to use when you're looking for specific items, as in the product ID example, or when you want to fetch a customer address. In those cases, the closest match usually doesn't help you and can even introduce embarrassing errors. (Whoops! You mistyped the product ID, and Numbers inserted the data for the closest match—so instead of a shipment of burger buns, a vat of cheese-flavored ice cream is winging its way to your local takeout place.)

To look up the product ID, an exact match is called for, which means that you finally have all the arguments you need to search for the price of the product with the ID BAC24. The final formula looks like this:

```
=VLOOKUP("BAC24", ID:Price, 3, FALSE)
```

As usual, things get much more interesting when you replace the "BAC24" search value with a cell reference, letting you look up values based on what you type into your spreadsheet. For example, this whole discussion started with a promise that it would help you complete your shipment to the local takeout restaurant. You can do this by putting a packing-list form on one sheet of your document and stashing your product table on another. By adding lookup formulas to this form, you can enter just the product's ID, and Numbers will fetch the product's name and unit price from the product table, entering them for you automatically. With those values in place, you can use them and refer to them like any other value. In the packing list, for example, enter the product ID, and the Price column figures the final value. Figure 20-17 shows the result.

You can add an IF function to your VLOOKUP formula so that it performs this data-collecting errand only when a product ID has been supplied. If you don't do this, VLOOKUP tries to find a match using an empty value, returning either an irrelevant row or an error. In row 2, for example, the condition for this check would be:

```
NOT( ISBLANK($A2) )
```

This literally means, "Is cell A2 not blank?" but, when translated to something a bit more graceful, asks, "Is there a value in cell A2?" If yes, do the lookup. If not, insert an empty value. The final IF function looks like this:

```
=IF( NOT( ISBLANK($A2) ), VLOOKUP( $A2, $ID:$Price, 2, FALSE ), "" )
```

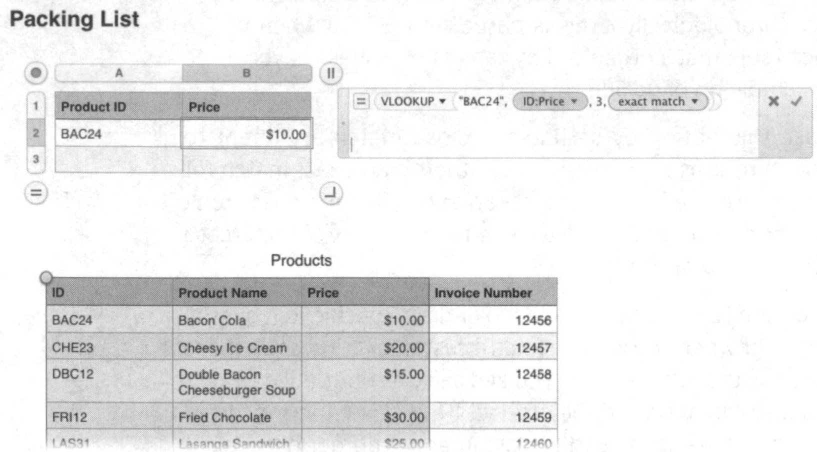

Packing List

FIGURE 20-17

This packing-list form looks up product names and prices when you enter a product ID. For example, typing BAC24 into cell A2 of the upper table fetches the price listed in the Products table. You can also add lookups to a form on one sheet to fetch data from a reference table on another.

■ MATCHING TEXT WITH VLOOKUP AND HLOOKUP

When you're doing a lookup for an exact text match—like finding the name of a product, company, or client—both VLOOKUP and HLOOKUP let you use wildcards in the search-for argument (see the box on page 579). This can save time by letting you find a match without having to type each and every character of your search value, which gets tiresome when you're trying to look up the address, for example, of "Abracadabra Excalibur Kitchen Appliance Company, Inc."

In that case, setting your search term to "abra*" does the trick. Similarly, in the packing-list example you just saw, you could type "ba*" into the Product ID column, and the lookup function would still fetch the price of the Bacon Cola. You can also build the asterisk directly into the VLOOKUP request by adding it to the cell value. For example:

```
=VLOOKUP( $A2 & "*", $ID:$Price, 3, FALSE )
```

NOTE Numbers allows wildcards only in exact-match lookups; you can't use them in close-match searches (see page 584 for a discussion of the difference).

Doing this makes it more likely that you'll create a search value with more than one match, though that can happen with any search value, with or without a wildcard, text or otherwise. No matter what, though, the lookup functions always return just one result. If there are multiple matches, Numbers picks one of them and hands it back to you; if you're searching for numerical data, for example, it returns the largest value that's less than the search value. When you absolutely *must* look up multiple rows that match a search value, filters (page 502) are your best option.

■ MANAGING "LEFT LOOKUPS"

As described earlier, VLOOKUP can return cell values only to the right of the search column. In the Products table shown back in Figure 20-17, this restriction means that you can't look up a product name to get the product ID. The only values available to you when searching in the Product Name column are the cells in the Price and Invoice Number columns.

When you need to look up a value to the left of the search column—a *left lookup*—you have a few options. First, of course, you can simply move the result column to the right of the search column (see page 498 for info about moving rows and columns). If that's not an option, you can use the LOOKUP function or combine the MATCH and INDEX functions—topics that you'll learn about in the next few pages. Finally, you can also fall back to an ugly but effective kludge: Put a *copy* of the values you want to find in a brand-new column to the right of the search column.

For example, to look up a product name by searching for an invoice number, you'd add a new column to the product table, using a cell reference in each cell to grab its value from the Product Name column, as shown in Figure 20-18, which includes a Product Name Copy column.

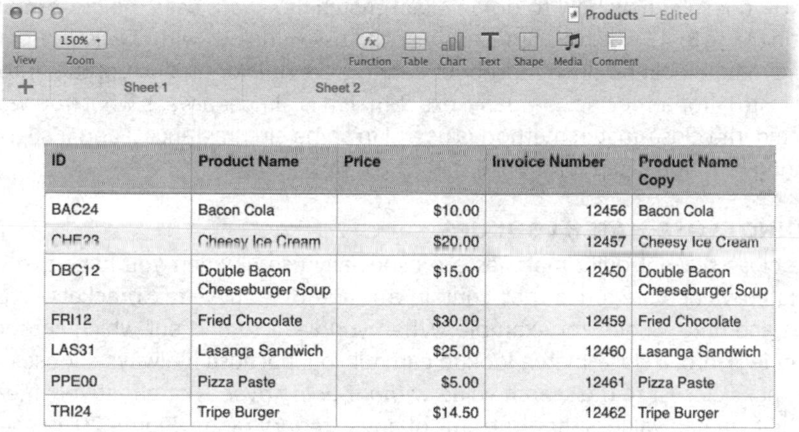

ID	Product Name	Price	Invoice Number	Product Name Copy
BAC24	Bacon Cola	$10.00	12456	Bacon Cola
CHE23	Cheesy Ice Cream	$20.00	12457	Cheesy Ice Cream
DBC12	Double Bacon Cheeseburger Soup	$15.00	12450	Double Bacon Cheeseburger Soup
FRI12	Fried Chocolate	$30.00	12459	Fried Chocolate
LAS31	Lasanga Sandwich	$25.00	12460	Lasanga Sandwich
PPE00	Pizza Paste	$5.00	12461	Pizza Paste
TRI24	Tripe Burger	$14.50	12462	Tripe Burger

FIGURE 20-18

To create a clone of the Product Name column, add a new column to the right edge of the table. In all the new column's body cells, add a simple formula that sets the cell's value to the Product Name cell in the same row.

Now VLOOKUP has a column it can work with when you search the Invoice Number column. To fetch the product name for the invoice number 12457, for example, this formula does the trick:

```
=VLOOKUP("12457", Invoice Number:Product Name Copy, 5, FALSE)
```

Now, though, you have two matching columns—a potentially confusing situation and certainly one that wastes valuable pixel space in your sheet. Sweep the new column under the rug by choosing Hide Column from its reference tab drop-down menu. Even with that column hidden, the lookup function continues to work on its values. (For more on hiding rows and columns, see page 499.)

Using LOOKUP for Easier (but Inexact) Matches

The LOOKUP function is an alternative to VLOOKUP and HLOOKUP, offering advantages (and one significant disadvantage) over those two functions. LOOKUP lets you choose *any* result column or result row from which to fetch a value, no matter what range you choose for your search column or search row. This sidesteps VLOOKUP's left-lookup problem and also dispenses with figuring out the column or row offset for the result cell, giving you a simpler overall syntax. You give LOOKUP three arguments:

```
=LOOKUP(search-for, search-where, result-values)
```

The first argument, *search-for*, is the search value you want to match, and the second argument, *search-where*, is the cell range (usually a column) where Numbers should look for that search value. When LOOKUP finds a match, it returns the value in the corresponding position in the cell range of the third argument, *result-values*.

This straight-to-the-point format is a big improvement over the relatively indirect arguments of the VLOOKUP and HLOOKUP functions. To find the product ID of the shipment of Cheesy Ice Cream in Figure 20-16, for example, simply enter this:

```
=LOOKUP("Cheesy Ice Cream", Product Name, ID)
```

There's a catch, though, and it unfortunately disqualifies LOOKUP from many uses: LOOKUP doesn't know how to do an exact match. It *always* uses the close-match method (page 584), which also means you can't use wildcards with LOOKUP. For the most common lookups like the product catalog example or finding contact info or order history for a specific company, exact match is almost always what you want. That said, the close-match method is useful in some circumstances, and it's worth exploring how you can put it to use.

■ DOING CLOSE-MATCH LOOKUPS

These close-but-not-quite matches are especially useful when you have a set of graduated-value categories that contain a range of values—tax brackets, grade scales, and date ranges, for example. When you want to find out which category a value falls into, a close-match lookup can tell you, because it always chooses the value that's closest to the search value *without going over*. That effectively means that the matched value is the "bottom" of any category range. Figure 20-19 shows examples of close-match search results.

As shown in Figure 20-19, one of the uses for a close-match lookup is to find the corresponding letter grade for a percent score. Head back to the classroom, where you can help the instructor instantly assign letter grades based on students' final scores. To do that, add a table to hold the grade scale and then add lookups to the Grade column, as shown in Figure 20-20.

Figure 20-20 uses the LOOKUP function to find the letter grades in the column. To find Stewart's grade, for example, this is the formula:

```
=LOOKUP(B3,If your score is this much or more…,Letter Grade)
```

if you make this much or more....	Tax rate
$0.00	0%
$7,825.00	10%
$31,850.00	15%
$77,100.00	25%
$160,850.00	28%
$349,600.00	33%

	A	B
1	If your score is this much or more...	Letter Grade
2	93.3%	A
3	90.0%	A-
4	86.6%	B+
5	83.3%	B
6	80.0%	B-
7	76.6%	C+
8	73.3%	C
9	66.6%	C-
10	63.3%	D+
11	60.00%	D
12	0.0%	F

FIGURE 20-19

You can use a close match to find where a value belongs in a graduated set of categories. Because a close match finds the closest value equal to or less than the search term, this lets you look up categories based on the bottom value, or "start," of each category: The start of a new tax bracket, the start of a new project phase, or the start of a new grade level, for example.

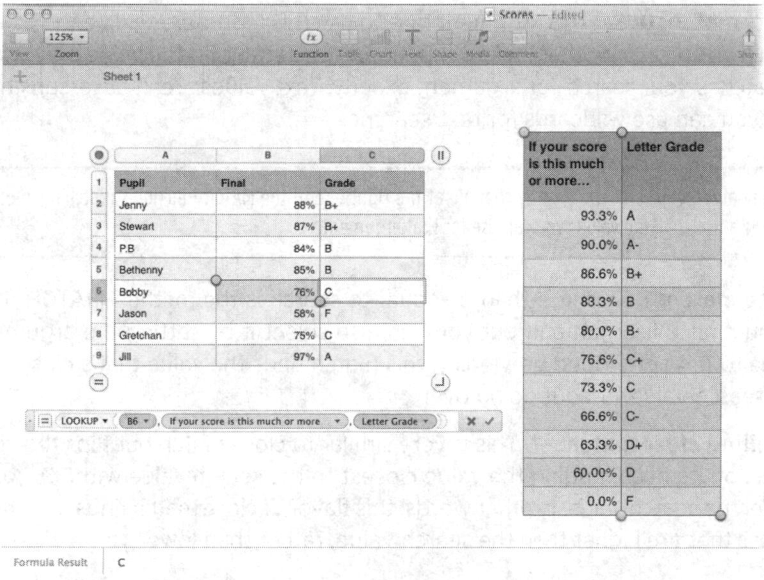

FIGURE 20-20

When you add a grade-scale table to a grade-book document, a simple LOOKUP function lets you find the letter grade associated with each score. Here, the selected grade is found by using the student's final score for a close-match lookup. The closest match for Bobby's 76% grade is 73.3%, a C. (He'd need to earn another 0.6 percentage points to achieve a C+.)

Pupil	Final	Grade
Jenny	88%	B+
Stewart	87%	B+
P.B	84%	B
Bethenny	85%	B
Bobby	76%	C
Jason	58%	F
Gretchan	75%	C
Jill	97%	A

If your score is this much or more...	Letter Grade
93.3%	A
90.0%	A-
86.6%	B+
83.3%	B
80.0%	B-
76.6%	C+
73.3%	C
66.6%	C-
63.3%	D+
60.00%	D
0.0%	F

LOOKUP ▼ B6 ▼ If your score is this much or more ▼ Letter Grade ▼

Formula Result | C

Using MATCH and INDEX to Fetch Values

When you have to do a left lookup *and* you need to do an exact match, then LOOKUP, VLOOKUP, and HLOOKUP all let you down. The solution is to turn to the MATCH and INDEX functions, which can fetch *any* cell value in your spreadsheet without the restrictions of the other lookups. However, this combination is a bit more complicated to construct; that's why using the other lookup functions is typically more appealing when they'll do the trick.

Combining MATCH and INDEX turns your lookup into a two-man job, where each function handles a separate task. MATCH finds the location of the search cell in your table, and then INDEX uses that info to retrieve the value you're after. In this section, you'll see how to use these functions to do a left lookup to look up a product ID by matching its associated product name, using the product-list example you saw earlier (Figure 20-16 on page 583).

The first step is to find the matching row in the table's Product Name column. That's a job for MATCH, which specializes in finding a specific value in a row or column. MATCH accepts three arguments:

```
=MATCH(search-for, search-where, matching-method)
```

The first argument, *search-for*, is the value you want it to find, and the second argument, *search-where*, is the range of cells where you want Numbers to look. MATCH can look in only one direction—along a row or along a column—which means that the range for the second argument must be a straight line of cells within a single row or column. You can use a column reference, for example, or specify a range of cells.

The final argument, *matching-method*, tells Numbers how to match the search value, and takes one of three values: 0, 1, or –1.

- **Exact match: 0.** Set this argument to 0 to use this method. Just like the exact-match option in the other lookup functions, this setting finds a value only when it matches your search-for argument exactly. Text values aren't case-sensitive, and you can use wildcards for text searches.

> **TIP** Remember, you can click the tiny triangle at the right end of the MATCH function's matching-method capsule to see a list of all the values you can use for that argument.

- **Close match: 1.** This less-than-or-equal-to search is the method MATCH uses if you omit this argument, but you can also select it by setting the argument value to 1. As described previously, this match finds the value that's closest to the search value without going over.

- **Modified close match: –1.** This is very similar to close match but flips the condition on its head, finding the value closest to the search value without going *under* the search value. In other words, this flavor of close match finds matching values that are higher than the search value, rather than lower.

NOTE If MATCH doesn't find a match, it returns an error message.

To find the location of the row in the Products table that has an exact match for the product name Fried Chocolate, for example, the following MATCH function does the trick:

```
=MATCH(B5 Product Name, find value)
```

As Figure 20-21 shows, however, the match doesn't yet tell you much, resulting only in the inscrutable number 5. (The example in Figure 20-21 replaces the "Fried Chocolate" string with a cell reference.)

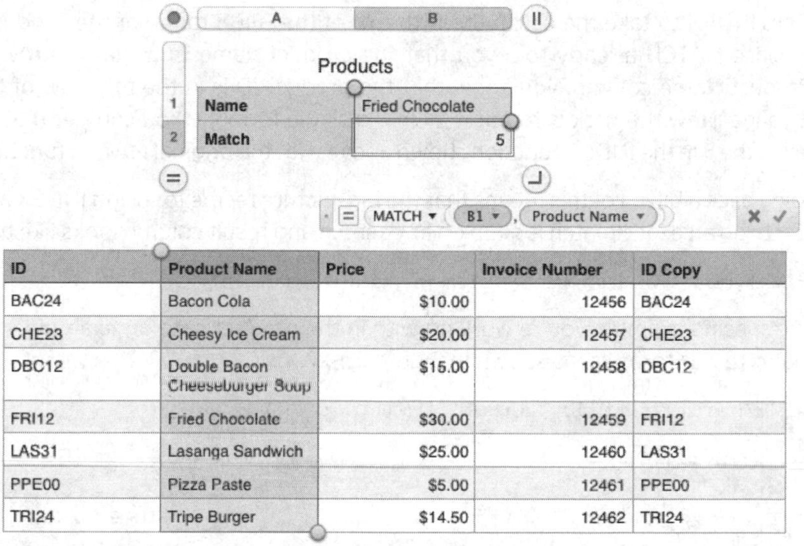

FIGURE 20-21

The MATCH function in cell B2 of the upper table searches cells in the Product Name column in the lower table, finding a match for the "Find" value in cell B5. Here, the result of searching for Fried Chocolate is 5, which indicates that there's a match in the fifth cell in the Product Name column.

The 5 result offered up by MATCH refers to the matching cell's location in the range (in this example, the Product Name column), counting from the top (or from the left when you're working with a row). That means the cell you're after is in the fifth row in this column. That's mildly interesting, but it doesn't do much for you on its own, since the value you're actually after is the product ID for Fried Chocolate. That's where INDEX comes in.

The INDEX function returns the value of any cell you want when you supply its row/column coordinates within a range. Since MATCH told you the row of the cell in the Product Name column (B2:B8 range), that gives you enough info to tell INDEX the coordinates of the cell next door, which holds the product ID you're after.

The INDEX function accepts three arguments. Well, OK, it accepts a fourth optional argument, too—an *area index*, a topic not covered in this book. For most common uses, only the following three are important:

```
=INDEX(range, row-index, column-index)
```

> **NOTE** The *column-index* argument is optional, and if you leave it out, Numbers assumes you want to work with the first column of your selection. When your range is a column—the most common case—that means that you can always leave off its argument.

For example, this combination of arguments gets you the cell you're after:

```
=INDEX( Products::B1:B8, 5 )
```

This tells INDEX to take the cell in the fifth row of the B1:B8 range of the Products table. Since MATCH already told you that the product name is in the fifth row of the Product Name column, you know that the product ID is in the fifth row of the B1:B8 range. Now the trick is to put it all into a single formula. You can get that by replacing the 5 in the INDEX function shown above with the original MATCH function.

Stepping back a bit, all of this means that the big-picture recipe for using INDEX and MATCH to do an exact-match lookup on any search and result column looks like this:

```
=INDEX(result-values, MATCH(search-for, search-where, 0))
```

For the specific example you're working with in the product-catalog example, that translates to this formula, as shown in Figure 20-22:

```
=INDEX('Products-1'::ID, MATCH(B1, Product Name,0))
```

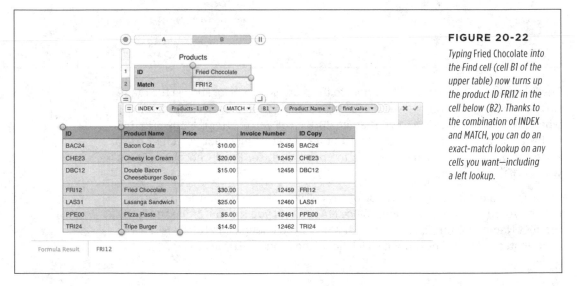

FIGURE 20-22

Typing Fried Chocolate *into the Find cell (cell B1 of the upper table) now turns up the product ID FRI12 in the cell below (B2). Thanks to the combination of INDEX and MATCH, you can do an exact-match lookup on any cells you want—including a left lookup.*

Other Lookup Functions

The lookup functions mentioned so far are the heavy hitters of spreadsheet lookups, but you can find several others in the Functions tab's Reference category. Table 20-3 summarizes a few of the most useful, and you can find complete details on these and others in the Functions tab's descriptions.

In this chapter, you've seen how Numbers can work all kinds of transformations on your data using functions. Now get ready for a whole new kind of metamorphosis: seeing your matter-of-fact data bloom into gorgeous graphs and charming charts. Chapter 21 teaches you how to put a visual spin on your spreadsheets.

TABLE 20-3 *More lookup functions*

FUNCTION	SYNTAX	DESCRIPTION
OFFSET	OFFSET(*base, row-offset, column-offset, rows, columns*)	Returns the value of the cell (or range of cells) that's a certain number of rows and columns away from another specified cell.
COLUMN	COLUMN(*cell*)	Returns the column number for a specified cell (or the formula cell, if no cell is specified). For example, =COLUMN(C2) returns the number 3, since C is the third column of the table.
ROW	ROW(*cell*)	Returns the row number for a specified cell (or the formula cell, if no cell is specified). For example, =ROW(B4) returns the number 4.
COLUMNS	COLUMNS(*range*)	Counts the number of columns in the range reference.
ROWS	ROWS(*range*)	Counts the number of rows in the range reference.

Charts: Giving Shape to Data

They call economics the dismal science, but iWork's stunning charts can brighten even the grayest numbers. When deployed correctly, graphic charts add energy and insight to your data. Bright colors, 3D effects, and effortless formatting—that's anything but dismal.

The trick is how to hang onto the "science" part while you're at it. The point of a chart is to clarify the message behind your data, showing visual trends and relationships that may not be immediately evident from staring at the numbers themselves. It takes care to create a graphic that does this well. Great charts tell a complicated story at a glance; poorly designed charts can confuse and mislead. (Perhaps you *want* to mislead—that takes a carefully designed chart, too!)

This is where iWork's remarkable chart features are both a blessing and a curse. Numbers is chock-full of options for decorating, labeling, coloring, shading, and even twirling your chart into just about any form you'd like. It's an impressive toolkit, and the results always look polished; you can create a chart in seconds that looks like a whole art department labored over it for hours. The problem is that it's easy to get so carried away with formatting the chart that you lose track of its message, sacrificing substance for flash. Your charts should be more than a pretty graphic or a splash of color in the annual report—they should enhance people's understanding of your data.

The good news is that you can have it both ways, creating gorgeous graphs that also enlighten. This chapter shows you not only *how* to use Numbers' chart tools, but also why and when. You'll learn about the various styles of charts that Numbers offers, how to integrate them with your tables, and how to format them with elegance. The chapter finishes with a review of where to pull back, showing you how a bit of restraint can lend greater sophistication and a sharper point to your charts. But, first, the basics.

NOTE   If you want to try some of the techniques described in this chapter, you can grab a sample source table (*sample_table.numbers*), complete with lots of data, from this book's Missing CD page at *www.missingmanuals.com/cds*.

■ Adding a Chart to Your Spreadsheet

In Numbers, charts help visualize data from one or more of your tables, showing all of a table's data or just a portion. Because table data feeds your charts, every chart is associated with a table, a link that you create when you first add the chart to your spreadsheet.

To add a chart, first select the table whose data you want to graph—the *source table*. The way you select the table matters: If you select all of a table's cells or select the table at the object level so that its eight selection handles are visible, Numbers adds a chart that includes *all* the table's data. If you select only a portion of the table's cells—even only one cell—then the chart shows the data in that selection. (As you'll learn on page 611, you can change the selection of charted cells anytime, so you're not locked into your original choice, but you can save yourself time by making the right selection from the get-go.) Figure 21-1 shows the striking difference between creating a chart based on all of a table's cells versus just a single cell.

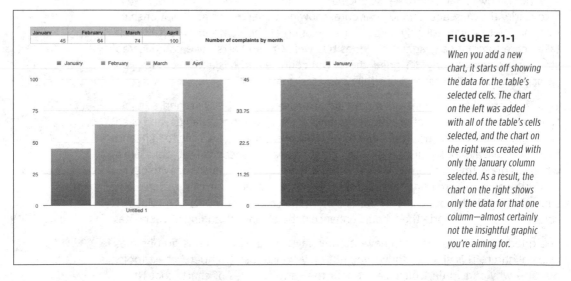

FIGURE 21-1

When you add a new chart, it starts off showing the data for the table's selected cells. The chart on the left was added with all of the table's cells selected, and the chart on the right was created with only the January column selected. As a result, the chart on the right shows only the data for that one column—almost certainly not the insightful graphic you're aiming for.

If the table or selected cells are empty, the chart will be blank until you add values. If no table is selected when you add a chart, Numbers adds a *placeholder chart* to your spreadsheet (like the one shown in Figure 21-3). Page 611 explains how to add data to placeholder charts.

With your table-selection strategy settled, click the Chart button in the toolbar, and choose the type of chart you'd like to use (Figure 21-2). When you click a chart type, Numbers adds the chart to your sheet.

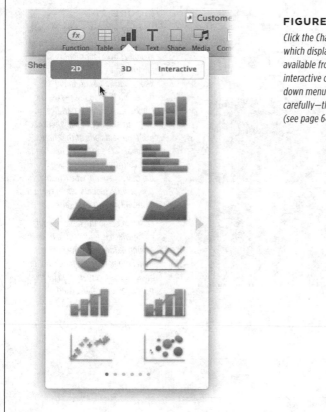

FIGURE 21-2

Click the Chart button in the toolbar to open this drop-down menu, which displays Numbers' various chart styles. (These options are also available from the Insert→Chart menu.) You can choose from 3D and interactive charts by clicking the buttons along the top of this drop-down menu. 3D and interactive charts are eye-catching, but use them carefully—they can distort your data to produce misleading results (see page 641).

Drag the chart wherever you'd like it to appear (you can even paste it into a whole different sheet), and resize it using its selection handles. To remove a chart, select it, and then press Delete.

NOTE Because a chart is dependent on its source table, deleting the source table rips the data from your chart, turning it back into a boring old placeholder chart.

Chart Parts

You'll learn about all the different chart types on page 601, but you first need to get acquainted with some of the anatomical terms for the different parts of charts.

As mentioned above, if you don't have a table selected when you add a chart to your spreadsheet, Numbers adds a placeholder chart like the one shown in Figure 21-3. Think of this starter chart as a floor model to help you get acquainted with how charts work in Numbers. It's a good place to start a tour of the basic features that all charts share.

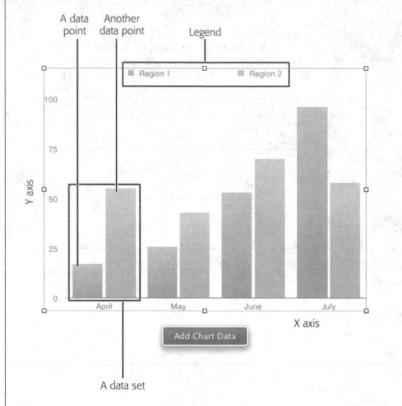

FIGURE 21-3

Numbers' placeholder column chart plots two data series (Region 1 and Region 2) over four months. The month names are listed along the x-axis, and values up to 100 are represented along the y-axis. The numbers behind the chart live in the chart's source table, where each row represents one of the chart's regional data series. The row header cells correspond to the labels in the chart's legend, which displays color keys to identify which column represents which data series.

Each number in the table is a data point, which is represented by a column in the chart. The numbers from both data series for each month are a data set, represented by the paired columns in the chart.

■ THE X-AXIS AND Y-AXIS

The *x-axis* and the *y-axis* are your chart's horizontal and vertical measuring sticks, respectively. All chart types except pie charts have x- and y-axes, which give your chart scale and context. One axis corresponds to either your spreadsheet's row or column headings, the *categories* of data you're charting; in Figure 21-3, for example, the column headings for months are charted along the x-axis. The other axis measures the *values* of your data—the number of visitors on different days, for example.

> **TIP** Numbers lets you choose the scale of the value axis (in Figure 21-3, that's the y-axis) as either linear or logarithmic. For mere mortals, linear is what you're looking for, and that's the standard setting. If you like yours logarithmic, select the chart, and then open the Format panel's Axis tab. Make sure the "Value (Y)" button is selected, and then open the Axis Scale drop-down menu and choose Logarithmic.

■ DATA SERIES AND DATA SETS

Charts construct a visual story from your data. Like every story, there's a certain series of events that combine to give the whole picture and produce the narrative. In charts, these narrative events are called *data points;* they're the individual data values from your table. As you saw back in Figure 21-1, a single data point doesn't make for much of a story. Instead, you have to display several data points about your subject in order to draw conclusions about it. Because you show a series of data about your subject, this subject is called the *data series*—the main character of your story.

The chart in Figure 21-4, for example, tells the story of Crazyland Wonderpark and its changing number of visitors over 7 months. The months are the data series because the data points are represented by a *series* of columns, one for each month. The simplest charts, like this one, have only a single data series. Figure 21-3, however, shows a chart with *two* data series. You can tell the difference between the two data series shown in that chart (at least, you can onscreen) because Numbers displays each one in a different color: It displays Region 1's info as blue bars, and Region 2's info as green bars.

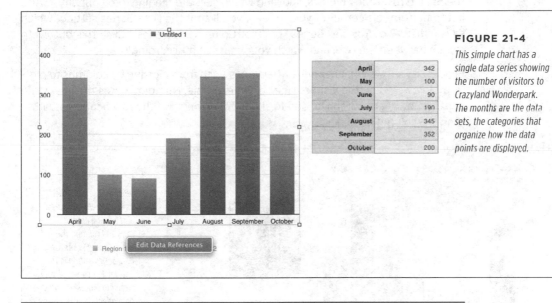

FIGURE 21-4

This simple chart has a single data series showing the number of visitors to Crazyland Wonderpark. The months are the data sets, the categories that organize how the data points are displayed.

> **TIP** When you include header cells in your source table, your chart becomes much easier to work with. In a standard chart, Numbers uses the table's header cells as the chart's text labels, making it immediately clear how the chart is displaying your data.

In both charts, the data points are organized by months. In chart-speak, the months are the *categories*, or *data sets*, of the chart. A data set is a collection of data points for all of the chart's data series. In the charts in Figure 21-3 and Figure 21-4, April is a data set, May is a data set, and so on.

All iWork charts display one or more data series, but they differ in how they display data points. Figures 21-3 and 21-4 both show column charts, which display data points as—you guessed it—columns. Other chart types, which you'll explore in just a few pages, draw these data points in different ways—as bars, pie slices, coordinates, points on a line, and so on. No matter how they render the data points, however, the bottom line is that charts all illustrate the same things: one or more data series, organized into categories of one or more data sets.

NOTE Scatter charts are the exception; although they have data series, scatter charts don't organize the data into data-set categories. For more on scatter charts, see page 614.

In the chart's source table, data series and data sets are represented by rows and columns. In Figure 21-3, the rows are the data sets (April, May, June, and so on), and the columns are the data series. But Numbers lets you flip this arrangement on its head, changing chart orientation so that the months are the data series, and the regions are the data sets. You do this by selecting the chart and then clicking its Edit Data References button. In the source table, a dark frame materializes around the related rows and columns, showing which cells are feeding into your chart. And in the bottom-left corner of your screen, you'll spot the Data Series setting, which says either "Plot Rows as Series" or "Plot Columns as Series." Click this button to switch between the two, and watch your chart shift accordingly.

Figure 21-5 shows what happens when you switch from plotting by columns to plotting by rows, using the visitors chart as an example. Numbers notes the new state of affairs by changing the legend to show the meaning of the row headings, rather than the column headings.

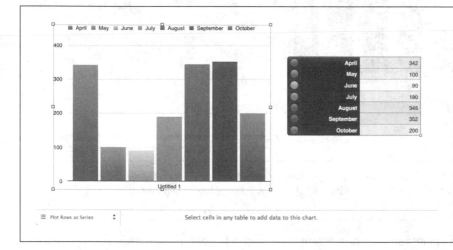

FIGURE 21-5

When you select a chart, its source table sprouts a dark outline around the rows and columns used in the chart. Click the Data Series button in the bottom-left corner of your screen to flip the chart's data orientation. Here, you see the visitor data from Figure 21-4 plotted with rows as series rather than columns as series.

■ **THE LEGEND**

Just like the legend on a map, a chart's *legend* shows what the lines, bars, and symbols in the chart represent. The legend displays the headings of the rows or columns containing the data series and can also display the color or symbol used for the data points on the chart. The legend is a separate object on your page—you can reposition or remove it without affecting the chart itself. When you move the *chart*, however, the legend moves along with it; the only way to position them independently of each other is to move the legend. To move the legend, select your chart, and then click the legend to select it. You can then use drag and drop to move the legend to a new position.

To hide the legend, select your chart and then open the Format panel's Chart tab. In the Chart Options section, turn off the Legend checkbox. To bring the legend back, simply turn this checkbox back on. You'll learn about editing the legend's text on page 618.

Numbers' Chart Types

The first key to creating great charts is picking the right kind of chart for the type of information you're presenting. Now that you've got the hang of how Numbers organizes its charts, you've got the info you need to choose what kind of chart to build. (See page 641 for advice on picking the right type of chart for your data.) Numbers offers 12 types of charts; throw in the 3D and interactive chart styles, and you've got 24 styles in all. That's a lot of options, and it's important to understand the strengths of each so you can make the right choice for your data. Here's a quick tour:

- **Column charts** are a good choice for showing simple results clearly. One data series produces one column, while two or more series allow you to compare those series back to back. In the chart below, for example, you can compare the various theme-park related stats over a 3-month period.

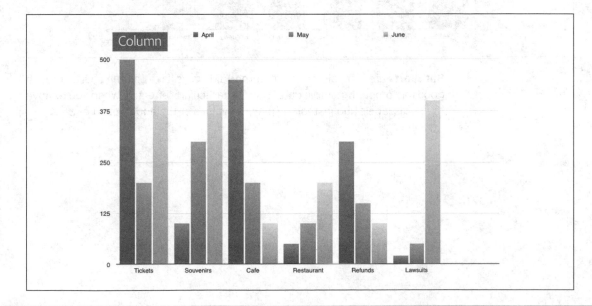

NOTE   For many chart types, the Format panel's Chart tab offers a custom set of options for formatting the chart's display. You'll find more details about formatting charts starting on page 626.

- **Stacked column charts** let you display the cumulative result of multiple data series, one on top of the other. The chart below shows the same data as the column chart on the previous page. Unlike regular column charts, stacked column charts do a poor job of comparing the values of each data series within individual columns, and even make it tough to estimate what those individual values might be. Because the emphasis is on the *combined* value of the data sets, use stacked column charts only when the individual values of the data series are less important than the overall combined values.

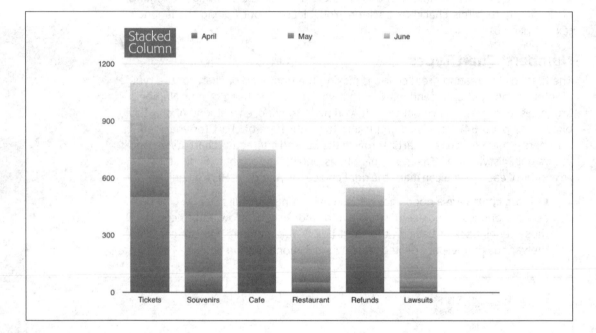

- **Bar charts** are just column charts turned sideways. Like column charts, they're good for comparing simple data. They're particularly effective when you remove the x-axis labels and instead display the values at the end of each bar.

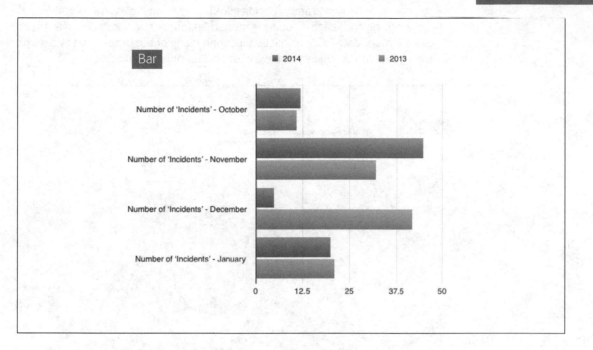

- **Stacked bar charts** line up multiple data series end to end to show their total values; they have the same pitfalls as stacked column charts.

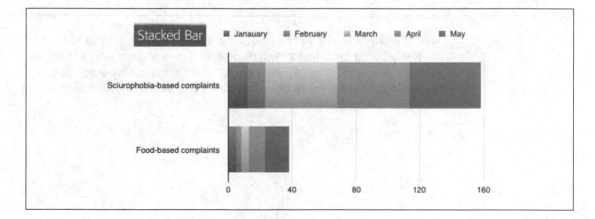

- **Line charts** are typically the best choice for viewing trends over time. These charts plot data as points and then join them with a line. They're very good for comparing or demonstrating relationships between multiple data sets (although they become confusing if you have more than four or five lines). Line charts can present more data in a compact space than many of the other chart types and are a good choice when you have a lot of data points to plot.

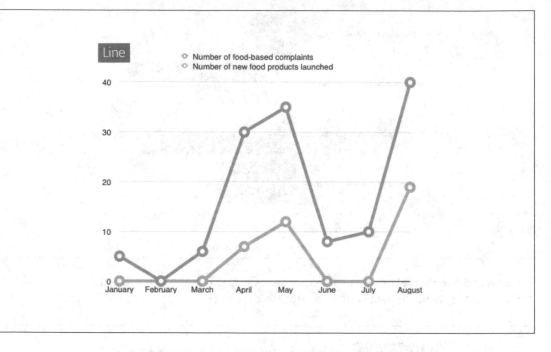

- **Area charts** are similar to line charts but fill in the space below the charted line with a background fill for each data series. Like line charts, area charts are good at tracking the change in data series' values over time. However, be aware that when data series cross, one of the series can disappear behind the other, making its data invisible.

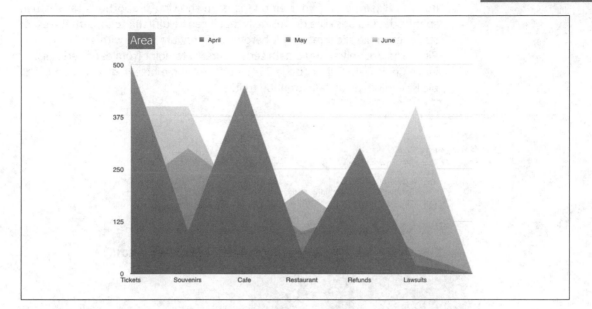

- **Stacked area charts** illustrate the combined values of multiple data series for each data set. Like stacked column and bar charts, these charts emphasize total cumulative value and, as a result, aren't great for showing specific values for individual data series. Because of the continuous flow of the chart data, however, they're better than stacked bar and column graphs at illustrating the changing importance of each data series from data set to data set.

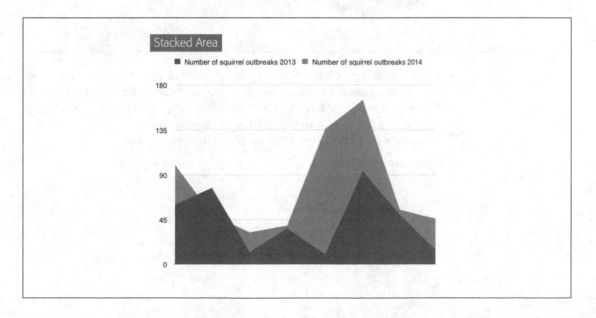

• **Pie charts** display percentages of a whole, like how many of each type of souvenir you sold last year. These charts work best when there aren't too many items to illustrate and your emphasis is on showing proportions rather than specific data values. The downside is that it can be difficult to discern the exact size of each pie slice, making it hard to differentiate slices with similar values. Pie charts use only a single data set: the first data point from each series listed in the Chart Data Editor (page 236). In the example below, one section of the pie is "exploded" to call attention to it.

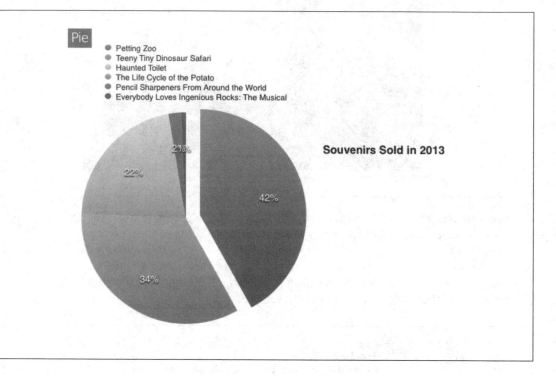

• **Scatter charts** plot individual data points and are useful for spotting trends within a large data set—as well as emphasizing *outliers* (data points that don't fit the overall trend). A favorite in scientific circles, scatter charts let you plot every data point to its own x- and y-coordinates, unlike other chart types where every data series has a value for specific data set categories.

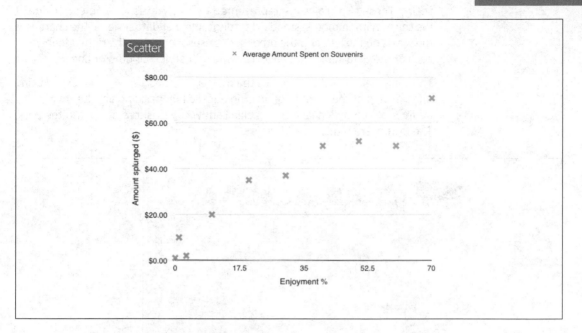

- **Mixed charts** display multiple data series in two chart styles: as column or line charts. Each series in the chart can have its own style. The chart below plots the number of squirrels roaming around Crazyland Wonderpark's petting zoo as a line chart and compares it to a column chart showing the number of visitors' lunches that have mysteriously gone missing.

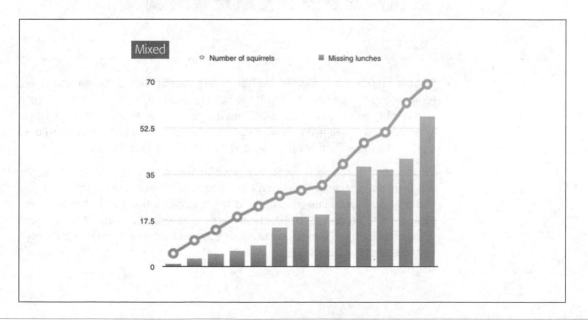

• **Two-axis charts** are mixed charts with a twist: One of the data series uses a different y-axis, which lets you display data that works in two different units or scales. These two scales are represented by two y-axes, one on either side of the chart. With Numbers' standard settings, the first data series in the chart uses the y-axis on the left, and the other series uses the one on the right. Meanwhile, each of the data series can have its own chart style—column or line.

The chart below further explores the mystery of the missing lunches, by using one axis to plot the number of missing packed lunches, and another to plot the number of yummy cheese-and-pickle sandwiches visitors bring into the park. The results are rather shocking.

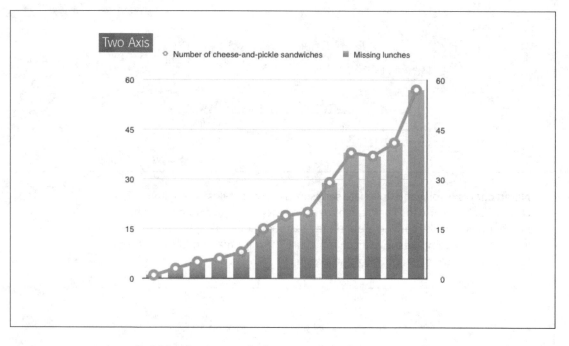

• **Bubble charts** are similar to scatter charts except that the data points are represented by bubbles. Not only do bubble charts look pretty, but they can also display an extra data series, taking the grand total to an impressive three. In addition to the familiar x and y values, a bubble chart can plot a third data series: z values, which are represented by the size of each bubble.

Bubble charts are handy when you need to squeeze in that extra data series but the points on your chart don't need to be an exact science (after all, you can't get an exact value from looking at the size of a bubble). In the following example, the number of products is displayed along the x-axis, the sales are displayed along the y-axis, and the percentage of total revenue is represented by the size of the bubbles.

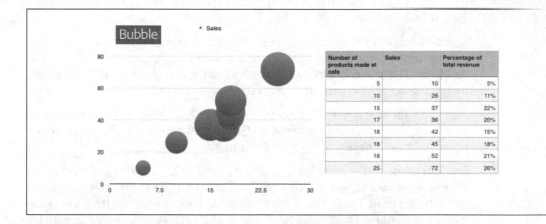

Number of products made at cafe	Sales	Percentage of total revenue
5	10	5%
10	26	11%
15	37	22%
17	36	20%
18	42	15%
18	45	18%
18	52	21%
25	72	26%

Switching Chart Types

Your very first decision when you add a chart to your spreadsheet is what kind of chart to add—in fact, making that choice is *how* you add the chart. Don't fret too much about making the wrong pick, though; if you later decide that your chart is more of a line chart than a column chart, Numbers makes it easy to switch via the Format panel's Chart tab (Figure 21-6). (Page 641 has tips on choosing the right chart type.)

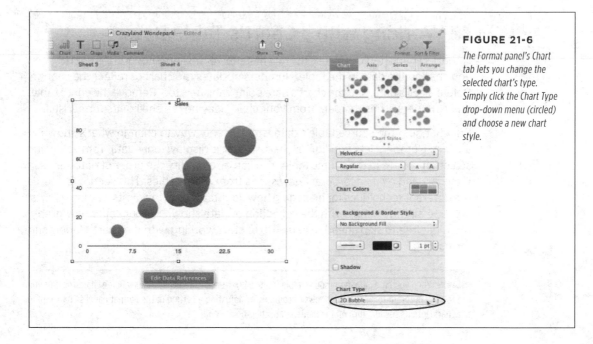

FIGURE 21-6

The Format panel's Chart tab lets you change the selected chart's type. Simply click the Chart Type drop-down menu (circled) and choose a new chart style.

To change the chart type, select the chart, go to the Format panel's Chart tab and open the Chart Type drop-down menu (you may have to scroll down to see it), and then choose a new chart. You can also choose a type from the Format→Chart→Chart Type submenu.

Numbers handles the switch between most chart types gracefully, but you might get unexpected results when you flip in or out of pie charts, bubble charts, and scatter charts. That's because these three types use the source table's data differently from the other chart types, which always plot every cell value as its own data point.

Pie charts, for example, illustrate only a single data set, so they show wedges for only the first row or column of the table. The first data point in each series is shown in the chart, and the rest of the table is ignored.

Scatter charts, on the other hand, use every cell's data, but treat *pairs of cells* as individual data points, with adjacent cells combining to provide the chart coordinates for each data point. The first cell is the x-axis value, and the second is the y-axis value, giving the chart the coordinates to plot. Scatter charts, in other words, require the source table to be organized entirely differently from the other chart types, and you shouldn't expect to switch easily with other chart types—at least, not if you expect the results to make sense. For more on working with scatter charts, see page 614.

Finally, bubble charts represent *three* sets of data rather than the usual two, meaning that at least one dimension of your data is likely to end up lost in translation (see page 617 for more on bubble charts).

■ Working with a Chart's Table Data

A chart's source table provides the raw material for the info shown in the chart. When you change the data in the table, Numbers updates the chart to reflect the change. Delete a cell's data, and the chart's data point vanishes, too. Remove the entire table, and Numbers strips the data from your chart, leaving it a shell of its former self.

But changing the source table's data isn't the only way to change what's shown in a chart. Numbers lets you limit a chart so that it displays only data from a specific selection of cells in the source table. You can also modify the order of data series in the chart and even incorporate new series from other tables. This section explores the different techniques for managing how your table data makes its way into charts. If you're already happy with the collection of data shown in your spiffy new graph, then feel free to skip ahead to page 618 to start working with the chart's labels and formatting.

TIP When you hide data in the source table (page 649), Numbers typically hides it in the chart, too. But you can tell the program to chart hidden rows or columns by adjusting a setting in the Format panel's Chart tab: In the Chart Options section, turn on the Hidden Data checkbox.

Adding Data to Placeholder Charts

As you learned earlier, if you don't have a table selected when you add a chart, Numbers adds a placeholder chart to your spreadsheet like the one back in Figure 21-3 on page 598. Since the chart doesn't have any data to use, it simply contains generic data that doesn't mean anything. (Placeholder charts look kind of faded and washed-out compared with charts that contain real data.) To give it some data to work with, click the Add Chart Data button below the chart. Your cursor sprouts a little column-chart icon to make it clear that you're hunting for chart data. Use these techniques to select table cells and add their data to your chart:

- Click individual cells.

- Drag across a range of cells.

- Select one cell, and then grab the selection handle in its bottom-right corner, and drag it across additional cells.

- If the "Plot Columns as Series" setting is selected (page 611), you can add an entire column to your chart by clicking that column's header. (If the column doesn't have a header, you can click the empty space directly above the column to achieve the same affect.)

- If the "Plot Rows as Series" setting is selected (page 611), you can add an entire row to the chart by clicking the row's header.

Choosing the Charted Cell Range

As you saw on page 596, you can choose the cells you want to chart when you first create a chart, but you can also change this selection at any time. Whittling down the set of charted cells is especially useful when you want to chart only the calculated totals of a table, for example, or zoom in on just two or three data series to do a focused comparison.

Say you want to put the average scores each product achieved in the taste-testing sessions into a graph so you can see at a glance how each foodstuff fared. You have a table containing all the scores from your different taste testers, but you want to chart only the grades in the table's Average row. That means the chart should have a single data series (the average score). To do that, you need to tell Numbers to chart only the Average row. Fortunately, that turns out to be a simple process.

When you select a chart, Numbers highlights the charted cells in the source table, outlining them. To edit these cells, click the Edit Data References button that appears beneath your chart. The outline around the cells now sports a circular handle at its bottom-right corner that lets you grow or shrink the collection of selected cells; drag the handle to change the selection's size. As you drag, the chart updates to display the selected values. Figure 21-7 shows how the selection box looks when charting the Average row. (If you want to try working out averages yourself, download the file *Averages.numbers* from this book's Missing CD page at *www.missingmanuals. com/cds*.)

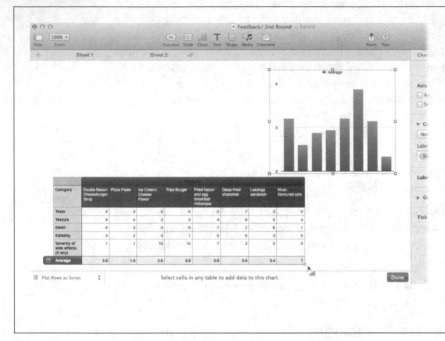

FIGURE 21-7

The chart shows the data from the body cells of the table's Average row. The source table indicates this by highlighting those cells when you select the chart. The circular handle at the bottom right of the selection box (where the cursor is positioned) lets you resize the box by dragging.

Here, the selection box has been sized and maneuvered to include only the cells containing the foods' average scores. The Data Series button in the bottom left of the screen shows that the chart uses rows as its data series.

The only wrinkle is that the circular handle can drag only the bottom-right corner of the selection box; the top-left corner of the selection remains fixed. That means that you can expand the selection down and to the right, but not up or to the left. If you want to select cells that are above or to the left of the box, you first have to move the selection box and *then* resize it:

1. **Select the chart and then click the Edit Chart References button (if you haven't already).**

2. **Put your cursor over the selected cells so the cursor turns into a four-headed arrow.**

3. **Drag the selection box so that its top-left corner contains the top-left cell whose data you'd like to include in the chart.**

4. **Drag the circular handle so that the box's bottom-right corner contains the bottom-right cell you want to include.**

Removing Data Series from a Chart

Moving and dragging a selection box to choose a cell range works well when all of your cells are in a tidy block. But what if you want to chart only selected data series, and they don't live next door to each other? Numbers lets you surgically remove data series from your chart without affecting the original data in the source table.

Say that you're charting the progress of the Crazyland Wonderpark baseball team. You've got all the stats for each player but want to do a head-to-head comparison of just two of them. In this scenario, each set of stats is a data series. To remove one set of stats from the chart, select the chart so that a dark border appears around the cells in the source table, as shown in Figure 21-8. Each data series also has a dark label with a little colored button in the center (the button corresponds to the color that represents this data in the actual chart). To remove a set of stats, click its label to select that set of cells, and then press Delete.

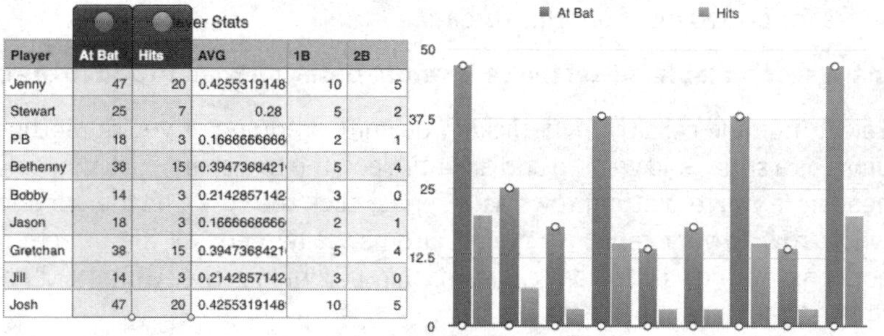

FIGURE 21-8

When you click a chart's Edit Data References button, Numbers highlights all the cells that feed into your table and surrounds them with a dark frame and a label. To remove an entire column's or row's worth of cells from your chart, click the dark label above or next to those cells, and then press Delete. Don't worry—the cells remain intact in your source table. To add more data to your chart, click individual cells, drag across a range of cells, or click a column or row header to add the entire row/column's worth of data to your chart.

NOTE If you're plotting columns, the dark labels appear above the columns' headers; if you're plotting rows, the labels appear to the left of the rows' headers. (If the table doesn't include column headers, the labels appear where the headers *would* be. If your table doesn't include row headers, then you'll need to drag across all the cells in a row to add the entire row's worth of data to your table.)

Numbers removes the data series from the chart (in this example, all the data points in the selected column). The data remains untouched in the source table but is no longer included in the chart. Repeat this process for every data series you want to remove.

TIP If you later decide to re-add the data series to your chart, you can do so by selecting the chart, clicking the Edit Data References button, and then either clicking the header of the table column or row you want to add, or dragging across a group of cells (hop back to page 438 for a detailed look at the different ways to select cells).

Adding Data Series from Other Tables

You can combine data series from more than one table, which lets you create a visual summary of information from several tables in your spreadsheet. A simple example: You've been hard at work analyzing the relationship between missing lunches and what kind of sandwiches visitors are bringing into the park, and you've got the results stored in two separate tables—one has the figures for potted meat sandwiches on white bread, the other for cheese-and-pickle baguettes. You'd like to combine the stats from both into a single chart. Here's how to do it:

1. **Create a chart from one of the tables.**

   In this example, doing so gives you half the data you want to chart: the data series for potted meat on white bread.

2. **In the second table, select the cells whose data you want to add to the chart.**

   Select multiple cells by Shift-clicking or Shift-dragging. If you're plotting columns as a series and want to add an entire column to a chart, click that column's header. If you're plotting rows as a series, click the row's header to add that whole row to your table. Numbers automatically feeds all the selected cells, columns, and rows into your chart, mashing them together with the data from the first table into one chart.

3. **To check what cells are feeding into your chart, select the chart, click the Edit Data References button, and you'll see that cells in two different tables light up.**

> **NOTE** You can't mix and match plotting columns as data series and plotting rows as data series. When you choose to "Plot Rows as Series" in the bottom-left corner of your screen, you change the settings for *all* the tables that feed into your chart. If you want to use the columns from one table and the rows from another, you'll need to juggle the data around in your original tables.

If your table data doesn't fall into your chart as you expect, you may have to fall back to editing the chart's cell references manually to get the data series organized. See the box on page 615 for details.

Changing the Order of Data Series

Unless you tell it otherwise, Numbers displays your chart's data series in the order they appear in the source table. That means you can only change the lineup by shuffling the rows or columns in the source table (see page 498 for details about moving rows and columns).

Working with Scatter Charts

Scatter charts interpret and display the source table's data differently from other charts. Every *other* chart type clusters data points together into data sets, displaying all of your sales results for 2013, for example, then 2014, then 2015, and so on. Every data series has a value for each of these data sets, so the result is very structured: a one-to-one comparison of each data series.

Working with a Chart's Cell References

This section describes lots of marvelous mousework that you can do to collect and shape the data for your chart—drawing boxes around the data cells, dragging from other tables, slicing out specific data series. When you make these selections, Numbers is really just keeping a list of cell references to include in your chart. Every time you add or remove cells to be charted, Numbers updates its internal list of cell references, organizing them by data series.

When you have a chart selected, the Format panel's Series tab lets you open the hood and monkey around with these cell references to change the cells used for any data series. You can replace all or part of a data series with a different row or column of data. This is useful, for example, when you have fresh info for a single data series, perhaps from a different table, and want to swap it into the chart without editing the original source table. This is also the only way to update cell references when the source table is located on a different sheet—if you created a chart on one sheet, for example, and then moved it to another, leaving the source table behind.

To edit a chart's cell references, select the data series you want to edit by selecting your chart and then clicking one of its data points (a column, bar, area, or line for the series). Numbers adds circular handles to all the chart's data points for that series to indicate that they're selected. Next, open the Format panel's Series tab (shown in Figure 21-13 on page 620) and click the Data heading to expand that section (if it isn't open already). The Data section contains two fields: Value and Name. Select the capsule in the Value field that represents the range you want to replace, and a selection box appears around the corresponding cells in the source table. You can then either drag this selection box to a new location or use its handles to add and remove cells from the range.

If you prefer to do things manually, click the Value field and then type your cell references directly into the Formula Editor that appears. You can also use a series of cell or range references; just put commas between each one. No matter what method you use, these cells can be from any table in your spreadsheet. When you make changes, Numbers updates the chart, using the new data for the series.

The Name field lets you display the name of the series in the chart (page 619 covers this in more detail).

Scatter charts, however, are just that—scattered. They dispense with the orderly presentation of bar, line, and area charts and instead sprinkle data points willy-nilly across the chart canvas. Every data point is actually made up of two values: the x-axis value and the y-axis value. The chart puts these two values together to plot each data point, independent of the rest. This type of chart is particularly good for plotting large data sets and finding correlations and patterns in a big cloud of data.

To make this work, scatter charts treat two source-table cells as one data point, requiring two rows or columns for a single data series—one x value and one y value. To show multiple data series, you add additional two-column or two-row pairs of cells to the source table. Figure 21-9 shows an example of a scatter plot with two data series.

When you create a scatter chart or select the cells that it should use, be sure that you always have an even number of columns or rows—every x value needs a corresponding y value—or some data series won't display at all. It's a good idea to enter and organize your x and y values into a table before creating the chart. The x value is always on the left of the pair when you're organizing data series in columns and on the top when you're organizing by rows. (The chart in Figure 21-9, for example, uses columns as data series.) Remember that you can switch between using rows or columns as data series by clicking the chart's Data Series button in the bottom-left corner of your screen (see page 599 for a refresher).

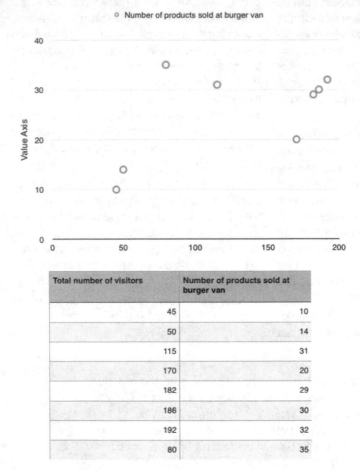

FIGURE 21-9

This scatter chart (top) has two data series—the number of products sold at the burger van, and the total number of visitors—which are represented in the source table (bottom) in two separate columns.

Here, the x value represents the total number of visitors, and the y value is the number of products sold at the burger van. Plotting the two together helps you see the correlation between the total number of visitors and how many sales the burger van makes.

Total number of visitors	Number of products sold at burger van
45	10
50	14
115	31
170	20
182	29
186	30
192	32
80	35

By default, scatter graphs share the same x values. This fact isn't obvious when you use a two-column table as the basis for your chart (as in Figure 21-9), but when you're dealing with three or more rows or columns, Numbers' Share X Values feature quickly becomes useful. For example, say you're studying the correlation between the number of squirrel-based incidents and the growing number of unaccounted-for coffee beans in the burger van's inventory. (You've had a word with the manager, and he's promised to beef up security.) You take measurements at regular intervals for your entire sample of 100 terrifyingly caffeinated squirrels. The x value—the time when the measurement was taken—is the same for all entries, so it makes sense to share this value among all measurements.

To see this feature in action, create a scatter chart based on more than two columns or rows of data. When the Share X Values option is left on, the scatter chart uses the first column or row as the x values and the rest of the chart as the y values for the data series. If the chart is set to use columns as data series, for example, then the first column holds the x values for all the entries, and every remaining column holds the y values for each data series.

This option, in other words, uses a single row or column for each data series—with one additional row or column to hold the x value for all the series. In the caffeinated squirrel experiment, each twitching squirrel would be a data series, each with a single row or column showing the measurement taken at each interval.

This approach makes for easier data entry in your source table—you're not repeating the same info over and over again—and also makes the table data easier to read, letting you scan across a single line of data to see the results for each sample period. However, you can turn off Share X Values at any time by selecting your chart, clicking its Edit Data References button, clicking the Data Series button in the bottom-left corner of the Numbers window (see Figure 21-10), and then turning off Share X Values.

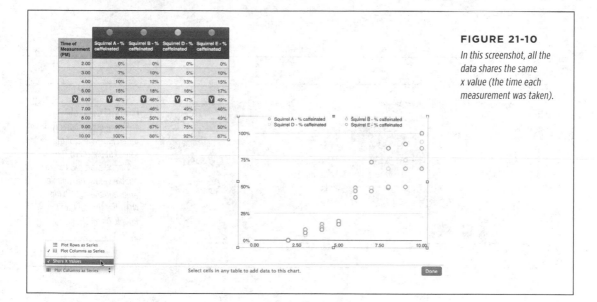

FIGURE 21-10

In this screenshot, all the data shares the same x value (the time each measurement was taken).

Working with Bubble Charts

Bubble charts are a variation of scatter charts, but each entry has *three* data series, not just two. Figure 21-11 shows an example of a bubble chart and its source table.

Numbers automatically represents your third data set with the area of the bubbles, but you can choose to represent this via the bubbles' diameter instead, by opening the Format panel's Series tab, clicking the Bubble Data heading to expand that section (if it isn't open already), and then clicking the drop-down menu, and then choosing Bubble Diameter (Figure 21-12 shows an example of the same chart with the two different settings applied.) Also in this section, you can tell Numbers to add bubbles representing negative values to your chart by turning on the "Show negative bubbles" checkbox.

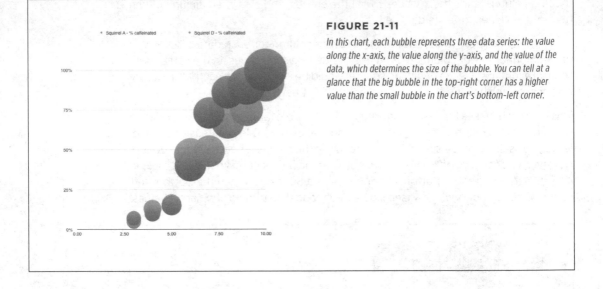

FIGURE 21-11

In this chart, each bubble represents three data series: the value along the x-axis, the value along the y-axis, and the value of the data, which determines the size of the bubble. You can tell at a glance that the big bubble in the top-right corner has a higher value than the small bubble in the chart's bottom-left corner.

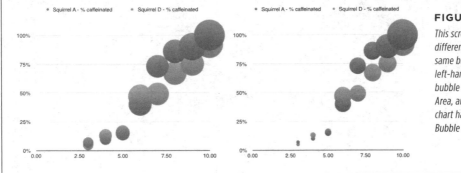

FIGURE 21-12

This screenshot shows two different versions of the same bubble chart. The left-hand chart has the bubble data set to Bubble Area, and the right-hand chart has the data set to Bubble Diameter.

■ Editing Chart Text and Labels

After laboring to collect your data and spin it into a beautiful chart chock-full of insights, don't forget to tell your reader what it means. The text in your chart—the title, the legend, and the data labels—is very nearly as important as the data itself, since it's the text that says what those bars, lines, and scatterplot dots represent. When your chart goes to 11, its text should concisely answer the question, "Eleven what?"

Just be sure not to overdo it—too many text labels can choke a chart with needless clutter. (See page 640 for tips on avoiding this and other kinds of "chartjunk.") Add just enough text to explain your data and stop there. The Format panel's Chart tab lets you add a variety of text elements, including a title, legend, axis titles, and axis data labels.

Chart Titles and Legends

Like tables, every chart has a name, even if it isn't displayed onscreen. To make the title visible, select your chart, open the Format panel's Chart tab, and turn on the Title checkbox. Your chart will now proudly display the word "Title" above it. To edit this placeholder, click the title once to select its text box, and then click it again to place your cursor inside the text box, ready to type a more illuminating title. You can format your title text in the Chart Title tab, which contains the usual text-formatting options (see page 466 for the lowdown on formatting text). To hide the title, simply turn off the Title checkbox. (You can recover the title anytime, by turning this checkbox back on).

Each chart's legend is a separate object that you can manipulate independently of the chart. The legend is like a cousin of the iWork text boxes you know and love: You can adjust its fill and stroke (border), give it a shadow, or change its text using the settings in the Format panel's Style tab; or change its size and position with the Arrange tab. Simply click a chart's legend to display these tabs.

The legend displays the labels for the chart's data series. When you first create a chart, Numbers uses the source table's header cells to figure out the names for each data series. If the data series' rows or columns don't have header cells, Numbers uses the inspiring names Untitled 1, Untitled 2, and so on. Either way, you can change these names by selecting your chart, clicking the legend once to select it at the object level, and then clicking it again to place your cursor inside the text. Don't worry—editing the legend has no effect on the source table's header cells.

You can also change the label for a data series by selecting the data series in your chart. (To do so, select the chart and then click one of its data points—a column, bar, or whatever; Numbers selects all the points in that series.) Next, open the Format panel's Series tab and click the Name field to launch the Formula Editor so you can type a new label (see Figure 21-13).

Initially, the Name field contains the cell reference of the header cell Numbers used as the legend's label or the text "Untitled [#]." Since you're working in the Formula Editor, if you want to write a label rather than using a cell reference, you have to put the label's text in quotes. Instead of typing a name directly, you can add a cell reference to the Name field, telling Numbers to use the cell's value as the label: Click the Name field, clear out the Formula Editor, and then click the cell whose value you want to use; press Return or click the Formula Editor's checkmark when you're done. Either way, Numbers updates the chart's legend with the data series' new name.

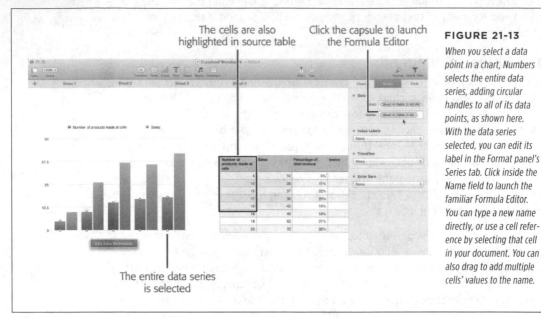

The cells are also highlighted in source table

Click the capsule to launch the Formula Editor

FIGURE 21-13

When you select a data point in a chart, Numbers selects the entire data series, adding circular handles to all of its data points, as shown here. With the data series selected, you can edit its label in the Format panel's Series tab. Click inside the Name field to launch the familiar Formula Editor. You can type a new name directly, or use a cell reference by selecting that cell in your document. You can also drag to add multiple cells' values to the name.

The entire data series is selected

To dismiss the legend, select the chart, open the Format panel's Chart tab, and turn off the Legend checkbox.

NOTE You can't remove the legend if it's selected at the text or object level, or remove it by pressing Delete. So make sure you have the chart selected at the object level before trying to turn off the Legend checkbox.

Axis Titles and Labels

The Format panel's Axis tab lets you add titles and labels to a chart's x- and y-axes to help viewers understand exactly what the axes represent.

NOTE The Axis tab appears only when you have a chart selected at the object level.

The *value axis* is the y-axis in column charts, line charts, and area charts, and the *category axis* is the x-axis because it displays the data-set categories. For bar charts, the situation is reversed. In scatter and bubble charts, which have no data-set categories, both the x- and y-axes display values. (Pie charts don't have axes, so the Axis pane doesn't appear for that chart type.)

NOTE For most charts, the Axis tab contains two buttons: "Value (Y)" and "Category (X)." However, in some instances you may see "Value (X)" and "Category (Y)" buttons instead (for example, when working with a bar chart). The following sections assume you're seeing the "Value (Y)" and "Category (X)" setup, but just be aware that these two buttons may occasionally switch their X and Y labels.

To add axis labels, head to the Axis tab and select either the "Value (Y)" or "Category (X)" button at the top of the tab, depending on which label you wish to edit. Then turn on the Axis Name checkbox, as shown in Figure 21-14. To remove an axis label, turn off the corresponding Axis Name checkbox.

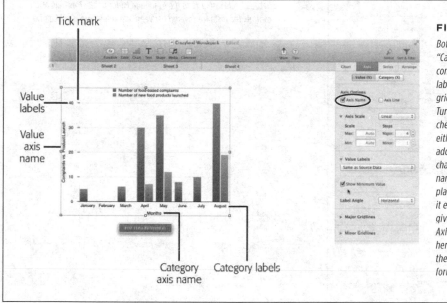

FIGURE 21-14

Both the "Value (Y)" and "Category (X)" settings contain options to show labels, tick marks, and gridlines on your charts. Turning on the Axis Name checkbox (circled) in either group of settings adds a text box to your chart with a placeholder name. Double-click the placeholder name to make it editable, and Numbers gives you access to the Axis Title tab (not shown here), which contains the usual array of text-formatting options.

To hide or display labels along the value axis, open the Format panel's Axis tab, select the "Value (Y)" button, and then open the Value Labels drop-down menu (Figure 21-15). Numbers initially sets this menu to "Same as Source Data," which uses the same formatting as the cells in your source table. But if you want to use another format, you can pick from Number, Currency, Percentage, Fraction, Scientific, Date & Time, or Duration. (These are the same options you encountered when you learned how to format table cells, so head back to page 473 if you need a refresher). Page 624 explains how to adjust the angle of value labels. To hide the chart's value labels, choose None.

NOTE The Value Labels drop-down menu appears only in the "Value (Y)" settings, so if you can't find it, make sure you're not in the "Category (X)" settings by mistake!

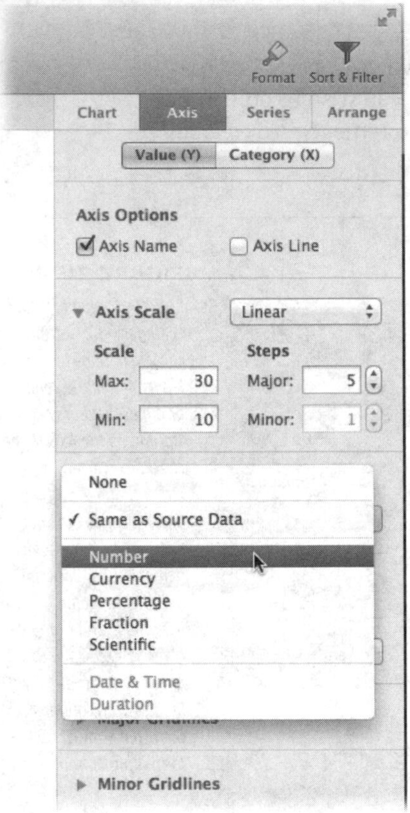

FIGURE 21-15

The Value Labels drop-down menu lets you control the measurements that appear along a chart's y-axis. For example, if you're displaying a currency, you can choose Currency from this drop-down menu. If you're happy with the way the data is formatted and displayed in your table, leave the Value Labels menu set to "Same as Source Data."

If you're working with logarithmic scale (page 598), you'll see a Decades field rather than the Major and Minor fields. This field also controls the distance covered between one value label and the next.

You can also choose the maximum and minimum values displayed on the axis. Make sure the "Value (Y)" button is selected, and then click the Axis Scale heading to expand this section (if it's not expanded already). The Max and Min fields control the maximum and minimum values shown along the axis (see Figure 21-16). If you leave these fields set to Auto, Numbers automatically adjusts the chart's scale to fit the data values displayed, but it always sets the minimum value to zero—unless any of your data points are less than zero, in which case, Numbers sets the minimum to a negative value. You might want to customize these settings in order to, for example, begin the chart at a higher value when all your data points are much higher than zero, or to display a higher range than your largest data point (to show how much fundraising is yet to be done to reach your goal, say). If you don't want to display the minimum value at all, turn off the Show Minimum Value checkbox circled in Figure 21-16. You can control the leaps your axis makes between one label and the next by adjusting the Major and Minor fields.

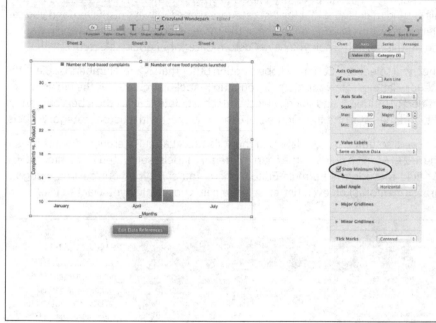

FIGURE 21-16

Control where your chart begins and ends by altering the Max and Min fields. To adjust the interval between one label and the next, use the Major and Minor fields. Set the value to Auto if you want to show both the maximum and minimum values in your chart. Make sure the Max value is evenly divisible by the numbers in the Major and Minor fields, or you'll end up with awkward value labels such as 33.333 and 66.667. Here, the chart begins at 10 (the Min value) and ends at 30 (the Max value).

You can label your chart's data sets with their series labels by clicking the "Category (X)" button at the top of the Axis tab, and then turning on the Series Names checkbox. This checkbox adds the data series labels to every data point (these are the same labels that appear in the chart's legend).

> **TIP** For a cleaner-looking chart, it's a good idea not to show the minimum value when it's zero (so turn off the Show Minimum Value checkbox). But if the minimum value is something other than zero, you owe it to your readers to include this value label so they can discern the chart's baseline value.

Also in the "Category (X)" settings, you can add category labels to your chart by opening the Category Labels drop-down menu and choosing any option other than None. Take your pick from these choices:

- **Auto-Fit Category Labels.** When you have lots of labels jostling for space on the x-axis, selecting this option can prevent the axis from getting overcrowded. This option is selected by default.

- **Show All Category Labels.** Displays—you guessed it—all the category labels. If you have lots of data, this can make your x-axis a very busy place.

- **Custom Category Intervals.** When space is short or you don't need to label every data set, you can control the number of category labels by selecting this option and then adjusting the "Show every # categories" field to space out the labels along the axis.

The final option in the Category Labels drop-down menu is Show Last Category. This setting makes sure that the last category name is always displayed, and you can select this option *in addition* to one of the three listed above. You'll usually want to turn on this setting when you have Custom Category Labels selected.

When you select any Category Labels option other than None, Numbers displays the category labels from your table (if you didn't label up your chart, the labels will be Untitled 1, Untitled 2, and so on). Select your chart, double-click the label you want to edit, and then start typing. Figure 21-17 shows a chart with custom category labels.

You can also edit category labels in the Axis tab's Label References field shown in Figure 21-17, which holds all the chart's category labels, separated by commas. Click this field to open the Formula Editor, where you can type your desired category names (in quotes) or, even better, select a cell whose value you want to use.

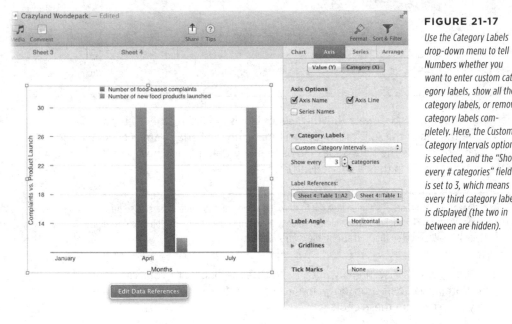

FIGURE 21-17

Use the Category Labels drop-down menu to tell Numbers whether you want to enter custom category labels, show all the category labels, or remove category labels completely. Here, the Custom Category Intervals option is selected, and the "Show every # categories" field is set to 3, which means every third category label is displayed (the two in between are hidden).

Turning on more than a few of these labels can make for a mighty crowded x-axis. Fortunately, you can ease the congestion by displaying the labels at a different angle. For example, when you select a column chart, open the Axis tab's "Category (X)" settings, and turn on the Series Name checkbox, Numbers adds the series name for *every* column—but there's almost never enough room to fit all of those names horizontally along the x-axis. The result is that the labels crowd together in an unreadable jumble. The fix is to display the series names vertically or diagonally.

Select your chart, and then go to the Axis tab, click the "Category (X)" button, and choose an option from the Label Angle drop-down menu. If you want something more daring than the standard Left Vertical, Left Horizontal, and so on, choose Custom to get access to rotation controls so you can set your labels at a quirky 127-degree angle. You can change the angle of the labels that appear along the Y axis too, by clicking the Axis tab's "Value (Y)" button and then choosing from the Label Angle drop-down menu.

Data-Point Labels

With the exception of scatter charts, all Numbers charts can slap a value label on every data point to show its value, as you can see in Figure 21-18. To add such labels, select the chart, and then click the Format panel's Series tab to reveal the settings for that specific chart type. Open the Value Labels drop-down menu and select any format other than None. You can choose from the usual array of data formats, such as Percentage, Currency, Fraction, and so on (skip back to page 473 for a reminder of how each format works). If you're happy with the way your data is formatted in the chart's source table, select "Same as Source Data."

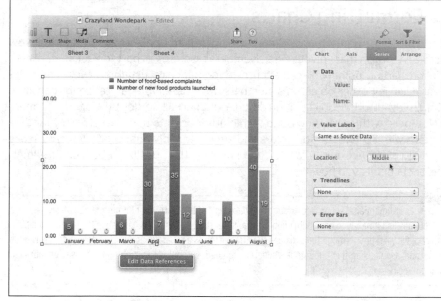

FIGURE 21-18

This chart uses value labels to display values inside each data point's column, an effective and more precise alternative to labeling the x-axis and making the reader estimate each value.

Once you've added value labels to your chart, you can set the position of the labels relative to the individual data points (bars in column and bar charts, points in line charts and area charts, and slices in pie charts) by opening the Series tab's Location drop-down menu and choosing from Right, Left, Top, Middle, Bottom, or Outside.

NOTE You can have different settings for the value labels in each data series. Just select the data point whose value label you want to edit (for example, a bar in a bar chart), and Numbers automatically selects the rest of that data series. Then open the Format panel's Series tab in the Format panel, and make your changes. For example, you could display one set of value labels as a percentage at the top of a bar, another set as a currency outside a bar, and so on.

Changing Text Styles

You can change the fonts for a whole chart at once by selecting the chart, opening the Chart tab, and then choosing a new font from the Chart Font section.

Change the fonts separately for axis titles, category labels, value labels, or the chart's title or legend by clicking one of those elements to select it and then opening the appropriate tab: Chart Title, Axis Title, the Axis Labels, or Style tab (depending on the element you selected). You can update only entire sets of labels at a time. So, if you highlight one item in the legend and set it to bold typeface, the other items in the legend acquire the bolding, too.

■ Formatting Charts

With your chart data organized and labeled, you're finally ready to add the wow factor. The graph that you get when Numbers first adds a chart to your spreadsheet is just a starting point—you can alter the appearance of just about every chart element. Like any other object in a Numbers document, you can resize it, reposition it, align it with other objects, and so on. But charts also get privileged treatment in Numbers, with formatting options that other objects don't have: Spin your data in space with 3D effects, add colors and effects to individual chart elements, make pie slices explode from the center, and fine-tune the position of bars and columns. This section tells you how.

TIP The Format panel's Chart and Arrange tabs have most of the controls for formatting a chart's appearance, and you may find it handy to have both open at once. To set this up, open the Chart tab in the Format panel, and then click View→Show Arrange Tools to open the Arrange tab as a separate, floating window. Drag this window to one side, and you can then dip into it whenever you need, without it ever getting in the way of your main editing screen.

Adding 3D Effects

Numbers lets you display your chart as a 3D diorama for your data, offering a slick presentation with a variety of textures that make the chart look like a physical object, with weight and presence. Eight of Numbers' chart types are available in 3D versions. (Sorry: Scatter charts, mixed charts, and two-axis charts don't have 3D versions.)

You can add a 3D chart by either clicking the toolbar's Chart button and making a selection from the 3D category, or clicking Insert→Chart and choosing one of the 3D options. Or, if you've already added a chart to your document, you can switch it to a 3D format by heading to the Format panel's Chart tab and clicking the Chart Type drop-down menu (you may have to scroll down to see it).

No matter which method you use to add a 3D chart, the Chart tab sprouts a new section: 3D Scene. Click the 3D Scene heading to expand that section, as shown in Figure 21-19. These settings let you change the chart's viewing angle to turn it three dimensionally in space, and add lighting effects and depth. A 3D scene controller also materializes on top of the chart in the canvas (see Figure 21-19); simply drag these curly arrows to rotate your chart. You can use either the controller or Chart tab settings to tilt and swivel the chart—they have the same effect.

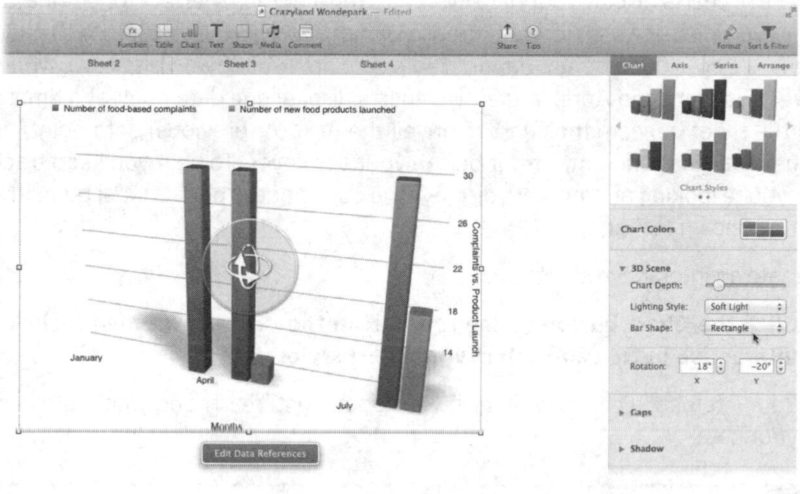

FIGURE 21-19

The Chart tab's 3D Scene settings let you spin your chart in space. The Chart Depth slider sends the chart back and forth in space, making it deeper or shallower. The Lighting Style drop-down menu lets you change the chart's lighting effects.

For pie charts, the Show Bevels checkbox rounds the edges of each pie slice to create a subtle boundary between wedges. Column and bar charts get their own special setting, Bar Shape, that lets you choose rectangular or cylindrical bars.

TIP To adjust the shadow cast by your 3D chart's elements, use the Chart tab's Shadow settings.

Tread carefully with these 3D effects: Although the result often looks remarkable, it doesn't always do your data any favors. By their very nature, 3D effects skew the perspective of the chart, changing its proportions to make some parts of the graph look larger than they are. So if your goal is to offer the most accurate view of your data, then 3D charts are *not* the way to go. But here's the thing: It's really *fun* to play with the 3D tool, and it's oddly satisfying to see Numbers spin and tilt your data with its sophisticated 3D modeling effects. And now here's some book saying that you shouldn't frolic with your charts in three dimensions. What gives?

The essential problem is that Numbers' chart data is only two dimensional; adding an artificial third dimension doesn't enhance your readers' understanding of the information. In fact, the skew and shadow of a 3D chart can actually obscure your chart's data by distorting its elements, making it difficult to accurately gauge data values. The bottom line is that these effects are window dressing—albeit incredibly impressive window dressing—that don't add substance to the chart. For all these reasons, 3D effects fall into the category of "chartjunk" (see page 640). But if you absolutely can't resist adding these effects to your chart, at least try to use 'em with restraint and keep the skewed perspective to a minimum: In the 3D Scene settings, keep the Chart Depth setting relatively low and keep the X and Y rotation angles relatively flat.

Working with Interactive Charts

Interactive charts display your data in stages, making them perfect for emphasizing the relationship between different groups of data, such as the sales from Q1 and Q2, expenses across the different departments, and how your gym visits have dwindled between January and April. Interactive charts display one data point at a time; you drag the slider beneath the chart to unveil the next (or previous) data point, making the data warp and move right before your very eyes. To help you keep track of what you're looking at, Numbers displays the current data point's label beneath the slider, as shown in Figure 21-20.

To create an interactive chart:

1. **Click the Chart button in the toolbar; in the drop-down menu, click the Interactive button and select your chart style.**

   Your interactive chart appears in your document, ready and waiting to accept your data.

NOTE If you want to convert an existing chart to an interactive one, do so by going to Format→Chart→Chart Type or clicking the Chart tab's Chart Type drop-down menu.

---

2. **Click the Add Chart Data button and add your source data.**

   Find your source table and drag to select a cell or range of cells to use. You can also add data from an entire row or column by clicking the header for that row or column. Select multiple cells by dragging across them.

3. **Once you've fed all the data into your chart, click the Done button in the lower-right part of the canvas.**

Now that your interactive chart is all filled in, grab the slider along the bottom of the chart to make your data dance.

TIP If you're dragging the slider and aren't getting the results you expect, you may have plotted columns when you meant to plot rows. Select your chart, click its Edit Data References button, and then take a look at the button in the bottom-left corner of the screen. If it's set to "Plot Columns as Series," then click it and choose "Plot Rows as Series" instead.

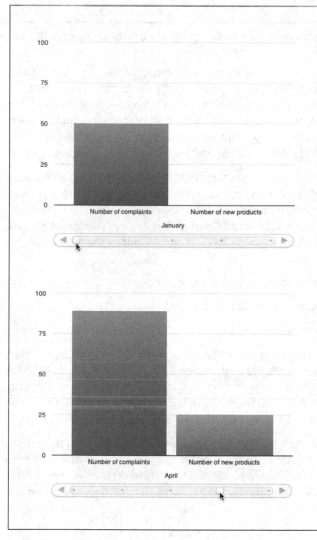

FIGURE 21-20

This chart shows how the number of complaints changes as new products launch throughout the year. Drag the slider right to see the next data point, or left to uncover the previous data point. The label beneath the chart reveals which data point you're currently looking at. These two screenshots show how the number of complaints changes from January to April, as different numbers of products launch. Drag the slider around to uncover data for the other months.

Try this interactive chart for yourself by going to this book's Missing CD page at www.missingmanuals.com/cds and downloading interactive_chart.numbers.

Adjusting Color, Shadow, and Opacity

The right combination of colors and opacity can add visual spark to your charts without distracting from their data. Every chart is made up of groups of objects that you can select and format in different ways. You can change the stroke, fill, and font color; choose a background color for the chart; or add elegantly subtle gradients to the bars of your data series.

When you select a chart at the object level so that its eight selection handles are visible, you can change the background color of the overall chart—the area that appears behind the data points.

NOTE This option is available only for 2D charts; Numbers doesn't let you set the background for 3D charts.

Open the Chart tab, and then click the Background & Border Style heading to expand that section (you may have to scroll down to see it). Open the drop-down menu at the top of that section, choose Color Fill, and then click the color well to choose from the available colors, or create your own by clicking the color wheel icon to launch the Color Picker. Alternatively, apply a gradient fill, advanced gradient fill, image fill, or advanced image fill. All these options are discussed in detail on page 348.

For the chart's data series elements—columns, bars, areas, pie wedges, and lines—Numbers provides a set of preselected palettes that you can use to quickly change the mood of the chart while making sure that the colors come from the same family. In the Chart tab, click the multicolored Chart Colors button, to open the Chart Colors drop-down menu shown in Figure 21-21. Then click one of the buttons at the top of this menu:

- **Colors** provides a selection of palettes with solid colors.

- **Images** gives you a selection of colored textures.

- **Textures** gives you a selection of textures.

If you prefer to craft your own color collection, you can use the trusty Color Picker to shade individual chart elements. Open the Color Picker by going to View→Show Colors. Then change the fill color of a column, bar, area, or pie wedge by dragging a color from the Color Picker's swatch or palette and dropping it onto the element to change; Numbers updates the chart's data points and legend with the new color.

If you're working with a 2D chart, you can add a stroke to outline the column, wedge, or line segment. Select the data series you want to outline, and then open the Format panel's Style tab and select a line style from the Stroke drop-down menu. You can then choose a new color using the Stroke section's color setting, or change the thickness using the "pt" field.

If you want to add a shadow effect to a data series in a 2D chart, select the data series in question, and then open the Chart tab and click the Shadow heading to expand that section. In the drop-down menu there, select Individual Series to add a basic shadow to the selected data series. You can then adjust the shadow's blur, offset, opacity, color, and angle (see page 199 for a recap on working with shadows). To add a shadow to all the data in your chart, select Grouped instead.

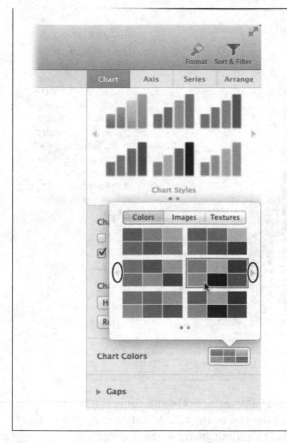

FIGURE 21-21

The Chart Colors drop-down menu lets you browse and select color palettes for your charts. To give a chart a color makeover, select the chart, open this menu, and then click your color scheme of choice. Don't forget to check the options in all three categories (Colors, Images, and Textures), and within each of those categories by clicking the left and right arrow buttons (circled).

You can also apply a shadow effect to a 3D chart by selecting the chart, opening the Chart tab, and then clicking the Shadow heading to expand that section. Apply a shadow by opening the drop-down menu and choosing On. You create a shadow effect in exactly the same way as for 2D charts—the only exception is that Numbers applies a shadow effect to *all* the data series in the 3D chart, to help maintain the illusion of depth. To remove a shadow effect, open the drop-down menu and select Off.

Formatting the X- and Y-Axes

Numbers lets you show or hide each of the chart axis lines, as well as add and format their labels, tick marks, and gridlines. Figure 21-22 gives you a tour of these elements.

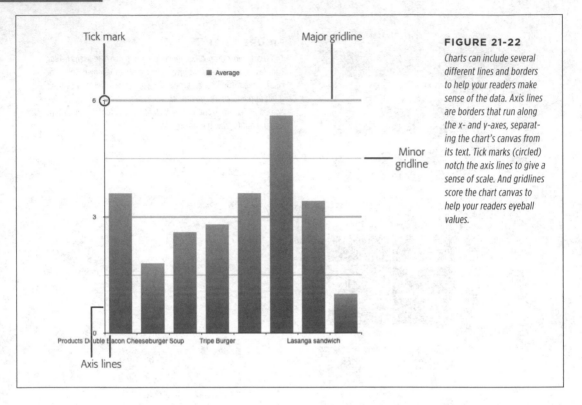

FIGURE 21-22

Charts can include several different lines and borders to help your readers make sense of the data. Axis lines are borders that run along the x- and y-axes, separating the chart's canvas from its text. Tick marks (circled) notch the axis lines to give a sense of scale. And gridlines score the chart canvas to help your readers eyeball values.

The Format panel's Axis tab is headquarters for these adjustments. Click the "Value (Y)" or "Category (X)" button at the top of the tab, and then use these settings menus to add or remove your chart's various marks and measures:

- **Axes.** Turn on the Axis Line checkbox to display the y- or x-axis, the lines that run along the left and bottom of the chart, respectively. Adding or removing an axis or border is a purely aesthetic choice—the axes on which the chart is built are there regardless of whether you can see their lines.

- **Tick marks.** Both axes have a Tick Mark drop-down menu that contains several choices for fine-tuning where the *tick marks* (scale markings) appear along the axis lines: Inside, Centered, and Outside. Alternatively, select None to remove tick marks completely.

- **Gridlines.** Gridlines jump out from their associated axis at a 90-degree angle, to make it easier for people to gauge the value of data points (for the value axis) or help separate the data sets (for the series axis). The category axis has a single set of gridlines that line up with its major tick marks; to turn it on, click the Gridlines heading to expand that section, and then choose a line style, color, and size for your gridlines (these options don't appear until you add gridlines to your chart). The value axis has both major and minor gridlines: Turn them on by clicking either the Major Gridlines or Minor Gridlines heading to expand that section, and then choose the line style, color, and size. To remove either set of gridlines, open the line-style drop-down menu and select None.

▪ FORMATTING THE VALUE AXES FOR TWO-AXIS CHARTS

Their name doesn't exactly make this clear, but two-axis charts actually have *three* axes for you to work with: the x-axis and two y-axes. When you select a two-axis chart, the Format panel's Axis tab gives you a separate group of value-axis settings for formatting the second y-axis, as shown in Figure 21-23. Click the "Value (Y1)" button to adjust settings for the left axis, or the "Value (Y2)" button to see settings for the right axis. The two have their own settings for titles, tick marks, gridlines, and value labels—including the number of value labels to display.

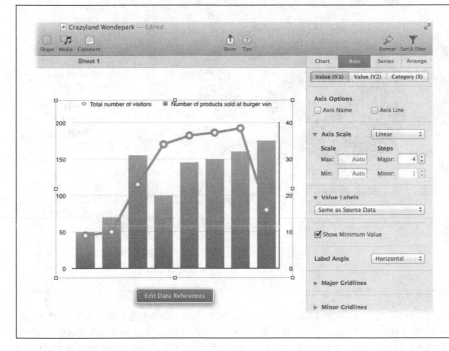

FIGURE 21-23

When you work with a two-axis chart, Numbers gives you an additional set of controls in the Axis tab to let you format each y-axis separately. The "Value (Y1)" options pull the strings on the left axis, while the "Value (Y2)" settings control the right axis. Two-axis charts always start off showing the values of the chart's first data series on the left (Y1) axis and the rest of the data series on the right (Y2). Here, the two axes have a different number of value labels, and the right axis sports a set of tick marks.

When you first add a two-axis chart, Numbers starts off by charting the first data series on the left y-axis (a.k.a. Y1) and the remaining data series on the right y-axis (Y2). You can customize these settings by choosing which axis you want each data series to use. To do so, select a data series by double-clicking one of its data points, opening the Format panel's Series tab, and making a selection from the "Plot on" drop-down menu.

Working with Pie Charts

Pie charts slice up your data differently from other chart types. These tasty charts show each piece of source data as a portion of a whole, representing each data point as a wedge of the pie. That means that pie charts have no x- and y-axes, and they can display only one data set—the first data set in the charted cells of your source table.

Practically speaking, that means the pie chart shows data only from the first row or column of the table's selected cells. If the data series are in rows in your source table, Numbers turns the first *column* into the pie chart, displaying the color keys next to your table's row labels. If the data series are in columns, Numbers turns the first *row* into the pie chart, showing the color keys next to the column labels. Each slice of the pie represents one of the data points in that set as a percentage of the total of that data set. Figure 21-24 shows how it works.

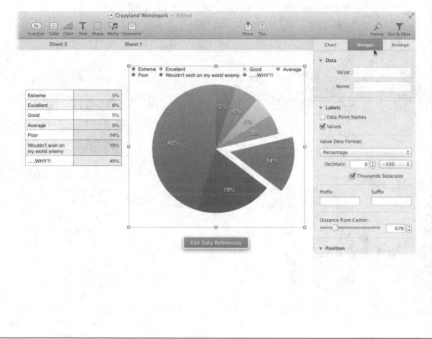

FIGURE 21-24

Pie charts can display only one data set. No matter how many data sets you choose in the source table, only the first one contributes to a pie chart—the others aren't included at all.

Here, the second column's values are charted. To choose a different data set, change the selection of charted rows (page 596) so that the data set you want falls into the first row. Or click the chart's Edit Data References button, and then use the Data Series button to switch the data sets from rows to column (see page 599).

Double-click a pie wedge to select it, and then drag the wedge to *explode* it, moving it away from the chart's center as if the slice has been carved out. People often use this technique to emphasize a certain segment (or a group of segments) of a pie chart to show, for example, what percentage of people loved their trip to Crazyland Wonderpark, as shown in Figure 21-24. You can also explode wedges using the Explode slider, described shortly.

In addition to exploding chart parts, the pie chart also gets its own custom Wedges tab in the Format panel, shown in Figure 21-24. Most of these settings apply to data series, the individual wedges of the pie chart. To apply your settings to all slices at once, select the chart at the object level so that its eight selection handles are visible; to make a change to just one wedge, double-click to select it (the name of the

Wedges tab changes to Wedge tab to indicate that only a single wedge is selected). Here's a rundown of the custom settings for pie charts:

- **Labels.** Click this heading to expand this section and get access to two check-boxes:

    — Turn on the **Data Point Names** checkbox to show the heading associated with this data in the original table. You can control the position of these headings using the "Distance from Center" slider that's lower down on the tab; dragging it to the right shoots the labels outside the pie, and dragging it left brings them back in.

    — Turn on the **Values** checkbox to display the data-point values for each wedge. Unless you change Numbers' standard settings, this value is a percentage of the whole instead of the actual numeric value of the data point. If you want to show the original value instead, choose a new data format in the tab's Value Data Format section.

- **Explode.** Use the "Distance from Center" slider in the Wedges tab's Position section to move the selected wedge(s) away from the pie. (Be careful not to confuse this slider with the tab's *other* "Distance from Center" slider, which is higher up on the tab).

- **Rotation Angle.** Spin a pie chart using the Rotation Angle setting. As you rotate the chart, Numbers keeps the labels right-side up as it spins the wedges around the wheel.

Spacing Bar and Column Charts

The Format panel's Chart tab (Figure 21-25) includes settings that control the bar spacing of column and bar charts (as well as their stacked siblings). Adjusting this spacing also adjusts the width of the bars themselves—Numbers narrows them to create extra space or widens them to fill in gaps. In other words, Numbers does what it can to work within the available space. If you find the bars getting too narrow, give Numbers more elbow room: Resize the chart by dragging its selection handles.

In the Format panel's Gaps section, the Between Columns setting determines the spacing—if any—between the bars within each data set. Zero percent means no gap, and 100 percent results in a gap equal in width to the bars. The Between Sets option controls the size of the gap between data sets, and here again a setting of 100 percent creates a gap as wide as one of the bars. It usually makes more sense to have little or no gap between bars and a larger gap between sets.

Formatting Data-Point Symbols

When you work with line, area, or scatter charts, the Format panel's Series tab lets you choose what symbol to use for the chart's data points. Select the chart at the object level, and then choose a symbol from the Data Symbols drop-down menu: circles, triangles, squares, or diamonds. (Choose None to keep a low profile and leave the data points unmarked.) The Size field next to the drop-down menu controls how big the symbols are; Numbers manages this automatically by default, but you can choose your own setting to make the symbols larger or smaller.

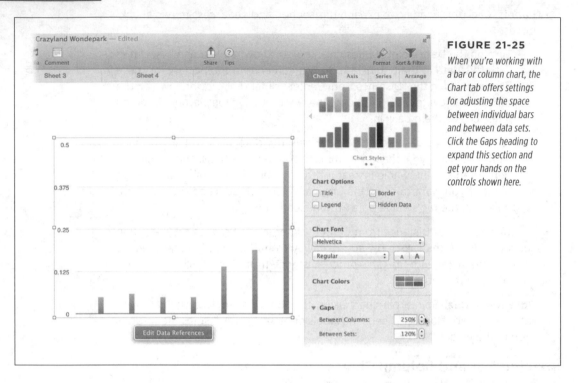

FIGURE 21-25

When you're working with a bar or column chart, the Chart tab offers settings for adjusting the space between individual bars and between data sets. Click the Gaps heading to expand this section and get your hands on the controls shown here.

For line and scatter charts, the Series tab also includes a Connection Lines drop-down menu, which lets you choose whether to connect the data points with straight or curved lines.

Choosing Chart Types for Mixed and Two-Axis Charts

Mixed charts and two-axis charts are the multitaskers in the Numbers chart family. Both chart types can display each data series in a different chart style: column, line, or area. In a mixed chart or two-axis chart, select a data series, and then open the Format panel's Series tab and choose the chart type in the "Show Series as" section (see Figure 21-26).

Adding Trendlines

When you have lots of data points, it can be difficult to spot the overall trend at first glance. *Trendlines* help clarify the direction of your data by applying a mathematical model that "fits" your data points, boiling them down to a single line. The resulting trendline is a path drawn across your chart as a kind of visual summary of one of your data series. In Numbers, you can add trendlines for any or all of your data series. There are many mathematical approaches to doing this, and Numbers gives you a choice of which model to use for each trendline.

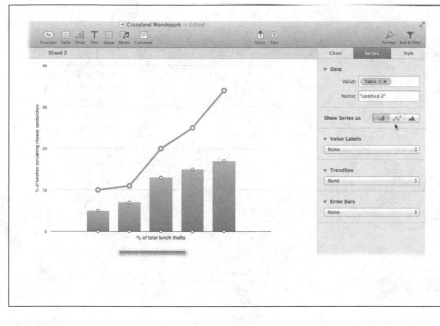

FIGURE 21-26

This mixed chart uses a column chart to show the percentage of total lunches stolen and a line chart to display the percentage of lunches containing cheese sandwiches.

Here, the "% of total lunch thefts" data series is selected, and the Series tab's "Show Series as" section tells you that this series is represented by a column chart. To change this series to a different type, click the appropriate "Show Series as" button (where the cursor is here).

> **NOTE** Trendlines aren't available for stacked charts or pie charts.

To add a trendline to your chart, select the data series you'd like to use by double-clicking one of its chart elements; to add trendlines to *all* of your data series, select the chart at the object level. Then, in the Format panel's Series tab, open the Trendline drop-down menu and select the type of equation you'd like to use to apply the trendline. The proper choice depends on the overall shape of your data values:

- **Linear.** Gives you a best-fit straight line, appropriate when your data follows a simple linear path, as shown in Figure 21-27.

- **Logarithmic.** Produces a best-fit curved line, appropriate when values increase or decrease quickly and then level out.

- **Polynomial.** Gives you a curved line that follows the peaks and valleys of your data, appropriate when you have rising and falling data. Choose the order of polynomial you want to use in the Order field that appears—increasing the polynomial adds more detail to the trendline. Order 4, for example, produces up to three peaks or valleys in the line.

- **Power.** Produces a curved line appropriate for data that tends to increase at a specific rate. You can use this option only for positive values—negative or zero values are a no-go.

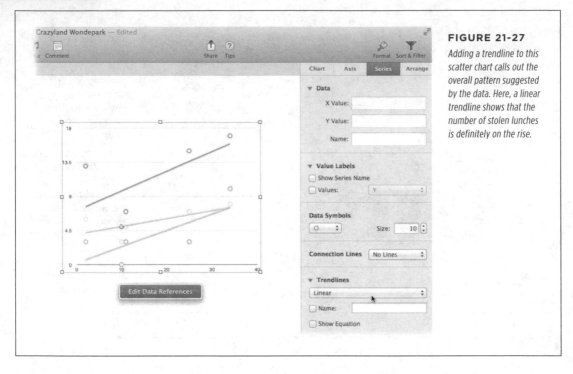

FIGURE 21-27

*Adding a trendline to this
scatter chart calls out the
overall pattern suggested
by the data. Here, a linear
trendline shows that the
number of stolen lunches
is definitely on the rise.*

- **Exponential.** Gives you a curved line appropriate for data that increases or decreases at increasingly faster rates. Like the Power option, Exponential can't be used with negative or zero values.

- **Moving Average.** This one acts like a line chart but draws its line through average data-point values. When you choose this option, use the Period field to tell Numbers how many data points you want it to sample for each trendline point. Numbers uses that number to cluster data points together in groups, and uses the average value as the trendline's points.

Numbers lets you add trendline labels to your chart, which means you can include the trendline in the chart's legend, show the equation that describes the trendline, or display the R-squared value for a trendline. (The R-squared value is a statistical measure of how well the trendline approximates the real data points; its fancypants name is the *coefficient of determination*. The value usually ranges from 0 to 1—the higher the value, the better the fit.) To add these labels, click a trendline to select it, and then open the Format panel's Trendline tab and turn on the Name, Show Equation, or R^2 Value checkboxes. The Name checkbox adds the trendline to the chart's legend; type the label's text into the neighboring field.

TIP The trendline's Name, Show Equation, and R2 Value checkboxes also appear on the Series tab.

Adding Error Bars

When you're charting measurements that may not be precise, you can indicate that by adding *error bars* to your chart. These are visual caveats that ride along with each data point to show the margin of error, warning the reader that the actual value could lie anywhere within the error bar's boundaries. You can add error bars to any kind of chart *except* pie charts, and you can add them to any or all of a chart's data series. To add them, double-click a data point to select its data series, or select *all* data series by selecting the chart at the object level. Then, in the Format panel's Series tab, open the Error Bars drop-down menu and choose how you want the error bars displayed:

- **Positive and Negative** displays full error bars, both above and below each data point.

- **Positive only** displays only the part of each error bar that falls *above* its data point.

- **Negative only** displays only the part of each error bar that falls *below* its data point.

Once you tell Numbers how to display the error bars, you get access to the Use drop-down menu, where you can choose from the following options:

- **Fixed Value** displays error bars with the exact same margin of error for every data point; you set that value in the field next door.

- **Percentage** displays error bars based on a fixed percentage of each data point's value; choose the percentage in the neighboring field.

- **Standard Deviation** displays error bars based on the standard deviation of your data set; choose the number of standard deviations in the adjacent field. *Standard deviation* is a statistical measure of how close or spread out your data values are. A low standard deviation indicates that the data points tend to be very close to the same average value, while high standard deviation indicates that the data vary wildly across a range of values.

- **Standard Error.** The *standard error of the mean* is similar to standard deviation but instead aims to show how accurately your data reflects the average value of "real-world" data—useful when polling a small sample of the actual population, for example. The standard error takes into account both the value of the standard deviation and the sample size: the standard deviation divided by the square root of the number of data points. This option always displays a smaller error margin than standard deviation, and in general, the larger the sample, the smaller the standard error will be. (Of course, choosing this option over standard deviation doesn't instantly make your data more accurate, even though it shows smaller margins of error; it's simply a different way to measure it.)

- **Custom Values** lets you set error bars based on your own criteria. In the Positive field, specify how far above the data points you want the error bars to extend;

in the Negative field, specify how far below the data points you want the error bars to extend. (You may only see one of these fields.)

NOTE For scatter and bubble charts, you get separate X Axis Error Bars and Y Axis Error Bars settings, which let you create separate error bars for each axis.

Once you've got your error bars in place, Numbers gives you lots of options for formatting them. Double-click the error bar in your chart to select it, and then open the Format panel's Error Bar tab, where you can adjust the error bar's stroke (outline) and endpoints, color, and shadow.

■ Avoiding Chartjunk

With all the tools, labels, decorations, and effects that you can add to Numbers charts, it's easy to get carried away. Marbled textures! Shadows! Gridlines! Tick marks! *Three-dimensional exploding pie charts!* Whoa there, eager chart-maker—you're burying your information under a pile of distracting effects.

Statisticians call this stuff *chartjunk*, unnecessary visual elements that make your graph tough to read or, worse, distort its shapes or perspective in ways that make your audience misinterpret the chart's info. Chartjunk is usually added with the best intentions—to make the chart pretty, to make it appear more "scientific," or just because the graphic tools are so much fun to play with. But don't lose sight of the reason you're making the chart in the first place: to convey complex information efficiently and in a way that makes underlying trends clear. If a chart element doesn't contribute directly to that goal—if it's merely ornamental—it's chartjunk. Let it go. Show off the data, not the chart.

Here are some common examples of chartjunk:

- **Shadows and 3D effects.** However you draw your graphs, the *data* behind iWork charts is two dimensional, drawn from a table of values. Faking a third dimension by adding shadows or perspective only distorts your graph's shapes without contributing meaning, as shown in Figure 21-28.

- **Ornamental shading.** Avoid complex patterns when coloring chart elements. Use the Chart Colors drop-down menu with restraint and avoid its noisier textures (looking at you, wood and marble texture fill).

- **Unnecessary text.** Titles, captions, and labels are important to describe what your chart is about, but pare them down to the bare minimum, giving readers what they need to understand the data, but no more.

- **Dense, dark, or heavy gridlines.** Gridlines, if used at all, should be a background element. When you have too many gridlines, or when they're too bold, they compete with the data points and make the chart difficult to read—the opposite of their intention. Consider whether gridlines are necessary at all, and if they are, make them skinny, light-colored, and/or low opacity.

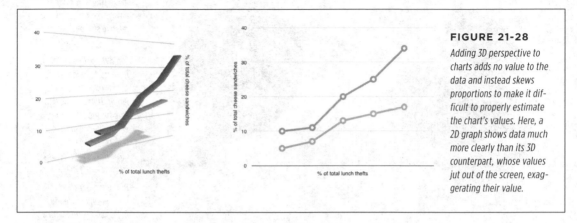

FIGURE 21-28

Adding 3D perspective to charts adds no value to the data and instead skews proportions to make it difficult to properly estimate the chart's values. Here, a 2D graph shows data much more clearly than its 3D counterpart, whose values jut out of the screen, exaggerating their value.

- **Fancy fonts.** Your chart's labels aren't the main event here—keep their fonts subdued and appropriately small.

Even though these elements and features are plainly distracting, something about them is irresistible. On the surface, they seem to lend a quality of slick professionalism. They just seem so...*fancy.* And it's addictively fun to tinker with the look and design of these charts. But keep in mind that heaping your charts with decoration doesn't give them extra authority or value—only the underlying information can do that. If your information is so dull that it requires vertigo inspiring 3D effects to make it interesting, then perhaps you're not sharing the right information—or maybe you're not presenting it the best way.

Choosing the Right Chart (or Table)

Every set of data tells a different story, and picking the right type of chart for that story is *critical* to communicating it effectively. Think twice before using a pie chart, for example. Although the goal of a pie chart is to illustrate proportions of values, it turns out that it's hard to distinguish the relative size of pie slices, particularly when they're close in value. This is especially true for 3D pie charts, which skew proportions. Column and bar charts do a better job of showing relative values, and with a more compact presentation, too, as shown in Figure 21-29.

It's even tougher to discern the difference between pie slices when you're asked to compare values in two separate pies. Here again, a column or bar chart makes the comparison clear, as shown in Figure 21-30.

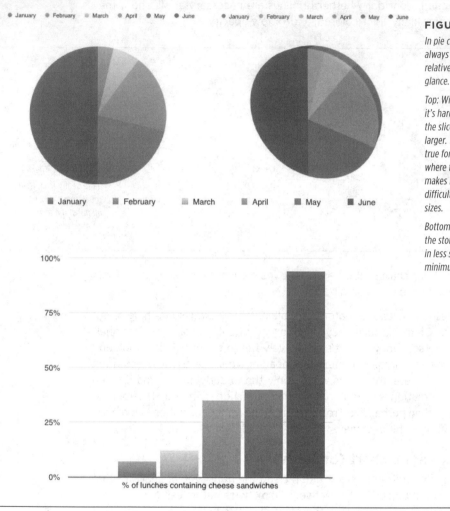

January • February • March • April • May • June   January • February • March • April • May • June

FIGURE 21-29

In pie charts, it's not always easy to judge the relative size of slices at a glance.

Top: Without value labels, it's hard to judge whether the slice for April or May is larger. That's particularly true for the 3D version, where the perspective makes it even more difficult to compare slice sizes.

Bottom: A bar chart tells the story more clearly, in less space, and with a minimum of chartjunk.

■ January   ■ February   ■ March   ■ April   ■ May   ■ June

% of lunches containing cheese sandwiches

Stacked charts present similar problems of estimation. Although they're useful in showing cumulative values for groups of data, it's difficult to visually gauge the values of groups within each stack. This is particularly true as you add more and more values to each stack—only the bottom element in the pile is easy to measure against the y-axis. When it's important to understand the relative values of each element at a glance, an *unstacked* chart is the way to go.

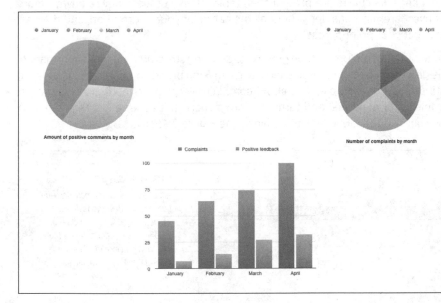

FIGURE 21-30

When you need to compare two data series, don't use two pie charts; it's difficult to quickly scan for value differences, and the relative proportions can be misleading. After a glance at these pie charts, you might think there was much more positivity in March than there was negativity, which sadly wasn't the case. Bar or column charts make it easy to see the differences.

The exception is area charts, where stacked versions are typically superior to their unstacked counterparts. An unstacked area chart is just a line chart with extra ink; in most cases, that means chartjunk. If the chart tracks more than one data series and their data lines cross, then one of the areas will obscure the other so that you can no longer see its data points (adjusting the chart's opacity can help with this, though). A line chart can often do the job better than an unstacked area chart, as shown in Figure 21-31.

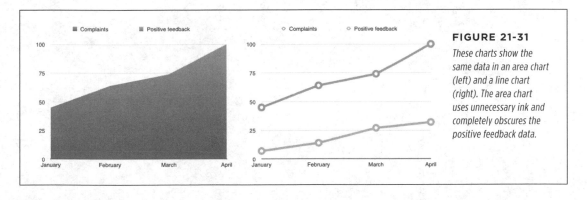

FIGURE 21-31

These charts show the same data in an area chart (left) and a line chart (right). The area chart uses unnecessary ink and completely obscures the positive feedback data.

TIP Unstacked area charts can be useful for drawing a contrast with other data as part of a mixed chart.

Finally, some data may simply be too thin to bother charting at all. Sometimes the best way to convey a set of numbers is just to show it in its raw form: in a table. After all, just because charts are prettier than tables doesn't mean they're always more effective. Carefully consider your goal, the nature of your information, and the best way to get your point across.

In general, tables are better than graphs for detailing structured numeric information, while graphs are better for indicating trends, making broad comparisons, or showing relationships. For example, data about complains vs. positive feedback is really just a simple list of numbers, and turning it into a chart isn't especially enlightening. A table could do the job just as effectively (see Figure 21-32).

Feedback	January	February	March	April
Positive	7	14	27	32
Negative	45	64	74	100

FIGURE 21-32

Tables often allow for more descriptive captions than charts do. When you're working with a small set of simple numeric information, a table can often convey a message with more clarity than a graphic.

None of this is to say that charts aren't useful, or even essential. On the contrary, a terrific graphic can be eye-opening and cut instantly through a vague cloud of data. Numbers gives you the tools to create exactly those kinds of charts and graphs. But those same tools can also confuse and confound when used carelessly. Like all great design, the process of creating a clear and simple chart is usually neither clear nor simple. Make sure you give the job the care and attention it deserves and, when in doubt, hold back on the eye-popping effects.

Designing Your Spreadsheet Report

From their very first appearance on personal computers in the late 1970s, spreadsheet programs have always treated numbers so...*seriously*. VisiCalc, Lotus 1-2-3, Microsoft Excel—these programs have all presented spreadsheets exclusively as relentless grids of rows and columns. This blandly straightforward approach has the benefit of putting an unwavering focus on the data: You've got *grids* of numbers, and you've got *charts* of numbers—and that's it. It's all about the data.

When Numbers came along, it introduced something completely new, and almost unthinkable, to the spreadsheet world: design. Numbers blows up the idea of the grid as the single defining design element of a spreadsheet document. While every other major spreadsheet program presents just one grid per worksheet, Numbers lets you have as many tables as you like, arranging them on the canvas wherever they suit you. Instead of treating graphics as an afterthought like other spreadsheet programs do, Numbers gives you the same effortless access to media and design elements that you find in Keynote or Pages.

As the previous chapters have demonstrated, Numbers' tables can work a grid with the best of them, giving single-minded attention to your data and calculations when that's what you're up to. But Numbers can also see beyond the data to the overall design of the *document*, making it easy to create eye-catching presentations. Apple's message: The fact that your data is serious doesn't mean you can't have fun with its design.

With Numbers, you can blend your carefully created tables and charts with a variety of multimedia elements to create rousing reports like the template examples shown in Figure 22-1. Using text captions, pictures, and even movies and audio, Numbers lets you illustrate your data with elegance. This chapter shows you how.

Recipe

HOW TO USE: Enter the number of people the recipe serves and how many you plan to prepare for. Then, enter your ingredients and amounts needed in the first two columns, using the pull-down menus for measurement types (for example, oz or cup). Finally, replace the sample instructions with your own recipe instructions.

The formula will scale the recipe for you. Match the measurement units for the scaled amount to get the proper conversion.

FIGURE 22-1

Numbers can create all the grids you want, but it can also create graphical reports with pictures, text, charts, shapes—even movies and sound. The Template Chooser (page 433) is a good place to browse for examples and inspiration. Here, the Recipe, Baby Record, and Party Planner templates offer three lively examples.

Sample Recipe

	Recipe serves	Prepared for
	4	8

Ingredient	Amount		Scaled amount	
Penne pasta	8	oz	1	lb
Olive oil	1	tbsp	2	tbsp
Sliced zucchini	1/2	cup	1	cup
Cooked, shredded	1/2	cup	1	cup

Shopping List

Ingredients	Have it	Quantity
Penne Pasta	☐	1 lb
	☐	
	☐	
	☐	
	☐	
	☐	
	☐	

Baby's First Year

September 7, 2014 at 6:29 am

Birth weight	7.9 lbs
Birth length	18.6 in
Birth head circ.	14.2 in
Location	Anytown, State

Height and Weight

Month	Height (in)	Weight (lbs)	Head Circumference (in)	Temp (F)	Notes
1	19.20	8.00	14.20	98.5	
2	20.10	8.20	14.99	98.5	

Budget Planning
KAREN'S BIRTHDAY

BUDGET			
Description	Per Person Cost	Fixed Costs	Total Costs
Site Rental		$300.00	$300.00
Decorations		$200.00	$200.00
Music		$150.00	$150.00
Food	$30.00		$540.00
Drinks	$20.00		$260.00

Number of Guests: 18

BUDGET OVERVIEW

■ Working with Objects

Good news! If you've made your way through the Pages or Keynote section of this book, you already know how to design a spreadsheet. Working with the sheet canvas in Numbers is nearly identical to designing a Keynote slide or building a page layout in Pages. Like both of those programs, Numbers clears a workspace for you and lets you arrange *objects* in that space. You even work with the exact same set of tools and building materials, since all iWork programs share a common arsenal of objects: pictures, text boxes, shapes, tables, charts, movies, and sounds.

By now, you probably know the drill: Click an object to select it; drag it to a new location on the page; resize it by dragging one of the selection handles along its border; and use the Format panel to add effects, borders, picture frames, and color fills.

As in Keynote, there's no such thing as inline objects in Numbers. Instead, all Numbers objects are *floating objects*, which you place on the sheet canvas independently of the rest. (You can, however, add images to table cells and other objects as backgrounds, as you'll learn on page 654.)

Because the details of adding and editing objects have been covered elsewhere in the book, this chapter covers the mechanics of each feature only briefly, pointing you to spots where you can find more substantive discussion. The main goal here is to spotlight the *possibilities* that these tools offer, inspiring you about just how different a spreadsheet can look.

First, though, let's be sure you know the fundamentals of working with objects. For a review of iWork's basic laws of object physics—how to select, move, and manipulate objects—head back to the description of working with objects in Keynote on page 312. To learn how to style and format objects with the Format panel, flip back to page 191, which explains modifying object styles in Pages.

Got it? Here's your assignment: The staff at Crazyland Wonderpark are lobbying for a monthly budget to fund some fun staff outings (they've got their sights set high; we're talking go-kart racing, cocktail-making classes, nights out at classy restaurants, and so on). They've worked up a budget, estimated the impact on staff morale, researched some potential activities, and collected a variety of facts and figures to bolster their case. All the info is collected in a big jumble of Numbers tables (Figure 22-2), and they think some thoughtful design may help them make their case better. In awe of your iWork abilities, your colleagues have come to you for help with the layout of the summary page and the detail pages within. Time to spring into action.

■ Identifying "Back Page" Data

Great reports, like sausages, are at their most delicious when you don't know every last thing that goes into them. Both go down easier if you're spared the gory details. In fact, the essential goal of most reports is to synthesize and summarize data rather than to catalog every last detail. So the first job of any document designer is to figure out the parts of your data you want to emphasize and which can be tucked away.

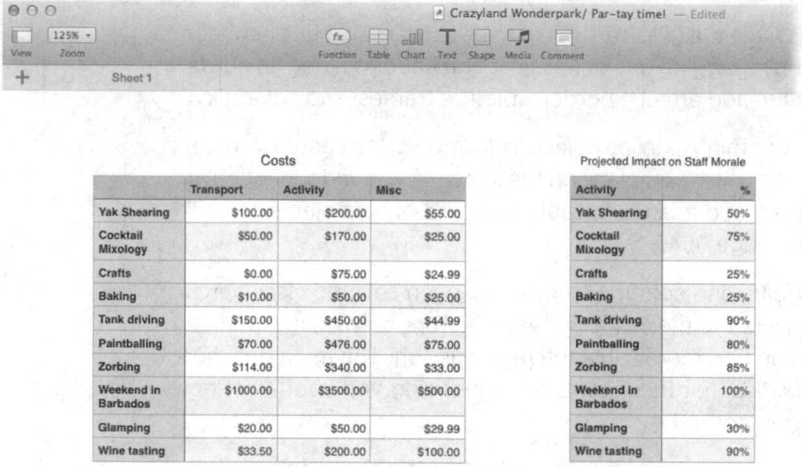

Costs

	Transport	Activity	Misc
Yak Shearing	$100.00	$200.00	$55.00
Cocktail Mixology	$50.00	$170.00	$25.00
Crafts	$0.00	$75.00	$24.99
Baking	$10.00	$50.00	$25.00
Tank driving	$150.00	$450.00	$44.99
Paintballing	$70.00	$476.00	$75.00
Zorbing	$114.00	$340.00	$33.00
Weekend in Barbados	$1000.00	$3500.00	$500.00
Glamping	$20.00	$50.00	$29.99
Wine tasting	$33.50	$200.00	$100.00

Projected Impact on Staff Morale

Activity	%
Yak Shearing	50%
Cocktail Mixology	75%
Crafts	25%
Baking	25%
Tank driving	90%
Paintballing	80%
Zorbing	85%
Weekend in Barbados	100%
Glamping	30%
Wine tasting	90%

FIGURE 22-2

The staff's spreadsheet contains the raw data for their presentation. It's got some summary data (projected expenses, impact each activity will have on staff morale, and a breakdown of the different activities they're dreaming of). As the designer, your job is to organize this data so that it's easy to understand, helping to forcefully make the staff's point.

Chances are, most of your spreadsheets involve totaling and subtotaling numbers to show bottom-line results. Particularly for a report's summary page—and often for inside pages, too—those final tallies are the numbers that matter. Depending on the type of document you're building, you may not even need to share the original raw data at all; at the very least, you can relegate it to one or more back sheets of your document. When you're ready to publish, you can then decide whether to print those sheets. If you're doing a scientific report on an experiment with thousands of measurements, for example, the data for those individual measurements should go on a back sheet while you put the summaries of your findings in sheets up front. Let Numbers sweat over your calculations in a back workshop while you parade the polished results around the showroom.

Your eager-beaver Crazyland Wonderpark colleagues have, alas, passed you a mountain of raw stats: many tables stacked into a single sheet. As you create their presentation report, you'll select the summary statistics to show on the front page, add increasing levels of detail on following pages, and create one or more sheets of "hidden" data that won't be published as part of the final result.

The decisions regarding what goes where typically evolve over the course of the design rather than all at once, but a few elements are usually immediately obvious. For example, the first thing the person who holds the power (and the purse strings) will ask is how much this hootenanny is going to cost. The front page should show a chart of the forecasted expenses. As it turns out, this front-page decision also determines one of the tables that will go to the *back* page. Read on.

Hiding Charts' Source Tables

Good candidates for your report's back page include tables that you plan to chart. As you learned in the last chapter, charts are always paired with a table. But including both the chart and its data is redundant and (often) unnecessary. You need the table *somewhere* in your document to keep the chart alive, but it doesn't have to be on the same sheet. Like the raw data described above, you can tuck charts' source tables on a back sheet and decide later whether to print them as part of your final report.

Here's the catch: You can't *cut* and paste the table to move it to a different sheet. If you do that, you temporarily remove the table from the chart and, when that happens, Numbers turns your chart back into a boring old placeholder chart, with no meaningful data. Instead, you need to *copy* and paste the source table to a new sheet, and then update the chart's cell references so that it references the duplicate source table rather than the original. *Then* you can delete the original table.

NOTE If you haven't already created a chart, you can copy and paste your table to your report's last sheet. Then create a chart on the first sheet, and you're free to add data from any table you want (even the one on the last sheet).

For example, say that you've created a new Summary sheet for your social-events presentation, and you've created a column chart to plot that all-important cost. Now you want to move the source table to a back sheet so that it doesn't clutter up the summary page (you want the result to look like Figure 22-3). To hide that source table, first create a sheet called Chart Data (page 446 explains how to add sheets), and then copy your source table onto that sheet. Then select the chart and click its Edit Data References button, open the Chart Data sheet in the Sheets bar, and select the cell(s) in the copied table. Be careful not to click anywhere except the Sheet tab and the table's cells, or Numbers will throw you out of "cell selecting" mode. When you're finished, click Done in the lower-right corner of the sheet canvas, and then delete the original table.

You're off and running with one organizational decision behind you. You've got a standalone chart on the summary page, and you've relocated one of the tables that the staff thrust upon you. Now to tackle the rest. The process for deciding what goes where always varies according to individual and project, but a good approach when you're getting started is often to dash off some brief text that defines what you're trying to do—a summary of findings or a statement of purpose. Even if this text doesn't wind up in your report, words often bring focus and help you identify the key data to highlight. For the summary page of the fun-loving staff's presentation, you'll start with a title and some brief proposal text. Click back to the Summary sheet and get ready to do some typing.

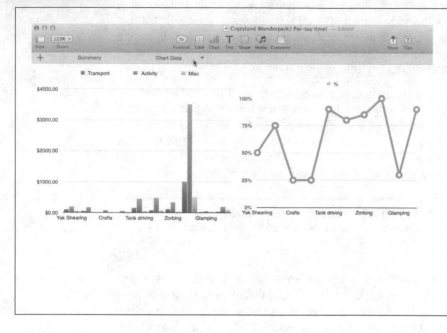

FIGURE 22-3

To safely move a chart's source table to a new sheet, copy the source table, paste it to the Chart Data sheet (where the cursor is positioned here), and then change the chart's cell references so they point to the duplicate table rather than the original. You're then free to delete the original table. This gives you a Summary sheet of glossy charts, and a separate sheet of cold, hard facts if your audience wants to dive into the nitty-gritty data behind the charts.

■ Adding Text

To add a *text box* to your spreadsheet, click the toolbar's Text button and choose a font style, or choose Insert→Text Box, and Numbers drops the object into the middle of the canvas, with the placeholder word "Text." Go ahead and type something a bit more expressive, as shown in Figure 22-4.

Numbers' text boxes work just like free text boxes in Keynote (page 322). Unlike every other object in Numbers, these objects have just two selection handles, one on each side. That means you can adjust their width but not their height. Numbers manages the height of text boxes automatically: As you type, the text box grows vertically to accommodate your prose. Likewise, when you delete text, the text box shrinks back down to size.

Use the Format panel and Fonts window to format and style your text. For more details about formatting text in Numbers, see page 466.

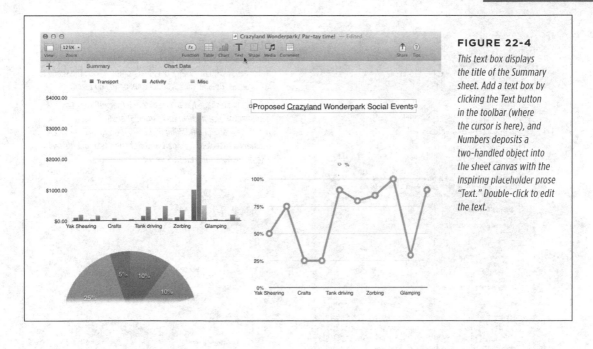

FIGURE 22-4

This text box displays the title of the Summary sheet. Add a text box by clicking the Text button in the toolbar (where the cursor is here), and Numbers deposits a two-handled object into the sheet canvas with the inspiring placeholder prose "Text." Double-click to edit the text.

■ Drawing Shapes

Text boxes work well for all kinds of text—titles, labels, captions, lengthy descriptions—but when you want text to have a bolder presence on the page, *shapes* make great alternatives. In fact, shapes are really just text boxes with a couple of special privileges: You can size shapes to any height you wish, and of course you can assign them any shape, giving you more flexible display options than a text box.

The ability to size a shape to any height adds an interesting advantage over text boxes because it lets you use the shape as a container for more than just the text inside. Figure 22-5 shows an example: The rectangle shape holds the proposal's intro text but also stretches to extend its border around a table of projected costs.

As hoped, the proposal text in this shape helps shed some light on the other elements that should appear on the summary sheet. The text emphasizes the social activities the Crazyland Wonderpark team are pushing for the hardest, suggesting that this cover page should include some content—perhaps some images or stats to prove that yak shearing really *is* the perfect team-building activity. Adding three columns to fill out the bottom-right corner of the page should work nicely, and here again shapes can help.

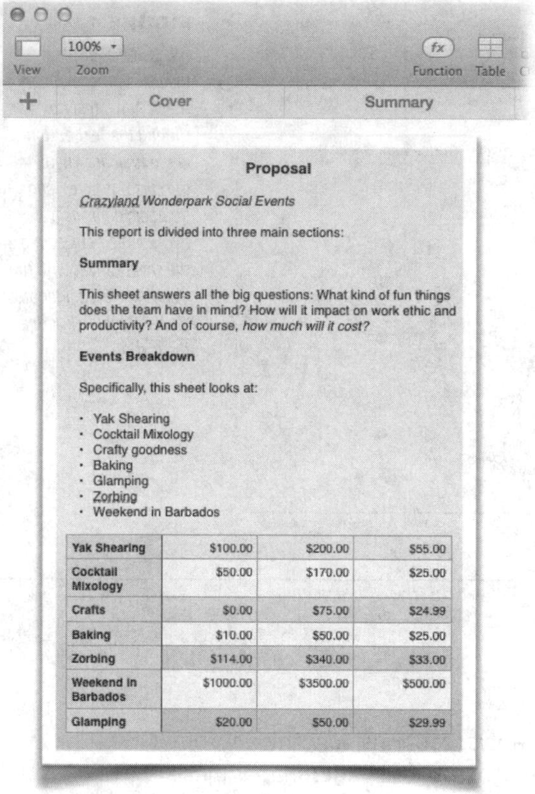

FIGURE 22-5

When you click the Shapes button in the toolbar, Numbers offers its collection of shapes. Pick one, and Numbers adds the shape to your canvas. Double-click inside the shape to add text.

This rectangle shape has a picture frame (page 198) and a gentle advanced-gradient fill (page 195) applied to it to give the impression of light falling on paper. The expenses table is positioned to look like it's part of the shape's text, but it's really a separate object floating above the shape.

Shapes can play lots of useful roles beyond glorified text boxes. They're especially versatile as background elements to provide a color, texture, or gradient behind one or more design elements. Figure 22-6 shows how shapes create three shaded columns as background for the content.

Of course, shapes are also useful simply as shapes. Add arrows or stars to call attention to certain elements of the design, or create your own custom shapes and squiggles to draw any form you want. From there, you can adjust the shape's border and fill, giving it a color, gradient, or image fill. For all the details about working with shapes, see page 168.

And hey, what do you know, highlighting the different activities with shapes and pictures rounds out the cover sheet for your report, shown in its full glory in Figure 22-7. The ever-attentive reader will also notice there's a new type of design element: photos and other graphics, which are the next topic in this chapter.

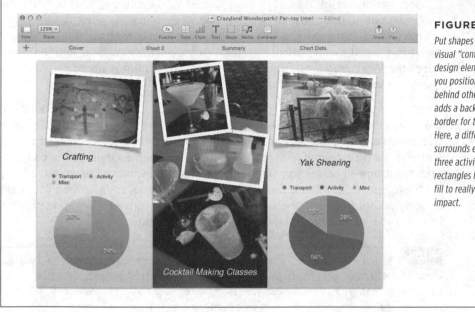

FIGURE 22-6

Put shapes to work as visual "containers" for design elements. When you position a shape behind other objects, it adds a background or border for those objects. Here, a different rectangle surrounds each of the three activities. One of the rectangles has an image fill to really make a visual impact.

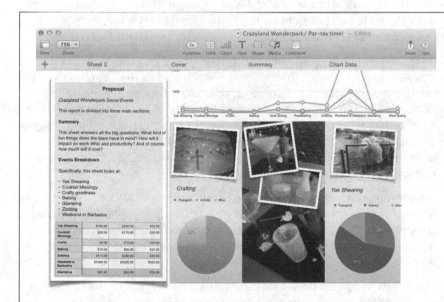

FIGURE 22-7

The final design of the proposal's cover page mixes intro text, a line graph, a smattering of important big-picture pie charts, a table, and eye-catching images. The whole thing works as a kind of magazine-cover intro for the detailed data presented within.

The source tables for all these charts are tucked away on the back sheet, so the audience isn't over-whelmed by rows of stats on the very first sheet.

■ Inserting Pictures

As you start designing the inside pages of spreadsheet reports, the content inevitably becomes denser, giving way to more traditional columns and rows of grid data. That makes the judicious use of design elements even more important, not only to set the tone of your report but also to add visual breaks for the reader, making it easier to digest the information. Pictures are especially helpful here, and Numbers, like all the iWork programs, gives you fast access to all photos stored in iPhoto, My Photo Stream, and iCloud.

To add a picture from iPhoto, My Photo Stream, or iCloud, click the Media button in the toolbar to summon the Media Browser (for a reminder on how the Media Browser works, hop back to page 5). Click the Photos tab, find the image you want to use, and give it a click; Numbers drops the picture into your document. You can then drag the image wherever you want. If the picture you want to use isn't in iPhoto, My Photo Stream, or iCloud, you can insert a picture from anywhere on your hard drive by selecting Insert→Choose and browsing to the file, or by dragging the file's icon into your spreadsheet from the Finder or your desktop.

> **NOTE** Be careful where you drop your photo when dragging from the Finder or the desktop. If you drop it onto a shape, Numbers turns that shape into an *image mask* for your picture, cropping the picture into the selected shape and removing the shape from your layout. More on image masks in just a moment.

In addition to the usual assortment of styles, shadows, reflections, and picture frames that you can add to most objects via the Format panel's Style tab, Numbers gives you some picture-specific editing tools:

- **Masks.** Add a mask to an image to crop it, specifying exactly what portion you want to show in your spreadsheet. Page 11 reveals the details behind the mask, or you can cut to the chase by selecting the picture, opening the Format panel's Image tab, and then clicking the Edit Mask button, or by choosing Format→Image→Edit Mask. You can also crop your picture along the contours of a shape by selecting the image, choosing Format→Image→"Mask with Shape," and then choosing one of the shapes from this list. Figure 22-8 shows the result of masking with a rounded rectangle and an oval.

- **Instant Alpha.** You can remove image backgrounds with iWork's Instant Alpha feature, which makes portions of your picture see-through, handy for creating cutout effects. Page 162 makes the feature completely transparent, or give it a try right away by selecting the picture and then choosing Format→Image→Instant Alpha (or by going to the Format panel's Image tab and clicking Instant Alpha).

- **The Adjust Image window.** Fine-tune your picture's color, contrast, and levels with the Adjust Image window, which gives you sliders to calibrate every aspect of your picture. Page 164 has the scoop.

FIGURE 22-8

The photo at top left has been cropped with the Format→"Mask with Shape" command, using a rounded rectangle to take the edge off its corners. A few other things are happening here, too: The bun image has been masked with an oval shape, a rectangle is providing the backdrop for the main body of the sheet, and this rectangle backdrop is also sporting a picture-frame border.

Adding Pictures to Table Cells

When you want to create a grid of pictures or otherwise add illustrations to your table, you can add images to table cells—kind of. When you drag a picture from the Finder or desktop into a table cell or paste a picture into a cell, Numbers adds it to the table as a *background image,* adding the picture as the cell's fill image. Any content in that cell appears on top of the picture, and the picture itself replaces any fill color or fill image the cell had before.

You can't resize, mask, or otherwise work iWork's normal picture magic on fill images, but you can adjust their display somewhat in the Format panel's Cell tab. Select the cell in question, open the Cell tab, and then click the Fill heading to expand this section. You'll find the Fill drop-down menu set to Image Fill, with the image set to the cell's picture. Pick a scaling method from the second drop-down menu to change how Numbers sizes the picture in the cell. The standard "Scale to Fit" option squeezes the whole image into the cell. For details about the other options and more about image fill, see page 196.

Working with Placeholder Images

If you've based your document on one of Numbers' built-in templates and the template includes pictures, it's easy to quickly replace those photos with your own without throwing the layout out of whack. Those pictures are almost always *media placeholders,* temporary stand-ins filling out the design until you make a better offer. You can tell for sure by taking a peek at the image's bottom-right corner; if the image is a media placeholder, it sports a gray icon. To add your own content to the placeholder, drag a picture from your Finder or desktop and drop it over the placeholder, or click the placeholder's gray icon to launch the Media Browser. Numbers automatically sizes, positions, and styles your picture to match the placeholder's layout. (This often means that the photo is masked, too; see page 11 for details about how to edit the image mask if you'd like to change how the picture is cropped.)

Reducing File Size

As the number of pictures in your spreadsheet starts to rival the number of table cells, you'll likely notice your document's file size expand. Images can be big, and when you add lots of them, they can weigh down the spreadsheet and make it difficult to send via email. When things get heavy, Numbers has a way to help trim down your document's size.

First, though, save your document; this technique won't work otherwise. After that, choose File→Reduce File Size to make Numbers cut any unused pixels from your spreadsheet. Here's what that means: Normally, Numbers keeps a copy of the full original image inside the document, which lets you shrink, enlarge, and mask the picture—and then later undo all that and return to the original image in its full glory anytime. Keeping that full-sized original, though, comes at a price: larger file size. If you've reduced or masked any of the images, the Reduce File Size command tells Numbers to get rid of the unused pixels. This saves space, but the catch is that Numbers no longer has the larger image should you decide to unmask or otherwise enlarge the picture in your document. The fix in that case is to throw out the trimmed image and then insert the original image all over again.

> **NOTE** You can reduce the file size for *all* images only—you can't pick and choose which media files get shrunk. The Reduce File Size command also reduces any sound and movie files in the document, clipping any unused portions.

When you select Reduce File Size, Numbers asks if you really want to proceed. When you click Reduce, Numbers applies the squeeze.

> **NOTE** Unfortunately, Reduce File Size doesn't do anything to reduce the size of images used as image fills, which includes all images you might have added to table cells. Only images sitting directly in the sheet canvas are affected by this command.

■ Adding Movies and Sound

Movies in a spreadsheet? Hey, if accountants can play a starring role at the movie awards, then surely you can award movies a starring role in your accounting spreadsheet.

Video might be useful in a product list, for example, to show a walk-around view of one or more listed gizmos, and a "screencast" movie demonstrating how to use a complex spreadsheet could be a useful training aid. In the case of the staff-nights-out proposal, what could be better than an audio interview with Ted at the burger van about how having a line-dancing class to look forward to will make him work at *least* 57.5% harder?

Adding movies or sound clips to your spreadsheet works just like adding a picture. Click the toolbar's Media button to open the Media Browser, and then click either the Music or Movies tab. The Music pane displays your iTunes playlists; the Movies pane shows your videos from iMovie, iTunes, iPhoto, and Photo Booth, as well as files and folders from your Mac's Movies directory. Click a movie to add it to your document. Alternatively, choose Insert→Choose and select the file to add, or drag a file from the Finder or desktop.

Click the audio icon or movie image to play the clip, and do the same to stop it. The Format panel's Movie and Audio tabs also offer play, pause, fast-forward, and rewind buttons you can use to control playback. These tabs also let you limit the clip to a certain passage and loop its playback. See page 175 for details.

> **TIP** To trim the file size of the movie and sound clips in your spreadsheet, see the previous section on reducing file size.

Speaking of Hollywood endings, you're no doubt anxious to find out how this chapter's little drama turns out. Do the hard-working staff at Crazyland Wonderpark get their line-dancing classes and sushi-making lessons after all? The only way to find out, of course, is to float the proposal and send it out there. That's the topic of the next chapter, which tells you how to share your spreadsheet in print and online. But first, let's take a look at how to create your own templates.

■ Creating Custom Numbers Templates

What's that, you don't feel so good? You've got a pain in your spreadsheet? Describe the symptoms: constant reformatting of chart colors and text styles; tedious application of the same familiar formulas; acute boredom with rebuilding the same handful of tables over and over again; accompanied by a throbbing ache at the temples. Friend, I'm afraid you've got a severe case of *time fritteritis*, a condition marked by terrible wastes of attention and mental energy. Happily, the treatment is painless, quickly applied, and features a 100 percent recovery rate: You need a custom template—possibly several.

Custom templates don't have to be complicated for you to feel their soothing effects immediately. Even creating your own custom *blank* template—an empty sheet—can be a huge timesaver if you prestock it with your preferred object styles and a savvy selection of reusable tables (packed with formulas, of course). Having your very own plain-vanilla starter document in the Template Chooser means you'll no longer have to spend ages tweaking colors and text styles *every time* you add a new chart or create a new document.

Templates become even more useful when you have forms that you or others fill out all the time: time sheets, invoices, expense reports, worksheets for calculating the odds of management letting you and your colleagues book that weekend social in Barbados—you know, the everyday stuff. When you have these go-to documents available in the Template Chooser, you've always got a fresh form at the ready. These templates can be as elaborate as you like—multimedia reports, statements carefully branded with your logo, or complex grade books that you need to fill in every semester. You could even create an order form that fills in product info by doing lookups (page 582) from a catalog on a separate sheet.

This chapter takes you through the process of building your own custom templates and adding them to the Template Chooser.

Anatomy of a Numbers Template

The deep, dark secret of Numbers templates is that they have no deep, dark secret. Templates are basically just regular Numbers documents that you happen to stash in the Template Chooser. When you create a template, you build a normal spreadsheet, load it up with tables, sprinkle in your design, and then choose File→"Save as Template," and confirm that, yes, you do want to "Add to Template Chooser." From then on, when you open the Template Chooser, you'll find your new template, along with any others you've created, in the My Templates category.

Your custom templates work just like Apple's built-in beauties: Open a document from the Template Chooser and you get a clone of the model document as a fresh, untitled file. The spreadsheet is in exactly the same state as when you saved the original template: All the content, formulas, functions, tables, pictures—everything is there as you saved it. Creating a template, in other words, puts your document into suspended animation, ready for you to revive as an entirely new document at any time.

Your custom templates don't need to contain any content: A template can create a completely empty sheet. This might not seem like much of a timesaver, but even blank templates come loaded with a bevy of styles that let you completely overhaul an object with the click of a mouse. In fact, creating a template like this is the *only* way to save custom styles for charts, objects, fonts, and everything else. Add a group of your commonly used chart settings to the Format panel's Style tab, and you're saving some serious time.

Even when you're whipping up a multi-sheet confection of elaborate tables and functions, creating and choosing these background settings for your template is nearly as important as the content itself. Specifically, every template—actually, every Numbers spreadsheet—contains detailed formatting instructions for displaying each and every object:

- **Document formatting.** The paper size and orientation (vertical or horizontal), and page-numbering settings.

- **Chart styles.** The Styles pane's collection of prefab chart formatting.

- **Text boxes, shapes, and connection lines.** Create new styles that let you apply text styles, fills, borders, shadows, and so on to new objects with a few clicks of the mouse.

- **Pictures and movies.** Configure shadows, reflections, opacity, and outlines, and save them as ready-to-use styles in the Format panel's trusty Style tab.

Building Your Own Template

Start by opening a spreadsheet—it can be a document you've created in the past or a completely fresh spreadsheet from the template of your choice. Whatever you choose, the idea is to start with a document that's already as close as possible to the template you plan to save. This spreadsheet will become the model document that you use as the basis for your template. Choose File→Save right off the bat to save the file. *Don't* choose "Save as Template" just yet—you're just saving this as a regular Numbers spreadsheet. Give it a name like Barbados Weekender Worksheet Model. This way, you can save the file periodically as you work on it, since you won't actually save it as a template file until you've completed your work on this model document.

Next, get your document and sheet settings squared away. Then go to File→Print and choose your preferred printer, paper size, and your page-numbering preferences. Now you're ready to start defining all the styles for the document's various elements: charts, text boxes, shapes, connection lines, images, and movies.

■ ADDING NEW OBJECT STYLES

What's the status of your Styles pane? Does it include all the chart styles that you use? Having the right set of prefab formats always helps, and it's worth taking a few minutes to get this part right. If you need a refresher about the Styles pane and the role it plays in creating crowd-pleasing objects, head back to page 175.

> **NOTE** The following instructions use charts as an example, but you create styles for all Numbers objects in exactly the same way—except tables. Sadly, you can't create new styles for tables. If you have a collection of settings you want to apply across multiple tables, your best bet is to add a table to your template, style it exactly the way you want, and then save that perfectly styled version as part of your template. Then, whenever you create a new document based on this template, you get a perfectly styled table that you can copy and paste to use multiple times throughout your document.

If you already have sample charts in place as working models for the chart styles you'd like to add, select them one by one, open the Format panel's Style tab, and then click the little arrows that appear in the Style pane until you reach a blank thumbnail with a + on it; click the + to save your style. Alternatively, save an object's style by selecting that object and then choosing Format→Advanced→Create [Object] Style.

If you'd like to create additional styles, add a new chart to the sheet and format the text, colors, borders, and so on, and then save the style as described above. If you want your template to be empty, then when you're done styling the chart, you can delete it and Numbers still remembers the style(s) you created.

■ **CREATING THE TEMPLATE'S CONTENT**

Armed with a bunch of snazzy new styles, you're ready to create the content that will actually appear in the sheet canvas, if you haven't already done so. Unless you're creating a blank template, this is where you polish off your spreadsheet's design to make it look the way it should when you or others create a new document based on your template.

Add your tables, including all the content, formulas, cell formatting, and placeholder data you want. Add any charts, text boxes, images, shapes, and other content on as many sheets as you like. Go ahead and name the sheets, tables, and charts. *Everything* you do here will show up in documents built from your template, so fix your spreadsheet up exactly the way you want it.

If the spreadsheet requires instructions, leave a note for others (or for yourself!) by adding a text box—even better, add a comment to the appropriate cell, or a sticky note to the surface of the sheet (comments are always visible when you create a new document from a template). See page 469 for more details about comments.

If you've added pictures or movies to your layout and you'd like to make it easy to replace those with other pictures, then turn them into media placeholders. Select the object, and then choose Format→Advanced→"Define as Media Placeholder." When you or others drop a picture or a movie on the placeholder, Numbers automatically drops it in, replacing the placeholder and formatting the new object to match the placeholder's size, position, rotation, graphic style—you name it. All set? You're ready to save.

Saving and Organizing Your Templates

Choose File→"Save as Template," and confirm that you want to "Add to Template Chooser." Then type a name for your new template, just as you'd like it to appear in the Template Chooser.

> **TIP** If you ever want to make changes to your template file, create a new document from the template, make your modifications, and then choose File→"Save as Template" again.

You don't *have* to save your template file to the Template Chooser—you can save it anywhere you like—but it'll show up in the Template Chooser only if you select "Add to Template Chooser." To save your template in another location (for example, on the desktop ready for you to email to your template-loving buddies), go to File→"Save as Template," but this time click Save. In the Save As dialog box, give your template file a name, some optional tags, and choose its location. When you're ready, click Save. This template won't show up in your Template Chooser, but you can add it at any time by locating the file in your Finder and then double-clicking it. A Numbers window appears, asking if you want to add this file to your Template Chooser.

This is also how you install a third-party template: Download the template file, double-click it and, when prompted by Numbers, choose "Add to Template Chooser."

Sharing Your Spreadsheets

You've got a spreadsheet loaded with stunning statistics, artfully crafted formulas, and insightful charts, all wrapped in an elegant design. You, dear reader, are an unstoppable number-crunching machine. You certainly shouldn't keep all that genius to yourself. When you've got your numbers nailed and your functions formulated, it's time to get your document out there. Whether you're printing the family investment plan for your husband, emailing an Excel file to your boss, or sharing your Little League team's stats online, this chapter covers all the ways Numbers can help slingshot your spreadsheet from your computer into the world.

In the next few pages, you'll learn how to print your document, save it in various file formats, share it with other iWork programs, and send it to the far side of the Internet. Let's get to it—the world awaits.

■ Printing Your Spreadsheet

Start a Numbers print job by choosing File→Print (or pressing ⌘-P), which transports you to Print Preview mode. If you're in a hurry, you can print straightaway by clicking the Print button at the bottom of the Print Preview tab. But, before you commit your spreadsheet to printed paper, you should do a bit of housekeeping. Select your preferred printer and paper size from the Print Preview tab (Figure 23-1), and then spend some time perfecting your document's layout.

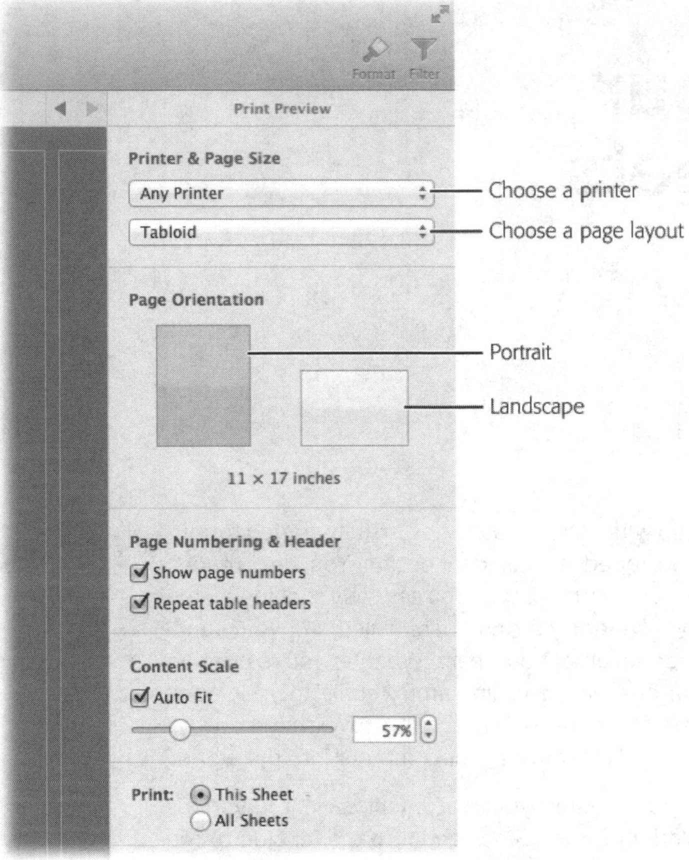

FIGURE 23-1

The Print Preview tab lets you select a printer and a paper size for your document. You can also choose the orientation of your page (landscape or portrait), and whether to show page numbers. If you have a table that spans multiple pages, you'll most likely want to keep the "Repeat table headers" checkbox turned on, so that the table makes sense on page 1 and subsequent pages.

While you're working on your spreadsheet, Numbers gives you an endless canvas where you can stretch out your tables, charts, and other design elements. Onscreen, at least, there's no such thing as a page break. But when you send those hundreds of columns and thousands of rows to a printer, page breaks become a reality. To avoid a situation where you print off a Numbers document and find that the last row of cells has slipped off page 1 onto page 2, Numbers' *Auto Fit* feature scales your document for you. This will usually give you the effect you want, but if you're not happy with Numbers' auto-fitting, you can scale your content manually by dragging the Content Scale slider in the Print Preview tab, or by typing a percentage into its accompanying field. As soon as you move the slider, Numbers turns off the Auto Scale checkbox.

Chapter 16 has more information about using Print Preview, starting on page 450.

When you've got your layout just the way you want it for the sheets you plan to print, you're ready to send it to the printer. If you plan to print just one of your sheets, select the This Sheet radio button near the bottom of the Print Preview tab. If you want to print all the sheets that make up your document, select All Sheets instead. (If you're unsure, you can browse through your sheets using the tabs in the Sheets bar.)

When you're ready, click the Print button at the bottom of the Print Preview panel. The Print dialog box opens, so you can make final tweaks to how your document will look on the printed page, as shown in Figure 23-2. If you want to print more than one copy of your document, for example, enter a number in the Copies box. To print something less than the whole shebang, enter a page range in the From and To fields, such as *4* to *8*.

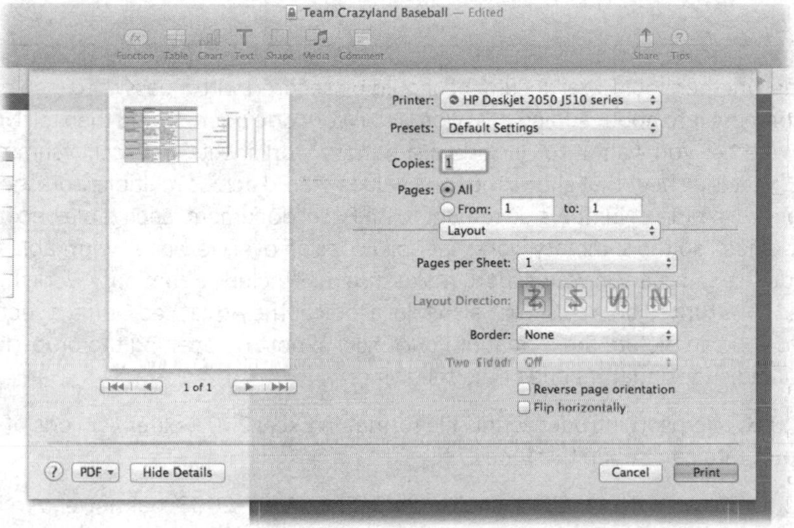

FIGURE 23-2

The Print dialog box gives you a preview of what you're about to print. (If your Print dialog box looks a bit slimmer than the version shown here, click the Show Details button.) You can use the navigation buttons below the preview image to flip through your pages. When you're satisfied with your print plan, click the Print button to commit your numbers to paper.

Ready? Click Print to send your spreadsheet to the printer.

■ Exporting to Other Formats

Paper is all well and good, but chances are that you'll share your document electronically far more often than you put it on paper. When you're sending a spreadsheet file to friends or coworkers who haven't yet discovered the joys of iWork, Numbers lets you save your document in a handful of other formats to allow even these poor souls to receive the benefit of your labor. You can save your spreadsheet for editing and viewing in Microsoft Excel, Numbers '09, or CSV format. You can also save your document as a read-only PDF file; this is the only option that will always look exactly like your original, but with the obvious drawback that it can't be edited. Each of these choices has its strengths and weaknesses, and this section explains them all.

NOTE You can also export your document as a Zip archive. See page 255 for more about exporting iWork documents in this format.

Saving an Excel File

The heavyweight champion of the spreadsheet world is, of course, Microsoft Excel. It's far and away the most popular spreadsheet program out there, which means that sooner or later, someone's going to ask for your spreadsheet as an Excel file. Numbers makes it easy to save a copy for Excel: Choose File→Export To→Excel, which opens the Export Your Spreadsheet dialog box.

TIP Suddenly gone off the idea of Excel, and want to export your document in a different format instead? Not a problem: You can jump among formats by clicking the tabs along the top of the Export Your Spreadsheet dialog box.

Decide whether your Excel document should be secured with a password (see page 243 for more info about adding passwords to iWork documents), and then tell Numbers whether you want it to "Include a summary worksheet." In Excel, a summary worksheet is a sheet that shows the total values stored across multiple worksheets. When you export a Numbers document to an Excel document, each table becomes a worksheet, so the summary worksheet provides an overview of all your tables. To include this summary in your export, make sure the "Include a summary worksheet" checkbox is turned on. You should also take a look at the Advanced Options section, where you can dictate the format of your Excel export by opening the drop-down menu and choosing from one of the following:

- **.xlsx.** Microsoft introduced this file format in Excel 2007; older versions of this program can't open this type of file.

- **.xls.** This was the standard file format in Excel 1997–2003, but newer versions of the program can open these files, too.

When you're ready to export, click the Next button. In the Save As dialog box, enter a name for your Excel file, enter some tags (see page 15 for a reminder about tags), and choose where to store your Excel document. (For details on *importing* Excel files, see page 449.)

TIP If you want to email your spreadsheet to someone, a faster route is to click the Share button in the toolbar, and then choose Send a Copy→Email. This opens the "Send via Email" dialog box. Although the Numbers tab is always selected, you can easily hop among the different formats by clicking one of the other tabs along the top of this dialog box. Select Excel (or PDF, or CSV), click Next, and Numbers creates a copy of the file in Excel format, launches Mail, and opens a new message with the file already attached.

That part's easy; it's the stuff that comes afterward that can be tricky. Numbers and Excel have very different ideas about how to format documents, and Numbers' export machinery often deals with this in disappointing fashion. The good news is that, when you're saving a fairly simple spreadsheet with basic formulas and functions, one table per sheet, the leap to Excel works well, giving you the results you'd hope for.

But when you've put Numbers through its paces to take advantage of its document-design acumen, the result doesn't always translate well to Excel, whose clunky design and formatting features simply can't keep up with Numbers. If your spreadsheet includes more than one table per sheet—one of Numbers' most fundamental features—the tables all get placed on separate worksheets in the exported Excel document. Other objects follow suit, scattering across several Excel worksheets. Even a single-sheet Numbers document can morph into many, many worksheets in Excel if it contains lots of tables, charts, or design elements. Bottom line: You wind up with a document that doesn't look much like the original.

Exported Excel documents include a cover-page summary saying that the file was exported by Numbers and that its tables now appear on separate sheets (see Figure 23-3). This cover sheet also offers links to the worksheets containing your various tables and objects. The introductory text ends with the less-than-reassuring caveat, "Please be aware that formula calculations may differ in Excel." Alas, these calculation lapses do happen sometimes, especially when you use relatively sophisticated formulas that include lookups (page 582).

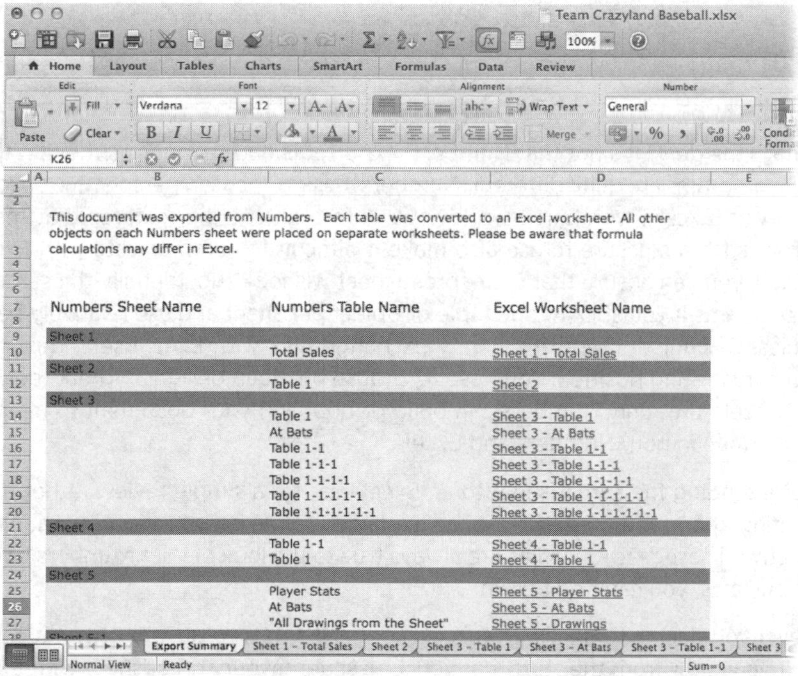

FIGURE 23-3

When you export a Numbers document to Excel format, the summary worksheet explains that the document came from Numbers and lists links to your tables, charts, and other objects—which are now scattered across several worksheets.

You can prevent Numbers from adding a summary sheet by going to File→Export To→Excel and making sure the "Include a summary worksheet" checkbox is turned off before going ahead with your export.

Despite the summary sheet's cautionary message and the occasional slip-up, the exported Excel files are typically usable—your data, formulas, and *most* functions make the trip intact. But the Excel version will almost certainly require some significant reformatting and head-scratching to piece together if you've used Numbers' document-design features to create your spreadsheet. Numbers does its best to let you know about these problems, showing warning messages like the one in Figure 23-4 after the export is complete.

FIGURE 23-4

When Numbers runs into compatibility issues while saving your spreadsheet as an Excel document, it details the problems in this window.

So what's the deal? It's not that Numbers' exporter is *bad* so much as the fact that the two programs are quite different. Numbers' design-focused perspective doesn't fit well with Excel's workhorse worldview. Unfortunately, the features that make Numbers such a pleasure to use also make it difficult to communicate with Excel. That said, you can ensure that your spreadsheet will look substantially the same in both programs if you stick to one table or object per sheet and use relatively basic formulas. Of course, if you frequently exchange files with Excel users, this puts you in a frustrating position: You have to choose between designing great-looking spreadsheets that only Numbers can build or hobbling your document to make it look the same in both Numbers and Excel.

If you're sending the spreadsheet to an Excel user for a simple review rather than for editing, then sending a PDF file (as explained in the next section) is a happier alternative. These read-only files are always true to the look of your Numbers document but, alas, you can't edit them.

However you decide to deal with this exchange, it's best to go into it with a game plan. If you know from the start that you'll be sharing your spreadsheet with Excel users, make the decision early on about whether you'll send a PDF or an Excel file. It's important to keep these considerations in mind when you plan to share with Planet Excel. Keep your spreadsheet simple while you're doing the back and forth, saving the design extravaganza for the very end when you no longer have to cope with the programs' differences.

Exporting a PDF Document

PDF (Portable Document Format) is the way to go when you don't need—or want—people to edit your spreadsheet. It's also ideal when you want to ensure that anyone can read your document no matter what computer or software he's using—even if he doesn't even have a spreadsheet program. PDF files are read-only, but they pay back this downside with their accuracy—they always look *exactly* like the original document. People can open PDF files with various programs, including the free Adobe Reader, which they can download from *www.adobe.com/reader*.

> **NOTE** While people using Adobe Reader to view your PDF can't edit the document, they *can* annotate it. The latest version of the program—Adobe Reader XI at the time of this writing—includes a whole host of markup tools on its Comment tab.

To export a copy of your spreadsheet as a PDF, choose File→Export To→PDF. Numbers shows you the options for exporting to PDF, shown in Figure 23-5.

FIGURE 23-5

The Export Your Spreadsheet dialog box's PDF tab lets you select the image quality and password options for the exported document. To require a password, turn on the "Require password to open" checkbox, and then create your password. (If you already password-protected your Numbers document by going to File→Set Password [page 243], you can either use that password or click the Change Password button to create a new one.)

The Image Quality drop-down menu lets you choose from three options, which also affect the size of the exported file (the better the image quality, the bigger the file).

Of course, this setting is important only if you actually have pictures in your document. Assuming that you do, here's what the options mean:

- **Good** reduces images to 72 dpi, which is appropriate for onscreen viewing but not great for printing.

- **Better** reduces images to 150 dpi—fine for printing on an inkjet printer, for example.

- **Best** doesn't reduce the images at all. Let 'er rip with the top-quality original images.

After you've chosen your settings, click Next to specify a name and location for the file, and then click Export.

Exporting a CSV File

CSV stands for "comma-separated values"—the lingua franca of the spreadsheet world. Any spreadsheet program can read this plain-text format, but that also means it's the lowest-common-denominator option. No graphics or formatting make its way into this kind of file, and every table is saved as a separate CSV file; Numbers creates a folder to save all these files.

To export a CSV file, choose File→Export To→CSV. (If you've applied a password to your document, Numbers warns that you can't password-protect CSV files.) To choose the text encoding to use in your document, click the Advanced Options flippy triangle, and then make your selection from the drop-down menu (see Figure 23-6). Numbers automatically selects "Unicode (UTF-8)," which should work with most programs. Click Next to choose a filename, tags, and location for the file, and then click Export.

FIGURE 23-6

The CSV tab of the Export Your Spreadsheet dialog box asks you to choose the text encoding for the exported file. Unicode is typically the way to go, but the menu also includes options for Western (Mac OS Roman) or Western (Windows Latin 1). Only old-school Mac and Windows programs are likely to want those formats, so you should choose them only when you run into problems getting a program to accept the Unicode-formatted file.

Saving Spreadsheets for Numbers '09

When you're sharing your document with friends who haven't gotten around to updating to the latest version of iWork, you can save the document in the iWork '09 format. As you might expect, doing this strips out any features that are new in iWork, including interactive charts, bubble charts, and star ratings.

To export your document as a Numbers '09 file, go to File→Export To→Numbers '09, choose whether your file should be password protected, and then click Next. By now, you know the drill: Give your file a name, a home, some optional tags, and then click Export.

■ Sharing with Pages and Keynote

One of the best features of iWork is how seamless all its programs feel. They share the same icons, tools, and even features, often making it seem more like you're using a single program than three separate ones.

You can swap tables back and forth between all the iWork programs, and with only a few caveats, they work just fine anywhere you send them. Pages and Keynote both understand formulas and functions, for example, so even sophisticated Numbers calculations make the transition to the other programs with no problem. When you copy and paste a chart, there's no need to do the same with its source table; clever Keynote and Pages always paste the chart's data into their own Chart Data Editor. To take a peek at this table, select a freshly pasted graph and click the Edit Chart Data button—voilà, all the data is waiting for you! (You can learn more about working with the Chart Data Editor on page 236.)

What Pages and Keynote *can't* do is maintain a link between the version of the chart or table in Numbers and their versions. If you make a change to a chart's source table in Numbers, for example, don't expect the chart to update in Keynote. Even if you copy a chart's source table into Pages or Keynote, the link between the two is broken. To change the data for a chart in Pages or Keynote, you need to use the program's Chart Data Editor.

■ Distributing Spreadsheets Online

You might've heard about this thing called the Internet—it's a pretty big deal. The Web and email have become essential ways to share documents of all kinds, and Numbers offers a few options for getting your document online and into the mix quickly. Apple's iCloud service offers a convenient way to review and collaborate on documents with a group, and Numbers' "Share a Copy" submenu has everything you need to quickly catapult your document over to Mail, Facebook, Twitter, and elsewhere.

Sharing via iCloud

When you're ready to share a budget plan with a group of colleagues, a team roster with your soccer team, or the plans for Crazyland Wonderpark's freshly approved social events program, iCloud makes for a convenient online venue. This web-based service is built right into Numbers and lets your group of invited reviewers check out your spreadsheet online, make edits, add comments, or download the document in a variety of formats.

When you share a document via iCloud, you're actually sending a link that recipients use to access your document online. When someone receives your link, they just need to copy and paste it into their web browser, and they're whisked away to an online version of your document. The really cool thing is that, although they're making edits online, you can see their changes in your Mac-based document. So, if your coworker has been busy updating your spreadsheet online while you were busy taking a nap, when you wake up and open your document, her changes are ready and waiting for you; clever Numbers for iCloud beams the latest changes straight to your Mac. This sharing is a two-way street: Any changes you make to a shared document on your Mac also appear in its online counterpart.

> **TIP** Getting the latest online changes beamed into your computer requires an active Internet connection. If you're working on a Numbers document with your online posse, it's a good idea to have your laptop permanently connected to the World Wide Web. This connection ensures that you have access to your collaborators' latest changes—and that they have access to yours.

Before sharing documents via iCloud, you need to create an iCloud account (see page 750). You also need to let your Mac know about your iCloud account, by entering your username and password as discussed on page 258. After checking these tasks off your to-do list, you're ready to take your Numbers documents online. To share a Numbers document via iCloud:

1. **Open the spreadsheet in Numbers, head to the toolbar and click Share→ "Share via iCloud," and then choose your sharing method (see Figure 23-7).**

   Remember, sharing a document via iCloud involves sending a link to other people, so this step lets you choose *how* you send this all-important link. You can send it via email, Messages, Twitter, or Facebook. If none of these channels float your boat, choose Copy Link and then paste the link wherever you want.

2. **If you haven't already saved this document to iCloud, do that now. (If you *have* already saved your document to your iCloud account, hop to step 3).**

   Depending on your exact situation, you'll see one of several dialog boxes:

   — If you've already saved your Numbers spreadsheet on your computer, Numbers tells you that you need to move it to iCloud, so click "Move to iCloud" and enter the usual info in the Save As dialog box. (Make sure you don't change the Where drop-down menu—leave it set to iCloud.)

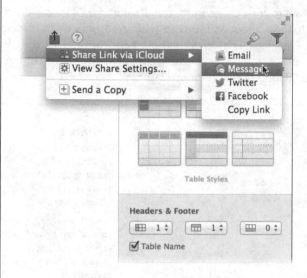

FIGURE 23-7

To invite people to view your Numbers spreadsheet on iCloud, choose Share→"Share via iCloud," and Numbers lists all the different places where you can send the link. If you have a different channel in mind (pasting the link into a Google Hangout, or sending it as a Facebook private message, for example), choose Copy Link, and then paste the link anywhere you like.

— If this is a new document you haven't saved at all, the Save As dialog box launches with iCloud already selected in the Where drop-down menu.

— If this is your first time sharing anything via iCloud, click OK in the dialog box that appears to launch the Save As box.

Whatever route you take to the Save As dialog box, make sure the Where option is set to iCloud, and then click Save. Annoyingly, when you click Save, Numbers closes the Share dialog box.

3. **Go to Share→"Share via iCloud," and then re-select your sharing method.**

   If you choose Copy Link, you're done—the link is stored on your Clipboard (page 36), ready for you to paste anywhere you like.

4. **If you're sharing via email, Messages, Twitter, or Facebook, make sure everything looks good, and then click Send.**

   If you chose Email or Messages, Numbers presents you with a pre-filled message or email. Check over the text, enter a recipient, and then click Send. Numbers fires off an email or Messages notification, letting your recipient know about your freshly shared spreadsheet.

   If you went the Facebook or Twitter route, check the text and then click Send. Numbers adds the link to your Facebook Timeline or Twitter feed. Just be wary of posting to social media sites, as the link will be much more public than if you send it directly to one person.

5. **To share your spreadsheet with even more people, or to send it to a different channel, make your selection from the Share→"Share via iCloud" submenu. Rinse and repeat.**

Changed your mind and want to cut a collaborator out of your life? Or is your document finally ready to send to the printers, and you can't risk any of your well-meaning but meddling collaborators making a final tweak without your knowledge? You can make a shared document private again by selecting Share→View Share Settings and then clicking the Stop Sharing button (Figure 23-8).

FIGURE 23-8

To turn a shared document back into a private document, choose Share→View Share Settings→Stop Sharing.

This dialog box also lets you send your document to new collaborators, or post it to extra channels, by clicking the Send Link button. To copy the link, put your cursor over the link as shown here, and then click the Copy Link button when it appears.

iCloud offers the same basic layout of your spreadsheet as Numbers for Mac, complete with the familiar toolbar-and-Format-panel combo. (See Chapter 30 for an overview of Numbers for iCloud.)

NOTE Collaborators don't need an iCloud account to edit the spreadsheets you share with them.

The way the document appears on iCloud is always faithful to your original layout—fonts, charts, and all—and looks just as it would if you were browsing it in Numbers for Mac. You may notice though, that there's no Save button; that's because iCloud saves all your changes (and shares them with your collaborators) automatically.

If you want to print a Numbers document that's been shared with you via iCloud, you have several options. You can generate a PDF and then print that document by going to Tools→Print; iCloud generates your PDF. Click Open PDF to open the document, and then select File→Print. Alternatively, you can download the iCloud document to your Mac and then print this copy. Choose Tools→"Download a Copy," and then select your format: Numbers, PDF, or Excel. Once the file has downloaded, open it and print as normal.

◼ Sending a Copy of Your Document

iCloud makes it easy to beam your document around the Web, gathering feedback and input from other people in the process. The downside is that when you share a document via iCloud, you're giving your collaborators the power to edit the one and only version of your document. This may not be a problem, but what if you're sharing your spreadsheet with a friend who's well known for his poor taste, and you have a sneaking suspicion he'll paint your tables orange and lime green? Or maybe one of your coworkers doesn't have the best grasp of technology, and it's a distinct possibility that she could accidentally delete your 15-page table? Or what if you just want to distribute your finished document, without giving anyone else the power to make changes. Does sharing *always* have to carry the risk of unwelcome edits?

Happily, the answer is "no." If you want to distribute your document while ensuring that your version remains untouched, you can share a *copy* of the document. This copy arrives on the recipient's computer, ready for him to review, or even for him to edit and then send back to you, so you can decide whether his changes are a good fit for your master document.

To send a copy of your document:

1. **Go to Share→"Send a Copy," and choose from Email, Messages, or AirDrop.**

2. **Choose your document's format.**

   You can pick from Numbers, PDF, Excel, or CSV. The rules are the same as when you export a document, so see page 663 for a reminder on the pros and cons of these different formats. Just make sure you choose a format your recipients can actually open!

3. **Click Next.**

   Numbers generates your file. If you opted for Email or Messages, Numbers creates a message with your document already attached; just enter a recipient, and then click Send. If you chose AirDrop instead, make sure your recipient is nearby and has AirDrop open in his Finder so he can receive your file (for more on using AirDrop, visit *http://support.apple.com/kb/ht4783*).

iWork for iOS

Pages for iOS

N ow that the wonders of the Internet age are available anytime, anywhere, having to boot up your Mac whenever you need to tweak an iWork document feels practically Victorian. Besides, you can't be at your Mac creating dazzling iWork documents 24/7. Eventually, you have to venture out into the 3D world (a.k.a. reality). This may even involve doing something boring like sitting on a bus, which is when an iDevice (that's shorthand for an iPad, iPhone, or iPod Touch) can be your lifeline, transforming a dull half-hour into a cheeky little iWork session.

Pages for iOS has got all your on-the-go word processing needs covered, whether it's jotting down a quick haiku about that unique, bus-fresh aroma, or creating multimedia documents bursting with images, graphs, and charts. (Quick reminder: iOS is the operating system that powers all of Apple's iDevices.) Pages for iOS is the most powerful and artistically satisfying word processor since, well, Pages for Mac. So boot up your iDevice of choice and get ready to experience the power of Pages on the go.

> **NOTE** This chapter—and the next two—focus on the *iPad* version of the iWork apps. That's because you're more likely to use the iOS apps on iPads than any other iDevice (it's hard to imagine that anyone would try to, say, write a dissertation on an iPhone or an iPod Touch). The apps work pretty much the same way on all three iDevices, though if you're on an iPhone or an iPod Touch, you may encounter slight differences from what's stated here.

■ Creating Your First Document

To get started, track down the Pages icon on your iDevice, and give it a tap. (If you need help installing the Pages app, check out page 799.) If this is your first visit to Pages, you see a Welcome screen (tap Continue) and then a Use iCloud screen (tap Later to ignore iCloud for now, or Use iCloud to connect the app to iCloud). Finally, on the Get Started screen, tap Use Pages to display Documents view (shown in Figure 24-1), a screen that contains thumbnail previews of all of your Pages documents (if any). Every time you launch Pages, the app takes you straight to Documents view.

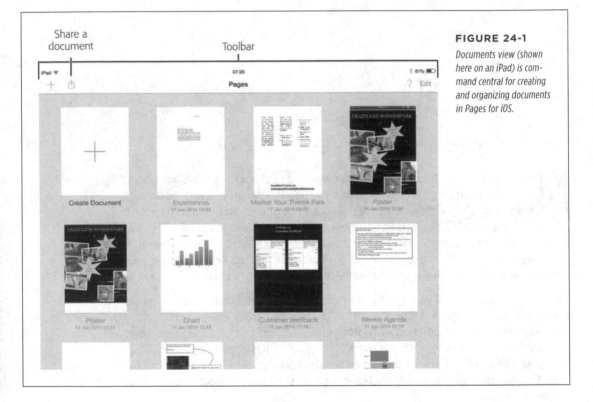

Share a document

Toolbar

FIGURE 24-1

Documents view (shown here on an iPad) is command central for creating and organizing documents in Pages for iOS.

Documents view is an important part of the Pages story. In addition to being your starting point for creating prose masterpieces, Documents view is also where you rename, copy, and delete documents. The box on page 679 has details.

> **TIP** When you're editing a document, you can hop back to Documents view in a jiffy by tapping Documents in the toolbar (and then jump back into any of your documents by tapping its thumbnail preview in Documents view).

If you haven't created any documents before, Documents view simply displays the message "No Documents. Tap to create a new document." Tap the screen to open the *Template Chooser*, which is described in a sec.

If you've already created some documents (or saved some to iCloud and connected Pages to your iCloud account [page 752]), then you'll see thumbnails of each document. To get from Documents view to the Template Chooser, either tap the thumbnail with the + on it, or tap the + in the toolbar and select Create Document.

ORGANIZATION STATION

Renaming, Copying, and Deleting Documents

In addition to being your starting point for creating prose masterpieces, Documents view is also where you rename, copy, and delete documents.

To rename a document, tap its title, enter a new one, and then either tap the blue Done button or tap anywhere outside of the title-editing box to save your title and hop back to Documents view.

To duplicate or delete a document, tap Edit in the toolbar, and then tap the thumbnail previews of all the documents you want to apply this change to. You can then tap either the + icon to duplicate them or the trash-can icon to delete them. Tap Done when you're finished duplicating/deleting.

You can also reorganize your documents in a couple of different ways. If you pull down on the Documents view screen, you'll see two buttons: Date and Name. Tap them to switch between sorting your documents by date and by name. Alternatively, tap Edit, and all your document thumbnails start wiggling. Tap all the documents you want to move, and then press and hold on one of the selected documents for a moment until they enlarge a bit; then drag the thumbnail to a new spot.

You can also create a folder containing several documents (similar to the way you can organize app icons into folders). Tap Edit to set the thumbnails wiggling, and then select all *but one* of the document(s) in question. Next, press and hold one of the selected documents, and then drag it onto the document you left out of your initial selection. Pages smooshes all the documents into a folder and then opens a title-editing box containing the name of that folder (the default is Folder, Folder 2, Folder 3, and so on). To give your new folder a more unique moniker, tap the title box and type away. When you've finished, either tap Done or tap anywhere outside of the title-editing box. To close the folder, tap anywhere outside of the folder's expanded box (the gray section).

To pull documents *out* of a folder, tap Edit in the toolbar, open the folder by giving it a tap, and then tap, hold, and drag files you want to remove. You can move multiple files out of a folder in one go by tapping each one's thumbnail so they're all selected, and then dragging them out of the folder. When you remove the last document from the folder, the folder vanishes.

When you're finished editing your documents and folders, tap the Done button to steady those shaking thumbnails and return to normal Documents view.

Choosing a Template

As you learned back in Chapter 1, the Pages experience is built around *templates,* which are essentially pre-made documents that contain handy placeholders. For example, the Real Estate Flyer template contains a big, eye-catching title and a sidebar with some dummy contact details. Templates let you create a new document by tweaking the placeholders, which is much less scary than a blank page. (If you *like* blank pages, you're in luck: Pages includes two Blank templates.)

As Figure 24-2 shows, just like in Pages for Mac, the Pages for iOS Template Chooser is divided into categories (Basic, Reports, and so on). Scroll to browse all the templates that Pages has to offer. If you're on an iPad, you can also click Show Categories in the toolbar and then tap a category to view only the templates that fall under that category. When you find a template you're happy with, tap its thumbnail to create and open a document based on it.

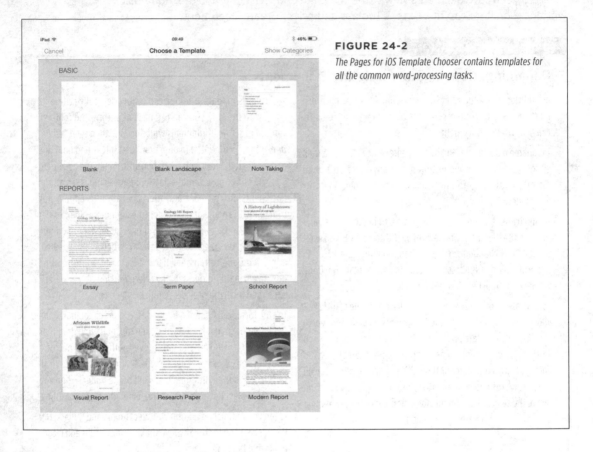

FIGURE 24-2

The Pages for iOS Template Chooser contains templates for all the common word-processing tasks.

Undoing Changes

You've got yourself a brand-new Pages for iOS document, and are probably rarin' to work on it. But before you dive in and start editing, it's important to know the escape routes you can use if you muck things up.

If you make a mistake while editing a document and need to undo your recent change(s), you have a couple of options. For a quick fix, either tap Undo in the toolbar, or give your iDevice a quick shake and then tap the Undo button that appears. If you change your mind about what you just undid, give it another shake, and you'll see a Redo button (sometimes, you'll see both Undo and Redo).

NOTE If you're wondering how to save your document, Pages for iOS saves all changes *automatically*, so you can call off your search for a Save button!

Document Setup

When creating multipage documents, you *could* style each page separately, but if they share any common elements, it's much easier to change the document's underlying *blueprint,* which affects all the pages in your document. To access a document's blueprint, first open the document, and then tap the wrench icon and choose Document Setup.

The Document Setup screen gives you lots of different options. Here are some of the most useful:

- **Headers and footers.** Tap either the header or footer bar, and then type out what you want to appear there, such as the document's author or title, or tap the Page Numbers pop-up to add a page number to every page in your document. You can choose from a range of page-number formats: 1, 1 of 12, Page 1, or Page 1 of 12.

- **Margins.** Change the margins for your entire document by dragging any of the arrows around the blueprint's perimeter to a new position.

- **Objects.** You can add the full range of objects to your blueprint (you'll learn all about objects in a sec) by tapping the + button in the toolbar and choosing from the drop-down menu. Any object you add appears on *every* page—and you can't delete it. This is useful if you have a background image you want to use throughout your document.

- **Change Paper Size.** Choose between US Letter and A4 paper sizes by tapping this option at the bottom of the screen.

Once you're happy with your changes, tap Done to return to your document, which Pages updates to reflect the changes you made to the blueprint.

■ Adding Objects

Along with templates, another familiar face you'll encounter in Pages for iOS are *objects.* Almost everything you add to a Pages document is an object: text, photos, shapes, and so on. To add an object to a document, tap the + in the toolbar and then pick the kind of object you want to add (see Figure 24-3).

The following sections explain the details of how to add objects to your documents.

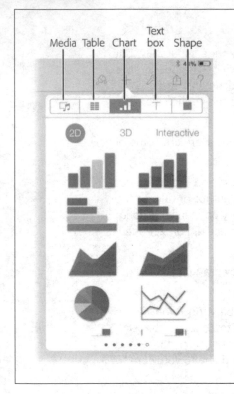

FIGURE 24-3

Add objects to your document by tapping the + in the toolbar, and then tap the button that represents the type of object you want to add: media (that's images, video, and audio), table, chart, text box, or shape.

Adding Images, Audio, and Video

To add an image, video, or audio clip, tap + and choose the media category. Strangely, although this category is the place to go to add images, audio, and video, the banner at the top of this submenu reads "Photos." Just ignore this banner, and choose either of these media hubs:

- **Camera Roll.** This is where your iDevice stores all your photos and other media.

- **My Photo Stream.** After you link Pages for iOS to iCloud (see page 752), you can use My Photo Stream, a service that gives you access to any media stored on other iDevices that are linked to your iCloud account. (For background reading on My Photo Stream, see *www.apple.com/icloud/features/photo-stream.html.*)

Tap either option, and then select an image, video, or audio clip to add it to your document. If you're adding a video or audio clip, tap its thumbnail, and then tap the Use button (on an iPhone or iPod Touch, this button is labeled Choose instead). You can also get a preview of the audio or video clip by tapping the Play button at the bottom of this drop-down menu. Page 694 explains how to work with images in Pages documents, and page 704 covers how to work with audio and video.

Adding Tables

To insert a table, tap the +, tap the table category, and then swipe left or right to view the different style options. Pages gives you loads of ways to customize a table once it's in your document, so for now just pick the combination of colors, borders, and headers/footers that's closest to what you want. Then flip to page 695 to learn how to work with Pages tables.

Adding Charts

When a table just won't cut it, tap the +, tap the charts icon, and then treat yourself to either a 2D, 3D, or interactive chart. Page 699 has lots more info about working with charts.

Adding Text

Word-processing documents let you add free-flowing text, but if you're dealing with a page-layout document, your text needs to be inside a text box. (Shapes, tables, and charts all work with text, too, but most of your "main" body text will go inside a text box.) To add a text box to your document, tap the +, tap the T icon, and then select the text that's formatted most like what you want. See page 15 for a discussion of page-layout documents vs. word-processing documents; and see page 688 for the full scoop on working with text boxes in Pages for iOS.

Adding Shapes

Tap + and then tap the square icon to see a selection of popular shapes and lines, as well as different *styles* for each shape (swipe left and right to see them). These styles are restricted to different background colors (also known as *fill colors*) and various border effects, but they're still handy shortcuts to getting the effect you crave.

You can edit shapes after adding them to your document, so simply tap the one that's closest to what you had in mind. Page 694 has the lowdown on working with shapes, and page 688 covers all your text-related options.

■ General Object Edits

This section takes a general look at working with objects before diving into the specifics of each object type. Regardless of what kind of object you've added to your document, here are some common controls you'll need to know:

- **Select.** To select an object, tap it once.

- **Move.** Select the object, and then drag it into a new position.

- **Resize.** To make an object larger or smaller, select it and then drag one of the blue handles that appears.

- **Lock/Unlock.** After going to the trouble of getting an object's size and positioning just right, you don't want to change it by accident and ruin all of your hard work. To make an object impossible to edit, *lock* it by selecting it and then tapping the paintbrush icon in the toolbar. In the pane that appears, tap Arrange→Lock; the object's resizing handles turn gray with little X's on them to indicate that you can't drag them. (You can't lock *every* type of object in every type of document; if you select an object and the Lock option isn't available, you're out of luck.) To make the object editable again, select the object and then choose Unlock from the mini toolbar that appears, or open the paintbrush menu and tap Unlock.

TIP If you're editing a document on your iPhone or iPod Touch, whenever you summon one of Pages' helpful panels by tapping the paintbrush, +, or wrench icon, you can return to your document by tapping the Done button or down-pointing triangle in the panel's upper-right corner. If you're on an iPad, simply tap anywhere outside the panel.

Whenever you select an object, you'll see a mini toolbar that contains some handy commands:

- **Copy.** Tap this button to copy the object to Pages' *Clipboard* (page 36), and then paste this duplicate to a new spot by tapping and keeping your finger pressed down on a blank area of your document; when you see the Paste button, tap it.

- **Cut.** Cutting an object copies it to your Clipboard *and* deletes the original; you can then paste the object in a new spot as described above. This is a handy alternative to dragging objects, particularly when you want to move them considerable distances.

- **Delete.** Removes the object from your document altogether.

- **Comment.** Tap this button to add a "sticky note" to the selected object. (One exception: You can't add comments to tables.) Type out your message, and then save it by tapping anywhere outside of the comment bubble—which also collapses (hides) the comment bubble. Collapsed comments still make their presence known by displaying a colored flag next to the object they're connected to. To open a collapsed comment, tap the object it's connected to, and then select Comment from the mini toolbar, or tap the comment flag itself.

  If your document is becoming overrun with comment flags, you can hide them (without deleting the comments) by tapping the wrench icon in the toolbar, choosing Settings, and then tapping the Comments switch to turn it off (it turns from green to white). To make the comment flags visible again, simply turn this switch back on. To delete a comment, open the comment, and then tap Delete in its bottom-left corner.

Move to Back/Front

As you learned in Chapter 7, when objects overlap, their *layers* determine the result. You can think of layers kind of like those transparent plastic sheets used with old-fashioned overhead projectors (remember those?) Each layer has an object on it, and all the layers combined create what you see in your document, just like you could combine plastic sheets on a projector. Objects on a layer that's higher up in the "stack" (in other words, closer to the front) overlap objects that are on lower layers.

To change where an object sits in this pecking order, first select the object. Then tap the paintbrush icon, choose Arrange, and then adjust the "Move to Back/Front" slider (Figure 24-4).

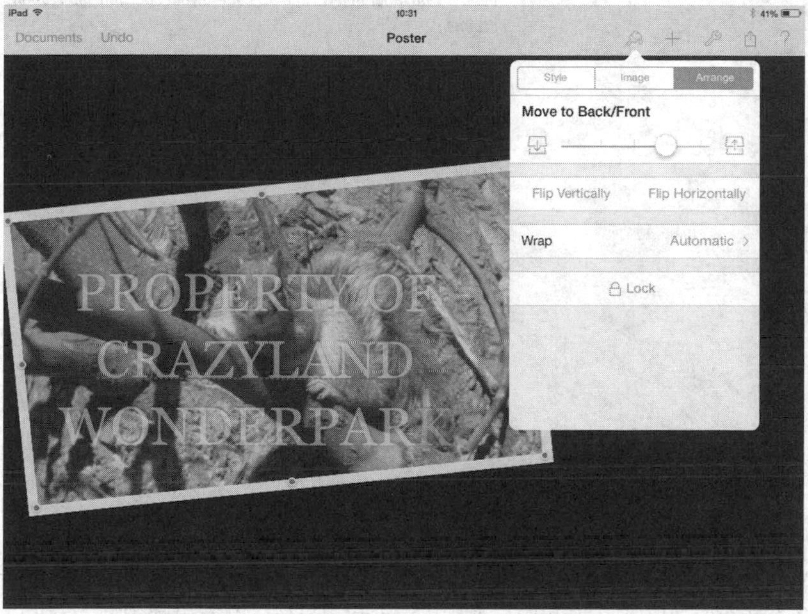

FIGURE 24-4

Mixing up layers lets you do things like create a watermark effect by sending an image to the very back layer of a document and putting text in front of it. Here, the text "Property of Crazyland Wonderpark" is on a higher layer than the squirrel image (meaning it's closer to the "front" of the document), so it overlays the image. You'll also notice that the text is see-through; the next section explains how to alter the opacity of your objects.

Adjusting Opacity

Objects arrive in your document completely opaque, but in some cases you may want to see through them to what's in the layers beneath then, as with the text in Figure 24-4. You can reduce an object's opacity by selecting it, tapping the paintbrush icon, choosing Style→Style Options→Effects, and then manipulating the Opacity slider. Dragging the slider to 0% makes the object invisible, while setting it to 100% gives you a solid object (everything in the layers beneath it is completely obscured).

> **NOTE** You can't alter the opacity of graphs and tables, but this is no biggie—you don't want people struggling to read your data, after all!

Text Wrapping

If you're going to add *any* text to your document, you need to think about how this text interacts with other objects. That's where text wrapping comes in. To get started, select an object you want to apply text wrapping to, and then tap the paintbrush icon and choose Arrange→Wrap (Figure 24-5).

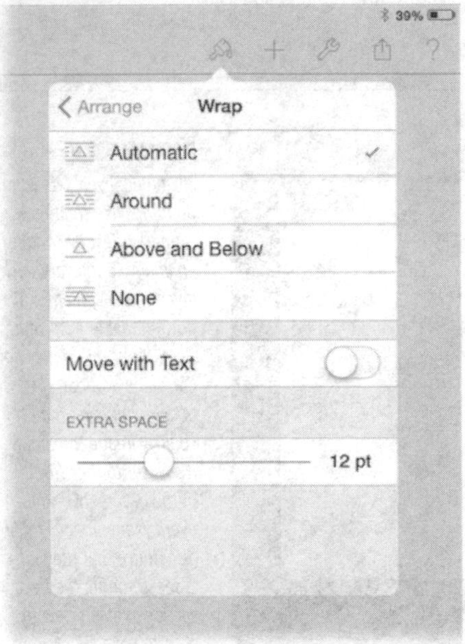

FIGURE 24-5

Text wrapping affects how free-flowing text interacts with objects in a word-processing document and how text inside a text box interacts with other objects in both page-layout and word-processing documents.

For text that flows above and below an object but not to its right or left, select "Above and Below." To make the text completely surround the object, opt for Around instead. To let Pages control wrapping, leave Automatic selected.

The Wrap menu's Extra Space slider controls how much space Pages inserts between the object and surrounding text. Set this slider to 0 for text that pushes right up against your object's borders, or a higher number to leave more room.

If you're working with a word-processing document (see page 15), you get an extra text wrap option: "Move with Text." To make an object shift to accommodate changing amounts of text (for example, if you delete a chunk of text above a shape, the shape moves up the page), tap this slider to turn it on (green). If you change your mind, you can anchor an object firmly to the page by turning this slider back off (white).

Using Guidelines

When you have multiple objects on the same page, you often want to align them. Happily, you don't need to dig out your old shatterproof ruler to get that perfectly aligned look, as Pages can supply a range of guidelines whenever it looks like you're trying to get your objects lined up (Figure 24-6).

To turn guidelines on (or off, if they're getting on your nerves), tap the wrench icon, choose Settings, and then adjust the following settings:

- **Center Guides** appear whenever the center of the selected object aligns with the center of another object on the page.

FIGURE 24-6

Flickering guidelines appear when you're dragging an object into a new position and that object is precariously close to aligning with other objects on the same page. To create that perfect alignment, follow the guidelines and drop your object into position.

- **Edge Guides** appear whenever an edge of the selected object aligns with the edges of any other object.

- **Spacing Guides** appear when two or more objects are equally spaced across the page. This is useful for creating neat rows of objects that are equal distances from one another.

> **TIP** When you're questing after that perfectly aligned object, you might find it helpful to display Pages' built-in ruler. To do so on an iPad, tap the wrench icon, choose Settings, and then tap the Ruler switch to turn it green. When you're done arranging objects, dismiss the ruler by tapping this switch again to turn it off. (On an iPhone or iPod Touch, Pages automatically hides the ruler to save precious screen real estate. Whenever you want to display the ruler, you have to tap the wrench icon and then choose Ruler.)

Styling Objects

When you're creating a document that's more about visuals than text (such as a poster), you may want to give your objects some extra pizzazz. Pages for iOS offers two methods for creating funkier objects: borders and effects.

To add a border to an image, movie clip, or shape, select the object, tap the paintbrush icon, choose Style→Style Options→Border, and then tap the Border switch to turn it on. Once you do that, you can customize the border by adjusting its color, width, and line style.

> **TIP** If you select an image, then the Style tab contains some ready-and-raring-to-go border styles, including effects that are impossible to create using the Color, Width, and Line Style settings alone. Scroll down to see the thumbnails that represent these styles, and then tap one to apply it to your image.

To add a basic border to a table, tap the paintbrush and select Table→Table Options, and then turn on the Table Outline switch. You can also add a basic border to some charts by selecting the chart, tapping the paintbrush icon, choosing Chart Options, and then turning on the Border switch (this setting isn't available for all chart types). Unfortunately, you can't customize chart or table borders.

You can also add shadow and reflection effects to shapes, text boxes, photos, and videos by tapping the paintbrush icon, choosing Style→Style Options→Effects, and then turning on the Shadow and/or Reflection switches. After adding a shadow, you can choose a shadow style using the thumbnails that appear. If you opt for a reflection, you can dictate how dramatic or subtle the reflection is by adjusting the unlabeled slider.

> **TIP** Don't have time to mess around with effects and borders, but still crave stylish objects? Every object has several ready-baked styles you can use. To see what's available for the selected object, tap the paintbrush icon, choose Style, and then tap any of the thumbnails.

■ Working with Text

Words are a big part of the Pages experience, and you can add them to many objects, including text boxes (obviously), tables, charts, shapes, and the free-flowing text of a word-processing document. To add text to an object, double-tap it to place your cursor inside. If the object contains placeholder text that's getting in your way, tap any word and Pages selects the whole placeholder; simply type to replace it.

To select a section of text, double-tap any word within it, and then grab the blue handles that appear and drag them across all the text you wish to change. Depending on whether you select a single word or an entire paragraph, a mini toolbar appears with some of the following options (on an iPhone or an iPod Touch, you have to click the mini toolbar's arrow buttons to see them all):

- **Replace** suggests replacements for the selected word.

- **Define** launches Pages' built-in dictionary. If Pages doesn't find a definition, then tap Search Web to perform a Google search for the selected word.

- **Highlight/Remove Highlight** adds or removes yellow highlighting from the selected text. This is a quick and easy way to draw attention to a particular passage.

- **Style.** If you've created the perfect combination of typeface, font size, color, and so on (more on that in a sec), you can apply this style to another piece of text. Select the text with the formatting you want to copy, and then tap Style→Copy Style. Then select a piece of text that will receive this copied style, select Style from the mini toolbar, and tap Paste Style; Pages updates the selected text with the copied style.

Basic Text Formatting

When you first start typing, Pages uses its standard text-formatting settings, but in a world of infinite possibilities, these settings won't always be right for your purposes.

There are two ways to format text. If you know what you want in advance, you can choose all your formatting *before* typing a single letter. Or you can apply changes to existing text by *selecting* it and then making your formatting changes. If you're working with the free-flowing text of a word-processing document, you format it by tapping the paintbrush icon and selecting the Style tab. If you're working with text in a text box, you make your formatting changes by opening the paintbrush menu and selecting the Text tab. Either way, you can choose from the following:

- **Bold, Italic, Underlined, Strikethrough.** To give your text a bold, italic, underlined, or strikethrough makeover, tap the B, I, U, or S button, respectively.

- **Alignment.** You can change the horizontal alignment of your text using the four horizontal alignment buttons indicated in Figure 24-7. If you're working with a text box, you get access to vertical alignment options, too: Open the paintbrush drop-down menu, tap the Style button, and then use the alignment buttons to create text that's top, middle, or bottom aligned. (See page 48 for more about aligning text.)

- **Paragraph Style.** Want perfectly formatted text in a hurry? Tap one of the ready-to-go paragraph styles in this menu (scroll to see all your options).

You can also change the color, font, and size of your text by tapping the very first option in the Style or Text tab (where it says "14 pt Helvetica" in Figure 24-7). Doing so displays the menu shown in Figure 24-8, where you can adjust these settings:

- **Size.** Tap the up and down arrows in this section to scale your text up or down, one point at a time.

- **Color.** Tap the color swatch to view the available hues. Swipe left and right to see all your options, and tap a color swatch to apply it to your text.

- **Font.** Tap this setting, and then select a new font from the menu. Most fonts are marked with an "i" that indicates there are some additional styles available for that font. These styles are usually restricted to Italic, Bold, Regular, or Condensed, but they're still handy shortcuts for getting the effect you want.

Tap a font's "i" icon to see what's available, and then tap a style to apply it to your selected text.

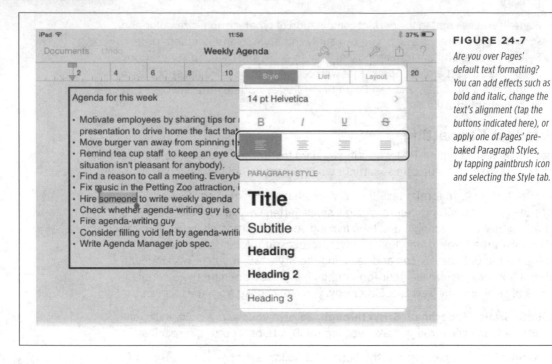

FIGURE 24-7

Are you over Pages' default text formatting? You can add effects such as bold and italic, change the text's alignment (tap the buttons indicated here), or apply one of Pages' pre-baked Paragraph Styles, by tapping paintbrush icon and selecting the Style tab.

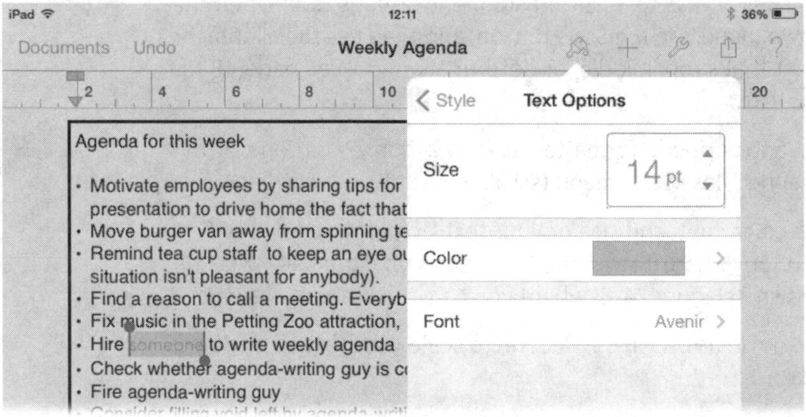

FIGURE 24-8

In the Text Options sub-menu, you can change the size of your font, its color, and the font itself.

Changing the Margins

Margins control where text begins and ends within the confines of an object. Margins give you a level of control over your text's positioning that's impossible to achieve with Pages' alignment buttons alone.

NOTE To adjust the margins for a whole document, adjust the document's blueprint as described on page 681.

You set margins using Pages' ruler. Double-tap an object to review its current margins, which are marked with arrow icons, as shown in Figure 24-9. (If the ruler isn't open, tap the wrench icon, choose Settings, and then tap the Ruler switch so it turns green. To display the ruler on an iPhone or iPod Touch, tap the wrench icon and then tap Ruler.)

FIGURE 24-9

Double-tap an object, and the ruler appears at the top of your screen. The current margins are marked with little arrows (shown here at 4" and 14"). To change the margins, drag the arrow icons along the ruler. All the text within the currently selected object shifts accordingly.

Tab Stops

A *tab stop* is the jump your cursor makes when you press the Tab key on your keyboard (see page 52 for details). Tab stops are useful when you're working on a document that requires custom spacing. To see the current tab stops in your document, double-tap any object and display the ruler as described in the previous section, or double-tap within the body text of a word-processing document. Tab stops appear on the ruler as triangles, circles, and diamonds, depending on the alignment settings for that particular tab stop (see Figure 24-10).

FIGURE 24-10

From left to right, the tab stop icons circled here represent right aligned, left aligned, center aligned, and decimal aligned. All tab stops initially have right alignment, but you can cycle through the different alignments by double-tapping the tab stop's icon.

You add tab stops by tapping the ruler. To change the position of a tab stop, simply drag it along the ruler. To *remove* a tab stop, drag its icon down, off the ruler. When you're typing, you can jump to the next tab stop by tapping the tab button at the top left of the pop-up keyboard.

> **NOTE** Sadly, if you're on an iPhone or an iPod Touch, the keyboard doesn't contain a tab key. So if you want to add room between pieces of text, you simply have to use the space bar. Hopefully Apple will add a tab key soon.

Creating Lists

Lists are useful for organizing information and making quick notes. Pages for iOS lets you create several types of lists by double-tapping to place your pointer inside a text box, shape, or the body text of a word-processing document, and then tapping the paintbrush icon. Select the List button, and then choose from the menu (see page 66 for more information about the different types of lists).

If you're not happy with your list's position on the page, you can change its left or right indent using the buttons at the top of the paintbrush menu's List tab (see Figure 24-11).

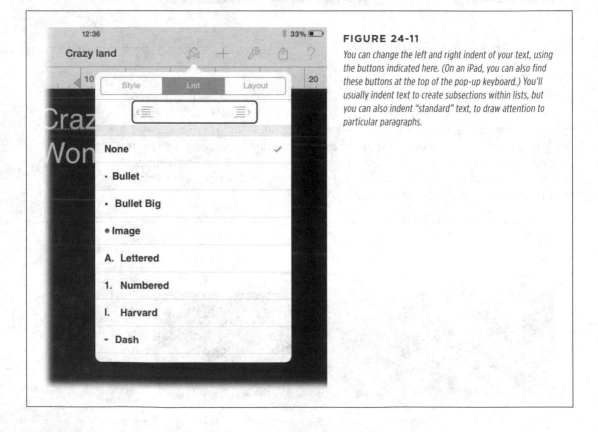

FIGURE 24-11

You can change the left and right indent of your text, using the buttons indicated here. (On an iPad, you can also find these buttons at the top of the pop-up keyboard.) You'll usually indent text to create subsections within lists, but you can also indent "standard" text, to draw attention to particular paragraphs.

Changing the Number of Columns

In Pages, text is arranged into columns, whether it's a single column that stretches across an entire object or multiple columns that divide up your content. Multiple columns are useful for breaking up dense chunks of text (as in newspapers and magazines). To increase the number of columns within an object, double-tap the object (or change the number of margins across an entire word-processing document by making sure no objects are selected), tap the paintbrush icon, choose Layout, and then tap the + and – buttons in the Column section. The maximum number of columns you can have is four.

NOTE You can't create multiple columns within every object that can hold text. Speech bubble shapes, for example, can hold only one column.

Adjusting Line Spacing

You can change the amount of space Pages inserts between each line of text, either within a single object or across your document as a whole. Increasing line spacing can make a text-heavy document look less intimidating, while decreasing line spacing lets you squeeze more text onto a page.

To change line spacing within an object, double-tap the object to place your insertion point inside it, and then tap the paintbrush icon, choose Layout, and then tap the arrows in the Line Spacing section. To change line spacing across an *entire* document (up to the next page break), simply make sure no object is selected before you adjust this setting.

Checking Spelling

Once you're happy with your text's formatting, it's time to start churning out those words! When you open Pages, the spell checker is already switched on, so as you type, you'll notice it swooping in and correcting common typos and adding a dashed red line underneath misspelled words. Tap any underlined word to view the spell checker's suggestions.

It's generally a good idea to leave the spell checker running, but it can get irritating if you're writing something that contains lots of custom words, such as the latest installment in your sci-fi epic. To turn the spell checker off, tap the wrench icon, choose Settings, and then tap the Check Spelling switch to turn it off.

TIP The spell checker is useful, but it doesn't help you understand what a word *means*. To access Pages' dictionary, double-tap a word and then select Define. If Pages comes up empty-handed, you can perform a Google search for the selected word by tapping Search Web. If you suspect the dictionary might be speaking a different language, tap Manage, and then browse the list of available dictionaries.

■ Working with Shapes

Page 683 taught you how to add shapes to your Pages documents. But what if none of the built-in shapes is exactly what you want? You can modify many of iWork's shapes by dragging their *green* selection handles (not to be confused with the blue selection handles that let you resize shapes). This doesn't work for all shapes, however; if you select a shape but don't see any green selection handles, that means you can't modify the shape.

You can also alter a shape's fill color. Tap the shape to select it, tap the paintbrush icon in the toolbar, and then select Style→Style Options→Fill and make your selection from the available colors (swipe left and right to see all the options).

Working with Connection Lines

As you may recall from Chapter 7, a *connection line* is a special type of shape that links two objects in a page-layout document. After you add a connection line, you can move either object and the line stretches and squashes automatically to keep those two objects linked. To link two objects with a connection line, tap both objects simultaneously so they're both selected (this can be a bit tricky, so it may take multiple attempts before you get the hang of it). When both objects are selected, tap the + in the toolbar, open the Shapes menu, and then tap the line in the submenu's upper-right corner (the line with the three dots).

If you're not a fan of the line's current shape, you can bend it or tell it to straighten up its act by tapping the line to select it, and then dragging the green handle in its center. The curve of the line changes, but the line remains connected to your two objects (Figure 24-12 shows all three selection handles).

Even when a line is tethered to two objects, you can move it without changing its curve or breaking that connection: Tap the line to select it and reveal its selection handles, and then tap and hold any part of the line *except* its selection handles, and then drag the line to a new spot. The connected objects move along with the line.

To disconnect a connection line from an object, tap the line so that its three handles appear, and then tap and hold one of the blue selection handles and drag it away from the object. This severs their bond, but your connection line is now free to start seeing another object. To connect your line to a new object, drag the disconnected blue dot onto the object you want to link. You may need to shift the line around a bit, but once the object is highlighted in blue, you're good to go: release the line, and the fickle connection line binds itself to this new object.

■ Working with Images

Pages may be a word processor, but unless you're writing something totally straight-laced like your resumé or an I'm-sorry-our-squirrels-stole-your-bagged-lunch letter, a few pictures can really liven up a document.

When you add an image to a Pages document (as explained on page 682), it's normal for portions of that image to wind up hidden behind an *image mask*. Image masks let you control how much of the picture is visible without resorting to anything drastic like cropping (see page 11 for details).

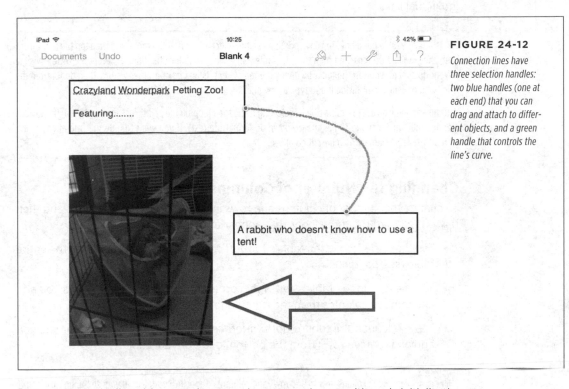

FIGURE 24-12
Connection lines have three selection handles: two blue handles (one at each end) that you can drag and attach to different objects, and a green handle that controls the line's curve.

Pages automatically adds a mask to any image you insert, although initially the mask doesn't hide any of the image. To take a closer look at a mask, double-tap the image; Pages displays its mask and the corresponding Mask slider. To alter the size of the image inside the mask, drag the slider right to make the image larger, or left to make it smaller. You can also control what part of the image is visible inside the mask by pressing down on the image and then dragging it into a new position. To change the mask itself, make sure the mask slider is visible, and then drag the mask's blue selection handles. Once you've got things looking good, tap an empty spot in your document to exit the mask and save your changes.

■ Working with Tables

Pages may be a word-processing app, but it can handle numbers, too, letting you create both tables and charts. You should use tables when your numbers can speak for themselves, or when you need to present a lot of data in a clear, structured way.

You learned how to add a table on page 683. Unless it's your lucky day, chances are that none of Pages' stock tables will have the combination of columns, rows, and layout options that you're looking for. Thankfully, Pages has everything you need to micromanage every part of your table, right down to the appearance of individual lines.

> **TIP** Every table has a title. To view your table's title, select any part of the table, and then tap the paintbrush icon, choose Table Options, and then turn the Table Name switch on. Once the boring placeholder title is visible in your document, you can change it by giving it a tap so that its text box becomes visible; then double-tap the title to place your cursor inside it and type a new one.
>
> You can add some pizzazz to a table title by selecting it and then tapping the paintbrush icon and using the various settings that appear (page 39 has the lowdown on formatting text). If you want to hide the title at any point, turn off the Table Name switch described above.

Changing the Number of Columns and Rows

To change the number of columns and rows in your table, select the table and then pay attention to the three icons that appear at its corners:

- Tap the circle icon in the table's *top-left* corner to cut, copy, or delete the entire table (see page 455).

- Tap the icon in the table's *top-right* corner to open a pop-up that lets you add and remove *columns* from the right edge of your table.

- Tap the icon in the table's *bottom-left* corner to open a pop-up that lets you add and remove *rows* from the bottom edge of your table.

> **NOTE** Page 699 explains how to add rows and columns to specific spots within your table, not just on the edges.

In addition to standard columns and rows, tables can include *header rows* and *header columns*, which usually describe the contents of that row or column, respectively. A header row runs along the top of your table, and a header column runs along the left-hand side. To edit a table's headers, select the table, and then tap the paintbrush icon, choose Headers, and then adjust the Header Rows and Header Columns settings. Changing either Header setting to 0 removes that header completely.

You can also add a *footer row*, which runs along the bottom of the table. Footer rows are often overlooked, but they're useful in lengthier tables, where the reader would have to scroll to see what's written in the header row. To add a footer row, tap the paintbrush icon, choose Headers, and then adjust the Footer Rows setting.

Creating More Colorful Tables

Changing a table's fill color is more complicated than with other objects, as you need to specify whether this change applies to a single cell, multiple cells, or entire rows and columns. To get started, select your table, tap a cell, and then drag the blue handles that appear so the blue box contains all the cells you want to change. Then tap the paintbrush icon, choose Cell ›Fill Color, and choose a color. If you create a color catastrophe, this is also where you can undo your mistake. To completely remove the fill for the selected cells, tap No Fill, or regain your table's original coloring by tapping "Reset to Style."

Another popular color setup for tables is *alternating rows*, where even rows are one color and odd rows are another, which can make tables easier to read. There are two ways to get this effect. You can highlight each row in turn and change its color; this method is tedious, but it lets you choose exactly what colors you want. Or you can tap the paintbrush icon, choose Table→Table Options, and then turn on the Alternating Rows switch; the downside is that you have no control over the colors Pages uses.

Changing Gridlines

If you have a specific vision for your table, Pages can help make it a reality by giving you control over the individual gridlines that make up your table. These are the gridlines you can modify:

- **Horizontal lines** between rows.
- **Header column lines,** which separate the cells in the header column.
- **Vertical lines** that separate columns.
- **Header row lines,** which separate the cells in the header row.
- **Footer row lines,** which separate the cells in the footer row.

To add or remove any of these gridlines, select any cell(s) in your table, and then tap the paintbrush icon, choose Table→Table Options→Grid Options, and then turn the various switches on or off. You can even remove all the gridlines, if you want (see Figure 24-13).

Adding Text to a Table

To add text to your table, just double-tap a cell and start typing. All of the standard text-formatting options apply, and you can change the text's size, color, or font by tapping the paintbrush icon and choosing Cell→Text Options.

> **TIP** You can set the font for an entire table in one fell swoop by selecting any part of the table and then tapping the paintbrush icon, choosing Table→Table Options→Table Font, and then making your selection.

As you type, the cell expands to accommodate your text. To prevent this expansion, select a cell (or several), and then tap the paintbrush icon, tap the Cell button, and then turn off "Wrap Text in Cell." Once you do that, when the selected cells are full, any extra text flows into the neighboring cells (text wrapping in tables is covered in detail on page 463).

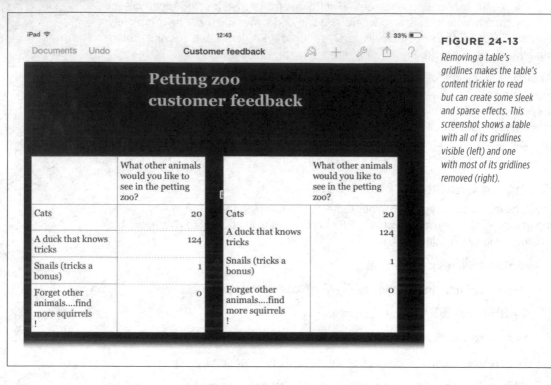

FIGURE 24-13

Removing a table's gridlines makes the table's content trickier to read but can create some sleek and sparse effects. This screenshot shows a table with all of its gridlines visible (left) and one with most of its gridlines removed (right).

Once you've entered some text in your table, you can tell Pages to resize a column or row so that all its data is visible, with no empty space, by tapping the column or row's *reference tab* (page 210), and then tapping Fit in the mini toolbar that appears.

At some point, you may also want to shuffle the data within each of your columns. Pages can sort your data in ascending order (A, B, C or 1, 2, 3) or descending order (C, B, A or 3, 2, 1). To tell Pages to reshuffle the data within a column, tap that column's reference tab, tap Sort, and then choose either Sort Ascending or Sort Descending.

Finally, you can tell Pages to apply some automatic formatting to the data you've just typed. For example, if you're creating a column of prices, you can tell Pages to give all your cells the Currency formatting, and Pages will add the currency symbol to each cell automatically. To apply this automatic data formatting, either tap a row or column's reference tab, select a single cell or highlight multiple cells, and then tap the paintbrush icon in the toolbar and choose Format. You can then pick from the available formats. Click the "i" symbol next to each format, to see additional options for that format (for example, do you want to display a $ or a £ in your Currency cells?). Data formatting is covered in more detail on page 216.

■ ADDING, DELETING AND MOVING ROWS AND COLUMNS

Imagine you've finished adding data to a table, only to realize that the first column would have worked better as the *last* column. Instead of retyping everything or messing around with the Copy and Paste commands, you can simply drag and drop the entire column (or row) into a new location within the table. To do so, tap the column or row's reference tab, or drag the blue handles to select an entire row or column, and then drag the row/column to its new position. Simple!

TIP If you had something less drastic in mind, you can move the contents of a single cell by tapping that cell once to select it at the cell level (if you see a blinking cursor inside the cell, you've selected it at the text level instead). Then press down and drag the cell into its new location. As you move the cell's contents, a blue outline shows where the contents will appear when you let go. You can move the contents of multiple cells by selecting a single cell, dragging its selection handles until all the cells you want to move are selected, and then dragging the whole shebang.

You already know how to add columns and rows to the ends of your table (page 696), but you can insert rows and columns in the middles of tables, too. To insert a column, tap the reference tab of the column directly *to the right* of where you want to insert it, and select Insert from the mini toolbar that appears. To insert a row, tap the reference tab of the row directly *below* where you want to add your new row, and tap Insert in the mini toolbar. If you realize your table has grown out of control, you can remove a particular row or column by tapping its reference tab and then tapping Delete in the mini toolbar.

■ Working with Charts

For data that dazzles, you need a chart. Charts deliver a visual punch that you can't really get with columns, rows, and numbers.

Pages for iOS has a full range of 2D, 3D, and interactive graphs that you can tweak to get exactly the effect you have in mind. However, before you get hung up on the visuals, you need to lay a good foundation and enter all the data that gets fed into your chart. (It's a dirty job, but someone's got to do it.)

Entering Data

When you add a chart to your document (page 683 explains how), Pages populates it with some placeholder data. To enter data of your very own, tap the chart, and then select Edit Data in the mini toolbar that appears. Pages responds by drawing back the curtain and showing you the plain old table that's behind your fancy chart.

To add or modify the table's data, select any cell and start typing. If you're on an iPad, you can use the Next keys in the pop-up keyboard to advance either one cell to the right or to the cell immediately below your current selection. When you reach the final cell in a row or column, one of the Next buttons turns into a New button, which you can tap to add an extra row or column. If you're on an iPhone or iPod Touch, simply tap each cell you want to edit. In many ways, this table functions exactly the same as the tables described in the previous section: You can cut, copy, delete, and insert rows and columns (see page 695 for more info).

When you're finished typing in those precious numbers, tap Done to return to your document.

> **TIP** The pop-up keyboard initially displays only numbers, but you can get your hands on the full keyboard by tapping the gear icon in the upper-left corner of the screen and turning on the Full Keyboard switch.

Rearranging Data

With all of this data flying around, what are the odds of you tripping up and entering your percentage of satisfied visitors on May *12* in the cell that's supposed to show the percentage of satisfied visitors on May *13* (wouldn't that be embarrassing)? If at some point you need to reshuffle your cells, tap the chart, choose Edit Data, select the cell (or group of cells) in question, and then choose either Copy or Cut from the pop-up. Next, tap the cell you wish to move the copied data to, and then select Paste when prompted.

Although you can apply the Cut, Copy, and Paste commands to an entire column or row, why not make things easier for yourself and *drag* the column/row into the new position instead? Simply tap and hold the column or row's reference tab (page 210), and then drag the row/column to a new spot.

> **TIP** Another way to adjust the data in your chart is to use a different data series setting. The box below explains what this setting does and how to change it.

Once you're happy with the data you've entered, tap Done and Pages takes you back to your chart, which updates automatically to accommodate these behind-the-scenes changes.

POWER USERS' CLINIC

Data Series

When you create a chart, Pages takes all the information within a single column or row and mashes it together to create a *data series* within your chart. A data series can be a slice of a pie chart, a point on a scatter graph, or a single bar within a bar chart. Basically, it's the way the different cells are grouped and represented within your chart. (See page 234 for more info.)

On the Edit Chart Data screen (to open it, tap the chart and then choose Edit Data), you can tell Pages whether your data should be grouped based on the column or the row it's in. To do so, tap the gear icon, and then select "Plot Rows as Series" or "Plot Columns as Series." If you're unsure which works best for your chart, experiment with both options.

Changing Chart Types

If you've been working on a chart for a while when it dawns on you that your pie chart would have worked better as a scatter graph, or that you should have opted for the 3D version rather than boring old 2D, you don't have to start from scratch: You can transform your chart into a new chart type with just a few taps.

To convert a chart, tap the chart to select it, and then tap the paintbrush icon in the toolbar. Tap Chart→Chart Options→Chart Type, and then choose a new type from the list of options.

> **NOTE** When you change chart types, all the chart's data and stylistic changes are preserved *unless* they're not compatible with the new chart type. For example, value labels (page 621) don't work in scatter graphs, so they get lost in translation. In most cases, what's lost isn't a big deal, so don't worry about this too much. But if you *do* lose something important when changing chart types, there's always the magical Undo command (page 680).

Adding Labels

If you're a fan of the less-is-more approach to chart building, then look away now! If, on the other hand, you think your chart would benefit from a few labels, then you'll be happy to know that Pages has a ton of labeling options. Select the chart you wish to label, tap the paintbrush icon, and then choose Chart→Chart Options to display the following settings:

- **Chart Title.** Add a title to your chart (so viewers know what they're looking at) by turning on this switch.

- **Legend.** A *legend* is the key that appears alongside your chart and tells viewers what all the different colors mean. A legend is pretty essential, so Pages turns this setting on automatically.

- **Value Labels.** If you suspect your chart's data isn't clear enough, you can annotate it with value labels that show exactly what numbers are powering each section of the chart (see Figure 24-14). Unfortunately, value labels don't work on all chart types: If you're working on an area, stacked area, bubble, line, or scatter chart, then you're out of luck.

When you add value labels to a chart, Pages displays the values exactly as you entered them in the chart's underlying table, unless you tell it otherwise. To get all bossy about your value labels, make sure your chart is selected, tap the paintbrush icon, choose Chart→Chart Options→Number Format, and then select from the following options:

- **Decimals.** This setting controls how many numbers are displayed after the decimal point. If you choose a Decimals setting that makes it so Pages can't display the full number, then it rounds value labels to the nearest full number. For example, if you change the Decimal setting to 1 and then enter a data value of 10.86, Pages displays that number as 10.9 in your chart.

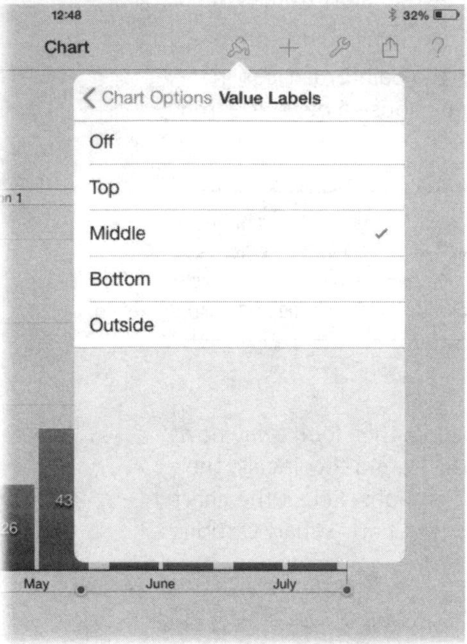

FIGURE 24-14

When you add value labels (like the numbers on each bar of this bar chart), Pages lets you choose where they appear in relation to what they're annotating. In this example, your options are Top, Middle, Bottom, and Outside, but the options vary depending on the type of chart you're editing.

- **Show as Percent.** Turn on this setting to convert your value labels into percentages.

- **Prefix.** This setting lets you enter the numbers, letters, or symbols that should appear *before* each value label, such as $.

- **Suffix.** This is where you type the numbers, letters, or symbols that should appear *after* each value label, such as %.

NOTE The Prefix and Suffix options aren't available for pie charts.

- **Separator.** Turn on this setting to display the thousands separator (1,000 satisfied visitors vs. 1000 satisfied visitors).

- **Negative format.** Pages can display negative numbers as either –100 or (100). Simply tap your preferred format.

Formatting Text

The text-formatting options for charts are limited, but you can make some sweeping changes to the size of the text and the font it uses. Making these changes can help ensure that your text stands out, or let you squeeze more info into a single chart. To make these adjustments, select your chart, tap the paintbrush icon, choose Chart→Chart Options, and then use the Smaller and Larger labels to change the size of the text. Tap Chart Font to choose a new font.

Adding Axis Labels

If your chart has an x- and y-axis (meaning it isn't a pie chart), you can fine-tune the labels and markings that appear along those axes. (Quick refresher: The x-axis is the horizontal one, and the y-axis is the vertical one.) This is pretty nitpicky stuff, but it can help make complex charts easier to understand.

To get control over either of the axes, select your chart, tap the paintbrush icon, choose either X Axis or Y Axis, and then pick from the following:

> **NOTE** Some of the settings listed here appear in the X Axis category but not the Y Axis category (and vice versa). They may also be listed in a different order here than what you see onscreen, depending on the type of chart you're editing.

- **Category Labels.** This setting lets you add or remove column header labels from your chart.

- **Label Angle.** This is where you can set the angle of your chart's labels, including some quirky options such as Right Diagonal.

- **Number Format.** Create some automatic formatting for your various labels by dictating how many decimal points are shown, whether Pages adds a prefix or suffix to each label, whether to include separators, and how negative numbers are displayed.

- **Axis Name.** Turn on this setting to add a placeholder title to your chart's x- or y-axis.

- **Axis Line.** This is an extra line that you can add to your chart to clearly separate the axis from the chart's content.

- **Major Gridlines.** These are the main lines that divide up your chart's content. Gridlines make a chart easier to read, but removing them makes the chart look cleaner.

- **Minor Gridlines.** These are the minor lines that divide up your chart's content.

- **Major Tick Marks.** These are extra markings that you can add along the x- or y-axis to make it easier to distinguish specific numbers at a glance, in even complex charts.

- **Value Scale Settings.** If your chart's data falls within a narrow range, you may want to tweak where the chart begins and ends, either to highlight the slight differences in your data, or simply to cut back on wasted space. To make this change, tap Value Scale Settings, choose either Maximum Value or Minimum Value, and then type in your value.

TIP   In the Value Scale Settings menu, you'll spot two mysterious-sounding options: Linear and Log. A *logarithmic scale* (Log to its buddies) is a measurement that uses a logarithm of a physical quantity (that's clear as mud, right?). If you're not thinking, "Yes, logarithm of a physical quantity, where have you been all my life?" then keep things simple by sticking with Linear.

Editing 3D Charts

When it comes to 3D charts, Pages has some extra settings that will make you the envy of all your chart-loving friends: *angle* and *depth.*

You can rotate a 3D chart to create the impression of looking at it from different angles. To do so, select the chart, tap and hold your finger down on the circular rotation button in its center, and then drag to tilt the chart in different directions.

You can also change the depth of your chart, which is essentially its 3D-ness: A depth of 100% makes the chart look as though it could jump right off the screen (OK, that's an exaggeration). To change the depth, select the chart, tap the paintbrush icon, choose Chart→Chart Options, and then adjust the Depth slider.

If you're working with a bar chart, you can also change the shape of its columns: Switch from rectangular to cylindrical and back again by opening the Chart Options menu and tapping the Column Shape or Bar Shape setting.

Interactive Charts

Interactive charts (page 628) are useful for showing how your data changes over time: Simply drag the slider that appears beneath the chart to watch your data shift. You edit an interactive chart's data in exactly the same way as 2D and 3D charts: Tap the chart to select it, choose Edit Data, and then edit and rearrange the underlying figures (see page 699 for a reminder). Once you've entered all your data, tap Done, and then drag the slider to see each data series in turn.

■ Working with Audio and Video

You can style a video clip the same way you style other objects in Pages, by adding a border, shadow, and/or reflection (page 688), and adjusting the video's opacity (page 685). However, you can also change *how* a video clip plays in your document. To do so, select the video, tap the paintbrush icon, tap the Movie button, and then choose from the following:

- **None.** Play the clip once through.

- **Loop.** Play the video on a continuous loop.

- **Loop Back & Forth.** Suspect your clip contains Satanic messages? This setting makes the clip play forward, then backward, then forward again on a continuous loop. Scary stuff!

If you're dealing with audio, you can either play the clip once or play it on a continuous loop—sorry, there's no back-and-forth option.

Sharing Your Documents

Once you're happy with your document, it's time to go public. To get sharing, make sure you're in Documents view, and then tap the Share icon in the toolbar (it's labeled in Figure 24-1). You then get to choose "Share Link via iCloud" or "Send a Copy."

> **TIP** The "Open in Another App" option is a handy shortcut for converting Pages documents to another format. Tap this command to choose Pages, PDF, Word, or ePub format.

"Share Link via iCloud" lets you—you guessed it—share a link to your document via Apple's iCloud service. Before you can use iCloud, you need to create an iCloud account (page 750), and then get the Pages app talking to your iCloud account (page 752). Sharing documents via iCloud is covered in full on page 256, but here's the short version: Tap the Share icon in the toolbar, tap "Share Link via iCloud," and then tap the document you want to share. You can then choose to share the link via Message, Mail, Twitter, or Facebook. You can also copy your document's link, ready to paste wherever you want, by tapping Copy. (When a document is shared via iCloud, Pages adds a green triangle to the document's thumbnail.)

The other sharing option—"Send a Copy"—lets you send a *copy* of your document to someone rather than the master. Tap this option and then choose from the following:

- **Message.** Send a copy via the Message app (you can learn more about Message for iOS at *http://support.apple.com/kb/ht3529*). Pages lets you choose a format for the copy: Pages, PDF, Word, or ePub. (If you're unsure what programs the recipient has at her disposal, PDF is always a safe bet). Pages then creates a message for you, with your copied document already attached. Just enter the name of your lucky recipient and tap Send.

- **Mail.** The most common way of sending a document to a buddy is via email. Tap the Mail button, pick a format, and iWork opens your email program with the document already attached to a sparkling new message.

- **iTunes.** Send a copy of your document to iTunes (you can find lots of info on iTunes at *www.apple.com/support/itunes*).

- **WebDav.** If you have access to a WebDAV server, you can transfer your documents by copying them to and from that server. (This is a pretty technical way to go, but if you're intrigued, you can learn more about it at *http://support. apple.com/kb/ht4283*).

If you want to let people modify your lovely document, it may be worth switching on Pages' change-tracking feature before you share. When change tracking is turned on, Pages highlights every addition to your document and shows every deletion as a strikethrough, so you can see exactly what has changed. Figure 24-15 explains how to turn on change tracking.

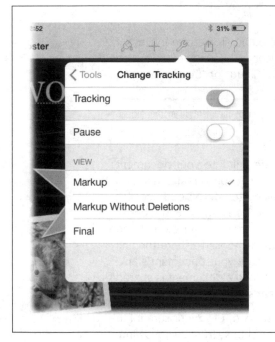

FIGURE 24-15

To access the Tracking setting shown here, tap the wrench icon and then choose Change Tracking. When change tracking is turned on, you can choose from Markup (Pages displays additions and deletions color-coded by author), Markup Without Deletions (Pages displays only new text), or Final (Pages shows you how the document will look if you accept all changes). You can also temporarily suspend change tracking by turning on the Pause switch; turn it off to resume change tracking.

You can't turn change tracking on once a document is shared. So if you want to use change tracking, make sure to switch it on in advance.

When you share a document, you don't need to make it public forever: You can return a shared document to your Fortress of Solitude by opening that document, tapping the Share icon in the toolbar and then choosing View Share Settings; Pages opens the Share Settings window. To stop sharing your document with all of your collaborators (this means barring everyone from accessing your document), tap Stop Sharing.

Printing Documents

You can print iWork documents from any printer that's set up to work with your iDevice. (The exact process for connecting your iDevice to a printer depends on the combination of printer and gadget you have. For instructions on how to connect a printer to your particular iDevice, boot up the iDevice and open the Safari web browser. Then go to Bookmarks→User Guide and search for *Print*.)

To print an iWork document, open the document, tap the wrench icon, and then choose Print→Printer (if you're on an iPhone or an iPod Touch, choose "Share and Print"→Print instead).

The app searches for any printers loitering in the area and then asks you to confirm that it's found the right one. Specify how many copies you want by tapping the + and – buttons, and then tap Print.

Set Password

Is your document top secret? If you're worried about competitors, enemies, or annoying siblings laying their peepers on your document, why not add a password for extra protection? (OK, so this section is about the *opposite* of sharing.)

To password-protect a document, tap the wrench icon in the toolbar, and then select Set Password. Enter and verify your password (Figure 24-16), and then tap Done (if you've had a sudden change of heart, tap Cancel instead). Once you've added a password to your document, a padlock appears next to its title in the toolbar.

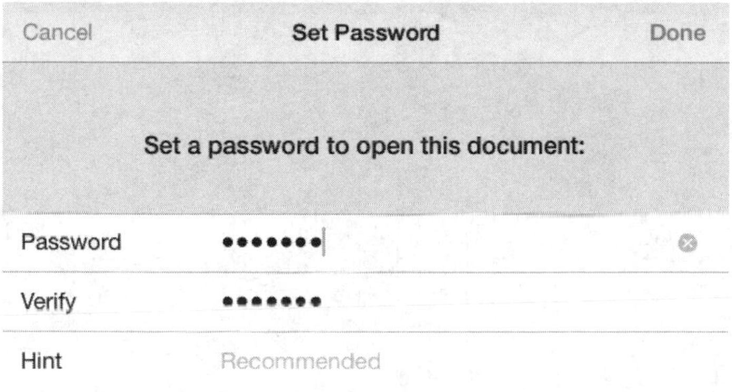

Cancel	**Set Password**	Done
	Set a password to open this document:	
Password	●●●●●●●	
Verify	●●●●●●●	
Hint	Recommended	

FIGURE 24-16

To add a password to your document, enter it in the Password field. You'll then need to repeat this password in the Verify field (just to make sure a typo hasn't wormed its way in). Finally, you can create an optional hint that Pages will display when you've entered your password incorrectly a couple of times.

To swap your boring old password for a more thrilling one, tap the wrench icon and choose Change Password. You then need to enter your current password in the Old Password field, and then type your new one in both the New Password field and the Verify field (and create a hint, if you want).

To remove your password, tap the wrench icon and select Change Password. You can then turn off the Require Password setting; enter your original password in the Password field, and tap Done.

Keynote for iOS

When a big presentation is looming, it's difficult to think about anything else. You may even wake up in the middle of the night in a cold sweat following a nightmare where you forgot your projector cable. When you're in the throes of pre-presentation panic, having your slides within easy reach at all times lets you whip out your iDevice (that's an iPhone, iPad, or iPhone Touch) and rehearse your presentation whenever those doubts begin to creep into your mind.

In this chapter, you'll learn how Keynote for iOS lets you carry your presentation with you wherever you go. It's perfect for running through your speech at every opportunity, and for making changes when a new idea unexpectedly pops into your head during your morning latte break.

NOTE   If you don't have Keynote for iOS yet, flip to page 799 to learn how to install it on your iDevice.

Also, like the previous chapter, this chapter focuses on the iPad version of Keynote, so you may see slight differences if you're using it on an iPhone or an iPod Touch.

■ Creating Presentations

To create your first Keynote presentation, find the Keynote app on your iDevice and give it a tap. What you see next depends on whether you've used the app before.

When you launch the Keynote app for the *first* time, you see a Welcome screen (tap Continue), and then a Get Started screen. To view any existing presentations that are knocking around on your iDevice, tap View My Presentations to open *Documents view* (covered in a sec). To jump straight in and create your first presentation, tap "Create a Presentation." Keynote launches the *Theme Chooser* (also explained momentarily).

> **TIP** If you've connected the Keynote app to your iCloud account (page 752), then Documents view contains any presentations you've created in Keynote for iCloud, as well as Keynote for Mac (assuming it's connected to your iCloud account). See page 752 for details on how to connect iWork for Mac to iCloud.

Every *subsequent* time you launch Keynote, the first screen you set eyes on is Documents view, which is a central hub where you can access all your Keynote presentations. (Keynote for iOS's Documents view screen looks almost exactly like Pages for iOS's Documents view screen, which is shown in Figure 24-1 on page 678.) To resume working on any presentation, tap its thumbnail. (To return to Documents view from the editing screen, tap Presentations in the app's toolbar—see Figure 25-1.) To create a *new* presentation from Documents view, tap the + icon in the toolbar and select Create Presentation, or tap the thumbnail with the + on it. Either way, Keynote responds by opening the Theme Chooser.

> **TIP** You can perform lots of additional useful tasks in Documents view, including renaming, copying, deleting, organizing (page 679), and sharing (page 705) your presentations.

As you learned in Chapter 11, all Keynote presentations are based on *themes*, which make it easy to achieve a uniform look and feel throughout your presentation. Each theme includes several *layouts* that typically contain a mix of placeholder bullet points, images, titles, and text. By selecting a theme and then choosing a layout for each slide, Keynote lets you build a complete, professionally designed presentation quickly and easily.

In the Theme Chooser, tap any theme to create a new presentation based on it. Because the presentation you create over the course of this chapter is going to advertise Crazyland Wonderpark's latest attraction, the terrifying Teeny Tiny Dinosaur Safari (quite possibly the world's most miniature dinosaur attraction), make sure you choose a suitably dark and dangerous theme. When you select a theme, Keynote whisks you over to the layout screen, which is described next.

> **NOTE** See page 281 for info on the Theme Chooser's Standard and Wide options.

A Quick Tour of Keynote

Keynote's layout screen (Figure 25-1) looks a lot like the layout screen in Keynote for Mac.

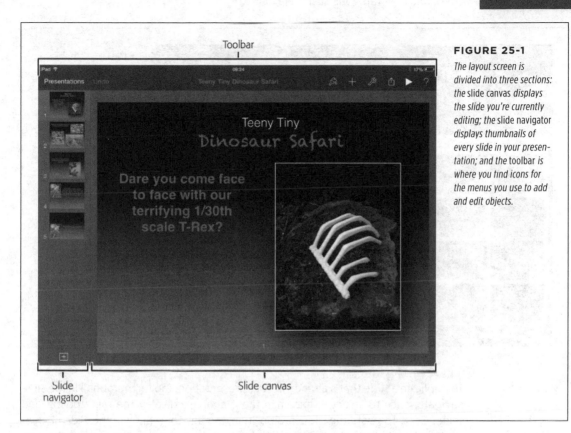

FIGURE 25-1

The layout screen is divided into three sections: the slide canvas displays the slide you're currently editing; the slide navigator displays thumbnails of every slide in your presentation; and the toolbar is where you find icons for the menus you use to add and edit objects.

The slide canvas displays the currently selected slide, and it's where you'll spend the majority of your Keynote time, adding and editing *objects*. Almost everything you add to a slide is an object, whether it's a text box, image, video, shape, audio clip, and so on. This consistency is a real time-saver, because once you know how to edit one object, you pretty much know how to edit them all. Hop to page 683 to learn all about working with objects.

The layout screen's slide navigator contains thumbnails of all the slides in your presentation. To edit a slide, tap its thumbnail in the slide navigator, and the slide appears in the slide canvas, ready for you to edit. To change the order of your slides, press down on a thumbnail in the slide navigator for a couple of seconds, and then drag it into a new position within the navigator.

Adding Slides

When you first create a presentation, it contains only a solitary title slide (see page 282 for info on Keynote's various slide layouts), but the Teeny Tiny Dinosaur Safari has way too much dinosaur-related awesomeness to squeeze onto one measly slide.

To add more slides, tap the + icon at the bottom of the slide navigator (see Figure 25-2), and then tap your desired layout.

FIGURE 25-2

To add a slide, tap the + at the bottom of your screen to open a menu that contains all the available layouts for your chosen theme. Each layout contains a different mixture of text, bullet points, and image placeholders, and uses a style that fits your overall theme. Each theme also contains a blank layout that gives you complete control over what goes where.

To duplicate a slide that's already in your presentation, tap its thumbnail in the slide navigator once to select it, and then tap it again to display the mini toolbar and select Copy. To paste the slide into position, tap any thumbnail in the slide navigator to select it, and then tap the thumbnail again and select Paste from the mini toolbar. You can then reshuffle your slides as required by dragging them around in the slide navigator.

To permanently remove a slide from your presentation, tap its thumbnail once to select it, and then give the thumbnail another tap and select Delete from the mini toolbar. If that sounds a bit drastic, choose Skip from the mini toolbar instead to hide the slide so it doesn't appear when you play your presentation (on an iPhone or iPod Touch, you may have to tap the mini toolbar's arrow buttons to see the Skip command). Keynote collapses the slide's thumbnail, so it appears as a white line in the slide navigator. To bring the slide out of hiding, tap the line representing that slide in the navigator, and then give it another tap and select Don't Skip.

When you need to customize a slide in a hurry, you can just replace its placeholder text and images with your own content. To replace the text, double-tap where it says "Double-tap to edit" (who'd have guessed?), and then start typing. To replace an image placeholder, tap the + in the image's bottom-right corner to launch the Media Browser; find the photo you want to use, and then tap it to drop it into the image placeholder (see page 694 for the skinny on working with images).

This is actually all you need to do to create a basic, fully functioning, Keynote presentation. Pretty easy, huh?

NOTE We all make mistakes. Fortunately, it's easy to undo mistakes in any of the iWork for iOS apps: Just tap Undo in the toolbar. (See page 680 for more info.)

Adding and Working with Objects

To add an object to your presentation, tap the + in the toolbar to launch a menu containing all sorts of funky objects (Figure 25-3). This menu works just like the + menu in Pages for iOS (see page 681).

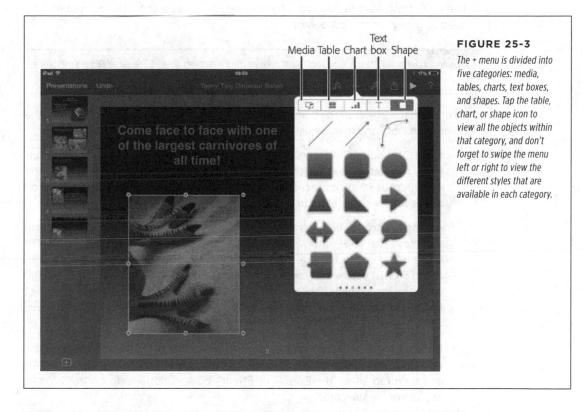

FIGURE 25-3

The + menu is divided into five categories: media, tables, charts, text boxes, and shapes. Tap the table, chart, or shape icon to view all the objects within that category, and don't forget to swipe the menu left or right to view the different styles that are available in each category.

TIP You can add text to tables (page 697) and shapes (page 694) by double-tapping the object you want to add text to and then typing away. Alternatively, you can add a few words to charts in the form of value labels and titles (page 701).

Selecting, moving, resizing, and locking objects works the same in Keynote for iOS as in Pages for iOS, so flip to page 683 for details.

When you have more than one object on a slide, you may want to align them in some way. Keynote's got you covered with handy guidelines that appear whenever you're resizing or relocating an object and other objects are loitering nearby. To switch Keynote's guidelines on, tap the wrench icon in the toolbar, choose Settings→Guides, and then tap any of the switches to turn them on. (See page 686 for details on the different types of guidelines.)

You can cut, copy, or delete an object by selecting it and then tapping Cut, Copy, or Delete in the mini toolbar that appears. If you select Cut or Copy, you can then paste the object into its new position by tapping an empty spot where you want to put the object, and then tapping Paste in the mini toolbar. You also add a comment to an object by tapping Comment in the mini toolbar (see page 684 for details).

■ FORMATTING OBJECTS

The paintbrush icon in Keynote's toolbar opens a menu that has everything you need to give your objects oomph.

> **NOTE** Formatting text is slightly different from working with other objects. See page 688 for a master class on creating beautiful text.

To unleash the power of the paintbrush, select the object you want to style, tap the paintbrush icon, and then adjust the following settings:

- **Style.** This submenu contains some quick-fix styles for when you want a perfectly formatted object without the fuss. These styles may not be particularly adventurous (don't expect to see much beyond different background colors) but as handy shortcuts, they're nothing to sniff at.

- **Arrange.** This submenu contains lots of options, but some of the most useful are "Move to Back/Front," which lets you control how your objects overlap with one another (page 684), and Lock, which lets you lock and unlock an object (page 683). If you're working with a text box, you can change its margins (page 690) and the number of columns (page 693). Depending on the type of object that's selected, you may also see Flip Vertically and Flip Horizontally options, which rotate the object.

- **Borders and Effects.** You can make an object more stylish by adding borders and effects (page 688). Tap the paintbrush icon, choose Style→Style Options, and then tap either the Border or Effects button, depending on the type of object you've selected.

If you're working with an image, you see an Image button in the paintbrush menu. Tap it to see settings that let you edit the image's mask (see page 695 for more info); turn sections of your image transparent with Instant Alpha (page 162); or switch the current image for a new one by tapping Replace.

◼ Animating Slides

What would a presentation be without animations? Whether you're adding transitions between slides or animating how objects appear onscreen and then exit the spotlight, your biggest challenge will be resisting the urge to cram Keynote's entire arsenal of animations into a single presentation. Just remember that an *occasional* animated flourish is more effective than objects flying in from every direction in bursts of flames, showers of confetti, and flashes of lightning.

Keynote offers two types of animations: transitions and object builds. To add or edit any animation, you need to be in "Transitions and Builds" mode; to switch to that mode, simply tap the wrench icon and select "Transitions and Builds."

TIP You can tell you're in "Transitions and Builds" mode because Keynote slaps a big blue banner across the top of the screen that says, "Tap a slide or an object to add an animation."

In this mode, Keynote clearly labels all animated objects with a number to identify the order of their animations and adds an orange triangle to the thumbnail of the slides you've applied transition effects to. When you tap an object's or a slide's thumbnail, a pop-up appears with the name of the animation you've applied. Because you haven't added any animations yet, no matter what object or slide thumbnail you tap, all of these labels read "None," as shown in Figure 25-5. The following sections show you how to change this!

Transitioning Between Slides

As you know from Chapter 13, *slide transitions* are short animations that take you from slide A to slide B. A slide's transition determines how that slide *exits* the screen. So if you apply a confetti transition to slide A, for example, it disappears in a festive burst of confetti, and then slide B appears. When used sparingly, transitions add neat flourishes to a presentation without distracting from the actual content.

To add a slide transition, make sure you're in "Transitions and Builds" mode, and then tap the thumbnail of the slide you want to apply the transition to. In the pop-up that appears, tap the + icon to display the Transitions menu (Figure 25-4). Tap the Effects button, browse through the various transitions, and then tap to make your selection. To see the transition in action, tap Play at the top of the menu. If you aren't thrilled by what you see, audition a new transition by tapping it in the menu, and then tap Play again. Once you've found an animation you're happy with, tap anywhere outside of the Transitions menu to close it (on an iPhone or an iPod Touch, tap Done instead).

NOTE The Magic Move transition (which is listed first in the Transitions menu) is different from the rest of Keynote's transitions. It's explained in detail on page 718.

If at any point you need a refresher on the transition, tap the slide's thumbnail in the slide navigator, tap the pop-up that appears, and then tap Play at the top of the Transitions menu. You can also play your presentation, complete with all its animations, by tapping the Play button in the toolbar (circled in Figure 25-4).

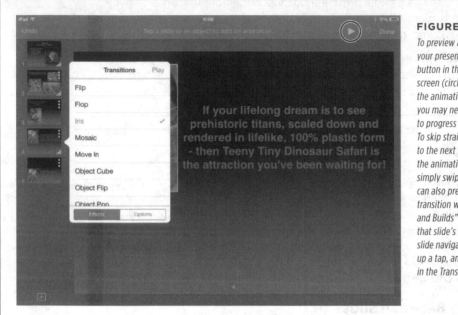

FIGURE 25-4

To preview all the animations in your presentation, tap the Play button in the corner of your screen (circled). (Depending on the animations you've applied, you may need to tap the screen to progress to the next slide. To skip straight from one slide to the next without seeing the animations you've added, simply swipe the screen.) You can also preview a particular transition while in "Transitions and Builds" mode by tapping that slide's thumbnail in the slide navigator, giving the pop-up a tap, and then tapping Play in the Transitions menu.

To change or modify a slide's transition, tap the slide in the slide navigator to see its animation label (like the one in Figure 25-5), and then tap the label's blue arrow icon within the label to reopen the Transitions menu.

Although you can take the slide transitions as they come, Keynote also gives you some options for customizing them. To see what's available, open the Transitions menu using the instructions above, and then tap Options. Depending on the transition you applied, you see some of the following settings:

- **Duration.** Stretch out or shorten the transition using the slider at the top of the Options menu (shown in Figure 25-6).

- **Direction.** If your transition is directional (for example, it swoops onscreen from the left side), you can control where it originates from using the wheel icon. Simply drag the blue arrow until it's pointing in the direction you want (see Figure 25-6).

- **Start Transition.** Unless you tell it otherwise, Keynote assumes that you don't want it to transition from one slide to the next until you give it the go-ahead by tapping the screen, so it automatically selects On Tap in this section. If you'd rather have your slide transitions trigger automatically after a certain period of time, tap After Previous Transition and then adjust the Delay slider.

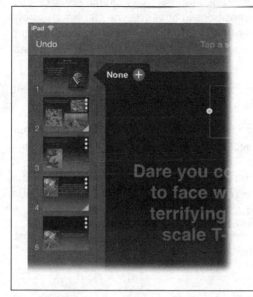

FIGURE 25-5

To check whether you've applied a transition to a particular slide, make sure you're in "Transitions and Builds" mode, and then tap the slide's thumbnail in the slide navigator. If you haven't yet added an animation to that slide, the label reads "None," as shown here. Tap the label's + icon to add a transition.

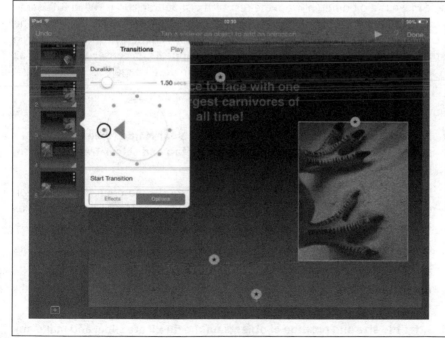

FIGURE 25-6

When you customize a slide transition or object build, you can specify which direction the animation originates from by dragging the arrow icon shown here until it's pointing in the desired direction. The blue dot (circled) indicates the current direction, just in case the arrow doesn't make things clear enough!

When you're applying lots of transitions, it's not a bad idea to reuse the same ones throughout your presentation to help create a feeling of consistency. If you've customized a transition, recreating that same animation across multiple slides can be time-consuming. But if you plan your transitions in advance, you can simply apply the desired transition to one slide, copy that slide, and then use these duplicates as the basis for the rest of your presentation (page 712 explains how to copy and paste slides).

After perfecting your slide transitions, tap Done at the top of the screen to exit "Transitions and Builds" mode and return to the normal slide-editing screen.

To delete a transition that you've applied to a slide, tap the slide in the slide navigator once to select it, and then give it a second tap and choose Transition in the mini toolbar that appears; doing so switches you to "Transitions and Builds" mode *and* launches the Transitions menu in one smooth move. In the Transitions menu, set the animation to None. (If you're *already* in "Transitions and Builds" mode, tap the slide in the slide navigator, tap the label that appears, and then choose None.)

> **TIP** You can quickly jump to the Transitions menu at any point by tapping the slide in the navigator to select it, tapping the slide again to display the mini toolbar, and then choosing Transition.

■ MAGIC MOVE

Magic Move is a bit different from the rest of the slide transitions. When the same object appears on two or more consecutive slides, using Magic Move makes the object appear to resize, rotate, or move—sometimes all three—into its new position on the subsequent slide. If more than one object appears on consecutive slides, all of the above applies to *all* the objects. (For more info, see page 356.)

To create a Magic Move transition, perfect the first slide in your sequence and then follow these steps:

1. **In the slide navigator, tap the first slide in your Magic Move sequence to select that slide, and then give it a second tap and select Transition from the mini toolbar.**

   Keynote switches to "Transitions and Builds" mode and opens the Transition menu. Bear in mind that, like all slide transitions, a Magic Move transition applies to the slide's *exit*, not its entrance.

2. **In the Transition menu, tap Magic Move, and then tap Yes to duplicate the slide.**

   A new slide appears in the slide navigator. Keynote automatically opens this new slide in the slide canvas, ready for you to edit.

3. **Alter the size and position of objects on the duplicate slide, and make any necessary text changes.**

Keynote is still firmly in "Transitions and Builds" mode, but you can make some limited changes to the duplicate slide, namely resizing and moving objects, and replacing any text by double-tapping it. To make more adventurous changes, you have to tap the Done button to return to normal slide-editing mode.

4. **Reopen the Transitions menu.**

Tap the slide's thumbnail once to select it, and then give the thumbnail a second tap and select Magic Move in the label that appears.

5. **In the Transitions menu, select Options and customize your slide transition.**

You see the usual array of settings that let you change the transition's duration, specify whether Keynote should trigger it automatically, and add an optional delay (see the previous section for details). You also see a "Delivery and Acceleration" option; tap it to see some settings that are specific to Magic Move:

— **Match Text.** Control whether the Magic Move effect applies only to objects or to individual words or characters by selecting By Object; By Word (Keynote moves words on slide A into their new position on slide B, creating the impression that your words are shuffling into a new order); or By Character (Keynote moves matching characters from slide A into their new position on slide B).

— **Fade Unmatched Objects.** Turn on this setting, and objects and text that aren't part of the Magic Move fade in gradually. Turn off this setting, and objects that don't match appear suddenly at the very end of the transition.

— **Acceleration.** This setting dictates the speed at which your matching objects move. Choose from None, Ease In (objects start out slow and then speed up as they approach their final position), Ease Out (objects start at full speed and then slow down), and Ease In & Ease Out (matching objects flick between accelerating and decelerating as they move across the screen).

As you edit your effect, you can preview it at any time by tapping Play in the Transitions menu.

6. **When your Magic Move transition looks good, close the Transitions menu by tapping anywhere outside it (or, on an iPhone or iPod Touch, tapping Done at the top of the menu), and then tap Done to exit "Transitions and Builds" mode.**

To see Magic Move in action alongside any other animations on your slide, tap the Play button at the top of the screen,

Adding Object Builds

If you want to draw attention to an object or stagger when your objects appear, *object builds* are where it's at. There are two types of object builds: *Build-in* effects control how an object arrives on a slide, and *build-out* effects control how it disappears from a slide. (See page 358 for detailed info on builds.)

To add an object build:

1. **In "Transitions and Builds" mode (page 715), tap the object you want to add the build to.**

   "Build in" and "build out" labels appear next to your object (see Figure 25-7). If you've already applied a build to that object, the label displays the name of the build.

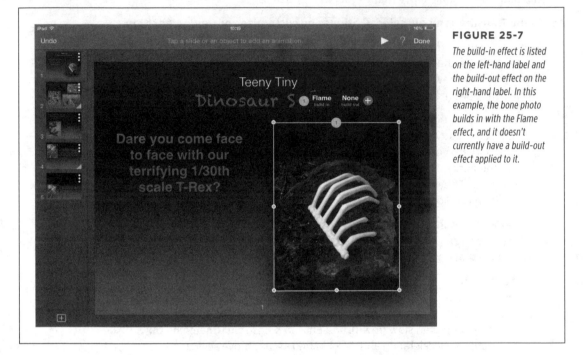

FIGURE 25-7

The build-in effect is listed on the left-hand label and the build-out effect on the right-hand label. In this example, the bone photo builds in with the Flame effect, and it doesn't currently have a build-out effect applied to it.

2. **Tap either the "build in" or "build out" label, depending on which one you want to add.**

   The Effects menu appears, with a long list of options.

3. **Review the available effects, and tap one to select it.**

   To see your selected effect in action, tap Play to preview it. If you're not thrilled by what you see, simply tap another effect and then tap Play again.

4. **To customize the build, tap Options, and then adjust the settings.**

   You'll see different options depending on which build you chose and whether it's a build in or a build out.

   Use the Duration slider to control how long the build takes. It can last anywhere from 0.10 seconds to 60 seconds.

Use the Start Build setting to tell Keynote to wait for your signal (On Tap) or play your build automatically after a set period of time (After Transition). If you choose After Transition, make sure you set the Delay slider to anything other than 0 seconds. You can also tell Keynote to start the animation simultaneously with the previous animation (With Build), or to start the animation immediately after the previous build comes to an end (After Build). You may need to scroll to see all of these options.

5. **When everything looks good, close the Effects menu by tapping anywhere outside it.**

Building Objects in Pieces

When you're animating a chart, table, or text (whether it's in a text box or a shape), you can stagger the animation so that the object builds—or dismantles—piece by piece. This can create some interesting visuals and is handy when you want to closely match what's displayed onscreen with the spoken part of your presentation.

To build an object in pieces, make sure you're in "Transitions and Builds" mode (if you're not, tap the wrench icon and choose "Transitions and Builds.") Select the object in question, and then tap either the "build in" or "build out" label that appears (depending on whether you want the object to appear or disappear in pieces, respectively). In the menu that opens, select an animation, and then tap the Delivery button. In the Delivery menu, you'll see some of the following options, depending on the type of object you selected:

- **For any object:**

  — **All at Once.** Applies the object build to the entire object.

- **For text:**

  — **By [block].** Stagger the object build based on each *block* of text (a block could be a paragraph, a heading, a bullet point, and so on); all the blocks must be within the same object in order for Keynote to animate them.

  — **By [block] Group.** Groups each block of text together with any subordinate text (such as an indented paragraph), and then applies the object build to each group in turn. Paragraph groups must be within the same object for Keynote to be able to animate them.

  — **By Highlighted [block].** When you apply this as a build-in effect, Keynote highlights each block of text as it appears within your object. When you apply this as a build-out effect, Keynote briefly highlights each block before it disappears.

- **For charts:**

  — **Background First.** When you apply this animation to a chart as a build-*in* effect, the chart's background appears before its data. Confusingly, when you apply this animation as a build-*out* effect, the data disappears before the background.

— **By Series.** Builds a chart one data series at a time. (A *data series* is a group of cells in your chart's underlying table; flip to page 234 for more info on working with these behind-the-scenes tables.) Exactly how this animation behaves varies depending on the chart type and the data; it can create effects such as pie charts that appear one slice at a time, bar charts that disappear one bar at a time, and so on.

— **By Set.** Builds a chart one *data set* at a time. (The definition of data set varies depending on the specific type of chart, but it typically corresponds to a single row or column in the chart's underlying table. See page 234 for more info.)

— **By Element in Series/Set.** Builds your chart one cell at a time.

• **For a table:**

— **Rows, Columns and Cells.** So you want to build a table one piece at a time? Brace yourself for a long list of variations on building your table per cell, per row, and per column.

Remember that you can see an animation in action by tapping the Play button at the top of the Build In/Build Out menu.

Changing the Build Order

When you apply object builds to several objects in a single slide, they play in the order you apply them. But this won't always be the order you had in mind—and even if it is, there's no guarantee that it'll look any good! If you're in normal slide-editing mode, you can change the order of your object builds by tapping any object that has a build applied to it, and then selecting Animate from the mini toolbar that appears. (If you're in "Transitions and Builds" mode, then just tap any object that has a build effect applied to it.)

TIP When you're in "Transitions and Builds" mode, you'll notice that Keynote adds numbers to all of your objects that have an object build applied, so you can see at a glance what order they'll animate in. Keynote adds an orange number for build-in effects, and a blue number for build-out effects.

At this point, it doesn't matter whether you tap the "build in" or "build out" label, so toss a coin or choose whichever label catches your eye. In the Transitions menu that opens, tap the Order button to see a list of every object you've applied an object build to, in the order these animations occur. Figure 25-8 shows an example of such a list and explains how to reorder the builds.

■ Creating Hyperlinks

When you're creating a viewer-guided presentation (see the box on page 724), hyperlinks are essential if your audience is ever going to get past the title slide. You can turn images, shapes, text boxes, and text into hyperlinks, and these links can transport the viewer to other slides within your presentation, to a web page, or even to his email program (the technical term for this process is *embedding* a hyperlink).

FIGURE 25-8

The Build Order menu goes to impressive lengths to make your running order clear: It includes all your object builds in a numbered list, and tapping any item in this list selects the corresponding object in the slide canvas. Also, in the Build Order menu, build-in and build-out effects are color-coded. To change the build order, simply press down on that effect in the list, and then drag it into a new position. For example, to make the text "Will you survive?" appear first on this slide, drag the fourth item in this list to the top of the heap.

To create a hyperlink, tap the wrench icon in the toolbar, choose Presentation Tools→Interactive Links, and then tap the object you wish to add the hyperlink to. Keynote displays a Link menu that contains submenus for each type of hyperlink:

- **Slide.** This submenu has everything you need to add a hyperlink that takes viewers from the current slide to any other slide within your presentation. To remove a slide hyperlink you added earlier, tap None.

TIP   Whenever the Link menu is open, Keynote adds a blue arrow to every object or piece of text that has an embedded hyperlink.

- **Webpage.** When the viewer taps an object or piece of text embedded with this kind of hyperlink, Keynote launches a web browser and takes him to the web address you specify. To create this kind of hyperlink, tap the Link box and then type the web address you want to send folks to. To remove the hyperlink, tap Remove Link.

FREQUENTLY ASKED QUESTION

Self-Playing or Viewer Guided?

There's more than one way to present your, um, presentation! You can keep a tight rein on proceedings by making Keynote wait for you to tap the screen before the next slide transition or object build kicks in. Alternatively, you can automate your presentation by setting time delays between each object build and slide transition, so you don't need to tap the screen at all. Finally, you can create a *viewer-guided presentation*, where the viewer uses hyperlinks to explore your presentation at her own pace (adding hyperlinks is covered on page 722). Viewer-guided presentations are useful when you're making your slides available to the audience after your talk.

Unless you specify otherwise (using the instructions below), Keynote assumes you want to control your presentation by tapping away at the screen. If you want an automated or viewer-guided presentation instead, you have to tweak some settings.

To create an automated presentation that requires absolutely no tapping, you need to tell Keynote how long it should wait between each slide transition and object build. To set these delays, tap the wrench icon in the toolbar, and then choose Presentation Tools→Presentation Type→Self Playing. Two new sliders then appear in this menu: Transition Delay and Build Delay; simply manipulate these sliders to create the desired delays. Keynote applies the same delay to *all* the slide

transitions and object builds in your presentation, but you can override these on a per-slide basis (page 715).

To create a presentation that the viewer navigates herself, tap the wrench icon in the app's toolbar, and then choose Presentation Tools→Presentation Type→Links Only. Of course, your next task is adding all the necessary hyperlinks so that your viewers can actually get beyond slide 1.

No matter which type of presentation you create, you can tell Keynote to play your slides on a continuous loop, rather than coming to a halt at the final slide and automatically returning you to the slide editing screen. Looping is handy when your presentation is background eye candy rather than something that's synchronized with your talk—for example, a photo slideshow of intrepid explorers bravely embarking on the Teeny Tiny Dinosaur Safari. To trap your audience in an endless loop of minuscule dinosaurs, tap the wrench icon and choose Presentation Tools→Presentation Type, and then turn on the Loop Presentation setting.

Finally, you can tell Keynote to restart your presentation from the beginning if it receives no input from you for a set amount of time. In the Presentation Type menu, turn on "Restart Show if Idle," and then choose how long Keynote should wait before starting again from the top.

- **Mail.** When the viewer clicks an object or a piece of text that's embedded with a mail hyperlink, Keynote launches the viewer's email program and automatically creates a new message, already addressed to the person of your choice. To create a mail hyperlink, tap the To box, and then type the desired email address. To remove a mail hyperlink, tap Remove Link.

TIP The easiest way to let people navigate a viewer-guided presentation is to tap the + icon, choose the shapes category, and then add arrows to each slide. (Be sure to flip one arrow so that it points "backwards.") Then embed these arrows with slide hyperlinks so they act as Back and Forward buttons, letting viewers hop between your slides.

After you've finished working on hyperlinks, you can return to the normal slide-editing screen by tapping the Done button in the toolbar.

■ Using Presenter Display

Keynote for iOS may be handy for reviewing and editing your presentation on the go, but you definitely don't want to use your iPad, iPhone, or iPod Touch's screen to present your masterpiece (imagine how much your audience would have to squint!).

When it's time to face your public, you can still use your trusty iDevice, but think big and connect it to a larger screen, whether that's a TV, a monitor, a projector, or any other compatible gizmo. With this kind of setup, your presentation can dazzle viewers on the big screen, while your iDevice displays a view called *presenter display*, which is visible only to you (more on this feature in a sec).

> **TIP** Want to get some feedback before showing off your presentation? You can send a copy to a buddy or share your document via iCloud. Check out page 705 for the skinny.

The type of video adapter cable you need depends on which iDevice and external screen you're using. For up-to-date information on compatible cables, Apple's website is the place to go: *http://support.apple.com/kb/HT4108*. (If you need help, check with your IT department.)

When you're ready to launch into your presentation, just plug your iDevice into the external monitor, tap the Play button in the toolbar, and you're off!

> **TIP** The Keynote for iOS app can turn your iDevice into a remote that can control a Keynote presentation on your Mac. For the lowdown, see page 385.

Adding Presenter Notes

Scribbling notes on a few cards is a recipe for disaster when, mid-presentation, you lose your place and have to shuffle through them. Keynote's presenter notes feature displays your notes alongside the corresponding slide, all within the privacy of your iDevice. The audience won't even know that you're having a sneaky glance at your notes.

To add notes to a slide, tap the slide's thumbnail in the slide navigator, and then tap the wrench icon and choose Presenter Notes. Keynote displays a sheet of virtual paper where you can type all the important stuff you want to remember during your presentation, as shown in Figure 25-9.

After you've finished making notes on one slide, you can tap any other slide in the navigator to repeat the process for that slide. Once you've made all your notes, tap Done to return to the slide-editing screen.

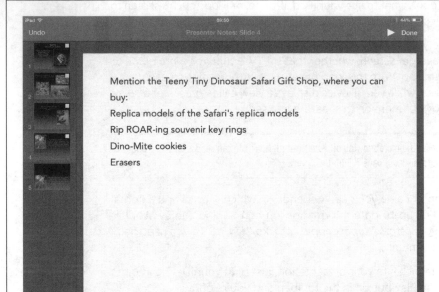

FIGURE 25-9

Presenter notes is a virtual notebook where you can jot down notes and prompts. And because it's visible only in presenter display, your audience is none the wiser!

Numbers for iOS

H aving to be at your Mac in order to create, access, and edit spreadsheets may seem like no big deal—after all, how often do mathematical formulas crop up in day-to-day life?

Actually, spreadsheets aren't just for when you're at your desk, crunching the monthly earnings and expenses, working on your tax returns, or keeping meticulous track of office supplies (although they're great at all of the above). Spreadsheets can also help you organize and analyze everyday data, such as who's paid his deposit for Curry Night or how many calories you have left for Friday night's big splurge. Once you're in the habit of using spreadsheets to make everyday tasks easier, you'll want those spreadsheets within easy reach at all times, regardless of whether you're on your Mac.

This chapter shows you how Numbers for iOS can help you keep track of facts, figures, and other assorted digits wherever you are, as well as how to subject your data to intense scrutiny using formulas and charts. So install the Numbers app as explained in Appendix A (page 799), and then read on!

NOTE Quick reminder: The images in this chapter show what Numbers for iOS looks like on an iPad. If you have an iPhone or an iPod Touch, the app looks a bit different on your smaller screen.

■ Creating a Spreadsheet

To get started with Numbers for iOS, track down the Numbers icon on your iPhone, iPad, or iPod Touch and give it a tap. The *first* time you launch Numbers, you see a snazzy Welcome screen; after taking a moment to appreciate the nice pictures, tap Continue. At this point, jump straight into the fun of creating your first spreadsheet by tapping "Create New," and Numbers opens the *Template Chooser* (Figure 26-1), where you can pick from a handful of templates.

> **TIP** If you haven't connected your Numbers app to your iCloud account yet, exit Numbers, and then go to Settings→Numbers, and then turn on the Use iCloud setting. You can learn more about connecting iOS apps to iCloud on page 752.

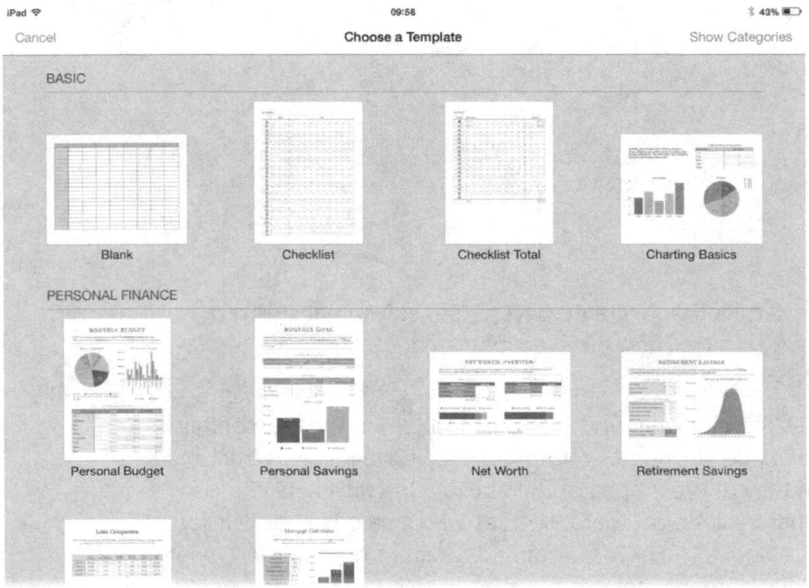

FIGURE 26-1

Just like in Numbers for Mac, the Template Chooser contains a selection of templates. Tap any template to create a new spreadsheet based on it. If you're not sure which one to choose, you can always go with Blank to create your spreadsheet from scratch. By default, Numbers displays all the templates you can choose from, but you can view the templates for a certain category only by tapping Show Categories (sorry—you don't have this option on an iPhone or an iPod Touch).

Things work a little differently every *subsequent* time you launch Numbers: The first screen you see when you launch the app is Documents view, which contains thumbnail previews of all your existing spreadsheets. Simply tap any thumbnail to open that spreadsheet. To create a new spreadsheet, tap the + icon in the toolbar at the top of the screen and choose Create Spreadsheet, or tap the thumbnail with the + on it; either way, Numbers opens the Template Chooser.

> **NOTE** Documents view is also where you can rename (page 679), share (page 705), copy (page 679), and delete (page 679) spreadsheets. If you're editing a spreadsheet and want to return to Documents view, just tap the word "Spreadsheets" in the toolbar. You can learn more about Documents view on page 678.

Regardless of how you got to the Template Chooser, the process of creating a spreadsheet is easy: Simply find the template that's closest to what you had in mind, tap its thumbnail—and that's it! Numbers takes care of the rest, generating a new document based on your chosen template. Each template contains a mix of different placeholder objects, such as charts, tables, text, and images, so often the only thing you need to do is enter your data.

> **NOTE** If you make a mistake while working on your spreadsheet, don't fret: Just tap Undo in the toolbar. See page 680 for more on undoing and redoing stuff in iWork for iOS.

■ Working with Objects

Almost everything you add to your spreadsheets is an object, whether that's an image, video, chart, table, audio clip, or shape. To add an object, tap the + icon in the app's toolbar, and then choose the type of object you want. The big benefit of everything being an object is that, once you know how to edit one type of object, you pretty much know how to edit them all. If you need a recap on editing objects, skip back to the pages listed below.

TOPIC	PAGE NUMBER
Selecting objects	683
Resizing objects	683
Moving objects	683
Cutting, copying, and pasting objects	684
Deleting objects	684
Locking/unlocking objects	683
Moving objects back/forward	684
Adding borders and effects to objects	688
Adding guidelines	686
Working with images	694
Working with audio and video clips	704
Working with tables	695
Working with charts	699
Working with shapes	694
Working with text boxes	688

Working with Sheets

In Numbers, each page is actually a *sheet*. When you have multiple sheets within a spreadsheet, they're divided into tabs that appear at the top of the document, in the *Sheets bar*. To add a new sheet, tap the + symbol on the leftmost tab; if you see the pop-up shown in Figure 26-2, then tap New Sheet.

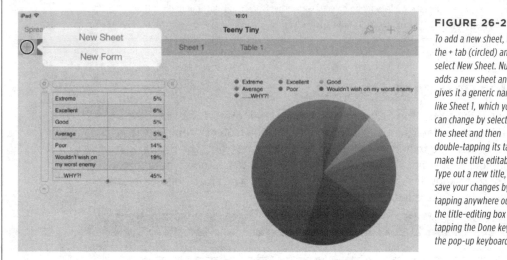

FIGURE 26-2

To add a new sheet, tap the + tab (circled) and select New Sheet. Numbers adds a new sheet and gives it a generic name like Sheet 1, which you can change by selecting the sheet and then double-tapping its tab to make the title editable. Type out a new title, and save your changes by tapping anywhere outside the title-editing box or tapping the Done key in the pop-up keyboard.

You can jump from one sheet to another by tapping the tabs in the Sheets bar. To reorder your sheets, press down on any tab and drag it into a new position. You can also duplicate a sheet by selecting it in the Sheets tab and then tapping it again and selecting Duplicate from the mini toolbar that appears. (Got too many sheets on your hands? The mini toolbar also gives you the option to delete the current sheet.)

Adding Data to a Table

Tables are one of the most common objects you'll work with in Numbers. Not only are tables useful for organizing data, but they're also the starting point for charts. After filling a table with lots of lovely data, you're just a few taps away from using that information to create an eye-catching chart.

Since you'll spend so much time working on tables, Numbers provides several keyboard layouts to help supercharge your data entry. Each keyboard layout is designed to make it easier for you to enter a particular kind of data, whether it's today's date or a complex mathematical formula.

To get started, add a table to your document as described on page 683. Then, to enter data into the table, double-tap a cell to open the keyboard—which is actually four *different* keyboard layouts in one. You can switch among the layouts using the buttons labeled in Figure 26-3. Pick the layout that corresponds to the type of data you're entering:

- **Numerical.** Use this keyboard layout to enter numerical data including currency values and percentages. It also includes some commonly used symbols such as checkboxes and stars (for rating things).

- **Time & Duration.** Use this keyboard to enter durations, dates, and other time-related data.

- **Text.** This layout is the standard keyboard you're used to. It contains letters, numbers, punctuation, and other assorted symbols.

- **Formulas & Functions.** While tables can make chunks of data easier to read, their real value lies in Numbers' ability to perform calculations on the data you enter into your tables. This keyboard layout includes all the numbers, symbols, and special operators you need to create formulas and functions that crunch complex strings of data.

Above the keyboard is the *input bar* where you enter your data, whether it's a long, complicated formula or something simpler like plain numbers or words. After entering your data, you can save it either by tapping anywhere outside the current cell or tapping the Done button next to the input bar.

NOTE When the Formulas & Functions keyboard is displayed, you'll see a checkmark and an X instead of the Done button (this is covered in a later section, so don't worry too much about it now).

And if you're using Numbers on an iPhone or an iPod Touch, you always see a green checkmark rather than a Done button; they work the same way.

The following sections explain how to use the input bar and the various keyboard layouts to get your info into Numbers.

Using the Standard Keyboard

There's nothing wrong with using the standard keyboard. If you want to enter some plain old numbers, letters, or punctuation, you can access this by tapping the T button labeled in Figure 26-3.

The standard keyboard actually has some alternate layouts of its own. The first layout you encounter is the alphabetic layout, but you can switch to a numerical layout by tapping the .?123 key (labeled "123" on an iPhone or iPod Touch). From there, if you're after a particularly obscure symbol, give the #+= key a tap to access the third and final layout. To get back to where it all began, tap the ABC key to return to the alphabetic keyboard.

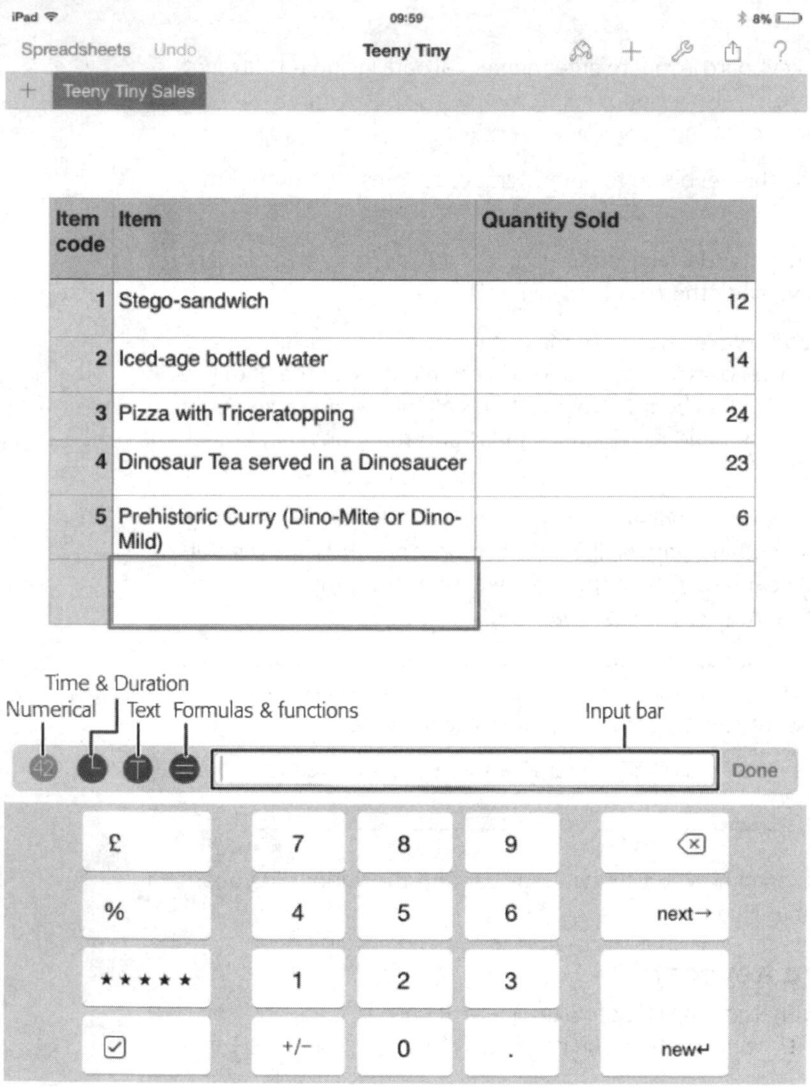

iPad 📶   09:59   ≉ 8% ▭

Spreadsheets Undo   **Teeny Tiny**   🖼️ + 🔧 📤 ?

+   Teeny Tiny Sales

Item code	Item	Quantity Sold
1	Stego-sandwich	12
2	Iced-age bottled water	14
3	Pizza with Triceratopping	24
4	Dinosaur Tea served in a Dinosaucer	23
5	Prehistoric Curry (Dino-Mite or Dino-Mild)	6

Time & Duration
Numerical   Text   Formulas & functions   Input bar

🟢 ⚫ Ⓣ ≡   [   ]   Done

£	7	8	9	⌫
%	4	5	6	next→
★★★★★	1	2	3	
☑	+/−	0	.	new↵

FIGURE 26-3

Tap any of these icons to access the corresponding keyboard layout: Numerical, Time & Duration, Text, and Formulas & Functions.

Entering Numbers, Currency, Percentages, and Checkboxes

The Numerical keyboard layout (tap the 42 button to display it; see Figure 26-3) makes entering basic numerical data a breeze by placing the 0–9 keys smack-bang in the middle of your screen and surrounding them with a few useful extras:

- **Currency symbol.** Exactly what symbol you see on this key depends on where you are. If you're in the UK, you get a £ like in Figure 26-3; if you're in the U.S., you see a $; and so on. Whatever your local currency, give this key a tap to transform numbers into cold, hard cash.

- **Percentages.** To turn a number into a percentage, tap the % key.

- **Star rating.** Nothing lets you know what's hot and what's not quicker than a star rating. Numbers lets you rate things on a scale of 1 to 5 stars. To create a star rating, enter a number from 1 to 5 that represents the number of stars you want to give, and then tap the ★★★★★ key. (If you're on an iPhone or iPod Touch, the key is marked with just one star, but it works exactly the same). If you type a number *higher* than 5 before tapping this key, Numbers converts it to 5 stars.

- **Checkbox.** Checkboxes let you see, at a glance, whether an item in your table has been bought, sold, or put in your suitcase so you're ready for that trip to the Bahamas. To add a checkbox, tap the checkbox key (labeled in Figure 26-4), and then tell Numbers whether the box should be turned on (True) or turned off (False) either by tapping the True/False checkbox in the input bar or by tapping the checkbox itself.

- **+/−.** Tap this key to turn the numbers in the currently selected cell from positive to negative, or vice versa.

Entering Dates, Times, and Durations

The Time & Duration keyboard is ideal for entering date and time info. To use this layout, tap the clock button labeled in Figure 26-3. As Figure 26-5 shows, on an iPad, this keyboard layout is dominated by two big buttons: Date & Time and Duration. (On an iPhone or an iPod Touch, these buttons are instead labeled with a calendar icon and an hourglass icon, respectively.)

TIP   If you want to enter today's date, you can save yourself some time by tapping the Date & Time button, tapping the "day" or "year" button in the input bar, and then tapping the Today key. When you do that, Numbers adds the date, month, and year to the current cell. And if you want to get *really* specific, you can tap "hour," "minute," or "second," and then tap the Now button to enter the current hour, minute, or second.

If you want to enter duration data instead (for example, the number of hours worked), tap the Duration button and the input bar updates to display all of Numbers' duration categories (weeks, days, hours, and so on). Make your selection, and the keyboard layout shifts to accommodate all the keys you need to enter this particular snippet of information. Thanks, Numbers!

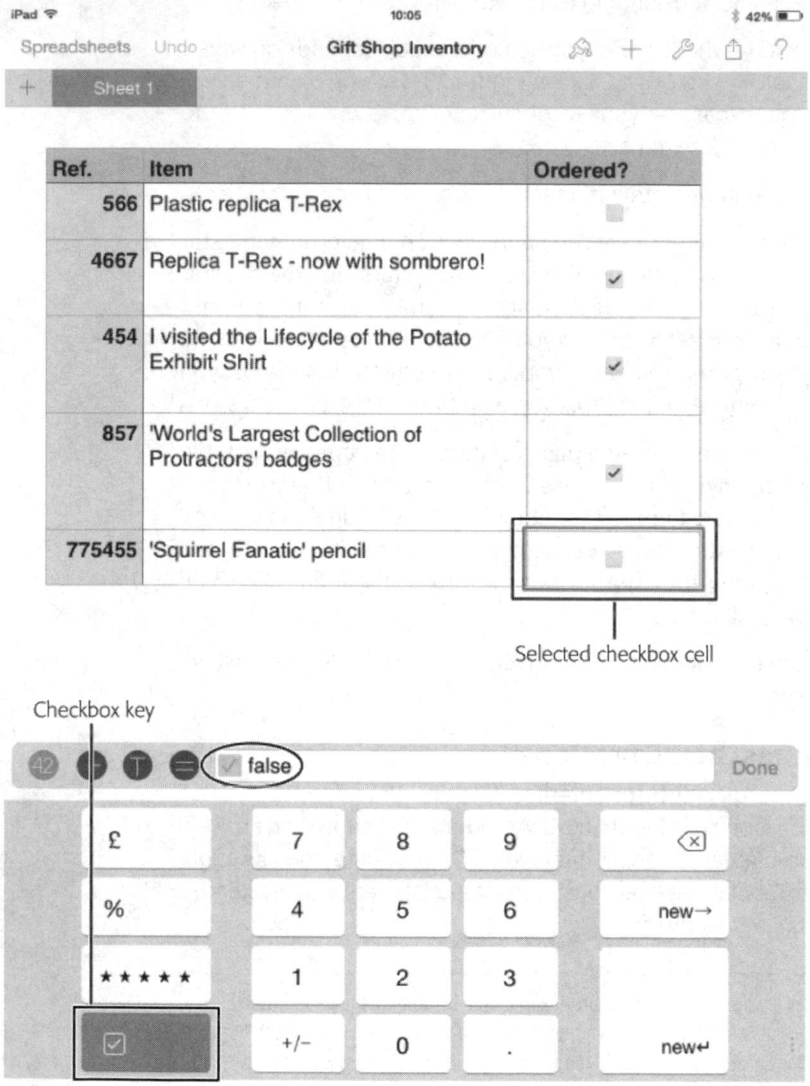

FIGURE 26-4

To add a checkbox, tap the checkbox key. All checkboxes start out turned off (a.k.a. False), but you can toggle between on and off by tapping the True/False checkbox in the input bar (circled), or tapping the table cell where the checkbox appears.

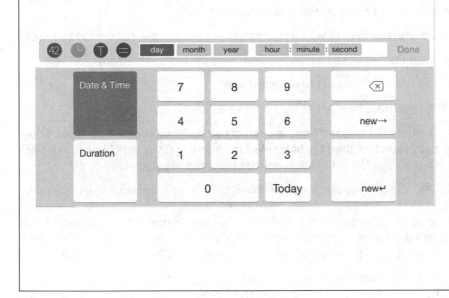

FIGURE 26-5

When you tap the Date & Time key, different date and time categories appear in the input bar, ranging from Year right through to Second. (On an iPhone or iPod Touch, you have to swipe left and right on the input bar to see all these options.) Tap any of these categories, and Numbers updates the keyboard based on your selection. Here, the input bar's Day category is selected and the keyboard includes numeric keys so you can specify a day of the month.

TIP The Formulas & Functions keyboard layout is covered in the following section.

■ Working with Data

Tables are handy for organizing data, and they make great starting points for creating charts. And as an added bonus, once you've fed all of your data into a table, you can perform calculations on it—which is where the Formulas & Functions keyboard layout comes in. Whether you're working out the grand total of a row or subjecting your data to more complex calculations, you can use the Formulas & Functions keyboard layout to really put your data through its paces.

Not only do formulas automate calculations, but if you tweak the data within your table at any point, your formulas also automatically *recalculate,* using the new data to provide you with an updated answer. So put that calculator away, as the next few sections show you how to use the Formulas & Functions keyboard layout to make your life more formulaic.

NOTE When creating formulas, you use *cell references,* which are basically a cell's column and its row. For example a cell in column D, row 4 has a cell reference of D4 (page 230 has more info about cell references).

Totaling Things Up

One of the most popular calculations is working out the grand total of a collection of cells, whether it's an entire row, a column, or even a group of random cells within a single table or spread across multiple tables. Once you've entered all of your data in a table, you're ready to work out the grand total:

1. **Double-tap the cell where the results of your calculation should appear.**

   Numbers displays its keyboard, with the familiar input bar above the keys.

2. **Tap the = button next to the input bar.**

   The keyboard switches to the Formulas & Functions layout.

3. **Tap the SUM key, and Numbers selects all the cells above the cell you origi-nally selected; drag the blue selection handles (they look like little circles) to select all the cells that should be included in your total.**

   The cells don't always have to be side by side, or even within the same table. To include nonadjacent cells, just tap the nonadjacent cells in question to sur-round them with a new set of selection handles. To help you keep track of which cells you select, Numbers assigns each set of selection handles its own color. If needed, you can drag these selection handles to select additional cells.

   Repeat until all the desired cells are selected. As you select cells, Numbers helps you keep track by updating the contents of the input bar to include all the selected cells' cell references.

4. **To save your formula and see your total, tap the checkmark button at the right end of the input bar.**

   Numbers performs its mathematical wizardry and the results appear in your table (Figure 26-6 shows an example). If you make a mistake, tap the Delete key until the input bar is clear (on an iPhone or iPod touch, this button has a left-pointing arrow with an X on it). And if you're on an iPad, you can exit the cell without saving your formula by tapping the red X next to the input bar (shown in Figure 26-6).

Adding, Subtracting, Multiplying, and Dividing

Totaling up a group of cells tends to be the calculation folks use most often in Num-bers, but sometimes you want to throw subtraction, multiplication, and/or division into the mix. These kinds of equations open the door to things like working out the average value of a group of cells, or subtracting the total you spent from the total you made. Here's how to write a simple formula that lets you add, subtract, multiply, or divide the data in two cells:

1. **Double-tap the cell where you want the results of your calculation to appear, and then tap the = button next to the input bar.**

   The Formulas & Functions keyboard layout appears.

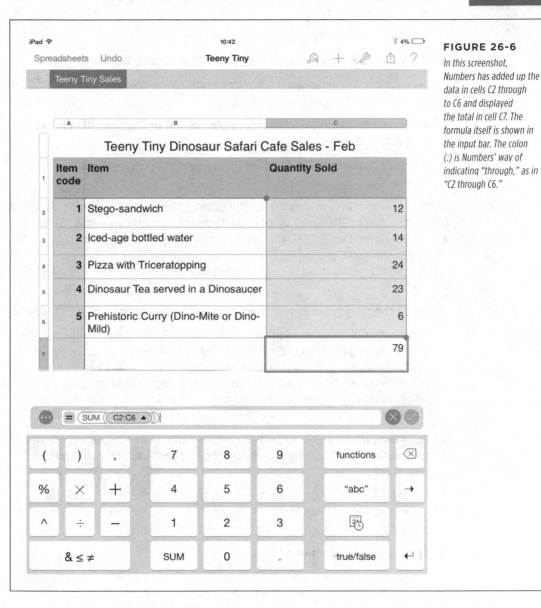

FIGURE 26-6

In this screenshot, Numbers has added up the data in cells C2 through to C6 and displayed the total in cell C7. The formula itself is shown in the input bar. The colon (:) is Numbers' way of indicating "through," as in "C2 through C6."

2. **Tap the first cell whose value you want to include in your formula.**

   For example, tap cell D3, and Numbers displays "D3" in the input bar to indicate that this cell is part of your equation.

3. **Tell Numbers how it should combine the value in the first cell with the second cell (which you'll select in step 4) by tapping the ×, +, ÷, or – key, or using an operator.**

See page 739 for an explanation on operators.

4. **Tap the second cell whose value you want to include in your formula.**

For example, if you tapped the + button in step 3 and then you tap cell D4, your equation will now look like this: D3+D4.

5. **When you finish creating your formula, save it by tapping the checkmark in the input bar.**

Numbers calculates the result of your formula and puts it in the cell you double-tapped way back in step 1.

Adding (or subtracting, or dividing, or multiplying) the values of two cells is a good start, but sooner or later you'll want to perform calculations on *ranges* of cells. For example, the formula C3:C9–D4:D12 tells Numbers to add cells C3 through C9 together, and then add cells D4 through D12 together, and finally subtract the second total from the first. To build this sort of formula, perform step 1 of the list above, and then:

1. **Select the range of cells you're going to use in the first part of your formula.**

Tap the first cell in your range to add it to your formula, keep your finger on the screen, and then drag across the rest of the cells you want to include in this part of your equation. For example, you could select cell D3 and then drag to encompass cells D4 and D5, too. When you do so, Numbers displays "D3:D5" in the input bar (remember, the colon means "through"). You can also tap a cell and then drag its selection handles to select a range.

2. **Tell Numbers how you want it to combine the values in the first range of cells with the values in the second range of cells (which you'll add in the next step).**

Tap the ×, +, ÷, or – keys or use an operator (see page 739). For example, if you want to add up the values in the two ranges of cells, tap the + key. In the input bar, your formula now looks something like this: D3:D5+.

3. **Select the second range of cells.**

For instance, tap cell C3, and then drag the selection handles so they're around cells C3, C4, and C5. Your formula now looks like this: D3:D5+C3:C5.

4. **Repeat steps 1–2 to add additional parts to your formula, if necessary.**

5. **When you finish working on your formula, save it by tapping the checkmark in the input bar.**

Numbers calculates the result of your formula and places it in the cell you originally double-tapped.

TIP See Chapter 19 for more about formulas.

Comparing and Contrasting Values

To compare and contrast the values of different cells, you use *operators* (comparison symbols) such as < (less than), > (greater than), and = (equal to).

For example, operators can tell you how cell A25's value compares to cell B25's value. Although this may not sound particularly helpful, imagine that A25 and B25 are cells that display the grand totals for their respective rows. By comparing these values using operators, you can get Numbers to crunch all of your data and spit out a neat little summary. In other words, you can ask, "Is everything in row A equal to everything in row B?" and Numbers will respond with "True" or "False." To work out the answer manually would take a fair amount of number-crunching, and you'd need to redo these calculations every time you made a change to the underlying data. But operators let you avoid all that work.

All the operator keys live in the Formulas & Functions keyboard layout (tap the = button labeled in Figure 26-3 to display it). To see them, tap the &≤≠ key. (Oddly, on an iPhone or iPod Touch, this key is labeled %≠≤ instead.) If you're unfamiliar with operators, Figure 26-7 shows you what each operator key means.

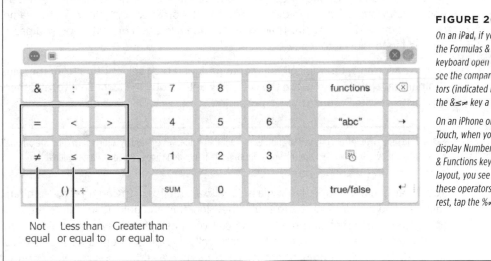

FIGURE 26-7

On an iPad, if you have the Formulas & Functions keyboard open but don't see the comparison operators (indicated here), give the &≤≠ key a tap.

On an iPhone or iPod Touch, when you first display Numbers' Formulas & Functions keyboard layout, you see some of these operators. To see the rest, tap the %≠≤ key.

To create a simple formula using an operator, double-tap the cell where you want your results to appear, and then:

1. **Select the cell (or range of cells) whose values you want to use as the first part of your formula, or type a numeric value into the input bar.**

   To select a range of cells, tap one cell and then drag the selection handles until all the desired cells are highlighted.

2. **Tap an operator symbol to add it to your formula.**

   For example, if you want to ask Numbers, "Is the value in cell C5 equal to..." you'd select cell C5 in step 1, and then tap the equal sign in this step, so your formula looks like this: C5=.

3. **Select the cell (or range of cells) whose value you want to compare to whatever you selected or typed in step 1, or type a numeric value.**

   For example, to ask Numbers whether the value in cell C5 is equal to the value in cell H8, you'd tap cell H8 to create the formula C5=H8.

4. **In the input bar, tap the checkmark button.**

   Numbers calculates the result of your comparison and displays either True or False in the cell you double-tapped before creating the formula.

> **NOTE** You can also use parentheses to create more complicated formulas. For example, the formula (C5+C20+D5)=F1:F10 asks Numbers whether the grand total of the values in cells C5, C20, and D5 is equal to the grand total of the values in cells F1 through F10. You can make things as straightforward or as complicated as you want.

Reusing Formulas

Unless you can't get enough of typing out operators, parentheses, and cell references, you won't be jumping up and down at the prospect of typing out the same formula time and time again. Thankfully, Numbers lets you quickly copy and paste an existing formula into a new cell.

To copy a formula, tap the cell that contains it, and then select Copy from the mini toolbar that appears. Next, tap the cell you want to copy the formula into, and then tap Paste→Paste Formulas when prompted.

> **TIP** To copy a *value* from one cell to another (even if that value was created by a formula), copy the original as described above, and then tap the cell you want to paste it into and choose Paste→Paste Values.

You'll notice that the copied formula isn't an *exact* replica of the original, as Numbers takes a good long look at the formula's new location and adjusts its cell references to match the columns and rows of the cell you paste it into. For example, if you copy the formula D1+D2 from cell D3 into cell F3, Numbers updates the formula to F1+F2. This kind of adjustment is called *mapping,* and it usually gives you the results you want. But if you need to make changes to the formula after you paste it, double-tap the cell where it lives, and all of its components appear in the input bar. You can then update any part of the formula by tapping it in the input bar and making your changes.

> **NOTE** If you want to preserve some, or all, of your original references (in other words, you don't want Numbers to do any mapping), then check out the Tip on page 741.

IWORK: THE MISSING MANUAL

What if you want to copy only a *snippet* of a formula? You could copy the entire thing and then delete the parts you don't need, but those kinds of manual tweaks can be nearly as annoying as creating the whole thing from scratch. Thankfully, Numbers lets you get picky about which bits of a formula you want and which bits get left behind. To copy *part* of a formula:

1. **Double-tap the cell containing the formula you want to copy.**

   The keyboard pops up and the full formula appears in the input bar.

2. **In the input bar, double-tap the section of the formula you want to copy.**

   Numbers puts selection handles around the section you double-tapped.

3. **If you want to copy more of the formula, drag the selection handles to highlight the sections you're interested in.**

   Unfortunately, you can't select nonadjacent sections of a formula. So if you want to copy just the beginning and end of a formula, for example, your best option is to copy the whole thing, paste it into the new cell, and then double-tap that cell and edit the formula to remove all the unwanted stuff.

4. **In the mini toolbar that appears, tap Cut or Copy; then exit the formula by tapping the X next to the input bar.**

   This step is important: If you tap any other cell while you have the input bar open, Numbers adds that cell reference to the input bar—probably not what you had in mind!

5. **Double-tap the cell you want to paste the formula into.**

   Numbers selects the cell and displays the input bar and keyboard.

6. **Tap the = button to display the Formulas & Functions keyboard layout, tap the input bar, and then select Paste.**

   Numbers pastes the part of the formula you selected into its new home. Tap the checkmark button to save your pasted formula.

TIP Most of the time, you'll be grateful that Numbers automatically updates your cell references when you copy and paste a formula, but occasionally you want to preserve some or all of those references. Although you *can* go back and change them manually, making those sorts of tedious adjustments will have you wondering why you bothered with copy and paste in the first place.

But don't forsake that Copy button just yet! You can *force* Numbers to keep its paws off your cell references when you copy and paste formulas. To do so, double-tap the cell where you created the formula, and all the formula's segments appear in the input bar. Look closely, and you'll spot a tiny triangle next to each cell reference. Tap this triangle to open a menu that contains a smorgasbord of sliders that you can adjust to tell Numbers which cell references to preserve and which ones are fair game. (See page 536 for more info on preserving cell references.)

Working with Built-In Functions

This section has covered some of the most commonly used formulas, but the fun doesn't end there! Numbers comes with over 250 functions that you can use in your formulas. There isn't room to cover *all* these functions here, but Numbers has a menu where you can learn more about every last function, and add them to your table with just a few taps. (See Chapter 20 for more about functions.) Here's how to access this menu:

1. **Double-tap the cell where you want the function to appear, and then switch to the Formulas & Functions keyboard layout.**

   To access this layout, tap the = button next to the input bar.

2. **Tap the Functions key (or, if you're on an iPod Touch or iPhone, tap the *fx* key instead).**

3. **In the panel that appears, tap the Categories button, and then tap any category to view a list of all the functions in it.**

   If you're unsure what a particular function does, you can find out more by tapping the "i" icon next to its name. Once you're done reading about the function, tap the category name at the top left of the panel to return to that category.

4. **Tap the name of a function to add it to the input bar.**

   Numbers adds the function to the cell you selected in step 1, and the function appears in the input bar. At this point, you can add more functions or cell references (page 230) as necessary.

> **TIP** With more than 250 functions to choose from, the Functions menu can be confusing if you're just out for a browse. Apple maintains an online list of all the functions Numbers has to offer, which is easier to navigate if you just want an idea of what's available: *http://help.apple.com/functions/mac/4.0.*

■ Using Forms to Supercharge Data Entry

While you *can* enter your data one cell at a time, doing so is super time-consuming when you need to enter lots of data. Imagine working your way through a row that's 32 cells wide—you'd have to do a ton of tapping, and the likelihood of putting a bit of info in the wrong cell is pretty high. There must be a better way...

To make large-scale data entry less frustrating and error prone, Numbers lets you enter data via *forms*. You can create a form for any table, and each form follows the same layout:

- A form is made up of multiple *records*.

- Each record corresponds to a single row within your table.

- Each *field* within a record corresponds to a single cell within your table.

That may sound complicated, but it's actually pretty easy to get the hang of once you start using forms. Figure 26-8, top, shows an example of a record, complete with fields.

With forms, filling out an entire row's worth of data is simply a matter of working your way through that row's record. Because each record is restricted to a single row, you're less likely to enter data in the wrong cell. Figure 26-8, bottom, shows a completed table.

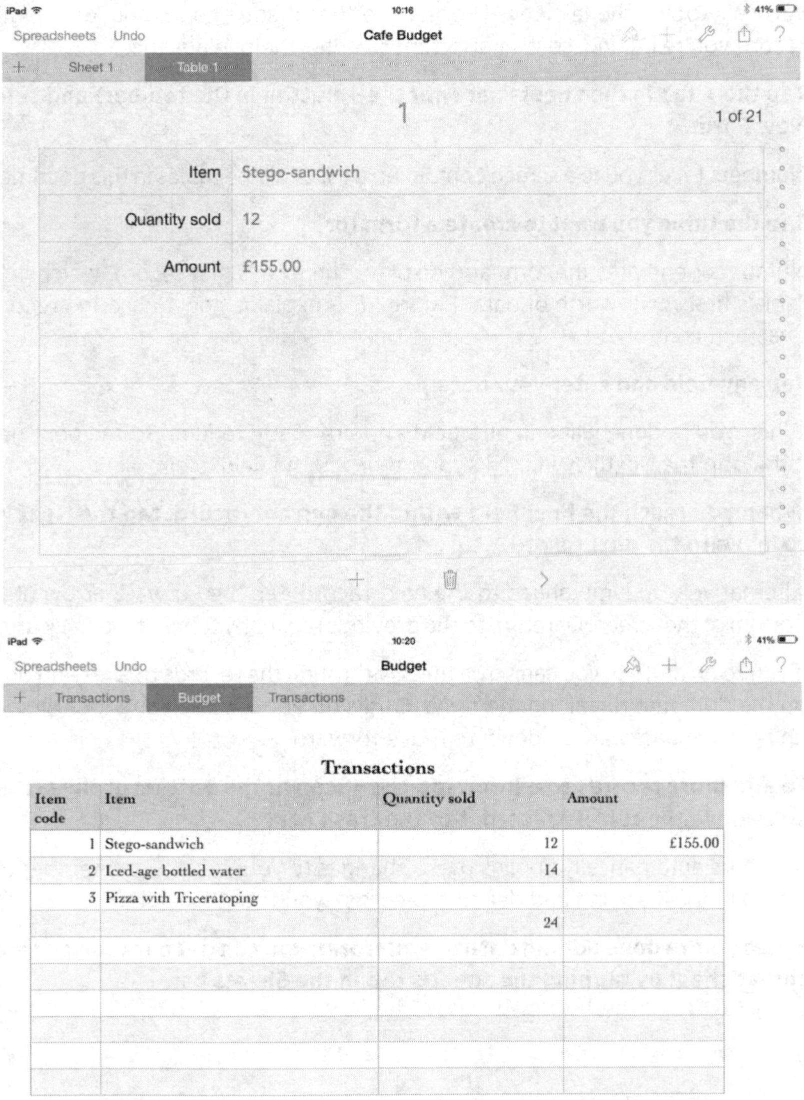

FIGURE 26-8

Top: This screenshot shows the record for row 1 of a table that contains three fields: Item, Quantity sold, and Amount (the Item Code value is the column header). You add data to a record (and, by extension, Row 1 of your table) by working your way down the record. Easy!

Bottom: After you enter data into the form's record, it appears in row 1 of your table, as shown here.

NOTE In the long run, inputting data into a form is quicker (and more accurate) than adding each piece of data to a table one cell at a time. However, because of the extra effort needed to *create* a form in the first place, it's rarely worth using a form if you're just entering a few scraps of data.

To get started with forms:

1. **Create a table (page 683), and then fill in all the cells in the header column and header row.**

   The header row runs along the top of your table, and the header column runs vertically down the left edge. Forms use these labels to let you know which record you're editing, so it's important to enter them in advance.

2. **Tap the + tab in the Sheets bar (*not* the + button in the toolbar) and select New Form.**

   Numbers takes you to a screen containing a list of all the tables in this document.

3. **Tap the table you want to create a form for.**

   Numbers generates the form and displays the form's first record, which is the table's first row's worth of data. Figure 26-9 explains how to use the record's onscreen controls.

4. **Tap any field and enter your data.**

   When you're done filling in one field and are ready to jump to the next field, either tap the Next key in the keyboard or tap the field itself.

5. **When you reach the final field within the current record, tap the Next key to move to the next record.**

   Alternatively, to jump ahead to the next record, tap the Forward arrow at the bottom of the screen. Or return to the previous record by tapping the Back arrow.

   If you're on an iPad, you can scroll quickly through the records by pressing down on the dots that run along the right-hand side of the screen and then swiping up to move backward or down to move forward.

6. **To add more records to a form, tap the + icon at the bottom of the screen. To remove the current record, tap the trash can.**

   Numbers automatically applies these changes to your table, so remember that you're not just adding and deleting records—you're adding and deleting *rows*.

7. **When you're done adding data to your form, you can get back to your main spreadsheet by tapping the sheet's tab in the Sheets bar.**

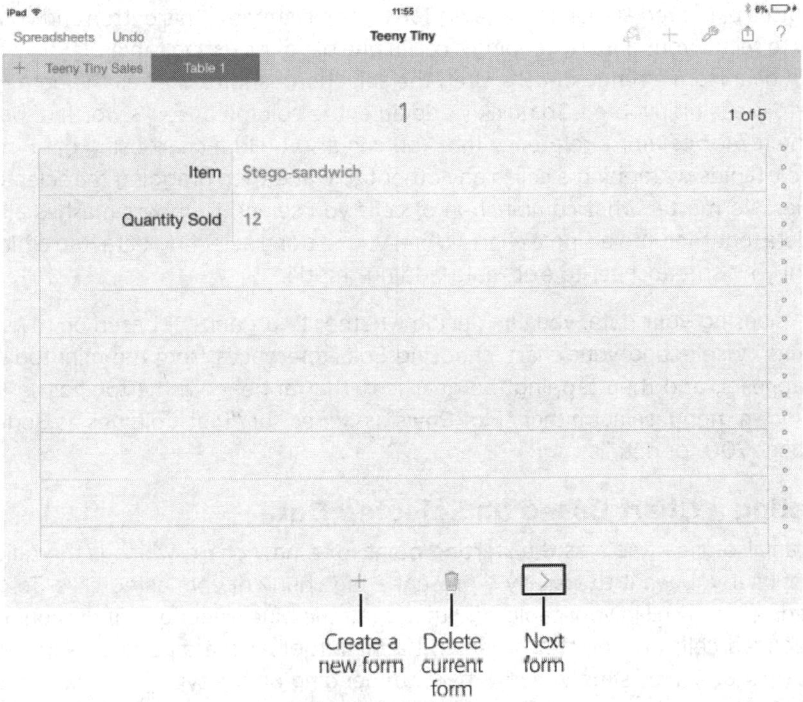

FIGURE 26-9

Here's the record from Figure 26-8 again. If you're on an iPad, you can move between records by dragging the dots along the right side of the record. And you can use the icons along the bottom of the record to perform tasks such as deleting and adding records.

Converting Tables into Charts

While charts and tables are entirely separate objects in Pages and Keynote, in Numbers the data for a chart *always* comes from a table. Not only does this fact make chart creation as easy as tapping the screen a couple of times, but it also lets you deliver a double-whammy of an easy-to-understand, visually appealing chart backed up with all of the related data organized into a table.

As the following sections explain, Numbers offers two methods of creating charts.

Creating a Blank Chart

You can create a blank chart first and then pick and choose your data from existing tables afterward. This method makes it easier to build a chart from data that's spread across various cells—and even various tables—because you can add the disconnected chunks of data in stages.

To create a blank chart and add your data afterward, you need to have created at least one table with data you want to use. After you've done that, tap the + icon in the toolbar; choose the charts category (the bar-chart icon); select 2D, 3D, or Interactive; and then tap any chart style to add it to your document. Your chart appears with a big button plastered across it that says "Tap to Add Data"; tap this button and you're ready to select your data by tapping a cell in one of your existing tables. If you want to add data from a range of cells, drag the selection handles until all the data you want to use is highlighted. To quickly add an entire column or row's worth of data, tap the row or column's reference tab. You can also build a chart using data from *multiple* tables by tapping a cell in any other table and then dragging the selection handles. No matter what combination of cells you select, Numbers mashes all of this data together into a single chart. When you're done selecting data, tap a blank area of your spreadsheet to exit "data-adding" mode.

After choosing your data, you can decide whether to organize it based on rows or columns by selecting your chart, choosing Edit References from the mini toolbar that appears, and then tapping the gear icon that appears in the toolbar. In the drop-down menu, select either "Plot Rows as Series" or "Plot Columns as Series" (see page 700 for details).

Creating a Chart Based on Selected Data

You can also use a table as the starting point for a new chart, which is the quickest option if you want to visually represent a big chunk of connected cells. To get started, select a cell in your table, and then drag the blue selection handles until all the required cells are selected. Then, in the mini toolbar that appears, tap Create Chart (this label may simply read "Chart," depending on the type of iDevice you're using). Find the type of chart you want to create, and give it a tap to add it to your spreadsheet. The chart appears, already filled in with your selected data.

Modifying a Chart's Data

Regardless of how you create a chart, at some point you may want to go back and change the data it contains, whether that means deleting data or incorporating additional cells into your chart.

To change the data that's included in a chart, select the chart, and then tap Edit References in the mini toolbar that appears. In your source table, Numbers highlights all the data that's represented in the chart by putting selection handles around it. You can grab any of these handles to add or remove cells, or add an entire row or column by tapping the corresponding header. You'll also notice a dark box next to all the columns and rows that are used in your chart. You can remove an entire column or row by tapping the colored dot within this dark box and then selecting Delete Series.

Numbers has more ways of modifying charts, such as adding value labels, changing the font, adding a legend, and more. These options work exactly the same as in Pages for iOS, so hop back to page 699 for details.

iWork for iCloud

PART

5

An Intro to iCloud

With iWork for Mac and the full suite of iWork apps for iOS, you can finally enjoy Pages, Keynote, and Numbers on your Mac *and* iDevices (specifically, iPad, iPhone, and iPod Touch). But sometimes, too much choice can be a bad thing.

Wouldn't it be great to have a centralized place to store the latest versions of all your iWork documents, and for that library to be accessible from any computer or mobile device? Shame that's just a pipe dream...

Actually, today's your lucky day, because there's one final member of the iWork family waiting to make your acquaintance: iWork for iCloud. Instead of hunting through your Mac, iPad, iPhone, and iPod Touch, you can simply open a web browser on any device (even a *Windows* computer), and then log into your iCloud account. Not only is the complete suite of iWork offerings—Keynote, Pages, and Numbers—waiting for you there, but all of your iWork documents are, too. Any document you share with iWork for iCloud is always just a login away.

What's more, when you connect any iWork app on an iDevice to your iCloud account, all the iWork documents you create within that app *automatically* synchronize with your iCloud account and vice versa. You can also save iWork documents you create on your Mac to your iCloud account, so they're available both on your Mac and via your iCloud account—and again, both versions of your document are automatically synchronized.

Picture the scene: You've managed to score a booth at the country's leading convention for underrated tourist attractions, but you overslept and in your panic you left those all-important flyers on the kitchen sideboard. Without your flyers, how can you convince the crowds that those pages of less-than-glowing online reviews are really just a big misunderstanding? Then you remember: You designed your flyer in Pages for Mac and saved it to your iCloud account! You boot up the nearest computer, log into iCloud.com, click the Pages icon, and your flyer is already waiting for you; all you need to do is print it out.

This chapter gets you up to speed with iWork for Cloud, from setting up your iCloud account to synchronizing all the iWork apps on your iDevices. You'll also learn how to save your iWork for Mac documents to your iCloud account.

■ Getting Started with iWork for iCloud

To learn about the history of iCloud, flip back to the "Sharing via iCloud" section that begins on page 256.

You're no doubt champing at the bit to experience iWork in a web browser. Here are the things you need to get started:

- **An Internet connection.** You knew that.

- **An approved web browser.** As you'd expect, iWork for iCloud runs in Apple's Safari browser (version 6.0.3 or later), but it also works in Google's Chrome (version 27.0.1 or later) and Microsoft's Internet Explorer (a.k.a. IE, version 9.0.8 or later). If you don't already have one of these browsers, grab one now (they're free):

  — **Safari:** *www.apple.com/safari*

  — **Google Chrome:** *www.google.com/chrome*

  — **Internet Explorer:** *www.microsoft.com/ie*

You also need an Apple ID (page 796 explains how to create one) and an iCloud account. You have to create an iCloud account on either a Mac or an iDevice (the following pages show you how). But once you've created your iCloud account, you're free to log into iCloud from a non-Apple device—yup, even a Windows computer.

TIP   If you create an iCloud account on a Mac, you still need to tell your iDevice(s) about your iCloud account (page 752) before their iWork apps can synchronize with iCloud. So if you use iWork on an iDevice, save yourself the hassle and just create your iCloud account on your iPad/iPhone/iPod Touch in the first place.

Creating an iCloud Account on a Mac

To get iCloud up and running on a Mac, the computer needs to be running OS X Lion (version 10.7.4) or later. To figure out which version of OS X your Mac has, go to →About This Mac; the box that appears lists the version number. If you're running a version earlier than 10.7.4, you need to visit *www.apple.com/osx* and purchase a newer version of OS X before you can use iCloud.

Once you're running a new enough version of OS X, go to →System Preferences →iCloud, enter your trusty Apple ID, and your iCloud account is ready to go. That was easy, wasn't it?

Creating an iCloud Account on an iDevice

The first time you turn your shiny new iDevice on, the Setup Assistant asks you to create an iCloud account. You should check whether you already *have* an iCloud account by going to your *home screen* (the one you see when you turn on or unlock your iDevice) and tapping Settings→iCloud to see if there's already an iCloud account listed. If not, you can create one now. But before you start, check that you're running the latest version of Apple's iOS software. Figure 27-1 explains how.

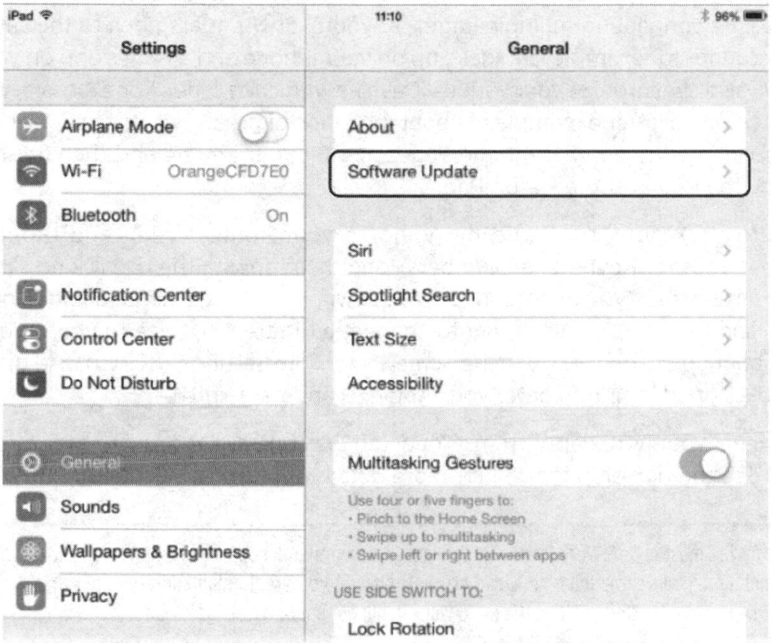

FIGURE 27-1

Check for iOS updates by going to your home screen and tapping Settings →General→Software Update (indicated). If you're up to date, you'll see a message saying so. If not, you'll see info about the update that's available. To install it, tap "Download and Install." Review the terms and conditions, and then tap Agree. (To save precious battery life, it's a good idea to connect your device to a power source while it updates.)

Once you're running the latest and greatest iOS software, you're ready to create an iCloud account:

1. **Go to the home screen and tap Settings→iCloud, enter your Apple ID, and then tap Sign In.**

   Whatever device you use, your Apple ID account remains the same.

2. **Read, and then agree to, the terms and conditions (twice!).**

   If you like to keep records of everything you agree to, tap "Send by Email" to forward a copy of the terms and conditions to your email address. Tap Agree to confirm that you accept them, and then (strangely) you need to confirm that you agree a *second* time before proceeding.

3. **Grant (or refuse) iCloud access to your location.**

   If you fancy using location-dependent features such as "Find my [iDevice]," which can help you track down your gadget if you lose it, you need to grant iCloud access to your location by tapping OK when you see the "Allow iCloud to Use the Location of your [iPad/iPhone/iPod]" message. (If you're unsure whether these features are right for you, see *www.apple.com/icloud/features* for more information.) After you tap OK, your iCloud account is good to go.

While you have your iDevice to hand, you might as well connect your iWork apps to your iCloud account. This connection means that any changes you make within your iWork for iDevice apps are automatically shared with their iCloud counterparts, and vice versa. By connecting multiple Pages, Keynote, or Numbers apps to the same iCloud account—for example, a Pages app on your iPhone and a Pages app on your iPad—you also synchronize your various iDevices with *each other*. For example, you can start writing a letter of complaint about the ration of green sweets to red sweets in your recent candy purchase in the Pages app on your iPhone and then finish it later using the Pages app on your iPad.

Link your iWork apps to iCloud by going to your home screen and tapping Settings→Pages (or Keynote, or Numbers), and then tapping the Use iCloud slider so that it turns green (you may need to scroll down the Settings menu to find Pages, Keynote, and Numbers). If you need to connect a different iDevice to your iCloud account, boot up the device, go to the home screen, tap Settings→iCloud, and make sure you're signed in (if not, enter your Apple ID and password).

To disconnect your iWork apps from iCloud, tap the app's slider again to turn it back to white. See the box on page 753 for more details about this process.

> **TIP** To get the most out of iWork for iCloud, connect all of your iWork apps on all your iDevices to the *same* iCloud account. (You could have separate iCloud accounts linked to different email addresses, but that can get confusing.) The more connected you are, the more value you'll get out of iWork for iCloud.

■ Connecting iWork for Mac to iCloud

Any document you create in Pages, Keynote, or Numbers for Mac can be saved to your iCloud account. The main benefit of saving an iWork for Mac document to iCloud is that, if your computer suffers a meltdown, your document is still safely stored online. It also means that you can access your document from any *other* computer by logging into your iCloud account. And, if you've connected your iCloud account to your iDevices as explained in the previous section, your document is also accessible from your iDevices.

Disconnecting from iCloud

If at some point you disconnect an iWork for iOS app from iCloud (either accidentally, or intentionally because Aunt Doris wants to borrow your iPad and you don't want her to see your iWork docs about the surprise birthday rave you're planning for her in Ibiza), the next time you launch the app, you're confronted with an accusative You're Not Using iCloud pop-up. Breakups can be tough, and when the beautiful relationship between your iDevice or Mac and your iCloud account comes to an end, the two parties need some pointers on how to handle their shared documents.

To keep a copy of the most recent version of any synchronized iWork documents on your iDevice, select "Keep on My [iDevice]." Alternatively, tap "Delete from my [iDevice]" to remove all documents synchronized with your iCloud account. If you

realize what a terrible mistake you've made, hit Continue Using iCloud to get your iDevice and iCloud account back together.

There are two ways to disconnect the iWork for Mac programs from iCloud. You can sign out of iCloud completely by going to → System Preferences → iCloud → Sign Out, at which point you see a warning that all documents stored in iCloud will be deleted from your Mac; click Cancel if you change your mind, or go ahead and break the connection by selecting "Delete from Mac." Or you can disconnect only the iWork programs from iCloud but leave other programs connected. Go to → System Preferences → iCloud, and scroll down until you find the Documents & Data category. Click the Options button next to it to see a list of all the iWork programs installed on your Mac. To break the connection between a specific iWork program and iCloud, turn off its checkbox, and then click Done.

To set up all this handy interconnectedness, you need to tell your Mac about your iCloud account (if you haven't already). Go to → System Preferences → iCloud, and enter your iCloud information.

The iWork for Mac programs don't save documents to iCloud *automatically*; you need to manually save or move a document to iCloud:

- To save a new Pages, Keynote, or Numbers document to iCloud, select File→ Save. In the Where drop-down menu, select iCloud, and then save your document as normal (enter a filename and click Save).

- To move a previously saved document to iCloud, choose File→Move To, and then select iCloud from the Where drop-down menu.

After that, your document appears both on your Mac *and* in your iCloud account. To open a document on your Mac that you saved to iCloud, call up the Open dialog box (either by launching the iWork program in question or, if it's already open, choosing File→Open). Then choose iCloud at the top of this dialog box (as shown in Figure 27-2), select your file, and then click Open. This document will also appear in Pages, Numbers, or Keynote for iCloud (depending on the type of document you've created).

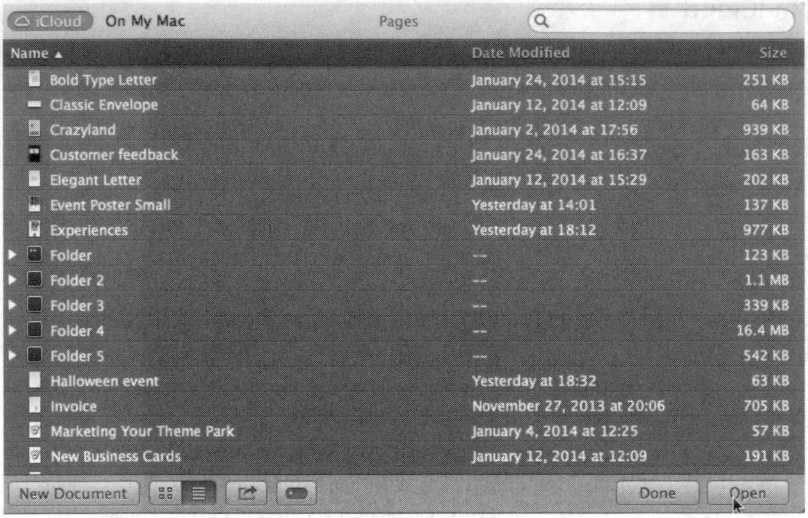

FIGURE 27-2

The Open dialog box lets you access documents saved to your iCloud account and to your Mac. Switch between the two using the buttons at the top of the dialog box.

Pages for iCloud

Picture the scene: You've just put the finishing touches to your 20-page freeform poem. All you need to do now is print it out, and you'll be the envy of everyone at tonight's writer's meetup. But before you have the chance to plug the printer in and rattle off a copy, the worst possible thing happens: Your computer suffers an epic meltdown, and you have to go to the meetup empty-handed.

In this uncertain world where computers fail and files can get corrupted or deleted, Pages for iCloud can be your safety net. No matter where you are on Earth, as long as you have an Internet connection, you can access your Pages documents. And, because your documents are stored on *Apple's* computers, not yours, you won't lose your documents even if your computer goes up in smoke. You can sleep a little more soundly at night knowing that.

Whether you use iCloud as your backup by syncing all of your Pages documents with your account or use iCloud as an online word processor in its own right, the bottom line is that if your important document exists in Pages for iCloud, you can use any Internet-connected computer (even a PC!) to log into your account, print off a copy, and wow everyone at the writer's meetup.

This chapter shows you how to create documents in Pages for iCloud, add objects to them, and share your documents with other people. Whether you're creating an entirely new document or continuing work on something you created earlier on your iPhone, iPad, or iPod Touch (your *iDevices*)—or even on your Mac—this chapter has you covered.

NOTE   If you haven't created an iCloud account yet, flip back to page 750. And if you need to link your Pages for iCloud account to any Pages apps that are knocking around your iDevices, flip to page 752. You can also save any documents you create on Pages for Mac to your iCloud account (see page 752), so they're accessible on your computer and online.

Accessing Pages for iCloud

Whenever you log into your iCloud account, the web-based version of Pages is right there waiting for you (how did it know you were visiting today?). To log into your iCloud account, open one of the compatible web browsers:

- Safari 6.0.3 or later

- Chrome 27.0.1 or later

- Internet Explorer 9.0.8 or later

TIP   If you don't already have one of the browsers listed above, you can download any of them for free thanks to the magic of the Internet. The quickest way to grab one is to launch your current browser, and then use your search engine of choice (google.com, say) to search for *download Chrome* or *download Internet Explorer*.

Once you have a compatible web browser installed, launch it and head to *www. icloud.com*. (This web page is your gateway to everything iWork for iCloud–related, so you might want to bookmark it.) At iCloud.com, you see a pop-up that kindly requests your Apple ID and password. Type in this info and then press Enter or click the gray arrow to log into your account. (You may be prompted to choose your preferred language and time zone; if so, pick the correct ones, and then click Start Using iCloud.) You can now choose from the three iWork apps: Pages, Numbers, and Keynote. Since you're perusing the Pages for iCloud chapter, click the Pages icon to go directly to Pages' *Documents view*.

NOTE   As mentioned above, you can use iWork for iCloud on Macs *and* PCs. So if you're away from home and have access to only your hotel's desktop PC, no problem. Launch Internet Explorer or Chrome and log into iCloud.com to work on your Pages documents. The only differences are minor: Instead of ⌘-clicking things, you right-click them; instead of the Return key, you press the Enter key; and instead of pressing ⌘-C to copy something, you press Ctrl+C. Aside from minor differences like that, everything works basically the same way. This book focuses on Macs, but as long as you keep these differences in mind, you should have no trouble using iWork for iCloud on a PC.

Documents View

Documents view (Figure 28-1) is where you access all the documents you create in Pages for iCloud, as well as the documents you create in any iOS apps that you link to iCloud, and any documents you create on your Mac and save to iCloud. If you've linked iCloud to the Pages app on your iPhone, for example, then this screen may be pretty full already. To open an existing document, double-click its thumbnail, and the document opens in a new window. To create a new document, click the big + sign.

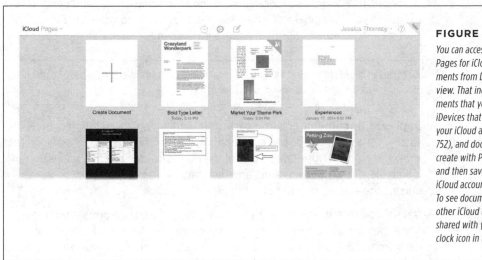

FIGURE 28-1

You can access all of your Pages for iCloud documents from Documents view. That includes documents that you create on iDevices that are linked to your iCloud account (page 752), and documents you create with Pages for Mac and then save to your iCloud account (page 752). To see documents that other iCloud users have shared with you, click the clock icon in the toolbar.

Opening and creating documents are the main tasks you perform in Documents view, but it has a few more tricks up its sleeve. To see what Documents view is capable of, click the gear icon in Pages' toolbar, and then select any of the following:

- **Create Document.** This is a more long-winded way to create a document. Unless you already have the gear menu open, it's much quicker to click the + sign on the first thumbnail in Documets view.

- **Upload Document.** Pages isn't fussy—it lets you upload and edit documents that weren't created in your iCloud account, or even in Pages at all. iCloud is more than happy to upload documents that are in Pages format, Microsoft Word format (.doc and .docx files), or text format (.txt). Select Upload Document, use the new window to zero in on your file, and then click Open to upload the file to iCloud.

- **Sort by Date/Name.** Documents view can quickly become a crowded place, especially if you connect lots of Pages apps to iCloud or if you save all your Pages for Mac documents to your iCloud account. You can bring some order to Documents view by arranging your files based on the date you last edited them or by their names. In most cases, arranging them by date makes sense, as your most recently edited ones float to the top, and that's the sort method Pages for iCloud uses unless you tell it otherwise.

You may notice that some of the options in the gear menu are grayed out; that's because you can use these commands only when you have a document selected. (If you haven't created any documents yet, page 760 tells you how.) So if you want to download, delete, or duplicate a document, click its thumbnail once to select it, and then click the gear icon and choose any of the following:

- **Download Document.** Downloads a copy of the document to your computer for safekeeping. When you click this command, Pages asks you to choose a format (Pages, PDF, or Word), so running this command is also a quick and painless way to change your document's format. Pick your preferred format, and Pages takes a moment to prepare your document before downloading it to your computer.

> **NOTE** You can download a copy of an open document from the document-editing window by clicking the Tools button in the toolbar and then choosing "Download a Copy."

- **Duplicate Document.** Makes a copy of the document, which Pages gives the catchy name "[original document name] copy." You should probably change that stinker of a name right away, so click the duplicate document's name to make it editable. Type a better name, and then tap the Return key or click anywhere outside the editing box to make the new name stick.

- **Delete Document.** Permanently removes the document from iCloud *and* from any Pages for iOS or Mac apps that are connected to iCloud. When you click this command, Pages asks whether you're absolutely sure you want to scrub this document from the face of the Earth. If you're feeling ruthless, click Delete; otherwise, give the document a reprieve by clicking Cancel.

- **Share Document.** Why keep a fabulous document to yourself? One of the really great features of iWork for iCloud is that it lets you invite other people to collaborate on your documents. When you share a Pages for iCloud document, any changes made by other people appear on your screen, and your changes appear in theirs. To share a document, click this command in the gear menu and Pages opens a window containing the web address other people can use to access your document in their web browsers. Pass the link around to your iWork collaborators by copying the link (click it and then press ⌘-C) and pasting it (⌘-V) anywhere you want (onto your Facebook wall, into a Google Hangout, and so on). To email the link directly to someone, click Email Link, which launches the Mail program with a fresh email already created, ready for you to fire off to the lucky recipient.

> **TIP** You can share an open document from the document-editing window by clicking the Share button in the toolbar. To stop sharing an open document, click this Share button once again, click Settings in the drop-down menu, and then click Stop Sharing.

- **View Share Settings.** Just because you shared a document when you were young and foolish doesn't mean it needs to stay public forever. You can kick everyone out of your document by selecting View Share Settings and then clicking the Stop Sharing button. From now on, only you can access this document.

- **Send a Copy.** This command is the topic of the next section.

Sharing Documents via Email

You can send a copy of your document to someone directly from iWork for iCloud via email, but there's a catch: You have to do it via Apple's iCloud Mail. (Alternatively, you can download a document to your computer and then use any email program to send your document as an attachment.) If you don't have an iCloud Mail account (that's any email address that ends in *@icloud.com*), don't worry—setting one up is easy.

To create an iCloud Mail account, you first need to switch Mail on in your Mac's System Preferences, so go to ¢→System Preferences→iCloud, enter your iCloud login details (see page 750 for instructions on creating an iCloud account), and then turn on the checkbox next to the Mail icon. As soon as you do this, Apple asks you to create an iCloud Mail address by choosing a username. If you already have an *@ me.com* or *@mac.com* email address, simply type in the part of the address before the @ symbol. If not, type out your desired username (you can't change it later, so choose wisely), click OK, and then confirm that you're truly happy with your new email address by clicking Create.

NOTE If you're a PC user looking to create an iCloud Mail account, you can't do so on your PC. You need to borrow an iDevice that's running iOS 5 or later, or a Mac with OS X Lion v10.7.5 or later. However, once you've created your account, you can set up Microsoft Outlook 2007 or later to work with iCloud Mail (*http://support. apple.com/kb/dl1455* has all the info you need).

Congratulations, you're now the proud owner of an iCloud Mail account! You can now share documents via iCloud Mail from a couple of different places:

- **Documents view.** Click the thumbnail of the document you want to share, and then click the gear icon and choose Send a Copy.

- **Document-editing window.** If you're editing a document when you're overcome with the burning desire to share it, click the Tools button, and then select "Send a Copy."

Regardless of the route you take, the results are the same: Pages asks whether you want to send the document as a Pages, PDF, or Word file.

TIP While Pages format is *your* first choice (obviously), if you're sending a document to someone who may not use Pages, play it safe and go with PDF, which works for everyone.

Choose a format, and Pages generates your document. When it's done, click the Email button to open iCloud Mail, which displays a pre-prepared email—with your document already attached! The only thing left to do is enter the recipient's email address, type out a friendly greeting, and then hit Send.

■ Creating a Pages Document

To create a new document, make sure you have Documents view open, and then either click the thumbnail with the big + or click the gear icon and select Create Document. Either way, Pages opens the *Template Chooser*. Just like in Pages for Mac, this is where you choose a template to base your document on (see page 4 for a refresher). Choose a template by double-clicking its thumbnail, and Pages creates and opens a new document based on that template.

In Pages for iCloud, documents open in their own separate windows (Figure 28-2 shows an example), while Documents view remains in the browser's original window. Documents view and the document-editing window(s) exist independently of each other, so if you close Documents view, your document-editing window couldn't care less. But it usually makes sense to leave the Documents view window open in the background while you create your documents in other windows.

> **TIP** If you close the Documents view window and need to bring it back, as long as you still have at least one document-editing window open, you don't need to go to the strenuous effort of typing *www.icloud.com* all over again. Instead, click the Tools button in the document-editing window's toolbar, and then choose "Go to my Documents." Voilà—Documents view opens in either a new tab in your main browser window or in a new window.

The handy thing about editing documents in separate browser windows is that you can have multiple documents open and visible at once (though you might need to drag and resize your browser windows to keep everything onscreen). To open additional documents, go to Documents view and double-click a document's thumbnail to open that document in its own window. The ability to look at multiple documents simultaneously is handy for comparing and contrasting, and you can even copy and paste objects and text between documents.

When you create a document, Pages names it the same thing as the template it's based on; for example, create a new document from the Blank template, and your document winds up with the riveting name Blank. To give your document a more exciting title, head to the Documents view window. Click the document's current name, type a better one, and then hit Return or click outside the editing box to save it.

Pages saves all of your changes automatically, so you don't need to worry about saving documents before closing them. When you're done, just click the red X in the corner of the document-editing window.

The Document-Editing Window

If you're a Pages for Mac fan, you'll feel right at home in Pages for iCloud's document-editing windows. At the top of the screen, you'll find a toolbar that lets you add objects such as images and shapes to your document. And on the right side of the window, the trusty Format panel with all of its tabs is present and accounted for. Just like in Pages for Mac, the Format panel displays different tabs depending on what's selected in your document. Figure 28-2 shows what this panel looks like when you have a shape selected.

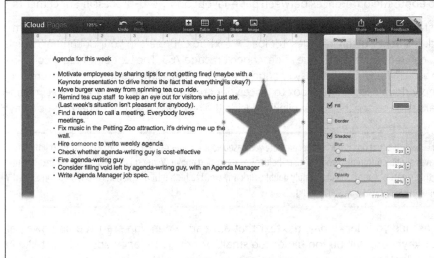

FIGURE 28-2

The Format panel changes depending on what object(s) or text are currently selected. This setup ensures that the Format panel always has everything you need (well, maybe not everything—it can't give you the recipe for the perfect meringue), and since it contains only relevant buttons, sliders, and checkboxes, it's uncluttered and easy to navigate, with nothing hidden away in strange nooks and crannies.

Sooner or later, you'll make a mistake or your cat will jump on your keyboard and delete half your document. Thankfully, Apple knows that mistakes and cat-related-accidents happen, so it includes an Undo button right in the toolbar. Simply click it to undo your most recent change (keep clicking it to keep undoing more changes). If you realize that undoing the "mistake" was actually a mistake in itself, then reapply the change by giving the Redo button a click (it also lives in the toolbar).

NOTE When you close a document, Pages saves all your changes *and you can no longer undo them.* So be sure to undo any unwanted changes *before* you click that X button!

Every time you open a document, Pages assumes that 125% is the magic number, at least when it comes to your zoom level. If it's mistaken, you can change the zoom level by clicking the 125% button in the toolbar and then selecting a new percentage. If you want to look at your document as a whole, choose a smaller number or select Fit Page, which automatically scales the document so the whole thing fits neatly onto your screen. If you want to really scrutinize the document's finer details, choose a higher number or select Fit Width, which gives you the maximum zoom possible while still displaying the full width of your document.

◼ Working with Text

Whether you're writing a quick Please Stop Drinking My Milk note to your roommates or the first few pages of a sci-fi novel about dinosaurs in space, all the words in a page-layout document go inside a *text box*. (In word-processing documents, words can go inside text boxes, too, but you can also have free-flowing body text—just click inside the main body of your document and start typing. See page 15 for more info about the differences between page-layout and word-processing documents.)

To start along the road to annoying your roommates (or to bestseller superstardom), click the Text button in Pages' toolbar. A text box appears in your document, which you can reposition and resize as described on page 765. The text box initially contains the word "Text," but it's easy enough to replace that with your literary masterpiece. Simply double-click a text box to place your cursor inside it. The word "Text" disappears and you see the cursor blinking inside the box, which is your signal to type away!

> **NOTE** If a text box is part of the template you based your document on (page 760), then its placeholder text behaves slightly differently from the placeholder text described above. To get rid of the placeholder text in a text box that's part of your template, simply double-click any word to highlight *all* the text, which then conveniently disappears as soon as you start typing.

Unless it's your lucky day, the text that appears when you start tapping away at your keyboard will be too big or too small, or not quite fancy enough. Just like in Pages for Mac, you use the Format panel's various settings to create text that you can be proud of. The various settings are generally very similar to the settings in Pages for Mac (sometimes even identical), though a few options aren't available in Pages for iCloud. This section gives a quick overview of formatting text in Pages for iCloud and lists the pages where you can find more details in Part One of this book.

Pages has two main methods of formatting text. If you're the super-organized type, you can make all of your formatting decisions in advance, so that when you start typing, your text is perfectly formatted. But if those creative juices are flowing, the last thing you want to do is muck around with menus, so you can type in your text and *then* do your formatting afterward. To give existing text a stylish new look, drag your cursor across the text to select it; Pages then applies any formatting changes you make to all the selected text.

Regardless of which approach you opt for, you make formatting changes in exactly the same way. Head to the Format panel, make sure the Text tab shown in Figure 28-3 is open, and then adjust the settings in the following sections:

- **Paragraph Style.** When you're in a hurry, click the button in this section to reveal a drop-down menu of pre-built *styles* that you can apply to your text. Each style has a unique combination of text coloring, size, and font—great for when you need perfectly formatted text right away. See page 77 for more info.

- **Font.** This section includes the following settings:
  - **Font family** (page 41). The first drop-down menu lets you select a font family (Helvetica, Futura, and so on).
  - **Typeface** (page 41). Choose from Regular, Bold, and so on (depending on the font family).

- **Bold, Italic, Underline, Strikethrough.** Click these buttons to create text that's bold, italicized, underlined, or has a line straight through it. You can apply more than one of these effects to the same piece of text.

- **Font size.** Use this setting to scale your text up or down.

- **Color.** Click the color swatch and choose from the drop-down menu.

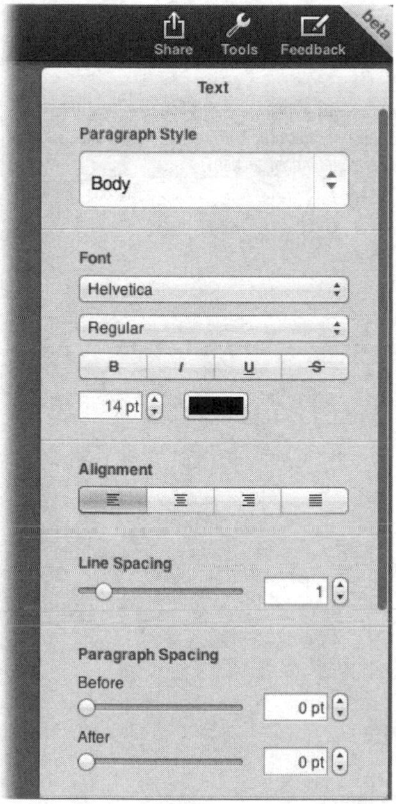

FIGURE 28-3

Use the settings in the Font section to change the appearance of entire paragraphs, words, or just single characters. You can use these controls to change text's font, typeface, size, and color, and apply effects such as bold and italic.

- **Alignment** (page 48) dictates where text sits horizontally and vertically within a text box and where free-flowing text sits horizontally in a word-processing document. The four Alignment buttons shown in Figure 28-3 control horizontal alignment (left, center, right, or justified). If you're working with a text box, you get a second row of alignment buttons that controls vertical alignment (top, middle, or bottom).

- **Line/Paragraph Spacing** (page 51). Spacing controls your text's position in relation to surrounding text. You can use the Line Spacing slider to change the amount of space between each line, and the Paragraph Spacing section's

Before and After sliders to control the space before and after each paragraph. (If you're not a fan of sliders, you can use the fields next to each slider instead.)

- **List Style** (page 68). This section (shown in Figure 28-4) lets you create—you guessed it—lists. Simply position your cursor where you want the list to begin (it doesn't matter whether you've already typed out the first item in your list), and then select an option from the List Style drop-down menu. Page 69 describes the various list formats.

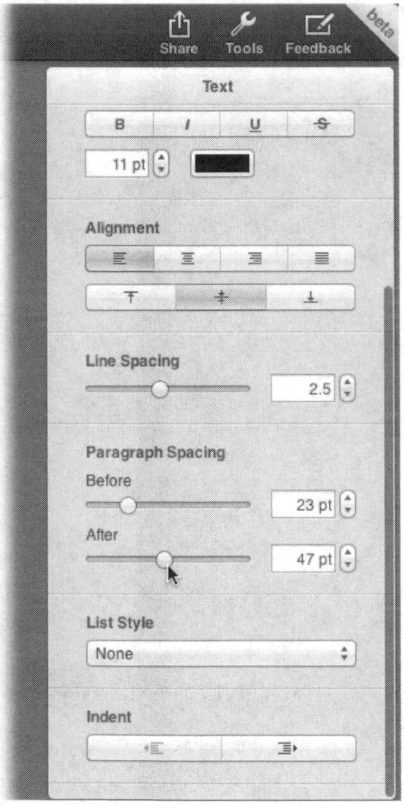

FIGURE 28-4

The Format panel contains so many settings you have to scroll to see them all. This screenshot shows the bottom half of the panel, which includes the List Style and Indent sections.

- **Indent** (page 57). If you're not happy with your text's horizontal positioning on the page, you can change its left and right indents using the buttons in this section.

Just like Pages for Mac, Pages for iCloud has a built-in spell checker to ensure that all of your documents are free of spelling errors. Whenever you make a spelling slip-up, the spell checker adds a dotted red line beneath the scene of the crime. To view the spell checker's suggestions, click the misspelled word, and then click one of the suggestions that appears. The spell checker is turned on from the get-go, but if you're making heavy use of perfectly legitimate words that the foolish spell checker refuses to recognize ("Crazyland Wonderpark," for example), its incessant underlining can get annoying. To turn it off, click Tools→Settings→Check Spelling (you can reactivate it anytime by repeating this process).

Page Count, Page Numbers, and Other Special Text Fields

Pages for iCloud also offers a few special kinds of text fields for page numbers, footnotes, and page counts.

NOTE If you need a reminder about how these fields work, skip back to the following pages: page numbers (page 120), footnotes (page 110), and page counts (page 120).

To add a page number or page count to your document, make sure your cursor is positioned somewhere that can accept text (for example, inside a text box or shape, or inside the body of a word-processing document). Then click the Insert button in the toolbar and select Page Number or Page Count.

To get iCloud to automatically add a page number or page count to every page of your word-processing document, you need to add these special text fields to the document's header or footer. To find a document's header or footer, put your cursor at the top or the bottom of your document until a gray box appears—this is the outline of the header or footer. Click to place your cursor inside it, and then insert a page number or page count as described in the previous paragraph.

TIP To quickly create multiple pages within a word-processing document, place your cursor inside the main body text where you want the current page to end and the next page to begin, and then click the Insert button in the toolbar and choose Page Break.

Finally, you can add footnotes to the main body text of a word-processing document. Place your insertion point where you want to create the reference for your footnote, and then click the Insert button and select Footnote. iCloud inserts your footnote's reference at the insertion point and takes you straight to the document's footer, ready for you to type out your footnote.

■ Working with Objects

If you've been reading this book from the beginning, you know what's coming next: *Everything in Pages is an object*. Just like in Pages for Mac, you use the same editing wizardry across all the different object types (text boxes, tables, shapes, photos, or whatever):

- **Select.** To select an object, click it once.

- **Resize.** Select the object and then position your cursor over one of the blue selection handles that appears around it. When the cursor turns into a two-headed arrow, resize the object by dragging the selection handle. In most cases, this method is accurate enough, but if it isn't, you can specify an exact size by selecting the object, opening the Format panel's Arrange tab, and then adjusting the Width and Height fields. If you're resizing an image, you'll usually want to leave the Constrain Proportions checkbox turned on, to prevent the image from getting stretched or squashed as you resize. If you make a mistake with your resizing and want to make the image look like it did initially, click the Arrange tab's Original Size button.

- **Move.** The quickest way to relocate an object is to drag and drop it to a new location (just don't drag the object's resizing handles, or you'll resize the object instead). If you want precise control over where an object sits on the page, select the object, open the Format panel's Arrange tab, and then use the Position section's X (horizontal) and Y (vertical) fields to adjust the object's location.

- **Delete.** Select the object, and then press the Delete key. (If you realize you've made a terrible mistake, simply click the Undo button to bring the object back.)

- **Copy.** Select the object and then press ⌘-C (Ctrl+C on a PC).

- **Cut.** To copy an object and delete the original, select the object, and then press ⌘-X (Ctrl+X).

- **Paste.** To paste an object that you've cut or copied, press ⌘-V (Ctrl+V), and then drag it to its new location.

- **Rotate.** Select an object and then head to the Arrange tab's Rotate section, which contains everything you need to create an askew or obsessively level object (see Figure 28-5).

- **Group.** As explained on page 154, grouping objects lets you apply the same change to multiple objects, which can save you some time. Before creating a group, you need to select multiple objects by Shift-clicking each one (which is also handy for performing general edits en masse, such as mass deletions). Then, in the Format panel's Arrange tab, click Arrange→Group. From that point on, whenever you click any of the objects within that group, Pages selects *all* the objects so they're ready for editing, as shown in Figure 28-5. If your group hits creative differences, you can send them their separate ways by selecting one object in the group (which selects them all), and then clicking the Arrange panel's Ungroup button.

- **Align.** When you're moving objects around, you'll often want to align them in some way, whether that's aligning them with each other or with the edges or center of the page. Rather than leaving you to guess and hope for the best, just like Pages for Mac, Pages for iCloud provides you with *guides,* flickering yellow lines that appear when you're moving an object around. To activate Pages' guides, go to Tools→Settings, and choose from the following:

  — **Center Guides** help you align the centers of objects with other objects or the center of the page. (These guides are turned on initially; the other kinds aren't.)

FIGURE 28-5

You can set the angle of an object using the controls in the Arrange tab's Rotate section. (The little dot inside the circle icon indicates the object's current angle.)

To create and break groups, respectively, use the Group and Ungroup buttons shown here. Any changes you make to a group of objects apply to every object within it.

— **Edge Guides** help you align an object's edge with the edge of another object or of the page.

— **Spacing Guides** appear when two or more objects are already equally spaced and Pages thinks you're trying to get additional objects lined up with similar spacing. These guides display the current distance between the objects Pages believes you're trying to align.

> **TIP** You can also align objects using their x- and y-coordinates, although this method is trickier because you need to know the coordinates you want to use. If you do, select the object, open the Arrange tab's Format panel, and then type the coordinates into the Position boxes.

Working with Shapes

To add a shape to your document, click the Shape button in the toolbar, and then choose from the selection of stars, arrows, lines, and other shapey goodness. Your options are basically the same as in Pages for Mac (page 168).

In a hurry but still want a shape you won't be embarrassed to show your friends? Pages has a handful of ready-made styles that you can try on for size. To apply a style to a shape, select the shape, and then click the Format panel's Shape tab. The different styles you can choose from appear as thumbnails at the top of the tab; click any style to apply it to your shape.

> **TIP** To use a shape as a hipper alternative to a text box, place your cursor inside the shape by double-clicking it, and you're ready to start typing. You can format this text in exactly the same way as text that lives inside a text box (page 761).

Shapes generally work the same way in Pages for iCloud as they do in Pages for Mac. Here's a quick rundown of your options, including cross references that point to where you can learn more about each topic:

- **Fill color** (page 192). To change a shape's fill color, select the shape and then head to the Format panel's Shape tab. Make sure the Fill checkbox is turned on, and then click the color swatch to its right to choose a new color. To completely remove the fill, simply select the shape and then turn off the Fill checkbox.

> **TIP** If you want your shape to have *some* color but still want to see what's underneath it (maybe your document's background image is so awe-inspiring, it'd be a crime against humanity to cover it up), you can change the shape's opacity. Select your shape, open the Format panel's Shape tab, and then adjust the Opacity setting. If you scale opacity down to 0%, the shape becomes completely transparent—and there's not much point in an invisible shape.

- **Borders** (page 198) give shapes a more fashionable edge. To add a border, select your shape, open the Format panel's Shape tab, and then turn on the Border checkbox. Pages displays settings for customizing the border (see Figure 28-6). The exact settings depend on what type of border you pick: a line border or a more extravagant picture frame border; use the drop-down menu at the top of the Border section to choose. With a line border, you can change the line's style (such as dashed or dotted), its thickness, and its color. With a picture frame border, you get the settings shown in Figure 28-6.

- **Shadows** (page 199) can really lift shapes off the page by creating a 3D effect. To add a shadow, select a shape, open the Format panel's Shape tab, and then turn on the Shadow checkbox. Doing so adds a basic, run-of-the-mill shadow to your shape and displays settings that let you adjust the shadow's blur, offset, opacity, angle, and color. They work the same way as in Pages for Mac.

- **Reflections** (page 199) can also create the illusion of depth and 3D-ness, by projecting a mirror image of your shape across the page. To add a reflection, select the shape, make sure the Format panel's Shape tab is open in the Format panel, and then turn on the Reflection checkbox. You can change the reflection's opacity using the familiar combination of slider, text field, and arrows. Unfortunately, you can't adjust the angle or location of the reflection—it always appears below your shape.

Working with Images

Shapes and text are a good start, but sooner or later you'll want to upload a photo of your cat, a self-portrait you took in your bathroom mirror, or a shot of the massive hamburger you ate for lunch. It couldn't be easier to add images to your Pages document: Just click the Image button in the toolbar, click Choose Image, and then track down the image file in the window that appears.

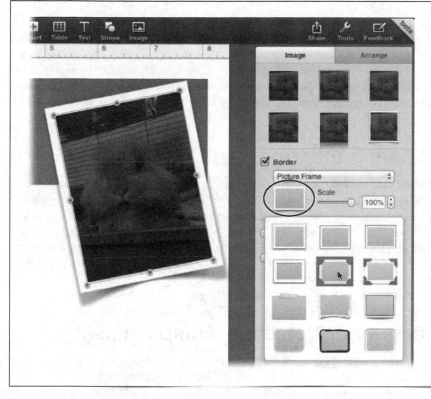

FIGURE 28-6

*Pages offers a selection of
frames ranging from fancy,
metal-edged ones, to an
effect that makes it look like
your shape or image has
been taped to the screen. To
go frame shopping, click the
frame thumbnail (circled), and
then click any of the frames in
the drop-down menu to add it
to your shape. You can make
the frame bigger or smaller
using the Scale slider or its
accompanying text field.*

> **NOTE** Image files can be no bigger than 2.4 megabytes in size. So if you see a dialog box telling you that
> your image was too large, switch to an image-editing program like iPhoto, make the image a bit smaller or lower
> its resolution, and then try again.

Just like with shapes, you can apply borders, reflections, and shadows to images using
the techniques described in the previous section. You can also change an image's
mask, which lets you create the impression that you've cropped the image without
actually making any permanent changes to it. Double-click any image to take a closer
look at its mask, and flip to page 11 for the details of working with image masks.

If you're in a hurry, why not use one of Pages' ready-and-raring-to-go styles? Simply
select your image, open the Format panel's Image tab, and then click any of the
thumbnails at the top of the tab to apply that style to your image.

Working with Tables

Tables are the perfect way to present large amounts of data in an easy-to-understand way. Tables are covered in detail on page 784, but here's a quick run-through.

You add a table to your document by clicking Table in the toolbar and choosing a table from the drop-down menu. Enter your data by double-clicking a cell and then typing. You can apply a selection of ready-made styles to your table via the Format panel's Table tab, where you can also change the number of headers and footers, as well as adjust the size of the text. To make more specific changes to the font used in different parts of your table, use the settings in the Format panel's Cell tab.

■ Printing Your Document

When you print a Pages for iCloud document, you're actually printing a PDF copy of it. (This doesn't have any impact on the master copy of your document—it's still safely saved in iCloud. PDF is just a format that ensures that your document will look the same no matter who opens it; see page 253 for more info.) To generate a PDF version for printing, click the Tools button in the toolbar, and then select Print. Wait a few moments while iCloud generates your PDF, click Open PDF, and then print it by selecting File→Print.

■ Password-Protecting Your Document

If your document needs a bit of extra protection, you can add a password to it by clicking the Tools button in the toolbar and then selecting Settings→Set Password. In the dialog box that appears, enter your password twice to prevent typos and, if you like, create a hint, which is useful if you're the forgetful type. Once you've entered all this info, click Set Password.

If you need to change your password at any point, go to Tools→Settings→Change Password, enter your old password, and then you're ready to create a new password: Click Change Password once you're done. To remove your password completely, go to Tools→Settings→Change Password, enter your old password, and then click Remove Password.

Keynote for iCloud

I t's a sad fact of life that inspiration strikes at the most inconvenient moments: when you're at the dry cleaner's, waiting in line at the post office, or wrestling a shark on the rim of an erupting volcano. When you finally settle down at your Mac with a fresh cup of coffee, tingling with anticipation at the thought of creating a Keynote presentation, inspiration is often nowhere to be found.

After wrestling a few half-decent slides out of your uncooperative gray matter, you head out on some mundane errand (like picking up the dry cleaning or checking that the perimeter is secured against zombies) and *bam*—inspiration strikes and you know exactly how to phrase that awkward bullet point on slide 72. Of course, by the time you're back at your computer, you can't *quite* recall the exact phrasing...

With Keynote for iCloud, rather than risking that perfect bullet point slipping through your fingers, you can borrow your buddy's MacBook or use Uncle Frank's PC, launch a compatible web browser (see page 750), log into iCloud.com (page 756), and the presentation you were working on in Keynote for iCloud is waiting for you. You make some changes, and then when you get home and hop on your Mac, those changes are reflected there, too. Handy!

Keynote for iCloud ensures that you can access all your presentations all the time. But what makes iCloud *extra* special is that it can actually link the version of Keynote that's on your Mac (see page 409 for more info) with the version that's on all your iDevices (page 752).

NOTE Quick reminder: *iDevice* is snappy shorthand for all the Apple devices that can run Keynote for iOS (specifically, the iPhone, iPad, and iPod Touch).

How does this work? Behind the scenes, any edits you make or documents you create in Keynote for iOS are shared with Keynote for iCloud, and vice versa. And if you have Keynote for iOS installed on more than one iDevice and the apps are all connected to the same iCloud account, then any changes are shared between the two apps (or three apps, four apps, and so on). You can also save Keynote for Mac documents to iCloud so that they appear in Keynote for iCloud, too (page 409 has the lowdown on saving Mac documents to iCloud).

You can access Keynote for iCloud on *any* computer that has Internet access. So imagine you get home and discover that your Mac has spontaneously combusted. No problem: Just dig out that old Windows laptop that's been collecting dust under your bed, use it to log into your iCloud account, and presto—there's your presentation, complete with all the changes you made on your Mac. With Keynote for iCloud in your corner, nothing can come between you and your presentation!

Keynote for iCloud is quite similar to Keynote for Mac. This chapter gives you an overview of how to use Keynote for iCloud and directs you to where you can learn more in other parts of this book.

> **NOTE** This chapter doesn't cover the nitty-gritty of connecting your iDevices to iCloud or creating an iCloud account. You can find that info on pages 752 and 750, respectively.

Creating a Presentation

You access Keynote for iCloud in exactly the same way as the other iWork for iCloud offerings: Launch a compatible web browser (they're listed on page 750), point it to *www.icloud.com*, and log in with your Apple ID and password.

Click the Keynote icon to launch Keynote for iCloud, and you arrive at Documents view, which looks almost exactly the same as Pages for iCloud's Documents view screen shown in Figure 28-1 (page 757). If you've linked your iCloud account to any Keynote for iOS apps or saved any Keynote for Mac presentations to iCloud, Documents view may already contain some presentations. Double-click a presentation's thumbnail to open it.

> **TIP** You can perform all sorts of useful tasks in Documents view, including downloading, duplicating, sharing, and deleting presentations. Flip to page 756 to see everything that Documents view is capable of.

Creating a presentation in Keynote for iCloud couldn't be easier: Click the big + sign that's labeled "Create Presentation." Doing so displays the Theme Chooser, which works just like the one in Keynote for Mac (page 280). Simply double-click the theme you want and Keynote creates a presentation based on it.

NOTE   You choose the size of your slides in advance. Choose from Standard (4:3 format) or Wide (16:9 format, which gives you a slightly stretched slide) by clicking the buttons at the top of the Template Chooser.

Your new presentation appears in a brand-new browser window (Figure 29-1 provides an overview). This is handy because it lets you have more than one presentation open. Simply switch back to the window where Documents view is displayed and open an existing presentation or create a new one, and that presentation appears in its own window. This is especially handy if you have two monitors connected to your computer—you can display one window on each screen.

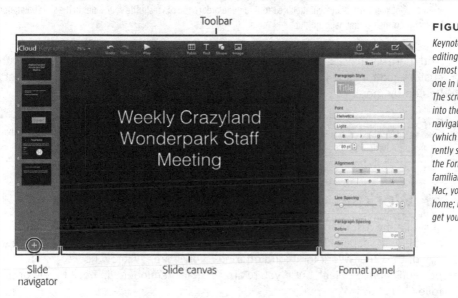

FIGURE 29-1

Keynote for iCloud's editing window looks almost exactly like the one in Keynote for Mac. The screen is divided into the toolbar, the slide navigator, the slide canvas (which displays the currently selected slide), and the Format panel. If you're familiar with Keynote for Mac, you'll feel right at home; if not, this book will get you there!

Depending on the layout you choose, the initial slide may arrive in your presentation with placeholder objects and text. To replace the dummy text, double-click it. To add images to your slide, go to the toolbar at the top of the screen and click Image→Choose Image. You can then select one of the image files that are hanging around on your computer to add it to your slide. To replace a placeholder image, click the icon in its bottom-right corner to launch a window where you can choose your own image.

The slide navigator displays all of your slides as thumbnails. Click any thumbnail to open that slide in the slide canvas so you can edit it.

To add a slide, click the + sign at the bottom of the slide navigator (it's circled in Figure 29-1). Keynote displays all the layouts that are part of your chosen theme; simply click your preferred layout. If none of these layouts fit the bill, use the blank layout instead (you may have to scroll down in the Add Slide menu to see it).

You can also copy an existing slide by Control-clicking its thumbnail in the slide navigator and then selecting New Slide (to create a new slide based on the selected slide's layout, containing the original layout's placeholder text and objects) or Duplicate (to create an *exact* duplicate of the selected slide—both its layout *and* any content you've added).

At some point you'll want to quietly bump off slides that have outlived their usefulness. To remove a slide, click its thumbnail in the slide navigator and then press the Delete key. You can also Control-click the slide's thumbnail in the navigator and then choose Delete.

TIP Not keen on your presentation's current running order? You can reshuffle your slides in the slide navigator by dragging their thumbnails around.

And there you have it, a basic (OK, *very* basic) Keynote presentation, complete with customized text and images as well as multiple slides. But Keynote for iCloud lets you do far more.

TIP Say you delete a slide and then immediately regret it. No problem—simply click Undo in the toolbar. See page 761 for everything you need to know about Undo and Redo.

■ Working with Objects 101

Just like the rest of the iWork crew, everything in Keynote for iCloud (whether it's an image, a shape, a text box, or whatever) is an *object*. If you've dipped a toe in any of the other iWork for iCloud offerings, you'll already know how to create that perfectly edited object, but if you're after a quick reminder, flip back to any of the following pages:

FOR MORE ABOUT...	...TURN TO THIS PAGE
Selecting objects	Page 765
Resizing objects	Page 765
Moving objects	Page 766
Deleting objects	Page 766
Copying, cutting, and pasting objects	Page 766
Rotating objects	Page 766
Grouping objects	Page 766
Aligning objects	Page 766
Adjusting an object's opacity	Page 768

Now that you know how to get an object just right, it's time to take the plunge and add some objects to your presentation.

As of this writing, you can't add audio and video clips to presentations in Keynote for iCloud. Also, if you open a presentation in Keynote for iCloud that you created in Keynote for Mac or iOS, you can't play any audio or video clips it contains. Apple claims that you'll be able to play such clips in iCloud "soon."

Adding Text to Slides

No matter how radical your presentation is, when you sit down to create a slide, some things are inevitable: You'll spend longer agonizing over slide transitions and animations than the actual content; you'll throw some crazy clip art into the mix to try to squeeze a laugh out of your audience; and eventually, there will be bullet points. There are *always* bullet points.

For those inevitable bullet-point situations (not to mention other types of text, like full sentences and paragraphs), click the Text button. Keynote drops a text box onto your slide, complete with a snippet of dummy text. If necessary, drag the text box into a new position. To resize the box, simply drag the blue resizing handles around its edge. Then double-click the text box to place your cursor inside it and start typing, and the box magically expands as you type.

TIP If rectangular and square text boxes are too restrictive for a free spirit such as yourself, you can use *shapes* as containers for text, too. Stay tuned for more about shapes.

Keynote, like all its iWork brethren, puts an emphasis on visual flair, so it's no surprise that you can turn plain old text into something dazzling (if you're the sort of person who gets dazzled by nicely formatted text, that is). The Format panel has a ton of options for customizing text, from font-based tweaks such as color and size, right through to sweeping changes like altering the line and paragraph spacing. Root through the Format panel yourself, or hop back to page 761 to read all about the formatting options iCloud offers.

Adding Shapes to Slides

Shapes play many roles in Keynote, whether it's an arrow pointing to a bullet point that's just too good to ignore or a gold star that drives home just how great your presentation truly is. But you can also use shapes as containers for text; for example, you can add a speech bubble that lets the cuddly cats in your images dispense their words of wisdom.

To add a shape to your presentation, click the Shape button in the toolbar and select a shape from the drop-down menu. (Don't worry if you're not thrilled about the color or shading of the shapes in this menu—you can easily change them. Simply click the shape that's closest to what you're after.) Keynote drops the shape onto your slide. You can perform all the usual object edits on the shape, such as moving or resizing it. For a recap of all your options, see the table on page 774.

Once you've finished editing your shape at the object level, you may want to make some stylistic changes, such as adding a border or changing the shape's color. The quickest way to give your shape a style makeover is to select it and then click any of the ready-baked styles at the top of the Format panel's Shape tab.

If you're after a style that'll make your audience sit up straight and pay attention, select your shape and then invest some time exploring the Format panel's Shape tab. The settings there let you change a shape's fill color, borders, shadow, reflection, and opacity; page 767 has the details. Figure 29-2 shows an example of what you can do.

FIGURE 29-2

Turn on the Reflection checkbox to add a faded mirror image of a shape. You can then change its opacity either by manipulating the slider (where the cursor is here), clicking the text field next to it and typing out a new number, or clicking the little arrow buttons.

> **NOTE** As already mentioned, shapes can be text containers, too. To add text to a shape, double-click the shape to place your cursor inside it, and then start typing. All the usual text-formatting options apply, so flip to page 761 for a run-through of all the funky things you can do with text.

Adding Images to Slides

Whether you're using a relevant image to reinforce your point, or using a picture of a llama on a jet ski to bring some fun to your three-hour presentation on *The World's Rarest Soil Types & Where to Find Them*, images are essential for creating a visually attractive and engaging presentation.

Adding images to a Keynote slide is a snap: Simply click the Image button in the toolbar, and then click Choose Image. This launches a window where you can hunt out the image on your computer and then upload it to your slide.

If you have the image file close by (saved on your desktop, for example), it may be quicker to drag it onto your slide. Just pay special attention to where you drop it:

- Dropping it onto a blank area of a slide adds it as a new object.

- Dropping it on a shape replaces the shape but uses the shape's dimensions as an image mask (see page 11 for more on image masks). So, if you drop the image onto a star, you end up with a star shaped image. Spend some time experimenting to see what effects you can create.

- Dropping it onto an existing image replaces the original and uses its dimensions.

Images are objects, so when it comes to performing edits such as resizing, rotating, aligning and so on, all the usual rules apply (skip back to page 756 for a recap). You can also tweak the image's style (would that llama on a jet ski have more pizazz if it were framed or had a shadow?) using the Format panel's Image tab. There you'll find settings for adjusting the image's border, shadow, reflection, and opacity; see page 768 for details.

TIP You can apply prebuilt styles to an image by selecting it and then clicking any of the thumbnails at the top of the Image tab. They may not be the most adventurous styles you can cook up in Keynote, but they're the quickest.

Adding Tables to Slides

Tables may not spring to mind when you think of presentations, but a simple table can be useful for backing up an argument with cold, hard facts. Generally speaking, it's a bad idea to include a large, data-packed table in your presentation and then expect your audience to read it as you're delivering your talk. But you may also want to include tables if you're planning to make your slides available to your audience after your presentation, for example by printing them off or by emailing them around (see page 759) so they can study the table at length.

To add a table, click the Table button in the toolbar, select the table that's the closest to what you had in mind, and then drag, resize, and restyle it as required. Page 784 takes a closer look at working with tables in iCloud.

■ Transitioning Between Slides

A transition is a short animation that plays whenever you move from one slide to the next—it's basically how a slide *exits* the screen. Whether you want a slide to pivot, twirl, or swoosh offscreen, Keynote for iCloud has all the effects you need to really liven up your presentation. Just be wary of cramming *loads* of different transitions into your presentation: If each slide swoops and spins onscreen from different directions, you may leave your poor audience feeling dizzy.

To apply a transition, click a slide's thumbnail in the slide navigator (remember: you're animating the slide's *exit*), and the Format panel displays the Slide Transition tab, which contains all your options. See Figure 29-3 for a peek at what's available.

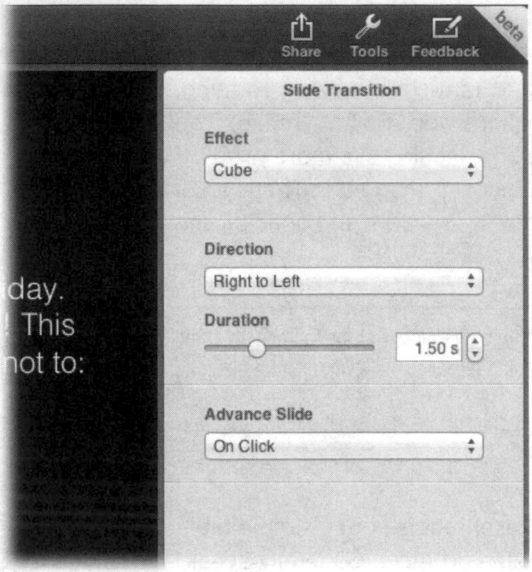

FIGURE 29-3

When you choose an option from the Slide Transition tab's Effect drop-down menu, other settings appear that are related to that effect. Here, the Cube effect is selected, and the Direction and Duration settings let you customize the effect.

As of this writing, you can't animate individual objects in Keynote for iCloud like you can in Keynote for Mac (page 354). So if you're itching to make your bulleted list appear one bullet point at a time, you'll have to use Keynote for Mac to do that—build-in and build-out effects aren't available in iCloud just yet. Also, the Magic Move transition (page 356) isn't currently available in Keynote for iCloud, either.

After you make a choice from the Effect drop-down menu, you can see your transition in action by clicking the Play button in the toolbar at the top of the screen. Keynote switches into Play mode (which you can exit by pressing Esc). To see your transition do its thing, give the window a click. If you're not happy with the transition, exit Play mode and then adjust the Slide Transition tab's settings until you find a transition that's more to your liking.

That's all you need to create a basic slide transition, but in typical iWork style, there are a couple of ways you can customize things.

Presentation running too long? Or are you struggling to find things to talk about and need to stretch your material out a little? You can change the duration of your transitions using the Slide Transition tab's Duration setting.

The second tweak up for grabs is changing how your transition is triggered. Keynote assumes you're the controlling type, so unless you specify otherwise, it waits for you to click the mouse before transitioning to the next slide. This type of trigger is known as On Click, but you can also tell Keynote to transition to the next slide automatically after a certain period. Automatic slide transitions work well if you've got your presentation timed down to the second or if you want your slideshow to rumble along in the background while you're presenting.

To change how your slide transition is triggered, head to the Slide Transition tab's Advance Slide drop-down menu. Choose Automatically, and then use the Delay setting that appears to tell Keynote how many seconds it should wait before triggering the slide transition.

> **TIP** However you customize your slide transitions, remember that you can see them in action anytime by clicking the Play button in the toolbar.

These are just the basics of slide transitions. For lots more info, head to page 351.

■ Sharing, Protecting, and Printing Your Presentations

Just like in Pages for iCloud, Keynote for iCloud makes it easy to share your presentations. Pages 758–759 have the details about inviting other people to collaborate on your documents and sending them copies via email. If you *don't* want anyone else's eyes on your document, you may want to add a password for extra security—page 770 has the scoop.

Alas, you don't have as many printing options in Keynote for iCloud as you do in Keynote for Mac. In fact, your *only* option is to print a PDF version of your presentation (see page 770). So, if you want to take advantage of Keynote for Mac's fancy printing features (page 399), you'll have to use the Mac version instead.

Numbers for iCloud

W e live in a crazy world, where you never know when you might suddenly need access to your spreadsheets. Maybe you're out and about when you spot the cappuccino machine of your dreams, but you need to review this month's expenses before splurging. Maybe you forgot to bring a printout of the spreadsheet proving your stellar attendance record to your dreaded performance meeting. Or maybe you bump into your childhood friend at the train station and she wants to know what you've been up to since high school (hey, there's no reason why you can't keep a spreadsheet of things like that).

Whenever unforeseen spreadsheet-related drama occurs, Numbers for iCloud gets you out of these tight spots by letting you access all of your Numbers for iCloud documents from any computer or iDevice with an Internet connection. (Remember, an iDevice is an iPhone, iPad, or iPhone Touch). In this chapter, you get up close and personal with Numbers for iCloud by learning how to create and edit spreadsheets.

NOTE If you connect the Numbers for iOS app to iCloud, then your spreadsheets are available the second you log into Numbers for iCloud. If this sounds like a good deal, check out page 752, which shows you how to connect iOS apps to iCloud. Likewise, if you've been saving and sharing your Numbers for Mac documents to iCloud, those spreadsheets will be waiting for you, too (see page 670 for more info).

And remember: You can use all the iWork for iCloud apps (Pages, Keynote, and Numbers) on Macs *and* PCs. See page 756 for info on the minor differences you'll encounter if you're on a PC.

■ Creating a Document

The first step to becoming a spreadsheet ninja is logging into your Numbers for iCloud account. (No iCloud account? No problem! Page 750 explains how to create one.) Launch a compatible web browser (page 750), and point it to *www.icloud. com*. Log into your account, and then click the Numbers icon to hop straight into *Documents view.* Figure 30-1 explains how to create a new document from there.

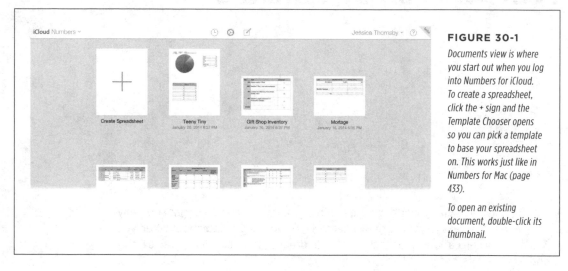

FIGURE 30-1

Documents view is where you start out when you log into Numbers for iCloud. To create a spreadsheet, click the + sign and the Template Chooser opens so you can pick a template to base your spreadsheet on. This works just like in Numbers for Mac (page 433).

To open an existing document, double-click its thumbnail.

Documents view is also where you can upload PDFs and Excel spreadsheets to Numbers for iCloud (along with any Numbers documents that are floating around on your computer, like ones you received via email, or that you downloaded). To upload one of these files, click the gear icon in the toolbar, select Upload Spreadsheet, and then choose the file to upload. Or, if you have the file somewhere close by (on your desktop, say), simply drag it onto your web browser and drop it into Documents view.

If you want to download a file from iCloud, click the spreadsheet's thumbnail in Documents view, and then open the gear menu and select Download Spreadsheet. You can then choose from Numbers, Excel, or PDF format. Pick your favorite, and Numbers downloads the file in your format of choice.

The other features of Numbers for iCloud's Documents view work just like in Pages for iCloud (except that most commands include the word "Spreadsheet" rather than "Document"). For an overview of how to duplicate, delete, rename, share, and sort spreadsheets, flip to pages 757–758.

Adding Sheets to Your Document

As you learned on page 446, Numbers spreadsheets are made up of sheets. Spreading your content across different sheets breaks it up into easy-to-digest chunks and lets you create clear divisions within your content. For example, a Budget spreadsheet might contain one sheet for earnings and one for expenses.

Adding more sheets is easy: Just click the + tab above the sheet canvas. Numbers gives the new sheet an uninspired title like Sheet 1. To trade this Dullsville title in for something more exciting, double-click the title, type a better one, and then save your change by clicking anywhere outside the tab or by pressing Return.

Once you start adding sheets, at some point you'll want to delete them, too. To delete, Control-click (right-click on a PC) the sheet's tab, and then select Delete Sheet; the sheet becomes a distant memory.

■ Working with Objects

Everything you add to a spreadsheet is an object, whether that's an image, table, chart, or shape. Happily, once you know how to edit one type of object, you pretty much know how to edit them all. Page 765 has all the info you need on performing object edits such as resizing and moving. You can also change an object's angle, group and ungroup objects to perform time-saving mass edits, and get objects perfectly aligned (page 766).

> **TIP** If you make a mistake during an object-editing frenzy, such as deleting an object by accident, don't fret. Numbers lets you undo your recent changes by pressing ⌘-Z on a Mac (Ctrl+Z on a PC), or by clicking the Undo button in the iCloud toolbar.

Although every spreadsheet is created with a full cast of placeholder objects and text, sooner or later you'll want to add objects of your very own. The following sections give you an overview of working with the various object types—except for tables. These are so important in Numbers that they get their own section, which begins on the next page.

> **TIP** No matter what kind of object you're working with, Numbers has a handful of ready-made styles that your object can try on for size. Depending on the object, these styles could include anything from border effects to different colors. To apply a premade style, select the object, and the styles appear as thumbnails at the top of the Format panel's leftmost tab—if you select a shape, this is the Shape tab; if you select a table, it's the Table tab; and so on. (Quick reminder: The Format panel is the pane on the right side of the Numbers window, just like in Numbers for Mac; see page 435 for a refresher.) Click any style's thumbnail to apply it to your object.

Working with Text Boxes and Shapes

Numbers' main focus may be on graphs and tables, but without any text, graphs and tables are just a bunch of boring old lines. To add a text box to your document, click the Text button in the toolbar. Then double-click the text box and start typing.

You can also use shapes as containers for text. See page 767 for the lowdown on adding shapes and how to use them as text containers. While you're there, you might want to learn how to apply a stylish border, reflection, or other neat effect to your shape.

iWork is all about style, so it's no surprise that Numbers for iCloud doesn't restrict you to boring text. You can use the Text tab on the right side of the Numbers window to change the font; adjust the text size; pick the text's color; apply a bold, italic, underlined, or strikethrough effect; and change the text's alignment and spacing.

If you're itching to beautify your text, page 762 covers formatting text in both text boxes *and* shapes. And page 764 has the lowdown on spell checking.

Working with Images

It may seem like all Numbers cares about are facts and figures, but it knows how to have a good time, too. You're welcome to add images to your spreadsheets to spice things up. Click the Image button in the toolbar, click Choose Image, and then pick the image you want to add. You can perform all the usual edits to the image, such as resizing and relocating it (page 765), and make stylistic changes, such as adding borders and shadow effects (page 768) or changing the image's mask (see page 769).

■ Working with Tables

Tables are, without a doubt, the most important part of Numbers. Tables are such a big part of the whole Numbers experience that, no matter which template you choose when you create your document, you get a placeholder table at no extra cost! This section shows you how to turn that bland old placeholder into something wild and unique (well, as wild and unique as it's possible for a table to be, anyway).

Generally speaking, you work with tables in Numbers for iCloud just like you work with them in Numbers for Mac. This chapter gives you a brief overview, points out any discrepancies, and tells you where you can find more information earlier in this book.

Before entering your own data in a placeholder table, you'll want to remove any dummy data that's already there. You can remove it on a cell-by-cell basis by clicking a cell and then hitting the Delete key, or drag over the table to select the cells you want to clear, and then press Delete. Rinse and repeat until all the placeholder data is no more.

If you take an instant dislike to the table(s) that arrive as part of your template, or if you want to invite even more tables to the party, you can add a blank table to your spreadsheet by clicking the Table button in the toolbar and then selecting one of the options in the drop-down menu.

All tables have a title—although this title may not be visible. If your table's title is hidden, you can make it visible by opening the Format panel's Table tab (shown in Figure 30-5) and turning the Name checkbox on. After that, you can type a new title in the text field next to the checkbox. To hide the title, simply turn off the Name checkbox. Doing so doesn't delete the title—you can recover it anytime by turning the Name checkbox back on.

Regardless of whether a table arrives as part of your template or you create it yourself, you change the table's appearance and data in exactly the same way:

- **Adding rows and columns:** Just like in Numbers for Mac, tables in Numbers for iCloud have handles at each of their four corners. The handles look a bit different than in Numbers for Mac (see Figure 30-2), but they work the same way:

  - To add a new column to the right edge of your table, click the handle in the table's top-right corner; to add multiple columns, drag this handle to the right instead.

  - To add an extra row to the bottom of your table, click the handle in the table's bottom-left corner; to add several rows, drag the handle downward instead.

  - To add columns and rows simultaneously, drag the handle in the table's bottom-right corner: As you drag downward, extra rows appear, and as you drag to the right, extra columns appear.

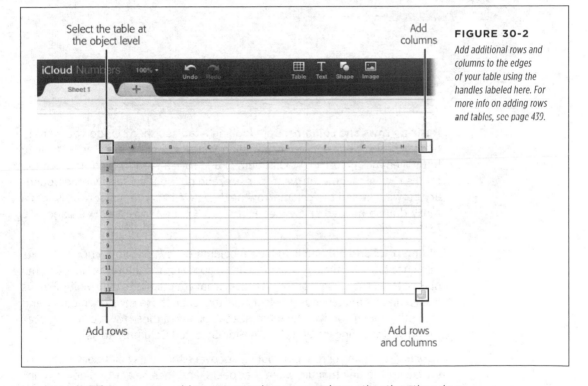

Select the table at the object level

Add columns

Add rows

Add rows and columns

FIGURE 30-2

Add additional rows and columns to the edges of your table using the handles labeled here. For more info on adding rows and tables, see page 439.

But what if you want to add a row or a column somewhere other than the edges of your table? The key to creating a column or a row in a specific location is the table's *reference tabs* (Figure 30-3). Reference tabs work the same way in Numbers for iCloud as they do in iWork for Mac—they just look slightly different in the two versions; see page 437 for a refresher.

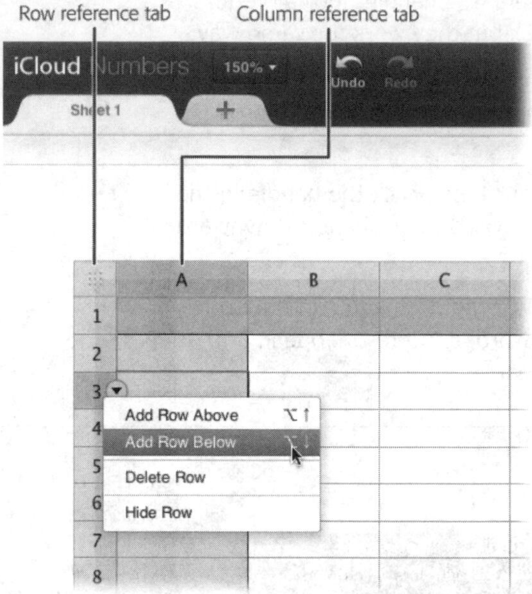

FIGURE 30-3

Use the table's reference tabs to tell Numbers where to add a new column or row. Put your cursor over the reference tab where you want to insert a row or column, click the tiny triangle when it appears, and then choose an option from the drop-down menu. For rows, you can choose between Add Row Above and Add Row Below; for columns, your options are Add Column Before and Add Column After.

- **Resizing rows and columns:** Data looking a tad squished? Or do you want to fill that pesky white space by spreading your table out a bit? The answer to both dilemmas is resizing your columns and rows. Head to the reference tab for the row or column you want to resize, and put your cursor over the boundary between it and the column/row next to it. When your cursor turns into a funky double-headed arrow (see Figure 30-4), drag to resize. See page 496 for more info.

- **Hiding rows and columns:** To hide a column or row, put your cursor over its reference tab, click the tiny triangle when it appears, and then click Hide Column or Hide Row. The column or row vanishes from your table. To hide multiple rows and columns simultaneously, select cells that span those rows or columns, and then put your cursor over the reference tab of any of those rows/columns, click the arrow that appears, and choose Hide Selected Columns/Rows.

  To *unhide* a column or row, put your cursor over either of its neighbors' reference tabs, click the tiny triangle when it appears, and then select Unhide Column/Row. To uncover *all* hidden rows, put your cursor over any row's reference tab, click the triangle, and then select "Unhide All Rows." If you're hunting for hidden columns instead, head to any column's reference tab, click the arrow, and choose "Unhide All Columns." See page 499 for more on hiding and unhiding table elements.

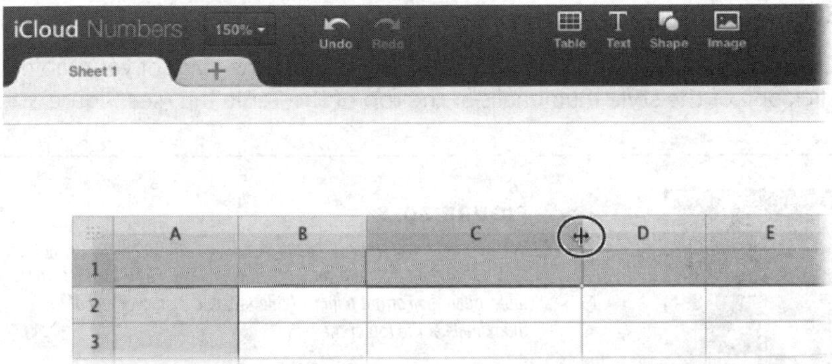

FIGURE 30-4

To resize a column, put your cursor over the boundary between it and its neighbor to the right. To resize a row, place your cursor over the boundary between it and the row beneath it. When the double-headed arrow appears (circled), drag to resize.

- **Deleting rows and columns:** To delete an *empty* row, drag the table's bottom-left handle across the rows you want to remove. To delete an *empty* column, drag the top-right handle across the columns to remove. To delete empty rows *and* columns, drag the bottom-right handle. To delete columns or rows that contain actual content, you'll need to hold down the Option key as you drag one of the handles.

  To delete a specific row or column (one in the middle of your table, say), put your cursor over its reference tab, click the tiny triangle when it appears, and then select Delete Row or Delete Column. To delete multiple rows or columns, select cells spanning the rows or columns earmarked for removal, and then go to one of their tab references and choose Delete Selected Rows/Columns. See page 490 for more info.

- **Moving rows and columns:** To move a column or row around your table, click that column or row's reference tab once to select it, and then drag it to its new home. Page 498 has more about moving table elements around.

- **Sorting table data:** You can reorder the data within a column, based on the contents of each cell in that column. Put your cursor over the column's reference tab, click the tiny triangle when it appears, and then select Sort Ascending (that's either A, B, C or 1, 2, 3) or Sort Descending (C, B, A or 3, 2, 1). See page 500 for more info.

- **Adjusting headers and footers:** Most tables in Numbers have a header row and/or a header column (page 492), and some also have footer rows (page 495). To add or remove headers and footers, go to the Format panel's Table tab and use the drop-down menus in the Headers & Footer section (shown in Figure 30-5). To freeze a header row or column so that it remains onscreen no matter how much you scroll (page 494), select Freeze Header Row or Freeze Header Column from the appropriate drop-down menu.

- **Merging table cells:** To merge a group of adjacent cells, select all the cells you want to smoosh together (they have to be adjacent), and then open the Format panel's Cell tab and click the Merge button. To resume treating merged cells as individuals, select the merged cell, and then click the Cell tab's Unmerge button. See page 464 for the full story on merging and unmerging.

- **Colorizing table cells:** The quickest way to change the color of your table is to click one of the style thumbnails at the top of the Table tab (see Figure 30-5).

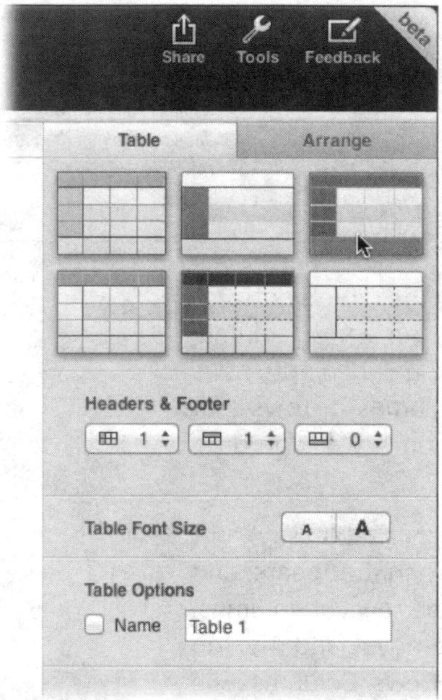

FIGURE 30-5

Numbers has several ready-baked styles that you can apply to your tables, including different color schemes. To apply a style, select the table, open the Format panel's Table tab, and then click any of the thumbnails at the top of the tab.

To use a color that's not included in any style, or just to harness the full power of the rainbow:

1. **Select the cell(s) to apply the new color to.**

   Either click a cell, drag to select a whole bunch of cells, or select an entire row or column by clicking its reference tab.

2. **In the Format panel, click the Cell tab and turn on the Fill checkbox.**

   A color swatch appears next to this checkbox.

3. **Click the swatch and choose a new color.**

   Numbers applies this color to all of your selected cells.

Adding Data to Tables

Your table is now a fetching shade of sunshine yellow, interspersed with rows of lime green, and has the right number of rows, columns, headers, and footers. Isn't it time to add some data to your perfect canvas?

You can add data to your table by double-clicking a cell and typing, but if you're entering a particular *type* of data, for example percentages or currency, typing out those supporting characters (such as $ and %) quickly becomes downright annoying. Happily, Numbers lets you specify the kind of data you're entering by choosing a *data format*. Data formats include currencies and percentages, as well as more unusual options like star ratings and steppers. Not only does specifying the data format save you time, but it helps you easily achieve a consistent format across all your cells.

To choose a data format, select all the cells you want to format by dragging over them, or select a whole row/column by clicking its reference (Shift-click to select multiple columns/rows). Then open the Format panel's Data tab and select your preferred format from the Data Format drop-down menu (see page 473 for a rundown of all the options). The Format panel then displays settings for fine-tuning your chosen format (for example, if you choose Currency, you can tell Numbers whether to use a $ or £ and so on). Figure 30-6 gives you an idea of some of the extra options you can choose from.

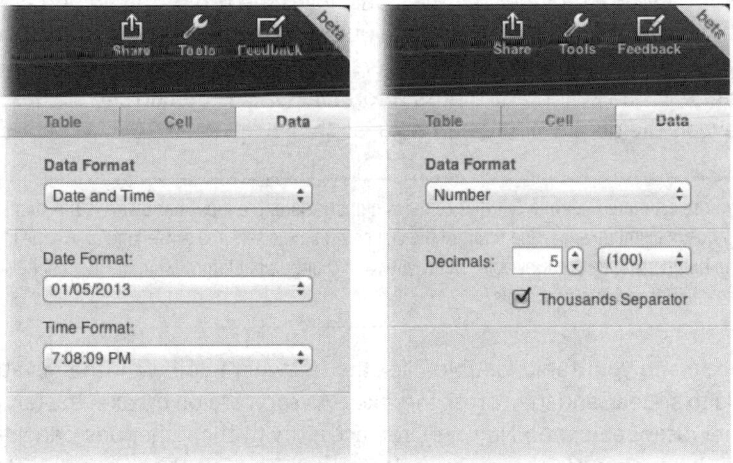

FIGURE 30-6

Depending on what you select in the Data Format drop-down, you'll see different data formatting options. This screenshot shows a couple of examples.

TIP Just like Numbers for Mac, Numbers for iCloud includes *autofill* (page 483), a handy feature that can help you quickly enter lots of data. The only difference between the two versions is that, in Numbers for iCloud, you autofill by dragging the selection handle in a cell's bottom-right corner rather than the yellow fill handle you get in Numbers for Mac).

If the text in your table is forcing you to squint, or it's so big that you feel like you're being shouted at, you can crank up or scale down all the text within the table. Simply click anywhere in the table to select it, and then open the Format panel's Table tab and click the Table Font Size buttons.

If this method isn't exact enough for you (if you know your text should be precisely 12 points, say), don't worry. Numbers lets you change the text size for a single cell, group of cells, or even on a per-word or per-letter basis. See page 761 for the low-down on formatting text.

Formulas and Functions

Think of formulas as your own personal accountant, crunching all of your data, doing sums, comparing and contrasting cells, and serving up the answers you're looking for, all wrapped up in a neat little bow (OK, the bow's a bit of an exaggeration). This may sound a bit over the top if your goal is simply to create a table that tracks how many vacation days you've got left at work, but formulas and functions are useful for these day-to-day tables too, not just for hardcore number-crunching.

Formulas (Chapter 19) and functions (Chapter 20) work almost exactly the same in Numbers for iCloud as they do in Numbers for Mac. However, the two versions of the program are laid out slightly differently, so a quick tour is in order.

In Numbers for iCloud, the *input bar* that runs along the top of the editing area is your key to formulas and functions. When you select a cell, its contents appear in the input bar. If the cell contains plain numbers or letters, the input bar looks pretty much the same as the cell, but if there's a formula lurking behind the scenes, the input bar reveals the details of your formula, as shown in Figure 30-7.

NOTE If you select more than one cell that contains numeric data, the input bar displays the sum, average, minimum value, maximum value, and count of the values within the selected cells—kind of like the Instant Calculation bar in Numbers for Mac. However, in iCloud, you can't change what information the input bar displays or drag formulas out of it and into your table.

To add a formula to your table, double-click the cell where you want the results of your formula to appear, and then press the = key. As soon as you press =, the familiar Format panel disappears, and Numbers replaces it with the Functions panel, and the Formula Editor appears above your selected cell. The Functions panel contains all the functions you need to build all sorts of funky formulas, so spend some time poking around in it (see page 229 for details). When you find a function you want to use, double-click its name, and Numbers adds it to your formula. (You can also add a function by selecting it and then clicking the Insert Function button.) When your formula looks good, press Return or click the Formula Editor's checkmark.

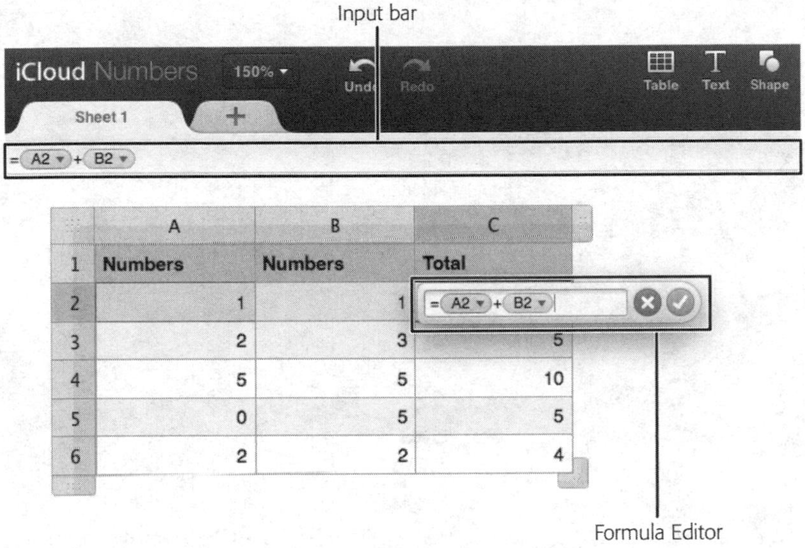

FIGURE 30-7

If you select a cell that's powered by a formula, the full formula appears in the input bar. This formula adds the value in cell A2 (1) to the value in cell B2 (1), so the data that ultimately appears in the selected cell (C2) will be 2. (See page 527 for the lowdown on cell references.)

TIP If you're unhappy with your formula, double-click its cell to reopen the Formula Editor. Then press the Delete key to remove the offending sections. Remember to press Return or click the checkmark to save your changes.

Chapter 19 has *tons* more info about the Formula Editor (page 523) and formulas in general, so if you want to be a formula master, that's the place to turn. And Chapter 20 covers the Functions panel and explains how to use Numbers' most helpful functions.

■ Sharing and Printing Presentations

Just like the other iWork for iCloud offerings, Numbers for iCloud lets you invite other people to collaborate on your spreadsheets. Page 758 has everything you need to know about sharing iCloud documents.

To print your spreadsheet, you need to generate a PDF version of it and then print out that PDF (see page 770). Or you can download a copy of your Numbers for iCloud document (see page 758) and then print out the downloaded document.

TIP As page 770 explains, you can also password-protect your document for extra security.

Appendix

APPENDIX A:
Installing and Upgrading iWork

Installing and Upgrading iWork

Installing iWork on your Mac or iOS device is a fairly straightforward process—essentially, you grab both sets of apps from the App Store, which comes preinstalled on your Mac or iDevice (see the box below). This appendix explains the details of the installation process, as well as how to install iWork for iOS apps on multiple iDevices, how you might be entitled to free iWork apps, and how to keep your apps up to date.

But before you can install iWork anywhere, you need an Apple ID.

What's with All the App Stores?

It's easy to get confused by the different App Stores that Apple runs. Here's the lowdown:

Apple's App Store is an online store where you can download apps for your iDevice. To download apps via the App Store, you use the App Store *app* that comes preinstalled on your iDevice.

The iDevice App Store is different from the *Mac* App Store that you see in your Mac's Dock. You use the Mac's online App Store to (surprise, surprise) purchase programs that run on your Mac.

If you're wondering where iTunes fits into all of this, iTunes is an app that contains the iDevice App Store and lots of other music- and entertainment-related goodies. You can use the iTunes store to download things such as TV shows and movies directly to your iDevice. (See *http://support.apple.com/kb/HT1491* for more on using iTunes with your iDevice.)

In this appendix, the only App Stores you need to worry about are the ones that come preinstalled on your iDevice and Mac.

■ Creating Your Apple ID

Your Apple ID is your key to everything Apple has to offer. Whether you're logging into iCloud.com (page 750), purchasing Pages for iOS from the App Store, or reserving the latest MacBook at your local Apple retail store, you need an Apple ID. If you're already wielding your Apple ID like a pro, skip ahead to page 798.

> **NOTE** Even if you're downloading the iWork apps as freebies, you still need a valid Apple ID.

Apple IDs are free to create; all you need is the following:

- **An Internet connection.**
- **A web browser.**
- **A working email address.**
- **A computer-type device.** Your Apple ID remains the same regardless of the device you use to create it on. However, creating an Apple ID requires a fair bit of typing, so it's far easier to create your Apple ID on something that boasts a computer-sized keyboard—like, say, a *Mac*.

If you already have an Apple ID but can't remember how to log into it, see the box below for help.

FREQUENTLY ASKED QUESTION

Recovering a Lost Apple ID or Password

Help! I know I already have an Apple ID, but I've forgotten my username and/or password. What should I do?

Say you created an Apple ID account when you bought your Mac but now can't remember your username. To prove to your poor, neglected Apple ID account that you still care, open your web browser and point it to *https://appleid.apple.com*. There, click the "Find your Apple ID" link, enter your info (name, address, email—the usual), and then click Next. Verify your identity either by answering the security questions you created when you set up your Apple ID (hopefully you haven't forgotten you mother's maiden name along with your password!) or by requesting that Apple send a password-reset email to your *rescue email address*.

(Rescue email addresses are a handy way of recovering your Apple ID when you've forgotten your password. You can cre-

ate a rescue email address when you first set up your Apple ID, or you can add a rescue email address to an existing account [covered on page 798]. If your Apple ID account has a rescue email address, the latter option tends to be the most straightforward.)

After answering the security questions or following the instructions in the email Apple sent to your rescue email address, you can create a new password and resume using your Apple ID.

If you know your Apple ID username but have forgotten your password, head to *https://appleid.apple.com*, click the "Reset your password" link, and then enter your Apple ID. Next, prove your identity by answering your security questions or asking Apple to send a password-reset email to your rescue email address.

To create an Apple ID, check that you're connected to the Internet, launch your web browser of choice (Safari, perhaps), and then head to *www.appleid.apple.com*. This website (shown in Figure A-1) is your go-to spot for all Apple ID–related activity, so it's worth bookmarking.

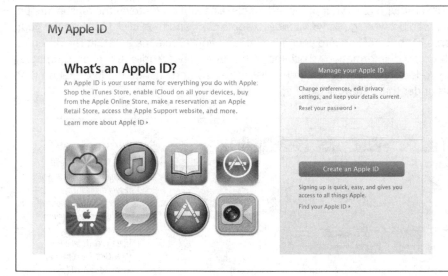

The Apple ID website has everything you need to manage your account. From here you can create an Apple ID, update an existing account, and learn more about Apple IDs. To do some background reading before signing up, click the "Learn more about Apple ID" link.

To create your ID, click the big blue "Create an Apple ID" button, and then enter all of your info, including your security questions and answers, date of birth, and full name and address. You can also create an optional (but advisable) rescue email address; the box on page 796 explains how it can come in handy.

TIP The email address you enter when creating your Apple ID serves as your username, so choose an active, genuine email address that you can remember. It's always a good idea to use your main email address (the one you use most often, if you have more than one) for something as important as an Apple ID.

After entering all of your information, scroll to the bottom of the screen and click Create Apple ID. Apple responds by firing off an email to the address you entered. This email contains a Verify Now link that you need to click before you can access your Apple ID. So log into your email account, open the "Please verify..." email, and then click the Verify Now link. Alternatively, you can copy the link and paste it into your browser.

TIP Apple ID emails tend to arrive pretty quickly, so if your verification email doesn't make an appearance within a few minutes, be suspicious. Check your email account's Spam and Trash folders, and if it's *still* nowhere to be found, double-check that your Internet connection is working.

Apple is a polite global corporation, so expect to receive a cheerful "Thank you for creating your Apple ID" email. As soon as this email pops into your inbox, your Apple ID is good to go.

■ MODIFYING YOUR APPLE ID

At some point, you may need to change the info associated with your Apple ID account. Maybe you moved, changed phone numbers, or want to add five random-ized hieroglyphics to your password for extra security. Whatever the reason, fire up your web browser, go to *www.appleid.apple.com*, and then click the "Manage your Apple ID" button. Log into your account, and you'll see a menu listing the different categories of information associated with your account (addresses, phone numbers, and so forth). Click any item in this list to review and change the information that falls under that category (see Figure A-2).

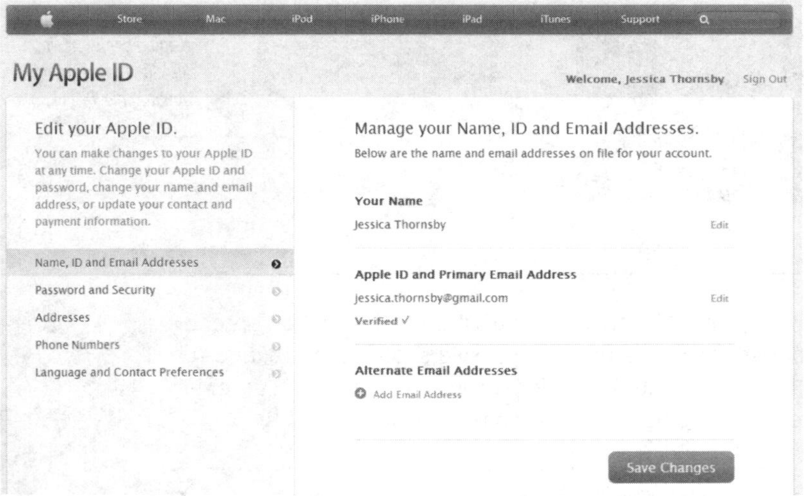

FIGURE A-2

Log into your Apple ID account and select any cat-egory in the list on the left to review all the info that falls under that category. To make a change to any item, click its blue Edit link. Click Save Changes to make your edits permanent. Depending on the info you're editing, you may also spot an Add button that lets you add more information, such as a second email address.

You can add a rescue email address or change the address you're currently using by selecting "Password and Security" in the left-hand menu, verifying your identity by entering your security information, and then scrolling down to the Rescue Email Address section. There, you can add, edit, and delete rescue email address info.

■ Installing and Updating iWork for Mac

If you're the owner of a new Mac (specifically, one purchased on or after October 1, 2013, that arrived with OS X Mavericks installed), you can get all three of the iWork for Mac apps for *free*. (You can check what version of OS X your Mac is running by going to →About This Mac; Mavericks is version 10.9).

To install iWork on the Mac, launch the App Store by clicking its icon in the Dock. In the Search bar in the upper-right corner of the App Store, type the name of the app you're looking for (Pages, Keynote, or Numbers—or type *iWork* to search for all three). As you type, a drop-down menu shows a list of suggestions; when you spot the one you're after, click it to perform a search based on that word or phrase.

Alternatively, type out your full search term and then either hit the Return key on your keyboard or click the little magnifying glass in the Search bar.

The Search page shows all the apps that match your search terms. To view more information about each app, click the app's thumbnail or title, and a page dedicated to that app opens, complete with customer reviews, screenshots, and similar apps you might be interested in. To go ahead and purchase the current app, click the blue price button to turn it into a green Buy App button. Click this button once again and, if you aren't already signed into your Apple ID account, the App Store asks for your Apple ID and password. Enter this information, click Sign In, and the App Store downloads the app of your choice.

Once the download is complete, launch the app by opening the Finder window, going to the Applications folder, and double-clicking the app's icon.

To check for updates to the iWork apps, open the App Store and click the Updates button in the toolbar at the top of the window. The Updates screen lists all available updates for the apps on your Mac. For each update you want to install, click the Update button (or click Update All to download the whole shebang).

Reinstalling iWork Apps on Your Mac

If you accidentally delete the iWork apps or get a new Mac and want to reinstall your favorite apps on your shiny new machine, you can reinstall any apps you've already bought—as long as you're using the same Apple ID. To reinstall an app, open the App Store and make sure you're using the correct Apple ID by going to Store→View My Account. Once you're certain you're logged into the right account, click the Purchases button at the top of the window to see a list of all the apps you've bought with the current Apple ID account.

To install any app you've purchased but, for whatever reason, don't currently have on this machine, click the Download button that appears next to that app.

■ Installing iWork for iOS

With your Apple ID all set up, you can get your hands on the iWork apps for iOS. To get started, ensure that your iDevice is connected to the Internet, and then go to your *home screen* (the main screen you see when you turn on your iDevice) and tap the App Store icon (it's blue). If you don't see the App Store icon on your home screen, swipe the screen from left to right, and then, in the Search field that appears, type *App Store.* If you *still* can't locate the App Store app, see Figure A-3 for instructions on how to coax it out of hiding.

Getting the iWork Apps for Free

If you're the owner of a shiny new iDevice—one that you bought and activated after September 1, 2013, and that runs iOS 7—then you're in luck: You can get the iWork apps for free.

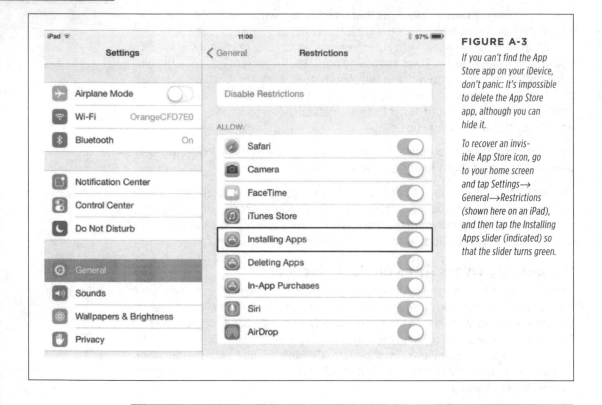

FIGURE A-3

If you can't find the App Store app on your iDevice, don't panic: It's impossible to delete the App Store app, although you can hide it.

To recover an invisible App Store icon, go to your home screen and tap Settings→ General→Restrictions (shown here on an iPad), and then tap the Installing Apps slider (indicated) so that the slider turns green.

NOTE Sadly, simply updating your iDevice to run iOS 7 *doesn't* mean you get the iWork apps for free. For example, if you bought an iPhone 4 in 2012 and have updated it to run iOS 7, you can't get the apps for free because this offer applies only to iDevices purchased after September 1, 2013. (If you have an iPhone 3GS or older, or the original iPad, your gadget can't even run iOS 7, so it doesn't matter when you buy and activate these iDevices.)

If you're curious which version of iOS your iDevice is running, go to Settings→General→About and look for the Version item. The first number listed there indicates your version of iOS: 6 means you have iOS 6, 7 means you have iOS 7, and so on.

To claim your freebies, ensure that you're hooked up to the Internet, and launch the App Store on your iDevice. A helpful Apple Apps window appears featuring all the apps that you can download for free—including Pages, Keynote, and Numbers. (If you don't see this window, read the box the next page.) Simply tap Download All, and your iDevice downloads all these apps without charging you a dime. Thanks, Apple!

Where Are My Freebies?

So you've got yourself a new iDevice that meets Apple's criteria for getting the iWork apps for free (see page 799). But what if you launch the App Store app and you don't see the Apple Apps window described on page 800?

It could be that you accidentally dismissed this window in the past. Thankfully, you haven't lost the chance to score some freebies. To claim your iWork apps, open the App Store, scroll to the bottom of the screen and, in the Quick Links section, click the "New to the App Store?" button. Scroll to the bottom of this screen, and then tap the "Apps Made by Apple" button. Voilà: all the iWork apps are waiting for you, complete with fetching Free buttons. Tap any of these apps to download them.

Buying the iWork for iOS Apps

If you're not one of those lucky devils who can get the iWork apps for free (see page 799 for details), it's easy enough to buy them using the App Store app that comes installed on your iDevice. If you're new to the App Store, the good news is that it's fairly easy to get the hang of. If you haven't already, launch the App Store by going to your home screen and tapping the App Store icon. After that, your next task is to find the app you want to purchase:

1. **Tap the Search box in the upper-right corner of your screen, and then start typing the name of the app you're looking for.**

    As you type, a drop-down menu appears with suggested search terms; the menu updates automatically as you type more letters. Type *iWork* to review all App Store entries that fall under the iWork banner, or type *Pages, Numbers,* or *Keynote* if you have one app in mind. If you make a mistake when typing and want to start from scratch, tap the X in the Search box.

2. **Continue typing until the correct term appears in the drop-down menu, and then tap to select it. (If the term you want doesn't appear in the drop-down list, simply tap Search after you finish typing.)**

    The App Store displays the items that match the term you selected or typed (see Figure A-4). The search results are displayed based on how closely they match your search query, starting with the most relevant.

> **NOTE** When searching for iWork apps, you may stumble upon iWork *templates* created by members of the Apple community. If you like the look of any of them, see page 276 for info on how to install downloaded templates.

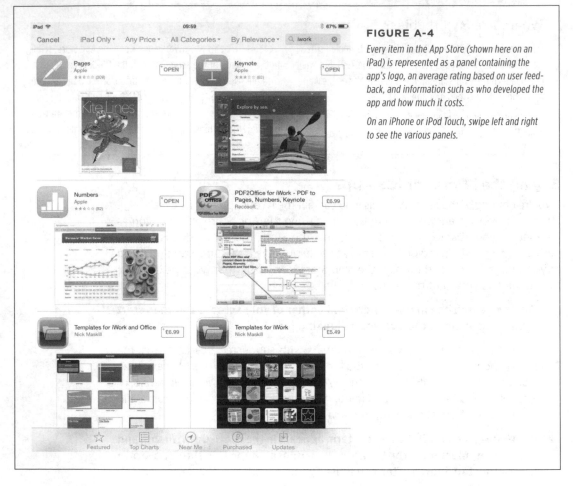

FIGURE A-4

Every item in the App Store (shown here on an iPad) is represented as a panel containing the app's logo, an average rating based on user feedback, and information such as who developed the app and how much it costs.

On an iPhone or iPod Touch, swipe left and right to see the various panels.

3. **Once you find the app you want, tap its panel to learn more (Figure A-5).**

   Before parting with your hard-earned cash, carefully review all the info about the app, particularly the comments left by satisfied (or dissatisfied!) customers. Reading through the reviews is the easiest way to get a sense of how good the app really is.

4. **Tap the app's price once to turn it into a green Buy App button; tap this new button, and then enter your Apple ID and tap OK.**

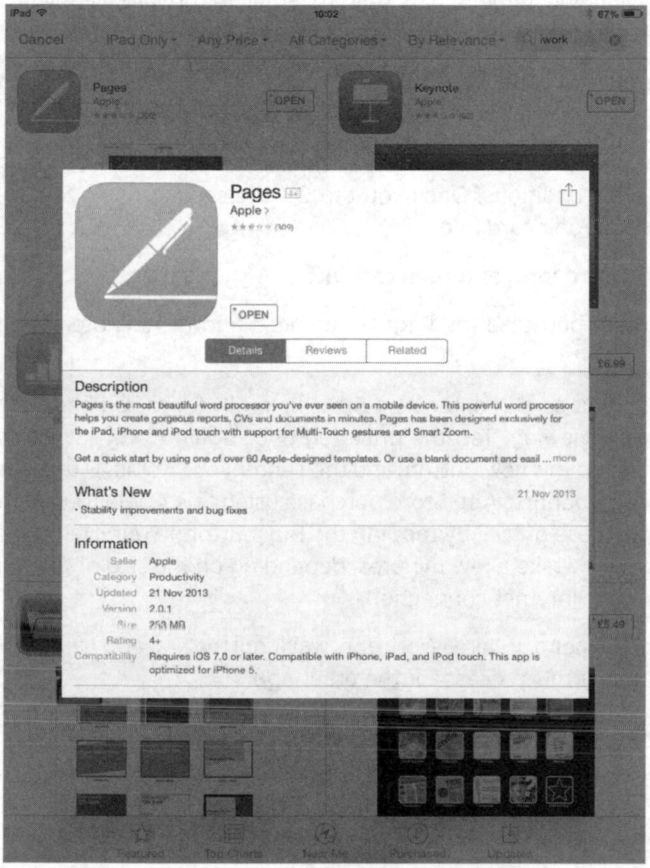

FIGURE A-5

Tap any app's panel in the App Store to learn more about it.

The Details tab (shown here) offers additional screenshots, information on what's new, and any hardware/software requirements.

If you've bought apps before, your iDevice starts downloading the app (you may need to enter your Apple ID username and password), and you can skip to page 804. However, if this is your Apple ID's first foray to the App Store, Apple helpfully informs you that "This Apple ID has not yet been used in the iTunes store." If you see this message, you need to enter your credit card info, so tap Review to get started, and then follow these steps:

1. **The App Store automatically detects your location, so verify whether the Store's guess is correct, and then tap Next.**

   The App Store generally does a decent job of zeroing in on your country and/or region, but you can change the default location by tapping the name of the country or region it displays. Scroll through the list of alternative locales, and then tap one to select it.

2. **Grab a strong cup of coffee and plow through the whopping 33 pages of terms and conditions.**

If you're using the App Store for work-related purposes and need to keep a record of everything you agree to, tap Send By Email to forward a copy of the terms and conditions to the email address associated with your Apple ID.

3. **Agree to the terms and conditions by tapping Agree, and then confirm your 100%, unwavering agreement by tapping OK a second time.**

Apple is a bit paranoid, so you have to *twice* confirm that you've really, *honestly* read the terms and conditions. Once you tap OK the second time, you see a screen for entering credit card info.

4. **Enter your credit card info, and then tap OK.**

You're now ready to purchase the Pages, Numbers, and/or Keynote apps for your iDevice.

After you enter your credit card info, the App Store helpfully takes you back to the app you were originally viewing. Tap the price tag once again to turn it into the green Buy App button; tap this new button, and then enter your Apple ID username and password. (If this is your first App Store purchase using this Apple ID, you may need to make your purchase official by tapping the Buy button.) Your iDevice then installs the app, which may take a few minutes, depending on the size of the app's file and the speed of your Internet connection.

If you're hankering for a second or third iWork app, wait until the first app has finished installing, and then repeat this process for the other app(s).

Installing iWork on Additional iDevices

After you download your first iWork app, you can use it on a second iDevice (or third, or fourth...) at no extra cost. The only catch is that both iDevices have to use the same Apple ID account. That's because Apple wants you to use the app on *your* iDevices, but not anyone else's. For example, you can download the Pages app and install it on your iPad and iPhone, but you can't also install it on your cousin's iPhone, your coworker's iPod Touch, and so on.

To install a previously downloaded iWork app on another iDevice, boot up the second gadget, go to your home screen, and then tap the App Store icon. Scroll to the bottom of the App Store and check whether you're already logged into an Apple ID account. If you're logged into an account but it *isn't* the one you used to purchase the iWork app, tap the "Apple ID: [username]" button, and then tap Sign Out. After that, tap Sign In, enter your Apple ID info, and then tap OK. You then see a bar containing several options at the bottom of the App Store screen (see Figure A-6).

TIP If this is your first time using this Apple ID on this iDevice, you may encounter a Verification Required message. Tap OK, and you're ready to continue.

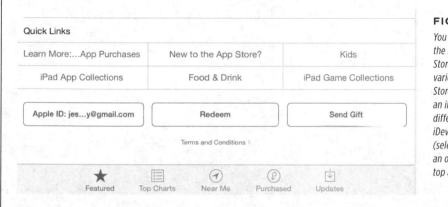

FIGURE A-6

You can use the bar at the bottom of the App Store to flit between the various sections of the Store (shown here on an iPad; you may see different sections on other iDevices). The Featured tab (selected here) provides an overview of Apple's top apps.

Tap the Purchased icon to view all the apps you've downloaded using the current Apple ID. (If you don't see this icon, tap Updates and then, on the Updates screen, tap Purchased.) Each downloaded app is represented by a panel, so tap the panel for the iWork app you want to install on the gadget you're currently holding. After reviewing the info about the app, tap the little cloud icon where the price tag button usually is. Your app is now downloaded and installed on this iDevice, too—at no extra cost.

Keeping the Apps Up to Date

From time to time, Apple releases free updates to the iWork apps. To check whether there are any updates for the apps on your iDevice, open the App Store app, and then tap the Updates tab in the bar at the bottom of your screen. On the Updates page, Apple lists all the available updates for all your apps. To download any of these updates, tap the Update button that appears next to each app.

Index

E

editing

3D charts (Pages for iOS), 704

cell references (Numbers), 531–533

documents (Pages for iCloud),
760–761

drag-and-drop method, 37–38

equations, 66

Formula Editor (Pages), 229–232

formulas (Numbers). *See* formulas
(Numbers)

in full-screen view (Pages), 28

masks (Pages), 12, 160

master slides, 416

photos (Keynote), 332–334

shapes, 173–174

table cells. *See* cells (Numbers)

text in iWork, 32–37

text in Keynote, 323–326

text in Pages, 6–8

effects (slide animation)

building movies, 367

building text, 360–362

chart building, 363–365

Effects drop-down menu, 293

Effects menu (Transitions tab),
353–354

object (slide transitions), 354–355

table building, 362–363

text, 355

email

linking slides to, 345

sending Pages documents via, 256

sending presentations via, 410

sending slideshows via, 408–409

Send via Email dialog box, 260

sharing documents via iCloud Mail,
759–760

EndNote program, 113

**Energy Saver (system preferences),
390**

Enhance button (images), 165

ePub format, 254–255

equation editors, 66

error bars (Numbers charts), 639–640

errors, formula (Numbers), 537

EVEN function, 554

**Excel files, saving spreadsheets as,
664–667**

exporting

documents (Pages). *See* document
exporting (Pages)

Keynote to Keynote '09, 402

Keynote to PowerPoint, 401–402

slideshows to PDF files, 405–406

slideshows to QuickTime movie,
403–405

slideshows to web pages, 407–408

slides to image files, 405–406

spreadsheets to different formats,
663–669

exposure slider (images), 164

extended desktop setup, 382

F

files

document sections vs. separate
(Pages), 114

importing from other programs
(Pages), 18

importing into Numbers, 449–450

reducing size of, 167–168, 334–335,
339, 656

saving as templates (Pages), 263

tagging (Pages), 15

fill handles, 226, 183, 532, 581

filling objects with images, 196–199

**filtering rows (Numbers tables),
502–506**

FIND function, 559–561

Find My Mac feature (iCloud), 258

Find & Replace

basics (Pages), 85–89

dialog box (Pages), 27–28

Numbers spreadsheets, 505–506

first-line indent marker, 58–59

**Fit Width/Fit Page settings (Pages),
25**

**Fit Width to Content setting
(Numbers), 497**

FIXED function, 563–564

flipping objects, 183–184, 314–316

floating charts (Pages), 234–235

floating objects

applying Mask with Selection
command to, 162

floating text boxes and, 153–154

grouping, 190

iWork

THE MISSING CD

There's no
CD with this book;
you just saved $5.00.

Instead, every single Web address, practice file, and piece of downloadable software mentioned in this book is available at *missingmanuals.com* (click the Missing CD icon). There you'll find a tidy list of links, organized by chapter.

Don't miss a thing!
Sign up for the free Missing Manual email announcement list at missingmanuals.com. We'll let you know when we release new titles, make free sample chapters available, and update the features and articles on the Missing Manual website.